Kim Stanley Robinson
Maps the Unimaginable

CRITICAL EXPLORATIONS IN SCIENCE FICTION AND FANTASY
(a series edited by Donald E. Palumbo and C.W. Sullivan III)

1. *Worlds Apart? Dualism and Transgression in Contemporary Female Dystopias* (Dunja M. Mohr, 2005)

2. *Tolkien and Shakespeare: Essays on Shared Themes and Language* (edited by Janet Brennan Croft, 2007)

3. *Culture, Identities and Technology in the Star Wars Films: Essays on the Two Trilogies* (edited by Carl Silvio and Tony M. Vinci, 2007)

4. *The Influence of Star Trek on Television, Film and Culture* (edited by Lincoln Geraghty, 2008)

5. *Hugo Gernsback and the Century of Science Fiction* (Gary Westfahl, 2007)

6. *One Earth, One People: The Mythopoeic Fantasy Series of Ursula K. Le Guin, Lloyd Alexander, Madeleine L'Engle and Orson Scott Card* (Marek Oziewicz, 2008)

7. *The Evolution of Tolkien's Mythology: A Study of the History of Middle-earth* (Elizabeth A. Whittingham, 2008)

8. *H. Beam Piper: A Biography* (John F. Carr, 2008)

9. *Dreams and Nightmares: Science and Technology in Myth and Fiction* (Mordecai Roshwald, 2008)

10. *Lilith in a New Light: Essays on the George MacDonald Fantasy Novel* (edited by Lucas H. Harriman, 2008)

11. *Feminist Narrative and the Supernatural: The Function of Fantastic Devices in Seven Recent Novels* (Katherine J. Weese, 2008)

12. *The Science of Fiction and the Fiction of Science: Collected Essays on SF Storytelling and the Gnostic Imagination* (Frank McConnell, edited by Gary Westfahl, 2009)

13. *Kim Stanley Robinson Maps the Unimaginable: Critical Essays* (edited by William J. Burling, 2009)

14. *The Inter-Galactic Playground: A Critical Study of Children's and Teens' Science Fiction* (Farah Mendlesohn, 2009)

15. *Science Fiction from Québec: A Postcolonial Study* (Amy J. Ransom, 2009)

16. *Science Fiction and the Two Cultures: Essays on Bridging the Gap Between the Sciences and the Humanities* (edited by Gary Westfahl and George Slusser, 2009)

17. *Stephen R. Donaldson and the Modern Epic Vision: A Critical Study of the "Chronicles of Thomas Covenant" Novels* (Christine Barkley, 2009)

Kim Stanley Robinson Maps the Unimaginable

Critical Essays

Edited by WILLIAM J. BURLING

CRITICAL EXPLORATIONS IN
SCIENCE FICTION AND FANTASY, 13
Donald E. Palumbo *and* C.W. Sullivan III, *series editors*

McFarland & Company, Inc., Publishers
Jefferson, North Carolina, and London

Quotations used by permission of Bantam Books, a division of Random House, Inc., and by permission of HarperCollins Publishers, Ltd.: From *Antarctica* by Kim Stanley Robinson, copyright 1998 by Kim Stanley Robinson. From *Blue Mars* by Kim Stanley Robinson, copyright 1996 by Kim Stanley Robinson. From *Fifty Degrees below Zero* by Kim Stanley Robinson, copyright 2005 by Kim Stanley Robinson. From *Forty Signs of Rain* by Kim Stanley Robinson, copyright 2004 by Kim Stanley Robinson. From *Green Mars* by Kim Stanley Robinson, copyright 1994 by Kim Stanley Robinson. From *Red Mars* by Kim Stanley Robinson, copyright 1993 by Kim Stanley Robinson. From *Sixty Days and Counting* by Kim Stanley Robinson, copyright 2007 by Kim Stanley Robinson. From *The Years of Rice and Salt* by Kim Stanley Robinson, copyright 2002 by Kim Stanley Robinson.

The editor of this volume, William J. Burling, died in March 2009 shortly after completing all of his duties on this book.

LIBRARY OF CONGRESS CATALOGUING-IN-PUBLICATION DATA

Kim Stanley Robinson maps the unimaginable :
critical essays / edited by William J. Burling.
p. cm. — (Critical explorations
in science fiction and fantasy ; 13)
Includes bibliographical references and index.

ISBN 978-0-7864-3369-8
softcover : 50# alkaline paper ∞

1. Robinson, Kim Stanley — Criticism and interpretation.
2. Science fiction, American — History and criticism.
I. Burling, William J.
PS3568.O2893Z75   2009   813'.54 — dc22   2009004966

British Library cataloguing data are available

©2009 Estate of William J. Burling. All rights reserved

No part of this book may be reproduced or transmitted in any form or by any means, electronic or mechanical, including photocopying or recording, or by any information storage and retrieval system, without permission in writing from the publisher.

On the cover: Kim Stanley Robinson (photograph by Ally Union); background images ©2009 Shutterstock

Manufactured in the United States of America

*McFarland & Company, Inc., Publishers
Box 611, Jefferson, North Carolina 28640
www.mcfarlandpub.com*

Table of Contents

Preface and Acknowledgments 1
Introduction 3

PART I. UTOPIA AND ALTERNATIVE HISTORY

1. Witness to Hard Times: Robinson's Other Californias
   (THOMAS P. MOYLAN) 11
2. "If I Find One Good City, I Will Spare the Man": Realism and
   Utopia in the Mars Trilogy (FREDRIC JAMESON) 48
3. Falling into History: Imagined Wests in the "Three Californias"
   and Mars Trilogy (CARL ABBOTT) 67
4. Remaking History: The Short Fiction (JOHN KESSEL) 83
5. *The Martians*: A Habitable Fabric of Possibilities (NICK GEVERS) . . . 95
6. Learning to Live in History: Alternate Historicities and the
   1990s in *The Years of Rice and Salt* (PHILLIP E. WEGNER) 98

PART II. THEORY AND POLITICS

7. The Density of Utopian Destiny in *Red Mars* (CAROL FRANKO) . . . 115
8. Falling into Theory: Simulation, Terraformation, and
   Eco-Economics in the Mars Trilogy (ROBERT MARKLEY) 122
9. Chromodynamics: Science and Colonialism in the Mars Trilogy
   (ELIZABETH LEANE) 144
10. The Theoretical Foundation of Utopian Radical Democracy
    in *Blue Mars* (WILLIAM J. BURLING) 157
11. The Politics of the Network: The Science in the Capital Trilogy
    (ROGER LUCKHURST) 170
12. Living Thought: Genes, Genres and Utopia in the Science
    in the Capital Trilogy (GIB PRETTYMAN) 181
13. "Structuralist Alchemy" in *Red Mars* (WILLIAM J. WHITE) 204

PART III. ECOLOGY AND NATURE

14. Ecological Newspeak (ALAN R. SLOTKIN) 227

15. Murray Bookchin on Mars! The Production of Nature in the
    Mars Trilogy (SHAUN HUSTON) 231

16. The Mars Trilogy and the Leopoldian Land Ethic (ERIC OTTO) . . . 242

17. Dead Penguins in Immigrant Pilchard Scandal: Telling Stories
    About "the Environment" in *Antarctica* (SHERRYL VINT *and*
    MARK BOULD) 257

PART IV. INTERVIEW AND SELECT BIBLIOGRAPHY

18. A Conversation with Kim Stanley Robinson
    (IRVING F. "BUD" FOOTE) 277

19. A Select Secondary Bibliography (WILLIAM J. BURLING) 292

About the Contributors   297

Index   301

Preface and Acknowledgments

As the editor of this volume, I have the pleasure of relating a few words about its origins and of thanking those involved in its development. This collection originated in a serendipitous way when, in June 2005, I contacted Kim Stanley Robinson via e-mail and out of the blue, to enquire if he would be interested in reading an essay I had published in *Utopian Studies* concerning the political ideas in *Blue Mars* (as included in the present anthology). He graciously agreed to read my piece and subsequently replied with what I would later learn were his characteristic generous and thoughtful responses. A brief continuing exchange soon brought out that someone else (whose identity I still do not know) had been considering editing a critical anthology on Robinson's work for several years before I entered the scene, but the project had bogged down. Sensing a moment of opportunity, I asked Stan (we were by this time on more familiar terms) to check with the "other editor" to see if I might take over the editorship, and the issue was soon decided in my favor. "Take over" is a misleading phrase. In fact, I started from scratch.

And so here I wish to record my first and primary debt, which is to Kim Stanley Robinson. Throughout the nearly three years of this project he has been enthusiastic, supportive and helpful in ways that extend far beyond mere professional courtesy and have exceeded my expectations time and again. Stan pointed me toward several possible contributors whose work I either did not know or appreciate as significant; communicated with possible contributors to assist me in encouraging them to join the roster; provided contact information for difficult to locate contributors; smoothed out copyright permission issues; and offered feedback when I struggled with complex situations, enabling me to reach positive outcomes. While my extensive e-mail relationship with Stan was an ongoing pleasure, the personal highlight came during late May 2007, when he graciously invited me and my wife, Deb, to his home in West Davis for an afternoon of stimulating conversation that will remain one of my fondest memories of this project. For the record, I must state that while Stan helped whenever and however he could, this anthology reflects my own vision, and all editorial decisions (and faults) are my own.

Several parties must be recognized for seminal assistance. Don Palumbo, my series editor with McFarland, has been receptive and helpful from our very first conversation at the International Conference for the Fantastic in the Arts in March 2006 down to the present moment concerning all stages of the proposal, development, and submission process. I am grateful also for a Summer Faculty Research Grant from Missouri State University during 2006 which allowed me the time and resources to conduct the initial bibliographical survey, to contact prospective contributors, and to prepare the proposal.

To Kit Hume I am thankful for putting me in touch with Stan Robinson in the first place. And, of course, I am grateful to those authors whose earlier work is reprinted here for their enthusiastic and timely participation. One of the great pleasures of this project was connecting with so many scholars who share a passion for Stan's fiction.

Several individuals went far beyond my expectations. To John Kessel, Phil Wegner, and Roger Luckhurst, authors who wrote new essays especially for this anthology, I am deeply thankful for such impressive contributions. To Gib Prettyman and the team of Sherryl Vint and Mark Bould I am grateful for providing superb, yet last-minute, contributions when two of the originally commissioned contributors suddenly had to drop out. Javier Martinez, the editor of *Extrapolation*, sent my way a totally unexpected new essay by Bill White that fit the collection perfectly, and has offered ongoing support and advice. Additional thanks to Gib Prettyman and Bill White for helping me to think through some finalizing details when the three of us served on a panel devoted to Stan Robinson's fiction at the 2007 Society for Utopian Studies conference in Toronto. Also at that conference was Tom Moylan, who deserves kudos for preparing his masterful essay for the present collection that combines material from two important earlier projects in a new and synergistic fashion, all the while dealing with serious health issues.

As always, I thank Deb and Amie for their patience, love, interest, and support during yet another of my extended projects.

—*William Burling*
February 2009

Introduction

> And so ... [the new society on Mars] can most help the home planet by serving as a way for you to see yourselves. As a way to map out an unimaginable immensity. Thus in a small way we do our part to create the great civilization that trembles on the brink of becoming.
> — Kim Stanley Robinson, *Blue Mars* [172]

Kim Stanley Robinson, recipient of multiple awards and honors, ranks among the most important of progressive science fiction and utopian authors. While his fiction has steadily attracted the close attention of leading critics and scholars such as Fredric Jameson, Tom Moylan, and Robert Markley, no critical anthology devoted to his work has yet appeared. The present volume therefore presents thirteen of the most noteworthy (and often influential) previously published essays, interviews, and reviews along with five newly commissioned essays that explore Robinson's contributions to and reputation within the fields of utopian and science fiction. Thus, rather than serving solely as a retrospective, the anthology adds substantively to the critical dialogue in its own right by establishing Robinson as an intellectual figure of the first rank and by defining the interpretive debate for the near future.

The essays were chosen based on the basis of several factors. First, the observant reader will note how many of these essayists quote each other's work, indicating the degree to which a sustained, coherent body of commentary in fact has already emerged. Thus I have tried to include as many as possible of the most widely cited and influential commentaries. Second, I have attempted to select essays covering as far as possible the historical chronology and generic range of Robinson's career, including essays addressed not only to the rightly famous "California" and "Mars" trilogies, but also to lesser studied works, such as his shorter fiction and novels such as *Antarctica* and *The Years of Rice and Salt*. Further the essays pay attention to the chronology of Robinson's career, from the beginnings in the early 1980s right up to the recently completed "Science in the Capital" trilogy. Also important was the need to consider the enormous intellectual scope of Robinson's work via a variety of theoretical constellations, from Bakhtin to Foucault to Bookchin to Greimas to Latour and many, many more. The Index alone reveals the remarkable range of connections established by the various essayists. And not without significance is the fact the authors in this collection come from four continents, attesting to the fact of Robinson's international stature and significance.

The collection is organized into four sections suggested by and relevant to Robinson's broad artistic agenda: utopia and alternative history; theory and politics; ecology and nature; and interview and bibliography. Each section is arranged chronologically by major themes and as such clarifies the development of the critical dialog while also paying attention to important milestones in Robinson's fictional output. The anthology concludes Bud Foote's groundbreaking interview with Robinson from 1994, and a current select secondary bibliography compiled by me.

The six essays in Part I, "Utopia and Alternative History," immediately focus on what are arguably many of the key thematic dynamics in Robinson's work. Tom Moylan in "Utopia Is When Our Lives Matter: Reading Kim Stanley Robinson's *Pacific Edge*" (1995) was one of the first critics to recognize Robinson's innovations respecting the critical utopian tradition in the California Trilogy, consisting of *The Wild Shore* (1984), *The Gold Coast* (1988), and *Pacific Edge* (1990). His contribution included here, "Witness to Hard Times: Robinson's Other Californias" combines the original 1995 essay with material from his later meditation on the trilogy in *Scraps of the Untainted Sky* (2000) and adds newer insights not previously published. Moylan offers a detailed close reading of the three novels which supports his claim that they "perceptively, and palimpsestically, test the formal possibilities of the sf genre, especially in its dystopian and utopian modes." Another influential commentator to recognize and advocate for Robinson's critical reputation is Fredric Jameson, his former teacher. Jameson regularly, though in the main only briefly, commented on Robinson's importance in other essays during the 1990s, but with the appearance of "'If I Find One Good City, I Will Spare the Man': Realism and Utopia in the Mars Trilogy," his only essay solely dedicated to Robinson's work, Jameson resituates the "hard sf" dimensions of Robinson's celebrated Mars Trilogy (1992–1996): "Besides all this, we need to insist on the way in which any first scientific reading of the Mars trilogy must eventually develop into a second allegorical one, in which the hard SF content stands revealed as socio-political — that is to say, as utopian." This essay, widely cited in Robinson scholarship, represents a milestone in critical understanding of the Mars Trilogy. Another recent and ground-breaking essay is Carl Abbott's "Falling into History: Imagined Wests in the 'Three Californias' and Mars Trilogy." Abbott establishes the thematic significances of the opening up of the American West and particularly of California, the latter being the ideological and geographical degree zero in Robinson's two most well-known trilogies. Robinson himself has remarked in various interviews that he thinks of himself as a regional writer, a major interpretive dimension well argued by Abbott.

The first section concludes with two new essays and an essay review. In "Remaking History: The Short Fiction," John Kessel, a distinguished, award-winning science fiction author in his own right whose *Corrupting Dr. Nice* (1997) Robinson himself has called "the best time-travel novel ever written" (as published on the novel's dust jacket) focuses on Robinson's neglected but thematically seminal short fiction. In commenting upon short stories from Robinson's early career as collected in *The Planet on the Table* (1986) and *Remaking History* (1991), he argues that virtually all of Robinson's short fiction is concerned principally with a critique of history as a constructive determinant of present-day societies, as a philosophical connection between the present and the future, and as an influence on moral action. Kessel insightfully identifies how Robinson interrogates history, histories, and historians by offering readings of alternate histories ("The Lucky Strike"), the lives of historians ("The History of the 20th Century, with Illustrations"), historical falsifications ("Vinland the Dream"), and future reconstructions of the past ("Remaking History"). Also insisting upon the notable significance of Robinson's short fiction is Nick Gevers' slightly revised version of an earlier review essay, "*The Martians*: A Habitable Fabric of Possibilities," which argues that "*The Martians* is best regarded not as a casual companion volume, as a pendant assortment of offcuts, afterthoughts, and miscellaneous paraphernalia, but rather as a metafictional commentary by Robinson on his own work, a justification of his art in the guise of a cycle of fictions."

Gevers further contends that the stories in Robinson's 1997 collection "embody utopia at their most fundamental level. Utopia structures them; it shapes their language, their subject matter, their sensibility." As such *The Martians* deserves close attention.

Focusing on an unjustly overlooked text is Philip Wegner's new essay, "Learning to Live in History: Alternative Historicities and the 1990s in *The Years of Rice and Salt*," which concludes Part I. Wegner argues that Robinson's recent *The Years of Rice and Salt* (2002) is an outstanding example of the science fiction subgenre of the alternative history. This strategy of literary estrangement—fusing together as it does one of the dominant literary genres of the nineteenth century, the historical novel, and what Jameson has theorized as its twentieth century successor, science fiction—is a privileged methodology for interrogating currently dominant epistemologies of history. Robinson's novel, Wegner argues, therefore challenges the post-historical sensibilities codified by Francis Fukyama's much-discussed essay, "The End of History," in order to teach its readers "the importance and indeed necessity of hope precisely in those situations where the possibility of any radical transformation of the status quo seems to have become once more distant." Connecting the novel to Robinson's earlier fiction, Wegner asserts that *The Years of Rice and Salt* "continues the work begun in his preceding *Mars* trilogy—[and] is thus analogous to that in the contemporary radical theoretical work of Jameson, Michael Hardt and Antonio Negri, Slavoj Zizek, Kojin Karatani, Jacques Derrida, Michael Löwy, Alain Badiou, Judith Butler, and others, and in the collective political projects of such groups as the counter-globalization 'movement of movements' and the World Social Forum, all of whom struggle to reinvent the project of radical social change—in short, the collective project of revolution—in a new historical context."

Jameson has remarked that the Mars trilogy "will surely be the great political novel of the 1990s" (*The Seeds of Time* 65). Accordingly Part II, "Theory and Politics," addresses the richly complex theoretical issues at play in Robinson's fiction. The first commentator, Carol Franko, established herself in the mid–1990s as an early leading Robinson scholar with a pair of articles in 1994 and 1995 (see bibliography). Her third essay on Robinson (from 1997) included here, "The Density of Utopian Destiny in Robinson's *Red Mars*," builds upon her earlier work. Drawing on M. M. Bakhtin's notions of dialogism, polyphony, and carnival, Franko argues that in the first two volumes of the Mars trilogy Robinson presents a richly complex spread of utopian political possibilities. Robert Markley's influential and widely cited 1997 essay, included here as "Falling Into Theory: Simulation, Terraformation, and Eco-Economics in the Mars Trilogy" (1997) was also among the very first essays to address in detail the depth and sophistication of Robinson's portrayal of the political intersection of ecology and economics, and went far toward clarifying and enhancing Robinson's importance as a proponent of viable eco-economic theory. Markley argues that Robinson's Mars trilogy is better understood as "historical simulation" than as "utopian longing." Markley emphasizes that "Robinson's oxymoronic phrase 'historical simulations' thus suggests his interest in reprogramming the mindset that divides nature from culture; rather than utopian longings, his trilogy offers a carefully nuanced thought experiment as a means to imagine the greening of science, economics, and politics." Unsurprisingly this essay has been widely cited, as has the next one. Elizabeth Leane, who has also published elsewhere on the importance of Antarctica to Robinson's work, in "Chromodynamics: Science and Colonialism in the Mars Trilogy," focuses on the ideological dynamics that are implicit in the complex dialectic of science and planetary colonization. Leane proposes that the novel presents a "momentous change in scientific attitude and practice" that "is based on a desire to accept the agency of the other—to nurture what Barbara McClintock has termed 'a feeling for the organism.'" These complexities are expressed symbolically in the trilogy via a metaphoric color strategy that Leane terms "chromodynamics," i.e., a blending of colors that "must always be combined, most always exist in concert, but ... can change, can interact dynamically." Robinson's innovations in scientific practice are paralleled by his interest in new political possibilities, a thematic that has received little specific but is addressed by my own "The Theoretical Foundation of Utopian Radical Democracy in *Blue Mars*," the only essay yet to have appeared that is exclusively devoted to Robinson's political thought, especially in his most overtly theoretical novel stressing the challenges of utopian politics, *Blue Mars*. This meditation on Robinson's utopian political model and Ernesto Laclau and Chantal Mouffe's *Hegemony and Socialist Strategy* (1985) combines literary analysis and political critique to suggest that while Robinson has never read *Hegemony and Socialist Strategy*, his theoretical model benefits greatly from the cross-textual comparison with Laclau and Mouffe's discussion, while their theoretical model of subject position politics, read in the light of *Blue Mars*, likewise takes on concrete specificity.

Two new essays offer rich interpretive insights regarding Robinson's recent Science in the Capital trilogy. In "The Politics of the Network: The Science in the Capital Trilogy," Roger Luckhurst, a major voice in recent science fiction scholarship, examines Robinson's recent work and offers a new suggestive strategy for interpreting Robinson's intervention on the effects of global warming. Luckhurst asserts that the novel sequence as represented "in the mimetic world of the present-day, ... forms [a] very different kind of writing from the technological sublime of *Mars* or the critical dystopia of *The Gold Coast*. I want to call this style *proleptic Realism*." Refining claims by critics such as Jameson and Moylan that Robinson's fiction is allegorical rather than realistic, Luckhurst attempts "to detach Robinson's Realism from any confusion with verisimilitude (that is, mistaking Realism for being merely realistic). Instead, Robinson's new form can be considered as part of a tradition of political writing that takes Realism to be the exemplary mode for conveying the totality of a society and the underlying contradictory forces that drive its social and ecological relations." He further extends the critical debate by pointing out that "the trilogy as a whole embodies much of the theory of science [Bruno] Latour propounded in *Science in Action* in 1987." Markley had earlier suggested Latour's influence, an influence acknowledged by Robinson, but Luckhurst here outlines what may well be one of the most important new developments in Robinson scholarship.

Also grappling with the complexities of Robinson's newest trilogy is the Society for Utopian Studies award-winning essayist Gib Prettyman's "Living Thought: Genes, Genres and Utopia in the Science in the Capital Trilogy." Stressing Robinson's awareness that any novel is necessarily a mixture of genres, Prettyman focuses on the significance of forms such as "the day-after-tomorrow" and "the utopian black comedy" and proposes the highly suggestive contention that "Robinson presents a genetic conception of genres and their roles in human life, both historical and potential. Under this model, genres are metaphorically equated with genes as basic building blocks that encode lived situations and reproduce cultural behaviors in the same way that genes encode evolutionary situations and reproduce biological traits." This emphasis upon generic form thus demonstrates that "genres are (as Marxist literary critics have long asserted) at once imaginative and material categories, complex material encodings of lived human experience—in short, 'living thought.'" Prettyman's notion of "genres as genes" thus both insists upon and clarifies the conditions of ideological closure which inform Robinson's, and indeed, all utopian fiction.

Concluding this section is William's White's "'Structuralist Alchemy' in *Red Mars*." Following up on a key passage in *Green Mars* which directly presents a structuralist meditation on the rich connotative complexities of color imagery, White argues that Robinson's representation of A. J. Greimas's "semantic rectangle" *within* the text of the novels in turn can be reflexively applied *to the novels* themselves, especially in interpreting and defending the trilogy's dramatic paradigm shift, which some commentators have criticized as an artistic flaw. White's essay is therefore an important "narrative analysis that explores the 'actantial' dimension of *Red Mars*; that is, how characters come to embody or instantiate those discursive structures," in particular, the significance of "John Boone." The essence of the argument is that "the multiplexity of *Red Mars* and its sequels can be viewed as the product of the various tensions and sympathies emerging from the entanglement of myth and irony." White seeks, therefore, "to explode that dualism, to reveal and help make sense of the intricate discursive constitution of the Mars trilogy in particular and science fiction more broadly."

While all of the essays in this anthology in one way or other address ecology, Part III, "Ecology and Nature," emphasizes the centrality of this thematic to Robinson's entire artistic project. Alan R. Slotkin's "Ecological Newspeak" examines how Robinson's neologisms "enhance his ideas and themes," especially his commitment to "humanity's relationship with nature and its need to live in harmony with the natural world." Though among the shortest essays in this anthology, Slotkin's work well demonstrates the massive intellectual density and rigor on Robinson's fiction, with regard to attention to ecological issues as well as skill with language. This "intellectual density" is also the subject of Shaun Huston's "Murray Bookchin on Mars! The Production of Nature in the Mars Trilogy." Huston establishes the theoretical influence of Bookchin's thought on Robinson's trilogy, especially with respect to "third nature," a concept that theorizes the condition in which "humans realize their potential as 'nature rendered self-conscious.'" Robinson, Huston argues, "takes the question of third nature into new contexts for examination," particularly "one not marked by an attempt to subsume the rest of nature into the human fold." In "The Mars Trilogy and the Leopoldian Land Ethic" Eric Otto suggests further philosophical resonances in Robinson's fiction with the thought of Aldo Leopold, one of the twentieth century's most important ecological pioneers. While Leopold is not directly acknowledged by Robinson as an influence, Otto's essay establishes the potent latent legacy of Leopold's ecological philosophy, in that the Mars trilogy serves "to construct a viable model for ecological sustainability and an egalitarian relationship between all of nature's components."

The final essay in Part III is among the most dynamic, provocative, and closely-argued analyses of Robinson's ecological thought yet to appear. Sherryl Vint and Mark Bould's "Dead Penguins in Immigrant Pilchard Scandal: Telling Stories about 'the Environment' in *Antarctica*" situates Robinson's fiction within the "recent re-examination of Marx's conceptualization and treatment of nature and of attempts to develop a 'green' Marxism." They argue that all such science fiction "walks a very difficult line, trying to reconcile divergent red and green politics which should be mutually supportive, especially in the ongoing crisis of environmental destruction and mass extinction caused by capitalist social relations." Founded on a careful and generally sympathetic analysis of Robinson's fiction, their essay has wide-ranging prescriptive implications: "our aim is to more broadly point to the status of non-human nature as one of the sites of social justice that requires further thought in Marxist analyses." Thus "[a] materialist analysis requires that we include non-human nature in our demands for social justice, and we fear that even work as environmentally sensitive as Robinson's is not sufficiently attentive to such matters." Vint and Bould "thus draw attention to one of the key aporia in attempts to bring together environmentalist and Marxist perspectives: the loss of focus on non-human life as an end in itself rather than as a means to human ends." This essay challenges Robinson and all other writers to recognize the fundamental distinction between "landscape" and "environment," especially the severe limitations of purely human-centered solutions to global issues which ignore or downplay "non-human nature in our demands for social justice." Humanity, they assert, must develop a new relationship with nature, and they challenge authors of progressive utopian fiction to tell "more stories ... [that] feature far more radical coalitions among humans and non-humans."

The book concludes with two additional items. The first is Bud Foote's seminal "A Conversation with Kim Stanley Robinson," published in *Science Fiction Studies* (1994). Of contemporary science fiction authors, Robinson is among the best at using the interview format both to publicize his work and to provide meta-commentary upon it. The Foote interview exemplifies precisely such a document, and we should not be surprised to learn that it is quoted by many of the authors in the present anthology and widely in the greater body of discourse on Robinson. Rounding out the anthology is a select secondary bibliography that I have compiled to provide a convenient "first stop" for those wishing to read further into the extant scholarship, but also to acknowledge the other excellent essays that I was not able to include here.

Part I. Utopia and Alternative History

1

Witness to Hard Times: Robinson's Other Californias*

Thomas P. Moylan

I. Science Fiction, Dystopia, Utopia

"I'll stay right here and write another book."
— Kim Stanley Robinson, *The Wild Shore*

While his eutopian Mars trilogy is perhaps better known, Kim Stanley Robinson's Three Californias Trilogy, set closer to home, is itself a significant production in the history of utopian and science fiction.[1] In these explorations of American society in the late 1980s, Robinson created three parallel futures of the Southern Californian landscape that perceptively, and palimpsestically, test the formal possibilities of the sf genre, especially in its dystopian and eutopian modes.[2] Over six years, while the Mars project was gestating, he moved from a post-holocaust, apocalyptic narrative in *The Wild Shore* (1984), written in the vein of an Orson Scott Card or David Brin; to a near-future dystopian account in *The Gold Coast* (1988), closer to the sensibilities of Philip K. Dick and Samuel R. Delany; and on to the eutopian *Pacific Edge* (1990), which Edward James has called the most interesting literary utopia since Samuel R. Delany's *Triton* even as it invokes the communitarian spirit of Ursula K. Le Guin's thought experiments.

In each book, with the social reality mapped and challenged in the iconic setting, the discrete narrative follows a younger and older man as they cross generational barriers and engage in conversation about society, personal life, and the vocation of the writer, while they simultaneously confront the political and personal crises of their particular spacetime variation.[3] Each volume, then, gives us a self-reflexive meditation on its own conditions of production as the writing undertaken by its protagonist gives us the text, or at least the concept of the text, that we are reading. In the first two volumes, the young man decides on the mode of writing he must do to be true to himself as well as be a responsible political agent in his society. In *The Wild Shore*, Henry, at old Tom's urging, narrates his travels and experiences in the new frontier of a devastated Orange County; in the military-corporate-consumer society of

---

*This essay combines two earlier pieces and adds new material. The first source is "Utopia Is When Our Lives Matter: Reading Kim Stanley Robinson's *Pacific Edge*," *Utopian Studies* 6.2 (1995): 1–25. Reprinted by permission of *Utopian Studies*. The additional older material is from *Scraps of the Untainted Sky: Science Fiction, Utopia, Dystopia* (Boulder, CO: Westview Press, 2000). Reprinted by permission of Westview Press, a member of the Perseus Books Group.

The Gold Coast, Jim sets poetry aside to record the history of a dystopian Orange County; but in *Pacific Edge* it is the older man (the "Tom Barnard" that appears in all three works) who works out the literary and political theory of what is essentially the critical utopia in his journal, and then joins the revolution that produces the utopian society in which his grandson Kevin lives and names the text we are reading. Interestingly, in the last volume, the younger man, Kevin, is not a writer but a skilled carpenter in the post-revolutionary town of El Modena.

This extended meditation on the inter-relationships between writing, political analysis, and personal/collective engagement begins in the relatively quiet narrative of *The Wild Shore.* Set in 2047, wherein the other world powers (under a UN dominated by Russia) have put an end to the threatening force and arrogance of the United States by way of a mass neutron bomb attack that devastated the social infrastructure and state apparatus, Robinson's first study of an alternative space overlayed on his familiar Southern Californian reality is not overtly dystopian or eutopian. Instead, he opts for the ground-clearing approach of post-holocaust sf as he explores the complementary processes of a community coming alive and a young man coming of age, especially as a writer. After this opening tale on the terrain of his California, he moved on to the more systemic utopian texts of the next two books — as they develop the familiar double move of negation in the second volume and anticipation in the third.

Robinson's narrative in *The Wild Shore* focuses on a group of young people in their community in the Onofre Valley, located on the Southern California coast between the former Los Angeles to the north and San Diego to the south. Over the span of an eventful summer, he traces the lives, and decisions, of Henry (Henry Aaron Fletcher: with its resonances of Thoreau, the *Bounty* mutiny leader, and the baseball player Hank Aaron) and his friends (Steve, Gabby, Kristen, and Mando) as they come to terms with their lives in this devastated but gradually awakening society. Along with this group, he introduces the character of Tom Barnard, who appears in each of the volumes: here, Tom is an 81-year-old survivor of the UN attack and serves as wise man and teacher to the small community, especially as mentor to Henry and Steve. In the iconic setting that enfolds this narrative, Robinson gives us details of this harsh yet nascently hopeful future: the California they live in is a string of scattered communities gradually rebuilding after the UN attack sixty-three years earlier (see *WS* 203). Faced by an America that was a "giant" that "swam through the seas eating up all the little countries — drinking them up as it went along," the UN forces took action with 3000 neutron bombs and halted the power of this "killer whale" (*WS* 198). The resulting short-term radiation destruction of the infrastructure and the decline of the population meant that there were no longer "enough Americans left alive to add up to a nation at all, much less the strongest on Earth" (*WS* 43). Living off the ruins and leftovers of the past but also developing agriculture, fishing, and crafts to build new lives, the people of the Onofre Valley are, for Robinson, the optimum example of a viable alternative in this future. They live in a cluster of family homes scattered through the valley and are creating a healthy community on the edge of scarcity — doing so in an echo of Le Guin's Annarres, even as theirs is not yet a eutopian space. To their north, the "scavengers" still live off the detritus of urban LA, and while they are crafty traders they have not built viable communities. To the south, the people of San Diego have managed to re-build in a more technologically advanced way, but they have done so under the authoritarian leadership of a dictatorial mayor and his cronies and henchmen. In the western sea, based on the island of Catalina, the Japanese, as the UN protectorate force, maintain control over the broken mainland, monitoring it to be sure the old nation does not rise again.

The political crisis that drives Robinson's main line of narration arises when the San Diegans rebuild the old railway lines to the north (in a twist on the destruction of those lines in the 1950s by the oil-automobile-defense interests who then built the military-industrial-consumer behemoth that became the Southern California suburbs with their endless freeways). Ostensibly to reopen links between communities, the actual purpose of the rail project is one of extending the domination of the San Diego mayor in a strategy of "super-patriotism" that aims to build an "American resistance" in the mode of postwar American militarism (an option often reprised in post-holocaust sf of more right-wing persuasions). In the meantime, Henry and Steve are rankling against the stasis in their own community and yearning to look, and travel, outward. As Henry puts it, "it seemed to me that we were ... stuck so far in history that we couldn't move but one way when we were struck by events. How I wished we could be clear and free to move where we would" (*WS* 73). In their explorations outside the valley, they discover the new railway; and it is their resulting encounter and contestation with the San Diegans that moves the political and personal storylines forward. Initially, after hearing Henry and Steve's news, the Onofre community wants to embrace uncritically the new power, and apparent revival, of an "American" entity, from the south; but gradually, with Tom's warnings and Henry's interventions, they come to see the rail project and its hyper-patriotic politics for what they are. With help from democratic elements in San Diego who depose the mayor and end the jingoistic agenda of their community, the people of Onofre destroy the railroad tracks. In their stead, they link up with the San Diegans to develop radio technology (in another echo of Le Guin's *The Dispossessed*) and thus restore a communications link while holding off on any rail connection until local democracy is stronger and able to refuse centralized power, be it Japan, the UN, or a resurgent America.

The outcome to Robinson's tale is not revolution or social transformation, but rather revelation and reawakening—and writing. The new consciousness and political agency embraced by the Onofre and San Diego communities mark an initial step that could, if all went well, open the way to a fuller political development with more utopian potential. And at the creative register, this reawakening, this new view of the world becomes the focus of Henry's first writing project.

In the years leading up to this intense summer, Henry and his friends have been rediscovering literacy under Tom's gentle urging. At its end—while Steve sails off to discover the larger world; Kirsten and Gabby settle into their lives; and Mando tragically dies—Henry opts for the craft of writing and creates the very book we are reading. His experiences in this time of crisis have had their effect, and he struggles to come to terms with his new knowledge and perspective. In an echo of the epistemological work of sf itself, he reflects on his new insights:

> Before my trip south Onofre was just home, a natural place, and the houses, the bridge and the paths, the fields and the latrines, they were all just as much a part of it as the cliffs and the river and the trees. But now I saw it in a new way. The path. A broad swath of dusty dirt cutting through the weeds, curving here to get around the corner of the Simpsons' garden, narrowing there where rocks cramped it on both sides.... It went where it did because there had been agreement, when folks first moved to the valley, that this was the best way to the river from the meadows to the south. People's thinking had made that path.... People I knew had thought that bridge, and built it [*WS* 164].

In this initial recognition of a process of cognitive mapping, Henry undergoes a gestalt switch: "When you've changed you can't go back. Nothing looks the same ever again" (*WS* 165). Consequently, as he confronts the shame and anger, the sadness and hope, embedded in these days of crisis, he takes Tom's advice that writing will further understanding and he begins to fill the pages in Tom's gift of a blank book with his account of the events of this time of renewal.

Struggling to write, "stitching" his thoughts together, getting lost in his tale, yet pressing on, "the day came when the tale was on the page" (*WS* 370). With only a few pages left to finish up, Henry again reflects on the process and product of his effort:

> Here I've taken the trouble to write it all down, and now I'm done and I don't have a dog's idea what it meant. Except that most everything I know is wrong, especially the stuff I learned from Tom. I'm going to have to go through everything I know and try to figure out where he lied and where he told he truth, I've been doing that already with the books I've found, and with the books he doesn't know I borrowed from him, and I've found out a lot of things already [*WS* 376–377].

In this self-reflexive passage, he realizes that his gestalt shift has enabled him to comprehend a great deal about the wider world in which he lives even as he also savors his more immediate knowledge of his local area and the lives of his friends and neighbors. This realization has a positive effect on his future as a writer; for as he reaches the last page, his hands stiff, his words "all big and scrawling," he closes the book and prepares to do another, without hesitation. His very next sentence, and the last line of the book, is simply this: "I'll stay right here and fill another book" (*WS* 377). The writer, Henry, chooses to work on — as does the writer Robinson.

After completing this first study of an alternative, sf, version of his familiar reality, Robinson started again and wrote another two books: but now he worked more fully in a utopian mode, first entering into a dystopian imaginary and only then exploring a eutopian one. *Gold Coast* is still about his California; but its social map is fully realized and analyzed, and rendered more darkly, than that of *The Wild Shore*. It probes the totalizing processes of power, exploitation, and cooptation in a disconcertingly "normal" dystopia, even as its slim narrative of hope unfolds in the insights and commitments, and writing, of its protagonists. In yet another breakthrough summer, young Jim realizes at the end of *The Gold Coast* (after finishing the history of Orange County, *Torn Maps*, that threads its way through *Gold Coast* itself) that the book he has written may not be big or great, but it is his. He has done his best to capture how the people of his California are struggling to face their lives in this brave new world. As with Henry, Jim is uncertain about his work: "Clearly, he'll never be able to resolve his ambivalence regarding his hometown and the generations who made it"; it is impossible, he realizes, to "separate out the good from the bad, the heroic from the tawdry" (*GC* 388). And yet, he has effectively traced the complexity of these apparent polarities in his historical account. Book done, Jim decides to get on with his life, and drives off to find Hana, in a closing act of personal, yet resoundingly social, if not yet political, hope. For Jim's history, and Robinson's novel, there is a fullness to the text that expresses both authors' realization of what is there as well as their recognition of what could be, of their acknowledgment and critique of their societies, and most of all of their stubborn sense of the transformative hope that resides in the daily lives and commitments of the people they know.

Finally, switching fully into the eutopian register in *Pacific Edge*, Robinson wrote of the post-utopian community of El Modena and its continuing challenges, now met more effectively in an alternative space that already constructs and nurtures a new social system and a new humanity. By *Pacific Edge*, however, the self-reflexive mode of writing has moved from personal memoir through local history to revolutionary/utopian anticipation. Now it is Tom — facing his own gestalt shift when he is incarcerated in a detention camp on his return to the U.S.— who, caught in the belly of the beast, sets aside his abstract idealism and chooses the form of the critical utopia. Having evolved his creative strategy in the pages of his journal, working between a meditation on utopian writing and an analysis of the historical situation, he decides to write about the hard realities about him in a way that does not settle for the terrible present but rather teases out the utopian potential from the concrete situations of the people involved. Significantly, in this final volume of the trilogy, Robinson ends not with the older man's act of writing but with young Kevin's own epiphany and his decision to re-engage with everyday life in the utopia of El Modena, as he comes alive both politically and personally, making a new start in his own summer of 2065. And yet, it is Robinson's act of writing that has brought us at last to Kevin's renewed world.

Robinson's Three Californias Trilogy offers us both a set of case studies of sf/utopian writing strategies and an accumulative intervention into the terrible realities of late 1980s American society. The volumes were a substantial work in their own right, even as they also were the maquettes that led the way to the Mars trilogy. As he threaded his way between an investigation of the politics of form and a cognitive mapping of the historical conjuncture and its political imaginaries, he took us, and his own writing, from apocalypse to dystopia and ultimately into eutopia.

II. *The Gold Coast*

> There comes into being, then, a situation in which we can say that if individual experience is authentic, then it cannot be true; and that if a scientific or cognitive model of the same content is true, then it escapes individual experience.
> — Fredric Jameson, "Cognitive Mapping" [349]

1.
   After *Wild Shore*, with its post-apocalyptic narrative and setting, and before the eutopian *Pacific Edge*, Robinson turned to the dystopian narrative of *The Gold Coast*. He did so, however, in a textual strategy that drew on the sensibility of the classical dystopia, the noir pessimism of cyberpunk, and the stubborn hope of the critical utopia. On first reading, a reader might miss the dystopian and noir qualities that lurk beneath the textual surface and find only a postmodern world that is disconcertingly "normal," even to the extent of banality — as Robinson delves into the quotidian details of individual lives in this Other California in a style that accords with elements of the work of both Philip Dick and Samuel Delany. Although it is set in the near future of the 2040s (almost a hundred years after the founding of NATO), the tone of his genre-blurring tale of planetary capitalism as it plays out in the centers of corporate power and in the struggles of everyday life is — as in the other two volumes — that of a realist coming-of-age narrative, but one helped along with the additional discourses of history and poetry. Despite its deceptively innocent, almost presentist, ambience, Robinson's text is a carefully crafted dystopian effort in cognitively mapping the cultural logic of a system dominated by the Reaganite military-industrial complex in the years just before the historic shift of 1989 when the U.S. became the infamous "victor" of the Cold War. Indeed, as the hopeful, resistant elements of the narrative unfold, this work becomes an early example of what has come to known as the critical dystopia.[4]

2.
   Caught within the simultaneously sped-up and impoverished society produced by an ever more greedy corporate-governmental system, the young Jim McPherson and his twenty-

something friends try to find meaning and satisfaction in lives reduced to the needs and pleasures of an emptily commodified moment; while Jim's father, Dennis, fights to survive in a defense industry that has no need for his skill or idealism as it neglects quality production and political principles in favor of the accumulation of profit and power. As Jim confronts the political and creative challenges in his life, and his father eventually escapes the machinations of a corporate world that cares nothing for his work, their braided stories articulate a modest utopian hope in the ability of people to learn the scope of the new capitalist world and forge independent and politically committed lives in the social and geographical gaps of a system that shows no signs of changing. In addition to the iconic details and narrative spine of this dystopian world, Robinson self-reflexively explores the discursive functions of emancipating memory (social and personal), totalizing analysis, and — as in the other books — the craft of writing as they contribute to the processes of cognitive mapping and political activism.

Certainly, this alternative world of the twenty-first century is one that realistically represents the agendas of the U.S. military, the defense industry, and the government that were hegemonic in the mid–1980s. Even though the Cold War economy still provides the primary source of profit and power, other opportunities abound in new U.S. military actions in "Arabia" (Bahrain) and Southeast Asia (Thailand, Burma) and in the collateral challenges brought about by the expansion of a Reaganesque space defense system, the rearmament of Japan, drug wars in South America, and the other "forty odd wars currently being fought" with "obsolete equipment" (11). As in the Vietnam years, it is obvious that a "guns and butter" social policy is not working. Consequently, the daily lives of those who are not securely employed within the privileged sectors of the economy are shaped by a degraded environment, minimal employment, limited housing, and the mindless experiences of commodity consumption. Robinson encapsulates this social reality in his microcosm of Orange County (which "sprang Athena-like, full blown from the forehead of Zeus Los Angeles") by reducing his gaze to the local only to expose it as a fractal image of this world of militarized corporate capitalism. In an early statement of the book's concern with the processes of history (which anticipates and negates the assertions of Francis Fukuyama), Jim ironically but astutely observes that

> Orange County is the end of history, its purest product. Civilization kept moving west for thousands of years, in a sunset tropism, until they came to the edge here on the Pacific and they couldn't go any farther. And so they stopped here and *did it*. And by that time they were in the great late surge of corporate capitalism, so that everything here is purely organized, to buy and sell, buy and sell, every little piece of us [3].

Later in his working draft of the history of the county, Jim locates the causes of this dystopian degradation in the postwar engines of the peace-time military and the consumer economy (signified by Camp Pendleton and South Coast Plaza). As he recounts, the build-up in the aftermath of World War Two transformed the area when the "war machine" dominated its geography and economy; for the "military-industrial infrastructure was built, and left in place, and it provided work for the thousands of men who returned after the war, with their new families; they came, and bought houses built by the construction industry that had been so well primed by military construction" (264). Fed by the fear of communism and the satisfaction of consumer goods, the county boomed in employment and population. Gradually, acres of orange groves were replaced by strip malls and subdivisions; and by 2020 the number of malls had increased again, with "many square miles ... roofed and air-conditioned" (322). The new malls were fed by more elevated freeways which added another layer to the ones already in place, and the synergistic outcome was an "autopia" that endlessly cycles around itself. However, with the implosion of the national economy under the pressure of endless military adventures, the quality of life collapsed: an expanding population and limited space led to shared housing and the subsequent end of the suburban dream of a private home; the shrinking domestic economy produced fewer jobs and resulted in aimless youth and frustrated middle-managers; and the ecological diversity and beauty of the region was devastated by unproductive land and water speculation that consumed the last of the state forests. Embodying the "ultimate expression of the American Dream," this "over-lit," over-built, over-consumed, post-suburban reality may seem so familiar to U.S. readers that it will not be read through the distancing lens of dystopia, but simply taken as a realistic portrayal of life at the end of the twentieth-century. Formally, however, it is fully dystopian as it delivers a future-bearing cautionary tale by way of its detailed cause and effect analysis of an extrapolated society that no longer nurtures and stimulates its people but rather constitutes, as E. M. Forster described in his 1909 dystopia, an unseen social machine intent only on its own carcinogenic growth.

This cognitive map of Orange County configures the social matrix that Jim, his father, and his friends negotiate, either to acquiesce in its seductive routines (which are as "tracked" as the electromagnetic guidance system that replaced the gasoline-powered automobile) or to reach, at least individually if not yet collectively, for an alternative existence that is shaped by the social dream of a self-determined and fulfilled humanity rather than an economy intent on reifying and commodifying everyone and everything. Coming from different perspectives, two of Jim's friends bespeak the dystopian nature of their society in their own evaluations and responses. More resilient and resistant than the others, Tashi, who eventually leaves for the outlands of Alaska, manages to live on the edge of the system by working occasionally as a "car brain" mechanic and living in a tent "on the roof of one of the big condotowers in the Newport Town Center," growing his own vegetables, using the water facilities of the partly abandoned building, and enjoying a great view of the ocean, the "blue plain to the southwest" (98). His home, as he argues, symbolizes his ecological analysis of the society and his independent response to it. In a 1980s reprise of Forster's protagonist Kuno in "The Machine Stops," he explains to Jim that the "less you are plugged into the machine, the less it controls you.... Since most jobs are part of the machine, it follows that you should lead a life with no need for money. No easy task, of course, but one can approximate, do what is possible" (98).[5] At the other extreme, Jim's ambulance-driver friend, Abe Bernard, knows he is hopelessly entangled in the cogs of the machine as he drives its freeways to rescue its wounded. However, he at least understands why he can't act more independently, for he realizes that the quotidian has consumed him. Time flies by "in a haze of undifferentiated activity," and "his shifts on the job all blur together" (118). Like Kevin Lynch's disoriented urban dweller and Fredric Jameson's under-informed late capitalist subject, Abe sees that he and others like him no longer posses the perspective of the "long-term time scale" (118). A skilled and concerned paramedic, he remembers all the crashes, the rushes to hospitals, and the agonies of patients in some remote corner of his mind; but in his waking life, "the recollection mechanism is firmly turned off" (118). Unlike Tashi who uses the counter-logic of ecology to map his cannily resistant place in the larger system, Abe has no alternative framework by which he can locate himself so that he can gain control over his life and work. With memory suppressed and daily existence divided between being exhausted on the job and stoned afterward, he can no longer triangulate his position in a system that drains him at work and leaves him empty in his down time.

In this uncannily normal dystopian world, twenty-seven-year-old Jim McPherson begins to emerge from his immediate dreamscape and find his own way. As a well-interpellated subject of his time, he passively — and, in a Lukacsian sense, typically — survives by working two part-time jobs, going to parties heightened by designer drugs, cruising the freeways with his friends, drifting in and out of sexual "alliances," guiltily relating to his parents and uncle. And yet, through some sort of interpellative slippage, he knows that he is deeply unhappy and unable to take charge over any part of his mundane life. An apparent misfit who is not exceptionally strong or skillful, he teaches a few English classes at the community college and works as a clerk in a real estate office, but the passion that offers a way to dislodge himself from the system lies in his own creative work. He clumsily tinkers at musical sampling (combining the "slow parts" of Beethoven's five late string quartets into one tape), and he tries writing poetry (which in desperation he subjects to a randomized computer program). However, he attains a higher degree of creative energy and quality in his work on the history of Orange County. When his current ally, Virginia, comments that people "never think about how things got this way," Jim realizes that he is one of the remaining few who at least tries (31). As did Henry and his gang in the first volume, Jim and his friends go on nocturnal archaeological forays, digging through concrete parking lots to uncover fragments of life before the maze of strip malls, condotowers, subdivisions, and multi-layered freeways obliterated the decentralized towns, orange groves, and desert ecology. On his own, he compiles archival evidence of the way things were — accumulating old histories, visual artifacts, and his uncle Tom's stories. Three walls of his room are covered with maps of Orange County: one from the 1930s, one from the 1990s, and a contemporary one which shows the county "gridded and overgridded"; and orange crate labels with their pastoral images of a non-existent moment of peace and plenty hang on the bathroom wall (63).

Jim, however, knows that this supposedly healthier past is "out of reach" (64). Instead of dwelling nostalgically on its loss, he eventually writes its history, eight chapters of which are scattered through Robinson's text as a meta-commentary that frames the developing counter-narrative (and thus Henry's memoir in *The Wild Shore* is taken into a new level in the history of this volume). Five of the chapters portray a lost "utopian" world of ecological beauty and relative social well-being and end with the words "all that went away" (117, 224, 242); while three others narrate the instrumentalizing lead-up to the dystopian present and end with the words "none of that ever went away" (264, 295, 323). Clearly, Jim's intent is not to escape into the static icons on the end of orange crates. Instead, his maturing historical sense gives him the necessary critical distance to gain an empowering knowledge of the nature, pace, and consequences of change, and the human causes behind it. Finally, it makes this typical dystopian misfit want "to do something" to redress the exploitation and destruction of the land that his family has lived in for four generations (28).

The opportunity for meaningful action comes to Jim by way of a conversation with his friend, Arthur Bastanchury (whose roots in the region are marked by his family name which is also that of a major thoroughfare in the county). Engaging in political work that recalls the best of the 1960s opposition, Arthur is a "dedicated antiwar activist and underground newspaper publisher" (28). On his way to leaflet a shopping mall with fliers against the draft (reimposed by the "Gingrich Act"), he talks with Jim about the "sleepwalkers" who know nothing about the political situation and do even less (40). He alludes to Jim's historical research and challenges him to do more than indulge in what he mis-reads as a nostalgic obsession. Asserting that "what's needed is something more active, some kind of *real resistance,*" he reveals to Jim that he, and people he works with, have escalated their degree of activism by sabotaging weapons manufacturers based in Orange County (42). Although irritated by Arthur's "secretive righteousness," Jim is intrigued at the possibility of direct action and agrees to join Arthur the next time he leaflets a mall. During the distribution, Jim makes it clear that he wants nothing to do with terrorism, but he is drawn to Arthur's claims for the non-violent destruction of military property (65). Replaying the strategy of underground struggle of the African National Congress or the position taken by the American Catholic Left during the Vietnam War that "some property has no right to exist," Arthur argues that there is a "big difference between terrorism and sabotage," and he assures Jim that his group uses "methods that harm plastics, programs, and various composite construction materials, without endangering people" (65).

Yet, Jim demurs, holding to his reservations about violence. After another hassle with his father and another fight with Virginia, however, he tells Arthur that he is ready "to do something ... to help" (110). With a complex sets of reasons, hovering between personal frustration and political anger, Jim realizes that this is his

> chance to make some meaning out of his life, to strike back against ... everything. Against individuals, of course — his father, Virginia, Humphrey, his students — but he doesn't think of them, not consciously. He's thinking of the evil direction his country has taken for so long, in spite of all his protests, all his votes, all his deepest beliefs. Ignoring the world's need, profiting from its misery, fomenting fear in order to sell more arms, to take over more accounts, to own more, to make more money ... it really is the American way. And so there's no choice but action, now, some real and tangible form of *resistance* [110–111].

That night, Jim and Arthur collect their weapons from Arthur's covert connection and head for the parking lot of Parnell Airspace Corporation. They fire small, laser-guided missiles into the door of the company's physical plant. On impact, the bombs release a gas "containing degrading enzymes and chemical solvents ... and all the plastic, filaboy, reinforced carbon, graphite, epoxy resin, and kevlar reached by the gas" is "reduced to dust, or screwed up in some less dramatic way" (113). Back on the street, after damaging "ninety million dollars of space weaponry," Jim is elated at having finally "*done* something" (114). Looking at Jim with the "raptor intensity" of a typically opportunistic organizer, Arthur sums up the consciousness-raising consequences of direct action: "Take that first step, perform an act of resistance of even the smallest kind, and suddenly your perception changes. Reality changes. You see it can be done" (115).

Accepting Arthur's subsequent invitations, Jim takes part in attacks on the Northrop missile complex (174–177) and Aerojet North (186), and he looks forward to a third which will target a firm that makes "orbiting nuclear reactors" (244). At the end of each action, he utters his new slogan: "Here's to resistance" (177). Although this Californian sleeper appears to have awakened, the purity of direct action begins to fade as Jim begins to wonder about the network with which Arthur is affiliated. His first opportunity to learn more comes when his friend Sandy (a skilled chemist and the best producer of illicit designer eyedrop drugs in the area) takes Jim, Arthur, and the others to a party in San Diego hosted by his dealer friends, Bob Tompkins and his partner Raymond. As one of the larger drug distributors, Bob has invited Sandy down to discuss a once-off deal for a new line of designer aphrodisiacs that would bring him extra cash (cash he needs to pay the bills for his dying father who is hospitalized in the now commonly privatized medical system). As Sandy negotiates the deal with Bob, Jim overhears Arthur talking with Raymond and discovers that Raymond is the mysterious supplier behind the sabotage. Beginning with this conversation, the apparently unrelated plots of Jim and Arthur's political action, Sandy's drug dealing, and the corporate machinations experienced by Jim's father combine in a Dickensian web to reveal the underlying scheme that pulls all the action together and expresses the logic and practice that produces the society in which they all live.

In unfolding the layers of this mega-plot, Robinson adds another dimension to the cognitive mapping already at work in the iconic register of the text. Along with the account of the formation of militarized capitalism in his twenty-first century version of Orange County — in a version of one of Joanna Russ's recommended sf narrative strategies — he brings life to his provisional map through the discrete narrative of these braided life-stories as they thread their way through the iconic tapestry.[6] In fact, his piecemeal exposure of the "master plot" of the corporate executives, government bureaucrats, and renegade drug dealers more precisely replicates the necessarily incremental nature of this didactic aesthetic. True to Jameson's argument that no one person can correlate the truth of his or her experience within the systemic reality of late capitalism, no single character in Robinson's text is able to grasp the entire scope of the scheme that drives the basic crisis of the text, but each contributes bits that help to fill in the absent paradigm of the overall social map. Sandy, Dennis, and Jim work out separate pieces of the puzzle; but the full picture is only available to the reader who is in the privileged epistemological, and political, position to accumulate that collective knowledge and see it for what it is: namely, an embodiment of the logic of greed and power that informs the entire society. Self-reflexively, it is only through connecting the apparently independent actions of Sandy, Dennis, and Jim that the reader can follow a similar trajectory of discovery in order apprehend the overarching dystopian totality. Like the face of God (or Philip K. Dick's Absolute Benefactor in his short story "Faith of Our Fathers"), it can never quite be seen in its own right.[7] It is no surprise that the person who garners the first solid information about the larger scheme is Sandy. As the friendly drug-dealer of the sort associated with the counter-culture of the 1960s rather than the organized crime purveyors of the 1980s, he is a benign character who makes an honest living in the black economy. Working on the borderline of legitimate and illegitimate markets, moving imperceptibly between business and pleasure, and yet ultimately standing by his friendship with Jim and Arthur, Sandy is in the least fixed position and therefore the one who can more readily see the traces of the master plot in his canny peripheral vision, a vision he cultivates for his very survival. While Jim only hears fragments of Arthur's conversation at the Torrey Pines party, Sandy learns first hand from Bob that Raymond has become distracted from the drug trade by "other things." He finds out that Raymond's friends in Venezuela "were killed by some remotely piloted vehicles that the Venezuelan drug police had bought from our Army" and consequently he has vowed revenge on the U.S. military and defense industry: "He couldn't really declare war on the U.S. Army, but he's done the next best thing, and declared war on the people who made the robot planes" (149). Rather than political principles, it is personal revenge, and a continued interest in "keeping an eye out for profits," that has led him to import "little missile systems ... for sabotaging military production plants" and find "people who want these things done more than he does" (150).

Back in Orange County and checking with others in the "black economy's extended family," Sandy collects more rumors about the sabotage (182–185). From a friend and client, he hears that some believe the cause behind the attacks is even more insidious than Raymond's individual vendetta, for it appears to be a campaign of "industrial sabotage" undertaken by the corporations themselves in what could be "an intercorporations war" (185). When he and Tashi have to hide their illegal aphrodisiac shipment on the coastline below Jim's father's workplace, he also senses from Bob's interest that there is a connection with Laguna Space Research. And when he finally hears what Jim and Arthur have to say, he can confirm that they are indeed involved in the attacks. Yet, rather than expose his friends to unnecessary anxiety over what at this stage is still speculation, he refrains from telling them about Raymond's role and motivation. After more snooping — in the course of which he somehow forgets the corporate dimension — he believes he knows the "shape of the whole setup," as he sees that "Jim is working with Arthur, and Arthur is working for Raymond, and that Raymond is pursuing a private vendetta for private purposes — and perhaps making a profit on the side" (330). At this point, however, it is inconvenient to tell Jim and Arthur since they are preparing an attack on LSR that will have the desirable side-effect of covering Sandy's own retrieval of the abandoned drugs. Caught in a rush between loyalty and biz, he falls into a compromised silence that betrays his own generous qualities.

Sandy believes he knows the shape of the entire scheme, but he has actually only penetrated to the level of Raymond's personal involvement and never grasps the larger corporate role in the campaign. Jim's father, however, is in a better position to learn more about the corporate side of the plot. Working within the thriving defense sector, Dennis McPherson is unfortunately on the verge of losing his job at LSR, the small defense contractor whose parent company is "one of the world's corporate giants," Argo AG/Blessman Enterprises (21). With his experience and skill in engineering, he works meticulously on his projects; and because he can "see the larger patterns, where engineering touches both invention and administration," he also represents the company in Washington, negotiating proposals with the defense establishment (10). His commitment to quality, however, has angered his immediate superior, Stuart Lemon; for it has resulted in the company losing two projects because he was unable to keep his costs competitive with other companies. Lemon (a prime type of the privileged executive with financial and cultural capital) offers one last chance to Dennis when he returns from Washington with an Air Force "superblack" order for a small robot bomber to use against the Soviets. Dennis takes on the assignment of the "Stormbee" project, but his painstaking work is frustrated when the Air Force cancels the superblack status and opens the project to public bids. When Lemon reviews Dennis's revised budget, he asserts that it is "too high" because the "system [is] over-designed" (160).

Further up the line of power, Lemon's boss — Donald Hereford, president of LSR and a vice-president in the parent company — also assesses the bid in terms of profit and not product and orders Lemon to cut the production budget by "five percent, and the management and data costs by ten" (161). Despite the trimming, the project is awarded to Parnell Aviation (ironically, the company attacked by Jim and Arthur), and Dennis is furious because he knows Parnell cannot deliver at the cost it listed (180). Still thinking in terms of his liberal idealism — believing that his work inside the corporate structure can prevent war by producing well-designed weapons systems that will permanently discourage Soviet attacks — Dennis sees his deterrence logic and his reformist belief in the rule of law crumble when the project is finally lost in a court appeal in which the judge rules "in the interests of national security" (287). LSR's lawyer explains to Dennis that they had been unknowingly immersed in an internecine competition between competing managers and that the entire affair was "part of a campaign to pull the power of weapons procurement ... back completely in the Pentagon's power" (288). With his idealism shattered, Dennis admits that LSR was a pawn "in a battle between two parts of the Air Force" and the hegemony of the Pentagon, signified in the impenetrability of its "massive concrete bunker defended against all the world" (289, 291). He returns to California knowing that his days at LSR are numbered.

If the scheme around the Stormbee program exposes a layer of corporate logic to Dennis, the shadowy outline of the deeper, and more systemically insidious, level of causation is only available to the reader who follows the accumulating action as Dennis, Lemon, and Hereford confront the consequences of the terminated Stormbee contract. Even before the cancellation, Lemon knows that LSR is in danger, for the parent company has been demanding an increase in yearly profits and threatening to sell off the company if the new goals are not met (157). Later, in conversation with Hereford, he learns that the sabotage of neighboring companies might well be the work of corporate interests who are simply using the "local group of refusniks" to do the dirty work (257). Hereford—the hegemonic leader who has the widest view, and most control, of the power struggles—opaquely notes that company security had penetrated the campaign and found out that a "very large, very professional group" is at the root of it all (257); and he then implies that AG/Blessman itself might be that primary agent. In a description of "normal" corporate sabotage, the urbane and quietly powerful Hereford explains that a "company attacks others to harm their work and eventually damage their reputation for efficiency," but then another tactical twist occurs when "it attacks itself to keep suspicion away" (258). This information is already turning "tumblers" in Lemon's mind, but another drops into place when Hereford observes that the company in question "could use the attack on itself to get rid of something potentially damaging in and of itself" (258). He then orders Lemon to pull the security guards from the plant in light of the rumors that LSR will be attacked, ostensibly to save their lives. Lemon realizes that he's been sufficiently clued in to Hereford's plot to work with its effects in disciplining LSR, but he also is canny enough not to ask further questions. Looking at the "amused crinkle" in Hereford's eyes, he sees that the corporate leader knows full well what is going on, and what is at stake. In conversation some days later, Hereford "informs" Lemon that his security people have found the person hiring the activists—ostensibly Raymond—but again he only infers that the handler above Raymond can be found within AG/Blessman's own corporate headquarters (331).

Dennis's well-intentioned concerns about the fate of LSR intersect with this deeper plot after Hereford hears about the court ruling and orders Lemon not to appeal. The corporate leader argues that it is more important to preserve LSR's standing in the military-industrial hierarchy than to protect their own integrity, or their employees or the military troops using the weapons. As Hereford explains:

> If we win this one—force the Air Force to take back their award, and win the contract ourselves—then we've got the Stormbee system, sure. But we've also embarrassed the Air Force in front of the whole industry, the whole country. And if we do that, then Stormbee is the last program we can ever expect to get from the Air Force again. Because they'll remember. They'll do their best to bankrupt us [334].

Dennis, of course, is appalled at this account of raw corporate survivalism achieved at the expense of purpose, quality, and law. Embittered, he at last begins to see the operating pattern: "The whole operation, so neat, so efficient, so *real* looking, is all a sham, a fake.... Only the power struggles of certain people in Washington are real, and those battles are based on whims, personal ambitions, personal jealousies. And those battles make the rest of the world unreal" (335). Regarding himself as nothing more than "an extra in those battles," he closes his office door and goes home.

While he has learned more about the competitive dynamics behind the system in which he works and lives, Dennis still thinks like a liberal reformist and interprets everything in terms of a repairable personal or institutional dysfunction and not as an endemic result of the systemic logic itself. Closer to the center, Lemon and especially Hereford are more fully aware of, and complicit in, the actual maneuvers. When they review the situation after Jim's botched attack on LSR (which Dennis never realizes is his son's work), they implicitly understand that the damage which could have assisted in the downsizing of LSR did not occur. Less subtle than his comfortably powerful boss, Lemon comes out and asks if they should "stimulate another attack" (366), but Hereford deflects the suggestion: "Stimulate? Or simulate? ... No. The point is, we've been warned. So now it's our responsibility to see it doesn't happen again" (366). Successful damage or not, the attack has helped Hereford's cause, and he now has sufficient reason to close down LSR in California and move its design and production line to Florida. In a flash, he orders Lemon to fire the executive team, including Dennis, and he observes that Lemon should be happy that he too wasn't sacrificed. From his personal standpoint, Dennis simply experiences this ruthless restructuring as the end to his own career. However, the strategically positioned reader gets the picture of the systemic motive behind the entire set of actions. Simply put, Argo AG/Blessman Enterprises needs not only to survive but to triumph; and this economic and political "necessity" has driven the entire operation, setting in motion a series of events that brought untold damage to people inside the corporation and at large, only to guarantee that costs could be cut, power preserved, and position gained in the center of power.

3.

As Sandy, Dennis, and the corporate executives fix the dystopian social coordinates for the readerly eye, the counter-narrative line of Jim's search for meaning and purpose beyond his "hollow" and "fashionable" life offers at least a proto-political trajectory through which the system can begin to be critiqued, if not yet overturned and transformed (254). Even though the sabotage project has jolted him out of his malaise, Jim is further challenged through his interactions with those closest to him: his friends, his new lover Hana, and his father. When Sandy takes him along with Angela and Humphrey to Europe to escape the pressure of the interrupted smuggling deal — as with the travels undertaken by Henry and Steve in *The Wild Shore*—Jim finds it is an opportunity to see himself and his Orange County home against a broader canvas (225–38). After Humphrey's choice takes them to the French Disneyland and Sandy and Angela opt for Moscow, Jim suggests a visit to the historical sites of Cairo and Crete, thereby dipping back into the racially contested roots of Western reality. On a solitary walk, he gets lost in Cairo's streets and is overwhelmed by the poverty he encounters. Recalling Athol Fugard's play, *People Are Living Here*, he develops his own self-reflexive take on a "real world" that his encapsulated life in Orange County has not allowed. In Crete, he finds another comparative viewpoint on the history of Orange County as he looks critically back on it in terms of the strikingly different history of the quite similar landscape of this Mediterranean island. When he returns home, he realizes that the trip has further dislodged his sense of self and society, and he is filled with an increasing personal and political feeling of unease. With his working grasp of reality breaking down, he anxiously thinks about his situation in terms of the freeway mechanism that surrounds and shapes his meager life: "It's as if somewhere the program and the magnetic field keeping him on his particular track have been disarranged, fallen into some awful loop that keeps repeating over and over" (242).

Aware that he is developing a vertiginous perspective that will disruptively fuse his static existence with an expanding awareness of the history and social logic of his world, Jim experiences another epiphanic change when he meets and falls in love with Hana Steentoft, the art teacher in the classroom next to his at the community college. An artist and the most feminist and utopian character in the book, Hana has opted out of the party scene and committed herself to a form of art that rejects the fading fashion of postmodernism. Just as she challenges her "sleepwalking" students, she directs her utopian critique at Jim and urges him to take his creative work more seriously so as to focus his vision on "the open space left by the death of postmodernism" to "shape what comes next" (190). Accepting the challenge offered by Hana's more considered analysis, Jim begins to think again about how he can "make a difference" and help to change America: somehow — through the matrix of his writing, his resistance work, his teaching — he hopes to overcome the gap "between his desires and his achievements" (191). Yet, he hardly changes overnight; and in his waning foolishness he also learns negatively from Hana. When he brings her to one of Sandy's parties and his previous ally Virginia snubs her for not being suitably cool for their scene, he thinks Hana is wise and strong, and above such cultural pressures, and so he is shocked when he finds she has been deeply hurt by Virginia's response.

Embarrassed by his ignorance, Jim gains a better understanding of the power of social construction and interpellation, not at the level of theory but in the actual suffering of a loved one. He sees that

> no one can escape. You can pretend not to care about the image, but that's as far as the culture will let you get. Inside you have to feel it; you can fight it, but it'll always be there, the contemptuous dismissal of you by the Virginia Novellos of the world.... No doubt Hana saw that look and was perfectly aware of it, all the rest of the evening. And she did look different from the rest of the women there.... And now he had implied that she was so far out of the norm that she wouldn't have the common human response, wouldn't even notice, wouldn't even care [285].

Yet, even with this insight, Jim falters again when he is discovered by Hana while talking and holding hands with Virginia outside of a local restaurant. Guiltily he pulls his hand away, but the damage is done. Hana once more sees Jim caught in the web of a shallow social scene (see 310). In response, she turns away in anger and refuses to see or talk to him.

With Hana's rejection feeding his growing anxiety, Jim anticipates the upcoming raid on LSR with Arthur. Fearful that they may inadvertently hurt someone — as another sabotage group did in a raid in Silicon Valley — Jim nevertheless seizes the chance to keep acting, for he sees it as a way to forestall his impending psychic collapse. Before the attack, he visits his parents and predictably gets into yet another fight with his father. This time he crosses an emotional and political line when he accuses Dennis of being a maker of bombs and a purveyor of the very war mentality he is trying to stop. Dennis — who has just learned that his program was rejected — is already vulnerable and tries to explain his well-intentioned deterrence theory to Jim; but Jim will not listen and continues his rant. However, when Dennis plaintively cries out that the rejected Stormbee project was a "good" program, Jim hears the "fearful strain" in his father's voice, and he begins to feel Dennis's frustration and pain as his known world explodes. Consequently, Jim's anger momentarily "drains out of him, and he's amazed, even frightened, at what he has been saying" (345). Having now hurt his father as well as Hana, his personal and political anxiety grows, and he leaves the house in even more turmoil.

Tense and hyperventilating, Jim redirects his energy on the defense industry, seeing it as the prime cause of evil in the society — as a "malignancy making money in the service of death" (346). He launches into the night's action, but he also continues to think about his father's idealistic argument as he arranges to meet Arthur after picking up the missiles. Still ambivalent when he meets the four men who deliver the weaponry, Jim panics as a police cruiser sweeps into the parking lot. He runs, and two of the men chase him, perhaps believing he set up the arrest. Finding his car and telling the approaching policemen that the men are trying to steal it, he drives off, only to see Arthur standing with the other two men as the police pull up. Jim's diversion lets him get away, but he also knows Arthur will think he exposed the rest of the group to arrest. Having hurt yet another person, he begins his night of rage against the social machine, driving madly in a car filled with "six boxes of felony-level weaponry" (352). Dazed and confused, he feels he has "betrayed everyone he knows, in one way or another," but his guilt and fear give way to the secular fury that has brought him to this point. Sobbing and cursing, he cries to himself: "You know — you know — what should — be done — and you — can't — *do it*" (352).

Hesitation gone, he drives like a desolation angel to South Coast Plaza (where Virginia works) and fires a "Harris Mosquito missile with its Styx-90 payload" at the administrative headquarters of the mall (352). He sends another missile into the plate glass window of the First American Title Insurance and Real Estate offices (where he works with his friend Humphrey); and he fires another into the offices of the Orange County Board of Supervisors, the "crowd that has systematically helped real estate developers to cut OC up, in over a hundred years of mismanagement and graft" (353). Laughing manically, he strikes out at a Fluffy Donuts shop, another real estate office, a military microchip factory, and finally destroys the signs in the parking lot at LSR (353). Aware now that he "can't make OC go away, not with his idiot vandalism, not even by going crazy," he drives home, "still mindless with rage and disgust" (353). He trashes his apartment, destroys his music, kicks his books across the room, tears up his manuscripts, smashes his cheap video system, and pulls down his maps. Hearing a car approach, he runs out of the house and down the street. Along the way, he smashes more shop windows, but realizing that he is exposed as a rare pedestrian in autopia he jumps on a bus to Fashion Island. Still fuming, he picks up stones from a bonsai garden and prepares to throw them through the display windows of Bullock's and I. Magnin's. As he raises his arm, he is grabbed from behind and turns to see Tashi, who has fortuitously appeared like a Zen guardian angel.

Having just broken up with his long-time ally, Tashi is going through his own agonies, and when he takes Jim back to the tent to rest he suggests that they head off to the mountains. After a symbolic three days in the wilderness, they return to Orange County, refreshed in body and spirit. Tashi prepares to leave for Alaska; while Jim, who has calmed down and once again broadened his perspective, prepares to face the aftermath of his rampage. Back in his apartment, he gathers the torn maps and tapes them together in a synecdotal gesture of what he hopes to do with the shattered remnants of his own life. He picks up the scattered pages of poetry and history and looks at them with fresh eyes. With his apartment back in a strange new order, he visits home only to find his mother's note informing him that Dennis had been fired and that they have gone north to visit their small parcel of land near Eureka (in a geographic displacement that replicates the utopian trope found in many of the complementary dystopian films and fictions, from Ridley Scott's *Blade Runner* and Terry Gilliam's *Brazil* to Octavia E. Butler's *Parable of the Sower*). Feeling even more ambivalent about his actions against his father and LSR, he nevertheless resolves to "start up in a new way" (377). Visiting Angela, he learns that Sandy will survive the failure of the smuggling caper — escaping the wrath of his partners and the police — and that Arthur has disappeared. Again, he is uncertain, this time about Arthur and their actions. He respects Arthur's political commitment, but he is no longer sure that direct action is the way for him, even though he still agrees that "something has to be done, [that] there are forces in the country that have to be resisted" (380). Acknowledging for the first time that both Arthur and his father are, from their own standpoints, "right" in their views and actions, he realizes that neither his friend's participation in a singular social movement nor his father's reformism are right for him. He therefore decides that it is time he found his "own way, somewhere between or outside them — find some way that cannot be co-opted into the great war machine, some way that will actually help to change the thinking of America" (380).

With this resolution, Jim's activist turn against society that began with his foray into direct action reaches a new level of maturity and focus. Knowing that the system will be around for years to come, he decides that he can most effectively challenge its hegemonic lock by drawing on his particular skills and passions. On a personal level, he realizes that he needs to make amends with those he has hurt in his raging identity crisis, and he vows to reach out to his father and to Hana, but also to the other women he has scorned, Sheila and Virginia, and to his friends, Humphrey and Arthur, whose lives were damaged by his night of destruction. He plans as well to spend more time with his uncle Tom so that he can learn from his experience and wisdom. On a political level, he seizes on his writing as the basis for his real work. He has already realized that poetry, and the postmodern culture from which it stems, is not for him; and he concludes that it is "deliberately ignorant, concerned only with surfaces, with the look, the great California image ... the tired end of postmodernism, which makes utterly useless all his culturevulturing, because for postmodernism there is no past" (259).

Setting postmodern modalities aside, he thinks of the two writers most important to him, Albert Camus and Athol Fugard, and remembers that "both said that it was one's job to be a *witness* to one's times" (259). Jim, however, is humbled as he recalls the conditions under which both men wrote, for the "subjugation of Algeria" and "apartheid in South Africa" seem far more substantial than the situation in Orange County, at the geographical and historical edge of "the richest country of all time" (260). And yet, this is the place in which he can be a valid witness; and so he decides that his particular contribution will take the form of a history of Orange County, written in the form of a "collection of prose meditations" that follows in the poetic sprit of William Carlos Williams's *In the American Grain* (261). "How did it get this way" will be his question. His book will be his answer. If he cannot escape this deceptive dystopia, he can at least begin to expose it by giving life to the estranging and enlightening perspective of the long view of history. The painful steps of the past weeks have brought Jim to this realization of his vocation, and he returns to his apartment to begin his new life. After writing late into the night and falling into a sleep filled with wild dreams of recent events, he wakes up and looks over his finished pages. Happy with the new work, he decides to entitle the project *Torn Maps*. He packs up the finished copy, jumps in his car, and drives off to show it to Hana. The book ends in the midst of the journey, as he turns onto the offramp at Hana's exit.

4.

As Jim leaves the freeway, and re-engages with his writing and his life, the reader closes the book and is, hopefully, left with a bit more insight on the relationship between the structural coordinates of this extrapolated version of contemporary capitalism and the individual struggles of everyday life. Although Robinson's text begins as a disconcertingly familiar account of late-suburban alienation (replete with characters who are trying to make some sense of it all), it morphs into something else entirely as the details of the alternative world and the entwined narratives shatter the surface "normality" to reveal the anti-utopian logic of an economic and political system that privileges profit and power rather than a "healthy" and "caring" social alternative (see "Interview" 77). Bit by bit, from multiple points of view, the nature of this tightly sutured though apparently open society becomes increasingly clear, partially to some of the characters and as holistically as possible to the reader.[8] Even though elements traditionally associated with dystopias are missing (the classical array of authority figures, invasive surveillance, pervasive control, and outright terror; or the sf ambience of apocalyptic breakdowns or noir underworlds), *The Gold Coast* nevertheless offers its readers a dystopian view of the "friendly terror" of their own existence by fast-forwarding that reality just enough to expose both the dangers of the systemic logic that has produced the world in which they live and the limitations of the 1980s political tendencies of singular social movements and liberal reformism.

While the hegemonic narrative is dominated by the seemingly peripheral figures of Hereford and Lemon (as catachrestic personifications of the military-industrial complex), an open-ended counter-narrative of alienation giving way to critical awareness develops through the account of several characters whose lives are dispersed across the iconic tapestry of this alternative California. Foremost of course, Jim's crisis and coming-of-age offers the most direct instance of the dystopian sleepwalker who turns against the system; and here — as in the previous volume but now more intensively — Robinson engages in an acute intervention as he focuses on the challenges taken up by a straight white male protagonist who, in varying degrees of success, acts against his privileged subject position as he tries to forge a new form of personal and political existence.[9] Jim's story, however, is accompanied by several others that offer additional utopian "streaks" that survive in tactical spaces at the textual margins.[10] The relocations of Dennis and Lucy to Eureka and Tashi to Alaska point to peripheral enclaves that — even as they are still within the totality of planetary capital — could germinate a radical knowledge of, and perhaps opposition to, the cancerous system that the corporate couple and marginal eco-citizen have left behind. In another shadowy corner, Hanna (not unlike the political position expressed by Nili in Marge Piercy's *He, She and It*) also occupies a space at the margins of both the social mainstream and the postmodern opposition, even as she courageously and painfully reengages with everyday life on a regular basis.[11] Despite these counter-moves, however, the system is not seriously breached, much less changed. Instead of spaces or narratives of opposition, the reader encounters a set of proto-political moves that play out in the small changes of the daily lives of a few individuals who have torn open segments of the sutured reality that has produced and enclosed them. Not yet organized in a collective manner — and certainly not yet militant — Jim, Dennis, Lucy, Tashi, Hana, and even Arthur nevertheless begin the process of taking a second, more critical, look at their lives and their society.

Of course, the counter-narrative *in* the text reprises the counter-production *of* the text itself. Venturing out in the bleak years of the late 1980s, Robinson here takes his second step in his long term project of exploring the connections between sf and cognitive mapping, between creative fiction and the political imagination. In his third volume in this series, the eutopian *Pacific Edge*, and in work such as his Mars trilogy and *Antarctica*, he moves on to explorations of emerging modes of overt political opposition and new maps of liberated space; but in *The Gold Coast* he takes the interim step of searching for Utopia by way of an innovative critical dystopian text, with its militant pessimism that turns the wisdom of history and the commitment of daily struggle against the anti-utopian fear and loathing of radical political interrogation and transformation. As he later put it, he gave shape to a process of working within the insistent and troubled density of history itself, as it stands "between us and any decent society" ("Interview" 77). Like a Tantric Buddhism that reaches toward Nirvana precisely through the body that entraps the seeker, Robinson's dystopian narrative finds its own way to Utopia in stories of individuals who are developing new structures of feeling that will lead toward the collective movement needed for the political engagement and transformation that Utopia, and his own subsequent work, provisionally names.

III. *Pacific Edge*

1. Baseball, Memory, Utopia

> "Sorry about that, Kev," he said rapidly, "but you know I figured you'd want me to give it a try" [321].

The 1994 World Cup soccer final ended when Italy's Roberto Baggio, the 1993 Player of the Year, missed the net in the fourth round of penalty kicks that settled the scoreless, one hundred and twenty minute match against Brazil. After two years of qualifying play, six months of training, and a month of elimination rounds, the determination of the title came down to one Italian player against one Brazilian goalie. Time congealed into a critical moment. Baggio's entire season coalesced into one mis-timed downward arc that sent the ball sailing over the net. At that point, the extended holiday that is the World Cup ended, Brazilian fans around the globe began a carnival of celebration, and players started talking about "next time." For that one pointed moment, however, reality settled down to one man, one kick.

In the closing pages of Robinson's eutopian *Pacific Edge*, the protagonist Kevin Claiborne comes to his last time at bat for the El Modena softball season with a perfect hitting streak. In the bottom of the last inning, with two outs, his team, the Lobos, are down one run, with two on base. As he steps into the batter's box, "the world slips away" (320). The political and personal crises that have engaged Kevin all summer are forgotten, and time and activity spiral down to this instant of being in control, as Robinson puts it, "in the batter's pure moment of being, of grace" (320). In the next instant, Kevin hits a line drive to the outfield and slowly runs to first base as he watches the ball sail past his friend Hank, who is playing center field for the Tigers. In an "impossible" move, the forty-six-year-old Hank sprints, stretches, and catches the ball in a backhand stab. Confused and self-conscious, Kevin stops and laughs, distracted by the outcome. The game is over, the season is over, the hitting streak is broken. The teams, fellow townspeople and friends, congratulate each other and continue with their day-long party. The moment is over. Everyday life in Utopia goes on.

Baseball moments and metaphors run throughout this 1990 account of the third Orange County in Robinson's trilogy. The intense micro-universe of the game provides one of several iconic contexts for this multi-layered exploration of the dominant structures and practices of the new global order as well as the oppositional possibilities for social critique and utopian alternatives. For me at least, the baseball passages offer an oblique approach to two issues that Robinson closing text in the series text provokes: the opportunities and limitations of both personal and political control, and the social dynamics and political power of ritual.

Part of my readerly engagement stemmed from Robinson's evocation of boyhood delights and frustrations in long summers filled by seemingly endless baseball games. The unabashed, unfashionable, wholesomeness of his narrative contrasted sharply with that other, darker, intertext of pleasure and discomfort I associate with the more numerous cyberpunk sf written by men in the 1980s. In this light, *Pacific Edge* is a contemporary instance of a non-cyberpunk, engaged, male sf writer who is open to feminist sensibilities and issues and willing as well to explore utopian proclivities along with the tracing of the ubiquitous dystopian dimensions of the present that cyberpunk relishes. Unlike so many of the male cyberpunk writers who boldly and creatively faced the bleakness of their present moment while nevertheless reasserting a masculinity reinforced by the figure of their favored noir loner hero, Robinson's male characters (and here we can also bear in mind Henry and Jim from the first volumes in the trilogy) may in the short run be uneasy with themselves, but overall they are not unwilling to be a different sort of man, open emotionally and ethically to diversity and equality and, indeed, to the ambiguities of intersubjective identities and relations. As can be seen in his other work in this trilogy and beyond, Robinson's fictions steadily offer social frameworks that explore "a model of self-other relations that is ... based on the need for mutual recognition" of equal subjects (Franko, "Working the 'In-Between'" 193).

As he does in greater scale in the Mars trilogy, in this closing volume of his Three Californias Trilogy Robinson reasserts the critical utopian refusal to regard Utopia as an end in itself, seeing it instead as the very "road of history ... something we are working within, step by step" in a process that never ends ("Interview" 77). Moving beyond the apocalyptic and dystopian modes of *The Wild Shore* and *The Gold Coast*, in *Pacific Edge* he provides a eutopian framework from which he can, once again, offer us yet another layer of his holistic exploration of society and agency. He gives us yet another account of the globalizing economy and production and multiplex class struggle, but now he traces a more developed collective engagement that counters both planetary capitalism and liberal reformism by way of a fully eutopian (yet still difference-based) social struggle that connects the global system with local government and culture. As in the other volumes, Robinson's speculative fiction reaches fully into the realm of the personal even as it does the political. As Carol Franko has demonstrated, he opens up to a utopian vision that embraces the personal and social opportunities offered by "the alterity of the self and the subjectivity of the other" ("Working the 'In-Between'" 191).

While all the plot threads of *Pacific Edge* engage with this multi-layered exploration, from the personal to the public and back again, the baseball scenes provide a quick take that grounds the book's utopian psychology as it conjures up readerly memories. In El Modena's softball league, the friendly mixed-gender teams are already a significant step beyond the downside of my own experience with baseball: my childhood efforts included the pleasures of teamwork and achievement (terrible player though I was), but the interaction on the field also served as a disciplinary rite of male control by way of a discourse of compulsory heterosexuality (bad or un-hustling players were deemed fags and relegated to the margins of the group, most often in right field). Although Robinson's focus on the climactic moment of Kevin at the bat brings back the worst of these memories about performance, the sequence of events from the broken hitting streak to Kevin's later cleansing laughter as he relinquishes his need to keep a tight and singular control on his life transcends baseball as I knew it and turns it into a hopeful social drama. Beyond that, the celebration of the communal ritual of the game in this postmasculinist society revived the more fulfilling moments of group and individual joy that my own hours of summer play provided — and offered an anticipatory vision of the socially effective force of ritual as it plays out at the very end of the story. In this contradiction between the intersubjective, communal ritual of baseball and its anxious, performative dynamics of masculine power, Robinson gets at the utopian and dystopian sides of the experience of growing up male in postwar U.S. culture even as he sets the stage for the consideration of the role of the utopian impulse in the entire fabric of the social. In the structure of feeling that accumulates around the game, there is an ambience of frustration and freedom that casts a finer light on the entire narrative, thereby encouraging an openness to what else is in store for the reader/visitor in this utopia.

While the exploration of the limits and possibilities of intersubjective social relations is a powerful dimension of this closing text of the trilogy — as indeed they were in the first two — I find three other aspects that can be teased out of this narrative as important complements to Robinson's treatment of Utopia. One of these is the way the narrative strategies of the novel reconsider the literary utopian tradition itself in order to, once again, evoke a utopian impulse through the experience of a text that critically explores its own limits and possibilities as much as the present world situation. Another, building on that formal self-reflexivity, addresses the way the novel speculates on the relationship between global and local levels of analysis, critique, and action, especially as this operates through the ties between this volume's Tom Barnard story and that of his grandson, Kevin. Finally, both of these areas of exploration — the textual and the political — lead into a closing emphasis on the importance of political work in cultural spheres (in addition to action in the realm of the state and the economy) that returns to my opening questions of control and ritual and then broadens out to consider the possibilities for new spaces of opposition and change on the world map.

2. Writing Utopia

"Kevin, did it ever occur to you that there are more important things than softball?" [6].

There are, of course, more terrible conflicts in *Pacific Edge* than those found on the baseball diamond. Tom Barnard's internment and his epiphanic moment of commitment to working with a new Green Party for the long revolution against corporate hegemony, Kevin's campaign with his friends and allies to stop the exploitation of Rattlesnake Hill through Alfredo's misplaced desire for profit and power (inflected by a transnational corporate drive to restore its lost hegemony by buying out local entrepreneurs, and the sell-out of a compromised Green Party leadership), Tom's multi-phased life and final moments of drowning, and Kevin's failed love affair with Ramona (as one of several harsh losses of the summer): each and all of these contribute to the personal/political mix that constitutes the novel. However, as other critical utopian writers have done, Robinson develops his narrative in such a way that the complexities of history rather than the strict imposition of an abstract personal or public agenda (literary or political) engage the novel itself in the ongoing challenge of struggle and change. Individual control gives way to social process, and linear solutions give way to ambiguous but hopeful moments and trajectories imbued with utopian energies.

It is no accident, then, that the textual strategies of Robinson's eutopia continue the critical utopias of the 1970s. To be sure, Robinson invokes H. G. Wells' *A Modern Utopia* along with Delany and Le Guin, but the overall impact of the book is certainly in the spirit of the rethinking of the utopian impulse that has been in play for the past two or more decades. Although *Pacific Edge* is a text of its own time, it shares with the earlier critical utopias a politically informed willingness to meditate upon its own textual limitations and opportunities, to examine both the utopian society and the social situation from which it grew, to highlight the activism required for moving out of the dystopian present and into the utopian future, and finally to be unafraid of taking a hard look at the continuing imperfections and antagonisms in that new and open-ended version of the social.

Whereas Lyman Tower Sargent argues that critical utopias are no longer being written, I would approach the question a bit differently (see Sargent 10). I'd argue that the critical utopias — as formal expressions of a structure of feeling of their time — broke with the older modernist sense of Utopia as object, agenda or blueprint, and opted instead for an emphasis on Utopia as process or method. In doing so, they utterly changed the intertextual web of utopian writing. While to one degree or another embracing the anti-essentialist, anti-foundationalist stance now familiar in postmodernism, yet also rejecting its often attendant cynicism, the critical utopias of the 1970s launched a diverse attack on anti-utopian ideologies — those that rejected serious utopian efforts as unnecessary or unrealistic while substituting their own "utopias" (which circulated around claims for the end of ideology or history, or around hypostatized versions of the prevailing affirmative culture). Out of these challenges, the critical utopias offered narratives of better places which were simultaneously exposed to critical scrutiny lest they too slipped into the quicksand of common sense. After the historical moment of that critical intervention—and indeed intensified with the further degradation of social decency and responsibility in the 1980s—any utopian writer aware of the previous fictional works and sensitive to their negotiation of post-modern realities would be hard pressed *not* to write a literary utopia that was somehow "critical," not only of its own textual moves but also of what had come before, what was presently occurring, and even of what might next happen. Certainly, the *format* of the 1970s utopias was specific to the cultural moment, but their epistemological and formal strategies are alive and well in Robinson's work—in *Pacific Edge* but also in his Mars trilogy—as they are in the related mode of critical *dystopias* such as Piercy's *He, She, and It* or Butler's *The Parable of the Sower*.

The most direct attention to textual strategies in *Pacific Edge* occurs in the italicized journal entries that open chapters two through eleven. These brief commentaries—which we learn in chapter eleven are written by a younger Tom Barnard, now working as both the young man *and* the older man in this third volume—focus on the act of writing a literary utopia and the relationship of that effort to social revolution. Moving from personal musings to a complex reassessment of the current historical conjuncture, Tom charts his development from his youthful, isolated, and insulated, personal project to his later, committed integration of his roles of writer and lawyer as he aligns with the new Green Party to break the power of the transnational corporations. As did the writers of critical utopias, Tom does not abandon the utopian impulse: instead, he refunctions it as he ultimately decides that he will "not just write a utopia, but fight for it in the real world" (299).[12]

The first journal passage occurs in early March of 2012, fifty-three years before the setting of Kevin's story in the El Modena of 2065. Tom's wife and Kevin's grandmother, Pam, is doing environmental research in Switzerland, and Tom has taken the opportunity to quit his job as a lawyer in order to care for their daughter and write a utopian novel. Frustrated that his "real work" (as a public defender and as a lawyer for the shrinking Socialist Party) had accomplished little, he is taking the time to change the world in his own mind, to write a utopia as a way to clarify his beliefs and desires. However, even though he delights in the "pocket utopia" of Switzerland, he cannot avoid the strife of a world in economic and political crisis. As refugees pour across the Swiss border, the government responds in cool instrumental rationality with Stranger Control Laws that restrict residency, and for Tom and his family this results in the increasing pressure to leave the country. Immediately, Tom begins his rethinking of Utopia in the context of historical conflict as he concludes that "there's no such thing as a pocket utopia," no "little island of calm in a maddened world" (36).

Tom opens his next entry a month later with further thoughts on the impossibility of pocket utopias: islands of luxury exist in a world beset by misery, war, and hunger; but this is a schizoid, not a utopian, response. Swiss officials are making it very clear that Tom and his daughter Liddy must leave, and that Pam must follow once her fellowship ends. Crisis fills the pages in public and personal dimensions: the financial collapse of the Southern nations, the increase in civil wars, and the advance of environmental destruction are, of course, more enormous than the displacement the family will face, but the fear and dislocation experienced at the personal level are intense and frightening. Utopian hopes are fading on all fronts.

By entry three, Tom achieves a breakthrough in his understanding of Utopia. In an intertextual discussion of the narrator's journal in Samuel Delany's *Einstein Intersection*, he begins to come to grips with the relationship between utopian space, with its synchronic tendency to linger on already articulated alternatives, and historical disequilibrium, which diachronically displaces the product of the detached utopian imagination. The privileges of their family life in Switzerland and the luxury of utopian speculation tucked into the realms of the mind give way to the pain of personal disruption and anger at the world crisis. In his disillusionment, Tom reflects on the cheap escape from historical realities that singular utopias offer. He observes that by way of making a "clean cut, fresh start," utopian writing that simply breaks *from* the present falls into the same category of inauthentic existence as the geographical pocket utopia which severs itself from the rest of the world (as in the "utopias" Tom found in Switzerland or in his boyhood home in Orange County): "They don't speak to us trapped in this world as we are, we look at them the same way we look at the pretty inside of a paperweight, snow drifting down, so what?" (95). Consequently, Tom begins his work of re-definition. As he puts it, "we have to deal with history as it stands, no freer than a wedge in a crack" and from within that tenuous, critical space, Utopia can be refunctioned (95).[13] In this framework, Utopia is no longer

> the perfect end-product of our wishes, define it so and it deserves the scorn of those who sneer when they hear the word. No. Utopia is the process of making a better world, the name for one path history can take, a dynamic, tumultuous, agonizing process, with no end. Struggle forever. Compare it to the present course of history. If you can [95].

By entry four, the departure date for Tom and Liddy draws near, with Pam to follow in three to six months. As part of his review of the utopian genre, Tom has been reading Wells' *A Modern Utopia*, in which chapters of fiction alternate with essays that discuss "the political and economic problems we need to solve" (120–121). Unfortunately, the book is not in local libraries, and Pam very practically suggests that this implies some sort of formal failure on the part of the book to engage an ongoing readership. So Tom gives up on the essay genres, even though he is now clearly thinking about how to integrate current analysis and critique with the portrayal of a radical alternative.

Tom taps in his next entry while he is in flight back to the States. Still gestating his book, he is now thinking of utopian processes as an integral part of the wider spectrum of activist strategies: "Invent the history leading out of this world (please) into the world of the book" (147). He begins to connect the present and future social spaces by way of the immanent political action of forging the new society out of the shell of the old. The specific components of this process are also taking shape: some sort of collective agent and some set of strategies for structural change, which for Tom are still based in legal, governmental maneuvers. He speculates about remaking the law of the land, although his version still grows out of his own privileged position: "Say a whole class of Harvard Law School, class of '12 goes out to fill posts of all kinds, government, World Bank, IMF, Pentagon. Save the twenty-first century" (147). The only barrier to moving ahead with such a plan, Tom observes, is "inertia, ideology. Lack of imagination!" (147). And so, the power of utopian imagination becomes one of the material forces of his revolutionary project: he writes of history being redirected by a popular book (an Edward Bellamy reference?) and paraphrases Herbert Marcuse's observation that "one of the worst signs of our danger is we can't imagine the route from here to utopia" (148). He also begins to accept that what is actually empowering in the utopian impulse is the activity itself and not the idealized model: "Take the first step and you're there. Process, dynamism, the way is the life" (148). The end *is* the means.

At the point of landing at Dulles airport, Tom has abandoned the strategy of the traditional textual utopia and embraced a critical utopian attitude. On arrival, however, the situation worsens. Tipped off by the Swiss government, U.S. officials detain Tom as a suspected subversive, and when his mandatory physical indicates (falsely, purposefully) that he is HIV positive, he is held in an internment camp in Virginia. With Liddy sent off to grandparents and Pam in Switzerland, Tom waits out his incarceration in anger and frustration. History is pressing: "The problem of an adequate history bothers me still. I mean not my personal troubles, but the depression, the wars, the AIDS epidemic. (Fear). Every day everything is a little worse" (181). His own utopian effort, with its "cool detachment" rankles:

> Sometimes I read what I've written sick with anger, for them it's all too easy. Oh to really be that narrator, to sit back and write with cool ironic detachment about individual characters and their little lives because those lives really mattered. Utopia is when our lives matter [181].

In response, Tom begins to sketch out two possible scenarios — one with an Orange Country setting and one on Mars. Of course, the self-reflexive commentary at this point is immediate since Tom's locales are those of Robinson's own work: the California novels, of which *Pacific Edge* is the last and eutopian volume, and the Mars trilogy.

The next two entries written in the Virginia camp mark the collapse of Tom's naive hopes in his unexamined project. In both contributions, he faces up to the terror of the global order. While his appeal for release continues, he observes the suffering of those who are infected and dying in the camp, and he notes that the world is "getting bigger as it falls apart" (216). He makes no mention of Utopia. Tom's ninth entry is a crucial one: one in which, like a Prospero in reverse, he abandons his book, not to leave the world but to enter it. He comments: "All day I would sit there staring at the page, staring into the blank between my world and the world in my book. Until my hand would shake. Looking around me, looking at what my country was capable of when it was afraid. Seeing the headlines in the newspapers scattered around. Seeing my companions and the state they were in" (275). He responds by tearing up his notebooks: "No more utopia for me" (275). Left without vision or project, he is lost in the gap, the abyss, between what is and what could be, no longer in individual control. And then — as *Wild Shore*'s Tom Barnard did to Henry, and *Gold Coast*'s Tom did to Jim — history drives in its wedge as one of his dorm mates gives him a ballpoint and a lab notebook and asks him to start writing again: "You've got to tell what happens here! If you don't tell it, then who will? You got to, man" (276). From that instant, Tom's new project, now social rather than individual, begins. Combining what the reader can see as Henry's mode of memoir with Jim's history, and now reaching toward a full eutopian approach, he sets out to record the story of those in the camp, describing their suffering and their courage, but in so doing also tracking how Utopia emerges from these concrete dynamics of everyday life, and not from some set of abstract goals. He writes: "There is a place where people on the edge of death make jokes, they help each other, they share what they have, they endure. In this hell they make their own 'utopia'" (276).[14]

In the final entry, Tom has been released, now wiser and angrier. His first instinct is to pull his family together and to survive. However, in discussing the world crisis with his lawyer, who turns out to be a member of the newly formed Green Party, he is encouraged to join in the social revolution, and to put his utopian hopes into action. The lawyer asks him to look beyond privileged escape and to help the entire society and the world to endure. He challenges him to join others in Washington, D.C., and to help recast the legal structure, "the economic laws, the environmental laws, the relationship between local and global, the laws of property" (299). Tom sees there's plenty for him to do: "It didn't take all that much to convince me, really. Because I have to do something. Not just write a utopia, but fight for it in the real world — I have to" (299).

In this last entry, which expresses the choice of an "emerging utopia" over an "aristocrats' refuge," Tom's reorientation becomes a self-reflexive lesson in the text's utopian strategy (300). Instead of claiming a central, controlling role in his own singular narrative, Tom chooses to be part of a movement bigger than himself as he commits to the long revolution, to still be active but now in a collective effort attuned to the material dynamics of the process.[15] With such a reflection on utopian process breaking into the text on a regular basis, the narrative that results from the commitment made by Tom and others resonates with a sense of provisionality and movement, but not of absolute or abstract answers or agendas. In its completion, the linear account of Tom's experience in consciousness-raising serves as a device that informs the entire text. The journal entries thus foreground an open-ended utopian logic that insists on engagement with the present situation and careful attention to the manner in which historical struggles occur.[16]

3. The Global and the Local

"The world plays hardball, Claiborne" [41].

Pacific Edge's utopian interventions, of course, are not limited to its italicized sections. Again like the critical utopias, a feedback loop continues in the primary story by way of a dual narrative: expressed, on one hand, in the exposition of the contest between the present order of exploitation and suffering and the revolutionary challenge to the world system; and, on the other, in the portrayal of the utopian society as itself an imperfect, yet better existence. Drawing the two lines of conflict together are the synchronic and diachronic relationships of the global and local dimensions of the social: for the long term global revolution must occur before the local utopia of El Modena can flourish; yet, even in 2065, global and local oppositional practices must continue to work together if the utopian project is to remain viable.

Robinson's account of the process of global transformation begins with Tom's commitment to the movement led by the Green Party. In rethinking what needs to be done to end local injustice — based on his experiences with xenophobia and forced emigration in Switzerland, and repression and internment in Virginia — Tom realizes that singular efforts (as micropolitics or pocket utopias) are not sufficient. He sees that a larger scale of change is required, one that works through reciprocating relationships between the local and global. Focused by the organizational leadership of the Green Party and informed by a macro-analysis of the economic system, Tom and his co-conspirators embark on a two-generation, collective project. Also in anticipation of his narrative trajectory in the Mars trilogy, Robinson provides in the iconic background of this historic shift an overview of the new society and the steps taken to build it. In principle, the Green revolution refused the strategy of working toward a punctual revolutionary event in which power is seized and the entire system restructured once and for all: such idealized ventures seem more appropriate for the excitement of a baseball game rather than the complexities of history. In tracing the politics of the movement, Robinson meditates on the need to disperse control by means of a *structural* division of responsibilities among transnational and local units, and a *temporal* one that extends the larger political project into succeeding historical periods. In addition, theoretical and practical analyses and methods are drawn from a range of sources: including ecological, feminist, and Marxist theory and practice, as well as from sublated capitalist insights on self-interest and methods of market development. The resulting societal shift refuses an orthodox formation and opts for a mixed system based on ecological respect and restoration, human diversity and decency, and economic and political justice, within a democratically-regulated ethical balance of altruism and self-interest.

One of the first victories for the movement occurs in the 2030s "when the venture capital laws changed" so that speculation could be brought under social control. Later — twenty-eight years after Tom's final journal entry — the Green's intervention in the state apparatus achieved a substantial level of regulation over the corporations (251). The world-wide agreements of 2040 finally succeeded in dismantling the transnational companies and legislated legal size limits, to the effect of allowing nothing but smaller businesses that cooperated through carefully monitored public networks. This curbed corporate hegemony, but as the narrative points out, more needed to be done to prevent a regression to unfettered economic behavior and to heal the wounds of the past and re-distribute the social benefits for the future.

Tom's historical lecture on the university ship, *Ganesh*, sketches the events that moved the world situation toward Utopia. Contrary to retrenchment caveats (after 1968, and again after 1989) about the undesirability of a utopian thinking in terms of totalities or organizational leadership, and in a timely shift beyond the 1980s oppositional strategies of micro-politics based in single issues or identities, Robinson presents an argument for a renewed effort (albeit theoretically and politically aware of recent critiques and cautions, and of local needs and desires) to grasp analytically the pattern and consequences of transnational corporate exploitation. From there, he charts one scenario of an effort to work politically in a larger and more organized manner, in an extended series of carefully planned and propagandized stages, to replace that capital logic with a method that works from radically different economic, political, and cultural standpoints that develop out of each social conjuncture rather than from a priori assumptions. In describing the move from the Socialist to the Green Party as the primary public agent of change, Robinson registers the errors and mis-steps (and suppressions and defeats) of past political engagements; but he nevertheless takes a bold step (in the crucial year of 1990) toward reviving and re-articulating the possibility and scope of an organized transnational opposition.

In his shipboard talk, Tom's initial comments carry a radical populist tone as he characterizes the curtailing of corporations as being "like trust busting in Teddy Roosevelt's time" (282). However, in an earlier conversation with Kevin, he asserts that he "hated capitalism because it was a lie," and when he tells the students about governmental and popular hatred for the multinational cartels, his explanation becomes more complicated, indeed more Gramscian, in its analysis of political economy and its sense of the politics and culture required (55). For the key to success was the alliance of governmental and popular movements and the curbing of the unlimited economic activity enjoyed by the forces of a highly mobile capital and their state allies (283). This approach produced a steady and simultaneous engagement on the terrain of the state apparatus as well as that of the civil society — a studied project that resonates with the linkage of what Nancy Fraser has termed the "strong public" of legislative power with the "weak public" of social/cultural sensibility. As Tom describes it: "Governments hated multinationals because they were out of government control. People hated them because they made everyone cogs in machines, making money for someone else you never saw. That was the combination needed to take them on" (282).

The state component of the revolution includes several democratic socialist moves that were achieved by way of the "revolutionary power" (56) of legislation, and at least the threat of military and police force (284). Economically, basic resources such as water, energy, and land are nationalized to preserve the commons for social use (284); publicly owned and operated businesses help to produce social wealth and guarantee jobs to those who need them (91); military production is converted to civilian needs, with an emphasis on ecological restoration (57–58); market technologies (as opposed to ideologies) based on a tempered level of self-interest are encouraged, yet regulated to serve "the common good" (56, 284); individual wealth is restricted by income magnitude laws that guarantee, by way of redistributed social wealth, a minimum yearly amount of ten thousand dollars to every person but also cap earned income at one hundred thousand dollars (49); and individual taxation is democratically adjudicated so that people "can direct 60 percent of their taxes to whatever services they support the most" (91). Politically, some nation-states and many local governing councils retain a high degree of decision-making ability while cooperating within a transnational system directed by a democratized UN, wherein the General Assembly has replaced the Security Council as the focal point of power.

The civic/cultural component complements this economic and legislative apparatus as it embraces the ideological and subjective reconfiguration of the social articulated by ecological, feminist, and situated liberation movements. Diversity, decentralization, and self-determination provide the basis for the norms and customs of everyday life; and in this enlarged, non-exploitive, context, the California utopia's citizens are free to do as they wish. They are responsible for an ethical acceptance of the new social values and for the performance of an amount of socially necessary service, but they are also free to engage in the labor, the income level, and the life style of their choice.

This "quiet revolution" (282) was carefully planned and carried out over many years—in a version of what Ernst Bloch termed "temporal solidarity" (*Principle*, III 1174). The patient route was taken because of the extent and subtlety of the changes needed and in the interest of winning popular support along the way, not simply assuming control and imposing a new order. Nevertheless, and not surprisingly, the corporate powers reacted: "They bought people, courts, newspapers—they killed people," and they tried to buy poor countries to serve as havens. However, with action by UN and democratized national forces, the resort to safe havens was prevented and the unregulated flow of capital was stopped (283). Over the long term, a consensus was delicately forged, and the results led to a "revolution of all the people, using the power of government—laws, police, armies—against the very small executive class that owned and ran the multinationals" (283–284). Through careful analysis and strategic intervention, economic as well as political democracy was established, and the economic pyramid was altered: "We chopped the pyramid off and left only the constituent parts down at the base, and gave the function that higher parts of the pyramid served over to government, without siphoning off money, except for public works ... with wealth distributed in this way, the wars and catastrophes that would have destroyed the pyramid were averted" (285). Along with this new economic and political structure, a democratic and diverse culture also flourished. In short, "government mixed with business mixed with life styles" and produced the conditions for a utopian society (91).

Robinson then details this new culture when he presents the major plot line of the novel. As he previously did in the summer stories of Henry and of Jim, he gives us the tale of everyday life in the Orange County town of El Modena, as Kevin Claiborne and his friends live it in their summer of 2065. In this temporal shift across generations from Tom's narrative of global revolution to Kevin's story of a charged summer in a local, but not a pocket, utopia, Robinson's narrative takes a further step in this volume as it moves from a pre-utopian emphasis on historical change and radical re-perception to an exploration of the limits and possibilities of utopian life itself.

Located on the edge of the Sierra foothills, El Modena is a utopian town in a still evolving utopian world — one that has emerged "with a destiny of its own" as the scars of the age of greed begin to heal (21). In a letter back to Chicago, Oscar, the new town lawyer, gives the town a favorable economic review:

> Their system is a mix, combining a communalism of the Santa Rosa model — land and public utilities owned in common, residents required to do ten hours a week of town work, a couple of town-owned businesses in operation to use all the labor available, that sort of thing — with aspects of the new federal model: residents are taxed more and more heavily as they approach the personal income cap.... Businesses based in town are subject to the same sort of graduated system.... As usual in these set ups, the town is fairly wealthy.... From all the income generated, a town share is distributed back out to the citizens, which comes to about twice the national income floor [91].

Politically, the governing council attends to issues such as land use, resource allocation, and the local quality of life. The seven person group, with a rotating mayor, is balanced between two Green Party members (Kevin and Doris) committed to controlling growth and restoring the land and cultural life of the area, two Federal Party members (Alfredo and Matt) interested in renewing development, and three members (Hiroko, Susan, and Jerry) in a "fluctuating middle" (25).

Culturally, El Modena is a multi-racial, non-sexist, lively place that appears to have reached a stress-free balance of play and work. While coupled marriages still exist, people generally live in group houses which include married and single adults and lots of children. Restored and rebuilt housing is designed for maximum energy efficiency and with gardening plots that promote local, natural foods and beverages. Transport is generally limited to walking and bicycling; although communal cars can be used as needed, and ultralight planes are available for recreation. Physical exercise is a major part of the culture, for, as Oscar puts it, this is a place "where culture consists of a vigorous swim workout, followed by a discussion of the usefulness of hand paddles" (87). Daily life is punctuated by gossip, baseball games, and fairly frequent parties (where locally brewed tequila, wine, and beer are welcomed).

In general, the town seems on its way to an even brighter future, but, true to the form of the critical utopia, darkness falls when it becomes evident that some town members, Alfredo especially, are more interested in development, wealth, and power than in the new utopian ambience. Specifically, a bitter fight develops over the question of whether Alfredo and his company will be allowed to build a new commercial center on Rattlesnake Hill, the last remaining open land in the area. At this point, Robinson's account of the generational dynamics between the old activist and grandfather, Tom, and the "bioarchitect" and carpenter and grandson, Kevin, becomes significant. An important moment in the history of the relationship occurs when Tom passes on the responsibility for leadership to Kevin and his friends. When Kevin asks Tom to help with the battle for Rattlesnake Hill, Tom resists, claiming that his day has passed and that it is now Kevin's turn to take on the fight that "will never end" (56). Even though Tom asserts that it is now time for new, younger activists, he nevertheless comes "down out of the hills" to help (63), and through his old contacts in Washington he succeeds in discovering that Alfredo has become compromised — in "a Faustian bargain" (253) — by way of a secret deal with a Hong Kong corporation in his unexamined desire for wealth and power. In the end, however, Kevin and his friends have to carry on the battle when Tom dies before the research is released.

In the council battle over Rattlesnake Hill, Robinson provides the most public example of the persistence of greed and strife in this utopia, and he stresses the need for its citizens to remain democratically engaged in the real work of their society. The battle is foregrounded in the opening pages of the novel when, in a series of conversations, Kevin begins to reflect on the political sphere for the first time, since he will be entering the council as a new Green Party representative. In his conversation with Doris, he speculates on the relationship between the motivating force of values and actions (4). In a later conversation with Gabriela, he recalls an old school essay in which he debated the relationship between the pen and the sword (5); and in an interchange with Alfredo, he directly encounters a tension between work and play which will later play out in a very direct political form (7). Each of these binary insights fold in on themselves in the widening conflict as ideas, actions, and debates feed into the council fight. Even violence enters in when the overdetermined antagonism between Kevin and Alfredo over Rattlesnake Hill and Ramona explodes into a fist fight on the baseball diamond and when Tom's house burns down as a result of arson (the perpetrator of which is never discovered). The council debate continues, and gradually the group opposed to the development (Kevin, Doris, Oscar, Tom, Nadezhda, and others) uncovers the full story of Alfredo's complicity with a resurgent corporate powerhouse in Hong Kong and succeeds in winning the final vote on re-zoning. In pursuing this campaign, they learn about the ecology and politics of water in California, the politics of socialist decentralization as opposed to capitalist centralization, the economics of steady-state production and consumption in a restored landscape, as well as the need to be vigilant about the persistence of greed. In the activism of "all the business of running a small town, churned out point by pointing a public gathering," they work at the local level while always connecting that immediacy to the broader scheme of things: an experience that is "repeated thousands of times all over the globe" (27). "Real power" may well be found at the level of the town council, but only as it is understood as rehearsed and dispersed around the world, and brought back home again.

A key battle is lost near the end of the summer when the council votes 4 to 3 in favor of Alfredo's plan, with Jerry, the unpredictable "moderate," casting the deciding vote. A major reason for the defeat was the group's failure to disseminate information, to "win the battle of opinion" (141). At this moment, Tom's death by drowning slows down their access to the information on Alfredo's connection so that it is not available at the time of the meeting, and their television and door-to-door outreach is weakened by the lack of damning proof of the deal. As well, their political support is undercut when Jean Aureliano, the local Green Party leader, fails to support the public campaign against Alfredo in her desire not to offend Alfredo so that the Party could stay in office and pass their less radical proposals. This is a disappointing act of capitulation given that the Greens were the radical leaders of the revolution in the first place (see 260–263).

4. Ritual, Control, and Utopia

> All activity began to spiral down toward the ritual; more and more that was not part of it fell away and disappeared, until when one team took the field—first baseman rolling grounders to the infielders, pitcher taking practice tosses, outfielders throwing fly balls around—everything extraneous to the ritual was gone [9].

And yet, at this lowest political moment, when a significant battle is lost, it becomes clear that the war is not over. There are personal and public possibilities yet to be tapped. In particular, for the Hill to be saved, elements of everyday life in the culture of El Modena need to be connected with the immediate economic and legislative components of the issue at hand. At this point, the effective agency of social ritual enters the political scene—working, as

Franko has noted, as an empowering form of "social style" that achieves indirectly, in a communal dispersion of political control, what the direct confrontation with its more pointed efforts could not accomplish (204).[17]

The decision to draw on the power of ritual, by way of the memorial service for Tom, begins in a fairly traditional utopian fashion in Kevin's dreams and then moves outward to the event itself. After the disappointing council meeting, Kevin retreats to Rattlesnake Hill and falls into a dreamy sleep. A mysterious shape that has haunted his dreams all summer (one which, like the arsonist, is never fully explained) enters his dream for a brief moment and is followed by an image of a "crowd on the hill" (311). When he wakes to full consciousness (in an echo of William Morris rather than Wells), Kevin finds he has a plan. Out of the dream, on the powerful ground of the land in question, he plots the next move in the war to preserve not only the hill but also the quality of utopian life. The outcome is the memorial service for Tom, who was lost in the storm at sea. Doris casts a ceramic and bronze commemorative plate, with its own utopian message: "There Will Never Come An End To The Good That He Has Done" (311). Hank, in his role as minister, conducts the service; and all the townspeople attend. In his sermon, Hank links the sacredness of the hill with the contributions Tom made throughout his life: "All these trees we stand under were planted by Tom when he was a boy, to give this hilltop some shade, to make it a good place to come up and look around, take a look at the ocean or the mountains or just down to town. And he kept coming up here for the rest of his life. And we make this little grove his memorial. It was a place he liked, looking over a place he loved" (313). Hank then invites each person to strike a nail into the plate to fasten it to one of the sycamore trees.

As the nailing commences, Alfredo accuses Kevin of using the service as a political tool in the fight for the hill: "I should think you'd be ashamed of using your grandfather's death like this" (313). Kevin replies that Tom would have loved it, and that everyone would now consider the hill as an "inviolate" shrine: "Don't fuck with this hill any more, Alfredo. There's no one will like you if you do" (314). As if to punctuate Kevin's assertion, Ramona, recently reunited with Alfredo and due that afternoon to marry him, drives a nail into the tree: "That," Kevin muses, "would make the difference. Alfredo would never dare cross Ramona on an issue this charged" (314). The scene ends with Kevin telling Alfredo to build somewhere else and Alfredo stalking off.

What was lost in the strong public of the council was nevertheless won on the cultural front by way of the weak public experience of the service, in an instance in which social opinion became powerful enough to displace the legislative vote. In the deeply felt ceremony that braids together all the threads of the community, all its issues and hopes, the utopian potential of the community is protected. The political and the personal, the private and the public, are intertwined as each of the conflicts are resolved. As a relatively autonomous cultural formation, the service offers a good example of the utopian process as Sargent defines it: that is, as an instance of "social dreaming" that draws on fantasy (in the altered consciousness of night or, especially, day dreams) but also on consciously acknowledged human need, in what Sargent describes as the drive to secure "human psychic health" (5). The memorial service, then, derives from Kevin's *dream* as it is aligned with his *plan*. It is the combination of both elements (of what Ruth Levitas would understand as the joining of desire with hope) that produces the event's political effectiveness. Indeed, the service functions as a more spiritual form of Bakhtinian carnival — wherein what Michael Gardiner describes as "the mobilization of meaning" subverts asymmetrical and exploitative power relations (193). El Modena's ritual (like Bakhtin's carnival) offers an "enactment of utopian community, which helps create a transgressive or 'liminal' social space" in which the community rejects Alfredo's scheme and preserves the economic and political balance of the town while also carrying its vibrant culture into the future (Gardiner 171).

This celebration of the ritual for its sociopolitical force gives way to a closing narrative in which Robinson's treatment of the question of control helps further to clarify the way forward for the utopian process. In Kevin's own life, in its personal and political dimensions, control has been one of the challenges of the summer; and, in the process of his waking up to his own responsibilities and opportunities, Kevin's shifting character position helps to elucidate key components of everyday in the utopian society as well as that of the utopian narrative. Although Tom's history (from his birth in the symbolic year of 1984 to his death at 81 in 2065) includes the personal dimension of his family life, as poignantly seen in his retreat after Pam's death, his place in the novel primarily concerns the public, structural dimensions of the utopian impulse. In Kevin's story, however, an actually existing utopia consists of a mixture of public and personal concerns and behaviors. Kevin's love for Ramona, his close bond with Tom, and his doubled grief over Ramona's reunion with Alfredo and Tom's death are as much a part of his transformative summer as the struggle in the town council. Indeed, the council fight begins with Kevin's personal desire to save the childhood refuge that was "his hill" (43). Half asleep at his first meeting, he snaps awake when he senses that Alfredo is trying to slip something by in naming new members to the local water board, and he thereby begins the protracted campaign when his political conscience begins to stir (see 28–32).

At this point, the personal and political begin to coalesce in Kevin's feelings and actions. Even the metaphor for the political struggle comes from his love of baseball: "The world plays hardball. Sure, and he could handle it. But not Rattlesnake Hill!" (43). In this context, the baseball season, inflected by the pressures of his hitting streak, becomes a metaphor and a metonym for Kevin's emotional and political situation; it offers an immediate opportunity for Kevin to act out his transformation from a childlike insistence on control to a more considered and wiser grasp of the limits of that personal effort as well as the advantages of a more collective form of control. Described early in the book as "being nine years old forever" on the baseball field (but by extension throughout his innocent trip through daily life), Kevin is changed over the course of the summer (65). After waking from his dream on Rattlesnake Hill, and after a symbolically cleansing swim in the ocean, in the midst of his equally cleansing laughter, he at last begins to grasp the complexities of agency in this ecologically-valenced utopia.

In fleshing out the parameters of this utopian life, Robinson cautions that neither the local political fight in the town council nor the global fight, from Tom's time to the El Modena's present, are sufficient for doing what needs to be done. Here, the closing scenes of the memorial service and Kevin's end-of-summer insights suggest again that the mechanisms of control and ritual play a key mediating role in the social action needed for the continuation of the utopian impulse. Indeed, one way to read the narrative is as an extended initiation ritual — wherein the personal move to a new level of adulthood for Kevin is matched by the maturing of the utopian locale itself when struggle is embraced as an expected and normal activity. This transformation, as quiet as the social revolution Tom describes, turns on the issue of control. At 32, Kevin's innocence about love and politics is perhaps surprising (although a longer adolescence may well be a common, and positive, aspect of the new utopian life). He is slow to find a way to fight in council and slow to come to terms with his personal desires and losses. One reason for this conceptual and emotional sluggishness is his insistence on staying in control. This claim for the ability to call all shots in the face of adversity is perhaps best seen when he tells Tom and Nadezhda about Ramona's return to Alfredo. He begins awkwardly, but he gradually feels better about his very non-utopian manner of recapping the events of the summer:

> It felt good to tell it, in a way. Because it was *his story*, his and his alone, nobody else's. And in telling it he gained a sort of control over it he had never had when it happened.... What was valuable in the experience was that he had been out of control, living moment to moment with no plan, at the mercy of other people. What was valuable in the telling of the story was that he was in control, shaping the experience, deciding what it meant, putting other people in their proper place [255–256].

Kevin's reliance on control is also seen in an earlier passage when he begins the baseball season by constructing his persona as "third baseman Kevin Claiborne" in the linear narration of the game so familiar to young fans: "Third base like a razor's edge, third base like a mongoose among snakes; this was how the announcer in his head had always put it, ever since childhood" (10). And it is echoed later as Kevin realizes that he often speaks to his "own internal audience," the ideal receivers of his story, and his alone (305).

Kevin's claim to narrational control is, however, something other than a therapeutic gaining of perspective, for, in this very post-bourgeois society, it becomes little more than a defensive holding action over the plot and characters of his own life. From the utopian perspective, it is a contrasting throwback to an anti-utopian ideology of an individual, male, insistence on dominating personal, and indeed public, life.[18] This limitation in Kevin's consciousness evinces itself in his frequent figuration of women in general, and Ramona in particular, as animals. While such imagery could be regarded as some sort of psycho-physiological, indeed "cyborg," advance for humans who engage their bodily vitality, the objectification of one gender by another in these instances too easily reduces the objectified one to a lesser status, as some thing to be regarded and admired but not dealt with as an equal. On one of the first ultralight flights with Ramona, Kevin thinks of her as a "beautiful animal" who would, in some fantastic species transgression, bear their child (see 19), and later, while swimming with Ramona, he thinks of women in general as dolphins (133) — an observation grandfather Tom shares across generations when on the *Ganesh* he thinks of women being as "free as dolphins" (277). In addition to this obsession with her non-human vitality, Kevin consistently idealizes Ramona rather than accept her as she is: in falling in love with her again, he relies on his memories of their school day love, and at one point he thinks of her as embodying what he "loved most in women," thereby asserting a generic claim over female identity that flies in the face of the emancipated attitudes and behavior of the post-masculinist culture in El Modena (183).

So when at the end of this "sad utopia," Kevin confronts the losses of the summer — Ramona, Tom, the hitting streak, and possibly even Rattlesnake Hill — he totters in his social and personal immaturity on the edge of despair (Franko 204). Nevertheless, this *is* a utopian society, existing on the edge of peace and not of despair, and such personal and historical reversions to individual power have no lasting place in a society which infuses a very different order of subjectivity. Consequently, after some moments of indulgence, yet ultimately drawing on the strength of his more utopian construction and consciousness, Kevin abandons his private power play and embraces the "responsibility to otherness" that is so central to the values of his society (Franko 204). By way of the intense encounter in his dream and then by virtue of an almost Buddhist indulgence in laughter, he accepts the events of the summer, puts them in historical perspective, and gets on with his life in utopian reality — one in which social control is shared and distributed and individual dominance of any narrative or procedure is rejected (see Franko 207):

> His world and the wind pouring through it. His hands came together and made their half swing. If only Hank hadn't caught the last one. If only Ramona, if only Tom, if only the world, all in him at once, with a sharp stab of our unavoidable grief; and it seemed to him then that he was without a doubt the unhappiest person in the whole world. And at that thought (thinking about it) he began to laugh [326].

At that point the words end, and Robinson leaves his readers with their own experience of the gap between their present world and Utopia, but perhaps now enriched with more capacity for vision in the darkness.

5. Coda: Utopia and the New Global Order

> Kevin slowed down, approaching second. Confused. He had to laugh; he had forgotten how to leave the field after making an out. He stood there, feeling self-conscious. Game over, so there was no need to rush [320–321].

In his meditation on possible ways beyond the current impasse of the exploitative domain of global capital, on one hand, and the shrinkage of oppositional politics to the sphere of the micro or local, on the other, Robinson offers a larger utopian imaginary that can contribute to the growing sensibility of a new moment of social struggle. In this, as well as in his demonstration of the need to achieve a level of mediated social direction rather than unfettered individual power and in his reminder of the force of cultural formations and practices, Robinson generates a related but different version of what Benedict Anderson (referring to discourses of nation) has called "the framework of a new consciousness" (Anderson 65). Written at the moment of an exponential increase in the power of global capital and a diminution of national power as a potential base of regulation and opposition, Robinson's utopian text offers a social narrative that resonates with contemporaneous theories of post-national space.

As Arun Appadurai put it in his 1993 discussion of the possibilities of post-nationality, "local politics and global process affect each other in chaotic but not unpredictable ways, often outside the interactions of nation-states" and need new "complex, nonterritorial, postnational forms of allegiance" to move beyond that chaos (419, 418). While Appadurai does not sufficiently include the pervasiveness of capital nor the oppositional potential lingering in national/governmental structures in his analysis of this "chaotic" relationship, his exploration of emergent social formations that negotiate the global and local without necessarily making traditional use of the nation-state suggests one way to appreciate the creative, pedagogical, and political value of Robinson's effort to tell a tale of a movement and a society that defeats capital but also refuses the limits of the nation-state (even as it may yet work with discourses of nation or use elements of governmental power). That is, along with an array of transnational projects or movements (which Appadurai identifies as nongovernmental organizations, churches, philanthropic movements, terrorist movements, ecological movements, human rights movements, refugee networks, and even fashion — and one could add global labor movements and even divisions of transnational corporations themselves), cultural products such as *Pacific Edge*—and indeed the entire trilogy—also contribute to the new political momentum by way of articulating an engaged utopian imagination, working as an artistic/intellectual stimulus for grasping the social relations and processes of the emerging postnational series of linkages.

Indeed, the stimulation offered by *Pacific Edge* and the entire Three Californias Trilogy is not the work of utopian approach left over from an earlier era. In the 1990s, other utopian, narratives (including both eutopias and critical dystopias) were being published; and their appearance and reception may well indicate one way in which utopian writing has managed to preserve the insights of the critical utopias even as it moves to new utopian formulations in a new historical moment. In his eutopian Mars trilogy, Robinson again explores ways to develop new, post-national, social formations at the macro and micro levels that respond to the new global constellation of capital and the needed forms of opposition. For example, in *Green Mars*, volume two of the trilogy, a set of constitutional principles for Martian independence explicitly refuses to limit the new social order in terms of a singular "nation," at the planetary level, or even "nations," at the level of the locally diverse cultures and their cities. Instead, revolutionary Mars is imagined as a *world* with diverse *cultures*—with powerful economic, political, and cultural structures and practices, but none resembling the older forms of the nation-state (see 332–334). And in Piercy's critical dystopia, *He, She, and It*, the reader finds a contestation between transnational corporate zones, the utopian city-state of Tikvah, and the chaotic site of rejected peoples known as the "Glop," but not nations (indeed the one nation mentioned extensively, and seen as one that betrayed its own founding idealism, is Israel, which is now a derelict zone produced by the destruction of a nuclear bomb). The way forward on Piercy's dystopian planet involves an emerging alliance between the citizens of the liberated utopian city-state of Tikvah, the politically organized gangs of the extended space of the Glop, and other more limited enclaves such as the women in the Dark Zone of the former Israel. In *Pacific Edge* and these other utopian texts of the 1990s, therefore, the utopian sensibility appeared to be as strong as ever. However, not only did their search for new frameworks of consciousness and political organizing take place in terms of the challenges and problems of post-modernity, as did the critical utopias, but it also worked in the emerging spaces of a possible post-nationality, taking the ever persistent utopian process to its next stage as the new century approached.[19]

IV. Writing Utopia, 2007

> We have to find a way to free ourselves of the tenacious ghosts of the past that haunt the present and cripple our imagination, not only because of the question of scale and the fact that modern forms of representation and accountability are diluted and disoriented in the vast global territories but also because we ourselves have changed.
> — Michael Hardt and Antonio Negri, *Multitude* [308]

In a recent essay, published online as he was working on the third volume of his "Science in the Capital" series (*Sixty Days and Counting*, 2007; *Fifty Degrees Below Zero*, 2006; *Forty Signs of Rain*, 2005), Robinson briefly speaks of his penchant for trilogies:

> Why another trilogy? Well, mainly, I suppose, because it's a long [and] complicated story, and I like those. Trilogies are often just Very Long Novels, like Victorian triple-deckers; George Eliot's *Middlemarch* was first published in multiple volumes, but no one calls it a trilogy now. Some stories just need lots of pages to tell [it] right ["Imagining Abrupt Climate Change," online].

As readers, we have long benefited from Robinson's engaged efforts to tell it right.

Spanning the years from 1984 to 1990, his Three Californias Trilogy took its readers to the unfolding edge of sociopolitical debates and possibilities of the time while it also traced the ways each of its main characters endeavored to tell it right in their own writing. From the depths of Reaganite, neo-conservative, neo-militarist America to the dawning possibilities of the next decade (as they were just emerging in and against the intensified processes of global capitalism and ecocide), his three volumes generated critical maps as well as speculations on possible political moves that marked a step beyond, as well as through, the micro-politics of the 1980s. As with the Mars trilogy and the "Science in the Capital" books, Robinson wrote a deeply utopian set of parallel yet inter-related texts that explored the "impossible" future, the not yet of socio-political transformation. Indeed, his first trilogy opened the way for the other two both in its formal strategies and in its political speculations, always giving us an insight to politics as process, and to possible working scenarios within that process, but never settling for or coalescing into an overt plan or agenda. As such, Three Californias stands as an important creative and historical text in its own right as well as a foreshadowing of Robinson's later work.

Throughout these very long novels, as in his entire body of work, Robinson's accounts of the dawning consciousness of his protagonists and their responses to the crises of their time figure ways forward into a new political imaginary of opposition. While we are given social maps and alternatives (and in the later trilogies we get these by way of model constitutions and policy speeches as well as narrative) to generate a new utopian imaginary, we do so always within the creative energy of Robinson's literary web. As such, his extended fictions take us out of our world only to drop us back in by way of pleasurable and pedagogical maneuvers that can allow us to conclude along with Henry in *The Wild Shore* that "Nothing looks the same ever again" (165).

Notes

1. My appreciation to Kim Stanley Robinson for suggesting that I reprint both of my essays on his Three Californias trilogy, and to Bill Burling for agreeing. While I was tempted to write a third essay on *The Wild Shore* to complete my own trilogy, I've spared readers by touching on it briefly in my introduction. As products of their time, I've generally left the substance of the essays as they were, except for some shifting around for the introduction, some stylistic suturing to pull the parts into a new whole, and a trimming of endnotes. I thank Susan McManus for commenting on this new amalgam; and I am grateful to Carol Franko, Áine O'Brien, Kim Stanley Robinson, Jane Williams, and my *Utopian Studies* referees for their comments on the *Pacific Edge* essay; and Robinson, again, and Lyman Tower Sargent, Darko Suvin, and Phil Wegner for their comments on *The Gold Coast* chapter from *Scraps of the Untainted Sky*. I thank the Banff Centre for the Arts and George Mason University for research support on the first essay and Liverpool John Moores University and the National University of Ireland-Galway for support for the second.

2. In *Pacific Edge*, the character Oscar write a letter to friends in Chicago wherein he lists the "California writers" who represent one of these lines of theoretical insight: "Mary Austin, Jack London, Frank Norris, John Muir, Robinson Jeffers, Kenneth Rexroth, Gary Snyder, Ursula Le Guin, Cecelia Holland ... Muir's 'athlete philosopher,' his 'university of the wilderness,' these ideas infuse the whole tradition, and the result is a very vigorous, clear literature" (269). Robinson's Trilogy should be added to the list.

3. On the discrete and iconic registers of any sf text, see Moylan, *Demand the Impossible* 35–52.

4. Adding to the list of definitions he supplies in "The Three Faces of Utopianism, Revisited," Lyman Tower Sargent defines the critical dystopia as follows: "a non-existent society described in considerable detail and normally located in time and space that the author intended a contemporaneous reader to view as worse than contemporary society but that normally includes at least one eutopian enclave or holds out hope that the dystopia can be overcome and replaced with a eutopia" ("U.S. Eutopias" 222). For a fuller discussion of the critical dystopia, see Moylan, *Scraps*, "Chapter Six: The Critical Dystopia"; and Baccolini and Moylan, *Dark Horizons*, "Introduction: Dystopia and Histories."

5. For a reading of Forster's story as an early example of twentieth-century dystopia, see Moylan, *Scraps* 111–121.

6. See Joanna Russ's discussion of the "lyric" textual strategy — in which "images, events, scenes, passages, words, what-have-you" spiral "around an unspoken thematic or emotional center" (*To Write Like a Woman* 87); see also Moylan, *Scraps* 39–41.

7. For a discussion of Dick's story as dystopia, see Moylan, *Scraps* 173–177.

8. Robinson here anticipates the scope and method of the Mars Trilogy. In the *Foundation* interview, David Seed describes Robinson's work in the later trilogy as an *invitation* "into a new kind of holistic thinking to see how all sorts of different areas of knowledge might inter-relate"; Robinson agrees and connects Seed's description with his own embrace of the logic of ecological thought ("Interview" 78).

9. In developing his take on straight white masculinity, Robinson implicitly challenges the compromised soft-macho positions reinforced by a number of first wave cyberpunk works. On the cultural politics of white male struggles against material and discursive patriarchal power, see Pfeil; on resistance within male literary practice, see Schoene-Harwood.

10. Ildney Cavalcanti refers to Sarah Lefanu's observation in *Feminism and Science Fiction* that there is "a hidden utopian streak" in dystopian novels by women: "They contain an element of hopefulness that rests on a belief in the power and efficacy of women's speech" (quoted Cavalcanti 64n).

11. Regarding the political position Hana occupies, see Cavalcanti, who discusses Luce Irigaray's articulation of a critical space for women as it is "defined more in terms of strategic movement than fixed positionality" (Cavalcanti 66), or, as Rosi Braidotti puts it, as it works with "one foot in the system the other outside" (quoted Cavalcanti 66).

12. A few pages later, Robinson draws out his affiliation with the writers of the critical utopias as he invokes Le Guin by situating the environmental lawyer, Sally Tallhawk, in Kroeber College on the high desert campus of the University of California at Bishop (which, at the time Robinson was writing the novel, was itself only a "speculative" campus).

13. As Theodor Adorno put it: "hope is contradictorily tied to breaks in the form of predicative identity. Philosophical tradition had a word for these breaks: 'ideas' .... The ideas live in the cavities between what things claim to be and what they are. Utopia would be above identity and above contradiction; it would a togetherness of diversity" (150).

14. An intertextual link for me at this point is Tom Disch's *Camp Concentration*— that neglected sf work of the 1960s in which prison inmates are not only incarcerated but also experimentally infected with a mind enhancing, and fatal, strain of syphilis. The prisoners resist by using the force of mind they have gained through the experiment not only to take over the prison but also the bodies, and power positions, of the prison authorities. The book ends with them looking ahead to further conflicts with the authoritarian state. As in *Pacific Edge*, the effective political choice in Disch's narrative involves a move from private efforts for survival to a public, and collective, struggle to live as free humans: to fight, in history, for a utopian potential that can be teased out of the material and political contradictions of the present realities (to work with Bloch's concrete tendency and latency of the current conjuncture, rather than idealistically wishing or dreaming for a better time and place).

15. The revolutionary commitment of the female members of Tom's family is not foregrounded by Robinson, but it does feature in his broader picture of the movement. Three generations of women carry out their part of the larger effort in their work as scientists: Pam as an environmental researcher, daughter Liddy working on solar technology in space, and grand-daughter Jill doing medical work in Bangladesh.

16. Carol Franko's commentary is apt: for her, the book is "a utopian novel about a utopian novel that wasn't written"; she argues that Robinson's critique of the utopian genre is not a rejection of the acts of writing or reading such works, but rather a challenge to be "self-conscious about the strangeness of both activities" ("Working the 'In-Between'" 206).

17. Several other moments of ritual appear earlier in the novel and establish the validity of the memorial service as a meaningful event in a utopian community that values ritual and carnival. See the treatment of the "redneck festival" (109–116); Hank's party on the occasion of the Mars landing, in which Oscar has his vision (148–179); the drag races that Oscar and Doris attend (221–226); and the performance of *Macbeth* that Oscar and Kevin attend (271–272). Oscar—as both lawyer and trickster—plays a significant role in each of these events. Tom's service also recalls the memorial to the character Rabbit in Piercy's *Woman on the Edge of Time*.

18. I'm reminded here of Bron in Delany's *Triton*: a protagonist who is a decidedly non-utopian misfit in one of the most challenging of the critical utopias of the 1970s. Kevin's insistence on control may seem as anachronistic, but in the end he does not cling to the past as Bron does. Nevertheless, and contrary to Franko's generous account of Kevin as "privileged but not alienated," I see Kevin's immature desire to control his own narrative precisely as evidence of an alienation that he only overcomes when he faces up to the several personal and political adversities of the summer ("Working the 'In-Between'" 204).

19. My reading of *Pacific Edge* ends with references based in the theoretical/political context of 1994. However, the subsequent move into globalization/alter-globalization politics and theory, perhaps most powerfully represented by the work of Michael Hardt and Antonio Negri, is quite compatible with Robinson's analyses

in this closing novel of this first trilogy. Indeed, in his creative and cognitive way, he effectively anticipates this later historical, political, theoretical moment.

WORKS CITED

Adorno, Theodor W. *Negative Dialectics*. New York: Continuum, 1994.
Anderson, Benedict. *Imagined Communities: Reflections on the Origin and Spread of Nationalism*. London: Verso, 1983.
Appadurai, Arun. "Patriotism and Its Futures." *Public Culture* 5 (1993): 411–429.
Baccolini, Raffaella, and Tom Moylan. *Dark Horizons: Science Fiction and the Dystopian Imagination*. New York and London: Routledge, 2004.
Blade Runner. Dir. Ridley Scott. 1982.
Bloch, Ernst. *The Principle of Hope*. 3 vols. Cambridge: MIT Press, 1986.
Brazil. Dir. Terry Gilliam. 1985.
Butler, Octavia E. *The Parable of the Sower*. New York: Four Walls Eight Windows, 1993.
Cavalcanti, Ildney. "Articulating the Elsewhere: Utopia in Contemporary Feminist Dystopias." Diss. University of Strathclyde, 1999.
Delany, Samuel R. *The Einstein Intersection*. New York: Ace, 1967.
_____. *Triton*. New York: Bantam, 1976.
Dick, Philip K. "Faith of Our Fathers." *Dangerous Visions*. Ed. Harlan Ellison. Garden City, N.Y.: Doubleday, 1967. 175–204.
Disch, Thomas M. *Camp Concentration*. London: Hart-Davis, 1968.
Forster, E. M. "The Machine Stops." *Oxford and Cambridge Review* 8 (Michaelmas Term 1909): 83–122.
Franko, Carol. "Dialogical Twins, Post-Patriarchal Topography in Two Stories by Kim Stanley Robinson." *Science-Fiction Studies* (1995): 305–322.
_____. "The Density of Utopian Density in Robinson's *Red Mars*." *Extrapolation* (1997): 57–65.
_____. "Working the 'In-Between': Kim Stanley Robinson's Utopian Fiction." *Science-Fiction Studies* (July 1994): 191–211.
Fraser, Nancy. "Rethinking the Public Sphere: A Contribution to the Critique of Actually Existing Democracy." *The Phantom Public Sphere*. Ed. Bruce Robbins. Minneapolis and London: University of Minnesota Press, 1993. 1–33.
Gardiner, Michael. *The Dialogics of Critique: M. M. Bakhtin and the Theory of Ideology*. New York: Routledge, 1992.
Hardt, Michael, and Antonio Negri. *Empire*. Cambridge, Mass., and London: Harvard, 2000.
_____. *Multitude: War and Democracy in the Age of Empire*. London: Penguin, 2004.
James, Edward. "Building Utopias on Mars, from Crusoe to Robinson." *Foundation: The Review of Science Fiction* 68 (Autumn 1996): 64–75.
Jameson, Fredric. "Cognitive Mapping." *Marxism and the Interpretation of Culture*. Eds. Cary Nelson and Lawrence Grossberg. Urbana and Chicago: University of Illinois Press, 1988. 347–360.
Le Guin, Ursula K. *The Dispossessed*. New York: Harper, 1974.
Levitas, Ruth. *The Concept of Utopia*. Syracuse: Syracuse University Press, 1990.
Moylan, Tom. *Demand the Impossible: Science Fiction and the Utopian Imagination*. London and New York: Methuen, 1986.
_____. *Scraps of the Untainted Sky: Science Fiction, Utopia, Dystopia*. Boulder: Westview, 2000.
Pfeil, Fred. *White Guys: Studies in Postmodern Domination and Difference*. London and New York: Verso, 1985.
Piercy, Marge. *He, She, and It*. New York: Knopf, 1991.
_____. *Woman on the Edge of Time*. New York: Knopf, 1976.
Robinson, Kim Stanley. *Antarctica*. New York: Harper Collins, 1997.
_____. *Blue Mars*. New York: Harper Collins, 1996.
_____. *The Gold Coast*. New York: Tor, 1988.
_____. *Green Mars*. New York: Harper Collins, 1993.
_____. "Imagining Abrupt Climate Change: Terraforming Earth." Amazon shorts: Amazon.com [shortsmail@amazon.com]. Accessed 18 May 2007.
_____. *Pacific Edge*. New York: Unwin Hyman, 1990.
_____. *Red Mars*. New York: Harper Collins, 1992.
_____. *The Wild Shore*. New York: Ace, 1984.
_____, with David Seed. "The Mars Trilogy: An Interview." *Foundation: The Review of Science Fiction* 68 (Autumn 1996): 75–81.

Russ, Joanna. *To Write Like a Woman: Essays in Feminism and Science Fiction.* Bloomington: Indiana University Press, 1995.
Sargent, Lyman Tower. "The Three Faces of Utopianism, Revisited." *Utopian Studies* 5.1 (1994): 1–38.
_____. "U.S. Eutopias in the 1980s and 1990s: Self-fashioning in a World of Multiple Identities." *Utopianism/Literary Utopias and National Cultural Identities: A Comparative Perspective.* Bologna: COTEPRA, 2001. 221–231.
Schoene-Harwood, Bertolt. *Writing Men: Literary Masculinities from Frankenstein to the New Man.* Edinburgh: Edinburgh University Press, 2000.
Wells, H. G. *A Modern Utopia: A Sociological Holiday.* London: Chapman and Hall, 1905.
Williams, William Carols. *In the American Grain.* New York: New Directions, 1956.

2

"If I Find One Good City, I Will Spare the Man": Realism and Utopia in the Mars Trilogy*

Fredric Jameson

> Strictly speaking, Utopia is not a genre in its own right, but rather the socio-political sub-genre of science fiction.
> — Darko Suvin[1]

For those who still think that science fiction is about science, the Mars trilogy will certainly qualify. Not only are scientists and engineers among its principal characters; pages upon pages offer pocket disquisitions on a host of topics that surely qualify as hard science, most of it relating to terraforming: such as the biochemistry of rocks and solids; the dynamics of gases and the composition of atmosphere; aquifers and the release of water and other liquids; genetically engineered micro-organisms and genetically reconstructed DNA; radiation, light and heat; the food chain; the structure of topsoil; meteorology and the dynamics of wind and climate; botanical systems and classification; "string theory" and the unified field theory in physics; the mechanics of velocity in astronomical and military situations. Robinson manages to hold the non-scientific reader's interest and attention during these brief but ludic discussions, about which one would also like to hear the scientists' opinions or to browse through a collection of essays by the experts on his treatment of these specialized matters, which I take to be a mixture of state-of-the-art conceptualization and "speculation," mainstream or otherwise. It is true that the literary critic would here interpose the reminder that the novel offers a mimesis of science and scientific activity and not the thing itself. It is an aestheticist answer, which has always aimed at separating out the literary and "imaginative" from the referential ("real" science, "real" scientific texts and so on), but which in the present context has the disadvantage of bracketing the "cognitive" as such. Still even the "verisimilitude" of imitation necessarily has something to do with outside factors, and in particular the rapidly changing configurations of these various scientific fields in the real world.

More pertinent is, I think, the way in which these scientific facts and findings, presup-

---

*First published as "'If I Find One Good City, I Will Spare the Man': Realism and Utopia in Kim Stanley Robinson's Mars Trilogy." Reprinted from *Learning from Other Worlds: Estrangement, Cognition and the Politics of Science Fiction and Utopia*. Patrick Parrinder, ed. Liverpool, UK: Liverpool University Press, 2000. 208–233. Reprinted by permission of Liverpool University Press.

positions and activities are themselves staged: namely, as data and raw materials for the solving of problems, rather than as abstract and contemplative features of an epistemology or scientific world picture. Not only are "problems"—crises, dilemmas, catastrophes (has Sax thought about what to do if Burroughs was flooded?)—more dramatic than classic unresolved issues in theoretical science; but they also potentially give free rein to a different kind of imagination and a wilder set of propositions and puzzle-solutions. My favorite is Art Randolph's proposal for solving the population explosion: "I would give everyone alive a birthright which entitled them to parent three-quarters of a child.... He explained that every pair of parents would thus have the right to bear a child and a half; after having one, they could either sell the right to the other half, or arrange to buy a half from some other couple...."[2] There is thus a supplementary energy and invention to be admired in these solutions, above and beyond the "merely" scientific ones (unless indeed, the scientific ones are themselves aesthetically the result of just such ingenuity in the first place, something that non-scientists, with their reified respect for science as an absolute, are less often prepared to allow). At any rate, this kind of speculative problem-solving is obviously rather different from what one finds in a science fiction that offers a description of this or that kind of alien anatomy, a premise about the mechanism of this or that faster-than-light space travel, or a preview of developments in the universe several billion years from now. Indeed, the specifically SF motifs are here few and far between, and largely in the area of perception:

> To the east stood a number of rocket landing vehicles, each one a different shape and size, with the top of more sticking over the eastern horizon. All of them were crusted the same red-orange as the ground: it was an odd, thrilling sight, as if they had stumbled upon a long-abandoned alien spaceport [R 89].

But even here the next sentence puts us on the track of an idiosyncrasy (particularly when we remember that it is a Russian member of the First Hundred who is making the observation): "Parts of Baikonur would look like this, in a million years." Leaving aside a few wonderful Stapledonian excesses (the terraforming of Venus and the train-city Terminator on Mercury in the last volume), what look like science-fictional elements here are mostly temporal inversions, parts of early Mars looking old and museum-like, the great metropolis of Burroughs drowned under water in the last volume, inverted allusions to Terran ancient history—in particular to Crete—as those rise back up in Mars like a "return of the repressed." Is this then to say that the Mars trilogy is a more realistic kind of science fiction than what we ordinarily associate with space travel and emigration? Perhaps: but that is not quite the notion of realism I want to propose here.

Yet one more thing needs to be said about the kind of science we find in this novel: it is related to the overall problem of terraforming Mars, no doubt, but also has more general implications. Secondary themes hint at the secret of "problem-solving" here: the mockery of Sax's "monocausotaxophilia" (or, for example, "the love of single causes that explain everything"). But Sax himself is perplexed about prediction—"the interventions that worked, the interventions that backfired—the effects unintended, unforeseen, unnoticed"—particularly as far as Martian weather is concerned: "impossible to predict, even if one froze the variables and pretended terraforming had stabilized, which it certainly had not. Over and over Sax watched a thousand years of weather, altering variables in the models, and every time a completely different millennium flitted past" (B 336).

These structural unpredictabilities, based on chaos theory, have often been taken to be so many arguments against historical determinism, and assimilated to the anti–Marxian arsenal (in the name of some "freedom" and creativity at work at the very heart of Nature itself). Yet I think that "predictability" as such was never at stake here, and that we have here rather to do with that more fundamental structure of problem-solving in the Mars trilogy, which is not so much to be characterized in terms of *indeterminacy* as rather in those of *overdetermination*. The Althusserian concept[3] was indeed specifically designed to name what is finally not ultimately thinkable about historical conjunctures of this kind.

In other words, if all of Mars is one gigantic laboratory (and in another way it is, and we will also have to think about the novels from that perspective), then it is a unique laboratory in which the variables can never be isolated in the ordinary ways, but always coexist in a multiplicity which can scarcely be mastered by equations let alone by the computer itself. This means that whatever the scientific theme confronted — botany, biology, geology, physics, chemistry, astronomy — the projected solution to the imaginary problem will always involve the rehearsal of a specific kind of thinking to which we are not often accustomed, namely the grappling with what Althusser calls "complex overdetermined concrete situations"[4] which he also very specifically associates with history and above all with politics. It is therefore not only about the construction of a "biotic community" in topsoils that one might be tempted to exclaim (as Nadia does): "My God, it's like trying to get this government to work" (*B* 269): all of the scientific problems described in the novel, without exception, offer an allegory, by way of the form of overdetermination, of social, political, and historical problems also faced by the inhabitants of Mars.

This is, then, the sense in which science and politics are not (or not only) two separate themes in the Mars trilogy, which appear to alternate from chapter to chapter of the story of the planet's development; nor is it only a question of the inevitably scientific dimensions of any politics on Mars, nor even the increasingly obvious fact that scientific research today is itself a specialized form of institutional politics, over and above its implications for the more generally social and political. Besides all this, we need to insist on the way in which any first scientific reading of the Mars trilogy must eventually develop into a second allegorical one, in which the hard SF content stands revealed as socio-political — that is to say, as utopian.

We have to do, in other words, with the registers of reading and interpretation, and the way in which a shift between these two fundamental levels of nature and human collectivities tends to problematize each one in turn, and to send us back to the other. And this interpretative alternation also explains the more horizontal alternations in the text itself, its heterogeneities and the uneven sequence of great sheets of material — now the exploration of the landscape, now the grappling with political problems from Earth (the UN, the nation-states, the multinationals), now the brilliant set-pieces (the assassination of John Boone — "the first man on Mars" — the two revolutions, the falling of the space elevator as it wraps itself twice around the planet, great floods and fires in the tented cities, Sax's life disguised, then his rescue from the security new town, the search for Hiroko, the dramatic cures and dramatic deaths) ... so many distinct reading temporalities that are carefully juxtaposed, in a kind of distant echo of the narrative heterogeneities of the classical utopias themselves, the discovery in space or time, the encounters, then the guided tours and explanations, to which here correspond the innumerable visits to different kind of communities and settlements all over the new planet. Sheer length, sheer reading time, is crucial here in order to develop an *analogon* of historical time itself, as its overdeterminations slowly evolve across the longer Martian years, which the device of the longevity treatment prevents from forming into generations (or perhaps at best only three generations whose time is unsettled in a politically problematic way — a Bénard instability? — by the irregular immigration of Earth-dwellers). It is something of a scientific laboratory experiment in its own right, for human collective history knows rhythm and a logic radically distinct from the normal biological life span, and its paradoxes and unknowabilities stem as much from that incommensurability as they do from the other one that opposes biological individuals to larger multiplicities. The Mars trilogy then experimentally extends the lives of its viewers and participants in order to make them coeval with their own history, at the same time that it projects an original collectivity—the first settlers, the so-called "First Hundred"—as a collective protagonist or multiple subjects for that history itself; and this is also the moment to observe that the three books form a single narrative and constitute a single novel, rather than a genuine trilogy (like Robinson's Orange County books), let alone a series on the fantasy model. The shifting adjectives of the titles then correspond to stages in the development of the planet itself—first reddish rock, then covered by green plant life, and finally bathed in water and wrapped definitively in the great Martian oceans. (What the colors stand for here, and their political implications, we will see later.) Meanwhile, the later theme of the memory problems of the survivors, and the relationship of memory to the structure of the brain, is a kind of decorative projection of the structural or narrative device, what we will in a moment call its autoreferential inscription, and belongs to something like the modernist structural traits or features of the Mars trilogy.

Yet categories like "modernism" or "realism" have never seemed particularly compatible with so peculiarly generic a classification as that of Utopia (or Utopian discourse, the Utopian text), and we need to clarify them before we can work our way back to the more central issue of the relationship between science fiction and utopia that the Mars trilogy so insistently raises. One is tempted to think indeed that the hidden agenda behind predictably aimless and academic distinctions between realist and modernist utopias has more to do with the question about the possibility of a "postmodern" utopia, that is, about the possibility of utopias today as such, than it does with genre theory. In any case the classificatory categories in question themselves seem uniquely "modern," and not very relevant to More or Cyrano, let alone to the fantastic as such in general.

Rather than marshalling various traditional or *a priori* conceptions of realism, it seems best to begin with the Mars trilogy's own answer to this question, which can surely be glimpsed in Sax's musings about the way he thinks of science:

> I try to understand. I pay attention to things, you see, very closely. As closely as I can. Concentrating on the specificity of every moment. And I want to understand why it happens the way it does. I'm curious. And I think that everything happens for a reason. Everything. So, we ought to be able to tease those reasons out. When we can't ... well, I don't like it.
> It vexes me. Sometimes I call it ... the great unexplainable [*G* 12].

What is important in this rambling statement is less the issue of causality (about which the question of single versus multiple causes will be crucial enough in a different context, as we have already seen above) than it is the evocation of resistance: external reality organizes itself into a problem or even, at some lower limit, into an event as such, whose nature poses a problem only insofar as it raises a question about its own coming into existence in the first place, about the very why of its happening. This problem then, in the name of external reality or the world itself refuses an answer and eludes a solution: and I will want to suggest that it is very precisely this kind of "resistance" of a phenomenon posited as external and independent which defines the situation of literary realisms as well, and needs to be their effect when they succeed in becoming realism in the first place.

It is a "definition" which has the advantage of adapting to a variety of contents and historical situations, including the traditional ones: namely that realism has something to do with observation, with social documentation, with the rise of journalism and the "construction" of the ephemeral or actuality, and so forth. It also moves us away from the standard history-of-ideas notion of the central role of the emergence of modern science; and this is perhaps less paradoxical than it may at first seem, since the very observation about science with which we began already amounted to an attempt to describe science in terms of a whole range of other activities, or, in other words, to assimilate science to non-scientific activity and daily life as such. Science thereby becomes only one of the by-products of this increasingly specified "resistance" of reality, and not particularly even the primary agent, in a process we would do better to describe in terms of secularization.

For it is secularization as such which forestalls the easier answers of the theological or the traditional, the symbolic or the mythic; the latter's absence both confirms the autonomy of the problematic object and accounts for the creative frustration of the questions asked of it. At same time, this initial moment of secularization also precludes the development and deployment of subjectivity as such, and of the intricate dilemmas of projection and anthropomorphism, the confusions that result when we are able to begin wondering about the very source of the answers themselves: the mark of a humanization and socialization so extensive that Ann puts it, "we'll wonder ... why when we look at the land we can see anything but our own faces" (*R* 142).

Is this to say that the realistic moment must always betray a certain naïveté, a certain absence of reflexivity, an attention to the object too rapt to register the operation of our own mental categories in the process? In that case, or so the canonical account runs, realism's sequel modernism will date precisely the emergence of that new reflexivity and categorial consciousness. It is a reproach (or at least a historical diagnosis) which ought presumably also to be extended to language itself in order to gauge the extent of this precarious situation and the fragility of the realist moment in general. For the very unexplainable, in Sax's sense, the evocation of those problematic entities outside ourselves whose density refuses to answer our questions, the crucial event or occasion of the unsolvable mystery as such — these are all constructions of the realist's language, and presumably, particularly when we have to do with a novel, stands as a human artifact constructed in advance, after the fashion of the classic mystery novelist who initially devises a sequence of events designed to be as provisionally unintelligible as possible. In that case, literary realism is a trick and a deceit, which has to collapse as soon as the idea of fiction dawns on its reader. The unexplained presumably has to lie outside of language; even if the very illusion of the unexplained and the unexplainable is itself produced by language in the first place. And this is even more visible when we come to the most philosophically ambitious fictions: the tree root, for example, in Sartre's *Nausea*[5] which is supposed to stand for the absolute Not-I, and to resist and unveil the feebleness of the adjectives with which we try to seize and evoke it. Is the existential narrative still a realism, then? I think so, but it comes at the moment in which the various initial realisms have passed over into ontology; it is an ontological realism, as we shall see in a moment.

What threatens our belief in realism today, and yet perhaps stimulates newer and even more desperate forms of realism, is our widespread conviction (which owes as much to Sartre as to anybody else) about the "constructedness" of reality as such — the constructedness of scientific fact fully as much as of social institutions, the construction of gender and of the subjective fully as much as that of the objective categories through which we intuit the allegedly still real world. In that case everything is human, and the formerly unexplainable, the formerly contingent and resistant, will recede uniformly against the horizon of a complete humanization and a complete socialization, of the awareness of the omnipresence of praxis and production in the seeming autonomy of what lies outside us.

Thus, even the tree root must wane and fade away in its Being when we incorporate the longer historical view into our dealings with nature: in particular, a knowledge of the historical invention and production of plant life by emergent human society. At that point, then, presumably, everything we have hitherto considered to be natural and organic becomes as manufactured as the cityscape itself: and this is certainly a radical defamiliarization that much of science fiction has attempted to convey. If the tree and its roots are not the result of such ancient domestication, as it were the dogs among plant life, then this form tends to separate itself out, not as a messenger of some unknowable Being, but rather merely as a kind of archaic symbol:

> The Mediterranean tree, the tree of the Greeks.... Each tree was like an animal holding its plumage up into the wind, its knobby legs thrust into the ground. A hillside of plumage flashing under the wind's onslaught, under its fluctuating gusts and knocks and unexpected stillnesses all perfectly revealed by the feathering leaves [*B* 187].

On the other hand, one can also evoke a more dialectical construction, a production by the negative, as when even wilderness itself—"desert" in its archaic sense of the emptiness of people—waste, the radically non-human in earthly nature, is itself brought into being and generated by the emergence of the fact of the human—the jar on the hill—in its midst:

> It made the slovenly wilderness
> Surround that hill.[6]

This was Marx's great reminder to Feuerbach, when he invited him to look out on to the Roman Campagna:

> So much is this activity, this unceasing sensuous labor and creation, this production, the foundation of the whole sensuous world as it now exists that, were it interrupted for only a year, Feuerbach would not only find an enormous change in the natural world, but would very soon find that the whole world of men and his own perceptive faculty, nay his own existence, were missing.[7]

Behind the theory of social construction, therefore, lies praxis and human production itself, which makes a mockery of realism's staged mystery stories, its fictive astonishment at encountering the "resistance" of a reality it has itself cooked up in another avatar. The thought then drifts across the mind, like the proverbial cloud no bigger on the horizon than a hand, and in the form of what is as yet a merely speculative perplexity, whether precisely that production and its story, the very construction of otherness itself, the history of praxis and the resistances it must transform in its turn—whether those narratives at the second degree, or better still at the level of preconditions—might not yield a realism in their own right, comparable to yet different from the more familiar realisms whose secrets we have been trying to surprise. Production, praxis, even construction as such, in fact require the resistance of some initial raw material, diffused through the situation which itself takes shape only under the pickaxe of the original project: it is a formula that combines both requirements, that of the confrontation of an unyielding set of elements, to be inventoried and described, that of the human pressure that will gradually give them names and the appearance, if not yet of a city, at least of its quarry and foundation pit, an immense building site whose future skyline is still unknown.

This is, at any rate, the ambiguous space in which the Mars trilogy is uniquely positioned, wedged in between the moments of otherness and production, between geology and biology, rock and plant, impact crater and tented village. Time is inscribed, in this spatial novel, as the marker of "emergent properties" (*B* 343), of the radically unexpected and unpredictable, which is to say of contingency and ontological resistance in the realm of temporality and of change itself; hitherto static descriptions of the outside world are thus already secretly historical:

> The flowers were mounted on little mossy cushions or florettes, or tucked among hairy leaves. All the plants hugged the dark ground, which would be markedly warmer than the air above it; nothing but grass blades stuck higher than a few centimeters off the soil. He tiptoed carefully from rock to rock, unwilling to step on even a single plant. He knelt on the gravel to inspect some of the little growths, the magnifying lenses on his face-plate at their highest power. Glowing vividly in the morning light were the classic fellfield organisms: moss campion, with its rings of tiny pink flowers on dark green pads; a phlox cushion; five-centimeter sprigs of bluegrass, like glass in the night, using the phlox taproot to anchor its own delicate roots ... there was a magenta primrose, with its yellow eye and its deep green leaves, which formed narrow troughs to channel water down into the rosette. Many of the leaves of these plants were hairy. There was an intensely blue forget-me-not, the petals so suffused with warming anthocyanins that they were nearly purple — the color that the Martian sky would achieve at around 230 millibars, according to Sax's calculations on the drive to Arena. It was surprising there was no name for that color, it was so distinctive. Perhaps that was cyanic blue [*G* 150].

Here the very colors are events in their own right, the yellow eye of the primrose "looks back at you" (Rimbaud), the unnamed blue almost speaks to you, like a word on the tip of the tongue. Color is here on Mars already defamiliarized and made strange, pre-prepared for further dramas of meaning, as we shall see. Meanwhile, the various traits themselves hover on the strategic fault line between the symbolic and the contingent, between meaning and being: blocking off a space of undecidability which is unexpectedly narrative:

> So he dove back into studying plants. Many of the fellfield organisms he was finding had hairy leaves, and very thick leaf surfaces, which helped protect the plants from the harsh UV blast of Martian sunlight. These adaptations could very well be examples of homologies ... or they could be examples of convergence.... And these days they could also be simply the result of bioengineering.... There was a biotique lab in Elysium, led by a Harry Whitebrook, designing many of the most successful surface plants, especially the sedges and grasses, and a check in the Whitebrook catalogue often showed that his hand had been at work, in which case the similarities were often a matter of artificial convergence, Whitebrook inserting traits like hairy leaves into almost every plant he bred [*G* 160].

Art then, rather than nature: the hairy leaves are like the traits of style of a distinctive painter, which help to authenticate this or that doubtful canvas. Now suddenly otherness falls away, and we have to do with the mediation of human artifacts, to be scrutinized not for natural laws and evolutionary processes but rather for intentions and forensic responsibility. Indeed, all this later unexpectedly comes to life in a different way, when Harry Whitebrook appears on the scene in person, in flesh and blood so to speak (*B* 214); he has moved on to experimentation with animal life, and rather large animal life at that, and Ann thinks of assassinating him, as one of the great criminals of terraforming. Yet the apparition has a rather different effect from this mystery-story one: rather like those rare moments in the novel when God, or the Author, make their appearance in person — the visit to the corporate office at the end of Frank Norris's *The Octopus*, or the desperate appearance in the writer's study of one of the doomed characters of Miguel de Unamuno's *Mist*— more than a mere figure in the carpet this, a kind of ultimate chance to ask the ultimate questions, to unravel the fabric of the universe by tugging on this tantalizing loose thread. It is what the Romantics called Irony, in the heightened or sublime sense of the I behind the not-I — the lantern bobbing through the woods towards the cabin in which the terrified characters of C.D. Grabbe (in *Scherz, Satire, Ironie, und tiefere Bedeutung*) attempt to hide, warning the audience, as the curtain is about to fall, that the newcomer is in fact Grabbe himself, "the author of this damned play!" Yet such Romantic Irony is rarely understood to be the logical outcome of any really consequent realism: here, I believe that its ghostly presence rather marks the fault line between realism and something else, which I will call ontology and into which the inventory of otherness and resistance can logically develop, when realism is conceived in a religious or metaphysical mode. It is an outcome which will not surprise students of film theory, where the ontological strains both in Bazin and in Kracauer have a religious solemnity and promise a "redemption of physical reality."[8]

This ontological alternative is more difficult to project and to achieve in narrative literature as such, where an approach to the visible and the tactile is mediated by language and must generally be keyed by interpretive signals (thus Heidegger's examples are mainly those of lyric poetry).[9] In the Mars trilogy, however, and in science fiction generally, it is the possibility of separating off the elements of human labor from the underlying conditions of Being itself which makes both dimensions available for celebration. Thus it has been observed about *Robinson Crusoe* that its mythical status of origins, of an absolute new beginning and the philosophical blank state of human culture and civilization, depended on some initial prestidigitation: not only is the island occasionally visited by other people and cultures, but above all Crusoe himself is able to salvage a good deal of Europe from the shipwreck, and to stock his island refuge in advance with a variety of tools and materials, in other words with stored human labor. But this inventory is not only obvious, it is foregrounded in the Mars trilogy, where to the Whitmanesque list — "an Allen wrench set, some pliers, a power drill, several clamps, some hacksaws, an impact-wrench set, a brace of cold-tolerant bungie cords, etc., etc." (*R* 96) — a wholly different preview, a synthesizing perspective, is added: "'You know what this is,' Nadia said to Sax Russell one evening looking around her warehouse, 'it is an *entire town*, disassembled and lying in pieces" (*R* 96). Crusoe's atomized individualism makes it hard for him to feel about his laden yet doomed ship what disassembling the *Ares* suggests to its settler-passengers: "like dismantling a town and flinging the houses in different directions" (*R* 78). Crusoe must meanwhile produce his own internal division of labor: the *Ares* brings a collective one with it, and Mars itself generates whole new kinds of tasks, competencies, métiers and vocations (my favorite is the new art of "cliffside trail-making" which Nirgal encounters in the course of his joggings and ramblings around the planet [*B* 368]). "Terraforming" then retroactively includes all those implements, all those receptacles of human value, and it becomes the fundamental dividing line between realism as the narrative of human praxis and ontology as the traces of Being itself: two formal or generic possibilities, which thereby reinforce each other, insofar as production requires some preexistent being on which to do its work, while Being itself can be detected only in the spaces that human praxis spares, in the evanescent chance at origins that time and history inexorably efface.

It is therefore scarcely surprising that the trilogy should inscribe this its structural condition of possibility within the narrative itself: it is something like the modernist feature of this "realistic" text, its mode of autoreferentiality in other words, of designating its own unique process of production, and reproducing the form of the text within its themes. In something of the same fashion we have already observed the way in which the theme of the longevity treatment as it were authorizes the length of the trilogy itself and replaces the latter's temporality within its narrative, in the form of memory and forgetfulness and the structure of the brain. Terraforming now finds its internal marker and as it were its interpretant and its organ of resonance in the allegorization of two specific characters, Ann and Hiroko, who become the symbols and monuments, larger than life, of the pro and the con of this new productive process. It is true that all of the central characters gradually become allegorized in similar ways — "in the arguments on Earth, many people began to use the colonists' names as a kind of shorthand for the various positions" (*R* 151) — so that their collective relations project the intricate political constellations and multiple oppositions of the work, while individually they survive and redouble themselves over the course of the narrative, becoming their own legends or — what is probably more significant in a work in which long-range communication is also a significant issue — their own media images. Yet perhaps some supplementary word should be offered here about the talents and "specialties" of this particular writer, whose affinity for individual sports like skiing is also evident in other works and has its bearing on the veritable anthology of physical modes of appropriating the planet here. What must also be mentioned in that respect is the unique narrative sociability he shares with Pynchon and Delany, the preference, over states of individual introspection (although not, as we have seen, of perception), for collective zaniness and the manic interaction of a host of different characters, in a gamut that ranges from the late-night party all the way to revolution itself.

At any rate, it is clear that tension between the characters is a precondition for such moments of collective euphoria and the gift of tongues.[10] Multicultural liberals (like John Boone) are opposed to Machiavellian operators (like Frank Chalmers, for whom politics "was all damage control" [*G* 422]), themselves both opposed to professional mediators (like Art Randolph, responsible for the original Dorsa Brevia declaration and then the first constitution itself), all of their forces and positions then recirculated through the women characters, Mars' first president and first engineer Nadia Chernesheysky (along with that of her eventual partner the anarchist Arkady Bogdanov, her name offers a properly utopian autoreferentiality), and the first leader of the expedition, Maya Toitovna, whose public interventions throughout the first two hundred years offer a political fever chart of Martian history. The "semiotic rectangles"[11] with which Michel occasionally tries to sort out the "temperaments" of his patients among the First Hundred are perhaps not complicated enough to do justice to the multiple interactions between them and the constant evolution and reorganization of those interrelationships themselves at higher levels; a process which not only reconfirms the doctrine of "emergent properties" but perhaps in its own way also offers abstract cross-sections of "overdetermination" at fixed stages in its own trajectory.

The characters can also be typologized and allegorized, because their specializations are required for the novel's heterogeneity, passing from the various sciences (Sax Russell) to architectural and urban construction (Nadia) and on to politics (Maya or Frank). But the principal structural allegory develops around two central figures who are both marginal to the central historical movement of things and indispensable to the struggle over meanings which is also a part of that movement. Both are in that sense forces of negativity, Ann Clayborne because she herself implacably personifies refusal and opposition, Hiroko because her ultimate incarnation and avatar seems to have become absence itself: she negates empirical reality in the spirit of an ideal, while Ann seeks to undermine it in the political activism of an opposition to activism and an attempt to end history itself in a different way, by bringing change and "progress" to a halt.

For terraforming ought to constitute the utopian moment par excellence of this grand historical adventure, a global equivalent of that "flowering tree" which signaled the passage from winter to spring in Morris' *News from Nowhere*,[12] as its protagonist woke out of the sleep of his miserable "historical" London. But even if the inspection of plant life is one of the keenest events in this trilogy, the celebration of the coming of life is scarcely unanimous. Ann is the place of this particular great refusal, which it is essential to grasp as an affirmation as well and the very space of the alternative, if not indeed the original ontology. "A mask of anger," she is also a figure of desperate mourning and silence; her misery and unhappiness persists throughout her surface activities, as geologist and also *de facto* party chief— they are the most tangible expression of the irreversible loss which is also the colonization of Mars. And it is no doubt this persistence of a grief that cannot be resolved that makes her into more than an allegory of melancholy in its most morbid Freudian sense; her gaunt and unappeasable face suggests that she is ridden and inhabited by the incubus of a characterological defect which the others want to explain psychologically: "I think it is a denial of life. A turning to rock as something she could trust. She was mistreated as a girl, did you know that?" (*B* 44). Indeed, she comes to stand for death, from which she herself escapes by merest accident ("the long runout"— *G* 100; the enforced longevity treatment— *B* 83; the emergence unscathed from the hopeless civil war— *B* 27). Yet perhaps this is to mistake the irrevocability of death for a rather different kind of historical irreversibility— the fact that Mars is henceforth tainted and can never be returned to any pristine state, no matter what conservationist movements spring up as a second best in Ann's wake.

Indeed, one's impression is that the "original" planet speaks less often directly to its settlers than their own future projects for it: it must come as a pause and a shock in order to be seen:

> truly giant walls flanked him on both sides, dark brown slabs riven by a fractal infinity of gullies and ridges. At the foot of the walls lay huge spills of ancient rockfall, or the broken terracing of fossil beaches. In this gap the Swiss road was a line of green transponders, snaking past mesas and arroyos, so that it looked as if Monument Valley had been relocated at the bottom of a canyon twice as deep and five times as wide as the Grand Canyon. The sight was too astonishing for John to be able to concentrate on anything else, and for the first time in his journey he drove all day with Pauline [the computer] off [*R* 236].

Does this very astonishment not confirm Ann's suspicion that the First Settlers "have never even seen Mars" (*R* 160), but only their own faces, their own projections, even in the guise of life forms engineered and implanted by human beings? Ann's "mistake had been in coming to Mars in the first place, and then falling in love with it. Falling in love with a place everyone else wanted to destroy" (*R* 490). It would be wrong to think of her relationship to this planet as some purely aesthetic or contemplative one, however: for she is in a way its historian and the student of its archaic palimpsest: "To see the landscape in its history, to read it like a text, written by its own long past: that was Ann's vision, achieved by a century's close observation and study, and by her own native gift, her love for it" (*B* 79). Here too the romance of causation and the story of production transform so many visual and natural curiosities into deep time:

> the fantastic pressures engendered by the impact had resulted in all manner of bizarre metamorphoses, the most common being giant shattercones, which were conical boulders fractured on every scale by the impact, so that some had faults you could drive into, while others were simply conical rocks on the ground, with microscopic flaws that covered every centimeter of their surfaces, like old china ... shattercones that had landed on their points and stood balanced; others that had had the softer material underneath them eroded away, until they became immense dolmens; giant rows of fangs; tall capped lingam columns, such as the one known as Big Man's

Hardon; crazily stacked strata piles, the most prominent of them called Dishes in the Sink; great walls of columnar basalt, patterned in hexagons; other walls as smooth and gleaming as immense chunks of jasper [*G* 421].

I think that the philosophical debate is thus poorly posed if we stage it in terms of the death wish, or of "a desperate attempt to stave off the present moment; to stave off history" (*B* 79), since the reading of the historical record is inscribed in such ontological meditation, and even the contemplation of Mars's pristine surface in that sense offers materials for "a poem that includes history," as Pound liked to put it. Heidegger is there, meanwhile, to show that the "opening onto Being" need not be exclusively restricted to the inorganic or to rock surfaces; although we need to juxtapose his accounts with the august later poetry of MacDiarmid:

> All is lithogenesis — or lochia,
> Carpolite fruit of the forbidden tree,
> Stones blacker than any in the Caaba,
> Cream-coloured caen-stone, chatoyant pieces,
> Celadon and corbeau, bistre and beige,
> Glaucous, hoar, enfouldered, cyathiform ...
> I must begin with these stones as the world began.[13]

It seems to me that the only way to do justice to this significant philosophical component of the trilogy is to grasp the anti-humanism inherent in all ontology, from the religious varieties all the way to secular ontologies like that of Heidegger. We have not done with the great debates around humanism that were conducted in the 1960s, even though such official themes seem to have receded into the archives of fashion. But we cannot yet assess this anti-humanist ontology until we take account of its great alternative, the "areophany" of Hiroko, who stands for greenness — viriditas — and life, and whose vitalism thus seems to oppose Ann's death urge in all respects: "Life is so much spirit, Hiroko used to say. It was a very strange business, the vigor of growing things, their tendency to proliferate, what Hiroko called their green surge, their viriditas" (*G* 153). Yet even this identification with the organic and the biological is somewhat discredited in advance by the presence of genetic engineering (just as the claim to Being of rocks was by their history).

Yet just as life does not simply run parallel to the organic and to dead matter, so also Hiroko's story is scarcely symmetrical to that of Ann; and if the latter becomes a political symbol (and a virtual allegory), Hiroko's transmutation into a virtual (Mars) goddess is both comparable and yet very different indeed. Nor does her modest first appearance as a rather withdrawn Japanese botany expert, nor even the lush arrangements of her spaceship farm (or the rumors about her "male harem," a collection of alleged sperm donations from members of the crew), presage the surprise of her disappearance, along with a whole breakaway group of followers, including a stowaway from Earth (the legendary Coyote-to-be). But the significance of this secession is enhanced by evidence of long and careful planning: caches stored around Mars' surface and undetectable from the air, and the wondrous sanctuaries underneath the ice, in which bamboo structures nestle among greenhouses ("the green world inside the white," as Nirgal thinks [*G* 7]), slowly project the image of a genuine alternative world ("they probably wanted to get free of us. Make something new. What you and Arkady say you want, they really wanted" [*R* 226]), and generate utopia within the utopia of the Mars colony. They also invest her person with an authority not far from superstition; so that the staged reappearances at crisis moments in the planet's history are politically influential as well as dramatic:

> A string of three sand-colored dirigibles floated up the slope of the volcano. They were small and antiquated, and did not answer radio inquiries....
> When their gondolas popped open, and twenty or so figures in walkers stepped out, a silence fell. "That's Hiroko," Nadia said suddenly over the common band [R 332].

Hiroko is thus the leader of a social and political sect, but also an authority figure for the larger Green movement; her well-nigh legendary status is meanwhile to be understood as the component of a cultural politics as well, as when she systematically develops and encourages a kind of Mars ritual during the great organizing congresses: "Hiroko ... seems an alien consciousness, with entirely different meanings for all the words in the language, and, despite her brilliance at ecosystem design, not really a scientist at all, but rather some kind of prophet" (*G* 115). Yet it is not particularly any personal ambition that is involved (we are told again and again of her impersonal relationship to her followers and her children, her relative indifference to individuals) but rather the sense, conscious or unconscious, that social cohesion is cemented, as the term suggests, by *re-ligio*, and therefore that the unique relationship the settlers need to develop to Mars must be sealed and strengthened by a ritual attachment to the planet of the type that some Terran ecological and feminist groups have tried to develop around the mythic entity of Gaea. (The appearance of "feral" community of intentionally primitive hunters on Mars also suggests Ernest Callenbach's inclusion, in *Ecotopia*, of an archaic ritual of rivalry and physical violence as a collective steam-valve: in the Mars trilogy, however, the feral merely designates one alternative possibility among others, as, indeed, does Hiroko's "new religion.") All this is of course heightened by the mystery of her disappearance and presumed death in the firestorm at Sabishii; after which her reappearance, to rescue Sax in the snowstorm (*B* 57), is only the first in many rumored sightings, on Earth itself, back on Mars and even in the outer planets and satellites.

But it is obviously as the spiritual leader of the Greens that the figure of Hiroko takes on an ideological meaning comparable to Ann's. No doubt we need to gloss these political terms, about whose traditional Terran meanings the Mars trilogy has some tricks to play on us. For if Earth's ecological movements have come to be designated as Green, it takes but a little reflection to understand that the comparable movement of conservation on Mars will be called Red; and that it is Ann's extreme or radical position, that the original Mars should be maintained in its pristine shape, without breathable atmosphere or plant life, that is the truly "ecological" political ideology. On Mars, then, the "Greens" are the party of progress and as it were of development in its bad, industrial sense: they stand for the "terraforming" of the planet and the loss, as it were and as we have seen above, of its ancient Being and meaning; never mind for the moment that there are clearly a whole range of technologies available to do this, and thus a whole range of Green ideologies and Green versions of "respect for the planet" (the most frequently mentioned compromise, unacceptable to Ann herself— until the very end?—being the proposal to limit breathable atmosphere up to a certain distance alone, so that above that mark the Martian landscape will retain its original desolation and impact formations). Hiroko's notion of "viriditas" can thus be seen as a kind of ideological compensation: the construction of an image of Martian life that might win the same kind of ecological adherence and loyalty as Ann's more obvious and literal appeal to what really once was. (But it should be noted that, latterly, Ann herself feels the ideological and political need to invent a Red version of "viriditas," a viriditas of rock (*B* 558), a paradoxical concept that seemed physically realized in advance by the green glow of Uranus [*B* 434].)

Still, Ann's "Reds" are a violent bunch, whose advocacy of "armed struggle" will certainly suggest Terran analogies, while Hiroko's "Greens" remain as vitalist as any of those so designated on Earth. I think we should not exaggerate the narrative temptation to reconcile these positions in some final, ideological "happy ending": it is true that something analogous is acted out on that symbolic level of color on which we have commented, in one of the novel's most striking descriptions:

> Right next to the pond were patches of dark green succulent leaves, dark red at their edges. Where the green shaded into red was a color he couldn't name, a dark lustrous brown stuffed somehow with both its constituent colors. He would have to call up a color chart soon, it seemed; lately when looking around outdoors he found that a color chart came in handy about once a minute. Waxy almost-white flowers were tucked under some of these bicolored leaves, Farther on lay some tangles, red-stalked, green-needled, like beached seaweed in miniature. Again that intermixture of red and green, right there in nature staring at him [B 54].

But the name for this unnamable color is Utopia, which stares insistently back at us from the Mars trilogy just as it does at Sax.[14] The utopian text is not supposed to produce this synthesis all by itself or to represent it: that is a matter for human history and for collective praxis. It is supposed only to produce the requirement of the synthesis, to open the space into which it is to be imagined. And this is the spirit in which the various political "solutions" of the Mars trilogy are also to be evaluated: that they are numerous, and contradictory or even irreconcilable, is I believe an advantage and an achievement in a contemporary utopia, which must also, as Darko Suvin has pointed out, stage an implicit debate with the objections and ideological and political prejudices of its readers.

Indeed, Suvin's originality; as a theorist of both SF and utopias all at once, is (among other things) not merely to have linked the two generically; but also to have conjoined the SF and utopian critical tradition with the Brechtian one, centering on estrangement (the so-called V-effect); and to have insisted not merely on the function of SF and Utopia to "estrange," to produce a V-effect for the reader from a normal "everyday" common-sense reality, but also to do so "cognitively" (a no less Brechtian component of the definition). The reassertion of the cognitive means, as we said at the outset, a refusal to allow the (obvious) aesthetic and artistic status of the SF or utopian work to neutralize its realistic and referential implications: so we do want to think about "real" science when we read these pages (and not only about the "mimesis" of science in the bad dismissive sense Plato gave that term), and by the same token we want to be able to think about "real" politics here and not merely about its convincing or unconvincing "representation" in these episodes, which dramatize our ideological objections and resistances to Utopia fully as much as they satisfy our impulses toward it. Unlike the "monological" utopias of the tradition, which needed to dramatize a single utopian possibility strongly because of its repression from Terran history and political possibility, this more "polyphonic" one includes the struggle between a whole range of utopian alternatives, about which it deliberately fails to conclude.

If the Mars trilogy is "realistic," then, on the strength of its inner reinvention of production as such, and "modernist" insofar as it then systematically designates that process of production as such, we must also insist on its properly utopian structure as a kind of "world reduction" in which not merely breathable atmosphere but custom, human relationships and finally political choices are pared down to the essentials and represented in a kind of zero degree. It is an argument that can be staged negatively, by an analysis of one of the great generic set-pieces of this narrative of coexisting worlds, and one which in genuine modernist fashion designates the utopian genre by its very exercise, namely the obligatory return tourist trip to Earth itself (which can be compared to the more central journey in Le Guin's *The Dispossessed*, and also to the equivalent in Brian Aldiss' quite different and non-utopian *Helliconia* trilogy). Here indeed, we find estrangement effects within the estrangement effects, and as it were in a *mise en abyme* that according to Gide's formula inverts the thematics of the surrounding work with a kind of telescopic precision. Here "terraforming" is still central — that is to say the existence of a layer of breathable atmosphere — yet its Terran equivalent suddenly becomes more vivid than the not insignificant accompanying problem of gravity (into which the Mars settlers slowly seem to grow):

> The air was salty hot, clangorous, heavy.... There was a doorway glowing with light. Slightly dizzy with the effort, [Nirgal] walked out into a blinding glare. Pure whiteness. It reeked of salt, fish, leaves, tar, shit, spices: like a greenhouse gone mad [*B* 139].

A landing in the Caribbean is evidently calculated to enhance the senses in general, assaulting them with the masks and costumes of Carnival and the sound of steel bands, and also with the lushness of green vegetation; yet the most "bodily" of all the senses seems the most strategically symbolic in its dominance:

> the rank stench was suddenly cut by the smell of tar on the wind.... The sweet scent [of a flower necklace] dashed with the stinging salt haze. Perfume and incense, chased by the hot vegetable wind, tarred and spiced.... The stench was of a greenhouse gone bad, things rotting, a hot wet press of air and everything blazing in a talcum of light [*B* 140].

This sensorium acts out the coexistence of multiplicities, and heightens the existential shock and conjunction of simultaneities that in the thinner, poorer air of Mars are carefully separated out from one another: as a figure for Earth's population crisis, it also emits a utopian afterimage of some Martian solution. At any rate, it is aesthetically as well as politically unsurprising that it is precisely this structural parallelism that Nirgal should point out in his first address to the Terran welcomers:

> "Mars is a mirror," he said in the microphone, "in which Terra sees its own essence. The move to Mars was a purifying voyage, stripping away all but the most important things. What happened in the end was Terran through and through ... we can most help the home planet by serving as a way for you to see yourselves. As a way to map out an unimaginable immensity" [*B* 141].

It should be added that this position is by no means shared by all the parties on Mars itself; and also that the theme of "immensity" is itself something of a defamiliarization, since so much about Mars — "Olympus Mons, the tallest mountain in the solar system" (*R* 86) or the canyons we have already seen which dwarf our own Grand Canyon — has been evoked in gigantistic terms (along with the accompanying mythologies of Big Man and Paul Bunyan, and, by inversion, the "little red people"). Now, however, unexpectedly, Nirgal in the Alps comes to "the sudden knowledge that Earth was so vast that in its variety it had regions that even out–Marsed Mars itself — that among all the ways that it was greater, *it was greater even at being Martian*" (*B* 159). These spatial and dimensional paradoxes are also, I think, hints about the peculiar reading methods we need to develop in order to navigate the structural peculiarities of utopian estrangement, which must separate us decisively from Earth before returning us to it.

Indeed, if it were not too clever by half it could be suggested that the other fundamental political preoccupation of the work is in this respect itself rather autoreferential. For it is important to understand that the debate over terraforming, and the symbolic opposition between Ann and Hiroko, is only one of the political axes around which the social and revolutionary drama of the book is fought: the other having to do with the independence of Mars from Earth, a durable Heinlein or SF theme[15] which is deepened here by the more utopian consideration of a whole change of self and the emergence of a New Martian on the order of Soviet New Man — the issue, in other words, of a cultural as well as a political revolution.

We must indeed here recall the structural precondition of that social "blank slate" upon which traditional utopias wrote their text: the radical separation of Utopia from historical reality, whether in the "great trench" dug by More's Utopus, or the ancient, now forgotten bloody revolution which ended capitalism long before the beginning of Morris' *News from Nowhere*, or even the planetary flight that, in a few dilapidated spaceships ferries Odo's followers across to the unpromising twin planet Anarres. But in the Mars trilogy this gesture remains suspended and incomplete: and the space elevator — brought down in one of the most spectacular revolutionary episodes (it wraps itself twice around the planet like a broken necklace) and then perpetually rebuilt, in Robinson's answer to Niven's *Ringworld* and so many other "floating islands" — is the persistent emblem of the threat of Terran politics and intervention, and the dilemmas of autonomy and "delinking" on Mars as well. In the traditional utopia it was the emblematic trench which "ended History"; here it is the attempt repeatedly to begin history over again which is the very subject of the work, and the other issue on which the various political parties and movements (some twenty are listed at *B* 100) must necessarily take a stand. There is thus material here for any number of combinations, so that in the long run the Greimas rectangle would seem to be more appropriate, after all, than dualisms of the Red/Green type (or even of Nirgal's green/white distinction: "in archetypal terminologies we might call green and white the Mystic and the Scientist ... but what we need, if you ask me, is a combination of the two, which we call the Alchemist"(*G* 13). What complicates all these logically possible combination and permutation schemes is the movement of History itself, which slowly modifies the fundamental situations and crises themselves. On the one hand, the issues surrounding terraforming are themselves transformed when a minimal atmosphere is acquired and a botanical biosphere is set in place (and also when the first big cities have been established): not only does the idea of returning to the "original" planetary conditions come to seem conservative as well as unrealizable, the thawing of the aquifers and the dramatic unleashing of the great floods foretell the definitive emergence of some irreversibly blue Mars. As for the other axis, which relates the settlers to Earth itself and its power structures, here two changes on both sides modify it ceaselessly. Mars becomes populated and urban, and its younger generations take the premise of Martian independence for granted, so that, after the second — more officially successful — revolution to that effect, political debate turns around the degree to which even a token emigration should be allowed and Earth's many dilemmas publicly acknowledged. But the very nature of Terran power has also evolved and been restructured over this period: an initial United Nations surveillance is undermined by the evolution of multinational corporations into trans- and then finally meta-nationals, with only a few enormous groups left, themselves divided into the traditional capitalist-rapacious ones and a new more experimental type of corporate power more dependent on the World Court (the Praxis group), at the same time that the status of the nation-state begins to oscillate perilously between the nominal flag-renting countries and the few economic giants, later displaced by the immensely populated states, particularly China and India, which support Martian independence at the same time that their overpopulation threatens it. The intricacies of these developments are then intensified by the threefold crisis of famine, the longevity treatment and its social consequences, and finally the break-up of the West Antarctic ice sheet and the disastrous rise in Terran sea level. Yet the Mars trilogy does not narrate this grim series of unresolvable crises in any direct or chronicle-like fashion;

rather, we learn to read it indirectly off Martian developments themselves and deduce the shifts in the Terran power structure from the modification of political constellations which are the response and the result on Mars itself. It is a system which allows a novel disposition of the utopian and the dystopian, if you like: the latter reserved for the seemingly inevitable degradation of Terran conditions, the former the invention of a range of political positions in that "realm of freedom" which is the Martian public sphere.

It would not be possible to sort the immense proliferation of groups and movements out without distinguishing between the political, the social and the economic levels as such; and indeed on some first general assessment it becomes clear that groups can emerge around concerns centered in any one of these three areas. The political ones are most likely to have come into being in response to the crises of Terran geopolitics outlined above, while the social groups are more likely to organize around what have come in postmodernity to be called "lifestyle" issues. And surely one of the vocations of the Mars trilogy is to have projected a "blank slate" so immense that an unimaginable variety of such social micro-systems can be housed: the descriptive or botanical level of the allegory indeed gives us the clue here:

> The closer he looked, the more he saw; and then, in one high basin, it seemed there were plants tucked everywhere.... The diversicolored palette of the lichen array; the dark green of pine needles, bunched spray of Hokkaido pines, foxtail pines, Sierra junipers. Life's colors. It was somewhat like walking from one great roofless room to another, over walls of stone: a small plaza; a kind of winding gallery, a vast ballroom; a number of tiny interlocking chambers; a sitting room. Some rooms have krummholz bonsai against their low walls, the trees no higher than their nooks, gnarled by wind, cut along the top at the snow level. Each brand, each plant, each open room, as shaped as any bonsai — and yet effortless [G 71].

The niches correspond to the varieties of social life, and ask us to fill them and to strain the utopian imagination itself for their tangible specification. One is reminded of Deleuze's celebration of the niches of life forms in Fellini: "The honeycomb-presentation ("alvéoles"), the cubicled images of huts, niches, cabins and windows."[16] On the other hand, from any postmodern perspective centered on the "new social movements" or on micropolitics, the social experimentation here scarcely knows the frenzied baroque formations one finds, extensively, in Bruce Sterling's *Schismatrix*, or, intensively, in Delany's *Trouble on Triton* (Olaf Stapledon, the great precursor in this respect, was perhaps reacting against racist ideologies, rather than anticipating this more properly 1960s' spirit). Alongside these utopian objections, then, the Mars trilogy also draws on a variety of cultural ones, after the initial Cold War "superstate" division of power of the *Ares*, it is a variety of Terran "cultures" in the national and anthropological sense we are given to observe, from Arabs to Swiss to Japanese and South African (with Sufi interludes and Cretan overtones): indeed, few novels can have projected a global post-coloniality of such range and dimensions, in a spirit so alien to U.S. parochialism and commodity universalism.

As for the economic, to turn our attention to it is at first to recall a certain initial bemusement at Darko Suvin's language (in the generic definition that we have taken as a motto): a "socio-political sub-genre" ... but why not a socioeconomic one? Or does he mean to imply, on the one hand, that the "economic" is a rather late mode of thinking and interpretation in human social and political thought and thereby in utopian thought as well? Yet utopias from Plato to More have specified an absence of private property as one of their defining characteristics. Or, on the other hand, does Suvin imply that some structural blindness of the utopia to economics as such betrays the fundamental limitation of the form? Or betrays the fundamental limitation of narrative itself?

Yet there is no lack, in the Mars trilogy, of socialist and cooperativist alternatives and ideologies, among which anarchism and Bogdanovism hold the pride of place, but also the Mondragon cooperatives in Spain. New economic systems are pioneered, the so-called "eco-economics," an elaborate calculation of value in terms of calories (*R* 268–270, *G* 316–317, *B* 117–118, *B* 240); or more rudimentary gift or barter economies ("it's a sort of two-track thing, where they can still give all they want, but the necessities are given values and distributed properly" (*G* 34). In the old days, the revival of these various schemes and their ideological authorities could often be shown to be an anti–Marxist strategy and a deployment of "utopian socialism" in exactly the spirit of Marx's critique of it. Today, it seems more likely to serve as a kind of collective Left anamnesis and a reflowering of elaborate and varied Left traditions and alternatives that were historically undeveloped, not least owing to the hegemony of Marxism itself.

Leninism does not in fact loom large here, although we are told about the existence of paleo–Marxist communes and splinter groups; but I think that has as much to do with revolutionary strategies as it does with Marxian economics; and indeed the debate about the nature of revolution itself is unsurprisingly one of the central themes of this trilogy which tells the story of several of them. In that respect, the word does seem to be confined to a very narrow sense indeed when we are told repeatedly by significant characters that revolution as such is outmoded, and is indeed itself a Terran concept ("it never even worked on Earth, not really" [*R* 315]) and are offered various substitutes, such as the notion of "phase change" from physics (*G* 497). The Leninist revolutionary party seems, however, to be the main target here, as political movements on Mars are grasped in terms of the dynamics of mass demonstrations, as in the Iranian revolution, where so great a percentage of the population is on the streets (*B* 598) that the only alternative for the power structure would be, as Brecht famously put it, "to dissolve the people and elect another one." Yet this politics of the mass movement yields splendid Eisensteinian images, such as the immense line of people against the sky, leaving the drowned city and thus also symbolically "walking away" (*G* 523) from the old system, the old way of life.

What identifies the Mars trilogy as a utopia, nonetheless, rather than a political novel about recurrent revolution as such, is the place of its unexamined premise, which in the traditional utopian text is to be found in the great trench itself, the separation, as has been said above, from everyday Terran reality. The politico-economics of Mars is here and throughout mainly anti-capitalist, although it should be noted that the liberal corporatist ideology of the Praxis meta-national is given a more sympathetic hearing than it may deserve. Yet private property has already disappeared from the Martian environment, or, rather, was never implanted there in the first place. This is, then, the sense of the so-called *Werteswandel*: "right here on Mars we have seen both patriarchy and property brought to an end. It's one of the greatest achievements in human history" (*B* 346). Yet it is an achievement that must constantly be renewed, since one of the latest political problems is the wave of Terran immigrants who cannot be assimilated because they have not absorbed such changes (the issue of some properly cultural revolution). And it is also a structural presupposition of this utopia, since we do not ever witness its evolution as a narrative event; perhaps indeed we could not do so. Yet utopia as a form is not the representation of radical alternatives; it is rather simply the imperative to imagine them.

Afterword

Of the many other things that could be said about the Mars trilogy, I want only to add this one which responds, as one always must, to Robert C. Elliott's test of the imaginative qualities of a given utopian text, namely their capacity to imagine properly utopian art works.[17] I do like the mysterious town of Medusa, in which solid blocks of whitish rock are surrounded by statues: "small white figures stood motionlessly between these buildings, on white plazas ringed by white trees" (*G* 265). But that is a relatively uncharacteristic note in this mainly "realist" utopia. So I prefer to submit this one:

> Mangalavid was showing the premiere performance of an aeolia built by a group in Noctis Labyrinthus. The aeolia turned out to be a small building, cut with apertures which whistled or hooted or squeaked, depending on the angle and strength of the wind hitting them. For the premiere the daily downslope wind in Noctis was augmented by some fierce katabatic gusts from the storm, and the music fluctuated like a composition, mournful, angry, dissonant or in sudden snatches harmonic: it seemed the work of a mind, an alien mind perhaps, but certainly something more than random chance. The almost aleatory aeolia, as a commentator said [*R* 293].

NOTES

1. *Metamorphoses of Science Fiction* (61).
2. Kim Stanley Robinson, *Green Mars* (1994; 69). Henceforth, all references to the trilogy — also including *Red Mars* (1993) and *Blue Mars* (1996) — are given within the text with the abbreviations *R*, *G* and *B*.
3. See Louis Althusser, *For Marx*, especially chapters 3 ("Contradiction and Overdeterrnination") and 6 ("On the Materialist Dialectic").
4. Ibid. 217: an "unevenness (in dominance) of the ever-pre-given complex whole."
5. Jean-Paul Sartre, *La Nausée*, in *Ouvres romanesques*, pp. 150–160 (journal notation beginning 'Six heures du soir').
6. Wallace Stevens, "Anecdote of the Jar," in *The Palm at the End of the Mind* (New York, 1967), ed. Holly Stevens, p. 46.
7. Karl Marx and Friedrich Engels, *The German Ideology* (Moscow, 1976 [1845–1846]), p. 46.
8. André Bazin, "The Ontology of the Photographic Image," and Siegfried Kracauer, *Theory of Film: The Redemption of Physical Reality*.
9. Heidegger, *Unterwegs zur Sprache*.
10. I must also note its opposite, in the frozen and chaotic results of the first floods: "The landscape itself was now speaking a kind of glossolalia" (*R* 495).
11. See A.J. Greimas, *On Meaning*.
12. "It was winter when I went to bed last night, and now, by witness of the riverside trees, it was summer, a beautiful bright morning seemingly of early June" (Morris 3).
13. Hugh McDiarmid, "On a Raised Beach."
14. "But where is socialism?' Dvanov remembered, and peered into the murk of the room, searching for his thing" (Andrei Platonov, *Chevengur*, 79); and see the discussion in my *The Seeds of Time*, pp 73–128.
15. As, classically, in Robert A. Heinlein's *The Moon Is a Harsh Mistress* (1966).
16. Gilles Deleuze, *Cinema, II* (89).
17. Robert C. Elliott, *The Shape of Utopia* (1970).

WORKS CITED

Althusser, Louis. *For Marx*. Trans. Ben Brewster. London: Verso, 1977.
Bazin, André. "The Ontology of the Photographic Image." In Bazin, *What Is Cinema?* Trans. H. Gray. Berkeley: University of California Press, 1967. 9–16.
Deleuze, Gilles. *Cinema, II*. 1985. Minneapolis: University of Minnesota Press, 1989.
Greimas, A. J. *On Meaning*. Minneapolis: University of Minnesota Press, 1987.
Heidegger, Martin. *Unterwegs zur Sprache*. Pfullingen: Neske, 1959.
Jameson, Fredric. *The Seeds of Time*. New York: Columbia University Press, 1994.
Kracauer, Siegfried. *Theory of Film: The Redemption of Physical Reality*. New York: Oxford University Press, 1960.
MacDiarmid, Hugh. "On a Raised Beach." In *The Faber Book of Twentieth-Century Scottish Poetry*. Ed. Douglas Dunn. London: Faber, 1992. 56–57.
Marx, Karl, and Friedrich Engels, *The German Ideology*. 1845–1846. Moscow: Progress Publishers, 1976.

Morris, William. *News from Nowhere*. 1890. London: Routledge & Keegan Paul, 1970.
Platonov, Andrei. *Chevengur*. 1928–1929. Ann Arbor: Ardis, 1978.
Sartre, Jean-Paul, *La Nausée*, in *Ouvres romanesques*. 1938. Paris: Gallimard, 1981.
Stevens, Wallace. *The Palm at the End of the Mind*. Ed. Holly Stevens. New York: Knopf, 1971.
Suvin, Darko. *Metamorphoses of Science Fiction*. New Haven, CT: Yale University Press, 1979.

3

Falling into History: Imagined Wests in the "Three Californias" and Mars Trilogy*

Carl Abbott

Red Mars is Kim Stanley Robinson's highly-praised science fiction novel published in 1993.[1] Its pivotal section carries the title "Falling into History." More than two decades have passed since permanent human settlers arrived on the red planet in 2027, and the growing Martian communities have become too complex to be guided by simple earth-made plans or single individuals. The section centers on John Boone, an explorer-hero ("the first man on Mars") and charismatic co-leader of the first one hundred settlers. As he spends three years wandering and visiting scattered settlements, he finds that Martian society is outgrowing his capacity to comprehend and direct.

> He had been on the road for years now ... cutting ribbons at the opening of one thing or another — a town, a well, a weather station, a mine, a mohole — and always talking, talking in public speeches or private conversations, talking to strangers, old friends, new acquaintances ... and all in an attempt to inspire the people to figure out a way to forget history, to build a functioning society. To create a scientific system designed for Mars, designed to their specifications, fair and just and rational and all those good things. To point the way to a new Mars! And yet after every year that passed, it seemed less likely ... events were out of control, and more than that, out of anyone's control.[2]

Robinson is a novelist who takes history seriously. The fall into history is the transition from the carefully controlled circumstances of a single contingent of first-comers to the intractability of multiple groups, peoples, values, and agendas. It is the collapse of the open-ended possibilities of a new place into the constrained situations of historicity — the concatenation of habits, hopes, and vested interests that characterize any society. In the words of critic Robert Markley, Robinson imagines a situation in which utopian schemes are inevitably "undone by the distance between the idealized operations of a frictionless system and the wear and tear of embodied, historical experience."[3]

Robinson himself is a Californian, raised in Orange County in the 1950s and 1960s and now living in Davis. One of the most popular and honored science fiction writers of the last

---

*First published as "Falling into History: The Imagined Wests in Kim Stanley Robinson's 'Three Californias' and Mars Trilogy," *Western Historical Quarterly* 34.1 (Spring 2003): 27–47. Copyright by the Western History Association. Reprinted by permission.

two decades, his reputation is based on two trilogies that hold mirrors to multiple historical experiences, prominently including that of the American West. The books that describe "Three Californias"—*The Wild Shore, The Gold Coast, Pacific Edge*—are explicitly regional, imagining alternative futures for Orange County over the twenty-first century. *Red Mars, Green Mars,* and *Blue Mars* constitute a single densely written novel of the settlement of the red planet over two centuries that transposes many of the problems of the American West to a new setting ("a triple decker in the old style," says the author).[4] Robinson is thus a distinctively western writer whose books are imagined discussions of the very stuff of western history, the inhabitation of "empty" places and their transformation into unexpected sorts of communities. He himself has commented: "I think of myself as a Californian writer more than I do a science fiction writer, and would be happy to be grouped with the California writers. To be grounded in that way, even regionalized, would be a very good way of giving some physicality or heft to the inclination of science fiction to be otherworldly by being set in the future."[5]

It is not surprising that a California/western writer may also be a science fiction writer. Americans have long projected political and cultural hopes on the West in forms that range from geopolitical boosterism to communitarian experiments. And we have been particularly eager to burden California with often contradictory roles as arcadia, utopia, and featured player in the collapse of civilization.[6] Science fiction is a natural extension of such western discourse, reinscribing the hopes and fears that shaped stories of the nineteenth- and twentieth-century West onto settings that stretch even more broadly across space and more deeply into time. Indeed, for many writers of speculative fiction, the western experience of the United States has served as a template for fictional futures. The result, at times, is a seamless connection of centuries—a common set of stories that link the historical past to the imagined future.[7]

Americans have long found it easy to apply the capacious frontier metaphor to realms beyond the stratosphere. Most television viewers know of the Starship *Enterprise*, which boldly voyages through "space: the final frontier" in endlessly recycled episodes of *Star Trek*. Closer to home, Disneyland juxtaposed the rocketships of Tomorrowland and the coonskin caps of Frontierland.[8] *Star Trek* creator Gene Roddenberry drew on a rich heritage of space adventure stories in crafting his television series (originally conceptualized as "wagon train to the stars"). "Space operas" as western horse operas with ray guns were a staple of pulp magazine fiction in the 1930s and 1940s. The Buck Rogers and Flash Gordon movies of the same era even inspired a Gene Autry serial called *The Phantom Empire*, in which Gene alternates between singing cowboy duties and captivity by ray-gun wielding Thunder Riders from the 100,000-year-old subterranean "scientific city" of Murania. The new *Magazine of Fantasy and Science Fiction* and *Galaxy* magazine, both started in the 1950s, still appeared on cheap paper but were conscious efforts to elevate the genre, with *Galaxy* editor H. L. Gold advertising that there would be no westerns disguised as science fiction in *his* pages.

More recently, the idea of a "high frontier" for American ingenuity and enterprise has been a political project. The rhetoric of John F. Kennedy connected the New Frontier to the goal of a manned mission to the moon, and former astronaut John Glenn later invoked the image of space as "the modern frontier for national adventure."[9] In the 1970s, Gerard K. O'Neill gave the metaphor an engineering twist with his detailed proposal for a high frontier of inhabited artificial satellites. The U.S. National Commission on Space in 1986 described the settlement of North America as a prologue to the space frontier. Lobbying organizations and publishers continue to keep alive the idea that the necessary next frontier will be space exploration, translating an old maxim into upward the course of empire takes its way.[10]

Robinson himself challenges these well-worn conventions by emphasizing community rather than heroism, civic life rather than adventure, and environmental management rather than economic opportunity. His trilogies address both the scientific-industrial politics of the high frontier and the literary formulas that underlie this political project. By taking seriously the possibilities of a cooperative commonwealth, both in *Pacific Edge* and in the Mars books, he questions the inevitability of capitalist economies. His attention to the dynamics and problems of social inclusion and exclusion undercut the easy nationalism of the earthly and unearthly frontiers. His attention to settlement and society contravene the dynamic of perpetual change that is embedded in the frontier myth.

I have two specific goals in this discussion: (1) to explore the ways in which Robinson as a western American author understands history and pivots his narratives on issues of historical interpretation, and (2) to examine how he incorporates into his fictions some of the familiar tropes and interpretations of the American western experience. The larger, implicit subject is the incorporation of western American history into popular culture, viewed through the ways that Robinson uses and transforms issues central to historical understanding and interpretation of the American West and other European settlement frontiers. In particular, we can gain new insights into the meaning of the West in American minds by examining how Robinson has dealt with such issues as the future of urbanization, the possibilities of intentional communities and of economic cooperation, governance on a settlement frontier, the responsibilities of leadership in a democracy, the clash between raw nature and human use of the landscape, and the political tensions between colony and imperium. There is, I believe, much in Robinson's projections of future historical change that incorporates or echoes the critical thinking about environment, conquest, inequality, and community associated with the "new western history" with its emphasis on the multiplicity and complexity of events and the contingency of narratives.[11] Reading his work may make us more sensitive participants in this historical conversation and give us greater understanding of how increasingly complex ideas about the American West are entering the world of popular culture.

Kim Stanley Robinson explicitly defines science fiction as historical in character — as articulated narratives that can be seen as anchored at their origins in "real" times and circumstances. "In every science fiction narrative," he writes, "there is an explicit or implicit fictional *history* that connects the period depicted to our present moment." That is to say, science fiction is narrative that starts with or assumes the historical present and writes it forward. In a different interview, he makes a parallel point in calling science fiction "the history that we cannot know." Readers can assume that a plausible sequence of events might lead from their present to the events in the story and can observe how the writer varies the assumptions behind those events. Science fiction is thus a set of thought experiments, as Martian society is itself characterized during one of the political debates in *Green Mars*.[12]

Robinson's definition differentiates true science fiction from many of the books and videos that sit on the science fiction shelves in libraries, bookstores, and Blockbuster video outlets. Science fiction is not cheerful Harry Potter fantasies nor dark vampire melodramas; it is not extra-terrestrial monster-slaying tales, sword-and-castle-in-a-different-universe romances, nor space operas set in some other galaxy a long time ago. Instead, Robinson aligns himself with hard science fiction writers who have crafted explicit future histories such as Robert Heinlein, David Brin, and Ken MacLeod and with so-called cyberpunk writers like William Gibson and Bruce Stephenson who project the near future of an electronically linked and mediated society.[13]

Robinson argues the virtues of historical fiction as a counterpart of science fiction. In comments on the work of historical novelist Cecelia Holland, he states that historical fiction and science fiction share the challenge of making intelligible the inner workings of alien cultures, and thereby illuminating our own cultural and social values. He also shares Holland's interest in politics — in the ways that people wield power and the ways that the powerless can resist the powerful. It is therefore possible "to write historical fiction for the same reason one writes science fiction: to take advantage of the psychological power of the estrangement effect, which in pulling readers momentarily out of their ordinary world views, gives them the chance to see things anew."[14]

In comments on his own work, Robinson places himself on a map of literary influences anchored by Joseph Conrad's socially-embedded adventures and Thomas Pynchon's ability to ground surreal narratives on the foundations of existing times and places. Several of Pynchon's purportedly mainstream novels — particularly *The Crying of Lot 49* and *Vineland* — deal with oddly off-kilter Californias that start out as places that we can recognize but drift inexorably into places of the imagination. The oppressor state that lurks beneath the sunny California surface in *Vineland* looks like the dark future that has been explicitly avoided in *Pacific Edge*. In the course of the Martian narrative, the center of gravity slowly shifts from the challenges faced by individuals to the complexities of bringing change to living societies. This is the same progression that we see in Conrad from the isolated protagonists of *Almayer's Folly* and *Lord Jim* to the complex colonial society described in *Nostromo* and the ambiguities of revolution as analyzed in *The Secret Agent*.[15]

Robinson is a theoretically sophisticated writer. He earned a master's in English from Boston University and a doctorate from the University of California–San Diego, where he worked with the influential literary scholar Fredric Jameson, perhaps best known as the critic who deconstructed the Westin Bonaventure Hotel in Los Angeles in "Postmodernism: The Cultural Logic of Late Capitalism."[16] His dissertation examined science fiction writer Philip K. Dick, whose work anticipated the shifting viewpoints of postmodernism and includes the story that Ridley Scott turned into the movie *Blade Runner*.[17] As a licensed but non-practicing academic, Robinson is fully aware of the traps in seeing history as sets of analogies, which mislead us as often as they help — although the unpacking or deconstruction of historical analogies is central to his Mars fiction.[18] In *Red Mars*, for example, John Boone tries to warn unhappy settlers that they are not the exact equivalent of the "hardy pioneer colonists" of 1775 and that changed circumstances make it impossible to reenact the American Revolution. In *Blue Mars*, the crafters of a new Martian constitution pick carefully among the numerous analogies from the political travail of twentieth-century Earth.[19]

Robinson also turns history-writing and the politics of memory into one of the motifs of his novels. A central character in *The Wild Shore* is the village storyteller, who manufactures a useable past for the survivors who eke out a livelihood from farming and fishing along the Southern California coast. Still a teenager when the bombs fell, he creates an imaginary career, adds three decades to his life, and spins tall tales into a half-accurate history to inspire the post-disaster generations. *Pacific Edge* alternates a communitarian present in the year 2065 with excerpts from a diary that touches on the political struggles that led to that particular set of social and economic institutions. The author of the diary is the same individual as the storyteller in the other book, living through a different future.

In the Mars trilogy, Robinson uses the science fiction gimmick of longevity treatments to maintain the members of the first-hundred settlers through two centuries of Martian history. Their own changing understanding of the present in light of their (and others') reinterpretations of the past becomes one of the themes and driving factors for the second and third volumes. Robinson models the problems and selectivity of historical memory and history writing in the memories of these characters. They habitually search the past for historical comparisons to understand the new Martian politics and society — usually with little success. They worry that they are forgetting the meaning of their own lived past. They repeatedly contemplate the character of historical understanding and stand bemused or infuriated when they find themselves reinterpreted as characters in history books or even in opera. The stories they tell about their own pasts become factors in the shaping of their present and future.[20]

The first trilogy, written in the 1980s, imagines three very different futures for Orange County, California. *The Wild Shore* describes a village climbing back to tribalism after the neutron bombing of the United States. The historical record is truncated, and the survivors are too busy toiling for food and shelter to sift historical fact from fiction. The Southern California of *The Gold Coast* is a straight line projection of an overcrowded "condomundo" where alienated young people do designer drugs with eyedroppers, drive automobiles with electronic guidance systems, and toy with terrorism against the transnational corporations that twist their coils around every activity. In *Pacific Edge*, the alternative is a federation of ecologically sensitive communities organized around the "small is beautiful" precepts of Ernst Schumacher and the principles of social ecology and mutual aid articulated by political philosopher Murray Bookchin.[21] Americans have used the political process to gradually rein in corporate America and focus self-government at the local level, although each community remains part of a larger world economy.

Social scientists and planners have developed increasing sophistication about the differences between forecasts and scenarios. Forecasts are quantified analogies that may use sophisticated mathematics but that still succeed or fail on the accuracy of their assumptions; the most important question about forecasts is why and how much change is likely to *change*— that is, what factors are likely to alter present short-term trends, rates, and structures.[22] In contrast, scenario builders attempt to consider possible interrelationships of technical, economic, social, cultural, and political factors. Scenario building in one sense is history on fast forward. Focused on the future, it utilizes disparate pieces of information within a broad context to create an understandable narrative. It may produce surprises, stimulating imaginative construction of alternative possibilities. And it welcomes the techniques of narrative to give body and presence to future possibilities; planners increasingly think of their task as "persuasive storytelling" that links the present to a future.[23]

Robinson demonstrates that his Orange County fictions are precisely these sorts of alternative scenarios by building in specific continuities across the books, a characteristic that he reinforces with a reference in *Pacific Edge* to Lawrence Durrell's Alexandria Quartet of novels that retell the same story from four points of view. Like much historical writing, the stories are grounded on the importance of place — a particular stretch of coast from Point Dana to San Onofre, the ridges and canyons that trail off the Santa Ana Mountains. The protagonist in each is a young man who matures, in part, by attracting and then failing to hold a strong woman. Each book makes it clear from the roster of characters that Orange County in the twenty-first century will be as much Latino as Anglo. The character Tom Barnard appears in each book at the end of a very different but logically derived life. The storyteller of *The Wild Shore* and the diary keeper of *Pacific Edge*, he ends his life in *The Gold Coast* in a nursing home, reminiscing to occasional visitors. And the books share an explicitly historical motif of digging up the past. Each opens with a group of friends wielding shovels — trekking to abandoned San Clemente to loot a grave for imagined treasure in *The Wild Shore*, digging beneath the street for the fun of discovering relics of the twentieth century in

The Gold Coast, cheerfully sharing required community work on a street project in *Pacific Edge*.

The trilogy is a set of variations on the common trope of "seeing the future in California." An imposing scholarly literature examines the ways in which greater Los Angeles served through the twentieth century as the summary or shorthand for the American future, the place to get a preview of things to come. More than half a century ago, Carey McWilliams argued that California was twenty years ahead of the rest of the nation. Los Angeles, claimed Neil Morgan in 1963, was "the center of gravity" in the westward tilt that was creating the America of tomorrow in the West of today. Postwar critics called Los Angeles "the ultimate city," the "prototype of the supercity," the "leading city." Richard Elman was a bewildered New Yorker who traveled to Compton, California, in 1967 "with the thought in mind that this was the future."[24]

In recent years, yet another scholarly generation has declared greater Los Angeles as the prototype for the twenty-first century city. A "Los Angeles School" of urban studies now argues, essentially, that we have in the SoCal metropolis a new urban form and dynamic that is postmodern. Its cityscape and spatiality, its economy and social ecology—all are fragmented, flexible, fluid—not so much formless as constantly in reformation. As expressed by Allen J. Scott, Michael Dear, Edward Soja, and others, this is a metropolis that exemplifies not its past but a coming future. And it is a metropolis where Orange County may seem to manifest the newest of the new as a post-suburban exopolis that can only be understood through fragmentary snapshots.[25]

Place—the Orange County setting—thus matters as the key to the trilogy's impact as well as serving as a factor in each narrative. It seems unlikely that a Fort Wayne trilogy or a Preble County, Ohio, trilogy, no matter how carefully done, would attract the same readership. As Robinson has agreed, Orange County's role as an "awful paradigm for the future ... could not be replaced by just any American city or suburb."[26] All three of Robinson's futures gain resonance as subtle departures and challenges to the standard dystopian Los Angeles of *Blade Runner* and the fictional variations on a Los Angeles apocalypse that Mike Davis recently summarized in *The Ecology of Fear*.[27] Davis roots his dark vision in *City of Quartz* in the collapse of hope in his Southern California hometown of Fontana. In contrast, Tom Barnard in *Pacific Edge* explicitly identifies the California of *his* childhood in the 1980s as a "pocket utopia."

> California when I was a child was a child's paradise, I was healthy, well fed, well clothed, well housed, I went to school and there were libraries with all the world in them and after school I played in orange groves and in Little League and in the band and down at the beach and every day was an adventure, and when I came home my mother and father created a home as solid as rock, the world seemed solid! And it comes to this, do you understand me—I grew up in utopia.
>
> But I didn't. Not really. Because while I was growing up in my sunny seaside home much of the world was in misery, hungry, sick ... I had been on an island...
>
> And if-if! if someday the whole world reaches utopia, then that dream California will become a precursor, and sign of things to come, and my childhood is redeemed.[28]

To get to that dream is to engage in politics, for the challenges and processes of democratic self-government set another theme that cuts across the three books and leads toward the second trilogy. *The Wild Shore* contrasts local town-meeting democracy and the strongman government that emerges from the ruins of San Diego. The second and third books contrast unsuccessful and successful ways to undercut the military-industrial complex. Slapdash terrorism in *The Gold Coast* turns out to be not only ineffective but corrupted by corporate power. *Pacific Edge* foregrounds the process of representative democracy—lobbying, bargaining, the use and abuse of bureaucratic rules to advance local interests. In the background narrative, improvements have been achieved incrementally, with political mobilization and organizing over multiple decades. In the intense local debate over developing a portion of the town's remaining open space, change again comes by increment through lobbying and votes in the town council.[29] Taken together, the books are an examination of how history happens as well as what history might mean.

The Mars trilogy is panoramic in scope and written from multiple points of view. The books follow the development of Martian society from first settlement by a team of 50 Russians and 50 Americans, through debates over environmental change, immigration, the development of multiple cultures, efforts at political independence, two rounds of constitution-making, "international" negotiations, generational conflicts, and changing social values. The structure is a series of long sections that take the viewpoints of key figures from the first hundred or their descendants. Taken together, the three volumes array the points of view of ten characters across thirty-two sections that average about sixty pages each.[30] The approach is reminiscent of John Dos Passos's *USA*. Another comparison is a contemporary writer whom Robinson cites as an influence: Peter Matthiessen, author of the Florida frontier trilogy *Killing Mister Watson*, *Lost Man's River*, and *Bone by Bone*.[31]

Robinson's vision of this future clearly draws on the history of North America. The narrative is premised on the technological capacity to "terraform" Mars (in effect making pastures of plenty from dry desert lands). In the tasks set for the original one hundred settlers are echoes of Jamestown and Philadelphia, Astoria and New Archangel; in the careful selection of the settlers for skills and temperaments are parallels to the schemes of nineteenth-century utopian socialists. Evolving experiments in political independence and self-government drive the story. Complicating the political history are conflicts between "reds" and "greens," the factions in this case ironically reversed from our current usage—the reds representing those who desire to leave Mars unaltered "wilderness" and the greens those who wish to adapt it to human use.

The titles—*Red Mars*, *Green Mars*, *Blue Mars*—trace the success of terraforming through massive engineering interventions to raise the ambient temperature and atmospheric pressure, to bring water to the surface, and to introduce plants and animals bioengineered from earth originals. There is careful and fascinating detail about the terraforming process—options, choices, setbacks, side effects, accomplishments. The technical dimension is reminiscent of the cetology and whaling lore in *Moby Dick*, and Robinson himself argues that "there is no intrinsic reason why scientific detail cannot be as interesting as the stage business of a chase scene."[32]

By imagining a first-hundred settlers equally divided among Russians and Americans, Robinson can draw on two structuring metaphors from nineteenth- and twentieth-century history. One is the promise and problems of socialist revolution against the power of capital. The second is the possibilities and processes of community-building in new lands. The first is the big, dramatic framework. The second underlies Robinson's projections of the evolution of everyday life on the high frontier. Both metaphors tie the hypothesized history of Mars to repeated falls into history—the failures of Russian socialism and French revolutionary utopianism; the transformation of New England between the 1630s and the 1680s, of Utah from the nineteenth to the twentieth century, or of any new place that wriggles free from the expectations of its founders.[33]

Red Mars, the first volume, pivots on the possibilities and failures of revolution, and it is full of the intertextuality that literary critics enjoy. A key character among the first hundred is Arkady Bogdanov, a charismatic revolutionary who preaches independence from Earth and helps to trigger a failed revolution in 2061 (the Martian equivalent of Russia's 1905 revolution). Martians regroup and try again successfully in 2127 with much better organization—think October 1917—when the oppressive regime is under external stress from eco-catastrophe on Earth. Bogdanov the character bears the name of a real Bolshevik leader, Alexandre Bogdanov, author of his own science fiction novel, *Red Star*, about the establishment of socialism on Mars. Referenced as well is Nikolai Cherneshevsky's feminist utopia of the 1860s, *What Is to Be Done?*[34] The phrase is modified for the section on failure of the first revolution in *Red Mars* (as "What have we done?!") and for the first section on constitution-making in *Green Mars*; the heroine of the constitutional convention is Nadia Chernyshevsky, another of the first hundred.

History in the Mars narrative is always conditional and mutable. It is made through the articulation of ideas, public debates, power plays, assassination. It is balanced between structure and agency, culture, politics, and economics. It is "whole, nonrepeatable, and contingent." It escapes the power of Bogdanov, Boone, his rival Frank Chalmers, or earth-based corporations to direct and shape. It shows the messiness of human life—there is always "more history, more trouble, between us and any decent society" Robinson commented in a 1996 interview.[35]

By *Green Mars* and *Blue Mars*, the increased complexity and density of cultures and institutions and "history" make action more problematic and complex. The heroes are now the constitution-makers, and by implication the scientists who help to create an inhabitable Mars. No single narrative can now contain the multifarious history. The model of the Russian revolutions drops away, for no simplifying theory works, in favor of Madisonian political compromises. The meat of the process of community formation is engaged conversation, engaged politics. The key events are now the forging of a revolutionary compact after the first failure ("What Is to Be Done" in *Green Mars*) and the establishment of formal government after a successful breakaway from Earth control ("A New Constitution" in *Blue Mars*). Nadia, the builder of engineering works and constitutions, emerges as the story's new hero.[36]

Robinson's Mars books are written explicitly against two alternative uses of Mars as frontier. One is the reinscription of the North American conquest narrative onto Mars in fantastic fictions that pay no attention to the science of transportation or settlement. Edgar Rice Burroughs kicked off the genre with "Under the Moons of Mars," in which western American John Carter takes refuge in an Arizona cave to escape Apache warriors, only to find himself on "Barsoom" (his name for Mars) facing much the same situation in a landscape that looks quite southwestern. Carter, whom Burroughs seems to have modeled on the protagonist of Owen Wister's *The Virginian*, continued his Martian adventures in a dozen books over several decades. The John Carter books were the implicit foil for Ray Bradbury's blithely unscientific but very self-conscious inversion of the same story in *The Martian Chronicles*, with episodes of genocide, labor exploitation, wasted landscapes, and ghost towns.[37]

From the opposite side of the science/humanities divide is a technologically specific literature that bundles hard science and entrepreneurial values to proclaim Mars as the most practical high frontier. Aerospace engineer Robert Zubrin zeroed in on the next planet out in *The Case for Mars*, invoking the spirit of Frederick Jackson Turner to proclaim that a new Martian frontier would help recapture the soul of America and, in turn, sparking formation of the Mars Society.[38] Recent science fiction novels that focus exclusively on dramatizing the technology of Mars exploration include planetary scientist Geoffrey A. Landis's *Mars Cross-*

ing and Zubrin's own *First Landing*. Both use that simplest of plots: the stranded explorers who must strike out across country with undaunted courage and work as a team to save themselves. Zubrin also puts his understanding of the American past into the mouth of Kevin McGee, the historian who accompanies the mission:

> I'm a historian, and I know that a society cannot have progress, or growth, or hope, unless there is an open frontier. That's what made America in its frontier days such a powerful engine of progress for all humanity.... We became the most creative nation in history, because we could see the infinite potential of the human mind.... We don't build new cities any more, and so we've begun to think of ourselves not as builders of our country, but as mere inhabitants. Our frontier has been gone too long, and now our nation is losing its spark.[39]

Robinson, too, is a historian of sorts, and one who is less likely than Kevin McGee to make most readers of the *Western Historical Quarterly* cringe. His fiction is suffused with an awareness of the American West as a historically shaped place. Where the Orange County books present possible extensions of western history, the Mars books adapt and utilize the themes and tropes through which Americans have come to understand that history. These themes illustrate and drive the action, and they are themselves challenged or interrogated by the dynamics of the fictions. And, most intriguingly, they are framed in ways that show familiarity with the themes and criticisms that the so-called new western historians were elaborating in the same years that Robinson was writing. These concerns have been summed up by Patricia Limerick with a series of "c" words: conquest, continuity, convergence, and complexity, to which we might add capitalism and community (with nods to William Robbins and Robert Hine).[40]

As the American West has been, the Martian frontier is projected as a place of often rapacious resource development. The theme of conquest, which is central to the new western history, takes the form of the conquest of nature. The first hundred begin with exploration and road building. Subsequent settlers construct high speed transit lines, build dams, and dig mines. They tap geothermal heat, pump out aquifers, and seed bioengineered plants to add weight, heat, and oxygen to the Martian atmosphere. With no building codes and environmental regulations in place, large corporations dig and run, build company towns on the cheap, and play workers of different nationalities against each other.[41] Like the Mountain West, Mars is an urban frontier of gateway cities and production cities from which miners and eventually agriculturalists spread outward: Sheffield stands in for a port city like San Francisco, Burroughs for an industrial city like Denver, Serenzi Na for a mining town like Butte, Bradbury for small agricultural cities like Grand Junction.

The history of the American West is testimony to the momentum of engineering technology, the easy step from can do to should do. So too is Martian history. The power and nearly inexorable appeal of terraforming technologies is similar to the American impulse to apply more and more technology to capture and deliver western water. In fact (the twentieth century) and in fiction (the twenty-second century), we see the ramp up from smaller to larger projects, the aesthetic attraction of the technical intervention, the promise of better life, the opening of land to settlement and use. Technical papers at a terraforming conference morph easily into grant applications from ambitious scientists.[42]

The terraforming project brings out contrasting environmentalisms of preservation and utilization. The ideas of western irrigation utopians like William Smythe echo in the American advocates of use. They find allies among the Russians, who are also development advocates, reflecting their own national history; the experience they bring is that of intensive exploitation of Siberia and Central Asia. We also hear the voices of preservationists who try to understand Mars in its own terms. In a landscape that has never before supported human beings, there is no way to deny that wilderness and other concepts through which we understand the physical settings of human life are socially constructed.[43] At one point of a debate over the future of the planet that recurs through the entire trilogy, scientist Sax Russell argues that "the beauty of Mars exists in the human mind. Without the human presence it is just a collection of atoms.... It is we who understand it and we who give it meaning." American ecologist Ann Clayborne, who longs for an unchanging Mars, counters that to truly see Mars requires "fitting into it as it is, and worshiping it with our attention." Another character "humanizes" Mars by devising the "aerophany," a "landscape religion, a consciousness of Mars as a physical space suffused with kami, which [is] the spiritual energy or power that rested in the land itself." More concretely, the protagonists later come to understand the irony of protecting the natural setting from resource development by selling its attractions for tourism.[44]

As in the American West, the place itself takes on the role of actor and influence. We hear echoes of western visionaries such as Gary Snyder, whom Robinson lists as a favorite poet.[45] The Marsscape looks like the California desert, Monument Valley, the Painted Desert. It is "a Utah of the imagination." Characters look like "weatherbeaten sodbuster[s]" and a scientific outpost like "a desiccated café in the Mojave." Settlers reproduce the flora and fauna of a southwestern canyon in a Martian valley that is tented over to hold in atmosphere.[46]

The idea that a frontier is a social safety valve acts as an exogenous force driving the story. Mars functions as a symbolic (even if not practical) release valve for an Earth collapsing from environmental stress. Crowded countries put in their claims for Martian land and resources, and illicit immigrants arrive despite official quotas and limits. Everyone knows that another planet cannot really relieve pressure at home, but home governments are unwilling to give up the fiction. The planet is linked inextricably to the history of Earth, becoming a cauldron where multinational immigration reproduces old ethnic identities and cultures in desperately pure forms.

Robinson thus incorporates into the narrative the idea of high frontier as safety valve, but he depicts this as a belief that is no more accurate for Mars than it was for western North America. The willingness of national governments on Earth to peddle the myth of a safety valve complicates the politics of environment and independence. Demands from back home constrain decisions on Mars about the pace of terraforming, for "millions on Earth wanted to come to Mars, to the 'new frontier,' where life was an adventure again." As the settlers later move toward a first revolution, Frank Chalmers notes one of their problems: "Did you see that program aired on Eurovid about all the open land on Mars? ... It was like a real estate ad." John Boone uses the imagery of frontier outpost to inspire settlers to common purpose and Arkady Bogdanov uses the rhetoric of a free and open frontier to recruit settlers from the U.S. to his revolution — both efforts that end in failure.[47]

The result is that the safety valve fails on both demographic realities (the mismatch between tens of thousands of immigrants and billions on the home planet) and on cultural conflict. Arkady Bogdanov's vision of inventing a new Martian culture from scratch crashes against the persistence of cultural differences among immigrants from Switzerland and India, the United States, Arab nations, and many other cultures. So does John Boone's alternative hope of easily blending the best ideas of Earth into a new society. Here is the theme of convergence from the new western history, an exploration of the ways in which a "white" frontier (pioneered in this case by Americans and Russians) is complicated by the arrival of immigrants from very different cultures, just as the presence of Native peoples and the arrival of Latinos, Chinese, Japanese, Filipinos, and many others has complicated the development of an Anglo-American West. The constitution makers struggle to reconcile respect for cultural peculiarities with universal rights, hoping at best for "a lot of different cultures coexisting."[48]

Questions of resource use and community come together in the relations between Earth and Mars, metropolis and colony. Central to the action is the clash between local autonomy and the domination of outside capital and corporations, another of the central issues of the new western history.[49] Beyond the direct tensions of capitalists and workers, Robinson argues that the global and local are interdependent because local opportunities are always embedded within larger structures. Mars cannot exist without a viable Earth. The societies are linked through cultural heritage and information exchange. The web of economic and cultural connections remains too strong to allow isolated purity. As Americans discovered after 1783 and again after 1815, the web of connections that tie new settlements to their places of origins are not easily severed or ignored.[50]

To be sure, one temptation in the face of pressure from Earth is to light out for the country in a repetition of a romantic version of western America. Nirgal, the epitome of the first Mars-born generation, reaches for the outback when things get too crowded.[51] So does the narrative's wildcard, a stowaway on the original voyage who makes the first hundred actually one hundred and one. He takes on the identity and role of the North American trickster Coyote. ("Coyote is out there in the back of the hills, breathing the air already and doing what he wants, the bastard.")[52] He travels the backlands organizing for economic separateness and political separation, and he argues passionately against connection to the past, but his influence gradually wanes.

As in the American West, such individualism contrasts and clashes with very specific sectarian versions of community. The empty Marsscape invites secular and religious utopian colonies. In the demimonde beyond corporate control, and between revolutions, are colonies and communities of Sufis, Baptists, Quakers, and Rastafarians. There are followers of Rousseau, adherents of Fourier, and, in another academic joke, acolytes of Foucault.[53] There are also radical Marsfirst ecoterrorists and mystical Mars-worshipers in the self-contained community of Zygote, concealed under the south polar ice. Hiroko Ai, the prophet of aerophany, explains the intention to John Boone:

> We have a vision of what life on Mars can be. We could see it wasn't going to go that way. We have been proved right by what has happened since. So we thought we would establish our own life.... We want to try it, to show by experiment how we can live here. Someone has to show what you mean when you talk about a different life, John Boone. Someone has to live the life.[54]

In fact, heroic individualism is replaced not by utopian experiments but by the merits of civic life. Robinson's alternative for Mars is also the great alternative for understanding western America: frontier as community building. The course of the Mars books problematizes end-state utopias. (This is also why the Russian model drops away.) The future must be found in the unruly and morally complex processes of community making, not in intellectualized schemes. We have, I think, a fictionalized version of Stanley Elkins's and Eric Mc-Kitrick's meaning for Frederick Jackson Turner's frontier in the challenges of working together and Robert Hine's search for western community in the bonding of people with place.[55]

The pivotal figures of the trilogy remain John and Nadia, the people who talk. The true solution is to build civil society through conversation. Mars at its best, says critic Carol Franko, is "an argumentative and interdependent confederation of diverse communities."[56] Boone seeks utopia through dialog, and the speech in which he sums up his ideas about forging a new Martian society pulls together and packs together thoughts and suggestions that he has picked up in years of conversation. Nadia and her supporters seek stability through negotiation. They work the hallways during political meetings and do the hard work of community organizing. Franko references literary theorist Mikhail Bakhtin and the literary-linguistic idea of "dialogism" in which meaning emerges from the continual interaction among people, their words, their actions, and their unspoken ideals.[57] In Bakhtin's view, novels establish their worlds by setting multiple voices in interaction, allowing their characters to form new meanings from the play within and between persons and words.

These theoretical statements return us as well to the ideas of *Pacific Edge*, where utopia is also a "process of making a better world, the name for one path history can take, a dynamic, tumultuous, agonizing process, with no end."[58] This preferred Orange County is a utopia achieved through legislation. Political participation matters, the process is more important than the end state, and victories can be real even if small and sometimes morally ambiguous. In Robinson's view, "utopia has to be rescued as a word, to mean 'working towards a more egalitarian society, a global society.'" Utopia is "a road of history, something we are working within."[59]

Like many contemporary writers in the social sciences and cultural studies, Robinson wants to explore the challenges that face conscious community building and the deliberate construction of civil society. As do many historians, he structures his narratives around the discords between utopian expectations and the practical compromises of an ethnically and culturally mixed society. These are the same concerns that animate Mikhail Bakhtin's criticism and make his ideas relevant, for Bakhtin's work is an effort to reinvigorate the political functions of fiction and to explore the ways in which literary texts must be understood in the context of their culture. In response to critics who suggested this connection, Robinson introduced an explicit reference to Bakhtin in *Blue Mars* as a way to argue that no one voice can be authoritative in a complex society.

A number of readings of Robinson's work are possible within this framework of social meaning. Science fiction critics, for example, tend to see both trilogies as reviving the critical utopias that flourished in the ferment of the 1970s, especially among writers with sympathy for that decade's feminist analysis. Ursula Le Guin, Marge Piercy, Joanna Russ, and Samuel Delany are examples of such New Wave science fiction writers whom Robinson acknowledges as influences.[60] Socialist critics focus on the exposition of the "gift economy" in the Mars narrative as an alternative to capitalism. And, to be sure, the books devote substantial attention to the possibilities and problems of an economy based on the principle of sustainability, or seeking to make one's impact on natural systems neutral in the long run.[61]

I remain intrigued by the western history reading. The Orange County volumes are explicit efforts to think through possible contingencies of western American development. We can contrast their postmodern orientation to incremental change with Ernest Callenbach's earlier and "modern" vision of a comprehensive and enlightened acceptance of Ecotopia.[62] The echoes of North America on the Martian frontier are also so pervasive that they need to be acknowledged and understood as critical commentaries on the American experience. At the same time, much of the new western history has itself been a political project, concerned to surface and legitimate alternative voices and understandings, to expand the public sphere, and to criticize the effects of unequal power.

Robinson and many new western historians have been probing the same questions — the power of capital, the imperatives of technology, the roots of community in shared action, the tensions between planetary and parochial values, the moral complexity of social choices, the power of past choices to constrain and direct the present.[63] Martians repeatedly try to build new societies innocent of history and fail each time. The books are thick with people, surrounding the protagonists with a dense supporting cast who have their own goals and points of view, thereby mirroring the constraints on real historical actors.[64] As a foundation for all of these topics, the theme of continuity is everywhere in the trilogies as each generation deals with an ever more complicated and historicized present, just as it is present in the minds of newer western historians. To swipe a turn of phrase, they come out of something in the same intellectual soil, out of the same American effort to probe the past in order to maintain a critical hope for the civic future.

NOTES

Note: Page numbers to the Mars trilogy refer to the Bantam Spectra paperback edition. The books in this trilogy are *Red Mars* (New York, 1993), *Green Mars* (New York, 1995), and *Blue Mars* (New York, 1997). The books in the "Three Californias" trilogy, in sequential order, are *The Wild Shore*, *The Gold Coast*, and *Pacific Edge*. References to *The Wild Shore* (1984; reprint New York, 1995) and *Pacific Edge* (1990; reprint New York, 1995) are to the Orb paperback editions. References to *The Gold Coast* (New York, 1988) indicate the St. Martin's Press version. Kim Stanley Robinson is the author of both series.

1. *Red Mars* won the annual Nebula Award of the professional organization of science fiction writers. *Green Mars* won the Hugo Award from science fiction fans.
2. Robinson, *Red Mars*, 283.
3. Robert Markley, "Falling into Theory: Simulation, Terraformation, and Eco-Economics in Kim Stanley Robinson's Martian Trilogy," *MFS Modern Fiction Studies* 43 (Fall 1997): 775.
4. David Seed, "The Mars Trilogy: An Interview," *Foundation: The Review of Science Fiction* 68 (Autumn 1996): 76.
5. Kim Stanley Robinson, letter to author, 14 August 2001.
6. William A. McClung, *Landscapes of Desire: Anglo Mythologies of Los Angeles* (Berkeley: University of California Press, 2000) and Mike Davis, *City of Quartz: Excavating the Future in Los Angeles* (New York: Verso, 1990).
7. Insightful studies of the connections between science fiction and the American uses of standard literary genres and sensibilities such as the romance and the gothic novel include David Ketterer, *New Worlds for Old: The Apocalyptic Imagination, Science Fiction, and American Literature* (Garden City, NY: Doubleday, 1974); David Mogen, Scott P. Sanders, and Joanne B. Karpinski, eds., *Frontier Gothic: Terror and Wonder at the Frontier in American Literature* (Rutherford, NJ: Farleigh Dickinson University Press, 1993); Gary Westfahl, *Space and Beyond: The Frontier Theme in Science Fiction* (Westport, CT: Greenwood, 2000); David Mogen, *Wilderness Visions: The Western Theme in Science Fiction Literature*, ed. Daryl F. Mallett, 2d ed. (San Bernadino, CA: Borgo, 1993); Gary K. Wolfe, "Frontiers in Space," in *The Frontier Experience and the American Dream*, ed. David Mogen, Mark Busby, and Paul Bryant (College Station: Texas A&M University Press, 1989), 248–63; Beverly J. Stoeltje, "Making the Frontier Myth: Folklore Process in a Modern Nation," *Western Folklore* 46 (October 1987): 235–53.
8. Michael Steiner, "Frontierland as Tomorrowland: Walt Disney and the Architectural Packaging of the Mythic West," *Montana The Magazine of Western History* 48 (Spring 1998): 2–17.
9. John Glenn quoted in Ray A. Williamson, "Outer Space as Frontier: Lessons for Today," *Western Folklore* 46 (October 1987): 259.
10. Gerard K. O'Neill, *The High Frontier: Human Colonies in Space* (New York: Morrow, 1976); U.S. National Commission on Space, *Pioneering the Space Frontier: The Report of the National Commission on Space* (New York: Bantam, 1986); Harry L. Shipman, *Humans in Space: 21st Century Frontiers* (New York: Plenum, 1989).
11. The "new western history" is a catchall term for a disparate set of scholars whose work emphasizes the costs as well as benefits of the European occupation of western North America and the continuities between the nineteenth and twentieth centuries in the American West. It also involves concern for multiple ideas about the meaning of the western experience and careful attention to voices that were under represented in early versions of regional history, such as women, wage workers, immigrants, and people of color. Representative publications include Patricia Nelson Limerick, *Legacy of Conquest: The Unbroken Past of the American West* (New York: Norton, 1987); Richard White, *"It's Your Misfortune and None of My Own": A History of the Amer-*

ican West (Norman: University of Oklahoma Press, 1991); Patricia Nelson Limerick, Charles E. Rankin, and Clyde A. Milner, II, eds., *Trails: Toward a New Western History* (Lawrence: University Press of Kansas, 1991); Clyde A. Milner II, Carol O'Connor, and Martha Sandweiss, eds., *The Oxford History of the American West* (New York: Oxford, 1994).

12. Kim Stanley Robinson, "Notes for an Essay on Cecelia Holland," *Foundation: The Review of Science Fiction* 40 (Summer 1987): 54; Bud Foote, "A Conversation with Kim Stanley Robinson," *Science-Fiction Studies* 21 (March 1994): 52; Robinson, *Green Mars*, 376.

13. This is not to say that Robinson shares Heinlein's Ayn Randish political philosophy or the viewpoints of the cyberpunks, whom he characterizes as an expression of the 1980s mentality of "caving to capitalism and concentrating on how to get one's own without worrying about the larger picture ... going with the flow of the world supermarket." Thomas E. Jackson, "Interview with Kim Stanley Robinson," *The New York Review of Science Fiction* no. 117 (May 1998): 15. Ken MacLeod states that "history is the trade secret of science fiction, and theories of history are its invisible engine" in his introduction to the U.S. edition of *The Star Fraction* (New York: Tor, 2001), 11.

14. Robinson, "Notes for an Essay on Cecelia Holland," 60. Robinson's most recent book, *The Years of Rice and Salt* (New York: Bantam, 2002), is an alternative future novel set on an earth where 95 percent of Europe's population perished in the Black Death, leaving Asian civilizations to contend for global hegemony.

15. Thomas Pynchon, *The Crying of Lot 49* (Philadelphia: Lippincott, 1966) and *Vineland* (Boston: Little, Brown, 1990); Joseph Conrad, *Almayer's Folly: A Story of an Eastern River* (New York: Doubleday, Page, 1895), *Lord Jim: A Tale* (Edinburgh: W. Blackwood, 1900), *Nostromo: A Tale of the Seaboard* (New York: Harper and Brothers, 1904), and *The Secret Agent: A Simple Tale* (New York: Harper and Brothers, 1907).

16. Fredric Jameson, "Postmodernism, or the Cultural Logic of Late Capitalism," *New Left Review* no. 146 (July-August 1984): 53–92.

17. *Blade Runner*, dir. Ridley Scott (1982). Other of Dick's fictions were the seeds for the films *Total Recall*, dir. Paul Verhoeven (1990), based on the story "We Can Dream it for You Wholesale," originally published in *Fantasy & Science Fiction* (April 1966) and *The Truman Show*, dir. Peter Weir (1998), based on *Time Out of Joint* (Philadelphia: Lippincott, 1959).

18. See Ernest R. May, *"Lessons" of the Past: The Use and Misuse of History in American Foreign Policy* (New York: Oxford, 1973); Richard E. Neustadt and Ernest R. May, *Thinking in Time: The Uses of History for Decision Makers* (New York: Free Press, 1986); Peter Stearns, "Forecasting the Future: Historical Analysis and Technological Determinism," *The Public Historian* 5 (Summer 1983): 31–54; Otis L. Graham, Jr., "The Uses and Misuses of History: Roles in Policymaking," *The Public Historian* 5 (Spring 1983): 5–19.

19. Robinson, *Red Mars*, 348; Seed, "Mars Trilogy," 79.

20. See Robinson, *Green Mars*, 540–2, 359; Robinson, *Blue Mars*, 678, 713. Also see Carol Franko, "The Density of Utopian Destiny in Robinson's *Red Mars*," *Extrapolation: A Journal of Science Fiction* 38 (Spring 1997): 56–65; Markley, "Falling into Theory," 788. Robinson's understanding of history is far different from Isaac Asimov's adolescent image of a mathematical calculus of historical forces in the Foundation novels. Sax Russell, the scientific genius behind terraforming, searches for a "science of history" to explain the rise of social conflict but gives up in the face of historical contingency. (See Robinson, *Green Mars*, 205–6.) Robinson's use is also different from that of science fiction writers who frequently adopt metahistorical cycle-of-civilization models from Gibbon, Spengler, Ibn Khaldun, and other macrohistorians as mechanical devices to structure grand narratives of far futures. Indeed, Robinson has his own fun with such models by introducing the Martian historian Charlotte Dorsa Brevia who in the 2170s publishes a "dense multivolumed analytical metahistory" that explains Martian society as the logical result of millennia of contest between existing and emergent social and economic systems that eventuate, conveniently in the 2170s, in a new democratic age. (See Robinson, *Blue Mars*, 482–4.) Her work sounds like nothing if not Hegel and Marx writ large.

21. Shaun Huston, "Murray Bookchin on Mars! The Production of Nature in Kim Stanley Robinson's Mars Trilogy," in *Lost in Space: Geographies of Science Fiction*, ed. Rob Kitchin and James Kneale (London: Continuum, 2002), 167–79.

22. Andrew M. Isserman, "Projection, Forecast, and Plan: On the Future of Population Forecasting," *Journal of the American Planning Association* 50 (Spring 1984): 208–21.

23. Larry Hirschhorn, "Scenario Writing: A Developmental Approach," *Journal of the American Planning Association* 46 (Spring 1980): 172–83; Peter Hall, *Great Planning Disasters* (London: Weidenfeld and Nicolson, 1980); James A. Throgmorton, *Planning as Persuasive Storytelling: The Rhetorica Construction of Chicago's Energy Future* (Chicago: University of Chicago Press, 1996).

24. Carey McWilliams, *California: The Great Exception* (1949; reprint Westport, CT: Greenwood, 1971); Neil Morgan, *Westward Tilt: The American West Today* (New York: Random, 1963), 107; Christopher Rand, *Los Angeles: The Ultimate City* (New York: Oxford, 1967); Arthur L. Grey, Jr., "Los Angeles: Urban Proto-

type," *Land Economics* 35 (August 1959): 232–42; Werner Hirsch, "Los Angeles: Leading City? A Leading City," in *Los Angeles: Viability and Prospects for Metropolitan Leadership*, ed. Werner Z. Hirsch (New York: Praeger, 1971), 237–41; Richard M. Elman, *Ill-At-Ease in Compton* (New York: Pantheon, 1967), vii.

25. Allen J. Scott and Edward W. Soja, eds., *The City: Los Angeles and Urban Theory at the End of the Twentieth Century* (Berkeley: University of California Press, 1996); Michael J. Dear, Greg Hise, and H. Eric Schockman, eds., *Rethinking Los Angeles* (Thousand Oaks, CA: Sage, 1996); Rob Kling, Spencer Olin, and Mark Poster, eds., *Postsuburban California: The Transformation of Orange County Since World War II* (Berkeley: University of California Press, 1991).

26. Kim Stanley Robinson, letter to author, 14 August 2001.

27. Mike Davis, *The Ecology of Fear: Los Angeles and the Imagination of Disaster* (New York: Metropolitan Books, 1998).

28. Robinson, *Pacific Edge*, 300.

29. Tom Moylan, "'Utopia is when our lives matter': Reading Kim Stanley Robinson's *Pacific Edge*," *Utopian Studies* 6, no. 2 (1995): 9.

30. There are five sections for Nadia Chernyshevsky, the engineer and political leader; five for Ann Clayborne, the ecologist and advocate of red Mars; five for Sax Russell, the scientist; five for Nirgal, the second generation leader; four for Maya Toitovna, the charismatic and manipulative leader of the Russian contingent; two for Frank Chalmers, the political pragmatist; two for Michael Duval, the psychiatrist; two for Art Randolph, the political facilitator; one for John Boone; and one for Zo Boone of the third generation.

31. The three novels in John Dos Passos's *USA* trilogy are *The 42nd Parallel* (New York: Harper and Row, 1930), *1919* (New York: Harcourt, Brace, 1932), and *Big Money* (New York: Harcourt, Brace, 1936); Peter Matthiessen, *Killing Mister Watson* (New York: Random, 1990), *Lost Man's River* (New York: Random, 1997), and *Bone by Bone* (New York: Random, 1999).

32. Jackson, "Interview with Kim Stanley Robinson," 18.

33. We can also read "falling into history" as reference to the biblical fall from innocence in Gen. 3–4. *Red Mars* is structured around the rivalry of American leaders John Boone and Frank Chalmers, in effect the senior and junior brothers. In the flash forward that opens the book, Chalmers arranges Boone's assassination and thereby recommits the sin of Cain.

34. John Newsinger, "The Martian Trilogy," *Monthly Review: An Independent Socialist Magazine* 49 (December 1997): 53–5; Alexander Bogdanov, *Red Star: The First Bolshevik Utopia*, ed. Loren R. Graham and Richard Stites, trans. Charles Rougle (Bloomington: Indiana University Press, 1984); Nikolai Cherneshevsky, *What Is to Be Done?* trans. Michael R. Katz (Ithaca, NY: Cornell University Press, 1989).

35. Seed, "Mars Trilogy," 77; Robinson, *Green Mars*, 220.

36. It is interesting to note that Greg Bear's *Moving Mars* (New York: Tor, 1993) also pivots on the politics and politicking of anti-colonial revolution, although it gives greater importance to a technological means for accomplishing the aim of independence.

37. Edgar Rice Burroughs, "Under the Moons of Mars," originally published in *All-Story* magazine (1912), and republished as *A Princess of Mars* (Chicago: A. C. McClurg, 1917); Owen Wister, *The Virginian* (New York: Macmillan, 1902); Ray Bradbury, *The Martian Chronicles* (Garden City, NY: Doubleday, 1958); Gregory M. Pfitzer, "The Only Good Alien Is a Dead Alien: Science Fiction and the Metaphysics of Indian-Hating on the High Frontier," *Journal of American Culture* 18 (Spring 1995): 51–67; Richard Slotkin, *Gunfighter Nation: The Myth of the Frontier in Twentieth-Century America* (New York: Atheneum, 1992); Paul A. Carter, *The Creation of Tomorrow: Fifty Years of Magazine Science Fiction* (New York: Columbia University Press, 1977), 60–9.

38. Robert M. Zubrin and Richard Wagner, *The Case for Mars: The Plan to Settle the Red Planet and Why We Must* (New York: Free Press, 1996); Markley, "Falling into Theory," 779.

39. Robert Zubrin, *First Landing* (New York: Ace, 2001), 240–1; Greg A. Landis, *Mars Crossing* (New York: Tor, 2000).

40. Patricia Nelson Limerick, *Something in the Soil: Legacies and Reckonings in the New West* (New York: Norton, 2000), 18–21; William Robbins, *Colony and Empire: The Capitalist Transformation of the American West* (Lawrence: University Press of Kansas, KS, 1994); Robert V. Hine, *Community on the American Frontier: Separate But Not Alone* (Norman: University of Oklahoma Press, 1985).

41. Robinson, *Green Mars*, 228.

42. Ibid., 213, 459–61, 475.

43. William Cronon, ed., *Uncommon Ground: Toward Reinventing Nature* (New York: Norton, 1995).

44. Robinson, *Red Mars*, 177, 179, 229; Hal K. Rothman, *Devil's Bargains: Tourism in the Twentieth Century American West* (Lawrence: University Press of Kansas, 1998).

45. Jackson, "Interview with Kim Stanley Robinson," 15–8.

46. Robinson, *Red Mars*, 40, 183, 261, 245; Robinson, *Blue Mars*, 275; Robinson, *Green Mars*, 364, 425.
47. Robinson, *Red Mars*, 170, 389, 380, 425.
48. Robinson, *Green Mars*, 337.
49. For a discussion of this, see Robbins, *Colony and Empire*.
50. Moylan, "'Utopia is when our lives matter,'" 8, 19; Seed, "Mars Trilogy," 77; Robinson, *Blue Mars*, 23.
51. For a time he becomes an isolated homesteader, reenacting another model of the western American experience.
52. Robinson, *Green Mars*, 48. Western American mythology is also reproduced in the afterlife of John Boone. His reputation, after his death, becomes legend and conflates with tales of Paul Bunyan on Mars ... who in turn encounters a Martian Big Man a hundred times larger yet than Paul and Babe. Robinson, *Red Mars*, 386.
53. Markley, "Falling into Theory," 782; Robinson, *Green Mars*, 230, 326.
54. Robinson, *Red Mars*, 374.
55. Hine, *Community on the American Frontier*; Stanley Elkins and Eric McKitrick, "A Meaning for Turner's Frontier: Part I: Democracy in the Old Northwest," *Political Science Quarterly* 69 (September 1954): 321–53.
56. Franko, "The Density of Utopian Destiny in Robinson's *Red Mars*," 60.
57. Robinson, *Red Mars*, 378–81; Franko, "The Density of Utopian Destiny in Robinson's *Red Mars*," 61. Mikhail Mikhailovich Bakhtin was a Russian literary critic and philosopher (1895–1975) who worked during the Soviet era. His work first came to the attention of American scholars at the end of the 1960s. There is a very substantial enterprise devoted to translating Bakhtin's fragmentary works from Russian and interpreting them in terms of literary theory and epistemology. Bakhtin wrote sympathetically about the historian's imagination (e.g., the work of Marc Bloch) and opposed metahistorians like Spengler who treated societies as fixed units rather than open and constantly changing constructs. There are interesting parallels between the ideas of Bakhtin and those of political philosopher Jurgen Habermas, who has emphasized open dialogue within a public sphere as the foundation of democratic society.
58. Robinson, *Pacific Edge*, 95; Carol Franko, "Working the 'In-Between': Kim Stanley Robinson's Utopian Fiction," *Science-Fiction Studies* 21 (1994): 191–211; Moylan, "'Utopia is when our lives matter,'" 4, 11.
59. Foote, "A Conversation with Kim Stanley Robinson," 56; Seed, "Mars Trilogy," 77.
60. Ursula K. Le Guin, *The Dispossessed: An Ambiguous Utopia* (New York: Harper and Row, 1974); Joanna Russ, *The Female Man* (New York: Bantam, 1975); Marge Piercy, *Woman on the Edge of Time* (New York: Knopf, 1976); Samuel R. Delany, *Triton* (Boston, 1976). See Jackson, "Interview with Kim Stanley Robinson," 17.
61. Another use of the western experience is the settlers' concern to develop cultural strictures against potlatching, or the use of excessive gifts to obtain moral leverage over and above the needs for everyday life. See Robinson, *Green Mars*, 291–3.
62. Ernest Callenbach, *Ecotopia: The Notebooks and Reports of William Weston* (Berkeley: Banyan Tree Press, 1975).
63. The index of Patricia Limerick's *Something in the Soil* (see note 40) has twenty-one subtopics listed under American West; seventeen of them, from "accumulated memories and stories of" to "tourism in," are also applicable to "Three Californias" and the Mars books.
64. My thanks to Amy Bridges for this insight.

4

Remaking History: The Short Fiction
John Kessel

> I have always been fascinated by history, as almost all science fiction writers are. For a long time, I've been saying science fiction itself is a historical genre: every text has within it (implicitly or explicitly) a history that runs back to now. To make a quick distinction between science fiction and fantasy — at least a first cut — science fiction is set in the future with a history that runs back to now, and fantasy dispenses with that connection and takes place in some historical bubble space of its own.
> — Kim Stanley Robinson, *Locus* interview, April 2007

Since 1990 the vast majority of Kim Stanley Robinson's fiction (with the exception of *The Martians* (1998), a series of vignettes associational to his Mars trilogy) has been at the novel length. It is a fair bet that Robinson's reputation as a writer will stand or fall on such massive works as his "California Trilogy" (*The Wild Shore, The Gold Coast, Pacific Edge*) his "Mars Trilogy" (*Red Mars, Green Mars, Blue Mars*), *The Years of Rice and Salt*, or his recent global warming trilogy. But in that first decade of his career, Robinson established himself as a first-rate creator of stand-alone short stories. Most of this short fiction has been collected in the omnibus volume *Remaking History* (1994) which merges the contents of two earlier collections, *The Planet on the Table* (1986) and an earlier, shorter volume also titled *Remaking History* (1991).

Robinson's early work comprises a significant body of first-rate science fiction, and shows forth themes that he was to explore in more scope in his novels. But these stories are not "warm-ups" for novels; they are works of art in their own right, and stand among the finest American short science fiction of the 1980s.

Not all of KSR's short fiction is about history, but much of it does relate to sf as a historical genre. The most obvious are his excursions into alternate history, but these form a relatively small number. More often, KSR uses historical events as a jumping off place, or the story turns into an examination of theories of history and the historical process itself. A natural consequence is that many of these stories deal with moral choice within these historical contexts. Do individuals bear responsibility for historical events? How much power does individual moral choice have? Do we despair at changing the world?

Another, related concern is the contrast between the large view that history forces on us, and the lives of individuals and groups living at some particular moment within that large sweep of events and movements. At times the contrast is not to human history but to natural, even geologic forces of time that overwhelm our short lives. This ties in with theological overtones — though it is little remarked upon, Robinson is surprisingly engaged with religion. Finally, KSR's concern with history leads to exploration of utopia and anti-utopia.

Kim Stanley Robinson attended the Clarion Writers' Workshop in 1975, and soon after published his first stories in Damon Knight's original anthology *Orbit*. Among them, "Coming Back to Dixieland" and "The Disguise" both bespeak a lively young imagination investing futuristic settings with awareness of traditional art. His chatty first person narrators are ingratiating but not particularly compelling. There is a sense in which KSR in these early stories is forcing his interest in the characters, and in the non–sf subject matter — in the case of "Dixieland" traditional jazz (one of the characters is directly modeled after the great New Orleans saxophonist Sidney Bechet), in the case of "The Disguise," Jacobean drama — into the framework of future-scene science fiction.

But with "Venice Drowned," which appeared in *Universe* in 1981, Robinson brought his sf background and his interest in humanistic story values fully into balance. "Venice Drowned" tells the story of Carlo Tafur, a boatman in a future Venice that is slowly being inundated by rising seas. Already most of the glorious buildings of our time are partially or fully under water, yet still the daily life of the city goes on as Venetians live in the upper stories of crumbling buildings or build anew on the roofs of older ones. Carlo is hired by some Japanese who seek to retrieve old works of art from an inundated church and take them to Japan. By aiding them in this appropriation, is Carlo betraying his people and culture? When a storm arises, should he let them die? In the end Carlo survives the storm and goes to rescue the divers, concluding, "Let them have what was under the water. What lived in Venice was still afloat."

What impresses about "Venice Drowned" is the union of character, speculative setting, and human story. The story raises the abstract issue of cultural appropriation without resorting to stereotypes or propaganda. With it KSR began a stretch of stories that were like a baseball hitter on a hot streak.

"Black Air" (1983) won the World Fantasy Award for short fiction. Set in 1588, it is a work of magic realism about a seventeen-year-old West African boy, Manuel, impressed into the Spanish Armada. It gains force from the irony that we know the disaster the Armada is sailing toward, but Manuel does not. Manuel comes close to dying from a fever, after which he is able to see men's souls hovering as flames above their heads. The natural events of the armada's ruin are woven with miraculous images, as when, in the midst of a battle with English raiders, Manuel sees a vision of Saint Anna in the rigging, and she deflects the course of a canon ball and saves his life.

The story turns on whether these images are hallucinations or visions of a spiritual world beyond the physical. As do other KSR stories, "Black Air" follows a small individual caught up in large historical events, set against a still larger, and mysterious, natural or spiritual world. Do our lives take place, as the Church insists, against a reality invisible to us? Is this invisible reality what the Church says it is? What place do our human realities take in that reality? Do our decisions have consequences? A crucial scene in the story comes when Manuel and other seamen are summoned to a secret ceremony in the bowels of the ship. The "mass" scene in the bowels of the ship quotes from mystical apocalyptic imagery and asserts the possibility of magical transformation. "I assume the appearance of a refiner's fire, purging the dross of forms outworn ... when thou hast been tried as by fire, the gold of thy soul shall be cleansed, and visible as fire: then the vision of thy Lord shall be granted unto thee, and seeing Him shalt thou behold the shining one, who is thine own true self" (227).[1]

Fra Lucien preaches that Christ is in all men. An armada sent to act in the name of God is acting under false pretenses. But when Manuel, at the end of the story, the ship wrecked in a storm off the western coast of Ireland, assumes that since he is Christ, he can walk on water, he almost drowns.

"Black Air" is beautifully written, funny, tragic, and ultimately mysterious. It marked KSR's first profound use of historical materials, his liberation from sf furniture, and looked forward to the fully realized work of the mid–1980s.

Theories of History

In these 1980s stories, KSR began, first implicitly, then explicitly, to address different theories of history and moral choice. The paired stories that deal most directly with these subjects, published at the beginning and the end of this stage of his career, are "The Lucky Strike" (1984) and "A Sensitive Dependence on Initial Conditions" (1991).

"The Lucky Strike" is an alternate history story that begins on Tinian Island in the Pacific in 1945. The viewpoint character, Captain Frank January, is the bombardier on a B-29 named *The Lucky Strike*. The story begins with a scene where, because of a mishap on a test flight, Captain John Tibbits' plane the *Enola Gay* and its crew crash. Consequently, *The Lucky Strike* is selected to make the raid on Hiroshima with the first atomic bomb.

With increasing tension, the story delineates the preparations for the mission, and January's misgivings about it, which culminate in his deliberately missing the target on the bomb run, causing the A-bomb to fall on an uninhabited area. January is accused of treason and court-martialed, found guilty, and at the end of the story is executed. But because of his decision and the belated support it gains, at first from a minority of Americans, a movement against the arms race and the Cold War develops which leads to the abolition of nuclear weapons and a vastly different postwar world.

The story slowly develops January's character to make plausible his remarkable decision of conscience. He is not presented as some larger-than-life hero acting on eternal principles so much as a man with a particular personal history that enables him to see alternatives to the course of action everyone around him, including those in authority, views as necessary. KSR is expert at teasing the moral implications out of descriptions without preaching. For example, when the crews are shown a film of the first atom bomb test at Alamogordo, which evokes stunned horror from January, the scientist briefing them reveals his lack of a moral imagination when the best he can say in reaction to the men's shocked silence is, "It's big, all right" (145). He tells the airmen that the fireball produced is hotter than the sun; several scenes later, January walks out of a building and, "The heat of the tropical sun — ninety-three million miles away, wasn't it?— pulsed painfully on the back of his neck" (149).

Carefully, KSR builds the story to January's moment of moral decision. All of Robinson's short fiction, whether directly related to history or not, presents arguments against quietism, even when his characters are struggling with situations so large that any individual action cannot hope to alter the outcome. Individuals must take moral responsibility. This is most beautifully enacted in the end of "The Lucky Strike" when, court-martialed and convicted, January is sent before the firing squad. In smoking a last cigarette with the priest, Patrick Getty, sent to speak with him before he is executed, January asks,

"They load one of the guns with a blank cartridge, right?"
"Yes," Getty said.

"So each man in the squad can imagine he may not have shot me?"

"Yes. That's right."

A tight, unhumorous smile was January's last expression. He threw down the cigarette, ground it out, poked the priest in the arm. "But I <u>know</u>."

What does January know? He knows that they are fooling themselves; they are fooling no one. They are all responsible. How does he know this? Because at the end of the execution, he will be dead. It does not matter how social or political structures, how political and historical theories, try to move that responsibility away from the individual. The parable of the firing squad demonstrates that the end point of any historical situation is the act: it is always there and cannot be escaped. Therefore, what each of us does is vitally important and cannot be passed off to some intellectual or social structure behind or above us. This is an almost Old Testament vision of personal responsibility.

Seven years later, KSR was to return to the materials of "The Lucky Strike," re-examining the degree to which individuals are morally responsible for the large movements of history, in "A Sensitive Dependence on Initial Conditions" (1991). "A Sensitive Dependence...," more essay than conventional story, uses the events of "The Lucky Strike" as a jumping off place for a discussion of theories of history, and a series of wildly different scenarios developing out of the attempt to bomb Hiroshima. The theories of history KSR elucidates are the "covering law" model, the "sufficient conditions" model, the "necessary conditions" model, the "weak covering law" model, the "great man theory," and the "chaos theory" model.

Is history determined by large social forces, or by individuals who bend history to their own purposes, or by some other mechanism that is not so easily parsed? If history is dependent on large social and economic forces, then we might despair at ever having any effect on it — the future is determined and nothing we can do, for good or ill, can change it. If great men can change it, then the future may be mutable, but is still not controllable. If history is a chaotic system, then it is sensitively dependent on initial conditions — that is, a very small, seemingly insignificant alteration can have huge effects later. Unpredictable ones. The famous chaos theory parable is of the butterfly that flaps its wings in China and causes tornados a week later in Kansas. Again we have no control.

But KSR ends in the same place he arrived at in "The Lucky Strike": regardless of whichever historical theory we accept, humans still must make moral choices. In a state of ignorance, even within a complex system whose parameters no one can ever entirely know, we are forced to decide whether or not we will behave as if our actions have consequences. "We have to choose, that is life in time.... There are few covering laws. Initial conditions are never fully known. The butterfly may be on the wing, it may be crushed underfoot. You are flying toward Hiroshima" (451).

Epistemology

Robinson's Ph.D. dissertation was published as *The Novels of Philip K. Dick*. In it KSR discusses the famed "reality breakdown" as a fundamental of Dick's fiction. In novels like *Eye in the Sky, The Man in the High Castle, The Three Stigmata of Palmer Eldrich, Ubik*, and a dozen others, what the characters have supposed to be a dependable sense of the "real" completely collapses. In general, KSR's own fiction does not depend heavily on such ontological questions, but a number of Robinson's stories do raise epistemological issues with regard to reality, most often in the context of characters discovering frauds or mistakes of interpretation.

In what is otherwise a Sherlock Holmes pastiche set on Mercury, "Mercurial" (1985), a digression on art forgery, points out how the forger must take into account the historical conditions that created the art in order to create a plausible history for his fake work. The implication is that we may not be able to trust history itself, since it is a bunch of tales told to us, and those may not be true. The past does not exist outside of our recordings of it, and those recordings are at best subject to interpretation, and at worst, to manipulation.

"Vinland the Dream" (1991) takes up the issue of historical forgery directly. A party of archeologists are excavating the purported Viking settlement at L'Anse aux Meadows, Newfoundland. Evidence has turned up to suggest that this is not a genuine settlement, but an elaborate fraud established in the late 18th century. The story consists primarily of a debate between an unnamed professor, the lead researcher, and an unnamed Canadian minister come to view the site. The professor is disconsolate at the evidence that the site may be a fraud, and speculates as to who might have established it and why. The female minister observes, and in the end suggests that perhaps the site's authenticity does not matter to us as much as does the story of a Viking settlement of Vinland. History is a story people tell about the past. "And fictions, dreams, hoaxes — they are also stories people tell. True or false, it's the stories that matter to us. Certain qualities in the stories themselves make them true or false...." (371–2).

The professor protests. The truth matters. We want more than stories from history, "We want something ... that the past doesn't have. Something secret, some secret meaning ... something that will give our lives a kind of sense" (373).

In "Remaking History" (1989), a low-budget film company run by lunar colonists is making a movie about the 1980 Iran hostage crisis during the Carter administration. But as the story progresses we discover that these colonists live in an alternative future in which the secret rescue mission President Carter mounted to retrieve the hostages from the Iranian embassy in Tehran succeeded. As a result, Carter was re-elected in 1980, with dozens of repercussions both large and small, including the fact that in this world John Lennon was not shot in December 1980. The actors and producers of the movie, in the course of the filming, debate what or who was responsible for these events working out the way they did. Is this a result of heroic action by individuals, or of the weight of countless decisions, and accidents, out of any person's control? The irony is that in our reality, all this ended in failure.

"The Translator" (1990) is a comedy on the inability to communicate, and the role of the translator as fraudulent mediator between cultures. The story might well be based on the proverb, "The translator is the traitor." This story questions the relationship between language and truth, between the signified and the signifier — but here the signifier is a desperate trickster acting according to his own motives. Owen Rumford is the mayor of a small human outpost on the planet Rannoch. One day two alien spaceships land near the town to take up a "ritual war" that they wage every few hundred years. The aliens use Rumford as their translator; Rumford understands very little of their languages and has only a clumsy mechanical dictionary to help him negotiate between the hostile races. His sole purpose in acting as go-between is to get the aliens to postpone the war — which would exterminate any humans on the planet — until after he is gone.

The story is very funny in suggesting the cultural differences, and the resulting linguistic habits, of the hippo aliens and the bird aliens. No real understanding between them is possible. So instead, Rumford defuses the situation by lying shamelessly to both sides. But in order to lie convincingly he must understand their purposes and cultures well enough to make up convincing false translations on the fly (using a computer dictionary for the aliens' languages that is by no means reliable or unambiguous in its renderings of the meaning of the aliens' terms). Rumford succeeds, but his success is only a stopgap, and the dues will be paid later—but at least Owen won't be there to pay them.

Historical frauds appear also in *Icehenge* and *The Wild Shore*. In all these cases the question is not of the fundamental nature of reality, but structures of human belief based on evidence that may or may not be trustworthy. Robinson proceeds on the assumption that there is a fundamental reality, though we may never have unambiguous evidence enough to remove all doubts about authenticity. For example, those aliens are going to come back in a hundred years, bearing weapons, regardless of Owen's linguistic gymnastics.

The closest KSR ever comes to presenting a Dickian vision of unstable reality is in one of his more obscure stories, "Ridge Running" (1984). The story, a realistic contemporary account of three mountain climbers in the Sierras, has no overt fantastic elements. Of the three climbers, Brian is gung-ho for macho climbing, Pete is not into such strenuous exertion, and Joe, their old friend, is recovering from brain damage resulting from an injury and has an incomplete grasp of language. At one point they open a box of notes left by previous climbers, and the wind blows the notes away. Does that mean the experience, no longer documented, no longer exists? "'Just think, all over the United States the memory of this peak has popped right out of twenty people's heads'" (89).

But the moment is a joke, and it passes. The larger question of the story is, what is going on in Joe's broken brain? What is reality for him? Is it any less real than the reality of Brian and Pete? To what degree does the existence of the world depend on linguistic constructs?

The Large vs. the Small

But regardless of what the three men see and believe, there is the overwhelming power of the mountains that makes such human-centered speculations about reality seem beside the point. This contrast between the culturally constructed historical world and the world of nature is taken up in many other KSR stories, and looks forward to the Mars novels, which might be said to be KSR's most elaborate exploration of individuals within the sweep of history, set against the backdrop of the overwhelming natural world. In story after story Robinson delineates some large world of ideas, of historical events, of huge, slow natural phenomena, and sets against these, in the foreground, ordinary, frail, completely human beings.

In "Ridge Running" he chooses to switch viewpoints between the three men climbing the Sierras. But the strongest Robinson stories use the close third person viewpoint to put us into the perspective of a single protagonist. KSR enforces the closeness through his style; for example, he frequently uses sentence fragments that present themselves as snatches of thought directly from the mind of the central character. His 1986 story "Down and Out in the Year 2000" begins,

> It was going to be hot again. Summer in Washington, D.C.—Lee Robinson woke and rolled on his mattress, broke into a sweat. That kind of a day [452].

"Down and Out..." tells of a few days in the life of Leroy Robinson.[2] KSR's title recalls Orwell's *Down and Out in Paris and London,* and like Orwell, he seeks to present certain hard realities that the science fiction reading public is loath to recognize. Lee and his partner Debra live in poverty, Debra is too sick to work, and Lee has no money to get her medical care. At a time when cyberpunks were presenting people in "the street" as romantic outsiders in black leather and mirrorshades, KSR shows real poor people, cut loose by a collapsed social welfare system, struggling to make a living. Like so many cyberpunk protagonists, Lee is a criminal, but instead of hacking into multinational corporate databases or performing sabotage on government agencies, his crime is growing and selling marijuana, a finger bag at a time. The mundane details of his desperate existence put the lie to the romantic image of dealers common in sf and elsewhere. There is no moral judgment made on Lee's dealing. He's doing what it takes, and not harming anybody doing it.

His trouble comes when someone raids his secret marijuana plots, hidden in various deserted buildings. Reduced to searching the coin returns of pay phones, seeking credit from shop owners who cannot help him, digging into dumpsters, his salvation comes when he turns to begging on the street, playing a kazoo.

KSR's poor are not perfect, and not simply victims. Lee's neighbor Rochelle, who used to be a nurse, helps take care of Debra, and Victor, a street beggar, lends Lee the kazoo. By the end he gets enough money to feed Debra and himself, and makes plans to replant his dope and get a harmonica and learn to play it.

Aside from its unsparing picture of the near future, the story functions as a commentary on 1980s science fiction. In the mid–1980s, a lot of heat (and some light) was generated by Bruce Sterling's critical flyer *Cheap Truth*, chief propaganda organ of the cyberpunk movement in SF. A number of critics in *CT* singled KSR out for criticism, asserting that his fiction wasn't real science fiction, concentrated too much on conventional literary values, and was even in some way counter-revolutionary. In response, KSR inserts a takedown of cyberpunk clichés into his story.

A number of Lee's friends hang out in "Fish Park" watching a portable TV, making mocking comments about the shows. On one channel is a melodrama that bears more than a passing resemblance to William Gibson's *Neuromancer*:

> Johnnie said, "That be Sam Spade, the greatest computer spy in the world."
> "How come he live in that shack, then?" Ramon asked.
> "That's to show it's a tough scuffle making it as a computer spy, real tough."
> "How come he got four million dollars worth of computers right there in the shack, then?" Ramon asked, and the others commenced giggling...
> ... Johnny said, "He's about to meet a slinky Afro-Asian spy...."
> Lee said, "I wonder why they're always Afro-Asian."
> Steve burst in, laughed. "So they can fuck all of us at once, man!" [459]

Tiring of this escapist fantasy they change the channel, get a brief news report about rioting in Los Angeles, but jump past harsh reality to another escapist fantasy that just happens to resemble Bruce Sterling's Shaper/Mechanist stories:

> "Cyborgs Versus Androids," Johnnie said ... "Lots of fighting..."
> "Yeah!" Steve exclaimed ... "I'm a cyborg myself, see, I got these false teeth!" [460]

The Fellowship of the Downtrodden

That lighthearted scene in Fish Park between the poor black men watching TV, and the way Rochelle and Victor quietly help Lee, find parallels in a half dozen other Robinson stories. When circumstances are almost unendurable in the worlds KSR delineates, he frequently gives us what I will call "the Fellowship of the Downtrodden." He does not sentimentalize the desperate — they still will work at cross purposes, and betray each other (for example, the unknown person who stole Lee's dope must have been one of his friends) but still there is a power that comes from brotherhood and sisterhood among the oppressed.

In general the importance of individuals against the large backdrops does not come from their holding some crucial place in a historical narrative, like January in "The Lucky Strike." Moral choice, which will have historical repercussions, is important, but typically KSR heroes, like Carlo in "Venice Drowned," are much smaller. Their very smallness is a source of their unity with others. When individuals band together, over and over in KSR's fiction, there is the possibility for fellow feeling, working in concert, altruism, and mutual support.

"A Transect" (1987), for instance, concerns contemporary South African racial politics and western indifference to them. The story moves back and forth between two men on different train trips, on different continents: a salesman taking the train home to New York from Montreal; a black South African taking the train from Johannesburg to his Bantustan "homeland." In the middle of the night, separated from their fellow passengers, somehow they meet briefly in the space between train cars. The salesman is worn out in the capitalist system, but does not recognize his ever present privilege until he meets the boy — then he sees it: "such incredible, excessive luxury — and this was just a train!" (488). The white businessman is troubled in his thoughts, oppressed by the continual pressure on him to make money; he sits in relative comfort in his coach seat but is totally isolated from those around him. The blacks, crowded into a hot, dirty car, nonetheless have a community. They banter with platform hawkers in the stations, mock each others' marriages, play music and sing songs (the performance of music in KSR stories is always a sign of the fellowship of mankind). But no one waits for them on the train platform when they arrive. The lonely businessman is at least greeted by his wife. The question of whether he is transformed by his brief encounter on the train is left open.

"The Lunatics" (1988) is predicated on this fellowship, but in this case the result is destruction: this is one of KSR's darkest stories. It tells of a rebellion by underground lunar slave miners. They live in perpetual darkness, and have had their memories erased, but still they organize, escape, and tunnel their way to the surface. The story climaxes when they use mining explosives to blow up a domed lunar city, then reach the surface for the first time, sit in the rubble and watch the stars and the earth in the sky. The fellowship of these miners is evoked as strongly as that of the kaffirs in "A Transect" but here the result is destruction, with little hope for amelioration in the aftermath.

Finally, "Glacier" (1988) presents a situation of political oppression in a future U.S. in the midst of a new ice age. A glacier is bearing down on Boston. Daily life goes on in the face of this monumentally destructive, beautiful force of nature that will eventually grind everything humans have created to powder. The story's hero, Alex, lives with his parents, liberal college professors in a U.S. society that has become increasingly repressive. Alex's father has moved from university to university, unable to get tenure. A man in a black coat spies on their apartment. His parents gather with like minded people, sharing food, intense conversation, poetry and music, yet another example of KSR's camaraderie of the downtrodden.

For teenaged Alex this is only the background of his life; he spends most of his time just outside of the neighborhood on the surface of the glacier. The juxtaposition of the huge, lovingly described glacier right next to urban Boston creates a surreal and unnatural contrast. Alex's family adopts a cat, which adapts to both them and the new environment. The story builds a series of parallels: the cat, Alex and his parents are all displaced but struggle to survive. The unstoppable force of the glacier parallels and contrasts the unstoppable drift of political repression. It moves slowly, encroaching, unavoidable. Yet life goes on, sacrifices are made, and people — and the cat — persevere. The family prepares to move again. Dad sells his books. Nature is alive and indifferent to human trouble and purpose. There are glaciers everywhere, even little ones in the puddles on the roof, in the corners of the concrete stoops Alex sits on.

Religion, Music, and Utopia

"The dystopian cliché of our times is just too easy," Robinson said in a 1996 on-line interview, "it no longer says 'Don't go this way' but rather 'This is the only way no matter what you do, so don't try to fight it.' That kind of dystopia is reinforcing of the status quo, it's a capitulation."

Certainly in these stories KSR deals with dystopian impulses, but at the same time attempts to see past dystopia, to avoid quietism in the face of the forces that threaten human existence. Stories from "Down and Out in the Year 2000" to "Glacier" serve as a warning, a corrective, and a testimony to human perseverance. Even in the worst circumstances, KSR presents a fundamental, willed optimism.

The source of that optimism is not religion, but in his story "The Part of Us That Loves" (1989) he comes as close as he ever does to presenting the answer to dystopian impulses in conventionally religious terms. This story (as does the early "Coming Back to Dixieland") also forcefully shows the human impulse to make music as our most vibrant expression of the utopian force within us.[3]

The story begins with a dramatized scene of Jesus reacting to news that John the Baptist has been killed. Then it is revealed that this is just the imagined vision of Naomi, a teenaged girl reading the Bible on the way to band rehearsal. She meets her friend Tom, a boy who is skeptical about Christianity. Just before a big concert, all of the band's instruments are stolen. The band leader makes them go on with make-do instruments. In a scene that recalls the climax of "Coming Back to Dixieland," the band begins to play, raggedly at first, and then comes together to play better than they ever have before. A miracle? Both Naomi and Tom agree it is, but what do we mean by a miracle? Is it just accessing some part of the human creativity that we normally do not reach? Or is it literally an in-spiration of some spirit of the Christian God?

This unifying spiritual impulse is what KSR sets in opposition to the individualism that rules so much libertarian-inspired sf, and that makes it impossible, in cyberpunk, to imagine an effective answer to those economic forces that tend toward dystopia. For Robinson, human beings are capable of miracles. And in almost all of the occurrences of the Fellowship of the Downtrodden, music, performed usually by a group, is a fundamental element. Scenes of music as miraculous healing force, elaborated to a greater or lesser degree, occur in "Down and Out in the Year 2000," "A Transect," "The Lunatics," "Glacier," and "Coming Back to Dixieland." If you are looking for the utopian moment in a KSR story, find the music.

One of the strangest expressions of the idea of utopian/dystopian contrast, the deadening weight of perfection, and the idea of music as humanizing influence, occurs in KSR's fable-like "Zurich" (1990). "Zurich" begins as autobiography. In the first person, the narrator (presumably KSR) tells how he must clean the apartment for a government inspection as he and his wife Lisa are to leave Switzerland after two years living in Zurich.[4] The story develops through comic exaggeration as the narrator gets increasingly obsessed with leaving the apartment spotless, to show the notoriously fastidious Swiss that an *Auslander* can live up to their demanding standards. The Swiss obsession with cleanliness, both admirable and frightening, becomes a metaphor for the denial of human fault, the desire to evade or expunge the mire of human fallibility.

The narrator, in the attempt to clean some recalcitrant dirty sheets, concocts a dangerous mixture of cleaners that infects his finger, giving him a Midas-like "cleaning touch": everything he touches instantly turns spotlessly white. He takes a tram into the city, gradually turning everything he touches an antiseptic white.

The one exception to his power occurs when a Latin American beggar gets onto the tram, wearing a colorful serape, and begins to play a bow-and-gourd instrument. The self-reliant Swiss passengers are uncomfortable and resentful of this imposition, with its implicit claim on their charity, until the man begins to sing.

> What a voice the man had! Suddenly the ridiculous twanging made sense.... That kind of singing is impossible to ignore or deny — we knew exactly what he was feeling, and so for a moment we were a little community. And all without understanding a word. What power the voice has to express what really matters! [526].

The passengers open up their wallets and purses and give generously to the beggar. As the narrator leaves the tram, having turned every thing and person on it milk white, he touches the singer. But instead of turning white the colors in the man's serape only glow brighter, and his eyes remain "black as obsidian" (527).

By the end of the story the narrator has turned everything in the city brilliantly white, and the lake and the mountains too. Yet the beggar still exists, representing something, both for good and for ill, beyond the reach of the perfecting impulse. "But from a distant street I could still hear that twanging" (528).

The Move to the Novel

By the mid–1980s KSR had completely mastered applying the methods of the classic 20th century modernist short story — the kind of story Joyce wrote in *Dubliners*, that O'Connor wrote in *A Good Man Is Hard to Find*— in the service of sf. The early first person viewpoint is for the most part put aside. In a third-person voice that moves supplely from detachment to close identification, KSR creates completely human characters, realizes settings in sensory detail, and evokes political or other themes through dramatic action. Of course Robinson was not the first to accomplish this — he had his precursors in Kate Wilhelm, Thomas Disch, Ursula Le Guin, Keith Roberts and dozens of others. But in "Venice Drowned," "Black Air," "The Lucky Strike," "Down and Out...," "Glacier," "The Translator," and "A Transect," he established himself as among the strongest of his generation of sf short story writers.

And yet in 1991, essentially, he gave up the short story. Why?

Well, for one thing the ability of a writer to make a living in science fiction at shorter lengths had by 1990 completely vanished. The novel is the only venue for commercial success in written sf. But I believe a further key to this abandonment can be seen in a number of the stories KSR published in the late 1980s. Stories like "The Lunatics," "Vinland the Dream," and "Remaking History" depend more on discussions and debates between the characters over history and politics, than on dramatic action. Robinson is less interested in fitting, or perhaps finds himself less able to fit, his discursive impulses within narrative. By the early 1990s, in "A Sensitive Dependence..." he is writing fiction in the form of essay.

Eventually he realizes that the answer is the novel, where, as we see in his Mars trilogy, he finds space to do both the discursive exploration and the dramatic realization of character that he could no longer easily contain in the short story.

However, one of his last stand-alone stories, 1991's "A History of the Twentieth Century, with Illustrations" is one of KSR's very finest. In it he manages to integrate both his dramatic and discursive skills into a powerful and disturbing narrative. Though it is not really a science fiction story, it is all about the historical perspective that science fiction writers attempt to bring to their observations of everyday life, and the fear that can arise from the feeling that we are trapped by destructive forces over which we have no control.

This story, set in the 1990s, begins when Frank Churchill, a Barbara Tuchman–like author of popular histories, suffering from depression after the breakup of his marriage, is commissioned to write a coffee-table book summing up the 20th century. Reluctant at first to take on this task, he travels to London and the British Museum where he immerses himself in research recalling the human-instigated disasters of the century, increasing in violence with our increased technological capacities. Ahead looms the threat of an even more horrible 21st century.

Isolated, unable to deal with these thoughts, Frank spirals even deeper into depression. He discovers an old volume titled *A History of the Nineteenth Century, with Illustrations*, published in 1902, which concludes with the lines, "I believe that man is good. I believe we stand at the dawn of a century that will be more peaceful and prosperous than any in history." The bitter irony of this statement, coming at the beginning of a century of unprecedented mechanized slaughter, sends Frank further into depression. He rents a car and drives north to Scotland, then flees farther and farther north into the Orkneys. He visits Neolithic ruins on the edge of the continent, facing the west and the storm-tossed Atlantic.

There he also faces the decision whether or not to despair completely and end his life. On the one hand, as a historian, he is all too aware of the persistence of human self-destruction. Atrocities go back thousands of years, as he reminds himself on seeing a Viking fortress in the Orkneys. We have learned nothing from our mistakes, yet our power to destroy has grown. "...[W]hat was implied for the next century was grim beyond measure. And with the technologies of destruction, practically anything was possible" (331).

On the positive side, the Neolithic ruins, with their evidence of everyday domesticity, show humans were the same then as now. They had same homely needs, desires, and ability to protect each other and thrive. Even when their culture perished, people went on. They exhibited bravery against the odds, as do the fishermen Frank sees going out into north Atlantic in midst of the storm (345).

In the end, Frank discards all his notes, and with them his personal and historical memories of disaster, and addresses a new, blank page in his notebook. Robinson's story ends, "'I believe that man is good. I believe we stand at the dawn of a century that will be more peaceful and prosperous than any in history.' Outside it was dark, and the wind howled" (341).

I suppose that these sentences, with their contrasting light and dark implications, can be seen (as of now) as the last words of Kim Stanley Robinson's career as a short story writer. The question of how anyone with a realistic understanding of human fallibility and our potential for destruction can imagine a positive future is one that Robinson has spent much of his career pondering. In his short stories he provides several causes for hope. In the novels he has written over the last fifteen years he has consistently pursued the themes of the short fiction, and found new ways to engage them, to powerful effect.

This is not to say that I expect KSR will no longer write in the short form. But I do expect, if he were to make an extended re-commitment to writing short fiction, the character of the stories, and possibly their form, would be different from that of the work of his first decade. I think he would have to re-invent the short story for himself, and I would look forward to seeing what results.

For now we have *Remaking History*, and that stands as a significant accomplishment.

Notes

1. The invocations given by Fra Lucien in the story come from the *Book of Tokens*, a metaphysical meditation on God, by Paul Foster Case, published by Builders of the Adytum, 1947.
2. The fact that KSR gives Lee, clearly a black man, his own last name is significant; in the mid–1980s, while his wife Lisa Nowell did post-doctoral work in Washington, KSR lived in the same apartment building on 16th Street where Leroy and Debra live in the story. KSR places himself elsewhere in the story when Lee encounters a white man sitting on the bench in the tiny "Fish Park" that the locals call their "living room": "The guy was white, young; his hair was blond and short, he wore wire-rimmed glasses..." (461). This young man looks exactly as KSR did when he lived in Washington D.C. in the 1980s.
3. KSR has spoken of his mother's devout religious beliefs. Also as a teenager Robinson trained to play the trumpet, and is a lover of traditional jazz.
4. KSR and his wife Lisa Nowell lived in Zurich for two years in the 1980s while Nowell worked as an environmental chemist for the World Health Organization.

Works Cited

Robinson, Kim Stanley. *Remaking History and Other Stories*. New York: Tom Doherty Associates, Inc., 1994.
_____. "Chop Wood, Carry Water" (interview). *Locus* 58.4 (Apr. 2007): 6, 58–60.
"Interview: Kim Stanley Robinson." *Science Fiction Weekly* 23.2 (17 June 1996). Cited 25 June 2007. <www.scifi.com/sfw/issue23/interview.html>

5

The Martians: A Habitable Fabric of Possibilities*
Nick Gevers

The chief justification for the existence of *The Martians*, Kim Stanley Robinson's fifth short story collection, is its status as a justification. The book is more than it seems—and it can only truly succeed if its less obvious qualities are recognized. So what is the semblance, and what is the reality?

What *The Martians* seems to be is a standard companion volume to a great serial magnum opus, similar to *The Dune Encyclopaedia* or *A Pliocene Companion* or *The Castle of the Otter*. Its twenty-eight sections complement or illuminate the vast human, political and environmental panoramas of Robinson's Mars trilogy (1992–6). Short stories and anecdotes fill gaps in the trilogy's record of major characters' lives. Quoted sections of imaginary Martian documents provide areological and constitutional background. Descriptive essays reiterate Robinson's passionate engagement with landscape and the dilemmas of its human inhabitation. Some of Robinson's best writing is to be found here. But this is not enough in itself to make this a major book. Of the stories here, only a few have the ability to stand on their own in a narrative sense, in particular "Sexual Dimorphism," "Exploring Fossil Canyon," and "Green Mars"—but the latter two have been published before, "Green Mars" as a title in its own right, so this collection offers few new examples of autonomous story-telling. Virtually all of these pieces are satisfactory only when read in close conjunction with the trilogy; their allusions and ironies succeed or fail on that basis. These allusions and ironies are copious, complex, and, fascinatingly, subversive yet affirmatory of much of the trilogy's material. Consequently, *The Martians* is best regarded not as a casual companion volume, as a pendant assortment of off-cuts, afterthoughts, and miscellaneous paraphernalia, but rather as a metafictional commentary by Robinson on his own work, a justification of his art in the guise of a cycle of fictions.

Such a justification is necessary because of the ideological ambition of the Mars trilogy. After all, Robinson there proclaimed an anarcho-syndicalist manifesto of great scope and idealism, one subject to many practical challenges: Could Mars really be terraformed into a utopian human home in under two centuries? Would capitalism really surrender so meekly? Would such a motley crew of fringe communities and volatile personalities really co-operate so successfully once independence was attained? To some extent Robinson's defense of his

---

*This essay first appeared as a book review of *The Martians* in *The New York Review of Science Fiction* (November 1999): 10–11. Copyright 1999 by the author, and reprinted by his permission.

assumptions in the trilogy itself has an unsatisfactorily naïve quality: in *Blue Mars*, Charlotte Dorsa Brevia's theory of history as progress to democracy and beyond can only be trusted on the basis of a profound Faith.

And aside from any doubts as to the viability of Robinson's anti-capitalist teleology as future history, there must be uncertainty as to how useful his eco-political blueprint is as a guide for present behavior, which he certainly intends it to be. How good a model for our next few decades, ones of global economic interdependence, overcrowding, and unemployment, is a narrative of the flight of a privileged (if idealistic) few to a planet millions of miles from the global economy, with vast open spaces, and a population inevitably made up of highly qualified experts whose employability is guaranteed? As in the cases of the not dissimilar *Pacific Edge* and *Antarctica*, the charge could be leveled that Robinson is proposing Libertarian escapism rather than a practical, universal responsibility to society and environment. In revising leftwards American SF's imperialistic myth of the Manifest Destiny of human interplanetary colonization, Robinson runs some risk of succumbing to the easy seductions of that myth. But *The Martians* is a very effective rebuttal of any such impression, a self-vindication of great skill, an audacious affirmation of Robinson's convictions and of the technical subtlety by which he represents them. The trilogy is validated.

This validation proceeds by two techniques: multiplicity of histories, and the fusion of utopia and narrative. The first of these is strongly anticipated by Robinson's short story or essay "A Sensitive Dependence on Initial Conditions" (1991; in *Remaking History*), in which, elaborating on the alternate-Hiroshima scenario of "The Lucky Strike" (1984; in *The Planet on the Table*), the narrator ponders multiple rival outcomes of the same event, and how these diverge or converge in the light of chaos theory and different theories of historical causation. In *The Martians*, various alternate futures jostle with the one set out in the trilogy, testing it, paralleling it, justifying it. The darker Californian futures laid out in *The Wild Shore* and *The Gold Coast* make the utopian option of *Pacific Edge* all the brighter by their contrast, in Robinson's Orange County trilogy; now, three other timelines cast supporting light on the one set out in *Red Mars*, *Green Mars*, and *Blue Mars*. One of these ensues on the non-colonization of Mars; two stories detail the cancellation of the great project, the terrible sense of failure and emptiness that this inflicts on one character who found fulfillment in the trilogy. The cruel ending of the second story, "Michel in Provence," is best understood in combination with Robinson's chronology for *Green Mars*; it makes the Martian adventure — the bold course — the only one worth undertaking.

The other rival histories obey this logic, and carry humanity to Mars, but in subversive variation. One sequence is the "Roger Clayborne and Eileen Monday" stories: "Exploring Fossil Canyon" (1982), "Green Mars" (1985), and the new tales "Arthur Sternbach Brings the Curveball to Mars" and "A Martian Romance." This is the version of Martian colonization that Robinson followed well before he finalized the precise scheme of the trilogy — the chronology is more open-ended, Mars' utopian development vaguer, although similar in many ways to the authorized version. Robinson's decision not to modify the early pieces — indeed, to sustain them as a separate history through additions — allows the reader both to understand much of the long-term genesis of his Martian undertaking, and to see a different, bitter end for terraformed Mars. In "A Martian Romance," the terraforming fails; this is Robinson acknowledging the criticism that his outline of areoformation might be untenable; but the determination of the characters to persevere even in the face of global winter makes clear the ability of idealism to overcome any setback. So utopian Mars will stand, if it takes two thousand years instead of two hundred. A fifth story, "What Matters," echoes Ray Bradbury's

"Night Meeting," as two similar men from the two different versions of Mars meet and converse in an eerie, unknowing dimensional crossover. And the third future history, a secret folkloric one, in the form of three brief episodes about the apocryphal indigenous "little red people" of Mars, implies that all the utopian goodwill of the human Martians is the product of quaint alien machinations — a mythic or intuitive declaration that utopia will out.

These divergences, then, paradoxically reinforce Robinson's central history. In other ways, that history comes under attack — as when, in "Sexual Dimorphism," a madman, despite living in utopia, succumbs to an atavistic delusion of gender difference; or as when, in "Keeping the Flame," Nirgal encounters relicts of the pre-utopian regime who would revive the bad old capitalist days of strip-mining and other ecological irresponsibility — but the alternatives are always patently monstrous. And as *The Martians* approaches its end, many of the poems in "If Wang Wei Lived on Mars," as well as the concluding story, "Purple Mars," broach a further history — an autobiographical one, that of Kim Stanley Robinson in the present. He is a poet experiencing landscape; he is a father coping with daftly uncooperative children. In his life, the components of the Martian utopia are already present. If they exist already, they can surely exist on a larger scale in the future. There is utopia now, on Earth, on Earth, on Earth, on Earth, on Earth...

This points to Robinson's other affirmatory technique: utopia as narrative. Virtually all of the sections of *The Martians*, if at times by negative example, embody utopia at their most fundamental level. Utopia structures them; it shapes their language, their subject matter, their sensibility. "The Constitution of Mars" and "Some Worknotes and Commentary on the Constitution, by Charlotte Dorsa Brevia" are obvious and didactic utopian exposition. But other pieces, notably "The Way the Land Spoke to Us" and "Four Teleological Trails," are opposite in manner, suggesting in subtle, understated terms how the topography of the planet itself can proclaim the lineaments of utopian thought. Short accounts of life in utopia, like "Saving Noctis Dam" and "Enough Is as Good as a Feast," illuminate in startlingly everyday terms the challenges and rewards of its way of life. And the stories featuring the trilogy's major characters intensify the earlier novels' sense of the emotional and intellectual vibrancy, the sheer energy, of the utopian enterprise: there is the volatile Maya's secret friendship, and Coyote's guerrilla nature, and Nirgal's identification with the wilderness, and Sax's fascination with the paradoxes of complexity. Even Jackie Boone, a largely negative figure in the novels, acquires a sudden deep humanity as her thoughts on her astonishing child Zo are revealed. Robinson caps the trilogy's triumphs of characterization with new emotional and ideological insights into his utopians; they live and breathe in the reader's mind, and so their society can too.

It may perhaps be appropriate, then, to see *The Martians* as a work after the pattern of Le Guin's *Always Coming Home* (1985). Many fragments, some quiet and domestic, some deeply reflective, some richly descriptive, some with great narrative energy, combine into a mosaic of a better, future civilization. This is the archaeology of the future: often slow and painstaking, but productive, detail by detail, of a rich and *habitable* fabric of possibility.

6

Learning to Live in History: Alternate Historicities and the 1990s in *The Years of Rice and Salt*
Phillip E. Wegner

> As long as man concentrates his interest contemplatively upon the past *or* future, both ossify into an alien existence. And between the subject and the object lies the unbridgeable "pernicious chasm" of the present. Man must be able to comprehend the present as becoming. He can do this by seeing in it the tendencies out of whose dialectical opposition he can *make* the future. Only when he does this will the present be a process of becoming that belongs to him.
> — Georg Lukács, *History and Class Consciousness*

Recent years have seen a resurgence of interest in the science fiction subgenre of the alternate history, or as the historians refer to their version of the practice, the "counter-factual narrative." In 2004, Philip Roth published to wide critical and popular interest *The Plot Against America*, an account of life in the United States in the aftermath of Charles Lindbergh's defeat of Roosevelt in 1940 and Lindbergh's efforts to keep the United States out of the war in Europe; and in 2007, there appeared to much acclaim Michael Chabon's *The Yiddish Policemen's Union*, a detective fiction set in a universe where Roosevelt's plan to establish a European Jewish community on the panhandle of Alaska had been enacted.[1] There are now even alternate histories of fictional universes, as 2003, for example, saw the publication of *Superman: Red Son*, a graphic novel that speculated on the consequences of the man of steel originally crash-landing in the Soviet Union.

Preceding these works, and far more ambitious in its reach and scope, is Kim Stanley Robinson's *The Years of Rice and Salt* (2002). The "point of divergence"— the moment when history begins to move along a dramatically different path — occurs much earlier in Robinson's novel, in the late 14th century, when a mutated form of the Black Death eradicates almost all of Europe's population, thereby removing Christianity and European modernity from the world historical stage. Indeed, the only Europeans we even see in the novel are the marginalized figures of exotic harem denizens and the inhabitants of the rural agrarian Orkney Islands (see *Years* 418 and 543). From this point, Robinson traces out an alternate history that extends nearly 700 years up to the last decades of the twenty-first century.[2] Robinson's novel is equally wide ranging in its spatial expanse, as the events take place throughout the Middle East, Asia, the space of Europe, and in the Americas, with only equatorial and southern Africa exempt from major actions in the novel. All these various times and places are brilliantly unified in this work into a single coherent and rich narrative.

However, perhaps the greatest achievement of this novel, and what will be at the center of attention in this essay, is the way it works to teach its audience, in a true Brechtian fashion, to think and hence to live history in new ways, to overcome the sense of paralysis and inaction that have been considered characteristic of postmodernism and to actively take control of our destiny once more — that is, to finally overcome the deep alienations of our long human prehistory and, as one character puts it, to "see for the first time what kinds of creatures we really are" (451). In this, Robinson's text comes to participate in a project shared by many of the great radical cultural figures of the historical moment that was the 1990s; and, to the degree that this moment is no longer our own, Robinson's work becomes more valuable than before. For most significantly, *The Years of Rice and Salt* teaches the importance and indeed necessity of hope precisely in those situations where the possibility of any radical transformation of the status quo seems to have become once more distant.

I.

There are three different strategies deployed in *The Years of Rice and Salt* by which these pedagogical labors unfold. The first takes the form of a careful and extended engagement with the expectations and possibilities of the generic form itself. In his classic essay, "Progress Versus Utopia; or, Can We Imagine the Future?," the cultural critic (and Robinson's teacher) Fredric Jameson argues that the genre of science fiction is a structural analogue and heir to the historical novel. The originality of both forms, Jameson maintains, lies in their capacity "for apprehending the present as history" (*Archaeologies* 288). The historical novel highlights the originality of what is in the early part of the nineteenth century the recent achievement of the imagined community of the modern nation-state by marking off its radical difference from those modes of collective social life that had preceded it. However, these earlier social forms are now understood to be part of the nation's determinate past, stages that must be passed through on the way to its realization. Science fiction — emerging in the late nineteenth century after, as Georg Lukács famously contends, the effectivity of the historical novel has considerably waned — reverses all of this, and now imagines the present as "the determinate past of something yet to come" (*Archaeologies* 288). Both forms thus bring into view for their readers the modern sense of a present that is swirling in the flows and eddies of historical time, emerging out of a past and giving way to a future that are both fully other to it.

Moreover, in both cases, this historicity takes on the force of necessity. The failure of the competing forces — for example, the cultural and social structures of the Scottish highland clans in Walter Scott's prototype of the genre — is represented in the historical novel as inevitable as the fate that befalls the heroes of any of the great tragedies (see Scott's short story, "The Two Drovers," for a concise expression of this dynamic). Science fiction, on the other hand, stresses that if things continue as they are — bringing into focus precisely "how things are in the present" being the real aim of the genre's portrait of an imaginary future — then such a destiny (usually an undesirable one) will be the result.

It is exactly this sense of historical determinism projected by both the historical novel and science fiction that is called into question in the hybrid form of the alternate history. Long a vital sub-genre of U.S. science fiction, achieving its first formulations in Murray Leinster's "parallel worlds" story, "Sidewise in Time" (1934) and L. Sprague De Camp's "nexus story" novel, *Lest Darkness Fall* (1941) and including such classics as Ward Moore's *Bring the Jubilee* (1955), Philip K. Dick's *The Man in the High Castle* (1962), and the Harlan Ellison–scripted episode of *Star Trek*, "The City on the Edge of Forever" (1967), this genre, through its register of the "what if" (what if the Roman empire did not fall? what if the Confederacy had won the Civil War? what if the U.S. had lost or had never entered World War II?), offers a vision of the present as the product of chance.[3] When it is most successful, the alternate history confronts us with the dizzying prospect that "what is" is in fact surrounded by an infinity of possible other worlds, other collective destinies whose lack of substantiality is simply a matter of accident. In this, the subgenre is deeply akin to the radical historical materialism of Walter Benjamin: "Against the history written by the victors, the celebration of the *fait accompli*, the historical one-way street and the 'inevitability' of the victory of those who triumphed, we must come back to this essential proposition: each present opens up onto a multiplicity of possible futures. In every historical conjuncture, there were alternatives.... In this case, the opening-up of the past and the opening-up of the future are intimately linked" (Löwy 115).

Moreover, as is the case in Moore's novel, the alternate history often suggests that the most seemingly incidental events can have monumental consequences for later developments. At the heart of *Bring the Jubilee* lies the conceit that there was a certain hill at the Battle of Gettysburg that might easily have been captured by the Confederate troops; their failure to do so produces all the subsequent history of which we are so familiar. Similarly in Terry Bisson's underappreciated *Fire on the Mountain* (1988), one character, upon reading *John Brown's Body*, the alternate history within the alternate history (a common device within the genre), exclaims, "Ridiculous! ... The author would have all of history hanging on one strand of rope with poor old Captain Brown" (154–5).

The consequences of this conclusion for how we consider our individual actions are then brought to the fore in Robinson's own early foray into the genre of the alternate history, the 1984 short story, "The Lucky Strike." In this work, Robinson explores what would have happened if the *Enola Gay* had crashed, killing its flight crew, before it had the opportunity to deliver its terrible payload on the Japanese city of Hiroshima on August 6, 1945. In its place, the backup plane, *Lucky Strike*, is ordered to fulfill the *Enola Gay*'s mission. However, the plane's bomber, Captain Frank January, makes the last minute decision to drop the first atomic bomb over an uninhabited forest region rather than the city center. Although January is court-martialed and executed for his actions, the effects of his action on later history are profound:

> [January] never would have guessed that so many people would join a January Society. He would never know of the effect the Society had on Dewey during the Korean crisis, never know of the Society's successful campaign for the test ban treaty, and never learn that thanks in part to the Society and its allies, a treaty would be signed by the great powers that would reduce the number of atomic bombs year by year, until there were none left [34].

The real lesson of the story is summarized for us by January: "'But now I've been thinking that if everybody were to live their whole lives like that, thinking that every move they made really was important, then ... it might make a difference.' He waved a hand vaguely, expelled cigarette smoke. 'You're accountable for what you do'" (37).

However, this also suggests one of the great potential paradoxes of the alternate history: for while it stresses the real significance of individual actions and seemingly insignificant events, when taken to its logical conclusion it presents a vision of history as fully independent of human intention and control. This tendency is exploited to its fullest in one of the other great alternate histories of the early 1990s, *The Difference Engine* (1991), co-authored by the two founding figures of the cyberpunk movement, William Gibson and Bruce Sterling. When one of the villains of the narrative worries that "since studying the writings of Karl Marx ... it has come to me that some dire violence has been done to the true and natural course of historical development," the central protagonist counters, "History works by Catastrophe! It's the way of the world, the only way there is, has been, or ever will be. There is no history — there is only contingency!" (301–2). If men make history, they do so, this novel argues, in ways they can never anticipate. And indeed, as Gibson and Sterling represent it, the seemingly incidental fact of the development of Charles Babbage's steam-driven computer ends up producing a radically different history, one wherein the British empire remains strong well into the twentieth century, and the USSR and U.S. never develop into the dominant global powers that they do in our world. In this way, Gibson and Sterling's fiction becomes a further element of the cyberpunk, and more generally high postmodernist, assault on the so-called *grand récits*, the master narratives of modernity, and the characteristic modernist efforts at social planning.[4]

However, to abolish history in this way is also to abolish the deeply modernist genre of science fiction from which the alternate history arises — and in this too, we see in *The Difference Engine* a continuity with the larger agenda of cyberpunk, wherein, Jameson notes, there occurs the collapse of "a formerly futurological science fiction ... into mere 'realism' and an outright representation of the present" (*Postmodernism* 286). Even more interesting, such a vision resonates with another even more infamous claim of the "end of history," that first advanced two years earlier by the conservative Hegelian Francis Fukuyama.[5] In this way, both cyberpunk and Fukuyama's narratives become crucial pedagogical weapons in the construction of an emergent neoliberal global hegemony, for which, as Margaret Thatcher first declared, there is "no alternative."

It is precisely this vision of the end of history that Robinson indirectly engages with in his contemporary mediation on the genre of the alternate history, "A Sensitive Dependence on Initial Conditions" (1991). Focusing upon the same point of divergence that was at the heart of "A Lucky Strike," Robinson offers in this work a reflection upon a variety of models of historical movement. In the end, Robinson refuses the zero-sum conclusion of Gibson and Sterling's work, and by extension that of much of postmodern thought, which posits the only choices as the stereotypical modernist totalitarian closure of rigid historical determinism or the postmodern free play of radical contingency. Rather, Robinson suggests, we should see these two extreme options as more akin to the quantum mechanical wave-particle duality: "The great man theory considers particles; historical materialism considers waves. The wave/particle duality, confirmed many times by experiment, assures us that neither theory can be the complete truth. Neither will serve as the covering law" (10). Instead, Robinson offers a much more dialectical conception of historical movement, amended as it is by the insights of the same chaos or complexity theory that is at the heart of *The Difference Engine*: "So the covering law is amended yet again. Explanations still require laws, but there are not laws for every event. The task of historical explanation becomes the act of making distinctions between those parts of an event that can be explained by laws, and those that cannot" (14). Robinson ultimately concludes that in every moment of individual choice, "the mind attempts the work of the historian: breaking potential events down into their component parts, enumerating conditions, seeking covering laws that will follow from the variety of possible choices. Alternative futures branch like dendrites away from the present moment, shifting chaotically, pulled this way and that by attractors dimly perceived. Probable outcomes emerge from those less likely" (16).⁶

It will be the goal of *The Years of Rice and Salt* to provide narrative substance to the vision of history offered in this short text. Thus, while the particular events are dramatically different in the richly realized world offered in Robinson's novel, there is still a sequence of historical developments similar to that in our reality: a scientific renaissance followed by (Chinese) first contact with the Americas, the development of steam technology, an industrial revolution, the outbreak of a global war (here imagined as a single 70 year "Long War" rather than our sequence of three "world wars" over the period of 1914–1989 — however, as in our own world, it too is a war "that no one won.... Everyone lost, and we have not yet recovered from it even now" [648]), the discovery of the atom bomb, and the eventual postwar collapse of the rigid state structures of one of the two major global powers.

Crucially, however, while the sequence may be similar, we are still free to interpret its significance in a variety of ways. These interpretations, one character will suggest late in the novel, are shaped by "more deeply hidden unconscious ideological biases" that in turn "can be teased out by identifying the mode of emplotment chosen to tell the tale" (*YRS* 635). There are four such modes of emplotment identified in the novel. The first is "romance, in which humanity struggles to work out its dharma, to better itself, and so generation by generation to make progress, fighting for justice, and an end to want, with the strong implication that we will eventually work our way up to the source of the peach blossom stream, and the age of great peace will come into being." The second, the "ironic or satiric mode," is the romance's inverse in which "everything that humanity tries to do fails, or rebounds against it, and the combination of biological reality and moral weakness, of death and evil, means that nothing in human affairs can succeed ... people who say it is all a chaos without causes" (636). However, far more interesting than these two "end-point extremes" are the two "mixed and partial modes," identified as tragedy and comedy: "In comedy the reconciliation is of people with other people, and with society at large." Tragedies, on the other hand, "make a darker reconciliation. Scholar White said of them, they tell the story of humanity face-to-face with reality itself, therefore facing death and dissolution and defeat. Tragic heroes are destroyed, but for those who survive to tell their tale, there is a rise in consciousness, in awareness of reality, and this is valuable in and of itself, dark though that knowledge may be" (636–7). The narrator of this paradigm then concludes by offering a call for a more synthetic historical vision: "Perhaps the way to construct a proper history is to inscribe the whole figure, and say that for the individual, ultimately, it is a tragedy; for the society, comedy. If we can make it so" (637). At this late juncture, the reader realizes that this synthetic vision has been advanced throughout the novel. The challenge offered to us as readers then is to adopt a similar bifocality in our own grasp of history.

Some readers will recognize that this mapping of the four modes of historical emplotment is taken from Hayden White's classic work, *Metahistory: The Historical Imagination in Nineteenth Century Europe* (1973). In a discussion of White's masterpiece, Jameson identifies the same combination championed by Robinson's novel as that found in the great dialectical thinkers: "Both Hegel and Marx, White tells us, achieved syntheses of Tragedy and Comedy: History is a comedy, all of whose individual moments are tragic" (Foreword xx). Jameson's essay also suggests that the positions described in the novel as the romance and satire modes are in fact more complex positions, named by him simply optimism (the synthesis of romance and comedy, "a conceivable but impossible synthesis") and pessimism (satire and tragedy, "the empty wiping out" of the first). This then leaves one final combination unaccounted for, that of satire and romance, along with their accompanying tropes of irony and metaphor (the tropes of tragedy and comedy in White's schema being, respectively, metonymy and synecdoche). This last position is the direct inverse of that of the dialectical thinkers, and is embodied for White, Jameson argues, in the figure of Nietzsche, who "begins with an identification of Tragedy and Comedy, which luminously eclipse each other and in their indistinction give rise to something else, which will be an Ironic sense of the powers of language that now once again release the great Metaphoric energies" (Foreword xx–xxi). It is, of course, the Nietzschean position that emerges as the dominant one in much of postmodern thought, including, I would maintain, in the cyberpunk alternate history of *The Difference Engine*: for in this last, it is precisely the ironic undermining of the earlier master narratives of modernity that then apparently creates the conditions for the desired comic resolution, figured here, much as in Gibson's earlier classic, *Neuromancer* (1984), by the new artificial intelligence, the All-Seeing Eye, that emerges at the novel's conclusion in this alternate world 1990s present. Here then we arrive at the real site of pedagogical and polemical engagement in Robinson's work, as it both challenges the postmodern common sense at work in cyberpunk and Fukuyama's essay and attempts to breath new life into the Hegelian Marxist vision of history and the radical project of global transformation that accompanies it.[7]

All this as well points toward the significant differences between the historical situations that are addressed in Robinson's two alternate history narratives I have discussed in this essay. "The Lucky Strike" is very much a fiction of the late Cold War period, a wish-fulfillment narrative wherein what has never happened is the massive global historical reality of the détente between the Soviet Union and the United States that seems to have blocked utterly the further development of history (and in this fantastic undoing of the Cold War blockage of history, the wish fulfillment structure of the narrative becomes identical with that of one of its most celebrated contemporary science fiction visions, the 1984 film, *The Terminator*).[8] However, in the moment of both *The Difference Engine* and *The Years of Rice and Salt*, the distinct period that I identify as that of the 1990s or the period of the "life between two deaths," this wish has been granted, as the Cold War has in fact come to an abrupt and unexpected conclusion. What Robinson's work makes so evident for us, however, is that such an Event has not, as the champions of neo-liberal capitalist globalization would maintain, brought history to an end, or made the older master narratives of human emancipation obsolete; rather it has created an opportunity for the latter's reinvigoration and reinvention. The project undertaken in this novel by Robinson — one that continues the work begun in his preceding Mars trilogy — is thus analogous to that in the contemporary radical theoretical work of Jameson, Michael Hardt and Antonio Negri, Slavoj Zizek, Kojin Karatani, Jacques Derrida, Michael Löwy, Alain Badiou, Judith Butler, and others, and in the collective political projects of such groups as the counter-globalization "movement of movements" and the World Social Forum, all of whom struggle to reinvent the project of radical social change — in short, the collective project of revolution — in a new historical context.

II.

However, this open transitional situation is a short-lived one, coming to an end just before the publication of *The Years of Rice and Salt* with the traumatic events of September 11, 2001. The new situation that then takes shape, the one in which we still live in today, is, of course, neither the post-historical world imagined in cyberpunk, Fukuyama's essay, or by the various champions of neo-liberalism, nor that of a new International or multitude envisioned in some of these other interventions.⁹ The response to the closure of such a moment of possibility is potentially another intense cycle of despair and paralysis, something similar occurring in Robinson's novel itself: "Well it was, as might be imagined after an end like that, a very discouraged and dispirited little jati that huddled together on the black floor of the bardo this time around. Who could blame them? Why should they have had any will to continue? It was hard to discern any reward for virtue, any forward progress — any dharmic justice of any kind ... the story ... had become instead a veritable charnel house. Why read on?" (305). A similar query is advanced nearly two centuries earlier in Hegel's own great meditation on history:

> When we contemplate this display of passions, and consider the historical consequences of their violence and of the irrationality which is associated with them (and even more so with good intentions and worthy aims); when we see the evil, the wickedness, and the downfall of the most flourishing empires the human spirit has created; and when we are moved to profound pity for the untold miseries of individual human beings — we can only end with a feeling of sadness at the transience of everything. And since all this destruction is not the work of mere nature but of the will of man, our sadness takes on a moral quality, for the good spirit in us (if we are at all susceptible to it) eventually revolts at such a spectacle. Without rhetorical exaggeration, we need only complete an accurate account of the misfortunes which have overtaken the finest manifestations of national and political life, and of personal virtues or innocence, to see a most terrifying picture take shape before our eyes. Its effect is to intensify our feelings to an extreme pitch of hopeless sorrow with no redeeming circumstances to counterbalance it [69].

It will thus be part of the project of Robinson's reinvigoration of an open dialectical view of history to develop a perspective from which such a question may be answered and the deep discouragement explicit within it challenged, a project that, as I will suggest in a moment, it also shares with some perhaps unexpected contemporaries.

I mentioned earlier that the spatial and historical scopes of Robinson's narrative are immense, encompassing a diverse range of characters and settings in a number of historical settings. Indeed, each of the ten books that make up this 658 page work could be read as short novels in their own right, each deploying a different form of presentation drawing upon some of the literary classics of our world. Robinson draws all of these disparate narratives together in a unique fashion. The central characters in each of the books are in fact the same figures, identified by the first letter of their name (B, K, and I being the most central), encountering each other again and again in their different incarnations:

> Jati, subcaste, family, village. It manifests differently. We all came into the cosmos together. New souls are born out of the void, but infrequently, especially at this point in the cycle, for we are in the Kali-yuga, the Age of Destruction. When new souls do appear it happens like a dandelion pod, souls like seeds, floating away on the dharma wind. We are all seeds of what we could be. But the new seeds float together and never separate by much, that's my point. We have gone through many lives together already. Our jati has been particularly tight since the avalanche. That fate bound us together. We rise or fall together [75].

In this way, the diverse stories and settings in the novel become chapters in a single extended novel whose plot is that of modern human history itself.

And yet, as this passage already suggests, the aims of Robinson's fiction are very different than those of the traditional novel. One character makes clear to us late in the book that we are not to read the novel as offering a defense of literal reincarnation: "No doubt Kirana was right to laugh. All the old myths were just stories. The only reincarnation you got was the next day's waking" (563). However, one lesson evident in all of Robinson's fictions is that "just stories" are of fundamental importance because the stories we tell shape how we conceptualize and in the end how we live in our world. Moreover, as the passage concerning the various modes of historiographic emplotment that I cited in the previous section also bears out, this pedagogical work is not only a matter of content but of form itself.

The way in which this particular work offers us a different pedagogy than that of the classical or realist novel is suggested near the very end of the book in a discussion of the allegorical significance of the formal device used to tie together the disparate events of the novel:

> Another way of rescuing the concept of reincarnation is simply to think of the species as the organism. The organism survives, and has a collective consciousness of itself—that's history, or language, or the twisting ladder structuring our brains—and it doesn't really matter what happens to any one cell of this body. In fact their deaths are necessary for the body to stay healthy and go on, it's a matter of making room for new cells. And if we think of it that way, then it might increase feelings of solidarity and obligation to others [654].

And yet, this is not quite the case of what goes on in this novel either, for while the device of reincarnation does turn us away from the classical novelistic concern with the fate of the monadic individual, the focus of *The Years of Rice and Salt* is not really on the deeply impersonal fate of humanity as suggested here (something perhaps more readily achieved in such science fiction modernist classics as Olaf Stapledon's *Last and First Men* and Andrei Plotanov's *Chevengur*). The scale of Robinson's narrative is in fact a more intermediate one, focusing particularly on the role of the collective of the group.[10] And throughout his work, Robinson's attention remains on one group in particular:

> Then there were the Sufis. Bismati watched his fellow scholars around the fire in the evenings, intent on a point of doctrine, or the questionable isnad of a hadith, and what that meant, arguing with exaggerated punctilio and little debater's jokes and flourishes, while a pot of thick hot coffee was poured with solemn attention into little glazed clay cups, all eyes gleaming with firelight and pleasure in the argument; and he thought, these are the Muslims who make Islam good. These are the men who have conquered the world, not the warriors. The armies could have done nothing without the word [129].

The central characters in Robinson's fiction are scholars, historians, mathematicians, philosophers, engineers, inventors, writers, and teachers — in short, intellectuals. One of the central aims of this book is to convey something of the deeply collective nature of intellectual work, its drama, and of its impact on historical development. Thus, we see a good deal of attention in the novel focused on discussion, exchanges of information, questioning and invention, while the actions of the leaders, political, economic, and military, occur off-stage. Indeed, one of the few political leaders we encounter directly in the text, the Kerala who founds the utopian Travancore Confederacy in India, is shown to be someone whose own deepest passion is intellectual work:

> and then he saw a group of Buddhist monks arranging charts of different elements in different families, depending on chemical and physical properties, all laid out in a very beautiful mandala, the subject of endless discussions in reading rooms, workshops, foundries and hospitals, everyone exploring even if they did not sail around the world, even if they never left Travancore, all of them anxious to have something interesting to tell the Kerala the next time he came by — not so the Kerala would reward them, though he would, but because he would be so happy at the new information. There was a look on his face everyone craved to see, and that was the whole story of Travancore right there [449].

Moreover, the reading experience of the novel is similarly one of this kind of intellectual exchange, as Robinson holds a series of different views and positions in front of us without rendering any simple judgment upon them: "Thus the bitter skepticism of the old woman, the stubborn hope of the old soldier, the insistent inquiry of Kirana, an inquiry that never got the answers she wanted, but forged on through idea after idea, testing them against her sense of things" (538). In this, Robinson's practice reveals a kinship with the learning plays of Bertolt Brecht: "Thus ultimately Brecht seems, rather, concerned with leaving that process open, and allowing the audience to have its own opinion and to frame its own moral, all the while attempting to suggest strongly — nay, even insist — that it cannot not do so" (Jameson, *Brecht* 107).

At the same time, the device of reincarnation works to instantiate a phenomenology other to that of our individual lives: "Everything took much longer than anyone had anticipated, and yet every few years everything was also somehow entirely different. The pulse of history's long duration was much slower than an individual's time" (626). Reincarnation thus attempts to enable its readers to experience for themselves something of these temporalities of history; and it thus serves in this novel as the equivalent of the "longevity treatments" of the Mars trilogy, of which Jameson has written,

> It is something of a scientific laboratory experiment in its own right, for human collective history knows rhythm and a logic radically distinct from the normal biological life span, and its paradoxes and unknowabilities stem as much from that incommensurability as they do from the other one that opposes biological individuals to larger multiplicities. The Mars trilogy then experimentally extends the lives of its viewers and participants in order to make them coeval with their own history, at the same time that it projects an original collectivity — the first settlers, the so-called "first Hundred" — as a collective protagonist or multiple subjects for that history itself [*Archaeologies* 396–7].

Robinson's gamble is that such a long view teaches, when it is truly lived, an essential historical patience. This is the advice the character B offers to K early in their second visit to the waiting room of history, the space between existences known as the "bardo" (a Tibetan word translated as "intermediate," "transitional," or "in-between" state): "The dharma is a matter that can't be short-changed, you have to work at it step by step, doing what you can in each given situation. You can't leap to heaven" (93). It is this advice the fiery and impetuous K refuses here — ""I shit on all that.... I'll be damned if I cooperate in such a horrible thing" (93) — and elsewhere in the novel, as she or he explodes into active rebellion in both the bardo and on the earth. However, such a revolutionary fervor untempered by a longer historical vision risks burning itself out when confronted with repeated failures, ultimately cooling into the embers of despair and passivity: "Bahram was hurt by this. 'It's you who give up on things,' he protested. 'Every time. That's what your cynicism is — you don't even try. You don't have the courage to carry on'" (307).

A similar counsel is offered to us in one of the other great radical political pedagogical texts of the period of the 1990s, the film *The Shawshank Redemption* (1994). The contrast between the visions of history in *The Years of Rice and Salt* and *The Difference Engine* that I discussed earlier is repeated in the opposition between *The Shawshank Redemption* and its far more commercially successful competitor released in the same year, *Forrest Gump*. *Forrest Gump* represents the earlier open cultural context of the 1960 as a nightmarish aberration, and works to reinforce the post–Cold War message that there is "no alternative" to the current global neo-liberal order. It does so by deploying a set of narrative strategies similar to those Evan Watkins describes as at work in the initial hugely successful advertisement campaign for the Mazda Miata: "The Miata ad strategy ... offers a past that was *always* yours, if over time dissipated, diffused, obscured, perhaps even taken away by vaguely malignant powers; but now it is in your power to repossess it, this time the way it ought to unfold, under the enabling sign of constructive energies available to you in much the same way they're available to the makers of the ad in their version of the construction as shown in the ad itself" (165). Conversely, *The Shawshank Redemption*, as with *The Years of Rice and Salt*, challenges this vision of historical closure, teaching its audience that another future is indeed possible if one adopts a proper historical perspective — patience and perseverance, a sense not of guarantees but of potential that only our efforts can bring to realization.

The film's central protagonist is the former wealthy lawyer Andy Dufresne (Tim Robbins) who, we learn early in the film, has been wrongfully sentenced to life in prison for the murder of his wife and her lover. Andy is in many ways the antithesis of the genial idiot Forrest Gump: he is very much an intellectual, deeply read, passionate about literature, art, and music: in one of the film's great set pieces, he plays over the prison loudspeaker system an aria from Mozart's *Marriage of Figaro*—a "progressive masterpiece of opera," which, Ernst Bloch writes, "simultaneously provides in the noblest enjoyment the most activating humane wishful image" (417) — a transgression for which Andy receives two weeks in the "hole." He also founds a library for the prison and serves as a tutor for those inmates seeking their high school equivalency degrees. As the narrative unfolds, it becomes evident that the prison, with its systematic exploitation of laborers and abusive and corrupt power structure, functions, as Michel Foucault famously described it, as a heterotopia, a space located within our reality that in turn mirrors back the larger social world, "to direct my eyes toward myself and to reconstitute myself there where I am" (179). The film effects a role reversal wherein the formerly privileged Andy becomes within this inverted mirror world the object of exploitation, his labor power used by the corrupt prison warden to enrich himself. Moreover, as Andy's comrade and the film's narrator, Ellis "Red" Redding (Morgan Freeman) points out, the system works to destroy any belief in the possibility of an alternative world: when Andy struggles to explain to his fellow inmates the utopian power of art to keep alive the memory of other possibilities — "that there are places in the world that are not made out of stone, that there's something inside that they can't get to, that they can't touch" — Red responds, "Hope is a dangerous thing, hope can drive a man insane. It's got no use on the inside. You better get used to that idea." And indeed, when Andy encounters a young inmate who has information that may lead to his freedom, the warden refuses to acknowledge it and has the young man murdered, throwing Andy into his darkest moment of despair. In this way, the film offers a devastating allegorical exploration of the realities and ideologies of contemporary capitalism.

However, as with Robinson's novel, the film also offers a pedagogy in another temporal phenomenology. Rather than developing this through Robinson's fantastic devices of reincarnation or life extensions, the film suggests that the heterotopic space of the prison itself generates another kind of temporality: as Andy explains to one of the younger inmates, "Prison time is slow time."[11] This slowing down of time enables the development of a more properly historical vision, one that in turn encourages the kind of careful slow labor necessary to create the preconditions for a sudden and to the outside world unexpected break with the status quo. After nearly two decades in Shawshank, Andy accomplishes exactly this transformation, by escaping and in turn bringing down the corrupt warden and his cronies. Andy was able to escape through a tunnel he had hidden for decades behind changing posters (a device also used to mark the passage of time, as each of the women on the poster — Rita Hayworth, Marilyn Monroe, and Raquel Welch — became emblematic of another decade passed), a tunnel that he had slowly and meticulously dug through the prison wall, working each night and depositing a pocketful or two of stone in the prison yard the following day.

It is no coincidence that Andy's escape occurs in the middle 1960s (and in a scene deleted from the final version of the film, we are reminded that when Red is paroled a year later, it is 1967's "Summer of Love"), for the film celebrates precisely the sense of open historical possibility represented by this historical situation. Indeed, at the film's conclusion, Red announces his own entrance into history proper, as for the first time in his life he experiences "the excitement only a free man can feel, a free man at the start of a long journey whose conclusion is uncertain." All this too suggests that the understanding of their present is in fact the same in both *Forrest Gump* and *The Shawshank Redemption*: both indirectly acknowledge that the end of the Cold War has created the potential for their moment to become another situation like that of the 1960s, but whereas the former warns against this explosive recrudescence of a sense of real freedom and possibility, the latter celebrates it.

This film and Robinson's novel thus both argue for the absolute necessity of the careful labor needed to cultivate Utopian hope. Late in the film, Andy writes to Red, "Hope is a good thing, maybe the best of things, and no good thing ever dies." And in their final appearance in the bardo, K says of B, "I don't know how you persist the way you do. You tire me too. All that hope in the face of calamity" (609). Both texts stress that such hope can sustain itself only by taking a long historical view necessary to recognize the often imperceptible transformative effects of our labors: "The past reproaches us! So many lives. Slowly we change, oh so slowly. You think it doesn't happen, but it does" (333). It is against the cultural pedagogy of the prison world, the world that suggests no real change is possible, that both texts stand. And upon such a view a tremendous burden rides: "You have to carry it — all the unborn lives to come depend on you! Without you the world would become a nightmare" (333).

III.

I suggested in the first section of this essay that *The Years of Rice and Salt*— and the same can be said of all of Robinson's work — differs from its cyberpunk contemporaries in its commitment to the older emancipatory paradigms of modernity, in whatever modified and revised form these may now exist. Similarly, Robinson's novel remains equally committed to the modernist project of science fiction, and it is here that the third level in the novel's historical pedagogy unfolds. In his classic study of the genre, Darko Suvin describes science fiction as "the literature of cognitive estrangement": "SF is, then, a literary genre whose necessary and sufficient conditions are the presence and interaction of estrangement and cognition, and whose main formal device is an imaginative framework alternative to the author's empirical environment" (7–8). If Suvin then goes on to note that this makes science fiction at once other to both nineteenth century realist fiction and to related forms of estranging fantastic fiction ("myth, but also from the folk (fairy) tale and the fantasy" [8]), we might also reverse this and suggest that science fiction is unique in that it draws upon the formal devices of the major fictional modes of both the nineteenth and early twentieth centuries. In a gloss on Suvin's definition of the genre, Jameson notes,

> Indeed, Suvin's originality as a theorist of both science fiction and Utopias all at once, is (among other things) not merely to have linked the two generically; but also to have conjoined the SF and utopian critical tradition with the Brechtian one, centering on estrangement (the so-called V-effect); and to have insisted not merely on the function of SF and Utopia to "estrange," to produce a V-effect for the reader from a normal "everyday" common-sense reality, but also to do so "cognitively" (a no less Brechtian component of the definition). The reassertion of the cog-

nitive means, as we said at the outset, a refusal to allow the (obvious) aesthetic and artistic status of the SF or utopian work to neutralize its realistic and referential implications [*Archaeologies* 410].

In short, Jameson shows how science fiction is a unique form of what we might call "realist (cognitive) modernism (estrangement)." Thus, whereas the classics of high modernism achieve these estranging effects through violations of formal expectations — and this was of the utmost importance to the originators of the concept of estrangement, Viktor Shklovsky and the Russian Formalists — science fiction estranges through its "realistic" content, a realism whose referent, as Marc Angenot points out, is an "absent" one, a true nowhere.

It is precisely through these operations of estrangement then that science fiction texts such as *The Years of Rice and Salt* teach us to think of what we take as most fixed and natural in our world as historical and the product of specific human energies. These estrangements occur in the novel on a number of different levels. Early on, we are offered this defamiliarized vision of the human body, represented from the perspective of K reincarnated as a tiger: "At his pace it was a long way. His body hung from his joints, and she saw how hard it must be to walk on two feet. Never a moment's rest, always balancing, falling forward and catching himself, as if always crossing a log over a creek. Shaky as a new cub, blind and wet" (99). Late in the novel, a "feng shui guru" offers the following reflection on the development of the city of Fangzhang, occupying the space of the San Francisco Bay area in our world and which as we had learned in an earlier chapter had developed here on the "northern peninsula ... all the way up to the peak of Mount Tamalpi" (458): "only geometric imbeciles would have located the city on the other side of the strait, aside from practical considerations of street platting, there is the intrinsic qi of the place, its dragon arteries are too exposed to the wind and the fog, it is best to leave it as a park" (644). A hundred pages earlier, Robinson offers us this speculation on why the peoples of Europe so readily succumbed to the plague centuries earlier: "They were pale because they were weak, or vice versa. Muzaffar has showed it, how the darker the skin, the stronger the persons. The blackest Africans are the strongest of all, the palest of the Golden Hoard are weakest. He did tests. The Franks were hereditarily incompetent, that was his conclusion. Losers in the evolutionary game of survival of the fittest" (575).

If these estranging transformations are examples of what Jameson describes as "fancy" in science fiction texts — wish fulfillments emanating from the individual subject and which reveal more about the author's desires than the larger social world he or she inhabits (although in their more collective dimension of "Utopian ideology" they do this latter as well) — they do help set the stage for the more significant acts of the estranging "Imagination" or "Utopian science" that occur in the narrative (*Archaeologies* 44–49). Perhaps the most important of these concerns the geo-political entity and form of community that have come in our modernity to be taken as the natural ones: for the failure of European civilization to develop as it does in our world into a position of global hegemony means that we have a modernity in the novel that is distinct from ours in the absence of what Benedict Anderson has famously described as the "imagined community" of the modern nation-state.

What this absence enables in this world is the development of a much more encompassing sense of belonging, one more along the current model of clashing "civilizations" made infamous by Samuel P. Huntington. Huntington too writes in response to the neo-liberal end of history thesis. As with Huntington, Robinson imagines these civilizations primarily along religious lines (and both authors too seem unsure whether "Africa" can be said to constitute a civilization in its own right). However, with the erasure in the text of Huntington's Western and Orthodox civilizations (Western and Eastern Europe), the map of civilizations offered to us is also a markedly different one. At the center of the novel, and increasingly engaged in a struggle for global dominance are the Chinese and Muslim civilizations, the latter ultimately coming to encompass much of what is in our world the Middle East, eastern and western Europe, Africa, and the east coasts of the Americas, before collapsing both as a result of its defeat in the Long War and its own rigid political structures. Of secondary significance, especially in the latter part of the novel, are the Travancori League, centered in Hindu India, and Hodenosaunee League of a North America where European incursion never occurs, thus enabling this confederacy of tribal groups to survive the belated attempts at conquest by both the Islamic and Chinese forces. Both then emerge in the aftermath of the Long War as major powers on the world historical stage.

At a number of places in the text, characters argue that history moves through violent moments of contact:

> History can be seen as a series of collisions of civilizations, and it is these collisions that create progress and new things. It may not happen at the actual point of contact, which is often racked by disruption war, but behind the lines of conflict, where the two cultures are most trying to define themselves and prevail, great progress is often made very swiftly, with works of permanent distinction in arts and technique.... No single civilization could ever progress; it is always a matter of two or more colliding [400].

These collisions define the major action of the novel. And yet the model presented here differs in a fundamental way from that of the neo-conservative Huntington: for the result of these conflicts is not in fact the ultimate "victory" of any one of these civilizations over its competitors. Instead, what we see is the formation of an increasingly complex syncretic cultural system, one that draws upon the strengths of each of the components: "Truly, you must become like these Sikhs you talk about, who combine what is best from the old religions, and make something new" (396). The reference to the Sikhs here also points out another central thread in the novel, as the best and strongest civilizations, the Indian Sikhs, the Native American Hodenosaunee, and the Japanese Buddhists are represented as those most flexible and open to external influences. (And indeed, the most difficult challenge to future development in the novel lies in the "old desert monotheisms" [523], of which Islam is of course here the major remaining figure.) It is these groups too, along with the intellectual cultures that I discussed earlier, that provide the model of a new global form of collective existence: "Meanwhile we continue to work with the Sikhs, treating them as chief allies and partners in what has become a larger Indian confederation of principalities and states. The unification of India on that basis is not something many people resist, because when it succeeds, it means peace" (442).

Robinson is deeply suspicious of any idealist attempt to force such a synthesis—this is why the project of the historian Ibrahim al-Lanzhou to demonstrate "the basic underlying identity of the teachings of Islam and Confucius" (381) is doomed to failure: "It was as though if he could only reconcile the two civilizations on paper, the bloody battles happening all around them would come to an end" (391). Rather, for Robinson it is a new synthesis that must be carefully and slowly hammered out on the ground, through the endless struggles, conflicts, compromises, and accommodations that in Robinson's presentation defines the sphere of the political at its most promising.

Robinson accomplishes a number of crucial goals with this estranging transformation. First, he shows us that any thinking about history is in fact also a form of thinking about space, as his work helps his readers further grasp the fact that space itself and our sense of spatial communal belonging are in fact the products of human activity, and that these spaces do change over time. (In this his work shares in what has been called the spatial turn in critical theory that emerged in the 1990s, deeply influenced, most centrally, by the spatial dialectic of the great social theorist Henri Lefebvre.[12]) Even more significantly, Robinson attempts to offer a sense of history as not a national but now a truly global phenomenon: indeed, late in the book, a young historian postulates, "All people who have ever lived on Earth have acted together to make global history. It is one story" (528). What has already been achieved in the fictional world of the novel is that which is only just coming into being in our world with the end of the period of the Cold War and the emergence of what has been popularly referred to as globalization. In effect, Robinson's entire novel functions as a form of what Jameson calls cognitive mapping, working to help its readers move beyond the old national model of belonging—a model that has witnessed a vicious resurgence in the aftermath of 9/11—and rather to think of themselves as part of a larger global reality. If there is a way forward, if there is to be a challenge to the stagnations of the present, then these hard lessons must be learned not only intellectually, but in the depth of our lived existences: "All the strands are beginning to weave together, you see. We have had to do it to survive" (649). And it is this kind of new conceptualization of our selves as members of common global community that is necessary if we ever hope to truly begin to live history in new ways. Perhaps the greatest brilliance of this novel lies in its effectiveness in conveying exactly this vital lesson.

Notes

1. For more detailed listing of recent alternate history fictions, see the Wikipedia entry, "Alternate History," at http://en.wikipedia.org/wiki/Alternate_history; Harry Turtledove's Introduction to *The Best Alternate History Stories*; and Karen Hellekson's useful study. For a discussion of World War II alternate histories, see Gavriel D. Rosenfeld. One of the more interesting discussions of Roth's novel is to be found in the exchange between Walter Benn Michaels and Michael Rothberg.

2. My essay has benefited from the study guide and timeline of the novel complied by Mark Rosa and found online at http://www.geocities.com/heiankyo794/tyoras-guide.html.

3. I draw here upon Hellekson's tripartite schema of the genre, one built upon the relationship between the moment of the break and the narrative locus: the "nexus story is an alternate history that focuses on a crucial point in history, such as a battle or assassination, in which something different happens that changes the outcome" (5); "true alternate history stories take place years after a change in a nexus event, which has resulted in a radically changed world" (7); and "parallel world stories," which "describe a number of alternate histories that exist simultaneously" (8).

4. I develop a reading of *The Difference Engine* further in "The Last Bomb." For a more extensive and deeply nuanced exploration of the representation of nineteenth century history in the novel, see Jay Clayton.

5. I discuss Fukuyama's essay, as well as number of responses to it, in "A Nightmare on the Brain of the Living: Messianic Historicity, Alienations, and *Independence Day*," in *Life Between Two Deaths*.

6. For a related vision of the radical potentialities of the alternate history, see Slavoj Žižek.

7. For another useful discussion of the conflict between the Nietzschean and Hegelian standpoints in contemporary critical theory, see Bruce Robbins.

8. See my "I'll Be Back: Repetitions and Revisions in the *Terminator* Films," in *Life Between Two Deaths*.

9. I discuss Gibson's response to this new reality in "Recognizing the Patterns."

10. Also see Raymond Williams' (whose concepts of emergent and residual are invoked in *Years* 640) classic essay on groups in history.

11. For another 1990s film that deploys a fantastic device akin to Robinson's to create an alternative historical phenomenology, see *Groundhog Day* (1993), a film I discuss in the Introduction to *Life Between Two Deaths*.

12. For further discussion of this turn, see my "Spatial Criticism."

Works Cited

Angenot, Marc. "The Absent Paradigm: An Introduction to the Semiotics of Science Fiction." *Science Fiction Studies* 6 (1979): 9–19.

Bisson, Terry. *Fire on the Mountain.* New York: Avon, 1988.
Bloch, Ernst. *The Principle of Hope.* Trans. Neville Plaice, Stephen Plaice and Paul Knight. Cambridge: The MIT Press, 1995.
Clayton, Jay. "Hacking the Nineteenth Century." *Victorian Afterlife: Postmodern Culture Rewrites the Nineteenth Century.* Eds. John Kucich and Dianne F. Sadoff. Minneapolis: University of Minnesota Press, 2000. 186–210.
Foucault, Michel. "Different Spaces." *Essential Works of Foucault, 1954–1984: Volume Two, Aesthetics, Methods, and Epistemology.* Ed. James D. Faubion. New York: The New Press, 1998. 175–185.
Gibson, William, and Bruce Sterling. *The Difference Engine.* New York: Bantam, 1991.
Hegel, Georg Wilhelm Friedrich. *Lectures on the Philosophy of World History. Introduction: Reason in History.* Trans. H. B. Nisbet. Cambridge: Cambridge University Press, 1975.
Hellekson, Karen. *The Alternate History: Refiguring Historical Time.* Kent, OH: The Kent State University Press, 2001.
Jameson, Fredric. *Archaeologies of the Future: The Desire Called Utopia and Other Science Fictions.* New York: Verso, 2005.
_____. *Brecht and Method.* New York: Verso, 1998.
_____. Foreword to *On Meaning: Selected Writings in Semiotic Theory* by Algirdas Julien Greimas. Minneapolis: University of Minnesota Press, 1987. vi–xxii.
_____. *Postmodernism, or, The Cultural Logic of Late Capitalism.* Durham: Duke University Press, 1990.
Löwy, Michael. *Fire Alarm: Reading Walter Benjamin's "On the Concept of History."* New York: Verso, 2005.
Lukács, Georg. *History and Class Consciousness: Studies in Marxist Dialectics.* Trans. Rodney Livingstone. Cambridge: The MIT Press, 1971.
Michaels, Walter Benn. "Plots Against America: Neo-Liberalism and Anti-Racism." *American Literary History* 18, no. 2 (2006): 288–302.
Robbins, Bruce. "Dive In!" *London Review of Books* 22, No. 21 (2 November 2000): 33–34.
Robinson, Kim Stanley. "The Lucky Strike." *The Best Alternate History Stories of the 20th Century.* Ed. Harry Turtledove. New York: Del Rey, 2001. 2–35.
_____. *A Sensitive Dependence on Initial Conditions* Eugene, OR: Pulphouse Publishing, 1991.
_____. *The Years of Rice and Salt.* New York: Bantam, 2002.
Rosenfeld, Gavriel D. *The World Hitler Never Made: Alternate History and the Memory of Nazism* (Cambridge: Cambridge University Press, 2005.
Rothberg, Michael. "Against Zero-Sum Logic: A Response to Walter Benn Michaels." *American Literary History* 18, no. 2 (2006): 303–311.
The Shawshank Redemption. Dir. Frank Darabont. Perf. Tim Robbins, Morgan Freeman, Bob Gunton, Clancy Brown, William Sadler, Gil Bellows, and James Whitmore. Columbia Pictures, 1994.
Suvin, Darko. *Metamorphoses of Science Fiction: On the Poetics and History of a Literary Genre.* New Haven: Yale University Press, 1979.
Turtledove, Harry, ed. *The Best Alternate History Stories of the 20th Century.* New York: Del Rey, 2001.
Watkins, Evan. *Throwaways: Work Culture and Consumer Education.* Stanford: Stanford University Press, 1993.
Wegner, Phillip E. "The Last Bomb: Historicizing History in Terry Bisson's *Fire on the Mountain* and Gibson and Sterling's *The Difference Engine.*" *The Comparatist* 23 (1999): 141–51.
_____. *Life Between Two Deaths: U.S. Culture, 1989–2001.* Durham: Duke University Press, 2009.
_____. "Recognizing the Patterns." *New Literary History* 38, no. 1 (2007): 183–200.
_____. "Spatial Criticism: Critical Geography, Space, Place, and Textuality." In *Introducing Criticism at the Twenty-First Century,* ed. Julian Wolfreys. Edinburgh: Edinburgh University Press, 2002. 179–201.
Williams, Raymond. "The Bloomsbury Fraction." *Problems in Materialism and Culture.* New York: Verso, 1980.
Žižek, Slavoj. "What if we don't act now?" *London Review of Books* 27, no. 16 (18 August 2005): 23.

Part II. Theory and Politics

7

The Density of Utopian Destiny in *Red Mars**

Carol Franko

> The contexts of dialogue ... extend into the deepest past and the most distant future.... Nothing is absolutely dead: every meaning will someday have its homecoming festival.
> — M. M. Bakhtin

Many things could prevent it; yet *Red Mars* and *Green Mars*, the first two novels of Kim Stanley Robinson's Mars trilogy,[1] suggest that it may be the destiny of human colonization and terraformation of Mars to develop into a utopian society that would resemble an argumentative and interdependent confederation of diverse communities. This utopia would entail a humanized Mars and a Mars-transformed humanity, flourishing through a dialogical general will and in a perpetually readjusting syncretism — syncretism being a term with a comparably vexed reputation as utopia.[2]

In the spirit of dialogism and syncretism, I want to preface speculations on how *Red Mars* (the first novel in the trilogy) narrates such a utopian destiny with a few quotations (taken from diverse sources) that put in play relevant themes: "Well, here we are" are the first words of the First Man on Mars — John Boone, originally from Minnesota and a main character in Red Mars to whose crucial speech acts I shall return; "If I could say we, ... I wouldn't be here" is a remark made by a Doris Lessing character to her psychiatrist (*The Golden Notebook* 235); "I speak and you hear me, therefore we are" is Francis Ponge rethinking Descartes (qtd. in Kristeva 45); it's also something that John Boone could have spoken to billions of viewers as he stepped onto Mars or that the psychiatrist of Doris Lessing's character could have replied cheerfully to her client; "The question 'who is talking' ... is also the question how many are talking" is Michael Holquist ("Introduction" xliv) on Mikhail Bakhtin's hybrid concept of dialogism, that literary-linguistic-anthropological concept that views subjectivity and semantics as emerging from the ongoing crisscrossing of meanings within and between persons and within and between words; "Speech affronts death" is a comment that Julia Kristeva makes on Socratic dialogue (52); and finally, "Geography is destiny" is reportedly Napoleon's explanation of his defeat in Russia; I found the phrase quoted in a book called *Women's Mysteries* (Downing 73).

These quotations raise issues crucial both to the story told in *Red Mars* and to utopian

---

*First published as "The Density of Utopian Destiny in Robinson's *Red Mars*." *Extrapolation* 38 (1997): 57–65. Copyright 1997 by The Kent State University Press. Reproduced with permission.

fiction in general — for example, the issue of "we" as endlessly problematic as well as both seemingly natural and surely necessary. Who are we, who speaks for our utopian hopes, and how is that done in a good way? And what is the geography of first-person plural — where and how is this "we-thing" going to happen? Utopian fiction typically aims to have a double effect on readers — getting us to see the constructed alienation and idiocy of much business-as-usual and then to affirm, perhaps even convert to, a better social arrangement that implicitly offers a ready-made sense of "we." As I consider how Robinson's novel is and does something related to but different from this simplified account of generic utopia, I will draw on several preoccupations of Bakhtin — beginning with his notion of dialogization, a term that refers to the way a discourse is revealed as participating in the contextual, constructed, intersubjective, and value-saturated nature of meaning.

In *Red Mars*, utopia keeps its function of "dialogizing" the common-sense wisdom of business-as-usual but is itself dialogized in several broad ways — first of all by those contingencies from which utopia is usually set apart: time and place. Thus in Red Mars utopia becomes an ongoing task within and in conflict with history, specifically twenty-first-century history, a task bound to and embodied in particular places and persons. This seemingly humbler utopia arguably reflects Robinson's ambitious view that utopia can become more tangible than a critical tool and an inspiring dream.[3] So he puts the struggle for utopia into a near-future story that could come true — a story informed by "hard" science in a way that has justly impressed readers and that renders in believable detail how humans soon might be settling on Mars. Further, he extrapolates how these possible scientific achievements complicate existing earthly political battles, social problems, and environmental issues. The result is that, as one reviewer of *Red Mars* exclaims, "Mr. Robinson makes the future seem not only plausible but already here,"[4] which doesn't mean that utopia is already here; yet *Red Mars* makes utopia an open contender for a human Martian destiny.

This assertion must be qualified and complicated. Beyond positing utopia as a possible struggle within history, Robinson further dialogizes it in two related ways — through his novel's dense and sometimes in-our-face intertextuality and through its plot that continually returns to a science-fictional Socratic dialogue.

Bud Foote aptly describes the self-conscious intertextuality of this novel: "Red Mars gives the reader an almost continual sense of itself as artifact, in its declaration that it is a story encompassing past stories which, in turn encompass still older stories" ("Notes" 65). Mars itself is the nexus of many of these embedded stories, from science fictions to fictional canals to ancient myths of Mars inspired by its redness and its erratic revolution around the sun. One of the vivid ways that Robinson alludes to past Mars stories is by repeating in different contexts the various names given to the red planet in many languages over the centuries. These litanies arguably become one of the ways that Mars itself becomes a speech actor, or at least an embodied and personified presence, in the novel's conversations.[5] Yet Robinson alludes to more than stories of Mars. So alongside references to science fiction authors like Ray Bradbury, Edgar Rice Burroughs, Philip Dick, and C. L. Moore[6] we find, for example, references to Tolkien's fantasy, a possible allusion to Virginia Woolf's first novel (in "The Voyage Out," title of second section, *Red Mars*), and quotations from the poetry of Jalaluddin Rumi, thirteenth-century Sufi writer and mystic whose quoted verse itself seems to rewrite the great chain of being from a perspective comparable to Darwinian evolution (see *Red Mars* 285–86). Another prominent source of the seemingly innumerable intertexts is Russian utopian fiction — including the famous *What Is to Be Done?*, written in prison in the 1860s by Nikolai Cherneshevsky and published serially through a mistake of the czar's censors.[7]

The thick allusiveness of Red Mars enacts Robinson's notion, expressed in a recent interview, that fiction is for him the crucial realm for the human activity of asserting and testing values. And that, in part, is what the intertextuality of *Red Mars* is doing — at the "meta" level, where the novel is a text relating itself to other texts and presenting all of these conversations to readers. That these intertextual conversations about values further dialogize the concept and hope of utopia is made vivid, for example, in the character of Nadia Chernyshevsky, whose last name as well as an acquired "title" allude not only to the Russian utopian novel *What Is to Be Done?* but also to the Mars novels of the American author Edgar Rice Burroughs. While the name Chernyshevsky clearly links Robinson's character to the Russian writer, she is also "nominally" associated with Burroughs. Her lover (Arkady Bogdanov, another allusively named character) impulsively dubs the unglamourous Nadia Princess of Mars, and the epithet sticks, suggesting an ambiguously ironic allusion to Burroughs's stories, which feature prominently a Princess of Mars.

One of the group of scientists called the First Hundred, whose scientific station is the first human settlement on Mars, Robinson's Nadia Chernyshevsky is an engineer who loves tools and troubleshooting and who builds and rebuilds many of the first dwellings and factories on Mars. Without losing her satisfaction in big projects, Nadia also comes to appreciate the wild beauty of pre-terraformed Mars. Two sections of *Red Mars* are told from Nadia's angle of vision: the Crucible, which details the first days of humans doing things on Mars, days that feature Nadia building the first dwellings and factories and acting as trouble-shooter for numerous other projects; and Senzeni Na, a later section, when things are going to hell politically and ecologically. Senzeni Na, also the name of a new mining town on Mars, is a Japanese phrase meaning "what have we done?" Indeed, as she finds herself involved in the politics of terraforming Mars and of a related revolution that she sympathizes with yet deplores, Robinson's Nadia Chernyshevsky is caught between the utopian question "what is to be done?" and the historical question "what have we done?" And her names are intertexts indicating that Robinson's novel is negotiating not only the same questions but also the ideological residue of earlier writings that have pondered what to do and what's been done.

On the one hand, Robinson's character represents progress in relation to her intertexts. Chernyshevsky's *What Is to Be Done?* features a likeable heroine who struggles against patriarchal marriage, works hard organizing sewing cooperatives and studying medicine, and is ultimately granted a vision of a utopian future that features equal rights, free love, and a technology, represented by the Crystal Palace, that is in harmony with both humans and nature. In Burroughs's novels, the Princess is often getting saved from worse-than-death and cannibalism by John Carter, the North American cowboy who becomes warlord and savior of Mars (Lawson 212–13). Robinson's "Princess" Nadia fulfills the wholesome, rationalistic feminism of *What Is to Be Done?* while leaving in the dust the more or less opposite approach to gender roles and sexuality inscribed in the Mars novels of Burroughs. Yet this doesn't mean that Robinson's novel escapes completely from the Burroughs world nor that his (post?)feminist character automatically brings along the rest of Chernyshevsky's utopian vision. On the contrary — Nadia is faced with the same issues as Burroughs's cowboy hero — control of the hostile Martian environment and of the social conflicts that apparently are "solved" in the Burroughs novels by continual warfare (Lawson 211). Furthermore, the desire for profit that inspired Burroughs to write lurid obsessive Mars stories (Lawson 208–09) is also fueling much of the colonization and terraforming efforts in Robinson's story — in fact the emerging bureaucratic center is a city named Burroughs. Instead of being a novelist as hopeful entrepreneur, the Burroughs on Red Mars consists of powerful and ruthless multinational corporations nominally controlled by a latter-day United Nations. Meanwhile, Nadia and others are confronted with revolution and with the need for a better way to build utopia; Chernyshevsky's novel is little help here, since the revolution that leads to its utopian dream is an understandably "self-censored" blank in his text (Suvin 248). Building a Crystal Palace on Mars is also a problem: Robinson's novel suggests that the planet first needs to be personified and consulted.

So by considering just one of Robinson's characters in relation to just a few of her intertexts, we fall into the ongoing dialogization of histories fictional and factual. "Falling into History" is the name of the longest section in *Red Mars*. It comes roughly halfway through the novel and is told from the perspective of John Boone, which brings us back to the first man on Mars (who also becomes one of the First Hundred colonists) and back to his first words: "Well, here we are."

I consider John Boone's life and death on Mars as that of a carnivalized Socratic hero seeking a syncretic solution and a viable sense of "we" for humans on Mars through the power of speech acts to produce "impact metamorphosis" (*Red Mars* 280)—a term from areology or Martian geology. The action plot of *Red Mars* is overlaid with ongoing, multifaceted debates in which John Boone and others practice a method of seeking knowledge that Bakhtin credits Socratic dialogue with inventing. In Socratic dialogue:

> The dialogic means of seeking truth is counterposed to official monologism, which pretends to possess a ready-made truth, and it is also counterposed to the naive self-confidence of those people who think that they know something, that is, who think that they possess certain truths. Truth is not born nor is it ... found inside the head of an individual person, [truth] is born between people collectively searching for [it], in the process of their dialogic interaction [110].

John Boone is not looking so much for truth as for a new and better social existence based in the physical realities of Mars and in what humans can do with those realities. He wants to help "create a scientific system designed for Mars, designed to their specifications, fair and just and rational and all those good things" (*Red Mars* 256). Geography is destiny, Boone might agree, although geography would become areology, because the "we" that he's seeking live on Ares, or Mars, not Earth. As he travels among the new settlements on Mars, Boone often thinks and speaks about the need for a plan[8]—certainly a desirable thing for a utopian social engineer—but what he excels at is not planning but dialogue, talking and listening to individuals and small groups, and then talking it out again in front of big groups. Thus his utopian goals are continually dialogized, and thus he is largely responsible for creating a crucial precedent—that the new human-Martian synthesis can be "born between people collectively searching for [it], in the process of their dialogic interaction." "That's how social life works," Boone explains to a friend (Hiroko Ai) who has chosen to pursue her plans for Mars in secret (338). With Boone the question who is talking is always the question how many are talking. Through his "active reception of the other's words" (as Bakhtin puts it), Boone makes speeches that are as much others' words as his own, so that these speeches are both the substance and the history of his interactions with several thousand people. For example, at a large gathering at the mountain Olympus Mons, Boone makes an impromptu speech (beginning, characteristically, "Look ... here we are on Mars" [341]) in which readers can find words and ideas (concerning, for example, a gift-based, ecological economics) of various settlers (Japanese, Sufis, Swiss, etc.) with whom Boone has had previous conversations. Moreover, in the same speech Boone continually uses metaphors from areology, thereby reminding his listeners of the specificity of place of their social experiment while also giving Mars a "voice" in the proceedings.

Boone makes his special contribution of beginning the forging of a human/Martian sense of "we" not only by talking and eliciting talk but also by often helping to make the whole process into a festival (like the episode at Olympus Mons) or carnival — this being the final Bakhtinian concept I'm going to use. Bakhtin argues that the cultural practices and attitudes that make up a carnival sense of the world are closely related to the Socratic seeking and testing of truths. To the Socratic method of informal and unfinalized discourse, carnival adds laughter, both smirking and joyous[9] (an emphasis on the corporeal, irreverent parodic rituals); and time — or, as Bakhtin puts this last component, the "core of the carnival sense of the world ... [is] the pathos of shifts and changes, of death and renewal" (124). In *Red Mars* the spirit of carnival embodies and historicizes the various episodes of the "world symposium" of John Boone and his many interlocutors (Bakhtin 293).

Even as this carnivalized "world symposium" dialogizes utopia — continually putting utopian goals into debate — it also fulfills the utopian function of unmasking and undermining the assumptions and rituals of business-as-usual. As Bakhtin remarks, Socratic speech "presumes a carnivalistic familiarization of relations among people who have entered the dialogue" (132), and these are not the kind of relations that the multinational corporations of *Red Mars* wish to foster. As the chief Martian talker, a Daniel Boone with a Frank Capra conscience, always ready to exploit his visibility as first man on Mars and no respecter of official authorities, John Boone becomes increasingly unpopular with various powers who do not view Mars as the birthplace of a new society but rather as a colossal mining venture and perhaps also as a place to send people from the overcrowded earth. Maybe Boone would have lived longer if he had taken the uncommunicative representatives of these powers more seriously. Instead, however, he "invests his entire self in discourse, and this discourse enters into the dialogic fabric of human life, into the world symposium" (Bakhtin 293).

"Speech affronts death" is Julia Kristeva's comment on Socratic dialogue, perhaps referring to how the philosopher kept talking until the poison took effect. And John Boone's speech acts arguably transcend the finiteness of his status as fictional character killed off in the first volume of a trilogy. *Red Mars* opens with one of the italicized passages that precede and sometimes intervene in each of its named sections. These italicized portions frame the chapters but also supplement them, interact with them, and sometimes "quote" them; and this opening section quotes one of John Boone's speeches (specifically, the last speech he makes on Mars) in which he speaks, as usual, in the human-Martian first-person plural. So with his words opening and framing Robinson's human-Martian epic, John Boone's speech arguably affronts death. Yet it is also true that death affronts and transforms the context of speech; John Boone's death renders the context of his speech overfull of destiny. That the special boon John brings to Mars is his gift for changing others and being changed by others through dialogue is not the first thing we learn about him. Before that, we know that he is killed one night after one of his speeches.

Orchestrated by one of Boone's oldest friends, and facilitated by the physical realities of life on red Mars, the murder occurs in the first titled section of the novel, called "Festival Night," which is a flash forward depicting events about twenty-five years after the First Hundred land on Mars. Everything that we later learn about John Boone's life in these twenty-some years is informed by the dramatic irony of our knowing the details of his mortality; this knowledge carnivalizes the hero, brings him down to earth (so to speak). Thus, for example, there is a poignant irony in that, during his ceaseless activity to speak/build utopia on Mars, we see Boone as the future victim of assassins hoping that Mars can escape the history of failed social experiments on Earth.

But the grim, historical "what have we done?" of Boone's death does not cancel out the "what is to be done?" of his and others' utopian hopes. Rather, Boone's death allows the central theme of utopian destiny to be named in such a way that it is both affirmed and "dialogized" or carnivalized. History is portrayed not only as ongoing murder but also as harboring the "active, accumulated memory" of a people (Bakhtin qtd in Schwab 117) — a memory that includes positive utopian impulses that imply the possibility of an alternative, better destiny. This theme is enacted in one of the carnivalesque episodes of *Red Mars*. During his travels around Mars, Boone comes across a community of Sufis who have made their home on an elevation formed by the "impact metamorphosis" (280) of a large meteor. As he debates, dances, eats and drinks with them, John and the Sufis are reciprocally inspired. John sees the Sufis as his Arab others/brothers and as a living embodiment of syncretic solutions — the latter not only because the Sufis have a syncretic religious tradition but also because they are scientists as well as mystics. The Sufis in turn see John as a fellow quester for more consciousness, embodying somehow both the quest and the successful realization of quest. In an episode that intensifies the dramatic irony but also enlarges the novel "beyond" it, an old Sufi woman foretells John's death, indicating that the death is not a failure but another stage of the quest (see 284–86 and 344–45). As if his encounter with the Sufis needed more significance, John has a thought about fiction. In his endless curiosity he tries to find out what the Sufis know of the different legends that are featuring Mars as BIG MAN and various other beings, but he realizes that they don't know. "He needed ... someone who could tell him how stories were born; but he had only these Sufis, grinning and weird, story creatures themselves. His fellow citizens in this new land" (285).

In this first volume of the Mars trilogy, John Boone is the character most concerned with developing a definition of "we" in relation to the "here" of Mars, and his death furthers this goal. Boone's death transforms the theme of utopian destiny in *Red Mars* — transforms utopian destiny in the sense of carnivalizing it — making it dense with time and change, death and renewal, and also dense with stories. Even as John thinks of how he needs someone "who could tell him how stories were born," he himself is a story being born — a story retold in various ways in *Red Mars* and *Green Mars*, the second volume. And of course he doesn't know this; he doesn't know that his speech will affront death in the sense that, by becoming a "story figure" himself in human-Martian history and folklore, he will continue to foster a human-Martian sense of "we" and will contribute to the creation of an "active accumulated memory" for humans on Mars, a memory to draw on for utopian hope and practice. Boone's character does not know this, and thus he has a comparably risky relation to a utopian destiny as "we" do, story creatures and fellow citizens, Robinson's readers.

Notes

1. The third novel, *Blue Mars* (1996) was published after the article was written.
2. William Reese defines syncretism thus: "From the Greek synkretizein ('to combine'). A term introduced by Plutarch to characterize the harmonizing efforts of the Neoplatonists. The term refers to the blending of philosophical doctrines from opposing schools, or religious doctrines from different faiths, in an effort to gain a unified point of view. In philosophy the term is usually pejorative, and the mixture of doctrines undistinguished, the common opinion being that superficiality is bound to result from syncretism" (564). In *Red Mars* Sax Russell, one of the First Hundred scientists keen on terraforming Mars and in conflict with "red" Mars advocates, introduces the term syncretism when he praises, with a little amusement, John Boone's speech at Olympus Mons (*Red Mars*, "Falling Into History"). In *Green Mars*, Sax himself is focused on as speech actor in process and as a syncretic thinker. Also in *Green Mars* we learn that Hiroko Ai is influenced in her utopian planning by accounts of a lost matriarchy of Crete — so possibly Hiroko puts the Crete in syn–Crete-ism.
3. See, for example, Bud Foote's "Conversation" with Robinson (60).

4. This review of *Red Mars* from the *Atlanta Journal and Constitution* is quoted inside the cover of *Green Mars*.
5. "The implications of [the] other as speaking subject need to be conceptualized as including more than humans, and as potentially being constituted by a speaker/author who is not the speaking subject but a renderer of the other as speaking subject" (Murphy "Prolegomenon" 45). Robinson arguably creates in *Red Mars* the synthesis of dialogism, feminism, and ecology that Murphy advocates. In Robinson's novel, Mars is rendered as a speaking subject in a number of ways: for example, through Hiroko and her group's areophany and through Ann Clayborne's defense of red Mars (over a terraformed Mars) and her experiences with the planet that press the limits of speech. The idea of carnival also applies: the carnivalized "grotesque body" of Mars is "a body in the act of becoming" (Bakhtin qtd in Holquist, *Dialogue* 89), a "body" that acts on and responds to the actions of humans.
6. Bud Foote points out that the opening of *Red Mars* is a deliberate rewrite of part of C. L. Moore's *Shambleau*, something that Foote confirmed in conversation with Robinson (see Foote, "Notes on" 65).
7. Also alluded to is the 1908 *Red Star*, the first Soviet utopian science fiction novel, written by Alexandre Bogdanov. In Bogdanov's novel the redness of the Red Star is ideological (as well as supposedly vegetable), since Mars is the setting of a communist utopia. Robinson's character Arkady Bogdanov is a shrewd, exuberant Marxist who lies to the screeners about his political commitments so that he can go to the red planet and who, for political reasons, is actually in favor of a "green," a terraformed, Mars — this being one example of the intertextuality of red and green in Robinson's novel.
8. The one hundred scientists who are the first Martian colonists don't bring a utopian blueprint with them on their spaceship; likewise, the novel does not give the impression that the author is only biding his time to eventually reveal the correct utopian solution. On the contrary, the self-conscious intertextuality gives the effect of a two-tiered conversation about utopia — between the characters and between the novel and its readers.
9. Frank Chalmers provides the smirking laughter of carnival, at least in "Festival Night," while Arkady Bogdanov (as well as Boone himself) provides much of the joyous carnival laughter in Red Mars.

Works Cited

Bakhtin, Mikhail. *Problems of Dostoevsky's Poetics*. Trans. Caryl Emerson. Minneapolis: University of Minnesota Press, 1984.
Bogdanov, Alexander. *Red Star: The First Bolshevik Utopia*. Ed. Loren R. Graham and Richard Stites. Trans. Charles Rougle. Bloomington: Indiana University Press, 1984.
Cherneshevsky, Nikolai. *What Is to Be Done?* Trans. Michael R. Katz. Ithaca: Cornell University Press, 1989.
Downing, Christine. *Women's Mysteries: Toward a Poetics of Gender*. New York: Crossroad, 1992.
Foote, Bud. "A Conversation with Kim Stanley Robinson." *Science-Fiction Studies* 21 (1994): 51–60.
_____. "Notes on *Red Mars*." *Science-Fiction Studies* 21 (1994): 61–66.
Holquist, Michael. *Dialogism: Bakhtin and His World*. London: Routledge, 1990.
_____. "Introduction." *Art and Answerability: Early Essays by M. M. Bakhtin*. Austin: University of Texas Press, 1990.
Kristeva, Julia. "Word, Dialogue and Novel." *The Kristeva Reader*. Ed. Toril Moi. New York: Columbia University Press, 1986.
Lawson, Benjamin S. "The Tune and Place of Edgar Rice Burroughs's Early Martian Trilogy." *Extrapolation* 27 (Fall 1986): 208–20.
Lessing, Doris. *The Golden Notebook*. New York: Bantam, 1962.
Murphy, Patrick D. "Prolegomenon for an Ecofeminist Dialogic." In *Feminism, Bakhtin, and the Dialogic*. Ed. Dale M. Bauer and Susan Jaret McKinstry. Albany: SUNY Press, 1991. 39–56.
Robinson, Kim Stanley. *Green Mars*. New York: Bantam Spectra, 1994.
_____. *Red Mars*. New York: Bantam Spectra, 1993.
Reese, William L. *Dictionary of Philosophy and Religion*. New Jersey: Humanities Press, 1980.
Schwab, Gabriele. *Subjects without Selves: Transitional Texts in Modern Fiction*. Cambridge, MA: Harvard University Press, 1994.
Suvin, Darko. *Metamorphoses of Science Fiction*. New Haven: Yale University Press, 1979.

8

Falling into Theory: Simulation, Terraformation, and Eco-Economics in the Mars Trilogy*
Robert Markley

> The world has become a giant science fiction novel which we're all coauthoring.
> — Kim Stanley Robinson, 1998

Utopia Revisited

In the Introduction to *Future Primitive: The New Ecotopias*, an anthology of "green" science fiction stories, Kim Stanley Robinson defines science fiction as "a collection of thought experiments that propose scenarios of the future.... They are historical simulations ... images, endlessly reiterated, [that] have come to form in our imagination a kind of consensus vision of the future" (Robinson, *Future* 3). In his own novels, as well as in this collection, Robinson presents alternatives to the genre's "consensus vision" of humankind "as the last organic units in [the] denatured, metallic, clean, and artificial world" of a cyber-engineered future. In place of this denatured vision, Robinson urges his readers to explore the utopian possibilities of "cobbl[ing] together aspects of the postmodern and the paleolithic" in a "future primitive" that might best be described as an ecocentric turn toward holism. This "future primitive," he implies, can serve as a powerful analytic to reveal — and indeed to gesture beyond — the forms of alienation that structure and are structured by the deep-seated antiecological values and assumptions characteristic of western thought (9–10). In this context, Robinson's Martian trilogy, *Red Mars* (1993), *Green Mars* (1994), and *Blue Mars* (1996), offers a sustained, theoretically sophisticated attempt to conjure into being a future that resists the romantic dystopianism of cyberpunk, the antitechnological bias of much "green" literature, and the blanket denunciations of capitalist technoscience that have become popular in some left-wing circles. Taken together, though, the three novels demonstrate just how complex a notion "utopia" can become. The "future primitive" that Robinson envisions both exploits and critiques what Don Ihde has called the "doubled desire" of technology. Historically, technology presents itself the essential means for humankind to adapt or to control nature and thereby improve

---

*First published as "Falling into Theory: Simulation, Terraformation, and Eco-Economics in Kim Stanley Robinson's Martian Trilogy." *Modern Fiction Studies* 43 (1997): 773–799. (c) Purdue Research Foundation. Reprinted with permission of the Johns Hopkins University Press.

the quality of life; however, the promises that technoscience makes — pleasure, plenty, and self-actualization — ironically seek to render it transparent. Massive investments of labor, capital, and resources, in other words, offer us enhanced versions of a "natural," pre-technological existence (Ihde, *Lifeworld* 75–6). In his Martian trilogy, the politics of this doubled desire lead Robinson to explore the consequences of people struggling "to yoke together impossible opposites" (Robinson, *Green* 229): mind and body, spirit and matter, nature and culture, and biosphere and technoscience. In the process, his novels call into question two of the constitutive fictions of modernity: the separation of nature from culture and the consequent privileging of contemporary technoculture at the expense of a devalued, technologically primitive past (Latour, *We Have Never* 99–100).

The Introduction to *Future Primitive* emphasizes that science fiction is a genre of ideas: Robinson argues that science fiction does not represent historical experience but generates simulations of what that experience may become. This distinction between representation and simulation is crucial to understanding his Martian trilogy as a theoretical intervention in late twentieth-century debates about ecology, economics, and technology, and it is worth noting the argument that Steve Shaviro makes. If representation, as Lacan suggests, is predicated on a fundamental lack, if it entails "the murder of the thing," simulation, he argues, "precedes its object: it doesn't imitate or stand in for a given thing, but provides a program for generating it" (Shaviro, *Doom* 17).[1] In Shaviro's sense, the "utopian" possibilities of science fiction occupy a register of simulation: they give imaginative form to the desire to think beyond the contradictions of historical existence, and, as the etymology of the word suggests, beyond our location in time, culture, and geography. Brought into the regime of representation, utopian schemes are always in the process, as Robinson suggests in a chapter title in *Red Mars*, of "falling into history," undone by the distance between the idealized operations of a frictionless system and the wear and tear of embodied, historical existence (Serres, *Parasite* 10–12). Utopias can best be understood, then, as expressions of their creators' (and their cultures') desires to imagine conditions which would allow humankind to transcend its *originary* alienation — an alienation, at once, ecological, political, and psychological that severs us from nature, from others, and from ourselves. Robinson's phrase "historical simulations" thus suggests his interest in reprogramming the mindset that divides nature from culture; rather than utopian longings, his trilogy offers a carefully nuanced thought experiment in the greening of science, economics, and politics.

As the titles *Red Mars*, *Green Mars*, and *Blue Mars* suggest, Robinson's future history focuses on the simulated science of terraformation — a science that exists only as a thought experiment, as the uncertain and arbitrary simulations designed to engineer a biosphere, sufficient at least for plant life, on Mars. Beginning with two short stories, "Exploring Fossil Canyon" (1982) and "Green Mars" (1985) and continuing after the trilogy in his collection of stories, sketches, and poems, *The Martians* (1999), Robinson uses the terraforming of Mars to rethink the complex relationships between planetary ecology, the interlocking systems that create and sustain the tenuous, seemingly miraculous conditions that allow life to flourish, and political economy, the distribution of scarce resources among competing populations and interests. At the conceptual center of this thought experiment lies what Robinson calls "eco-economics," his challenge to the default assumption that economics means the exploitation, degradation, and eventual exhaustion of natural resources — and the subsequent single-minded pursuit of more resources to exploit. On a world where the biosphere itself is being manufactured, notions of value make sense only to the extent that they erase distinctions between quantitative measures of labor and capital and qualitative contributions to social and ecological balance.

In this regard, Robinson radically revalues the science-fiction tradition of Burroughs, Brackett, and Bradbury; his literary and political touchstones becomes the utopian tradition represented by works such as Alexander Bogdanov's *Red Star* (1924) and Cyril Kornbluth's and Judith Merril's *Outpost Mars* (1953). Yet one of the strengths of the trilogy is its depiction of Mars as "a giant mountainous wilderness," in the experience of "red rock red dust the bare/ mineral of here and now" (Markley et al., *Red Planet* "interviews"; Robinson, *Martians* 385). In "Fossil Canyon," a tourist hiking through the canyon systems of the Valles Marineris, finds lava pellets that he initially mistakes for fossils. After the guide, Roger Clayborne (who reappears in two subsequent short stories), correctly identifies these "pseudofossils" as pellets from the eruption of Olympus Mons, Eileen Monday feels "a loss larger than she ever would have guessed. She wanted life out there as badly as ... the rest of them did" (Robinson, *Martians* 52). Roger and Eileen voice what become in the trilogy the "red" and "green" positions on colonizing Mars: the reds want to leave Mars in a nearly pristine — and lifeless — condition; the greens seek to terraform the planet to make it habitable by humans. The greens represent a spectrum of technological and political positions, articulating what are ultimately competing versions of planetary inhabitation: the utopias that hark back to the science-fiction paradises of the 1890s, a vast mining colony, a tourist haven, or even a new world that will supercede a worn-out Earth.

But in order to explore humanity's desires to conserve, exploit, and redefine the utopian possibilities for a spacefaring society, Robinson must distinguish his work scientifically, fictionally, and politically from the science-fiction traditions he has inherited. Whereas Larry Niven in *Rainbow Mars* (1999) populates the fourth planet with a century of imagined Martians, from H. G. Wells' octopoid cannibals to Edgar Rice Burroughs's giant green warriors, Robinson emphasizes a radical a break with such traditions. Standing on the surface of Mars, Eileen Monday recognizes that the experience of "red rock red dust" lies outside the literary and conceptual territory of twentieth-century planetology:

> All the so-called discoveries, all the Martians in her book — they were all part of a simple case of projection, nothing more. Humans wanted Martians, that was all there was to it. But there were not, and never had been, any canal builders; no lamppost creatures with heat-beam eyes, no brilliant lizards or grasshoppers, no manta ray intelligences, no angels and no devils; there were no four-armed races battling in blue jungles, no big-headed skinny thirsty folk, no sloe-eyed dusky beauties dying for Terran sperm, no wise little Bleekmen wandering stunned in the desert, no golden-eyed golden-skinned telepaths, no doppleganger race — not a funhouse mirror-image of any kind; there weren't any ruined adobe palaces, no dried oases castles, no mysterious cliff dwellings packed like a museum, no hologrammatic towers waiting to drive humans mad, no intricate canal systems with their locks all filled with sand, no, not a single canal; there were not even any mosses creeping down from the polar caps every summer, nor any rabbitlike animals living far underground; no plastic windmill-creatures, no lichen capable of casting dangerous electrical fields, no lichen of any kind; no algae in the hot springs, no microbes in the soil, no microbacteria in the regolith, no stromatolites, no nanobacteria in the deep bedrock ... no primeval soup [53].

The litany of science-fiction creatures and doppleganger races depopulates twenty-first century Mars, from Burroughs and Philip K. Dick down to the eco-niches that many scientists suspect may still harbor relics of the planet's Noachian past.[2] This depopulation is necessary to imagine how humankind might respond to an unmediated "nature," a pristine condition which would allow humanity to calculate — and take responsibility for — *all* the caloric, biogenetic, and chemical interventions in a dynamic environment. Eileen's Mars is a thought experiment, an experiment that never can be performed on Earth but that is a necessary starting point for considering the engineering and ethical implications of transplanting humans to a new world. In this respect, Mars becomes the site for a philosophical and political rethinking of the values and assumptions that underlie the discourses of ecology and, more generally, planetology.

In "Green Mars," Roger and Eileen meet two hundred years later (having benefited from the longevity treatments that play an important role in the trilogy) on a climbing expedition up the escarpment of Olympus Mons. Mars has been terraformed, and Roger treats the loss of the "red rock red dust" as "the visible sign of a history of exploitation," the reshaping of the planet to conform to human "history" rather than "topography" (192). In contrast, Eileen invokes Heidegger's "distinction between *earth* and *world*" in order to suggest that *all* experience is mediated: "'*Earth* is that blank materiality of nature that exists before us and more or less sets the parameters of what we can do.... *World* then is the human realm, the social and historical realm that gives earth its meaning'" (144). "Green Mars" fictionalizes the dynamic accommodation that must exist between these theoretical postulates. The ongoing deconstruction of this distinction between "earth" and "world" becomes, in effect, Robinson's contribution to a rethinking of the values and assumptions that define human representations of the natural environment. As he writes in the poem "Canyon Colour," "There, on a wet red beach —/ Green moss, green sedge. Green./ Not nature, not culture: just Mars" (364).

If "earth" is accessible only through the mediation of senses — not to mention the clothing, oxygen masks, ice boots, tents, and stoves that are necessary for mountaineering on any planet — this recognition does not mean a surrender to the imposition of human desires on a "blank" landscape, to the "projection" that Eileen had analyzed in "Fossil Canyon." At nineteen, on a Mars just beginning to be terraformed, Roger had experienced on "the great northern desert of Vastitas Borealis" an epiphanic moment in the wilderness:

> Light leaked over the horizon to the southeast and began to bring out the sand's dull ochre, flecked with dark red. When the sun cracked the horizon the light bounced off the short steep faces of the dunes and filled everything. He breathed the gold air, and something in him bloomed, he became a flower in a garden of rock, the sole consciousness of the desert, its focus, its soul. Nothing he had ever felt before came close to matching this exaltation, the awareness of brilliant light, of illimitable expanse, of the glossy, intense *presence* of material things [145].

As in the trilogy, such passages do not represent moments of psychological self-awareness but the collective experience of an environment that dissolves barriers between "self" and "nature." Yet as the hiss of the oxygen regulator reminds him, there is no idealized escape "back" to a garden, rock or otherwise, no choice to make that could sever earth from world. There is only an ethics of responsibility, of the values that the characters bring to the ascent of Olympus Mons. Roger's experience of "what it *feels* like to be in such wilderness" (206) is recaptured at the end of the climb when they reach the caldera of the tallest volcano in the solar system. It is this lived experience of finding oneself "'in the middle of such an heartless immensity'" that offers a means to think beyond the received opposition of humankind and nature. Robinson's invoking of Melville is suggestive: where Pip is driven mad by being left alone on the sea, Roger and Eileen represent the ongoing negotiation of "self" and "wilderness" as an opportunity to be explored rather than a battle to be fought or a horror to be avoided. Rather than the hostile Martian nature envisioned by Schuyler Miller in the 1930s and Ludek Pesek in the early 1970s, Robinson offers "the "most textured and varied evocations of a mapped Mars that literature has to offer" (Morton, *Mapping* 168–78).

Robinson's trilogy explores the possibilities of science fiction as a political thought experiment — notes towards a utopian future that have proved both a critical and popular success.[3]

Having established themselves on the fourth planet in *Red Mars*, the First One Hundred, the initial party of scientists sent to colonize the planet, fragment politically, socially, and geographically. After several years, a scientific team led by Vlad Taneev and Marina Tokareva develop a process to retard the onset of aging, then turn their attention to eco-economics as a means to integrate ecology and "its deformed offshoot economics" (297), to develop a system of value, in other words, that recognizes the feedback loops between the large-scale development of Martian resources and terraforming. In contrast to economics, "people arbitrarily ... assigning numerical values to non-numerical things," as Vlad puts it, eco-economics defines "efficiency [as] the calories you put out, divided by the calories you take in." An ethical imperative follows: "Everyone can increase their ecological efficiency by efforts to reduce how many kilocalories they use" (Robinson, *Green* 297, 298). Restricting consumption becomes a far more effective means to increase one's value to the system than accelerating production because production invariably strains scarce resources. Eco-economics, in this regard, calls into question the logic of capitalist production and, more generally, the ongoing exploitation of nature as the means to generate value. It acts as a historical simulation to suggest alternatives to the ever-increasing cycles of intensification and environmental degradation that Marvin Harris describes and that, as I have argued elsewhere, form the backdrop for the future histories written by Cyril Kornbluth, Judith Merril, Ray Bradbury, and others (Harris, *Cannibals* 5; Markley, *Dying*). As Robinson writes in a poem in *The Martians*, "in the/ Attempt to imagine Mars I came to see/ Earth more clearly than ever before" (382).

Robinson's fragile ecology-in-the-making on Mars thus serves as a fictional projection of late twentieth century eco-economic crises, a virtual space in which to imagine a society struggling through and toward "some kind of universal catastrophe rescue operation, or, in other words, the first phase of the postcapitalist era" (Robinson, *Blue* 63). His trilogy works on a variety of levels to imagine the conditions under which capitalism will evolve — haltingly, violently, uncertainly — toward an eco-economic future. What distinguishes these novels from other recent "thought experiments" about humanity's future on Mars is precisely his recognition that the unending profits envisioned by late (and future) capitalism require infinitely exploitable resources to escape the diminishing returns and declining living standards of intensification. As one of his characters, William Fort, the head of a metanational corporation that eventually metamorphoses into an umbrella of semi-autonomous collectives, declares, "Capital is a quantity of input, and efficiency is a ratio of output to input. No matter how efficient capital is, it can't make something out of nothing" (Robinson, *Green* 81). In this regard, the novels can be read as simulations that paradoxically remain open to stochastic self-organization, thought experiments that engage the contingencies on which most utopian aspirations founder: social unrest, economic competition, psychic crises, national rivalries, racial hatreds, official violence, greed, stupidity, and environmental degradation. As a richly imagined geophysical and political landscape, Robinson's Mars blurs distinctions between fictional and scientific simulations of terraforming, even as it allows readers to question the values on which current justifications for planetary engineering rest.

Scientific Speculation

Robinson's revaluation of the tradition of Martian science fiction is linked to his complex relationship to the scientific literature on terraforming that became an important subgenre of plans for the human exploration of Mars in the 1980s (Oberg, *New Earths*; Fogg,

Terraforming; McKay, Toon and Kasting, "Making," 489–95) He exploits the work of a number of scientists who have speculated about terraforming, but rejects the ideology of the frontier that Zubrin invokes (Zubrin, "Significance" 13–24; Zubrin *Case*). Terraforming, according to Martyn Fogg, one of its leading advocates, is the hypothetical "process of planetary engineering, specifically directed at enhancing the capacity of an extraterrestrial planetary environment to support life," and perhaps ultimately "to recreate an unconstrained planetary biosphere emulating all the functions of the biosphere of the Earth" (Fogg, *Terraforming*, 9).[4] In the case of Mars, the consensus candidate in the solar system for such planetary engineering, scientists have their work cut out for them. Mars' atmosphere is 95 percent carbon dioxide; its atmospheric pressure is about six millibars (little more than 1 percent of Earth's), its mean surface temperature is -56 degrees centigrade, it has no surface water, and because it has only trace amounts of oxygen, it has no ozone layer, so the surface is bathed in ultraviolet radiation (Fogg, *Terraforming* 202–03). Nonetheless, since the 1970s would-be planetary engineers have proposed a variety of strategies to create a biosphere on this forbidding terrain.

The minimalist approach, termed ecopoeisis by its proponents, stops short of full-scale terraformation; by augmenting the planet's greenhouse effect, some scientists believe that they can raise planetary temperatures, thicken and hydrate the atmosphere, and then seed the planet with genetically engineered anaerobic microorganisms to begin a long evolutionary process. But, as Fogg maintains, investing billions to provide a habitat for lichen makes little economic or scientific sense. Scenarios for no-holds-barred terraformation include creating a runaway greenhouse effect by introducing chloroflurocarbons into the atmosphere (the same pollutants that are compromising the ozone layer on Earth), thereby melting the polar ice and carbon dioxide caps, heating the planet, and outgassing carbon dioxide trapped in the regolith; "freeing" the water and ice that exist in subsurface deposits and in the polar caps by detonating thermonuclear explosions; placing giant mirrors in stationary orbits near Mars to increase insolation and warm the surface; and "harvesting" ice-rich asteroids from their orbits and propelling them onto collision courses with the planet, instantly thickening the atmosphere and providing water for plants to survive. "Oxygen availability does not limit our ability to terraform, Mars," Owen B. Toon, a leading expert on planetary atmospheres, argues, because it is "plentiful in the soils" (Toon, "Environments" 56). Citing "compelling evidence that Mars has a permafrost that is rich in water, Thomas Meyer and Chris McKay suggest that "it is possible to prepare breathable air, water, rocket propellant, fertilizer, and other useful compounds and feedstocks" from gases in Martian atmosphere (Meyer and McKay, "Using" 403, 399). Such *in situ* resource utilization (ISRU) would allow future colonists to relax "the need for tight closure, total recycling and complex toxicogenic filtering of the air supply ... , allowing the use of simpler semi-closed life support systems where losses could be continuously made up from freshly produced air supplies" (Meyer and McKay, "Using" 395). The overriding goal of these terraforming strategies is to create a biosphere by warming and hydrating the planet so that the same evolutionary processes that took place on precambrian Earth can occur — in exponentially accelerated fashion — on Mars.[5]

Significantly, one of the crucial texts on terraformation, cited almost reverently in the scientific literature, is a novel, *The Greening of Mars*, coauthored by two prominent scientists, James Lovelock, the originator of the Gaia Hypothesis, and Michael Allaby. Lovelock and Allaby turn twentieth-century swords (ICBMs) into plowshares (vehicles to carry chloroflurocarbons to Mars to augment the greenhouse effect), creating a carbon dioxide rich atmosphere that sustains wide varieties of plant life (Lovelock and Allaby, *Greening* 1984). In converting the nightmarish excesses and deadly byproducts of industrial civilization to benevolent uses, the novel provides the mythic origins for an imagined future, a parable of ecological restitution on a planetary scale: the authors' terraformed Mars exports the Gaia Hypothesis to the red planet, universalizing the balances and feedback loops of Earth's self-sustaining biosphere. As a thought experiment, the novel constitutes the ideational ground—the values, assumptions, and theories—upon which the emerging discipline of planetary engineering rests. In one respect, the simulated biosphere of Lovelock's and Allaby's twenty-third century Mars reinscribes, in scientific terms, late nineteenth-century views of the red planet as a bucolic paradise. More generally, the novel suggests the extent to which the science of terraformation relies on mythic archetypes of resurrection for its rationale.[6]

Even as such thought experiments—both literary and scientific—envision massive technological interventions to terraform Mars, their rhetoric invokes seemingly antithetical myths of humankind's relation to a terrestrial Nature: the idealized visions of restoration ecology and the endless generation of wealth through exploitation. Mediating this contradiction, I shall argue, is both the strategy and the rationale of Robinson's eco-economics. For its ecologically-minded proponents, terraformation is not the imposition of humankind's will on an alien environment but a heroic project to recreate conditions that existed three to four billion years ago when massive floods scoured the surface of a warmer and wetter Mars (Squyres and Kasting 1994, 744–49; Baker 2001, 228–36). As Chris McKay recently put it, "Mars lived fast, died young, and left a beautiful body—the Sylvia Plath approach to planetary science. We could play Ted and just ignore it, or we could do something better and bring it back to life" (Shirley 2004). This postmodernist vision of the Sleeping Beauty myth makes humankind's technological mastery of planetary engineering the equivalent of a magical kiss, and McKay advocates restoring Mars to a hypothesized indigenous biological, geochemical and hydrological cycles, with Martian microorganisms interacting with "restored" versions of its ancient atmospheric and surface environments (Shirley 2004). In Frederick Turner's 10,000 line epic poem *Genesis*, ecopoeisis on Mars is cast in an allusive language that blends epic conventions and Gaian ecology. Before terraformation, humankind encounters Mars in the twenty-first century as the abode of "a stunted and abortive chemistry,/ A backward travesty of life." Terraformed by dedicated science and mystical incantation, Mars becomes a self-sustaining biosphere, "an arch-oeconomy/ Dynamically balanced by the pull/ Of matched antagonists, controlled and led/ By a fine dance of feedbacks, asymptotic,/ Cyclical, damping, even catastrophic" (Turner, *Genesis* 7). As Fogg's enthusiastic praise of Turner's poem suggests, the mythos of biogenic resurrection plays a crucial role in constituting ecopoeisis as the fulfillment of our doubled desires for technology: planetary engineering creates a self-regulating biosphere in which humanity, and lower forms of life—"beetles and bacteria/ And molds and saprophytes," as Turner says—can start anew (Fogg 22–24). The myth of ecopoeisis as resurrection, though, might be called more accurately a form of ideological displacement: the terraformed Mars of the imagined future has not been restored to its pristine state but has become the vehicle to give scientific and poetic shape to fantasies of a prelapsarian terrestrial ecology.

If Mars terraformed becomes the scientific "confirmation" as well as the spiritual projection of Lovelock's Gaia Hypothesis, it is also the imaginary space of a new frontier, a technologized site for an updated manifest destiny. In promoting his Mars Direct scenario, Robert Zubrin forges explicit connections between the frontier thesis of Frederick Jackson Turner and the ideology of American-led terraformation (Zubrin, *Case* 295–306). "Without a frontier to grow in," Zubrin asserts, "not only American society, but the entire global civilization based upon Western enlightenment values of humanism, reason, science and progress will ultimately die" (303). Only Mars "has what it takes" to continue the march of progress toward a humanist salvation: "It's far enough away to free its colonists from intellectual, legal, or cultural domination by the old world, and rich enough in resources to give birth to the new" (298). Zubrin's libertarian rhetoric of self-actualization thus depends on the economics of resource appropriation, even as it evokes, as fellow enthusiast Turner puts it, "a project that will allow us to pursue beauty and truth on a grand scale" (Turner, "Life" 33–4). Terraformation is the signifier for the aesthetics as well as economics of plenitude.

Zubrin's romantic vision of the American frontier, however, is founded on dubious or simplified readings of American history that repress both the human and ecological consequences of conquest and colonization.[7] Liberty becomes a function of an idealized "New World" open to seemingly limitless exploitation of its resources. Projected into the future, this romanticized view of the frontier elevates the engineering strategies behind Mars Direct into a metaphysics of unlimited freedom founded on the exploitation of resources:

> If the idea is accepted that the world's resources are fixed, then each person is ultimately the enemy of every other person, and each race or nation is the enemy of every other race or nation. Only in a universe of unlimited resources can all men be brothers [304].

Zubrin's rhetorical movement from "the world's resources" to "a universe of unlimited resources" enacts the logic of a fantastic political economy in which terraformation — and the harvesting of resources from other worlds — becomes economically, socially, and politically essential to infinite growth and infinite freedom. For Zubrin, "Mars beckons" because capitalist and democratic values were "born in expansion, grew in expansion, and can only exist in a dynamic expansion." Whether one is a proponent of the Gaia Hypothesis or an investment banker, the effect of Zubrin's arguments is to reinforce the belief that humanity's only hope for the future is to repeat on Mars the cycles of spewing CFCs into the atmosphere, mining, harvesting crops and timber, and devastating wildlife that have compromised the earth's environment. The logic of terraformation, not surprisingly, thus requires new frontiers beyond the red planet. "The universe," Zubrin declares, "is vast. Its resources, if we can access them, are truly infinite" (304). Terraforming Mars becomes only the initial impetus to ratchet upwards the "two key technologies of power and propulsion" so that humankind can exploit the "infinite" resources of the outer solar system and beyond (Zubrin, *Entering* 127–222). Ironically, the logic of endless terraformation dictates that without the mind-boggling investments in technology to make accessible the "infinite" resources of new frontiers, humanity lapses into its default condition — the Hobbesian war of all against all. In Zubrin's mind, to terraform Mars — to render it both a biosphere and a commodity — is to reinvigorate ourselves psychically and to reverse the downward spiral of civilization.

The logic of the frontier that Zubrin sketches is founded on the anti-ecological assumption that "natural" resources are always and already marked as objects of exploitation and exchange. In this respect, he displaces onto Mars a vision of infinite resources that has led civilizations from one crisis of intensification to another until a dry, frigid, and almost oxygenless planet seems to many humanity's last best hope for survival. Not all commentators and scientists share Zubrin's enthusiasm for terraforming or his view of the American frontier. Jeremiah Creedon classifies the prospect of terraforming Mars as "grandiose" fantasy, like the Strategic Defense Initiative, that "belong[s] to a special kind of American virtual reality — a make-believe world full of things the public pays for but never sees." Terraforming, he adds, "falls short as science, [but] it does make great myth" (Creedon, "Mars" 36). Planetary engineering has critics in the scientific community, particularly when it is presented as a near-future project or a necessary consequence of colonization. The planetary astronomer David Grinspoon suggests that "terraforming will remain a purely intellectual exercise for the forseeable future," and therefore "anyone who suggests seriously that we embark on any of these [terraforming] schemes anytime soon should be institutionalized or forced to teach Freshman Astronomy at a large public university" (Grinspoon, *Venus* 337). More recently, he has conceded that as an intellectual and ethical exercise, "terraforming Mars is very good for us, and is maybe a first step towards attaining the kind of wisdom" that a century or so from now will be necessary to consider seriously planetary engineering (Shirley 2004). Projecting terraforming into the future makes it humanity's exit exam for graduating to the first phase of its new existence as a spacefaring civilization.

More like Grinspoon than Zubrin, Robinson does not define the "virtual reality" of terraformation in terms of new frontiers or a simplistic solutions to problems of overpopulation and environmental degradation on Earth. If Zubrin projects an idealized past into the future, Robinson calls into question the values and assumptions that have motivated previous colonialist enterprises. It is precisely this fantasy of the "mastery" of nature which eco-economics seeks to counter. At a crisis point in *Red Mars*, Frank Chalmers, the co-director of the mission to Mars and an inveterate politician, explains to the idealistic John Boone the logic of interplanetary colonization:

> "Why were we sent here in the first place, Frank?" "Because Russia and our United States of America were desperate, that's why. Decrepit, outmoded industrial dinosaurs, that's what we were, about to get eaten up by Japan and Europe and all the little tigers popping up in Asia. And we had all this space experience going to waste, and a couple of huge and unnecessary aerospace industries, and so we pooled them and came here on the chance that we'd find something worthwhile, and it paid off! ... And now even though we got a head start up here, there are a lot of new tigers down there who are better at things than we are, and they all want a piece of the action. There's a lot of countries down there with no room and no resources, ten billion people standing in their own shit" [352–53].

In Frank's mind, terraforming Mars is a fortuitous gamble, born of desperation, overpopulation, and the exhaustion of resources. His cynicism echoes throughout *Red Mars* as a counterpoint to both debates about the ethics of ecopoeisis and revolutionary struggles to determine who owns Mars and its resources. In one sense, the "utopian" project of Robinson's trilogy is to render such cynicism, as far as possible, a historical artifact, to replace the politics of desperation with a simulated future in which hard-won forms of cooperation, synthesis, and the dialogic unity of eco-economics wins out over a coercive political economy based on the control of scarce resources. In another sense, Mars, as it undergoes its sea-change from red, to green, to blue, offers its citizens (and the novels' readers) a means to rethink the individualistic and opportunistic values of the frontier.

The Martian Landscape

But it's a rough road to utopia. Robinson's trilogy is structured ideationally as a series of conflicts between competing visions of terraforming Mars and, therefore, opposing views of politics, economics, and social organization. During the course of two centuries (the longevity treatment developed by Vlad and his cohorts allows some characters, middle-aged in 2027 when *Red Mars* begins, to survive into the twenty-third century), the conflicts over terraformation mutate, grow sclerotic, and explode in revolutionary upheaval, anarchy, civil war, and repression. In one respect, his meticulous attention to political detail, to investigating the psychological changes that come over characters during decades of infighting, argument, and frustration, make Robinson seem more akin to Anthony Trollope than to, say, Ben Bova. The hero of his novels, nonetheless, remains Mars itself, particularly if one remains alert to the myriad ways in which humans—immigrants and then the native born—shape and are shaped by its outgassing regolith, thickening atmosphere, proliferating plant and animal life, and expanding oceans. In this respect, the evolving biosphere is not a backdrop for a tale of social evolution but an integral part of the complex workings of eco-economics.

The political, ecological, and philosophical conflicts in all three novels pit the opponents of terraformation, the Reds, against the champions of ecopoeisis, the Greens. In one sense, these struggles project into the future a debate already taking shape: the philosophical implications voiced by Chris McKay in advocating a minimalist ecopoeisis versus the enthusiasm some proponents exhibit for an all-out assault on lifelessness. "On earth," McKay notes, "the notion of life and the notion of nature are inseparable. But on Mars and in the rest of the solar system, life and nature are two different things. Mars appears to be a dead planet, yet it is undeniably a beautiful, valuable planet" (quoted in Kluger, "Mars" 74–75). In another, they reverse the valence of contemporary ecological discourse by making the most ardent proponents of planetary engineering the avatars of the mystical energy—"viriditas"—of life itself. In *Red Mars*, the key advocates of Red and Green philosophies, the geologist, Ann Clayborne, and the polymorphous scientific genius, Sax Russell, articulate their positions while the course of terraformation remains uncertain, "too big," as Sax says, with "too many factors, many of them unknown" to "model adequately" (171). In an effort to halt the terraformation of Mars, Ann sends private messages back to Earth, then must face her co-colonists, most of them terraforming enthusiasts. Her "tirade" consistently casts her opponents as careless children:

> "Here you sit in your little holes running your little experiments, making things like kids with a chemistry set in the basement, while the whole time an entire world sits outside your door. A world where the landforms are a hundred times larger than their counterparts on Earth, and a thousand times older, with evidence concerning the beginning of the solar system scattered all over, as well as the whole history of a planet, scarcely changed in the last billion years. And you're going to wreck it all.... You want to do that [the "mass alteration of the environment"] because you think you can. You want to try it out and see—as if this were some big playground sandbox for you to build castles in. A big Mars jar! You find your justifications where you can, but it's bad faith, and it's not science" [176–77].

At stake in Ann's comments is the moral relationship of humankind to the land. For her, the Martian landscape itself challenges anthropocentric and biogenic justifications for terraforming the planet; creating the conditions for life is purposeless because the geology of the planet is inherently valuable as a "historical record" of planetary and solar system history that dwarfs human technologies, intentions, and desires. If Red Mars is "a beautiful pure landscape," however, its purity can be appreciated only through human perceptions and values, through an aesthetic appreciation of its beauty and an intellectual, and even spiritual, recognition of the knowledge it offers.

In response to Ann, Sax emphasizes our inability to imagine beauty, or knowledge, or usefulness without giving in to a mystical anthropocentrism. His scientific defense of rapid terraformation heroicizes the irrevocable imposition by humans of a metaphysics of order on physical reality: "The beauty of Mars exists in the human mind," [Sax] said in that dry factual tone, and everyone stared at him amazed. "Without the human presence it is just a collection of atoms, no different than any other random speck of matter in the universe. It's we who understand it, and we who give it meaning" (177).

Sax's pronouncements suggest something of the attraction and limitations of his traditional scientific outlook, a worldview which evolves throughout *Green Mars* and *Blue Mars*. If Ann's defense of a "pure" Mars provokes a questioning of biocentrism, Sax identifies knowledge rather than the exploitation of resources as the ultimate rationale for terraformation. In this regard, his response to Ann becomes a kind of philosophical one-ups-manship; it is precisely human intervention which produces the "meaning" that structures even her celebration of an aesthetics and science of "pure" observation, an ideal of non-intervention. Yet Sax's insistence on the anthropocentric nature of meaning in the universe ironically reveals the accuracy of Ann's criticism: the basis of terraformation, of Baconian science itself, is an adolescent faith in human significance, a will-to-play (and play God) with the universe. For Sax, at least in *Red Mars*, science may be unpredictable and modeling techniques limited, but the mind remains capable of constructing knowledge by the inductive method, of developing experimental programs and then using the results to generate rather than simply recognize meaning in the cosmos.

These Red and Green philosophical positions — reiterated, modified, and contested during the course of the planet's transformation — mutate in response to the historical experiences of terraformation. The conceptual, political, and spiritual development of the trilogy, in this regard, may be described as the movement of Reds and Greens toward reconciliation; antagonists throughout the three novels, Ann and Sax become romantically linked at the end of *Blue Mars*, a measure of the operations of viriditas on both. The alchemical sublimate for the emergence of a blue Mars on which humans can walk, glide, and sail is the philosophy of Hiroko Ai, "the Japanese prodigy of biosphere design" (Robinson, *Red* 32), who articulates and embodies the holistic imperatives of a twenty-first century eco-theology. As the First Hundred branch out from their scientific station at Underhill and other settlers arrive from Earth, Hiroko and her followers leave for the southern hemisphere to further the ecopoeisis of Mars and to begin a communal existence which resists and transcends the antiecological, hierarchical efforts of transnational corporations to treat the planet as a vast mining camp. The isolation of this "Lost Colony" allows its members to survive the civil war of 2061, when corporate forces brutally quash attempts to establish an independent Mars, killing thousands, including many of the First Hundred.

Green Mars, which spans the decades after the war, might be seen as Hiroko's book because it is the moral force of her lived-philosophy of viriditas which brings together the scattered groups of the underground in a loose confederation and which eventually provides the rationale and moral authority for Martian independence. In the process, the nature of politics itself is transformed. At the beginning of this novel, Hiroko and her followers, including a generation of genetically engineered "ectogenes," have created a small utopia, Zygote, in an ice-dome under the south pole. As the spiritual leader of this society, she gives voice to a philosophy that seeks to unify microcosm and macrocosm and prepares members of the underground for their eventual re-emergence as a political as well as moral force:

> Look at the pattern this seashell makes. The dappled whorl, curving inward to infinity. That's the shape of the universe itself. There's a constant pressure, pushing toward pattern. A tendency in matter to evolve into ever more complex forms. It's a kind of pattern gravity, a holy greening power we call viriditas, and it is the driving force in the cosmos. Life, you see.... And because we are alive, the universe must be said to be alive. We are its consciousness as well as our own. We rise out of the cosmos and we see its mesh of patterns, and it strikes us as beautiful. And that

feeling is the most important thing in all the universe — its culmination, like the color of the flower at first bloom on a wet morning. It's a holy feeling, and our task in this world is to do everything we can to foster it [19].

Hiroko's celebration of viriditas inscribes the abstract principles of a scientific will-to-meaning (the Artificial Intelligence punned on in her name: Ai) on sensory experience. The greening power she invokes gestures toward a union of spirit and matter, a synthesis of organic complexity and the spiritual growth that attends the processes of technologically, genetically fostering ecopoeisis as the "supreme act of love" (19). As life forms spread across Mars, this moral and aesthetic imperative to create beauty becomes a sociopolitical complement to the attempts of the underground to move stochastically, intermittently toward a rough-hewn, evolving eco-economics. Viriditas, then, is not a simulation or thought experiment imposed on Mars but the embodied experience of participating in the evolution of green life on a red planet.

Throughout the trilogy, there are anticipations of the eventual reconciliation of Red and Green, of the alien landscape and the unforeseeable consequences of terraformation. Such anticipations, though, are scripted upon bodies and organisms, inscribed genetically, rather than articulated as abstract programs. This is the process of "areoformation," "an endeavor driven at a level below intention." Conscious political intentions and philosophical positions are acted upon and sublimated by the land itself, fostering complex processes of ideational as well as genetic evolution. The opening of *Green Mars* reads: "The point is not to make another Earth.... The point is to make something new and strange, something Martian.... All the genetic templates for [the] new biota are Terran; the minds designing them are Terran; but the terrain is Martian. And terrain is a powerful genetic engineer, determining what flourishes and what doesn't, pushing along progressive differentiation, and thus the evolution of new species" (13). In Robinson's descriptions of the landscape, Mars is sensed and felt as well as seen. The terrain acts upon its humans visitors, beginning a process of conceptual change before the effects of significant terraformation — heat, construction, and engineered life forms — take hold.

On an early expedition to the north pole led by Ann, Nadia, a Russian engineer, experiences the alien beauty of Mars; Robinson's description extends the strategies of aesthetic and psychological inquiry that had characterized Roger's epiphany in "Fossil Canyon":

> The sun touched the horizon, and the dune crests faded to shadow. The little button sun sank under the black line to the west. Now the sky was a maroon dome, the high clouds the pink of moss campion. Stars were popping out everywhere, and the maroon sky shifted to a vivid dark violet, an electric color that was picked up by the dune crests, so that it seemed crescents of liquid twilight lay across the black plain. Suddenly Nadia felt a breeze swirl through her nervous system, running up her spine and out into her skin; her cheeks tingled, and she could feel her spinal cord thrum. Beauty could make you shiver! It was a shock to feel such a physical response to beauty, a thrill like some kind of sex. And this beauty was so strange, so alien.... [S]he had been enjoying her life as it were a Siberia made right, so that really she had been living in a huge analogy, understanding everything in terms of her past. But now she stood under a tall violet sky on the surface of a petrified black ocean, all new, all strange; it was absolutely impossible to compare it to anything she had seen before ... [Robinson, *Red* 141–42].

For Robinson, who has digested seemingly all of the information available from the Viking missions, and then imagined the sensory overload of experiencing the planet's unearthly colors, massive dimensions, and weak gravity, beauty is both physical and geophysical, the product of the sublime engagement of human physiology and Martian landforms. Nadia's response to the alien beauty of violet skies and frozen silicate oceans is emblematic of the changes that Mars works on its colonists. The terrain itself suggests the inadequacy of frontier metaphors and economic rationalizations to describe areoformation, the changes wrought by the planet on humans as well by humans on the planet. Descriptions such as this one thus have a maieutic function: the impossibility of fitting Mars into paradigms imported from Earth forces characters to move beyond false historical analogies and, consequently, to take moral responsibility for the complex changes — socioeconomic as well as biospheric — initiated by terraformation. This responsibility is what ultimately distinguishes viriditas from corporatist models of terraformation as business investment and the passive worship of a romanticized Nature. Areoformation, another name for this responsibility, resists the acts of simplification and demonization that construct Mars — or the Earth — as a storehouse of materials and energies waiting to be extracted, priced, and marketed. In this light, the ebb and flow between Red and Green areophanies reveals the paradox that there is value in both the pristine terrain of Mars and in life spreading across and irrevocably altering the planet's surface and atmosphere. If viriditas in the abstract tends toward a kind of ecofeminist mysticism, it is constrained as practice by the geology itself, by what Sax refers to repeatedly as the "thisness" of specific forms of biospheric alchemy, of life evolving on and transforming the planet.

Rethinking History, Rethinking Economics

Terraformation provokes numerous reflections in the three novels on what settling Mars means in historical terms. These reflections extend the ethical and political dilemmas that Robinson explores in his earlier fiction, notably the short stories "The Lucky Strike" (1984), "A Sensitive Dependence on Initial Conditions" (1991), and the novel *Icehenge* (1984). To some extent, *Icehenge* anticipates both the political questions and literary strategies of the Mars trilogy; it marks as well Robinson's initial fascination with the fourth planet as a means to think through humanity's possible futures. *Icehenge* offers three linked narratives that deal with the consequences of a democratic uprising on twenty-third century Mars: it begins with the story of Emma Weil, a systems ecogeneticist, who returns to devastated colonies on Mars in 2248 rather than join the remnants of the defeated rebels on a desperate venture to become the first humans to venture beyond the solar system; the second narrative follows Hjalmar Nederland, an archaeologist, who in 2547 sets out to prove that the Martian rebellion was more than the anarchic rioting claimed by the colonial authorities; and the third section is narrated by Nederland's great grandson, Edmond Doya, who devotes his life to proving that Icehenge, a Stonehenge-like megalith found on Pluto, was *not* erected by the rebels on their way out of the solar system. Thematically, *Icehenge* examines the problems of memory, history, and autobiography in an age when people routinely live to be five hundred years old. Their attempts to authenticate Weil's journal — the only first-hand evidence that a social-democratic rebellion did occur — lead Nederland and later Doya to fantasize about meeting Emma, who becomes an imaginative projection of an ultimate truth or knowledge. The gap between such an idealized knowledge and the methodological problems of historical inquiry — shaped by the limitations of memory and the experience of trauma — fictionalizes the alienation of intellectual labor in the late twentieth-century. As a child, Nederland had survived the destruction of a rebellious Martian city: his path to self-realization lies in validating the ethical and political values of the rebellion. In contrast, Doya is a rootless and marginalized part-time academic, who seeks to debunk the very politics of memory that motivate his great grandfather.

In this context, *Icehenge* is a monument to competing reconstructions of the failed rebellion and, by implication, of the historical traumas of the twentieth century. On one level, the novel intimates that Icehenge was built by Emma (who apparently has reinvented herself and used her expertise to become a reclusive and mysterious billionaire) to commemorate the rebels and the democratic-socialist values that their quixotic voyage symbolizes. But this "revelation" is advanced at the end of the novel as only one of many reconstructions of the past. While Nederland believes that "history is made, because facts are not things" (88), his trust in the self-sufficiency of "things," of archaeological artifacts, is challenged by the controversies that swirl around Icehenge. In part, Nederland's dream is to recover an authentic history by excavating "one of the lost Martian cities" that he links to "all those cities that had been razed and abandoned by conquerors, Troy, Carthage, Palmyra, Tenochtitlan, [now] all resurrected by scientists and their work" (71). But this project of recovery gains a political authenticity only if this otherwise forgotten genocide can serve as a call to political action in the present. His interpretation of Icehenge as a testament to the legacy that "once all the Martians revolted together, and broke spontaneously toward utopia" anchors his belief that such a revolution could occur again (138). "To love the past," he contends, "is to become fully human" (165), but his great-grandson ends the novel by quoting a sensationalist author who claims that Icehenge was built by aliens: "In the beginning was the dream, and the work of disenchantment never ends" (262). The danger is that by adding the destroyed New Houston to such a list of lost cities, the significance of its destruction becomes a target for "the work of disenchantment," and a cynical and ultimately neoconservative resolution to the uncertainties of history.

To give into "disenchantment," however, is to risk precisely the senses — both political and ecological — of connectedness that animate the utopian rebels in *Icehenge* and, in *Green Mars*, Hiroko's settlement under the south polar icecap. In the earlier novel, politics and ecology are linked by the crew's efforts to create a closed, regenerative ecosystem onboard the jerryrigged starship. "We worked," writes Emma, "for hours and hours, mutating and testing bacteria, juggling the physiochemical processes, trying to make a tail-in-mouth snake that would roll across the galaxy" (41). The biochemical difficulty of creating such a closed system is a metaphor for the fate of the rebels on their voyage toward utopia, destruction, or a continuing historical struggle. In the middle section of *Icehenge* and more extensively in the trilogy, political conflict is implicated irrevocably in the terraformation of Mars. As Robinson has indicated, the fictional process of terraformation is not a blueprint for the future but a way to think about the interanimating logics of economics, ecology, and political power as they currently exist on Earth (Markley et al., *Red* "interviews," 2, 4, 5).

In *Red Mars*, *Green Mars*, and *Blue Mars*, various characters search fruitlessly for past analogues to explain present circumstances, and history itself comes to obsess many of them as they search for definitions, patterns, and meaning in human experience. On the initial voyage to Mars, John Boone and Phyllis Boyle, a true believer, debate the theological implications of history; later in *Red Mars*, while seeking a consensus on what form a new Martian society might take, John defines history as "what happened when you weren't looking — an unknowable infinity of events ... a nightmare, a compendium of examples to be avoided" (283–84). Decades later, Sax searches for a "science of history" to explain to himself the illogic of social stratification but must relinquish his inquiries, concluding that history is "nonrepeatable and contingent" (Robinson, *Green* 205–06). In the 2170s, Charlotte Dorsa Brevia, a product of an autonomous matriarchal commune, publishes a "metahistory," a "kind of master narrative," to explain the emergence of a "democratic Martian society" from the wreckage of the "dominance hierarchies" characteristic of both feudalism and capitalism (Robinson, *Blue* 393, 392). Her analysis of history tracks "a fundamental shift in systems" from the feudal-capitalist coercion of labor and monopolizing of profits to a "cooperative democratic economy" in which "everyone saw the stakes were high; everyone felt responsible for their collective fate; and everyone benefited from the frenetic burst of coordinated construction that was going on everywhere in the solar system" (Robinson, *Green* 393). Although Robinson's description of a democratic economy (like Zubrin's arguments for funding Mars Direct) requires access to additional resources and expansion throughout the solar system, he critiques theocentric and naively empiricist accounts of history for ignoring or marginalizing the complex effects of human needs, desires, and conflicts — and the spiraling cycles of intensification and the painful adjustments they dictate. Abstract systems and disembodied beliefs, in other words, represent an anthropocentric, masculinist belief in the superiority of ideas to the lived experience of history; such models invite disillusionment when they lead inevitably to violence, stagnation, and environmental degradation, leaving "ten billion people standing in their own shit."

Robinson's future history in the trilogy begins with an act of near-biblical betrayal: Frank Chalmers suborns the murder of his erstwhile friend and romantic rival, John Boone, by misrepresenting John's desire for a democratic Mars as a threat to the social and theological practices of a radical Arab faction. John, the first man to land on Mars, is an idealist, and his efforts to forge "a scientific system [of social organization] designed for Mars, designed to [the settlers'] specifications, fair and just and rational and all those good things" make him the ethical touchstone for the as yet unfocussed attempts in *Red Mars* to "point the way to a new Mars" (283). Frank's motives for the murder remain, to some extent, unclear even to him. Frank fears being cut out of the negotiations with Earth to revise the Treaty that governs interplanetary relations; he finds John's plans for Mars unrealistic, insufficiently attuned to "the ethnic hatreds, the religious manias" (16) that characterize an expanding, multi-ethnic Martian society; and he is jealous of John's continuing relationship with his former lover, Maya Toitovna, the leader of the Russian contingent of the First Hundred. Frank does not want authoritarian power but the authority to negotiate for Mars in its unending squabbles with Earth. His resort to murder — "Diplomacy by other means" (17) — testifies to the ethical confusion inherent in a politics that simply imposes Terran values and assumptions on Mars. Frank becomes a crisis manager without a vision, "empty, and cold in the chest" (400), bickering with Maya and constantly placating contending factions on Earth and Mars, trying to unify Mars by self-defeating strategies of playing one group off against another. He dies without having confessed to John's murder, but engaged in one of his few uncalculated, unselfish acts — saving Maya, Ann, Sax, and other refugees from the violence of 2061 during the massive floods triggered by the revolutionaries' sabotage of subsurface aquifers. Frank's death, then, coincides with the catastrophic reconfiguring of the landscape, the floods that alter "every single feature of the primal Mars," signaling irrevocably that "Red Mars was gone" (550). As he is swept away by the flood, the conventional notions that Martian politics can be micromanaged by Terran *realpolitik* — expediency, arm-twisting, and violence — are swept away as well.

The survivors of 2061 who continue the struggle toward eco-economics fall, then, not only into history but into theory, that is, into meta-explanations of the ongoing processes of areoformation. In *Green Mars*, Sax emerges as the hero of this quest to understand the complex transformations occurring on Mars. Part Four of the novel, by far the longest, is entitled "The Scientist as Hero," and tracks Sax's progress from the anthropocentric views of terraformation he voiced in *Red Mars* to his efforts to further the greening of the planet and its inhabitants. During the course of *Green Mars*, Sax is given a new face and new identity so that he can work above ground as a plant geneticist; is seduced by Phyllis, who represents the unholy alliance of Christian apologetics and capitalist ruthlessness; is unmasked by her; tortured and mind-probed to reveal what he knows about the underground; rescued by Maya and others; and then forced to struggle during a long rehabilitation to overcome the effects of a torture-induced stroke and relearn the intricacies of putting thoughts into words. Sax's efforts to regain his speech metaphorically underscore his emergence as a symbol and practitioner of a science committed to the ethical imperatives of viriditas and eco-economics. During his rehabilitation, Sax goes through extensive conversations with Michel Duval, the psychologist sent with the First One Hundred, who had saved himself from despair by joining Hiroko's group. For Michel, the scientist's job is

> to explore everything. No matter the difficulties! To stay open, to accept ambiguity. To attempt to fuse with the object of knowledge. To admit that there are values shot through the whole enterprise. To love it. To work toward discovering the values by which we should live. To work to enact those values in the world. To explore—and more than that—to create! [Robinson, *Green* 373].

Sax's response, "I'll have to think about that," testifies to his persistent professional dispassion even as he puts many of Michel's injunctions into practice. In the second half of *Green Mars* and in *Blue Mars*, Sax becomes a key figure in the development of a democratic Martian society, whether destroying Deimos so that it cannot be used as a base to attack the rebels during the second revolution against metanational authority, seeking to reconcile Ann and other Reds to the effects of terraformation, or developing an antidote for the memory losses that increasingly plague the aged survivors of two centuries of Martian history. Science, for Sax, loses none of its commitment to exploring the cosmos but, transformed and embodied, redefines the relationship between objective values and ethical commitment. Science creates rather than simply describes.

This reimagining of science necessarily informs and is informed by a rethinking of both conventional and revolutionary politics.[8] Even as it intervenes to ensure that the "whole enterprise" of settling Mars is "shot through" with egalitarian values, science provides a partial model for recasting politics so that decisions about immigration from Earth, resource management, and governance reflect its commitments to the "truths" of eco-economics. Few novels devote as much painstaking attention as *Green Mars* and *Blue Mars* to the complications and frustrations of political debate and compromise. In the former, the underground gathers at Dorsa Brevia to hash out a statement of principles that becomes the basis for Martian independence; in the latter, Reds, Greens, anarchistic collectives, and a range of ethnic and religious communities struggle to write a constitution that encodes the fundamental assumptions and values of eco-economics.[9] These political meetings are foreshadowed, in some respects, by the scientific conference on the progress of terraformation that Sax attends, in his new identity as Stephen Lindholm, in *Green Mars*. Initially eager to catch up on developments that have occurred during his years in the underground, Sax becomes increasingly dismayed by the politicization of science as different speakers plug the latest schemes of the corporations who fund their research: a "degraded dark zone invade[s] the heretofore neutral terrain of [the] conference" (199). This blasted ideal of disinterested scientific knowledge, though, re-emerges as the animating force behind the efforts of Maya, Nadia, Sax, and others to broker a ecologically sensitive politics for Blue Mars.

What finally succeeds at the constitutional conference is the process of compromise itself, a kind of utopia by committee. The realities of governing by eco-economic principles is fraught with conflict, but a free Mars evolves to meet crisis after crisis in the years following independence. Such agreements, though, are unthinkable without the terraformation of Mars: in 2061 the revolution fails because the rebels, in their domed structures, are easy prey to devastating attacks from space. At the end of *Green Mars*, when Reds mine the dikes that hold back one of Mars' new oceans, and, in the confusion of a transnational counterattack, detonate the explosives and send a flood racing toward the rebel stronghold of Burroughs, the entire population dons masks to filter the carbon dioxide remaining in the atmosphere and walks in the cold but thickened and oxygen-rich atmosphere seventy kilometers to safety. In the course of the three novels, the idealists, dreamers, and politicians are killed off: John, Frank, Arkady Bogdanov (Nadia's anarchist lover), and Phyllis. Hiroko disappears in a metanational attack at the end of *Green Mars*. The scientists — Vlad, Sax, and Nadia, who becomes the reluctant first president of Mars — and the nomads, notably the stowaway, Coyote, who survives for two centuries as trickster, jack-of-all-trades, roving ambassador to underground settlements, revolutionary, and party-goer — press on.

The ideal which survives revolutions, floods, conflicts, and conferences is eco-economics, the effort to find a means to live in concert with the realities of areoformation. At the constitutional convention in *Blue Mars*, Vlad defends eco-economics as "more democratic, more just" (119) than efforts by some of the younger generation to institute on Mars the verities of capitalist acquisition and ownership:

> If democracy and self-rule are fundamentals, then why should people give up these rights when they enter the workplace? In politics we fight like tigers for freedom, for the right to elect our leaders, for freedom of movement, choice of residence, choice of what work to pursue — control of our lives, in short. And then we wake up in the morning and go to work, and all those rights disappear. We no longer insist on them. And so for most of the day we return to feudalism. That is what capitalism is — a version of feudalism in which capital replaces land, and business leaders replace kings. But the hierarchy remains.... There is no reason why a tiny nobility should own the capital, and everyone else therefore be in service to them. There is no reason they should give us a living wage and take all the rest that we produce. No! The system called capitalist democracy was not really democratic at all.... History has shown us which values were real in that system [116–17].

Eco-economics rewrites the rules governing investment, capital, and labor. For economists, the conflation of feudalism and capitalism makes little historical sense, but Robinson insists on this identification at several points in the three novels (*Green* 85; *Blue* 392–93). In what amounts to an authorial endorsement of eco-economics, the narrator describes the effects of Vlad's speech in the rhetoric of Old Testament prophetic fury: "one of the ancient radicals had gotten mad and risen up to smite one of the neoconservative young power mongers" (120). Vlad emphasizes that ownership has been the guiding force of economic history — ownership defined as the unchecked and scientifically unsound privilege to treat common resources as private property. In contrast, the Dorsa Brevia accord recognizes "an economics based on ecological science. The goal of Martian economics," the document continues, "is not 'sustainable development' but the a sustainable prosperity for its entire biosphere" (*Green* 358). To charges that he is a utopian dreamer or the avatar of Terran socialism returned, Vlad reiterates the ecocentric principles of the Dorsa Brevia agreement: "the land, air, and water of Mars belong to no one, ... we are the stewards of it for all future generations" (119). This concept of stewardship challenges the logic of property common to both feudalism and capitalism; its refusal to commodify the resources which terraforming has produced means that the control of capital remains in the hands of those who produce it. As Vlad puts it, "in our system workers will hire capital rather than the other way around" (119). In one respect, the ideal of a self-regulating biosphere advanced by Lovelock and Allaby in *The Greening of Mars* is extrapolated in Robinson's eco-economics to the realm of sociopolitical organization. On Blue Mars, people not only try to live in harmony with a newly created biosphere, but participate in a open, evolving system of elaborate feedback loops, checks and balances, and safeguards to ensure that there are no threatening accumulations of capital by a "tiny nobility," a prospect as dangerous, Robinson implies, as a deadly buildup of atmospheric pollutants.

Terraforming and Its Limit Conditions

In all three novels, major characters—John, Frank, and Maya in *Red Mars*; Sax, Maya, Nadia, and Nirgal (one of Hiroko's sons) in *Green Mars*; and Nirgal, Sax, Maya, Ann, Jackie (John's daughter), and Zo (Jackie's daughter) in *Blue Mars*—wander the planet, at times almost aimlessly, working on various projects, meeting new settlers and old friends, and taking stock of the infinite changes being wrought on the planet and its inhabitants. In some respects, this rootlessness seems a necessary antidote to the bureaucracy, interference, and tyranny of metanational capitalism; in others, however, this nomadic existence testifies to the redefinition of notions of identity that the terraformation of Mars fosters.[10] In his travels, John comes to recognize that he was "probably wrong" to assume that "if he only saw more of the planet, visited one more settlement, talked to one more person, that he would somehow ... get it—and that this holistic understanding would then flow back from him to everybody else." The implicit politics of representation, of John's efforts to become the "articulator of all [the settlers'] hopes and desires" (*Red* 284), fails, in part, because it reinforces the alienation of social, ethnic, economic, and psychological descriptions of identity from the processes of areoformation, from the terrain itself. As John comes to recognize, Red Mars is already being transformed and transforming its inhabitants; character is interpenetrated by a sense of place, of geography, as well as by historical experiences and psychic traumas (Jameson, "'If'" 208–32). Nirgal, who (rather than his sometime lover, Jackie Boone) inherits John's role as the ethical consciousness of his generation, finds himself, more than a century later, rootless in the aftermath of independence. His disorientation marks both his recognition of and his resistance to the mutual inflections of identity, vocation, and place:

> All his life he had wandered Mars talking to people about a free Mars, about inhabitation rather than colonization, about becoming indigenous to the land. Now that task was ended.... It was hard to give up being a revolutionary. Nothing seemed to follow from it, either logically or emotionally.... On the one hand he wanted to stay a wanderer, to fly and walk and sail all over the world, a nomad forever, wandering ceaselessly until he knew Mars better than anyone else. Ah yes; it was a familiar euphoria. On the other hand, it was familiar, he had done that all his life. It would be the form, of his previous life, without the content. And he already knew the loneliness of that life, the rootlessness that made him feel so detached.... Coming from everywhere, he came from nowhere. He had no home. And so now he wanted that home, as much as freedom or more. A home. He wanted to pick a place and stay there, to learn it completely... [*Blue* 301].

Nirgal's efforts to turn farmer, however, are devastated by a dust storm, and he returns to a nomadic existence, for a time joining a tribe of hunter-gatherers, future primitives who roam Mars living off the terraformed land. His dilemma, in one respect, is that his "home"—Mars itself—is constantly undergoing alchemical transmutations: ancient craters fill with water and become seas, the population expands into previously pristine areas, the atmosphere thickens enough so that, with some genetic adjustments, humans can breathe the air without masks, and the sky evolves to various shades of an oxygen-rich reddish-blue. On Blue Mars, "home," like one's sense of self, is subject to areoformation. Nirgal, therefore, cannot be described as a "postmodern" self in the usual sense of that term; his subjectivity is a function of his political-spiritual calling as a spokesperson and exemplar of viriditas. His rootlessness is neither a sign of neurosis nor a hopeless quest for an absent ideal but the natural condition for settlers whose lives extend to centuries and for whom the "pharonic" projects (*Green* 438) of creating a new biosphere define, in effect, where they will be and who they will become. For this ectogenic *homo martialis*, one does not practice eco-economics so much as one becomes a function of its aerophonic energies. The generation of Martian natives which he represents marks the end of the classically conceived *homo economicus*, that phantom of endless self-aggrandizement, who must be banished for any ecotopia to thrive.

By the end of *Blue Mars*, Ann and Sax are lovers, the opposition of Reds and Greens subsumed by aerophonic blue. Mars has avoided a third interplanetary war and offered itself as a model for Earth as the mother planet struggles through crises of overpopulation, the result of the longevity treatment, and ecological devastation caused by the flooding of coastal regions when the Ross Ice Shelf in Antarctica is melted by volcanic eruptions. The trilogy ends on a beach with children eating ice cream and Ann willing herself to survive a bout of arythmia. The technologies of terraformation offer, ultimately, a vision of small-town life, or such a life experienced in an ecologically pristine equivalent of Santa Barbara: scenic beauty, good restaurants. Robinson returns his readers to the doubled desires of the technologies of terraformation — the utopian possibility of a future primitive beyond the ecological degradation and economic injustices of the late twentieth century. With Mars terraformed, the massive projects needed to transform the planet give way to a self-regulating biosphere; the true ecopoeisis becomes the creation of new forms of social as well as biological life. Robinson's 1700 page thought experiment finally presents itself less as a utopian dream than a falling into ecotopian theory — both a policy statement and a hard-won course charted to an imagined holism.

And yet terraformation remains a sequence of dynamic and unpredictable interactions between human intentions and irreducibly complex environmental changes, adaptations, and reconfigurations. Although the First One Hundred imagine Mars as "a blank red slate" on which, according to Arkady, they can "transform ... ourselves and our social reality," the planet ultimately proves recalcitrant. At the end of *The Martians*, Robinson returns to the romance of Eileen Monday and Roger Clayborne on a Mars on which terraforming has begun to fail: the planet is locked into an ice age that may require a re-engineering of the planetary environment. Blue Mars has given way to a deep freeze that redefines the limits and possibilities of the human experience on the planet. "Winterkill is winterkill," says Eileen, "but this is ridiculous. The whole world is dying" (349). Their ice boat trip across the frozen oceans of the north leads them back to the problems posed by terraforming that had sparked debates between the reds and greens throughout the trilogy. Hans Boethe, an areologist who had ascended Olympus Mons with them centuries earlier, offers a litany of ways that the ice age might be reversed:

> Bombs below the regolith.... A flying lens to focus some of the mirrors' light, heat the surface with focused sunlight. Then bring in some nitrogen from Titan. Direct a few comets to unpopulated areas, or aerobrake them so that they burn up in the atmosphere. That would thicken things up fast. And more halocarbon factories [352].

These "industrial" solutions are countered by Roger who reinvokes "ecopoeisis" as offering "less violence to the landscape" (352). This debate about re-terraforming Mars is not resolved, and "it begins to seem as if they are on an all-ice world, like Calisto or Europa"—or in Antarctica, the setting for Robinson's 1997 novel. The deep freeze on Mars both closes the trilogy and offers a meditation about the limitations of human intentions in environmental engineering or, more broadly, about humans' ability to transform nature into habitat. Even at the end of *The Gold Coast*, the second volume of his California trilogy, Robinson counters the dystopian vision of a landscape of triple-tiered highways and endemic pollution with a climb into the Sierra Nevada mountains that presents his hero the potential for both escape and renewal; as elsewhere in his fiction, mountain environments represent the possibility of a human relationship with the Earth that resists greed and ecological degradation. The view from the mountains provides the glimmer of a utopian—or at least a different—future from the one force-fed us by late capitalism. The reversal of terraforming in this final story, "A Martian Romance," however, is not experienced by the younger characters as a tragedy. In contrast to "the despair of the [environmental] crash" perceived by the older generation and the prospect that "warm[ing] things up again ... could take thousands of years," the young Jean-Claude "shrugs": "'It's the work that matters, not the end of the work.'" The story ends with his affirmation that even if "everything alive now will die, [and even if] the planet will stay frozen for thousands of years, ... there *will* be life on Mars" (360). This is not the affirmation of a "red" or "green" philosophy so much as it is a meditation on the bio-expansionism that is, after all, one of the generic bases of science fiction. The genre is refigured as an ethical commitment to the dynamic relationship between life and environment, a relationship that is transforming humans as humans transform the land. In this regard, while the experience of love, friendship, and dialogue are crucial to Robinson's achievement in the Mars trilogy, such experience is never divorced from the politics and ethics of being "visitors on this planet" (*Martians* 385), whether Earth or Mars. Love is finally defined by human efforts "to do something good something useful," by the complex relationships between "red rock red dust the bare/ mineral here of now/ and we the animals standing in it" (385). The ultimate challenge posed by planetary transformation is ultimately as much ethical as it is scientific.

Notes

1. On the logic of simulation and mathematics, see Markley, "Boundaries" 55–77.
2. In Robinson's short story "Discovering Life" (2000), the discovery of Martian microbes by astronauts on the planet short-circuits NASA's plans to begin terraforming Mars. "'Well, shit,'" one of the project scientists says at the end of the story, "I guess we'll just have to terraform Earth instead'" (Robinson *Vinland*, 153–64; quotation from 164).
3. *Red Mars* won the 1993 Nebula Award, *Green Mars* the 1994 Hugo Award. The Mars Society has adopted a red, green, and blue flag as a visual symbol of its members' hopes for the colonization of the planet, even though Robinson remains skeptical of the frontier mentality voiced by some promoters of Martian colonization. See Markley et al., *Red* "interviews" 3, 4).
4. Fogg's *Terraforming* remains the standard text in a growing body of "serious" scientific literature on terraforming; in his opening chapter Fogg surveys scholarship on terraforming through 1994. For important overviews of the technological and ecological problems involved in terraformation, see Averner and MacElroy *Habitability*; Oberg *New Earths*; McKay, et al., "Making" 489–95; Birch, "Terraforming" 331–40; Zubrin *Case*, 172–210; Jakosky *Search*, 160–5; Pollack and Sagan, "Planetary" 1992, 921–50; the essays collected from *Analog* in Schmidt and Zubrin, eds., *Islands*; Gerstell, et al., "Keeping" 2154–57; and the discussion in 2004 moderated by Donna Shirley. Robinson thanks Fogg and McKay in his Acknowledgments to both *Green Mars* and *Blue Mars*.
5. Fogg (1995) provides a comprehensive survey of various proposals and offers his own "synergic" approach

which applies all of these methods to create a carbon dioxide rich but significantly terraformed planet within two hundred years.

6. In his 1999 novel *White Mars*, Brian Aldiss, in collaboration with the noted mathematical physicist Roger Penrose, offers a utopian vision of human settlement on the red planet but resists the idea that terraforming will be an inevitable consequence of colonization. At the end of the novel, Aldiss adds a note from APIUM, the Association for the Protection and Integrity of an Unspoilt Mars. This statement contests many of the key points of the Founding Declaration of the Mars Society; attempts to turn the red planet "into something resembling a colony, an inferior Earth, ... would extend prevailing dystopian tendencies into the [twenty-first] century." Even though he disagrees vehemently with the terraforming dreams of Lovelock and Allaby, then, Aldiss shares an assumption that science fiction has a crucial role to play in shaping the values and assumptions that guide science itself. Inveighing against the "rape and ruination" of Mars, Aldiss envisions a treaty to protect the planet "as unspoilt white wilderness ... a kind of Ayers Rock in the sky" (323).

7. For ecological histories that challenge the traditional account of the frontier, see Crosby 1986; Crumley, *Historical* 1–16.

8. In a question and answer session at the Modern Language Association Conference (28 December 1998), Robinson reflected on his experiments in utopian fiction. In the utopian conclusion to his California trilogy, *Pacific Edge*, Robinson engaged in what he called a "sleight of hand," by putting the actual transformation from late capitalism to a democratic, environmentally rigorous and socially just society in the twenty-first century off stage. Rejecting a romanticized revolutionary call to action, Robinson characterizes himself as "a radical not really in favor of [armed] revolution." He describes his narrative technique in portraying the successful revolution in *Green Mars* as the application of the adage, "on thin ice skate fast." For his depiction of the incipient Martian utopia in *Blue Mars*, Robinson drew on scant historical models for alternative economies, including Lewis Hyde's *The Gift*; in 1998, he expressed the wish that he had used new work on "participatory economies" such as Herman Daly's *On Growth* and *Steady State Economics* and Lester Brown's *Full House*. See also Leane, "Chromodynamics" 83–104.

9. In *Antarctica* (1997), Robinson continues to explore the utopian structure of scientific practices, methods, and beliefs. The novel works towards the redefinition of a science in tune with the natural world and used against the excesses of capitalism, social injustice, and environmental degradation. As one of Robinson's characters puts it, "social justice is a necessary part of any working environmental program" (383). See particularly 322–7; 395–97.

10. On the decentered notions of subjectivity in Robinson's fiction, see Franko, "Working" 191–211, and Jameson, 208–32.

Works Cited

Aldiss, Brian, with Roger Penrose. *White Mars, or, The Mind Set Free: A Twentieth-First Century Utopia*. New York: St. Martin's Press, 1999.

Averner, Maurice, and Robert MacElroy, eds. *On the Habitability of Mars: An Approach to Planetary Ecosynthesis*. NASA SP-414, 1976.

Baker, Victor. "Water and the Martian Landscape." *Nature* 412 (2001), 228–36.

Birch, Paul. "Terraforming Mars Quickly." *Journal of the British Interplanetary Society* 45 (1992), 331–40.

Bogdanov, Alexander. *Red Star*. Trans. Charles Rougle; ed. Loren Graham and Richard Stites. Bloomington: Indiana University Press, 1984.

Creedon, Jeremiah. "Mars on a Billion Dollars a Day: Can We Hatch Life on the Red Planet?" *Utne Reader* 64 (July-August 1994), 34–6.

Crosby, Alfred W. *Ecological Imperialism: The Biological Expansion of Europe, 900–1900*. Cambridge: Cambridge University Press, 1986.

Crumley, Carole, ed. *Historical Ecology: Cultural Knowledge and Changing Landscapes*. Santa Fe: School of American Research Press, 1994.

Fogg, Martyn J. *Terraforming: Engineering Planetary Environments*. Warrendale, PA: Society of Automotive Engineers, 1995.

Franko, Carol. "Working the 'in-between': Kim Stanley Robinson's Utopian Fiction." *Science Fiction Studies* 21 (1994), 191–211.

Gerstell, M. F., J. S. Francisco, Y. L. Lung, and E. T. Aaltonee. "Keeping Mars Warm with New Super Greenhouse Gases." *Proceedings of the National Academy of Sciences* 98 (2001), 2154–7.

Grinspoon, David Harry. *Venus Revealed: A New Look Below the Clouds of Our Mysterious Twin Planet*. New York: Addison Wesley, 1997.

Harris, Marvin. *Cannibals and Kings: The Origins of Cultures*. New York: Random House, 1977.

Ihde, Don. *Technology and the Lifeworld: From Garden to Earth*. Bloomington: Indiana University of Press, 1990.
Jakosky, Bruce. *The Search for Life on Other Planets*. Cambridge: Cambridge University Press, 1998.
Jameson, Fredric. "'If I find one good city I will spare the man': Realism and Utopia in Kim Stanley Robinson's *Mars Trilogy*." *Learning from Other Worlds: Estrangement, Cognition, and the Politics of Science Fiction and Utopia*. Ed. Patrick Parrinder. Durham: Duke University Press, 2001, 208–32.
Judd, Cyril. 1952. [C. M. Kornbluth and Judith Merril.] *Outpost Mars*. New York: Ace Books, 1953.
Kluger, Jeffrey. "Mars, in the Earth's Image." *Discover* 13, no. 9 (September 1992), 72–6.
Latour, Bruno. *We Have Never Been Modern*. Trans. Catherine Porter. Cambridge: Harvard University Press, 1993.
Leane, Elizabeth. "Chromodynamics: Science and Colonialism in Kim Stanley Robinson's Mars Trilogy." *ARIEL* 33.1 (2002): 83–104.
Lovelock, James, and Michael Allaby. *The Greening of Mars*. New York: St. Martin's Press, 1984.
Markley, Robert. "Boundaries: Mathematics, Alienation, and the Metaphysics of Cyberspace." In Robert Markley ed., *Virtual Realities and Their Discontents*. Baltimore: Johns Hopkins University Press, 1996, 55–77.
_____. *Dying Planet: Mars in Science and the Imagination*. Durham: Duke University, 2005.
_____, Harrison Higgs, Michelle Kendrick, and Helen Burgess. *Red Planet: Scientific and Cultural Encounters with Mars*. DVD-ROM. Philadelphia: University of Pennsylvania Press, 2001.
McKay, Christopher P., Owen B. Toon, and James F. Kasting. "Making Mars Habitable." *Nature* 352 (1991), 489–95.
Meyer, Thomas R., and Christopher P. McKay. "Using the Resources of Mars for Human Settlement." *Strategies for Mars: A Guide to Human Exploration*. Ed. Carol Stoker and Carter Emmart. San Diego: Univelt for the American Astronautical Society, 1996, 393–442.
Morton, Oliver. *Mapping Mars: Science, Imagination, and the Birth of a World*. London: Fourth Estate, 2002.
Niven, Larry. *Rainbow Mars*. London: Orbit, 1999.
Oberg, James Edward. *New Earths: Transforming Other Planets for Humanity*. Harrisburg: Stackpole Books, 1982.
Pollack, J. B., and Carl Sagan. "Planetary Engineering." *Resources of Near-earth Space*. Ed. J Lewis, M. S. Matthews, and M. L. Guerrieri. Tucson: University of Arizona Press, 1993, 921–50.
Robinson, Kim Stanley. *Antarctica*. London: HarperCollins, 1997.
_____. *Blue Mars*. New York: Bantam, 1996.
_____. *Green Mars*. London: HarperCollins, 1994b.
_____. *Icehenge*. London: HarperCollins, 1984.
_____. *The Martians*. London: HarperCollins, 1999.
_____. *Red Mars*. New York: Bantam, 1993.
_____. *Vinland the Dream and Other Stories*. London: HarperCollins, 2002.
_____, ed. *Future Primitive: The New Ecotopias*. New York: Tor Books, 1994a.
Schmidt, Stanley, and Robert Zubrin, ed. *Islands in the Sky: Bold New Ideas for Colonizing Space*. New York: Wiley, 1996.
Serres, Michel. *The Parasite*. Trans. Lawrence Scher. Baltimore: Johns Hopkins University Press, 1982.
Shaviro, Steven. *Doom Patrols*. London: Serpent's Tail, 1996.
Shirley, Donna, moderator. "Terraforming Mars: Experts Debate How, Why, and Whether." Science Tuesday. http://www.space.com/scienceastronomy/terraform_debate_040727-7.html. Posted 26 July 2004.
Squyres, Steven and James F. Kasting. "Early Mars: How Warm and How Wet?" *Science* 265 (1994), 744–49.
Toon, Owen B. "Environments of Earth and Other Worlds." *Carl Sagan's Universe*. Ed. Yervant Terzian and Elizabeth Bilson. Cambridge: Cambridge University Press, 1997, 51–63.
Turner, Frederick. *Genesis*. Dallas: Saybrook, 1988.
_____. "Life on Mars: Cultivating a Planet — and Ourselves." *Harper's* 279 (August 1989), 33–4.
Zubrin, Robert. *Entering Space: Creating a Spacefaring Civilization*. New York: Tarcher/Putnam, 1999.
_____. "The Significance of the Martian Frontier," in *Strategies for Mars: A Guide to Human Exploration* . Ed. Carol Stoker and Carter Emmart. San Diego: Univelt for the American Astronautical Society, 13–24, 1996.
_____, with Richard Wagner. *The Case for Mars: The Plan to Settle the Red Planet and Why We Must*. New York: Free Press, 1996.

9

Chromodynamics: Science and Colonialism in the Mars Trilogy*

Elizabeth Leane

> Deal table in the middle, plain chairs all round the walls, on one end a large shining map, marked with all the colours of the rainbow. There was a vast amount of red — good to see at any time, because one knows that some real work is done in there, a deuce lot of blue, a little green.
> — Joseph Conrad, *Heart of Darkness*

Red Mars, *Green Mars*, and *Blue Mars*, the hefty volumes making up Kim Stanley Robinson's epic Mars trilogy, are only three of numerous recent publications, including novels, popularizations, and occasionally combinations of both, dealing with the planet Mars.[1] The following excerpts are taken from two such publications:

> There will be people on Mars long before the end of the twenty-first century. It's inevitable, and irresistible. It might happen before 2020. It could happen by 2011. Mars is our next frontier. The plans are being laid now, the missions designed. The technology exists. The latter-day equivalents of Magellan, Columbus and Cook, and all the other explorers of the age of European expansion, are preparing themselves [Walter 1].

> Plans are already afoot to send human beings to Mars. Behind these exciting possibilities lies a less worthy objective: an assumption that the Red Planet can be turned into something resembling a colony, an inferior Earth. [...]
> [...] Mars must become a UN protectorate, and be treated as a "planet for science," much as the Antarctic has been preserved, at least to a great extent, as unspoilt white wilderness. We are for a WHITE MARS! [Aldiss 323]

These two quotations appear to pull in ideologically opposing directions: while the passage from astropaleobiologist Malcolm Walter's *The Search for Life on Mars* seems to advocate an unreconstructed gallop towards the "next frontier," Aldiss concludes his novel *White Mars* (written with the aid of mathematician and popularizer Roger Penrose) with the demand that Mars be treated not as a colony, but as a "planet for science."[2] But can these two notions — Mars as a colony and Mars as a "planet for science" — be considered unproblematic opposites?

That colonialism and science are, on the contrary, fellow-travelers, is indicated by casual

---

*First published as "Chromodynamics: Science and Colonialism in Kim Stanley Robinson's Mars Trilogy." *ARIEL* 33.1 (2002): 83–104. Reprinted with the permission of the Board of Governors, University of Calgary, Calgary, Alberta.

reflection on the popular tropes of science — to seek new vistas, explore new fields, go where no one has gone before — and strongly supported by scholarly research. Historians of science have produced numerous demonstrations of the interdependent relationship between geographic exploration, commercial exploitation and scientific expedition in the last few centuries. "[F]or most of humanity," argue Paolo Palladino and Michael Worboys, "the history of science and imperialism *is* the history of science" (102; original emphasis).

Just as significant are recent critiques of scientific discourse which suggest not just a historical and commercial but also a discursive link between science and colonialism. Feminist science scholars in particular have been quick to note the parallels between scientific and colonialist metaphors of conquest: "The fantasies that attend [the] gendering of the production and reproduction of knowledge are at once sexualized and territorial (we speak not only of 'penetrating' or 'unveiling' nature's mysteries but of 'opening up new horizons' or 'pushing back the frontiers of knowledge')" (Jacobus, Keller and Shuttleworth 6). Many of these critics advocate the development of an alternative form (or forms) of science — a "feminist successor science," to use Sandra Harding's term — which might avoid patriarchal discourse and practice (146). This feminist science would presumably be an anti-colonialist science; for, as ecofeminists have pointed out,

> the relationship of exploitative dominance between man and nature (shaped by reductionist modern science since the 16th century) and the exploitative and oppressive relationship between men and women that prevails in most patriarchal societies, even modern industrial ones, [are] closely connected. [...] The devaluation of contributions from women and nature goes hand-in-hand with the value assigned to acts of colonization as acts of development and improvement [Mies and Shiva 3, 25].

One of the most stimulating of recent studies of the relationship between science, colonialism and patriarchy is Denise Albanese's *New Science, New World*, which focuses on the early modern period. Albanese states that "the repeated joining of the two topics in Renaissance texts makes clear that a rhetorical analogy exists between colonialism and science" (2). She treats science and colonialism as isomorphic modes of "power-knowledge, of conquest," modes which are "often mutually constitutive, interdependent, given their intermittent rearticulation within successive cultural formations" (59). Through her analysis of a number of seminal early modern texts, such as *The Tempest, Paradise Lost*, Bacon's *New Atlantis* and Galileo's *Dialogue on the Two Chief World Systems*, Albanese argues that this isomorphism can be connected in a complex way to the onset of the polarization of science and literature which has characterized the modern and postmodern periods. Writers such as Copernicus and Galileo, she suggests, by self-consciously employing "literary" forms to state their cosmological claims in order to avoid religious persecution, inaugurated a tradition in which "fiction" became defined in opposition to "fact," scientific truth-telling. This strategy, Albanese argues, replicated the strategies of colonial discourse: "as a consequence of the culturally productive mechanisms of opposition — particularly those mobilized by Renaissance colonialism — the emergence of modern scientific ideology in the seventeenth century resulted in the positing of fiction, of literary representation, as its binary (and prospectively devalued) opposite" (3). Like colonialism, and like patriarchy, science operates through a process of othering: just as the physical world is posited as object, as "other" to the observer, so literary discourse, a discourse of subjectivity, is othered, placed outside the realms of truth-telling.

The notion that the joint discourses of science and colonialism can be connected to the polarization of science and literature, fact and fiction, provides a particularly useful framework through which to investigate the Mars trilogy. Robinson writes within a genre which is itself riven by the literature/science split—"soft" knowledge versus "hard" knowledge. But also, as the name implies, science fiction by its very nature contests this split. Robinson has often been criticized for the "hardness" of his science fiction. John Gribbin, himself a writer of science fiction and a prolific popularizer of science, tells *New Scientist* readers that they would be better off perusing "the NASA manuals" than Robinson's *Red Mars*. This novel, Gribbin complains in his review, is "all science and no fiction." How Gribbin manages to overlook the highly complex maze of personality and politics that Robinson constructs in *Red Mars* remains a mystery. Nevertheless, for a trilogy which sets out to deal with immense political questions— where will we go next? how can we free ourselves from the destructive patterns of history? what forms might utopia take?—the Mars novels admittedly contain large passages dealing with detailed scientific description that seem to exceed the demands of the reality effect required by hard sf.

How can we read these detailed scientific passages as anything more than the maintenance of generic conventions and an established authorial style? How are we to integrate them into a novel which is explicitly, self-consciously political and explicitly, self-consciously postcolonial? From Wells to Welles, from Burroughs to Bradbury and beyond, Mars in science fiction has, perhaps more than any other location, been the site (or the source) of imperial desire and conquest. Robinson, by endowing his Martian landscape with the names of his literary forebears (Bradbury Point, Clarke and New Clarke, Burroughs, Sheffield), acknowledges this ancestry. His novels, like these earlier ones, represent primarily a narrative of colonization. The first settlement on Mars is referred to as a "colony" and its inhabitants as "colonists" (*Red* 193); later they are termed "'settlers'" and their children "'natives,'" and new visitors from Earth (or "Terra") are considered "'colonialists'" (*Green* 740). As this linguistic positioning indicates, they frequently argue over the politics of postcolonialism, both on Mars and Earth. These arguments are multifaceted: are humans justified in colonizing Mars, in terraforming its surface? Should Mars, once established, become independent from Earth? How might Mars interact with an Earth that has become a neocolonial, late-capitalist nightmare, with metanational companies acquiring "flags of convenience" by buying up their foreign debt? The whole trilogy can, from one perspective, be seen as an attempt to theorize, or, more accurately, to narrativize, a postcolonial dystopia on Earth, and a postcolonial utopia on Mars; its central problematic is whether the two can exist simultaneously and interdependently.

So what place has science in all this? Why the minutiae of geology, botany, atmospheric physics, biochemistry, quantum mechanics, genetics, neuroscience, superstring theory, hydrodynamics, and construction engineering, which even *New Scientist* readers might find tedious?

Previous commentators on the Mars trilogy have not overlooked this question. Fredric Jameson takes the trilogy's "pocket disquisitions" on science and technology as a starting point for his analysis, and bases his argument on the observation that "science and politics are not (or not only) two separate themes in the Mars trilogy" (208, 211). Rather, "all of the scientific problems described in [the Mars trilogy], without exception, offer an allegory ... of social, political and historical problems also faced by the inhabitants of Mars" (210–11). According to Jameson, the trilogy forces readers to alternate their interpretive frameworks, moving continuously between "nature and human collectivities," a process which tends to "problematize each one in turn, and send us back to the other." For Jameson, this goes some way towards explaining the trilogy's "heterogeneities and the uneven sequence of great sheets of material." Thus, "any first scientific reading of the Mars trilogy must eventually develop into a second allegorical one, in which the hard science-fictional content stands revealed as socio-political— that is to say, as utopian" (211). Moving from his observation of the socio-political import of the scientific problems in the trilogy to a discussion of the constructed nature of all knowledge and the ambiguous positioning of the trilogy between "otherness and production" (216), Jameson proceeds to a sophisticated examination of the relationship between science fiction, realism, and utopias.

Jameson's broad idea that the scientific problems explored in the trilogy have a role in the working through of socio-political problems in the novels is one that my reading here aims to develop. However, I also want to point to an aspect of the trilogy that is not dealt with in detail by Jameson. Although Jameson does discuss the political conflicts with which the trilogy is riven, his treatment of "otherness and production" is concerned largely with questions of ontology, realism, and representation that do not leave room for in-depth consideration of the postcolonial issues so central to the trilogy.

In the service of a fully politicized reading of the trilogy, Jameson's approach to its "hard" scientific passages needs to be supplemented by an acknowledgement of the discursive relationship between science and colonialism, and Albanese's identification of the connection between this relationship and the polarization of science and literature, of "hard" and "soft" knowledge. Specifically, I will argue that Robinson, working within a simultaneously "hard" and "soft" discourse, is able to point towards a form of knowledge that does not rely on the hard/soft binarism. Certainly, the "pocket disquisitions" on scientific and technical knowledge which pepper *Red Mars* are recognizably "other" to its "soft" narrative of politics and personality — it is this alterity which leads Gribbin to equate these passages with "the NASA manuals." As the trilogy continues, however, it is increasingly evident that the passages of scientific description are anything but "other" to the political (and personal) dilemmas which face the colonizers. Focusing particularly on the character of Sax Russell, Robinson's symbol of "hard," objective science, I will suggest that the gradual but momentous change in scientific attitude and practice displayed by this character can be read as the working through of a utopian vision of science — the kind of "successor science" which, according to feminist critics, is increasingly necessary.[3] This successor science, I will suggest, is based on a desire to accept the agency of the other — to nurture what Barbara McClintock has termed "a feeling for the organism" (qtd. in Keller 201).

In the Mars trilogy, Robinson develops the relationship between science and colonialism on a symbolic level through his use of tropes of color. His narrative is shaped by what, borrowing a term from quantum theory (itself arguably an area of "softness"— of uncertainty and observer subjectivity — within the "hardest" of sciences), we might coin his "chromodynamics." Physicists use this term to refer to that characteristic of quarks (the most fundamental of subatomic particles) associated with the strong force and termed, arbitrarily, "color." Quarks, like Mars, can be "red," "green," or "blue." The reason that I find "chromodynamics" an enabling metaphor here is that this theory states that a quark cannot exist alone, but only in combination with other differently colored quarks, as a component of another type of elementary particle, a hadron. A hadron such as the proton must consist of three quarks whose combination is "colorless" or "white." To produce "white," each of the three quarks must be a different "color": one "red," one "green," and one "blue."[4] Quantum chromodynamics thus insists that "colors" must always be combined, must always exist in concert, but combinations can change, can interact dynamically.

In the following I will argue that, while Robinson uses the color (or rather non-color) "white" to symbolically represent science, his is a whiteness very unlike that proposed by Aldiss. For Aldiss, whiteness seems to symbolize a desire to see blankness or emptiness — scientific objectivity and autonomy — where in fact there exists a blurred spectrum of motives, prior agendas, histories, politics, and personalities. For Robinson, a true utopian science must acknowledge these "colored" perspectives and maintain them in a dynamic union. In his first novel following the Mars trilogy, *Antarctica*, Robinson explicitly challenges (while acknowledging the lure of) the notion of a pure white "continent for science" unspoilt by politics.[5] Similarly, the Mars trilogy explodes the notion of a "planet for science." The trilogy is not a dry sample of hard sf on the level of "the NASA manuals," but rather an attempt to make the colored — the politicized — nature of science apparent, not in order to obliterate or ignore it, but to suggest a utopian chromodynamics.

Red and Green

Perhaps the most striking feature of the planet Mars as a site for a postcolonial narrative is the absence of indigenous life. At first glance, this might seem a convenient simplification, an avoidance of an essential issue of postcoloniality. A different view, however, is enabled by Albanese's observation that "the textual embodiment of the New World ... is the discursive counterpart of [the] state of nature: the condition of possibility for the emergence of 'science'" (6). One strategy of colonial discourse, she suggests, is to naturalize the colonized, to place the colonized in the same relationship to the colonizer as the natural world is to the scientist. Thus Robinson's emptying out of the site of colonization could be read as a literalization of this naturalizing impulse, an attempt to make the isomorphism of the colonial and scientific impulses explicit.

This emptying out is also, of course, a standard strategy of the utopian text. Jameson recalls the "structural precondition of that social 'blank slate' upon which traditional Utopias wrote their text: the radical separation of Utopia from historical reality." Jameson notes, however, that in the Mars trilogy "this gesture remains suspended and incomplete," and "the attempt repeatedly to begin History over again ... is the very subject of the work" (227). At one point in *Red Mars*, the unknown narrator muses on the "inertia" of history, and wonders what acceleration would be required to escape its gravity well (68). One aspect of this history which must be both escaped and repeated is the colonialist impulse itself; another is conflict arising from racial and cultural differences. The initial cold-war stand-off between the Russian and American members of the First Hundred colonizer-astronauts is soon replaced by a fracturing into myriad political, religious and racial groupings, as the various waves of immigrants arrive. Robinson is unafraid to show the continuance of various Terran racial stereotypes: Arab assassins; the inscrutable Japanese mystic (Hiroko Ai); the Russian anarchist (Arkady Bogdanov); the moody and passionate Russian beauty (Maya Toitovna); the heroic American astronaut, charismatic, confident, and idealistic (John Boone), and his counterpart, the unscrupulous American political operator (Frank Chalmers). Inevitably, with these stereotypes comes the continuance of racial and cultural conflict. Initially, this conflict exists between the multifarious immigrants on Mars, but it soon expands to interplanetary dimensions. And while the second-generation "natives" of Mars seem idealistically tolerant of their own ethnic differences, this tolerance comes at the expense of the othering of Earth/Terra itself, and a consequent hostility to Terran society and Terran immigrants, as indicated by the rise of the "MarsFirst" party.

The inescapable question central to this narrative is how to cease repeating the mistakes of the past, how to recognize and then to escape conflicting colors and move to a new synthesis, how to escape the inertia of history. The characters in the Mars trilogy are constantly trying to avoid comparing their situation with other revolutionary situations — the American War of Independence (a conflict symbolized by Red and Blue), the Russian Revolution (symbolized by Red and White), the whole history of revolutions. The Martians realize, furthermore, that the economic inequality that is engendered by capitalism is not separable from postcoloniality. The pragmatic Frank Chalmers points out to an Indian and a Chinese delegate to the first Martian conference that their need for land and resources on Mars is a result of "'resources that were taken from you without payment during the colonial years.'" When the Indian delegate remarks that "'in a very real sense the colonial period never ended,'" Frank replies, "'That's what transnational capitalism is: we're all colonies now'" (*Red* 460). As metanationals become more powerful than countries on Earth, effectively subsuming the governments of third-world nations, the discourses of capitalism and postcolonialism begin to blur. It is this dual heritage which the Martians want desperately to escape. Yet Maya, the Russian cosmonaut who co-captained the original voyage of the First Hundred, is (in her genetically prolonged old age) haunted by a sense of déjà vu, fearing that the second Martian revolution will merely repeat the violence and chaos of the first. History appears inescapable: "the present was a kind of past as well" (*Green* 672, 673). All the novels deal with people striking out for new territory, both physically and politically, determined not to repeat the mistakes of the past; but how is this possible, if striking out for new territory *is* a mistake of the past?

In Robinson's exploration of possible answers to this question, science plays an integral role. In *Red Mars*, the long passages of scientific and technological description may initially appear a respite from the political and personal intrigues of the colonizers. Certainly, they do appear to fulfill this function for the scientist characters such as Sax, Ann, and Nadia. Nevertheless, as the narrative continues, it becomes clear (as I will show) that this fulfillment is itself escapism based on naïve views of science. The increasingly complex understanding of scientific practices and attitudes developed throughout the trilogy intertwines with the continuing socio-political struggles, and the search for a synthesis of scientific approaches is interdependent with the search for a synthesis of political, racial and cultural views. This interdependence is inevitable, given that Martian science and Martian politics are primarily concerned with ways of encountering the other, whether this be data, a planet, or a people.

The interdependent narratives of postcolonial and scientific development in the trilogy are best characterized by the ongoing conflict, stretching the length of the trilogy, between the scientists Ann Clayborne and Sax Russell. It is Clayborne, the appropriately named geologist, who immediately laments the intrusion of humanity into the radically alien, radically beautiful Martian landscape: "...Mars will be gone and we'll be here, and we'll wonder why we feel so empty. Why when we look at the land we can never see anything but our own faces" (*Red* 190). Ann's desire is to read the planet's own history from its landscape and geological formations, "to read it like a text, written by its own long past" (*Blue* 98). She recognizes the impulse of the colonists to ignore this autonomous history and to recreate the colonized landscape in their own planet's image: to "terraform." Although Ann refuses the stereotypical colonial tropes, scorning as absurd "such simplistic analogies as ... the woman as planet," she does recognize terraforming as a form of bodily penetration, figuring the frozen oceans tapped from Mars' aquifers as "semen" (*Blue* 264–5). Thus Ann promotes a kind of ecofeminism, based on an appreciation, scientific and political, of "otherness." Because she sees this otherness constantly disregarded, written over, subsumed into sameness, she realizes that political activism is a necessary part of her scientific practice.

While Ann's position is ostensibly a politicized resistance to the colonialist impulses of science, it can also be read as a trust in the fundamental disinterestedness of science of the same kind Aldiss professes when he demands a "planet for science." Ann engages in a subtle form of doublethink in which she resists the impulse to view Mars as a mirror of Terran concepts and concerns, and yet is unable to see that in order to "read it like a text" she must submit it to these concepts and concerns. This becomes evident in her first major argument with Sax Russell, the stereotypically unemotional physicist, who emerges as one of the main advocates for terraforming, the Green who opposes Ann's Red:

> "The beauty of Mars exists in the human mind," he said in that dry factual tone, and everyone stared at him amazed. "Without the human presence it is just a collection of atoms, no different from any other random speck of matter in the universe. It's we who understand it, and we who give it meaning.... All those dumb sci-fi novels with their monsters and maidens and dying civilizations. And all the scientists who studied the data, or got us here. That's what makes Mars beautiful. Not the basalt and oxides" [*Red* 212].

Sax's point is that science, like literature, constructs Mars to the same degree as the giant bulldozers and air miners with which the colonizers build their early settlement. Mars is already written-over: by scientists, such as Giovanni Schiaparelli, who endowed its landscape with a hotchpotch of classical, religious, and mythological names, "a horrendous mishmash of the dreams of the past" (*Green* 155), and also by the sf writers whose names Robinson inscribes in his landscape, as they inscribed the Martian landscape in their texts. Mars was in the constant process of being both read and written over, before the terraforming even began: planet as palimpsest.

Ann, temporarily defeated by this argument, is only able to repeat her belief that humanity must concentrate on "fitting into" the universe rather than "turning it all into a mirror image of us" (*Red* 214). For Ann, Mars "is *its own place*" (*Red* 56; original emphasis). As the trilogy continues, around this belief spring up unidentified myths, such as that of the "little red people" (as opposed to the "little green men"). These mythical indigenes of the planet have their own name for Mars, "Ka" (in some dialects, "m'kah"), which, strangely, is echoed throughout many human languages: "*it may be that the planet itself suggests the sound in some hypnotic way that affects all conscious observers, whether standing right on it or seeing it as a red star in the sky ... maybe it's the colour that does it*" (*Green* 345–6; original emphasis). For Ann and her Red followers, Ka, the Red Planet, is a transcendental signified, an originary text, existing before and separate from human language and knowledge. Her despair becomes complete in the failed revolution of 2061, in which saboteurs flood the landscape by exploding aquifers: "The landscape itself was now speaking a kind of glossolalia," its stark redness replaced by a "white noise of despair" (*Red* 638, 654). She lives to see her position parodied when, in *Blue Mars*, her cause is taken to extremes by a younger generation, "religious fanatics [...] members of some kind of rock-worshipping sect" (27).

The argument between Sax and Ann is itself inscribed into the history of the planet, their opposing viewpoints becoming known as the "Russell program" and the "Clayborne position" (*Red* 202). The ensuing struggle between the Reds and the Greens, as they battle not only each other but a third postcolonial force, the exploitative Terran metanationals for whom "Mars is not a nation but a world resource" (*Red* 602), useful only as a source of minerals and a sink for Earth's overflowing population, becomes the framework around which the narrative is built. Complicating this standoff is the mysterious figure of Hiroko Ai, biosphere engineer, whose support for the Greens is not pragmatic but mystical, built around the concept of a life-force or "viriditas" which must manifest itself throughout the universe.

For Hiroko, the altering of Mars's atmosphere and surface is not terraforming, but rather "areoforming," a Gaia-like process in which the planet and its inhabitants evolve together, "*a complex communal response, a creative self-designing ability*" (*Green* 13; original emphasis).

These main advocates of a colored Mars, Ann (the Red), and Sax and Hiroko (the Greens), all begin the novel as scientists — scientists hand-picked to be part of the First Hundred, an elite scientific and diplomatic team. It is through the development of these characters, and in particular the working through of the longstanding impasse represented by Ann's Red and Sax's Green, that Robinson points the way towards an anti-colonialist ethos based on a new kind of science. Ann and Hiroko, ecofeminists divided over their attitude towards colonialism, are both opposed to the ultra-reductionist scientism represented by Sax, the particle physicist, the most stereotypical of the scientists.

In a trilogy in which each central character represents a particular value system, Sax is very clearly "the embodiment of the spirit of science" (*Blue* 193). He is mild, unemotional, and inexpressive, "as impassive as an owl, blinking as he looked over the readouts on the room's computer screens" (*Red* 45). His fellow-colonizers consider him a "parody of the scientist," and joke that his brain has been replaced by "the sum of a hundred hyperintelligent rats" (*Red* 286). Sax is filled with the desire for intellectual exploration and expansion, as his conversation with the psychologist Michel Duval makes evident:

[Michel:] *You conceive of science as nothing more than answers to questions?*
[Sax:] *As a system for generating answers.*
And what is the purpose of that?
... To know.
And what will you do with your knowledge?
... Find out more.
But why?
I don't know. It's the way I am [*Green* 502; original emphasis].

In his belief in exploration for its own sake, and also in his refusal to acknowledge any intrusion of values into his scientific research, Sax is ironically close to Ann, although he sees their positions as antithetical. When Sax realizes that Ann deliberately conceals scientific data to protect the planet, he interprets this as a sign of the distance between them: "Concealing data: he was shocked, she could tell. He couldn't imagine any reason good enough to conceal data. Perhaps this was the root of their inability to understand each other. Value systems based on entirely different assumptions. Completely different kinds of science" (*Red* 649). But the difference between Ann's and Sax's positions is not absolute at all: both allow for the entry of politics into science at one stage while denying it at another. Ann understands that science in practice is inevitably infused with political motivations, but cannot see that even in the abstract science constructs — and therefore colonizes — what it examines. Sax admits this latter point, but supports (at least initially) an idealized view of scientific practice as objective and untouched by personality or politics.

This seemingly slight divergence of Ann's and Sax's conception of science expands into fiercely opposed campaigns involving different gender politics and different attitudes towards postcolonial ethics. Ann sees the colonization of Mars as an invasion of the body; Sax enacts this invasion by supervising the drilling of moholes, enormous holes penetrating deep into the planet's interior, designed to release geothermal (or rather areothermal) heat into the planet's atmosphere. For Ann, the physical "mastery" of nature precludes its intellectual "mastery"; for Sax, these two forms of dominance go hand-in-hand. For Ann, the planet is its own place; for Sax, "The planet is the lab" (*Red* 312).

Green and White

The Mars trilogy, then, revolves around the ethics of exploring, colonizing, and changing a landscape void of human life, and an ethics based on science alone produces an impasse: the conflicting "Russell program" and "Clayborne position," the green and the red. However, the narrative does offer a means of moving beyond the terms of the Russell-Clayborne debate by pointing towards a rapprochement between science and another value system, and this rapprochement is symbolically suggested through chromodynamics.

The movement towards this rapprochement begins in the second novel of the trilogy, *Green Mars*, in which Nirgal, a Martian native and son of Hiroko who is brought up in a biosphere contained within an ice cave, sees the world in terms of "the green" and "the white." Throughout *Green Mars*, many binary pairs accrete around these colors, including life and death, animate and inanimate, animal and human, and, in the view of the psychologist Michel, "the Mystic and the Scientist." What is needed, according to Michel, is "a combination of both, which we call the *Alchemist*" (*Green* 27; original emphasis). Michel's words foreshadow the narrative: *Green Mars* describes not just the greening of Mars, but also the greening (in this new sense) of Sax Russell, "the current living avatar of the Great Scientist" (*Blue* 193). When Sax arrives on Mars, his one interest is terraforming the planet for human habitation, even if this must be done surreptitiously. In this utilitarian approach, he is not unlike the eighteenth-century explorer-scientists whom David Mackey describes in his *In the Wake of Cook*: "They were natural scientists, and the plants, animals and rocks which were the objects of their study, were evaluated in terms of their raw material potential. To such men it was axiomatic that overseas territories should provide sustenance for the rapidly expanding industries of England" (194). By the beginning of *Blue Mars*, however, Sax has undergone something of a conversion. Three experiences catalyze this change. The narration of each experience includes "pocket disquisitions" on science, but here it is clear that these disquisitions represent not merely the trappings of hard sf, but rather an attempt to show the reader alternative scientific visions.

The first steps towards Sax's conversion are described in the fourth section of *Green Mars*, tellingly entitled "The Scientist as Hero." It relates Sax's decision to emerge from the First Hundred's underground hiding place, with a new name and, thanks to plastic surgery, a new face, to continue his terraforming work. As the gregarious, relaxed Stephen Lindholm, Sax is forced to explore new dimensions of his personality. In his assumed position as a botanist, he is required to concentrate his somewhat dilettantish intelligence on a narrow range of plant life. In a scene heavy with symbolism, Sax encounters for the first time his botanical namesake, Saxifrage, "Rock breaker" (*Green* 222). Sax's very name suggests simultaneously the greening of the rocky red landscape, and the remote possibility of a move beyond this: the Arctic Saxifrage ends in "small pale blue flowers" (*Green* 223), and the word "sax" itself suggests the color of peace (Saxony blue or saxe blue). Through this and similar experiences, Sax seems to come to some understanding of what Hiroko calls "viriditas." He begins to *see* differently: "And it occurred to him that this vision was not a matter of accident [...] but the result of a new and growing conceptual understanding of the landscape." He thinks of the philosopher of science Thomas Kuhn, and realizes that he and Ann work within incommensurable paradigms: that the Mars he saw "was a function of what he believed, and what he wanted — it was *his* Mars, evolving right before his very eyes, always in the process of becoming something new" (*Green* 242; original emphasis). The physical world for Sax becomes, at this point, something more than a problem to be solved.

Not long after this, Sax, as Stephen Lindholm, attends an annual conference on terraforming. Here he is "supremely in his element" (*Green* 255). A scientific conference, for Sax, is like "a world outside time and space, in the imaginary space of pure science, surely one of the greatest achievements of the human spirit — a kind of utopian community, cozy and bright and protected. For Sax, a scientific conference *was* utopia" (*Green* 269; original emphasis). To Sax's horror, however, as the conference wears on, "science began to drift into politics" (*Green* 271), with the employees of various transnational projects each advocating a position indirectly supporting the relevant project. He is pained to see "science twisted so blatantly" (*Green* 272). It is a reasonably short step for him to see that science, like the Martian landscape, is always-already "corrupted" by human politics.

The second experience which pushes Sax towards this realization is his capture and torture by the transnational forces, during which he sustains brain damage. As part of his rehabilitation, he talks at length with the psychologist, Michel, outlining his view of science quoted above. Michel replies by suggesting a different conception of science:

> *We disagree. But either way, the scientist's job is to explore everything. No matter the difficulties! To stay open, to accept ambiguity. To attempt to fuse with the object of knowledge. To admit that there are values shot through the whole enterprise. To love it. To work toward discovering the values by which we should live. To work to enact those values in the world. To explore and more than that to create!*
>
> [Sax:] *I'll have to think about that* [*Green* 506; original emphasis].

Sax is clearly true to his word, because towards the end of the novel he emerges as a powerful force for the supporters of Martian independence, using his scientific skills in a targeted way to achieve political goals. He organizes the defense systems that enable the second Martian revolution of independence, and, in the third novel, negotiates a compromise between Green and Red wishes regarding terraforming, and makes a trip back to Earth in order to mediate the relationship between the colony and the "mother" planet. It is as though, having realized that science is inherently political, he also sees that he must use his science politically.

The third incident occurs when Sax, exploring the botany of the Martian landscape, becomes separated from his vehicle in a white-out (snow-storms being one of the results of his own terraforming project), and is rescued from death (and his vision of whiteness, of "pure" objective science) by the brief emergence of Hiroko, who has been presumed dead or in hiding. After this surreal, perhaps hallucinated, encounter with life-saving Green within a deathly white landscape, Sax experiences a surge of optimism; he feels as he felt when recovering from his brain damage, "as if sections of his brain were actively growing — the limbic system, perhaps, the home of the emotions, linking up with the cerebral cortex at last" (*Blue* 79). Later, watching a number of "[s]mall white rodents, sniffing around on the green of a sunken meadow," he interprets the scene symbolically as the release of the hundred lab-rats making up his brain: "Sax's mind, now free and scattered" (*Blue* 700). Scientist and Mystic, white and green, begin to merge in Sax, symbolizing the movement from a reductionist, ultra-rationalist science to one which appreciates "the peculiar symbolic logic of the limbic system" (*Blue* 49).

Utopian Chromodynamics

Science, then, is an integral component of Robinson's utopian vision in the Mars trilogy, but not science as traditionally conceived and practiced. Robinson's utopian science requires the openness to the "other" advocated by Michel, and the political self-awareness eventually realized by Sax. Sax's pre-conversion conception of the scientific conference as utopia is destroyed when he recognizes the ubiquity of political motives and perspectives. Yet even if this were not the case, Robinson suggests — even if a pure white "continent/planet for science" were possible — this would not constitute utopia. According to Arkady Bogdanov, the socialist activist who combusts towards the end of *Red Mars*, a scientific research station "'is actually a little model of prehistoric utopia, carved out of the transnational money economy by clever primates who want to live well'" (*Red* 402). Because this utopia is an island of order which feeds off the chaos of the surrounding dystopia of twenty-first-century Earth, it doesn't represent "'a true utopia'" (*Red* 403). For this reason, Arkady urges his colleagues to remake Martian society: "We are the first Martian colonists! We are *scientists*! It's our *job* to think things new, to make them new!" (*Red* 81; original emphasis). By the beginning of *Blue Mars*, Sax has taken up his catch-cry, urging Ann to "take history by the arm and break it — *make it*. Make it new" (34; original emphasis).

Arkady's view echoes feminist calls for a "successor science." Can Sax's conversion to Michel's way of seeing suggest the possibility of this new kind of science, a science which would temper its urge to explore with an appreciation of value and a need to "fuse with the object of knowledge," to use Michel's phrase quoted above? This wording is certainly closely aligned with the kind of science that Evelyn Fox Keller describes in her biography of the cytogeneticist and Nobel Laureate Barbara McClintock, in which McClintock suggests that the scientist must achieve "'a feeling for the organism.'" This corresponds to "[a] deep reverence for nature, a capacity for union with that which is to be known," attributes which "reflect a different image of science from that of a purely rational enterprise" (Keller 201). McClintock's science is one which insists on an openness before the material of study, a willingness to "'hear what the material has to say'" (198); an acceptance of its "otherness." This reverence is akin to a "form of mysticism — a commitment to the unity of experience, the oneness of nature, the fundamental mystery underlying the laws of nature." According to Keller, rationalism and mysticism — the white and the green — both underpin scientific history and practice (201).

The physicist Sax, originally the model of the ultra-rationalist, unemotional, masculinist scientist, ironically emerges in *Blue Mars* with a "feeling for the organism." He learns to practice the kind of science which values its objects' own separate existence as well as the acquisition of knowledge about these objects. In this sense, he not only merges his "white" with Hiroko's "green" — her mystical appreciation of all life — but also with Ann's "red" — her appreciation of the otherness of all objects, living and dead. It is only fitting that these two aged enemies, Ann and Sax, should become lovers by the end of the trilogy, each publicly expressing the other's original political viewpoint, both living "[o]n a brown Mars of some new kind, red, green, blue, all swirled together," both learning how to experience "life with the other" (*Blue* 779, 735). Robinson's wording here — "the other" rather than "each other" — is telling. Sax's conversion represents not only a personal reconciliation with Ann, but also a move towards a science which refuses the colonial and patriarchal impulse to naturalize and objectify the other.

This merging of colors does not, of course, automatically guarantee a harmonic solution to the trilogy's myriad political and ideological conflicts. The point of Robinson's chromodynamics is that it produces a dynamic, not a static, union. Discussing the brownish color which results from a red-green mix, unnamable on Sax's color chart, Jameson suggests that

> we should not exaggerate the narrative temptation to reconcile these positions in some final, ideological "happy ending": it is true that something analogous is acted out on [the] symbolic level of

color.[...] But the name for this unnameable color is Utopia, which stares insistently back at us from the Mars trilogy just as it does at Sax. The utopian text is not supposed to produce this synthesis all by itself, or to represent it: that is a matter for human history and for collective praxis. It is supposed only to produce the requirement of the synthesis, to open the space into which it is to be imagined [224–25].

The trilogy itself warns against easy harmonies: late in *Blue Mars*, Sax and Maya meet regularly to watch the sunset, using the color chart to find (or if necessary create) names for the various combinations of colors they see. While the scientific chart insists that red and green "'cannot be perceived simultaneously as components of the same color,'" Maya's artist's color wheel provides names for red-green mixes. Maya notes, however, that politically the union of red and green has occurred only in order to produce another opposition, the Reds joining with the Green "Free Mars" party to form an anti-immigration coalition, a united attempt to prevent further immigration from the increasingly crowded Earth. This action, Maya predicts, will lead to war on an interplanetary scale. Ironically, when Maya and Sax at last see a pure, immediately identifiable color, it is "blue, sky blue, Terran sky blue" (*Blue* 672–3). The utopian vision returns the colonists to their center and origin, Earth. It seems that history is not so easy to escape: the possibilities for conflict and peace in the solar system merely repeat the possibilities on Earth; or more optimistically, the possibilities represented by Robinson's narrative of Mars in the future are possibilities achievable in the here and now.

Thus, while Robinson's chromodynamics point to a possible utopian synthesis — of objective and subjective, science and literature, rationality and mysticism, habitation and conservation, unity and "otherness" — it is not an easy synthesis. The reader is unsure just what kind of science will be politically responsible, will abjure the patriarchal and colonialist discourse and practice which have marked it since the Renaissance. Robinson is no more able to describe in detail the nature of his "successor science" than is Harding or Keller. What he can and does do is make his readers experience different kinds of science, and more broadly knowledge systems, on the level of symbolism, of tropes of color, and also in the actual reading process. The long, painstaking descriptions of the physical world, presented alternately with equally painstaking descriptions of socio-political conflicts and negotiations themselves, represent a dialectical process, an attempt to rethink the "othering" of literature, and more broadly of "soft" or subjective knowledge, through which science initially defined itself. Gribbin, in his description of Robinson's novels as "all science and no fiction" reveals the same blinkered vision as Aldiss when he insists that Mars remain a pure white "planet for science." The Mars trilogy represents a utopian escape, not from Earth, but from this monochrome vision.

NOTES

1. These include, in addition to those publications mentioned in the text, popularizations such as John Brandenburg and Monica Paxson's *Dead Mars, Dying Earth* and Robert Zubrin and Richard Wagner's *The Case for Mars: The Plan to Settle the Red Planet and Why We Must*, and novels such as Jack Williamson's *Beachhead*, Frederick Pohl's *Mining the Oort*, Greg Bear's *Moving Mars*, Ben Bova's *Mars* and *Return to Mars*, scientist-popularizer William Hartmann's *Mars Underground*, Gregory Benford's *The Martian Race* and Larry Niven's *Rainbow Mars*.

2. *White Mars* appears to have been written at least in part as a response to the Mars trilogy, as Aldiss inscribes Robinson's name into his planet ("K. S. Robinson Avenue" [75]) in the same way that Robinson acknowledges his own forebears.

3. I am indebted here to Robert Markley, whose discussion of Sax's "emergence as a symbol and practitioner of a science committed to the ethical imperatives of viriditas and eco-economics" led me to focus on this aspect of the trilogy (790).

4. This is true of the group of hadrons termed "baryons"; a second group, termed "mesons," consist of two quarks. In a meson, a quark of a particular color is combined with an anti-quark, which carries the relevant anti-color (e.g., a "blue" quark will combine with an "anti-blue" anti-quark), again to form "white."

5. In the Mars trilogy, Robinson continually draws comparisons between the landscape and conditions in the Antarctic (particularly the Dry Valleys) and those of Mars. There is not space enough here to discuss *Antarctica*, but even a casual reading will reveal the extent to which this novel explores the recurring issues of the trilogy: the interconnectedness of science and colonialism, and the possibility of a utopian solution based on a merging of science and mysticism. See Leane, "*Antarctica* as a Scientific Utopia," for a more detailed analysis of these issues.

WORKS CITED

Albanese, Denise. *New Science, New World*. Durham, NC: Duke University Press, 1996.
Aldiss, Brian, with Roger Penrose. *White Mars or, The Mind Set Free: A 21st-Century Utopia*. London: Little, Brown, 1999.
Bear, Greg. *Moving Mars*. New York: Tor-St Martins, 1994.
Benford, Gregory. *The Martian Race*. New York: Warner, 1999.
Bova, Ben. *Mars*. London: Bantam, 1992.
_____. *Return to Mars*. New York: Eos-HarperCollins, 1999.
Brandenburg, John E., and Monica Rix Paxson. *Dead Mars, Dying Earth*. Shaftesbury, Dorset: Element, 1999.
Conrad, Joseph. *Heart of Darkness*. 1902. London: Penguin, 1988.
Gribbin, John. "Prizes for the Imagination." Review of *Red Mars*, by Kim Stanley Robinson, and other titles. *New Scientist* 13 March 1993: 47.
Harding, Sandra. *The Science Question in Feminism*. Ithaca: Cornell University Press, 1990.
Hartmann, William. *Mars Underground*. New York: Tor-St. Martins, 1997.
Jacobus, Mary, Evelyn Fox Keller, and Sally Shuttleworth, eds. "Introduction." *Body/Politics: Women and the Discourses of Science*. New York: Routledge, 1990. 1–10.
Jameson, Fredric. "'If I Find One Good City I Will Spare the Man': Realism and Utopia in Kim Stanley Robinson's Mars Trilogy." *Learning from Other Worlds: Estrangement and Cognition in Science Fiction and Utopian Literature*. Liverpool Science Fiction Texts and Studies 17. Ed. Patrick Parrinder. Liverpool: Liverpool University Press, 2000. 208–32.
Keller, Evelyn Fox. *A Feeling for the Organism: The Life and Work of Barbara McClintock*. New York: W.H. Freeman, 1983.
Leane, Elizabeth. "*Antarctica* as a Scientific Utopia." *Foundation : The International Review of Science Fiction* 32.3 (Autumn 2003): 27–35.
Mackey, David. *In the Wake of Cook: Exploration, Science and Empire, 1780–1801*. Wellington, NZ: Victoria University Press, 1985.
Markley, Robert. "Falling Into Theory: Simulation, Terraformation, and Eco-Economics in Kim Stanley Robinson's Martian Trilogy." *Modern Fiction Studies* 43.3 (1997): 773–99.
Mies, Maria, and Vandana Shiva. *Ecofeminism*. Halifax, Nova Scotia: Fernwood, 1993.
Niven, Larry. *Rainbow Mars*. New York: St Martins, 1999.
Palladino, Paolo, and Michael Worboys. "Science and Imperialism." *Isis* 84 (1993): 91–102.
Pohl, Frederick. *Mining the Oort*. New York: Del Rey, 1992.
Robinson, Kim Stanley. *Antarctica*. London: HarperCollins, 1998.
_____. *Blue Mars*. London: HarperCollins, 1996.
_____. *Green Mars*. London: HarperCollins, 1996.
_____. *Red Mars*. London: HarperCollins, 1993.
Walter, Malcolm. *The Search for Life on Mars*. St Leonards, NSW: Allen and Unwin, 1999.
Williamson, Jack. *Beachhead*. New York: Tor-St Martins, 1992.
Zubrin, Robert, with Richard Wagner. *The Case for Mars: The Plan to Settle the Red Planet and Why We Must*. New York, Free Press, 1996.

10

The Theoretical Foundation of Utopian Radical Democracy in *Blue Mars**
William J. Burling

One of the more promising literary utopias in recent years to offer a close and careful reconsideration of how the democratic political process might be redefined and thus revitalized is Kim Stanley Robinson's Mars trilogy. Robinson depicts in detail the establishment and development of what becomes a clear alternative to Earth's political and environmental quagmire, as the ever-increasing population of Martian colonists slowly formulates a radically new and empowering sense of politics. His extensive attention to the political process I read as something much more significant, however, than a mere literary fantasy, being rather a genuine contribution to the problem of democratic struggle in our time and place. In his many interviews Robinson has regularly made statements such as, "I consider my books to be a political work.... There's got to be a utopian strand, there's gotta be positive stories. You can criticize over and over again, but it also helps to have some vision of what should happen" (Smith). In particular the Mars trilogy is Robinson's attempt to comment on present-day Terran challenges. This thematic objective is stated by the character Ann Clayborne while visiting Earth in the third and concluding segment, *Blue Mars*: the Martian experiment was "a chance here to make something different. That was the whole point" (23). The point is reemphasized by Nadia's comment that the Martian government could well be employed as a role model for Terrans because it is "a small-scale model. Easier to understand" (148).

Despite Fredric Jameson's remark that the trilogy "will surely be the great political novel of the 1990s" (*The Seeds of Time* 65), however, Robinson's Martian political model has attracted little critical attention.[1] Phillip E. Wegner, for example, while asserting recently that Robinson has created an "important new utopian trilogy" (Wegner xx), offers no commentary, nor has Tom Moylan gone beyond applauding in general terms "Robinson's masterwork, the Martian trilogy" (*Scraps of the Untainted Sky* 320 n2). Shaun Huston, in a passing comment, suggests that Robinson's political model may be indebted to the work of Murray Bookchin, but presents no details (177).[2] A more detailed explication is Carol Franko's general theoretical meditation on the Martian political process in the first two-thirds of the trilogy (the concluding part had not yet appeared at the time of her essay), especially as it contributes to "the theme

---

*First published as "The Theoretical Foundation of Utopian Radical Democracy in Kim Stanley Robinson's *Blue Mars*." *Utopian Studies* 16 (2005): 75–96. Reprinted by permission of *Utopian Studies*.

of utopian destiny" (64). While her discussion certainly illuminates some dimensions of the polyphonic nature of the political process present in the first two volumes, Franko's application of Bahktin's notions of dialogism, polyphony, and carnival cannot be extended to the final volume of the trilogy, nor would such a methodology elucidate Robinson's precisely articulated Martian political vision. Perhaps the most useful commentary is provided by Jameson, who clarifies how "all of the scientific problems described in the novel, without exception, offer an allegory, by way of the form of overdetermination, of social, political and historical problems" ("If I Find One Good City I Will Spare the Man" 210–11). While his reading of the opposition between the actants of Hiroko as "virtual (Mars) goddess" and Ann as "political symbol (and a virtual allegory)" (222) goes far toward revealing the dialectical "political preoccupation of the work" (227), he specifically identifies only minimal elements from Ernest Callenbach's *Ecotopia* as possible parallels to Robinson's political vision (223), and names no other theorists.[3]

As we will see, *Blue Mars* visualizes in concrete fashion a political process that bears numerous affinities to the theoretical model of Ernesto Laclau and Chantal Mouffe as outlined in *Hegemony and Socialist Strategy: Towards a Radical Democratic Politics* (1985; hereafter *HSS*). The "radical democracy" advocated by Laclau and Mouffe finds its inspiration, of course, in Antonio Gramsci's concept of hegemony, but they extensively revise and extend Gramsci's insights. Drawing upon many theorists, but most notably the critiques of language, subjectivity, and historicity by Wittgenstein, Derrida, and Foucault, *HSS* differs considerably from previous Marxist theories of political process in redefining the "struggle" for freedom. While remaining faithful to a "socialist dimension, as it is necessary to put an end to capitalist relations of production, which are at the root of numerous relations of subordination," Laclau and Mouffe argue that "socialism is *one* of the components of a project for radical democracy, not vice versa" (178). This statement only begins to suggest the radical nature of their views. In a series of bold reassessments, they jettison several of the most foundational elements of classical Marxist thought, including the centrality of the "proletariat," the inevitability of the collapse of capitalism and the triumph of the socialist cause, and even the very notion of "scientific Marxism" itself.[4] The result is, they assert, "a form of politics which is founded not upon the dogmatic postulation of any 'essence of the social,' but, on the contrary, on affirmation of the contingency and ambiguity of every 'essence,' and on the constitutive character of social division and antagonism" (193). In short, they argue that a political process liberated from teleological assumptions allows, *even enables*, socialistic struggle to advance, and that the *process itself* can be one of the most empowering dimensions of a truly radical democracy.

The following essay seeks, therefore, to explore the striking affinities between the "radical politics" of *HSS* and the utopian political vision of *Blue Mars*. As Robinson has "not read the Laclau and Mouffe, nor even heard of it," however, the following essay, rather than attempting to provide the usual exegesis of a fictional work, will explore instead the political thought-praxis arising from considering both texts in combination.[5] Robinson's novel, as we shall see, provides a vivid concretization of Laclau and Mouffe's political theory while *HSS*, in turn, offers a means by which to understand and evaluate Robinson's utopian political experiment.

The Arena of Political Struggle

Blue Mars is quite specific as to the nature of the particular political situation in its opening pages. While the novel begins with a violent revolution which results in the expelling of Earth's UN paramilitary forces from nearly all of Mars and the creation of an opportunity for what all Martians hope will be complete Martian self-rule, this is no "typical" revolutionary situation like those of 1789 or 1917. The Martians have experienced a long history of progressive democratic process and have always enjoyed significant though not exclusive autonomy, and many of the colonists retain considerable sympathies for Earth despite the differences that led to the insurgence. The Martians, therefore, have not thrown off a tyrannical system of rule, but rather have responded to what they see as undue excesses on the part of the powerful Terran meta-national corporations that attempt to impose their will in insensitive and inappropriate ways.

Following their victory and liberation, the Martians have before them an absolute *tabula rasa*, but where anything is possible, everything is also potentially problematical. The two most important matters concern how to begin the process of establishing a system of government, and how to bridge a fundamental and apparently irreconcilable internal political rift. While many entities seek to promote their various agendas, the political situation is dominated by two groups. On the one side are the minority "Reds," who wish to severely limit or even to outlaw further colonization and to preserve unchanged the primordial Martian environment; on the other are the majority "Greens," who advocate regular but limited immigration from Earth and terra-forming of the planet to produce an environment hospitable to human inhabitation. A fragile and time-sensitive detente in the immediate aftermath of the revolution is thus the situation represented in the meeting of the congressional delegates in Part 3 entitled "A New Constitution," which I shall examine in some detail as it embodies most clearly many of the same points as presented in *HSS*.

This lengthy "constitutional congress" section depicts in detail the slow, laborious, and stressful hammering out of a process for discussion and then creating a constitution for Mars, and in so doing strikingly parallels two of the procedural fundamentals argued in *HSS*. The first is the precise classification of the political struggle itself. Laclau and Mouffe identify two types of struggles, the *popular* and the *democratic*. The "popular struggle" concerns the overthrow of an oppressive regime to promote political progress, is always and only two-sided, and involves the clash between two utterly irreconcilable groups, such that the creation of a unified society by negotiations between the opposing groups is impossible (e.g., the French Revolution). By contrast the "democratic struggle" arises only in advanced, capitalistic societies where a "variety of possible antagonisms" exists, many "in opposition to each other" (131), but in which the cause of freedom may be advanced through "a plurality of political spaces" (*HSS* 137). The Martians, in short, while they no longer have to answer to a tyrannical master (i.e., the popular struggle, such as it was, is concluded), must identify and root out the resilient mechanisms of oppression which threaten to replicate themselves in the new social order. And yet another set of problems must be solved, for social relations "do not answer to any single causal principle or logic of inconsistency" (103). On Robinson's Mars, the situation cannot be characterized as Earth versus Mars or any other simple binary opposition, and thus is *not a popular struggle but clearly a democratic one*. This essential assessment of the political situation is made clear by the identities of the many delegates to the "working session" that is convened to propose a model government. Literally scores of parties, groups, and population areas are represented, even to the point of including representatives from what one might presume to be the "enemy," i.e., Earth (*Blue Mars* 120–21), a point which has considerable significance and will be discussed in the next section.

In their general overview of the "democratic struggle," Laclau and Mouffe abandon two of the central tenets of the Marxist analysis that are mirrored in *Blue Mars*: the centrality of proletarian class struggle and the inevitability of the collapse of capitalism. On Robinson's

Mars literally dozens of subject groups, ranging from a few tens of people to many thousands, have long been pursuing widely diverging forms of religious, social, economic, and political arrangements, such as Bogdanovists, Bedouins, Christians, Muslims, Buddhists, Feminists, Eco-poets, communists, socialists, capitalists, and so on.[6] The subject identities and types of struggle are so multifarious (gender, environment, race, and so on) that proletarian "class" interests command no priority, instead being represented as one among many identities in the general process of democratic struggle. And as for the theoretical assumption of the collapse of capitalism due to its internal operating contradictions, Robinson intentionally complicates the situation. At the constitutional congress the "economic problem" looms over the entire process, and not until the matter is resolved by active debate and democratic political process is a peculiarly Martian system of "eco-economics" given birth. Hence capitalism did not in any sense collapse due to *economic* dynamics but was replaced via the *political process* (see next section). Without question, therefore, Robinson has depicted a terrain of *democratic struggle* which closely mirrors that delineated in *HSS*.

The Political Process

Though his depiction may be seen as a simple literary trick, a kind of naive leap of faith calling for a willing suspension of disbelief in assuming that such numerous and disparate parties will actually agree to sit down together, in fact Robinson shares one of the major premises of *HSS*. Laclau and Mouffe state that the political process is made possible by the agreement of the parties (i.e., in *Blue Mars* those attending the constitutional congress) to a *referential framework* (*HSS* 134), meaning a provisional set of shared beliefs. Laclau and Mouffe also insist on the proper understanding of what constitutes *identities*. These factors, once in place, generate the possibility of the political process, which they term the *field of discursivity*. This, when successful, results in an *articulation of antagonisms* leading to a *hegemonic formation*.

One of the crucial points required to grasp the novelty of the political process stressed in *HSS* concerns the definitions of the identities of both the whole group as such and the individual citizen. Indeed, without much exaggeration the case could be made that one of the central projects of modernity itself from Descartes forward has been the elucidation of new definitions of identity for both collective groups of citizens and the individual subject. The collective whole of the residents on Mars we would ordinarily think of as "Martian society," but Laclau and Mouffe propose the radical idea that *society* "is not a valid subject of discourse. There is no single underlying principle fixing—and hence constituting—the whole field of differences" (*HSS* 111). Thus all attempts to debate or determine "society's interests" are doomed to failure, because any given definition of a social body is nothing less than an incomplete, metaphorical construction: "the mere idea of a centre of the social has no meaning at all" (139). Therefore any notion of final, fixed social unity, which Laclau and Mouffe (via Lacan) term a *suture* (88n1), can never be achieved (cf. 111). We should not despair over the impossibility of suture, however, because "social division," though inherent in politics, actually provides "the very possibility of a democratic politics" (xiv). They propose, instead of "society," to use the term *social formation* to describe the collective population.

Likewise, the construction of the individual "subject" has been one of the most difficult yet important challenges in philosophical and political studies, for without some sense of individual identity, no gesture can be made toward establishing the individual's relationship with the larger social formation. To this end Laclau and Mouffe term the citizen the *agent*, who is, they argue, "ambiguous, incomplete, and polysemical" (121). The agent holds non-articulated positions termed *elements*, which are in flux and thus changeable.

In addition Laclau and Mouffe argue that the field of discursivity as political process is based upon "part of what Wittgenstein calls language game, which is an example of what we have called discourse" (108). By *elements* is meant the subject positions advocated by the agents, and Laclau and Mouffe are careful to emphasize that no element can "consolidate itself as a *separate position*" (122). This fundamental fluidity of agendas and positions "makes hegemonic articulation possible" (122), due to the fact that no party can claim absolute ownership or defining control of the resulting nodal points. Stanley Aronowitz describes this condition as "a micro-politics of autonomous oppositional movements, whether derived from production relations or not" (qtd. in Moylan, *Demand the Impossible* 208). Thus Laclau and Mouffe argue that because *nothing is fixed*, neither the positions of subjects nor their identities nor even any particular interests of society at large, then the political process as a field of discourse is enabled.

In *Blue Mars* the requirement of the "referential framework" is specifically emphasized by Robinson and consists of the acknowledgment by all parties of a pre-existing "master list of fundamental individual rights" (129). This master list had been steadily evolving since the days of the first colonists, is recognized by the delegates as specifically Martian, and includes categories in addition to the political. Despite the fact that "the exact nature of these rights was still a matter of controversy":

> the so-called political rights were generally agreed to be "self-evident"— things citizens were free to do, things governments were forbidden to do — habeas corpus, freedom of movement, of speech, of association, of religion, a ban on weapons — all these were approved by a vast majority of Martian natives... [129].

This master list is significant for what Robinson establishes as the groundwork from which the discussions can begin, and we shall return to this aspect below. Also of note is the fact that the citizens had already undergone a dress rehearsal for the congressional session in the creation of the Dorsa Brevia document, a kind of Martian political manifesto, produced many years earlier during a previous period of democratic struggle (*Green Mars*, Part 7, "What Is to Be Done?"). Thus the Martians had a referential framework already at hand which served them well in their time of need.

Also corresponding in *Blue Mars* to the requirements presented in *HSS* is the very fact of the wide range of participants, i.e., the heterogeneous social formation. Robinson represents numerous diverse and conflicting positions, the existence of which confounds any possibility of complete agreement on all points. Moreover, the various individuals (agents) on Mars have always co-existed in a condition of extensive and constant diversity and development in all arenas of social interaction. In other words, they are used to the idea of multiple perspectives, and genuinely respect the existence of such views. To this end the leadership decided early on that "we might as well be inclusive" by inviting to the congressional congress a representative from "any Martian group, as long as the group had had some tangible existence before the conference began" (119). Further, any who felt themselves excluded could petition to a committee "which allowed almost all petitioners to join" (120). These citizens were more prepared than any before them in human history: for twelve m-years (24 Earth years) they had been "working up plans for a government, in anticipation of a successful revolution," as demonstrated by the fact that the schools and the university "had taught courses in the matter" (120). The Martians are able and willing to engage in an utterly new kind of political process, which closely parallels Laclau and Mouffe's notion of the broad field of discursivity. In short, on Mars the citizens have the opportunity and the means to advocate for their own positions in a context of relative respect. This situation, though far from free of problems, nevertheless represents the possibilities of the radical democratic process as a site for personal and group empowerment.

Expectations and Outcomes

The third point specified in *HSS* and flowing logically from its premises is, nevertheless, one of its most radical components, namely, "the impossibility of an ultimate fixity of meaning" (112). Laclau and Mouffe, in clear distinction to many Marxist analysts, deny the existence of any inevitable historical destiny; rather, humanity must create new possibilities through struggle, and the results cannot be predicted. Thus there can be no privileged, *a priori* political goals. The best that can be hoped for, and such an accomplishment would be considerable, is a successful articulation of antagonisms resulting in "*the construction of nodal points which partially fix meaning*" (113). The establishing of a provisional *hegemony* therefore becomes the only possible goal and measure of political success and social agreement simply because the relationships and the identities of the antagonists and their differential elements are forever "incomplete and pierced by contingency" (110). Critics such as Alain Badiou argue that Laclau and Mouffe's insistence on indeterminate contingency is simply "feeble idealism, and a veritable renunciation of politics as independent thought-praxis" (115). Badiou's view minimizes or even overlooks, however, their core premises that *material interests are crucial* (109) and that "the separation between the economic and the political is hereby *eliminated*" by their project (120).[7] To summarize: in *HSS* the political struggle is *co-identical* with the economic, but successful political outcomes, in their view, are incomplete, contingent, and forever open to further articulation.

For Robinson, these elements of non-fixity, non-essentialism, and contingency reside at the center of the Martian political process. During the Martian constitutional congress, "everything was on the table" (*Blue Mars* 148) as they struggled with "turmoil ... and a barely contained confusion" (126), but everyone recognized that the moment was without precedent: "No — the truth was, they were in a new situation. There was no historical analogy that would be of much help to them now" (131). As for the enormous rift between Reds and Greens that had nearly caused civil war and that threatened to disrupt the congress, at last "the impasse was broken, or at least finessed" (156) by a series of concessions, appointments, and "grand gestures," in short, by a democratic articulation of antagonisms. The constitution resulting from this process was presented to and ratified by the population (158). The resulting hegemony, to employ Laclau and Mouffe's terminology, may be characterized as "nodal points which partially fix the meaning of the social in an organized system of differences" (*HSS* 135). We are left with the clear sense that the Martian constitution is not an ending but a beginning, a point reiterated as a thematic reminder near the conclusion of the novel: "*The negotiations would go on for years. Like a choir in counterpoint, singing a great fugue*" (*Blue Mars* 746).

The Shape of Radical Martian Democracy

We have seen how the dynamics of Robinson's Martian congress generally resemble the process described by Laclau and Mouffe. What remains is a consideration of some of the key components of Robinson's political program, and I operate from the premise that any utopian representation constitutes a special kind of literary endeavor wishing to contribute to the debate over the future of humanity, and thus willingly invites evaluation. Indeed, the whole project of this particular type of novel, which Moylan identifies as the *critical utopia*, is to "refer to something other than a predictable alternative paradigm, for at their core they [critical utopias] identify self-critical utopian discourse itself as a process that can tear apart the dominant ideological web" (*Demand the Impossible* 213). Thus, both Robinson's *Blue Mars* and Laclau and Mouffe's *HSS* promote the utopian, radical, democratic political project in at least four ways: the proliferation of political spaces; an insistence on necessary changes in the economic realm; the depoliticization of fundamental governmental processes and decisions; and the creation of a new "common sense" grounded on the twin premises that monetary profit is not the most important dimension of life and that individual rights can be defined and maintained only in the context of collective social relations.

First, Robinson's text resonates deeply with one of the key summary dicta of *HSS*: "The multiplication of political spaces and the preventing of concentration of power in one point are, then, preconditions of every truly democratic transformation of society" (*HSS* 178). We find that from the beginning of *Blue Mars* this enlargement of spaces is specifically designated indeed even named as such in a comment by the Red leader Clayborne, as having an important touchstone character: "Everything that increases the space within which we can create a new society is a good thing. Everything that reduces our space is a bad thing. Think about it!" (*Blue Mars* 23). Thus Clayborne's insistence must be read as a manifesto for the necessity of spaces for all positions.

The overall political culture of Mars seeks to balance the respective spheres of the state and citizen in a very proactive fashion so as to prevent the concentration of power in the state without completely enfeebling it. On this point we learn that Mars will not be divided into nations or states, but rather construct itself as a planet-wide political body that attempts to balance the interests and needs of the many semi-autonomous, tented city-states (the atmosphere is still not breathable at this point, though it does become so later). The problem is classic: "Too much [power for the central government] and it was back to a big centralized state," but, as Jackie Boone, a key character, points out, "too little ... [power] and there could be tents out there deciding slavery is okay, or female genital mutilation is okay, or any other crime based on Terran barbarism is okay" (128). The complete details of the solution are too extensive to examine here but comprise, as Robinson tells us, "an emphasis on local semi-autonomy," with "many checks against majoritarian rule," including a weak presidency and central government (154). The most powerful component in the governmental framework, surprisingly, is the judiciary, in particular the "Environmental Court," which eventually emerges as the single most important entity.

Second, as Laclau and Mouffe specify, democratic struggle presupposes necessary changes in the economic realm, as addressed in their insistence that "every project for radical democracy implies a socialist dimension, as it is necessary to put an end to capitalist relations of production, which are at the root of numerous relations of subordination." But they go on to surprise the reader by enlarging the issue: "this cannot mean only workers' self-management, as what is at stake is true participation by all subjects in decisions about what is to be produced ... [especially] ecological demands or demands by other groups which, without being producers, are affected by the decisions taken in the field of production" (*HSS* 178). In *Blue Mars* Robinson attends to these very aspects of relations of production, especially worker empowerment, and modifies the issues inherent in the "field of production" problem in light of Mars' fragile environment, such that "ecological demands" assume highest precedence. The most significant of these numerous economic issues as stressed in *HSS* is similarly articulated by Robinson at length throughout *Blue Mars* and ultimately "solved" by his presentation of a new form of "eco-economics."

In this depiction of a society that could "provide for everyone in an equitable way" (64), Robinson goes to considerable lengths to establish why capitalism must be severely refashioned to the point of being essentially unrecognizable. One major area concerns the impact of relations of subordination in capitalism on subject identity. Appropriately, the chief character in this regard in *Blue Mars* is Michel Duval, the psychotherapist, who frequently expostulates on a variety of identity implications, especially the damaging effects resulting from the interplay of capitalism and patriarchy. Duval deconstructs for fellow original pioneer Sax Russell the pernicious and oppressive operations of capital that destroy people's personal lives and family relations, creating a social condition that is "illogical, and even stupid. Brutal and stupid." What is needed, Duval offers, is "a shift back to the maternal ... to some kind of post-oedipal reintegration with nature, which we are still in the process of reinventing" (54). The effect of the capitalistic relations of production on subjectivity soon thereafter becomes one of the chief concerns addressed by the Martian political process.

The problem of reorganizing the relations of production are, of course, staggering, but Robinson does not avoid the challenge. The congressional discussions put off, perhaps even intentionally, any direct confrontation with the "problem" of the economy until it can no longer be avoided, and then it surfaces just when "in all the squabbling it was very hard to see any signs of growing accord" whatsoever (141). Instead of exploding the congress, however, the hardest of all the problems, the economic, becomes the catalyst which enables the successful creation of the new Martian world order.

In the process of showing how the Martians reach their decision, Robinson does not simply leap to consensus for a new economic order. He carefully shows how the justifications for the continuation of capitalism are flawed in two fundamental ways: the illusion of democracy in the work place and the disproportionate ownership of wealth. The relevant section in the novel consists of a debate between the characters of Antar, the pro-capitalist, and Vlad, the eco-economist. Antar begins with the assumption held by some Martian parties that the economic system, of course, will remain capitalistic. He then urges the creation of an utterly laissez-faire form of government, stressing the traditional libertarian view that the "real problem of society" is the meddling interference of an overbearing and restrictive government. This bedrock argument corresponds to the "negative" school of political theory identified in *HSS* (17273), in which government is *always* a problem, such that the smallest and weakest form is always preferable.

Vlad steps forward to obliterate Antar's case, first demystifying the exploitative dimensions of so-called freedom under libertarian capitalism. In a final emotional flourish, reminiscent of the voice of the speaker in Samuel Johnson's "The Vanity of Human Wishes," who cuts short the apparently endless false arguments for earthly happiness by sharply declaring "Enquirer, cease" (Johnson 92), Vlad cuts to the chase: "No! The system called capitalist democracy was not really democratic at all.... So. We must change. It is time. If self-rule is a fundamental value, if simple justice is a value, then they are valuable everywhere, including in the workplace where we spend so much of our lives" (*Blue Mars* 14344).

The second thrust of Vlad's remarks demolishes Antar's belief in the axiomatic notion that the capitalist owners of the means of production deserve their profits because they take all the risks. Vlad once again strikes to the heart of the matter by critiquing the essential structure of capitalism as "a version of feudalism in which capital replaces land, and business leaders replace kings" such that "five percent of the population owned ninety-five percent of the wealth" (143). Moving quickly as a result of this moment of absolute demystification and clarity, the Martians agree to embrace Vlad and Marina's socialistic system of "eco-economics" (141), the effect of which "will be democratic in a way capitalism never even tried to be" (144). In other words, Vlad proposes a new form of radical democracy where, as Laclau and Mouffe also argue (120), the political and the economic are no longer falsely understood as separate spheres of activity.

The great debate does raise, however, an important difference between the theoretical basis of Vlad's analysis of capitalism and that assumed by Laclau and Mouffe. Vlad's interpretation affirms Marx's theoretical model for understanding capitalism as an historical phenomenon with a knowable logic, points vigorously denied in *HSS*. Laclau and Mouffe argue, in their absolute theoretical demand for contingency, that "the life of society is ever more complex than the morphological categories of Marxist discourse" (26). Their view, therefore, that "Marxist theory cannot ... be thinkable only within a closed model" (27), is apparently not shared by Robinson.

Even in light of this important difference, Robinson's Martian "eco-economic" order addresses the main theoretical premises established by Laclau and Mouffe. For example, the means of production are returned to the workers: "all economic enterprises are to be small cooperatives, owned by the workers and no one else" (*Blue Mars* 144). The establishment of smaller worker-owned enterprises is not a return, however, to the pre-industrial cottage workshop system, for, as Raymond Williams has noted, socialism will be more complicated than capitalism, not simpler (cf. Jameson, *Postmodernism, or, The Cultural Logic of Late Capitalism* 336). On Mars the new order becomes "a complex system, with public and private spheres of economic activity" (*Blue Mars* 145) in a newly defined market paradigm which assigns government-directed "not-for-profit status to vital life-support matters" (146), guaranteeing equal access for all citizens to "housing, health care, food, education" (145). The establishment of a non-profit segment of the economy correctly recognizes and heads off the threat of scarcities which, in and of themselves, can create conditions ripe for abuses of power. On this latter subject Robinson has also taken a lesson, perhaps, from Ursula Le Guin's *The Dispossessed*, in which the anarcho-communistic society of Anarres struggles with massive material shortages that threaten the overall stability of their order and encroach upon personal freedom. As Carl Freedman insightfully points out, Le Guin, in turn, was responding to an argument first proposed by Leon Trotsky that "material privation not only sets quantitative limits to the achievements of socialism; it may qualitatively deform socialists values at their very core" (122).

The authors of *HSS* also assert that the economy must answer to all groups who are affected by production decisions including "environmental demands" (178). Their emphasis on democratically shared ecological control is strongly echoed on Mars by the creation of a new kind of judiciary. Unlike that on Earth, where only civil and criminal law is recognized, the Martian system contains a "double supreme court, one half a constitutional court, and the other half an environmental court, with members to both appointed, elected, and drawn by lottery" (154). The environmental court, of course, is "charged with overseeing the stewardship of the land, which was to belong to all Martians together ... there would not be private property as such, but there would be various tenure rights established in leasing contracts" (155). The court, in other words, would recognize and balance the needs of the social collective and the "rights" of the planet. These are only a few of the economic proposals envisioned by Robinson such that the economic system "aids us to reach the goals of more justice and more freedom" (147). And, indeed, the last paragraph of this monumental trilogy concludes with a final emphasis on and homage to the presumed success of the new economic order: "Nowhere on this world were people killing each other, nowhere were they desperate for shelter or food, nowhere were they scared for their kids" (761). In short, economic equality, Robinson argues, can produce a hitherto unknown degree of general social prosperity and stability.

Further, and despite the conventional arguments to the contrary, we see no signs of stagnation in human creativity and enterprise as a result of a socialized economy. In fact, Robinson refutes those nay-sayers who believe that humanity needs capitalistic economic competition in order to progress, and insists on quite the opposite by depicting an explosion of possibilities impossible under capitalism. The Martian eco-economic model eventually is adopted by all of humanity, creating the technological and material foundation for the colonization of the entire solar system and beyond by inspiring and enabling the ultimate human adventure and accomplishment, the first voyage to the stars, appropriately, to a Mars-like planet circling Aldebaran.

On the third point (depoliticization of government activities) Robinson's model strongly resembles the position taken in chapter 4 of *HSS* which attempts to refute the neo-conservative view that only experts can or should run a government, the effect of which "would be a depoliticization of fundamental decisions at the economic level, as well as at social and political levels" (*HSS* 173). Robinson directly addresses this issue in Charlottes response to Nadia's investigation of the problem of centralized power. She suggests that one "tactic is to deprofessionalize governing. You make some big part of the government a public obligation, like jury duty, and then draft ordinary citizens to serve for a short time. They get professional staff help, but they make the decisions themselves" (139). Charlotte also proposes decentralization of the government "because it creates lots of small minorities" and a complex set of checks and balances "so that the government's a kind of cat's cradle of competing forces." All of these strategies aim at "spreading power around to as many groups as you can" (139).

And one final point of overlap, and perhaps the most important, concerns the absolute need for "the construction of a new 'common sense'" (*HSS* 183), in that both *Blue Mars* and *HSS* attempt to theorize the crucial category of subject identity as it might develop in as yet unimagined historical and material conditions. On Robinson's Mars, in order to cut off the problems which emerge from a continuing persistence of "possessive individualism" (183), the citizenry comes utterly to support the belief that "economic rationality is simply not the highest value" (*Blue Mars* 145). This Martian requirement strongly echoes Laclau and Mouffe's contention that citizens must not align themselves entirely out of personal self-interest. Rather they must agree to the philosophy that "individual rights" are defined not "in isolation, but only in the context of social relations" (*HSS* 184). Thus one's personal "democratic rights must be understood, as ... rights which can only be exercised collectively, and which suppose the existence of equal rights for others" (184–85). The Martian constitutional congress considers at length the possible dangers of interest-bloc voting, or, as Robinson calls it, "majoritarianism," and offers several solutions, including the use of the "Australian ballot, where voters vote for two or more candidates in ranked fashion" (*Blue Mars* 139). In short, Martians learn to listen to and respect the opinions of others as a routine mode of behavior.

The "voting rights" proposal, though vitally important, is but one small part of how Robinson attempts to represent a new "common sense." Perhaps a more useful way to identify the heart of the issue is to recall Marx's observation in *Capital* that a "reign of freedom" will begin only when "the work imposed by necessity and external finality shall cease" (qtd.

in Sartre 34). At the time of the cessation of exploitative conditions of production, Sartre remarks "there will exist for *everyone* a margin of *real* freedom" resulting in the creation of "a philosophy of freedom" (34). Robinson's term for this "philosophy of freedom," one which he carefully establishes and expands throughout the entire Martian trilogy up to this point, is called *areophany*, a concept so complex and vast that it defies any simple definition, reaching as it does into many pockets of subjectivity, action, and implication. One is simply obliged to read the entire trilogy in order to perceive the overall richness and complexity of this particularized "philosophy of freedom" that represents how people will live in a world "beyond the sphere of material production proper" (Marx, *Capital*; qtd. in Sartre 34).

In this new condition of freedom, of areophany, the Martians move beyond the binary of Red or Green. As Russell and Clayborne conclude in a particularly epiphanic moment near the end of the trilogy, "Perhaps the combination should be called blue.... Brown isn't very attractive, and it reeks of compromise. Maybe we should be thinking of something entirely new" (*Blue Mars* 730). Their realization that compromise is unsatisfactory precisely mirrors the desired endpoint of Laclau and Mouffe's sense of radical democratic politics.[8] Hegemony is not a situation where merely the lowest common political denominator is achieved through compromise, but rather the forging of an entirely new type of consensus which moves through and beyond the previous status quo toward egalitarian possibilities. Establishing a hegemonic formation does not, *and must not*, require that any point essential to any agent's interests be given up or watered down. To do so would be to sacrifice the defining integrity of the agent and thus to diminish both that agent's identity and the corresponding *raison d'être* of the entire democratic process.

As these parallels strongly indicate, both Robinson and the authors of *HSS* offer proposals that form the foundation of what can well be called a utopian, democratic, radical, political vision.[9] Robinson's utopian novum, though it owes no direct debt to *HSS*, in a key sense fulfills Laclau and Mouffe's recognition of the necessity for utopian representation: "the presence of the imaginary as a set of symbolic meanings which totalize as negativity a certain social order is absolutely essential for the constitution of all left-wing thought" (*HSS* 190). Literary utopias, therefore, contribute in very real ways to the process of struggle by simply envisioning theoretical political alternatives.

Conclusion

Many detailed analyses of the possibilities for political struggle in the name of democracy stress the *goals* of such activity but do not identify or offer a *process* for political engagement. Michael Hardt and Antonio Negri in *Empire* (2000), for example, offer some suggestive areas for activism, but admit that the task, though "clear at the conceptual level, remains rather abstract. What specific and concrete practices will animate this political project? We cannot say at this point" (399–400). If political theorists cannot propose concrete political action, then can we wonder that average citizens of democratic countries feel discouraged when confronted with the perplexing realities of political struggle? Numerous challenges exist, such as the ever-expanding profit-driven interests of trans-national capitalism and the lack of a mechanism for corporate accountability at all levels. Likewise the creeping processes of commodification world-wide serve to redefine or erase meaningful personal and collective social identities and practices. And to make matters even more difficult, activists face increasingly restricted access to mass media.

Yet, as Robinson in *Blue Mars* and Laclau and Mouffe in *HSS* demonstrate, the very fact of the existence of the inherent instabilities, inconsistencies, and disagreements *even among capitalists* as to how democracy is defined and ought to operate serves to empower the agenda of those who struggle, once they fully understand the latent power residing in the essential indeterminacy of the democratic process. The curious, contradictory internal logic of capitalism demands that no outcomes can be predetermined or closed, including those of the political process itself. Jameson is certainly right to remind us that the Mars trilogy is first and foremost a literary utopia in form, and thus must be understood, therefore, "not [as] the representation of radical alternatives ... [but] simply [as] the imperative to imagine them" ("'If I Find'" 231). Therefore the *combination* of the theoretical premises of *HSS* and the literary representation of similar views in *Blue Mars*, in tandem, provide detailed, interlocking axes of radical political modeling which *concretely* strive to demonstrate how the "articulation of democratic antagonisms" could work in real historical circumstances. Thus *HSS* and *Blue Mars* provide further support to the Blochian principle of hope inherent in the struggle toward a better — but by no means guaranteed — future.

Notes

1. Hassler and Wilcox's recent *Political Science Fiction* (1997), for example, does not include any analysis of Robinson's work. The Mars trilogy may have appeared too late for inclusion, but neither are Robinson's earlier works discussed (specifically the "Orange County" trilogy) despite their considerable political content.

2. Environmental "politics" is also the focus of Eric Otto's reading of the Mars trilogy in light of Aldo Leopold's "land ethic" meditation in *A Sand-County Almanac*. See Otto, "The Mars Trilogy and the Leopoldian Land Ethic" in the present volume. Other important environmental implications are addressed by Shaun Huston, and Sherryl Vint and Mark Bould, also included in this collection.

3. Jameson also helpfully notes how many traditional utopias (e.g., those by More, Morris, Heinlein, Niven, and so on) posit "the radical separation of Utopia from historical reality," whereas Robinson's is placed within real (projected) time and retains "the persistent threat of Terran politics and intervention" ("'If I Find'" 227).

4. The longstanding, contentious, and extensive debate since the publication of their controversial theory is a subject of great interest but cannot be examined here. For a useful overview of some of the major positions, see Best and Kellner, *Postmodern Theory*, chapter 6.

5. Robinson, personal e-mail responding to my queries.

6. Four years before *HSS*, Stanley Aronowitz in *The Crisis in Historical Materialism* (1981) had outlined many of the same points for new radical political thinking from the Left that also appear in Laclau and Mouffe's study and that resonate deeply with *Blue Mars*. Moylan calls attention to and usefully summarizes the essence of Aronowitz's analysis: "The demands of this new [micro-political] block include the end to male supremacy and the emancipation of women, the autonomy of nature, the self-management of the workplace and living space, and the liberation of racial, ethnic, and linguistic groups" (*Demand the Impossible* 208). Interestingly, despite his reputation, and the fact of the close and useful agreement in *HSS* with Aronowitz's position, his work is not mentioned by Laclau and Mouffe, and neither is *HSS* mentioned by Moylan in his otherwise comprehensive *Demand the Impossible* (1986), the latter omission no doubt due to the timing of publishing overlaps. He does refer to *HSS*, however, in *Scraps of the Untainted Sky* (2000). Nevertheless, the clarity and consensus of these several studies resonate powerfully in light of Robinson's novel.

7. In answer to critics who assert that all political activity within the current democratic system is futile and even mystifying, we should bear in mind that Laclau and Mouffe's strategies for political activity not only seek to address immediate and pressing concerns and injustices, but also might serve to organize viable opposition to the current capitalistic status quo in other areas of social activity.

8. Jameson also argues that this idea of a new common sense, which he calls "change of self," is fundamental to the meaning of the Mars trilogy. His analysis focuses on Hiroko, rather than Russell, however, as the thematic binary opposite of Clayborne.

9. The Mars trilogy is not, of course, Robinson's first or only literary representation of a radically democratic political model. For an earlier and less sophisticated version, though still of considerable interest, see *Pacific Edge* (1990), the utopian third movement of his "Orange County" trilogy, where many of the sub-

themes of the Mars trilogy first appear, such as full empowerment for women and a foundational insistence on environmental awareness. As an analysis of the many thematic connections between these works is beyond the scope of the present essay, however, I will simply echo Moylan's excellent suggestion (*Scraps* 204, 320n2), that *Pacific Edge* serves as a rehearsal in schematic form of the central political issues in the Mars sequence.

WORKS CITED

Aronowitz, Stanley. *The Crisis in Historical Materialism: Class, Politics, and Culture in Marxist Theory*. New York: Praeger, 1981.
Badiou, Alain. *Ethics: An Essay on the Understanding of Evil*. Trans. Peter Hallward. New York: Verso, 2001.
Best, Steven, and Douglas Kellner. *Postmodern Theory*. New York: Guilford, 1991.
Franko, Carol. "The Density of Utopian Destiny in Robinson's *Red Mars*." *Extrapolation* 38 (1997): 5765.
Freedman, Carl. *Critical Theory and Science Fiction*. Hanover, NH: University Press of New England, 2000.
Hardt, Michael, and Antonio Negri. *Empire*. Cambridge: Harvard University Press, 2000.
Hassler, Donald, and Clyde Wilcox. *Political Science Fiction*. Columbia, SC: University of South Carolina Press, 1997.
Huston, Shaun. "Murray Bookchin on Mars! The Production of Nature in Kim Stanley Robinson's Mars Trilogy." *Lost in Space: Geographies of Science Fiction*. Ed. Rob Kitchin and James Kneale. London: Continuum, 2002. 167–79.
Jameson, Fredric. "'If I Find One Good City I Will Spare the Man': Realism and Utopia in Kim Stanley Robinsons *Mars Trilogy*." *Learning from Other Worlds: Estrangement, Cognition and the Politics of Science Fiction and Utopia. Essays in Honour of Darko Suvin*. Ed. Patrick Parrinder. Liverpool, Eng.: Liverpool University Press, 2000. 30343.
_____. *The Seeds of Time*. New York: Columbia University Press, 1994.
_____. *Postmodernism, or, The Cultural Logic of Late Capitalism*. Durham: Duke University Press, 1991.
Johnson, Samuel. *Samuel Johnson: The Complete English Poems*. Ed. J. D. Fleeman. Harmondsworth: Penguin, 1971.
Laclau, Ernesto, and Chantal Mouffe. *Hegemony and Socialist Strategy: Towards a Radical Democratic Politics*. 1985. 2nd ed. London: Verso, 2001.
Moylan, Tom. *Demand the Impossible: Science Fiction and the Utopian Imagination*. New York: Methuen, 1986.
_____. *Scraps of the Untainted Sky: Science Fiction, Utopia, Dystopia*. Boulder, CO: Westview, 2000.
Otto, Eric. "Kim Stanley Robinson's *Mars Trilogy* and the Leopoldian Land Ethic." *Utopian Studies* 14.2 (2003): 118–35.
Robinson, Kim Stanley. *Blue Mars*. New York: Bantam, 1997.
_____. *Green Mars*. New York: Bantam, 1995.
_____. *Pacific Edge*. New York: Bantam, 1990.
_____. Personal e-mail to William J. Burling. 30 June 2004.
_____. *Red Mars*. New York: Bantam Books, 1993.
Sartre, Jean-Paul. *Search for a Method*. New York: Vintage, 1968.
Smith, Jeremy. "Kim Stanley Robinson: The Ambiguous Utopian." *January Magazine* (on-line). http://www.januarymagazine.com/profiles/ksrobinson.html.
Wegner, Phillip W. *Imaginary Communities: Utopia, the Nation, and the Spatial Histories of Modernity*. Berkeley: University of California Press, 2002.

11

The Politics of the Network: The Science in the Capital Trilogy
Roger Luckhurst

Proleptic Realism

The trilogy *Forty Signs of Rain* (2004), *Fifty Degrees Below* (2005) and *Sixty Days and Counting* (2007) continually provokes the reader into asking questions about its genre status. For novels that track the tipping point of ecological disaster, where feedbacks accelerate and catastrophize climate change, there is surprisingly little catastrophe on display. The first two books delay their set-piece storms, and then mostly avoid large-scale descriptions of destruction for the intimacies of everyday survival and making-do in a small group of Washington insiders. This is not the celebratory nihilism of "the imagination of disaster" that Susan Sontag criticized. The third book resolutely refuses to culminate in either global apocalypse or triumph, ending instead as a traditional, human-scale comedy with a triple marriage. Comedy emerges not only from confounding the traditional trajectories of the disaster novel or the American apocalyptic imagination. Robinson also uses but challenges the conventions of the political conspiracy thriller, resisting what Richard Hofstadter long ago termed the "paranoid style in American politics" by allowing the democrats a victory. This series therefore refuses the dubious pleasures of the imagination of disaster, but it is not a pious ecological jeremiad either. Indeed, one suspects that some elements of the burgeoning ecocriticism movement would be suspicious of books that invested so heavily and enthusiastically in technological and bio-engineering solutions to climate change.

Readers expecting a utopian Robinson might also be flummoxed. In the past, Robinson used the trilogy form to explore utopian or at least critical dystopian possibilities in the California and Mars series. Science in the Capital does not appear to follow any trinitarian logic: no syllogism here. Rather, it tracks the same, unbroken reality, which is a recognizably contemporary America. The blank canvas of Mars is replaced by the precisely rendered topography of the institutional landscape of Washington, D.C. If there is a surviving utopian strand then it is a studiedly limited one. The radical thrust for reinvigorating the American polity comes not from the Marxian eco-economics of the Mars series, but impassioned speeches about the legacy of Abraham Lincoln or FDR's "bold and persistent experiment" of the New Deal. We are in a compromised and pragmatic utopia — if that is not a contradiction in terms — something like *The West Wing*'s alternative presidency to the neoliberal hegemony of the Clintons and Bushes.

I even wonder if this series can be called science fiction. There is a familiar notion that the acceleration of capitalism has colonized any imagination of the future, which has now been rendered as a managed market of risk assessment. In genre terms, we have a proliferation of near futures that can only intensify the destructive potentials of the present, something often identified with cyberpunk. Robinson's Mars trilogy seemed a defiance of this trend in its return to large-scale alternative future histories. Science in the Capital not only abandons this scale and alterity ambition, but gives us a recognizable contemporary America without any futuristic enhancements or extrapolated intensifications. George W. Bush is evidently in the White House in the first book and if Phil Chase's presidency takes us into the near future, it is one still hemmed in by the political forces of neoliberalism. It is "our" contemporary science and technology that has to deal with catastrophic climate change: there are no science-fictional mitigations invented in the course of 1,500 pages; they all sit inside the horizon of current scientific research. As Robinson himself has said, the series is "pretty conservative in its assumptions, and pretty realistic" (Robinson, "Chop Wood" 59).

Perhaps then we can follow Robinson and regard the series as a species of Realism, a term traditionally opposed to science fiction, but one that in fact regularly appears in commentary on Robinson. Tom Moylan's discussion of *The Gold Coast* regards it as part of a "genre-blurring" series that is both utopian and Realist to the extent that the books "do not easily go toward that better world. Rather, they linger in the terrors of the present even as they exemplify what is needed to transform it" (Moylan 199). In *The Gold Coast* leverage against complete saturation in the techno-capitalist environment of post-natural Orange County is provided by that traditional Realist resource: a history-writing that provides a genealogy of the depthless present. Jameson's dense discussion of the Mars trilogy initially emphasizes the same Realist imperative, to understand and explicate the causality of what Jameson terms, after Althusser, "complex overdetermined concrete situations" (Jameson 395). Yet Realism has been commonly considered a conservative and bourgeois art-form: the alleged ideological assumptions encoded in the very form of the "classic Realist text" were systematically dismantled by literary theory in the 1980s. Both Moylan and Jameson move Robinson quickly beyond the "traditional or *a priori* conceptions of realism" and towards allegory and utopia (Jameson 397). Science in the Capital makes this move more hesitant or difficult than ever, and where the text halts in the mimetic world of the present-day, it forms very different kind of writing from the technological sublime of Mars or the critical dystopia of *The Gold Coast*. I want to call this style *proleptic Realism*.

In one sense, it is faithful adherence to the science of climate change that restricts Robinson to very short-term projections from the empirical conditions of the immediate present. Weather is a chaotic and non-linear system, less and less predictable the longer the projections become. Predictions of the vectors and extent of climate change are, as the fourth United Nations Intergovernmental Panel on Climate Change reported in May 2007, "inherently unstable": only "scenarios i.e. internally consistent images of different futures — not predictions of the future" can be modeled (36). It is this degree of uncertainty that has consistently fuelled denials of the reality of climate change from outlier scientists, industry-funded think-tanks and the Bush administration. If part of the project of Science in the Capital is to widen and consolidate the consensus on the near-future catastrophic potential of climate change, then the novels strategically remain within a narrow range of projected models and possible mitigations in the face of political resistance from those who famously dismissed climate change as "liberal clap-trap" or "the greatest hoax ever perpetrated on the American people" (cited Mooney, 55 and 79). But it also means that the series exists in a curious transitional space between fact and fiction, accumulated evidence and future modeling, and in a contested arena where research proposals, empirical findings, market reports, science popularization, political strategy documents and science fiction can become very hard to distinguish from each other, since climate change discourse across the board must use prolepsis. Midway through the trilogy, listing increasing numbers of extreme weather anomalies, the narrator confesses: "The interactions were so complex, the feedbacks positive and negative so hard to gauge in advance, the unforeseen circumstances so potentially vast, that no one could say what would happen next to the global climate with any certainty" (*Fifty* 164).

Whilst this scientific problem is important, I want to detach Robinson's Realism from any confusion with verisimilitude (that is, mistaking Realism for being merely realistic). Instead, Robinson's new form can be considered as part of a tradition of political writing that takes Realism to be the exemplary mode for conveying the totality of a society and the underlying contradictory forces that drive its social and ecological relations. "The novel is the epic of an age in which the extensive totality of life is no longer directly given, in which the immanence of meaning in life has become a problem," the critic Georg Lukács argued (*Theory* 56). "The novel seeks, by giving form, to uncover and construct the concealed totality of life" (*Theory* 60). Lukács's defense of Realism has not offered much promise for science fiction criticism, based as it is on a reflectionist theory of representation and which laments the decline of the novel since 1848 into the decadent subjectivism of Modernism and other bastardies. Yet Robinson himself has always regarded science fiction as an inverted form of the historical novel, and if we can conceive of a proleptic Realism, a modeling of the present day tilted five minutes into the future, then Robinson can be understood to revivify some of the political ambitions of the form in two key ways. First, Science in the Capital aims to describe if not a complete social totality then at the very least a complex matrix of institutional forces that lie at the heart of the American political machine. Against the immense inertia of the forces controlling this matrix, Robinson engineers a plot that sets about re-directing its energies away from the cycle of destructive neo-liberal denial and towards a productive, ecologised capitalism. The books, in effect, construct a counter-hegemony out of actually existing elements of the American polity, and in a decidedly pragmatic rather than utopian mode. Second, Realism might help explain Robinson's decision to foreground character so extensively in the trilogy. Some critics have complained that the historical determinism of the Mars books rendered its characters "artificial" or "transparent," allegorical markers for abstract forces (Kerslake, 156). The surprise of Science in the Capital is the extent to which global warming recedes from the foreground for substantial chunks of each novel, apparently pushed aside for an extensive investigation of the psychic life of its principal characters. Science fiction is typically understood to de-emphasize character, but a theory of Realism might explain this initially curious focus.

Let's now examine these elements in more detail.

Only Connect!

The Science in the Capital trilogy was written in an era when the science reached more and more certitude about the human impact on climate change (first declared in the third IPCC report in 1995), and yet the political resistance in Washington reached an ideological peak. Despite the collapse of the Larsen B ice-shelf in 2002 or the New Orleans flood in 2005, George W. Bush consistently refused to acknowledge or even utter the words "climate change" until 2006. Even then, Bush countenanced no mitigations that would disrupt the accumulation of surplus value by American corporations. The Bush administration appeared at the end of a thirty-year development of antiscientific Republicanism that began with Richard Nixon's temporary abolition of the role of scientific advisor to the president and the expulsion of the National Science Foundation from the buildings adjacent to the White House in 1973.[1] Nixon remembered the formation of Scientists and Engineers for Johnson during the 1964 election campaign, a political intervention by concerned scientists that denounced the Republican candidate Barry Goldwater as a danger to the nuclear equilibrium of the Cold War. Nixon suspected that the scientific establishment was stuffed with Democrats after a number of embarrassments over ballistic programs and politicized appointments to the NSF, and so he worked to reduce their influence. Reagan's election was the first to tie evangelical Christianity directly into the Republican Party, so that Moral Majority views on creationism versus evolution were voiced by the executive, funding for abortion and HIV research was held back, and the fantasy science of the Strategic Defense Initiative was supported whilst the environmental effects of acid rain and CFCs were at first denied. In the 1990s, a new alliance of the religious right, industry lobbyists and Newt Gingrich's leadership of the House of Representatives intensified the ideological resistance to scientific authority. In 1993, The Advancement of Sound Science Coalition was set up, part funded by the tobacco firm Philip Morris to contest new findings on the effects of passive smoking. The front of attack was designed to be broad and apparently from grass-roots organizations which were funded to attack any science that threatened regulation or restriction in drugs, pesticides, or environmental health and safety. The aim of "sound science" was to contest scientific consensus by giving voice to contrary opinions, thus amplifying doubt and debate and delaying any binding, federal action. ExxonMobil began to fund research and reports issued by think tanks like the George C. Marshall Institute and the Heritage Foundation that contested the emerging consensus on climate change. Gingrich aided this design by abolishing Congress's Office of Technology Assessment and setting up a kind of free market of science advisors, thus ensuring that expertise was delivered in an adversarial context, where opposing opinion could always be hired. The adversarial conventions of news reportage also ensured that climate change remained "debatable" long after a scientific consensus had been established. The conservative agenda was aided considerably with the arrival of Fox News, which gave regular platforms to climate change contrarians.

The Bush White House explicitly used "sound science" tactics to refute IPCC findings on climate, ideologically suspect no doubt because they emerged from a United Nations body. One of the earliest acts of the new president in 2001 was to remove the head of the IPCC and install a more skeptical appointee (an act undertaken after the lobbying of ExxonMobil, Mooney claims). The administration has been consistently shown to intervene strongly on representations of climate change by government bodies. A National Academy of Sciences report in 2001 unfortunately reinforced IPCC findings. Since then, the White House has intervened to remove reference to this report, for instance from an Environmental Policy Agency document in 2003. In 2005, the press established that the presentation of climate change was being managed in the White House by an appointee from the American Petroleum Institute; he resigned, immediately to take up a post with ExxonMobil. In 2006, the NASA climatologist James Hansen revealed that the wording of his findings had been managed by NASA's public relations office. The shift to a very reluctant acknowledgement of human impacts and the need for mitigation only appeared late on in Bush's second term.

The popular novel could also be part of this conservative matrix. In 2005, Michael Crichton's conspiracy thriller about the false apocalyptics of the climate science, *State of Fear*, got him two hours of time with George W. Bush. The first appendix of *State of Fear* was called, without irony, "Why Politicized Science Is Dangerous." The book is a generic sound science attack on the vested interests behind climate change "junk" science.

Elements of this history are recounted by Robinson in Science in the Capital (in *Forty* 108ff; in *Fifty* 210ff). But whilst the anger of the trilogy is driven by this context, it is less interested in mapping the contours of what George Monbiot calls the "denial industry" and more committed tracing out the alliances and connections needed for a counter-strike to establish science at the core of Washington decision-making. Initially, Robinson uses clusters of characters to convey how science is done along the line from the outlying small laboratory to the White House advisory staff. Out in San Diego, Torrey Pines Generique is one of the bio-tech start-up laboratories that emerge between university and industry, public and private funding. The fragility of its finances (and thus its important research on proteomics) dramatizes the impact of venture capitalism on science, where the co-operation and transparency run up against private ownership, patent law and the profit motive. "Science didn't work like capitalism," one character reflects. "That was the rub, that was one of the rubs in the general dysfunction of the world. Capitalism ruled, but money was too simplistic and inadequate a measure of the wealth that science generated" (*Forty* 119). Venture capitalists eventually close the laboratory and disperse its team. When the facility is revived under a federally funded program, the functioning lab is fondly regarded as "a beautiful thing to behold. A bit of a Fabergé egg; fragile, rococo, needing sustenance and protection" (*Sixty* 359). Anna Quibler is a section head of the NSF, the model of a quantitative scientist, demanding statistical proofs and unable to engage with politicking or irrational argument. This does not stop her friendship with a group of exiled Tibetans, setting up the Khembali embassy in the offices shared by the NSF. Their new island nation disappears under the flood tides that breach its dikes in *Fifty* (just another startling sequence that reminds the reader of the Katrina hurricane). The Khembali role in the novel is to provide a provocative comparison between Buddhist philosophy and Western scientific method, proffering a holism of reason, spirit and affect that becomes increasingly important. Anna remains at NSF throughout the trilogy rather than moving into a White House role for the simple reason that "I like science more than politics" (*Sixty* 129). The head of the NSF, Diane Chang, recognizes that no such separation can be sustained in a period of emergency: her trajectory oversees the return of the NSF from an organization long marginalized by Nixon into the lynch-pin of federal and global mitigation projects. She shifts from the NSF to presidential science advisor: in this comedy, she will also marry and become First Lady. Charlie Quibler, Anna's husband, works as a part-time science advisor to the liberal Senator Phil Chase, first seen in Robinson's *Antarctica* and famously absent from Washington for much of the time, since he tracks climate change from the very edges of the world. In *Forty*, Charlie juggles child care with the dissatisfactions of Senate *Realpolitik*: he writes Chase's Climate Change Bill, a text termed "a narrative of the near future" (*Forty* 214), spars with the skeptical presidential advisor, memorably with the president himself, only to see the Bill dismembered by the Capitol's political machinery. By *Sixty*, Charlie has, with considerable ambivalence, become a full-time White House staffer for President Chase: he can now coordinate large-scale mitigations and lecture the neoconservatives of the World Bank about their rapacity, realizing with a shock that he has the power to decapitate its obstructive leadership.

Moving between all of these elements is Frank Vanderwal, the trilogy's pivotal character. A sociobiologist by inclination, Frank has moved from front-line laboratory research at the University of San Diego (with close contacts and shares in Torrey Pines Generique) for a one-year secondment at the NSF in Anna Quibler's department. He understands that such administration is part of the necessary system of social credit and co-operation in science, but is bored by doing meta-science and frustrated by the passivity and marginality of the NSF. He writes a denunciation of NSF policy for Diane Change as a final flourish to his resignation after a year, but this coincides with a personal crisis induced in part by a Khembali lecture on the limits of Western reason. Frank elects to stay at the NSF and in a central scene presents a manifesto of how the NSF might work to co-ordinate mitigations but also to reinject rational science into the core of Washington policy making. Frank advocates "optimodality," an ability to exist in radically separate and sometimes jarringly discontinuous social worlds. He thus moves between the lab-surfers of San Diego, meetings with Pentagon engineers, Buddhist philosophizing in tree-houses, friendships with homeless Vietnam veterans and fregan radicals, and high-level scientific discussions of thermohaline circulation and proteomics. Frank also becomes an object of interest for elements of the black-budget surveillance state in a sub-plot that hints at the substantial extent of an anti-democratic shadow government which has stolen elections by tampering with electronic vote counters. Scientists ally with democratic elements in the security agencies to ensure Chase is elected legally. To trace Frank is thus to trace out a limited but highly meaningful social totality, a matrix of power that fully intertwines science, society and politics.

When Frank presents his manifesto to the Board of the NSF, he justifies his radicalism by appealing to Thomas Kuhn's notion of "paradigm shift": "We do normal science. But as Kuhn pointed out, anomalies crop up. Undeniable events occur that we can't cope with inside the old paradigm" (*Forty* 289). But his conclusion is much more socio-political than Kuhn's largely internalist explanation of the history of science. "The way we have things organized now, scientists keep themselves out of political policy decisions.... But I say to hell with that! Science [is] the solution, not the problem. And so it has to *insist on itself*. That's what looks wild about these ideas, that scientists should take a stand and become a part of the political decision-making process" (*Forty* 292). In proposing to overturn the strategy of apparently preserving scientific "objectivity" by refusing to engage in everyday politics, Frank advocates abandoning the position taken by the scientific establishment since Nixon's punishment for Democrat-advocacy in 1964. This strategy has resolutely failed in the face of the ideological use of "sound science" by Republicans in the 1990s. Re-networking science to society in their own terms, Frank might well be regarded less a Kuhnian than a follower of the controversial science studies thinker, Bruno Latour. Indeed, the trilogy as a whole embodies much of the theory of science Latour propounded in *Science in Action* in 1987.[2]

In this book, Latour traces how a scientific theory or proposition might become accepted as a successful *fact*. Facts are not out there waiting to be discovered, in Latour's view, but are the end-product of a long process of intensive argument, experiment and counter-experiment. Latour begins with the scientific paper, examining how a statement stakes its claim by reference to powerful allies, methodologies, laboratories, published papers and authoritative rhetorics. He then builds a model that incorporates more and more elements that are mobilized to support the proposition, moving from the laboratory through allied research teams, funding bodies, funders from industry, government or the military, to educated publics, mass media communication, journalists, and so on. Latour's aim is to show that science does not take place in pristine laboratories where truthfulness is measured by their quarantine from the social world. Instead, science is always already thoroughly socialized, impure, messy and developed through "heterogeneous chains of association": "We are never confronted with science, technology, and society, but with a gamut of weaker and stronger associations" (100–1).

Considering the "big science" projects of particle accelerators and the such, Latour argues that "the harder, the purer the science is inside, the further outside the scientists have to go" to continue their projects (156). There is no such thing as "pure" science because these are the laboratories that have to seek the most funding, the most governmental and industry support. Science is therefore successful not to the degree that it isolates itself from society, but to the degree that it can be assessed by the "number of points linked, the strength and length of the linkage, the nature of the obstacles" (201). Latour's recipe for success is: only connect!

Robinson's trilogy is a Latourian manifesto for re-mapping the matrix of heterogeneous sources of power to accept the findings of climate science, countering the brilliant ideological exploitation of networks that has been demonstrated by the Right in blocking the facts of climate change. There is nothing more Latourian than the narrator's observation that "science wants to be boring, in that it wants to be beyond all dispute. It wants to understand the phenomena of the world in ways that everyone can agree on and share; it wants to make assertions from a position that is not any particular subject's position.... Complete agreement; the world put under a description" (*Forty* 78). This would be the arrival at undisputed fact: climate change as a *black box*, an undisputed assumption. The lesson is that climate change is what Latour calls a *tangled object*, uncertainly located between nature and culture (is it a man-made or natural variation?) and thus lying confusingly between object and subject, fact and artefact, and so has been inherently disputatious. Tangled objects "first appear as matters of concern, as new entities that provoke perplexity and thus speech in those who gather around them, and argue over them" (*Politic*, 22).

In the course of the trilogy, the scientists begin to understand the politics of the network and the primacy of messy political dispute. Following the flood of Washington that concludes *Forty Signs of Rain*, something the president calls an act of "climactic terrorism," Diane Chang galvanizes the NSF, "trying almost by force of will to make NSF a major node in the network of scientific organizations" (*Fifty* 176). The chains of heterogeneous associations get longer and longer (as do Frank's bewildering "To Do" lists that pepper the novels' progress). They begin to move outside the realms of the laboratory or science funding. Scientists even organize a notional presidential candidate in a "Social Science Experiment in Elective Politics," fully committing to an engagement with public politics for the first time since 1964. When they eventually swing behind Chase, withdrawing their candidate and thus helping to secure a Democrat election, the assemblage of allies stretches from the laboratory to the Oval Office. Charlie Quibler's lambasting of the World Bank neo-cons is thus part of the same complex assemblage or network alliance. Our small group of marginal characters are now in a position to terraform the Earth itself through the United Nations, pushing through a coherent mission architecture to orchestrate massive engineering projects.

Latour is a resolute pragmatist, working with a faux-naïf critical realism that he claims imposes nothing on his analysis, but merely follows the scientific actors themselves, the connections and the networks that they create. Latour is not interested in social explanations of science or ideology critique. He is opposed to the attempt to de-mystify or expose "real" conditions, as a Marxist might. Each network is distinct, each assemblage able to produce the terms of its own analysis. If true, this would render Latour indifferent to the political cast of any network: the Republican "sound science" matrix would be measured in terms of its greater or lesser pragmatic *success*. Clearly, Robinson has had a commitment to leftist critique: *The Gold Coast* wants to expose the connections that bind together Orange County's military-industrial-entertainment complex; Science in the Capital is a liberal, democratic manifesto for the politico-scientific transformation of the American polity. But this trilogy is also resolutely pragmatic, like Latour: it is a Realist depiction of a potential re-drawing of actually existing conditions, eschewing utopianism.

All of this makes the novels sound programmatic, a mechanistic study of ideological and institutional maneuvers — and to some extent they are. Robinson is a utilitarian writer: he has always insisted that "literature needs to be put to use" ("Chop Wood" 60), part of a politics of commitment rather than one of aesthetic autonomy. But as I have indicated, much of this exploration of the institutional matrix of science policy recedes into the deep background for large tracts of the trilogy, becoming instead the horizon for the exploration of character. This is not an evasion, however: what Science in the Capital demonstrates, particularly through the figure of Frank Vanderwal, is the way Realism understands character too as *network*.

Go Optimodal!

Frank Vanderwal is an impressively weird creation. He begins as a reductive sociobiologist, rationalizing much modern human behavior through evolutionary speculations confidently delivered as fact. Open plan offices reproduce the hominid experience of the savannah, playing Frisbee reanimates paleolithic hunting instincts, power plays in funding meetings reproduce primate struggles for group dominance. An early sign that this rationalism might have limits occurs when Frank's application of rational choice theory to the traffic on the commuter beltway cannot anticipate violent eruptions of road rage. Near the end of *Forty Signs of Rain,* Frank suffers a crisis in the midst of a Buddhist lecture: he believes that the maxim "An excess of reason is itself a form of madness" has been directed at him (235). "The scattered parts of consciousness occasionally assemble at once into a whole pattern," the narrator tells us (239). That this personal crisis coincides with Frank's re-commitment to the NSF and his call for an institutional paradigm shift indicates how we are to map the personal onto the collective. Reformulating subjectivity will itself be part of the conjunctural changes required in the permanent climate crisis of advanced capitalist societies. As Lukács argued, the hero of the novel "is not a personal destiny but the destiny of a community" (*Theory* 66). Since capitalist relations enforced alienation of self from others, Lukács then argued that it was only with the rise of Realism that "a fuller understanding of the life of the individual" could give rise "to a new kind of human self-awareness: man becomes aware of his nature as an ineluctably social animal" (*Contemporary Realism* 100–1).

Like character in any appropriately complex Realist novel, it is far from easy to map Frank's personal crisis onto the grander narrative of climate change. In *Fifty Degrees Below,* Frank's decisions become deeply odd. He abandons looking for a new apartment, lives in his truck, then in a tree-house, even through a bitterly cold winter that revives the snap ice age of the Younger Dryas. He seeks a "repaleolithization" of his life (42) in accord with Robinson's repeated dramatization of "going feral" or off map as an act of resistance or refusal of alienated modernity. Frank then celebrates "the parcellated life," the decision to embrace a "fully optimodal existence" (75) that sees him moving between entirely discrete social worlds, all the while connecting back together sections of a badly disordered community. This is a series of interactions that maps out a network, as total as late modern compartmentalization of the social world will allow. Just to reinforce Frank's status as an eccentric yet paradigmatic subject, an attack in the park leaves him with a broken nose and a subdural hematoma that renders him uncertain about the rationality or irrationality of any of his actions. He reads Antonio Damasio's *Descartes' Error,* understands that reason and affect must be thought together, and reconfirms his view that "perhaps a *passionate reason* was what was called for" (245). Optimodality appears to be an ideal of a new kind of subjectivity, then, but it begins to echo Frank's "To Do" lists that spiral out of control and which leave him paralyzed and unable to prioritize. The very last words of *Fifty Degrees Below* critique the optimodal life. Frank's Buddhist sparring partner warns him: "No! it is easy to live multiple lives! What is hard is to be a whole person" (520).

In *Sixty Days and Counting*, Frank experiences increasing paralysis with the disjuncture between his increasingly public and political role as a technocrat and the secrecy of his romantic entanglement with the black-ops agent Caroline, which brings the aggressive attention of rogue secret services. Frank now lives by excerpts from Ralph Waldo Emerson's works, posted daily on the net, limning the extent of the alienation of both man from nature and man from himself: 'It is the largest part of man that is not inventoried," one excerpt begins. "He is social, professional, sectarian, literary, and is this or that set and corporation. But after the most exhausting census has been made, there remains as much more which no tongue can tell. And this remainder is that which interests" (*Sixty* 99). The comic impulse of the trilogy is to seek resolution, at least of the personal stories that have interwoven across the texts, to use narrative to act to re-configure what oil-fuelled modernity has disfigured. At the characterological level, then, Science in the Capital seems to suggest that optimodality is the subjectivity of a time of crisis, but that the readjustment of nature and culture that comes from a committed ecological politics will allow a more holistic sense of self to emerge. Realism was always attacked by critical theory for its illusory "reality effect" and imposition of formal and narrative closure that re-confirmed ideological limits around possible character actions (see, for instance, Belsey). Proleptic Realism, however, cannot offer closure, hovering as it does in a finally indeterminable near future where the modeling of reality remains fundamentally incomplete. The conventions of comedy close the trilogy in a narrative concordance of union, but the reader recognizes the convention and also that this is only a temporary pause in an ongoing struggle with the immense inertias of late modern capitalism. Character can never be "complete," but the radical pressures on coherent subjectivity demonstrated in Robinson's extended portrait of Frank gives us a concrete determination of the forces in play.

Refuse the Apocalypse!

The historian Paul Boyer has tracked how a very particular, Protestant premillennial eschatology has come to dominate the American imagination. Of course, the American state was founded by sects driven by apocalyptic imaginings, but Boyer is interested in detailing the intensification of evangelical Christianity since the 1970s. This new wave of apocalyptic thinking has been consistently intertwined with ecology. The first Earth Day was held in 1970; in the same year Hal Lindsay published the Christian apocalyptic text, *The Late Great Planet Earth,* which bound together ecological crisis, nuclear catastrophe and the religious Armageddon. Lindsay's book sold over 28 million copies in America in the next twenty years. Successive presidents since Reagan have been members of these religious congregations, often producing serious concerns that eschatological beliefs are informing American policy. It is now virtually impossible to conceive of a serious presidential candidate who is not an evangelical, since America is now the most religious state on Earth. Lee Quinby has argued that "the convergence of general apocalyptic attitudes and a belief in the United States as the culmination of history is so thorough as to justify the term 'American Apocalypse'" (xvi).

Narratives of ecology can step directly into complicity with this sublime or rapturous discourse of the American Apocalypse: think about the spectacle of *The Day After Tomorrow*. In contrast, Robinson's trilogy not only sidesteps the genre of the disaster novel, but also the lure of ecological tragedy. Lawrence Buell has observed that "Apocalypse is the single most powerful master metaphor that the contemporary environmental imagination has at its disposal" (cited Garrard, 93). Yet Robinson follows an alternative tradition of ecological thought, and Science in the Capital might almost have been composed to fulfill the observations of Joseph Meeker's pioneering ecological text, *The Comedy of Survival*:

> Not every catastrophe is a tragedy, and not everything comic is humorous. Both tragedy and comedy arise from experiences of misfortune, but they respond to pain in very different ways.... The tragic mode of living requires that we perceive the world as a conquest among warring camps, that we make choices among them.... The comic way, on the other hand, is the path of reconciliation. When the usual patterns of life are disrupted, the comic spirit strives for a return to normalcy. The comic vision is not polarised, but complex: comedy sees many aspects simultaneously, and seeks for a strategy that will resolve problems with a minimum of pain and confrontation. The comic way is not heroic or idealistic; rather, it is a strategy for survival [14–15].

Robinson brings to ecology the engineer paradigm that traditionally suffuses American science fiction, but abandons the will to dominate or subdue nature often rehearsed there. Instead, the books seek compromise formations, mitigations that will restore an equilibrium between culture and nature. In many ways, this comic ecological vision completes my attempt to examine what a proleptic Realism might look like at a generic, narrative, and characterological level. As Meeker continues: "Organisms must adapt themselves to their circumstances in every possible way, must studiously avoid all-or-nothing choices, must seek alternatives to death, must accept and revel in maximum diversity, must accommodate themselves to the accidental limitations of birth and environment, and must prefer co-operation to competition" (20–1). This serves well as the manifesto of Phil Chase in his public political life but also Frank Vanderwal in the conjunctures of his public and private life.

In a key passage in *The Gold Coast*, the struggling writer Jim eventually rejects the postmodern style, "flashy, deliberately ignorant, concerned only with surfaces, with the look, the great Californian image, reflected in mirrors a million times" (259). Instead, he turns to the literature of commitment, of Camus and Fugard, and its utilitarian view of the text, the "ultimate test for literature, the most important question: Can it be turned to use? When you read a book, and go back out into the world: *can it be turned to use?*" (261). This pragmatic, instrumental measure suffuses the writing of Science in the Capital. If the vision of utopia is suspended here, I suspect it is because Robinson feels it is mainly a contemporary Realism that can best contribute to the sort of survival where utopian imagining becomes possible again, after the crisis induced by Republican denial has been solved.

Notes

1. Historical details in this paragraph derive from Greenberg, Monbiot and Mooney. It is worth noting that these science histories themselves demonstrate the political polarization of the "science wars": Monbiot and Mooney write from the left; Greenberg, whilst providing useful detail on the political history of science in Washington, actually argues hawkishly that Science has become a "clever, well-financed claimant for money" (1) that has triumphed over the politicians in the last thirty years.

2. I have written an introductory essay on Latour's work and its relevance for science fiction criticism elsewhere [Ed: *Science Fiction Studies* 33.1 (2006).] Given space, Robinson's ecological thought could be put in productive tension with Latour's *Politics of Nature*, but here I only want to sketch out how Robinson's trilogy can be read through Latour's pragmatic "actor-network theory" in *Science in Action*.

Works Cited

Belsey, Catherine. *Critical Practice*. London: Methuen, 1980.
Boyer, Paul. *When Time Shall Be No More: Prophecy and Belief in Modern American Culture*. Cambridge, Mass.: Harvard University Press, 1992.
Crichton, Michael. *State of Fear*. London: HarperCollins, 2005.
Garrard, Greg. *Ecocriticism*. London: Routledge, 2004.
Greenberg, Daniel S. *Science, Money and Politics: Political Triumph and Ethical Erosion*. Chicago: University of Chicago Press, 2001.
Hofstadter, Richard. *The Paranoid Style in American Politics and Other Essays*. London: Cape, 1966.
Intergovernmental Panel on Climate Change. "Summary for Policymakers," *Fourth Assessment Report, Working Group III*. <http://www.ipcc.ch>
Jameson, Fredric. *Archaeologies of the Future: The Desire Called Utopia and Other Science Fictions*. London: Verso, 2005.
Kerslake, Patricia. *Science Fiction and Empire*. Liverpool: Liverpool University Press, 2007.
Latour, Bruno. *Politics of Nature: How to Bring the Sciences into Democracy*. Trans. Catherine Porter. Cambridge, Mass.: Harvard University Press, 2004.
_____. *Science in Action: How to Follow Scientists and Engineers Through Society*. Cambridge, Mass.: Harvard University Press, 1987.
Luckhurst, Roger. "Bruno Latour's Scientifiction: Networks, Assemblages and Tangled Objects." *Science Fiction Studies* 33:1 (2006). 4–17.
Lukács, Georg. *The Meaning of Contemporary Realism*. GTrans. John and Necke Mander. London: Merlin Press, 1962.
_____. *The Theory of the Novel*. Trans. Anna Batock. London: Merlin Press, 1978.
Meeker, Joseph W. *The Comedy of Survival: Literary Ecology and a Play Ethic*. Tuscon: University of Arizona Press, 1997.
Monbiot, George. *Heat: How to Stop the Planet Burning*. London: Allen Lane, 2006.
Mooney, Chris. *The Republican War on Science*. New York: Basic Books, 2006.
Moylan, Tom. *Scraps of the Untainted Sky: Science Fiction, Utopia, Dystopia*. Boulder: Westview, 2000.
Quinby, Lee. *Anti-Apocalypse: Exercises in Genealogical Criticism*. Minneapolis: University of Minnesota Press, 1994.
Robinson, Kim Stanley. "Chop Wood, Carry Water." *Locus* 58: 4 (April 2007). 6, 58–9.
_____. *Fifty Degree Below*. London: HarperCollins, 2005.
_____. *Forty Signs of Rain*. London: HarperCollins, 2004.
_____. *The Gold Coast*. London: Futura, 1989.
_____. *Sixty Days and Counting*. London: HarperCollins, 2007
Sontag, Susan. "The Imagination of Disaster," in *Against Interpretation*. New York: Farrar, Strauss and Giroux, 1966. 209–25.

12

Living Thought: Genes, Genres and Utopia in the Science in the Capital Trilogy
Gib Prettyman

[U]nreasonable, nonsensical, unmethodical foreplay thus turns out to be an unavoidable precondition of clarity and empirical success.... [W]hen we attempt to describe and to understand developments of this kind in a general way, we are, of course, obliged to appeal to the existing forms of speech which do not take them into account and which must be distorted, misused, beaten into new patterns in order to fit unforeseen situations (without a constant misuse of language there can not be any discovery, any progress).
— Paul Feyerabend, *Against Method*

Critical evaluations of Kim Stanley Robinson commonly suggest that he is an important anomaly within prevailing intellectual or historical trends. Specifically, most critics argue that Robinson successfully addresses — or at least foregrounds — the worst impediments to utopian thought under postmodern capitalism. In 1994, Carol Franko argued that in contrast to trends of the Reaganite 1980s, "Robinson is one major writer whose eighties fiction suggests that ... utopian vision is not dead but perhaps hibernating, or mutating" (192). That same year, Bud Foote's early commentary on *Red Mars* noted that "In his concerns for the ecology, Robinson is very contemporary, but not contemporary SF" (61). The following year, focusing on *Pacific Edge*, Tom Moylan described Robinson's work as "a rare contemporary instance of a non-cyberpunk, engaged, male sf writer who is open to feminist sensibilities and issues and willing as well to explore utopian proclivities along with tracing of the ubiquitous dystopian dimensions of the present" ("Utopia Is When Our Lives Matter" 2). Moylan therefore identified Robinson with the tradition of the "critical utopia" initiated by the feminist sf writers of the 1970s.[1] In 2000, Fredric Jameson examined "the ambiguous space in which the Mars trilogy is uniquely positioned" between realism and "the radically unexpected and unpredictable" (*AF* 400–1), and in "The Desire Called Utopia" (2005) he asserted that the Mars trilogy "is only one example of a new formal tendency, in which it is not the representation of Utopia, but rather the conflict of all possible Utopias, and the arguments about the nature and desirability of Utopia as such, which move to the center of attention" (*AF* 216). "The Desire Called Utopia" explores the theoretical implications of such formal tendencies of utopian thought within the historical context of late capitalism, and as such represents a monumental contribution to the field of utopian studies. In this critical line one can glimpse the connections between Robinson's provocative oeuvre to date and a renewed interest in sf and utopia, as well as specifically between Robinson's fictions and Jameson's influential articulations of the formal nature and possibilities of utopia. In effect, Robinson's anomalous fictions have become exemplary of what utopian literature can (or can only) do in a postmodern world.[2]

The essay that follows contributes to this critical line by examining Robinson's experiments with genre in his most recent work to date: the "Science in the Capital" series *Forty Signs of Rain* (2004), *Fifty Degrees Below* (2005), and *Sixty Days and Counting* (2007).[3] I suggest that Robinson continues to challenge fundamental cultural norms — and to inspire critical theories of utopian thought — by exploring genres (in the widest sense) as thematic and structural elements in this complexly utopian project. Specifically, Robinson presents a genetic conception of genres and their roles in human life, both historical and potential. Under this model, genres are metaphorically equated with genes as basic building blocks that encode lived situations and reproduce cultural behaviors in the same way that genes encode evolutionary situations and reproduce biological traits. In addition to this metaphorical equation, however, the Science in the Capital series reminds us that from an evolutionary and biological perspective, human behaviors are literally engendered by genes that can be modified by sexual reproduction, by evolutionary mutation, and perhaps even by technological experiment and intervention. Therefore, the series represents genres, and indeed all human thought and culture, as living and evolving expressions of material — specifically biological and ecological — processes. Seen this way, genres are (as Marxist literary critics have long asserted) at once imaginative and material categories, complex material encodings of lived human experience — in short, "living thought" (1: 292).

Using this complex biological framework to (re)situate human thought and history, Robinson's Science in the Capital trilogy raises the possibility of modifying genres to express therapeutic restructuring of life under late capitalism. Through a series of interwoven narrative tropes — biotechnologies, new scientific paradigms and disciplines, liberating crises, and intellectual hybridizations — Robinson draws attention to the genetic function of genres and explores contemporary possibilities for modifying them. Forms of habitual thought are shown to engender recurring outcomes, and Robinson's narrative experiments (both thematically and formally) with ways of manipulating these embedded, embodied, and collective forms to produce healthier and more sustainable social outcomes, just as biotechnology experiments with genetic modifications in search of potentially powerful medical treatments or as environmental pressures stimulate genetic changes as evolutionary adaptations. Further pursing the analogy with biotechnology, Robinson's narrative also draws attention to the differences between *in vitro* achievements, which are significant only in a lab setting, and *in vivo* or real world accomplishments. Allegorically, this distinction between *in vitro* and *in vivo* solutions highlights the insufficiency of imagined political solutions without material "insertion techniques" that allow those modified structures of thought to be incorporated by living social organisms. Robinson imagines these genetic perspectives and generic experiments as "bold and persistent experimentation" in response to the systemic crisis of global capitalism. As such, they represent an imaginary deployment of a revolutionary science rather than a simple application of rationalistic "normal science." Simultaneously metaphorical and material, imaginative and "scientific," Robinson's narrative in effect shows the material role that the chaotic biodiversity of a properly "scientific" imagination must play in order for utopian representations to become social expressions and historical practices. Finally, I will suggest, this complexly biological approach to genre may represent a strategically postmodern "absolute formalism" (*AF*

213) and thus prompt further evolution in critical conceptions of utopianism under late capitalism.

Experiments in Genre

The generic experimentation of the Science in the Capital series is nothing new for Robinson, who by professional training and artistic temperament is keenly aware of the complex intellectual issues he faces as a writer of sf and utopia. Robinson's familiarity with contemporary scientific discourses is a frequently-noted feature of his work. Less often mentioned is his broad familiarity with social science and humanistic discourses, although it is well known that he studied with Jameson at UCSD and earned a Ph.D. with a dissertation on Philip K. Dick before turning full-time to fiction writing. Just as he has participated in contemporary scientific institutions by traveling to Antarctica and spending time at the National Science Foundation, Robinson has also participated in the scholarly discourse about sf and utopia — for example, as a featured speaker at the 2003 "Futures of Utopia" conference held in honor of Jameson's retirement as Head of the Program in Literature at Duke. Presumably Robinson is also the "Kim" mentioned along with several utopian scholars in the dedication of *Archaeologies of the Future* as Jameson's "comrades in the party of utopia." Such professional and institutional involvement gives Robinson's fictions an extremely productive artistic self-consciousness.

It can be argued that Robinson's literary field — science fiction, or sf and utopia, or however one defines it more specifically — demands such theoretical self-consciousness. Jameson suggests that what "uniquely characterizes" utopian literature "is its explicit intertextuality: few other literary forms have so brazenly affirmed themselves as argument and counterargument ... [or] so openly required cross-reference and debate within each new variant" (*AF* 2). Robinson very forthrightly shares his conceptions of the field and his oeuvre, which he refers to as "utopian fiction, defined very broadly" (Szeman 186). Robinson argues that "all science fiction has a utopian element" (Szeman 185), an observation that accords with scholarly emphasis on the genre of sf and utopia.[4] Partially this is because "The very name *science fiction* includes *science*, which is our world of facts, and *fiction*, which is for me the main repository of our values," so that sf "is an enjambment of facts and values in a way that our culture desperately needs right now" (Foote 53). Robinson further defines sf as "an historical genre, in that it takes place in our future. That is to say, from the fictional world of the novel you can follow its history back to us (or some moment of our past, in the case of the alternative history). The fictional history is related either explicitly or implicitly. If no history can be traced back, it may be some kind of fantasy novel, or something else, but it isn't science fiction as I recognize it" ("Wilderness, Utopia, History"). The utopian and the historical are then linked because "Science fiction is the history that we cannot know, the future history and the alternative history" (Foote 51).

More broadly, Robinson considers himself "a utopian novelist," which he emphasizes is already "a mix of genres" because utopian literature historically has not consisted of "novels per se." Thus "The old attack on utopias as boring is ... partly a result of them not being novels enough," and the innovation that scholars call the "critical utopia" results largely from making utopian concerns genuinely novelistic (Szeman 185). He is self-conscious about the differences between novellas, very short novels, novels, and very long novels, and he considers each to be in some ways a distinct genre (*Agony Column*). Robinson claims that he would like his texts to "have it both ways" by having them "stand as modernist novels" and also be "read by lab techs who have no training in literature" (Clarke 7). Thus he sometimes speaks of utopian fiction in pragmatic terms as "the thought-experiment which attacks social problems and suggests solutions, utopian goals, or envisions societies that we might then work towards" (Foote 55) and at other times stresses more aesthetic goals such as trying to create "an emotional train of thought like a piece of music" (Clarke 10). Ultimately these perspectives converge, as political engagement "simply makes for better novels, because they become attempts to portray whole societies and to understand the why of them" (Szeman 182).

Throughout these novelistic experiments, Robinson is acutely aware of the political urgency of his utopian efforts. He identifies himself explicitly as an "anti-capitalist American leftist" (*Agony Column*) and has argued eloquently and forcefully that contemporary capitalism is really "residual feudalism" (Szeman 182) or "liquid feudalism" (*Agony Column*) in which the division into lords and serfs is obscured by global markets. Therefore the capitalism he opposes is not "creation of capital" per se but "feudal control of capital" (Rohn). Globalization, "late capitalism's enmeshing of every culture on Earth, and the biosphere itself, into its system of strip-mining for short term gain," is "a malignant process, like a social cancer" (Jamneck). In opposition to the immense injustices of postmodern feudal capitalism, Robinson stresses the need for institutions on a human scale, ecological sustainability, and social justice. Because these things are impossible under global capitalism, and because each is necessary for the other, the struggle for them "is an anti-capitalist project in the end." But Robinson also hopes that "the real productive capacities of science, and the way science has to an extent 'scientized' the workings of society in the last century, will mean that science will prevail in the end; meaning the scientizing of capitalism into some post-capitalist order that is more just than the current one" (Rohn).

Given his self-conceptions about his oeuvre and its intended political effects, Robinson has made some provocative comments about genre in the Science in the Capital series specifically. He identifies the primary genre of the series as "day-after-tomorrow novels," or the "subgenre of science fiction sometimes called 'near-future science fiction'" (Szeman 181), akin to his Three Californias novels and *Antarctica* (with which it shares some characters). However, he also acknowledges that the series is generically diverse, saying that it has aspects of espionage novels and spy thrillers, that it is a political novel and a work of social comedy, and that it is "a mix of science fiction and present-day realism" (Gunn 2006, 2007; Locus). Early reviewers variously called *Forty Signs of Rain* and/or *Fifty Degrees Below* "science fiction environmental thrillers," a "novel of ideas that is also a social comedy," a "domestic novel," and "a glorious stew of disparate elements." Robinson says he wants readers to feel they are in one kind of novel, and then to fall through a "trap door" into another sort of novel—a science fiction novel (*Agony Column*). As if to embed that trap door effect in a generic distinction, he has also repeatedly referred to the series in interviews as "utopian black comedy." Obviously, then, Robinson's Science in the Capital trilogy raises many questions about its own genres—and, by extension, about the relationships of various genres to the overtly utopian ends that Robinson envisions for his self-consciously complex fictions.

Genres and Genes

The generic diversity of the series is amplified on the thematic level through connections between genes and genres. This connection is evident on the level of etymology, where both words (along with "gender") originate in Latin and Greek words for birth, origin, and species. Genre is thus at heart a biological metaphor, and Robinson's novels literalize that biological perspective through such thematic topics as biotechnology and genetic modification, sociobiology and evolutionary psychology, ecology and environmentalism, and new disciplines such as bioinformatics. Genres and other habitual forms of thought are related to biological and ecological processes both analogically and literally, allowing genres to be explored for their genetic function in social organisms. These thematic insights are also reinscribed into the novels as generic experiments with the narrative itself, in a process we could think of as Robinson's generic modifications. Both types of experiment — with thematic connections and with narrative forms — serve as political allegories for the material transformations in thought and habit necessary for a revolutionary break from late capitalism. Arguably, they also serve as direct political actions in the form of "bold and persistent experimentation" with contemporary forms of "living thought."

Early in *Forty Signs of Rain* we encounter the biotechnology of genetic modification through the story of the biotech start-up Torrey Pines Generique. Interestingly, the company name plays on the pun between genes and genres; the company is both generic (exemplary of its kind and unremarkable) and exotic (the faux French) in its commercial biotechnological (re)production. Literally, the company's genre is genetic modification. Scientists at Torrey Pines have engineered a genetic modification that expresses a desirable outcome: producing higher amounts of "good cholesterol" to fight heart disease (1: 33). However, despite its apparent materialization and potential power this demonstrable outcome remains essentially theoretical because in the real world — the world of complex organisms and human physiology, and also of venture capital, stock market perceptions, and the systemic demand for patents and profits — there is no method of "targeted delivery" for inserting the modification into "living bodies" (1: 37). "After all," the narrative elaborates, "the manipulations of gene and cell that they made were hardly ever done 'just to find things out,' though they did that too. They were done to accomplish certain things inside the cell, and hopefully later, inside a living body. Biotechnology, *bio techno logos*; the word on how to put the tool into the living organism" (1: 93–94). Here again, the connections between genres (*logos* as "-ologies" and codified discourses) and genes (as living codes and sources of organic "expression") are emphasized.

Meanwhile, the biotech industry is itself an expression of genres that function like living things in the material world.[5] When Torrey Pines is acquired by a larger biotech corporation appropriately named Small Delivery Systems (1: 257), it highlights the essentially biological metaphor by which corporate capitalism functions, a metaphor materially inscribed in the "legal fiction" that defines corporations as "artificial persons."[6] Both metaphorically and materially, two artificial persons (corporations) combine in an act of capitalistic evolution. Further emphasizing the genetic and evolutionary aspects of the merger, Torrey Pines is acquired solely to capture a successful algorithm — a gene-like mathematical instruction sequence — that belongs to the smaller company. This looks very much like the "desirable gene" version of evolution, where reproductive partners are supposedly chosen for their promising (and thus evolutionarily successful) genes. Under corporate capitalism, this algorithm is a potential genetic code for making money. Ironically, the scientific purpose of the algorithm is to decode genes; as a corporate possession, it will turn genes themselves (and by extension all life) into patents, private property, potential commodities, and corporate profits. Jameson has said of the Mars trilogy that "all of the scientific problems described in the novel, without exception, offer an allegory, by way of the form of overdetermination, of social, political, and historical problems also faced by the inhabitants of Mars" (*AF* 395–6). The same is true for the Science in the Capital series, except that the "inhabitants" in question are more clearly ourselves. The case of Torrey Pines Generique demonstrates the overdetermined pathologies of what Jameson terms late capitalism's "cynical reason." Here as elsewhere in the novels, genres are revealed to be forms of living thought with a material existence in the world.

The series develops these connections between genes and genres more explicitly. At the beginning of the "paradigm shift" that provides the novels' primary narrative thread, for example, Frank Vanderwal links genes to language. Playfully discussing the problems of translation with Deprung (whom we later discover is a reincarnated Buddhist lama), Frank accuses him of making up the key conceptual terms of his translations:

> But Deprung shook his head. "Not making things up. Re-creation, maybe."
> "Like DNA and phenotypes."
> "I don't know."
> "A kind of code."
> "Well, but language is never just a code."
> "No. More like gene expression."
> "You must tell me."
> "From an instruction sequence, like a gene, to what the instruction creates. Language to thought. Or to meaning, or comprehension. Whatever! To some kind of living thought" [1: 292].

Here Robinson draws attention to the material function of language as a gene-like instruction sequence that re-creates larger structures: thoughts, concepts, meanings, or even whole social organisms. This is something like the function that language has just served for Frank; a few lines from a lecture have already begun to spark a systematic restructuring of his entire life. This function is one of "living thought" because it involves encoding, reproduction, growth, and evolution of lived experience. Just as genes are evolutionary patterns that express characteristic proteins and biological structures, then, genres and other forms of thought can be understood as evolutionary patterns that express characteristic cognitive effects and social structures.

Robinson presents the utopian implications of the gene/genre comparison most provocatively in a meta-fictional interlude that begins the chapter "Broader Impacts" in *Forty Signs of Rain*. The passage begins with Marxist-inflected "decoding" of the "world system today" (echoing of course Robinson's own), which observes that what we call "capitalism" actually contains "buried residual patterns of feudalism and older hierarchies," and that "Everybody lives in an imaginary relationship to this real situation" so that we "only see what we think" despite existing "on a sidewalk over the abyss" (1: 343). "Imaginary relationship to this real situation" is a reference to Althusser's formulation of ideology, while "buried residual patterns" suggests bleak versions of history as social evolution and genetic fate. But the passage then shifts unexpectedly from these chilling and seemingly inescapable formulations to an even broader systemic perspective based on the metaphor of utopian change as a retrospectively miraculous genetic process:

> *There are islands of time when things seem stable. Nothing much happens but the rounds of the week. Later the islands break apart. When enough time has passed, no one now alive will still be here; everyone will be different. Then it will be the stories that will link the generations, history and DNA, long chains of the simplest bits—guanine, adenine, cytosine, thymine—love, hope, fear, selfishness—all recombining again and again, until a miracle happens*
> *and the organism springs forth!* [1: 343]

Here, Robinson suggests that history is made of repetitive stories and plots as DNA is made of repetitive genes and amino acids, and these endless mechanical combinations simultaneously encode what has been and (re)create what will be. Thus it is that utopian change—the springing forth of new social organisms — can be and indeed must be encoded in "the stories that will link generations." The model is one of evolution as punctuated equilibrium (reminiscent also of Kuhn's paradigms or Wallerstein's world-systems) where islands of normative near-stasis nevertheless result in periodic radical transformations. In the evolutionary framework of history, new organisms — biological and social — result from repetition and small changes within complex systems. Put in terms of sf and utopia, the "novum" or what Jameson calls "the Utopian form proper" are justified as simulated projections of evolutionary changes whereby the same old building blocks suddenly combine in new ways and "a miracle happens." Or, insofar as imaginative literature can alter genres to effect their "instruction sequence" on the model of genetic modification, perhaps utopian literature can materially engender dramatic changes such that "the organism springs forth."[7] The biological, ecological and evolutionary framework that links genes and genres reveals history to be composed of social "organisms" that encode, express, and replicate living thought, with all of the chaotic complexity and persistent vitality of life in the broadest sense.

From this point of view, all of the major plotlines of the series can be seen as explorations of potentially evolutionary or revolutionary changes to living thoughts in an island of time that appears to be breaking apart. The plight and perseverance of the Khembalis, the political efforts of Charlie Quibler and Phil Chase, the scientific and technological efforts led by NSF, and Frank Vanderwal's systemic ontological crisis — all are linked through the crisis of abrupt climate change and the effort to break with "business as usual" (1: 320). Each focuses in various ways on the systemic nature and living complexity of the crisis and the difficulty of "inserting" theoretical changes *in vivo*. Nevertheless, each plotline explores how concrete or even mundane actions — the ongoing "good work" beneath the dystopian "nightmare" of capitalist macro-political history (2: 527) — can potentially lead to systemic transformations. Specifically, they imagine modifying structures of habitual thought such that new social organisms would be expressed, with the goal of a sustainable social and material ecology designated "permaculture" (3: 367).

Modifying Scientific Genres

One problem blocking potential revolutionary changes is systemic habits of thought that are obviously flawed, but that people seem unable to change despite consciousness of the issues and knowledge of theoretical solutions. From the biological perspective, this is analogous to the problem of *in vivo* insertion in biotechnology, and it is a major problem for the technocrats trying to formulate scientific responses to abrupt climate change. As it turns out, however, the first genre that needs to be modified is science itself. Assessing the situation, Diane Chang, head of the National Science Foundation, quickly discovers that "ignorance of the situation has not been the problem. The problem is acting on what we know" (2: 82). Later she concludes "This is the real problem: we know, but we can't act" (2: 206). This assessment is echoed by Diane's scientific colleagues, Anna Quibler and Frank (2: 377), and becomes a central scientific as well as political problem in the novel: the postmodern problem of very complex systems.

The main narrative figure for this necessary transformation is Frank. At the beginning of the series, Frank is a habitually cynical scientist who believes his knowledge of evolution and biology allows him to know "the urtext underneath" every social practice (1: 30). Anna describes him as "Dissatisfied, cynical, sharp-tongued" and "unhappy" (1: 229). Frank's personal unhappiness is paralleled — semi-consciously on his part — with the cynical reason manifest in modern science: the subordination of scientific discovery and treatments to patents, the complexly artificial mechanisms of venture capital and stock prices and postmodern "markets" in general, the bottom line of windfall profits, and so forth. Despite his "scientific" awareness of the structural problems, however, Frank uses sociobiology as a form of social Darwinism. This is seen most clearly through Frank's repeated use of the sociobiological genre known as "Prisoner's Dilemma." Sitting in traffic on the Washington Beltway, for example, Frank sees "Primates in the driver's seat" (1: 125). This and all other social situations were "like a giant game of prisoner's dilemma,"

> the classic game in which two prisoners are separated and asked to tell tales on the other one, with release offered to them if they do. The standard computer model scoring system had it that if the prisoners cooperate with each other by staying silent, they each get three points; if both defect against the other, they each get one point; and if one defects and the other doesn't, the defector gets five points and the sap gets zero points…. In traffic, at work, in relationships of every kind — social life was nothing but a series of prisoners' dilemmas [1: 125–7].

Frank's almost brutal use of this generic reduction at the beginning of the series is contrasted (in Frank's own thoughts) with the example of Anna, whom he takes to represent "a female practice of science" (1: 17). Anna's example causes him "discomfort" for "the way her hyperscientific attitude combined with her passionate female expressiveness to suggest a complete science, or even a complete humanity" (1: 19). Ironically, this "reminded Frank of himself," not "the social self that he allowed others to see" but "his internal life as he alone experienced it." Frank too "was stuffed with extreme aspects of both rationality and emotionality," and because she "was too much like him" Anna "reminded him of things about himself he did not want to think about" (1: 19). Anna also explicitly challenges Frank's reliance on Prisoner's Dilemma, believing him "overly impressed by game theory. 'What if the numbers don't correspond to real life?' she asked him. 'What if you don't get five points for defecting when the other person doesn't, what if all those numbers are off, or even backward? Then it's just another computer game, right?'" (1: 255). Frank is thus abstractly aware of his alienation from himself, from his own thoughts and from pleasurable and healthy habits, but he is unable or unwilling to act on this awareness.

Frank's unhealthy and unscientific use of Prisoner's Dilemma demonstrates the danger of any form of habitual thought that is not thoroughly alive. More specifically, though, Frank's personal and institutional use of scientific genres is not sufficiently scientific — which points toward the need for a change in how "science" is conceived and practiced. Through the story of Frank and his transformation, Robinson suggests that for science to be potentially revolutionary or utopian, it first must change its own forms of thought significantly.

A major trope in the novels, therefore, is the embodied practices of science itself. Indeed, the term "trope" in biology refers to invariable responses by organisms to external stimuli, as for example when plants orient toward sunlight. Ironically, Frank uses this "scientific" trope in his own habitual way to characterize himself and the other scientists gathered to hear Rudra Cakrin's lecture "Purpose of Science from the Buddhist Perspective":

> These were people still interested enough in ideas to spend a lunch hour listening to a lecture on the philosophy of science…. Surplus time and energy, given over to curiosity: a fundamental hominid behavioral trait. The basic trait that got people into science, that made science in the first place, surviving despite the mind-numbing regimes of its modern-day expression. Here he was himself, after all, and no one could be more burnt out and disenchanted than he was. But still following a tropism helplessly, like a sunflower turning to look at the sun [1: 263].

Frank's reductive "scientific" version of life implies that nothing will ever change, that human behavior is a matter of genetic necessity. By extension, it implies that nothing can be done to change existing social arrangements — even though Frank himself, using what he thinks of as scientific skepticism, recognizes them to be "mind-numbing."

As it turns out, however, this time the tropism of scientific curiosity has led Frank to a lecture that sparks radically new thoughts and behaviors. The lecture is a turning point in Frank's life — and, by extension, in the proto-utopian history imagined in the novels. Midway through *Forty Signs of Rain*, Frank experiences a "paradigm shift" (1: 273) that causes him to renovate his life, including his scientific practices, in ways that feel more alive and promising to him. In terms of the biological context that I have been outlining, Frank's Buddhist lecture causes a generic mutation in his thoughts on the model of a genetic modification in DNA, and radically new habits result from the (re)combination of very old tropisms and forms of thought (in this case, scientific curiosity and the holistic spiritual ecology of Buddhism). Indeed, such genetic change occurs all the time, and from an evolutionary perspective (like Frank's sociobiology) or an ecological perspective (like Rudra's Buddhism), life is infinitely adaptable and changeable. Living thought is more in accord with this ecological diversity.

The thought that most directly engenders Frank's crisis is a kind of *koan* that is both resonant and dissonant with his experience: "An excess of reason is itself a form of madness" (1: 268). He recognizes that his use of sociobiology has been unhealthy, and has even become dangerously close to the cynical reason of global capitalism itself. At the same time, reason seems to him the only trustworthy method of discovery and guide to action: "Science was the gene trying to pass itself along more successfully" (1: 272). Following the recombinant implications of this dizzying *koan*, he finds himself returning to the trope of genes:

> Altruism, compassion, simple goddamned foolishness ... or else something real, a real force in the world, a kind of ... basic attribute of life, like the drive to propagate one's DNA to subsequent generations. A reason for being. Something beyond DNA. A rage to live, an urge to goodness. Love. A green force, *élan vital*, that was metaphysics, that was bad, but how else were you going to explain the data?
>
> An excess of reason wasn't going to do it.
>
> Genes, however, were very reasonable. They followed their directive, they reproduced. They were a living algorithm, creatures of four elements. Strings of binaries, codes of enormous length, codes that spoke bodies. It was a kind of reason that did that. Even a kind of monomania — an excess of reason, as the *koan* suggested. So that perhaps they were all mad, not just socially and individually, but genomically too. Molecular obsessive-compulsives. And then up from there, in stacked emergent insanities. Unless it was infused with some other quality that was not rational, some late emergent property like altruism, or compassion, or love — something that was not a code — then it was all for naught [1: 274].

As one result of this generic mutation in his thoughts, Frank begins to realize that he needs an organic, fully human approach to science — an approach he again associates with Anna: "The passionate scientist.... A scientist willing to take that best scientific attitude toward all of reality. Maybe that's what the old lama had been talking about. If too much reason was a form of madness, then perhaps passionate reason was what was called for.... It could be a religion, some kind of humanism or biocentrism, philabios, philocosmos" (1: 275).

As an active paradigm shift, this line of thought leads away from the institutional certainties (despite anomalies) of Kuhnian "normal science" and into the systematic uncertainties of "revolutionary science." Frank's paradigm shift lasts throughout the series and involves an experimental restructuring of all of his habits. In treating all of life like a *koan*, there can be no fixed "solution" but only an ongoing process of living thought. Robinson's novels suggest that revolutionary science, "the pure play of science" (Foote 56), is the most truly scientific practice. This is a model of ecological complexity, rather than abstract mastery of "reason" alone.

The painful organic transformation of revolutionary science is materialized with black-comic literalism when Frank suffers a brain injury that physically impairs his ability to make decisions. As with Sax Russell's brain injury in the Mars trilogy, Frank's injury forces him to consider his habitual thought processes from a very material as well as a very personal perspective:

> For a second he wasn't sure of anything. He thought back over the years, reviewing his actions, and wondered suddenly if he had ever been quite sane. He had made any number of bad decisions, especially in the past few years, but also long before that. All his life, but getting worse, as in a progressive disease.... What had he been thinking, how had he justified it?
>
> He hadn't. He hadn't thought about it; one might even say that he had managed to avoid thinking about it. It was a kind of mental skill, a negative capability. Agile in avoiding the basic questions. He had made up internal excuses, apparently. All at the unconscious level; in a world of internal divisions [2: 385].

In effect, the injury forces Frank to combine the habitually abstract observations of science with a fully-engaged emotional involvement, so that the understanding of material reality (the hallmark of the scientific method, properly conceived) is situated in the fullness of lived reality, rather than wielded as a "rational" tool. The scientific literature he reads confirms this "new model or paradigm, in which emotion and feeling were finally understood to be indispensable in the process of proper reasoning" (2: 248). Both Frank and Sax discover that becoming more fully-human and effective scientists is a never ending process.

Postmodern Sciences as Revolutionary Science

Re-conceiving scientific genres, then, is part and parcel of using the links between genes and genres in revolutionary ways. Fortunately, the narrative suggests, various new scientific disciplines, theories and methods are already pushing science away from "an excess of reason" in the form of mechanistic and reductive models and toward recognition and even quantification of lived ecological complexity. The narrative mentions examples such as chaos theory, econometrics, cascade mathematics, climate modeling, paleoclimatology, bioinformatics, and biostatistics. These theories or approaches might be thought of as postmodern sciences because of their recognition of "chaotic" systems, their emphasis on statistical probabilities and computer simulations, and their reincorporation of "late emergent properties" of a system into the system itself, as for example when measures of "consumer confidence" becomes themselves material factors of the economy.[8]

One example of postmodern science directly inspired Robinson to write the series: the paleoclimatology's discovery of "abrupt climate change" (*Agony Column*). As the narrative explains, ice cores taken from Greenland have confirmed that global climate can change abruptly, and that only eleven thousand years ago in the period known as the "Younger Dryas" the earth shifted from the same "warm-wet" pattern it has today to the "cool-dry-windy" conditions of an ice age in a period of only three years (2: 24). As a chaotic system, the global climate is a "complex of cycles" whose "interactions were so complex, the feedbacks positive and negative so hard to gauge in advance, the unforeseen consequences so potentially vast, that no one could say what would happen next" (2: 192–3). Chaotic systems like the climate or ecosystems can thus have "nonlinear tipping points" (2: 193) or "sensitive dependencies"

(2: 209) or "information cascades" (1: 324) capable of triggering the "butterfly effect" whereby minute factors have major effects on large systems. Abrupt climate change is thus a material confirmation of the reality and power of postmodern sciences like chaos theory. As such, it is simultaneously a warning about the imminence and severity of the global environmental crisis and a potential model for revolutionary changes triggered by apparently small factors. Both aspects — the new awareness of ecological crisis and the new models for revolutionary action — are crucial to Robinson's generic experiments in the Science in the Capital series.

Another example of new scientific thinking is Frank's primary field of bioinformatics, a relatively new and explicitly interdisciplinary field that brings modern computing and quantification abilities together with biology. Bioinformatics is closely associated with the Human Genome Project. Similarly, Anna Quibler's primary field is biostatistics, and Yann Pierzinski's complex bioalgorithms use such things as "cascading recombinant math" (2: 122) computer simulations, and symbolic logic in an effort to decode gene functions. In terms of genres as genes, computer modeling and simulation are appropriately postmodern examples of how consciousness can be reincorporated into material practice in quantifiable ways. Frank explains this in terms of Prisoner's Dilemma, where "the shadow of the future made all the difference" if the results of repeated trials could be recycled into the game in the form of "more elaborate strategies" (1: 126). Here again, these postmodern forms of scientific thinking are both warnings about the fragility and unpredictability of highly complex systems such as the environment, and simultaneously models for potential revolutionary change. Insofar as change — history — is not linear and cumulative, but instead dynamic and subject to abrupt transformation based on key tipping points or evolving computational consciousness, then utopian changes based on better strategies can be imagined in scientific terms.

Of course, as abrupt climate change shows, these postmodern sciences could signal dystopian near-futures just as easily as (indeed, more easily than) utopian ones. Computer-generated information already alters material structures not just in the future, but in the present through "markets" and other instrumental abstractions. Thus Frank later finds himself turned into a virtual commodity in a "virtual futures market" (2: 94) where some of the "investors" themselves are likely computer programs and the goals are surveillance, prediction, and political and economic control. In such a world, as Baudrillard has shown, "sign value" becomes a new material quality and the "hyperreality" of vast structures of simulations becomes more real than the erstwhile real.[9] The Science in the Capital series represents both utopian and dystopian potentials of such simulated realities. It is therefore important to realize that Robinson does not view genetic modification (or any other specific science or technology) as a magic bullet. Nor does he take the view that William Burling labels "scientific idealism" (10), the fantasy belief that science will inevitably and transcendently solve humanity's problems. Instead Robinson suggests that we can imagine "a sort of a leftist sociobiology" (Foote 56) and other forms of postmodern science as potential new intellectual genres that might contribute (either directly, or as metaphorical models) to generic modification of existing culture and the emergence of a permaculture.

Generic Modification

Given the context of postmodern sciences and the conception of genres as forms of living thought, we can now return to the various genres in play in the Science in the Capital series and see better how and why Robinson uses them. Robinson experiments with generic modifications that might express utopian outcomes and imagines how those generic modifications could be incorporated effectively into the living complexity of individual lives and social institutions. In doing so, he imagines postmodern hybrids that match biological and ecological complexity in ways analogous to postmodern science.

Robinson uses the crisis of abrupt climate change, for example, as both a reason and a means for generic experimentation. The crisis is an urgent and potentially utopian challenge to "normal" habits, and repeatedly in the novels we see a sense of giddy liberation resulting from crisis. The lab scientist Leo Mulhouse is "basically very happy" to be out in the big storm threatening the San Diego coast: "A public disaster, a natural world event; it put everyone in the same boat, somehow. In a way it was even inspiring — not just the human response, but the storm itself.... As if the wind had carried him off and out of his life" (1: 335). Building a sandbag wall against the flood in Washington, Frank "felt deeply happy, and looking around he could see that everyone else was happy too.... It takes something like this to free people to be always generous" (1: 374). After the storm, as Charlie Quibler escaped the flood, "Boats of all kinds dotted the long brown lake," and the "festival mood was expressed even by what people wore — Charlie saw Hawaiian shirts, bathing suits, even Carnival masks.... It looked as if something like Trinidad's Mardi Gras parade had been disrupted by a night of storms, but was reemerging triumphant in the new day" (1: 392). After the city endures a record freeze of fifty degrees below zero, big crowds walk out onto the "sudden new terrain" (2: 422) of the frozen Potomac and party "like Carnavale on ice" (2: 421). Even after his entire island country is flooded and destroyed, Deprung says, "I do not mind it. It seems to be good for people. It wakes them up" — a sentiment that Frank immediately understands (2: 213).

Taken together, especially in the context of Robinson's earlier work, we can see a genre here that we might call the "fortunate crisis." The genre serves several important functions in Robinson's narrative: it liberates people from their ordinary habits and modes of thought; it reminds people of the ecological big picture; it shows the ultimate contingency and vulnerability of the present order of things; it causes people to reassess their true needs and their relationship to "business as usual"; it frees people to be altruistic; it serves as a catalyst for experiment and for adoption of new habits. In effect, seen from the evolutionary perspective, crises are extraordinary environments that could shape genetic/generic changes. In all these ways, the fortunate crisis genre encourages the same kind of complex contingency as revolutionary science or postmodern science. In terms of genres as genes, the global environmental crisis is both a figurative and a literal bio-ecological context.

At the same time, as with science, there are habitual genres of crisis that need modification in order to escape business as usual. Reviewers who label the novels "environmental thrillers," for example, are alluding to popular genres (perhaps descended from gothic novels) in which a particular threat to the protagonist provides intense vicarious thrills for the reader before the necessary generic resolution. However, this genre of "thriller" is ultimately quietist, no matter how terrifying the specific threat involved. Robinson makes this point explicitly when (as often happens) interviewers ask him of global warming "is it too late" or "are we doomed?" This, as Robinson explains, is "not the right question to ask":

> If you reply "No, it's not too late," then there's an implied response, "Then I don't have to do anything." But if you say "Yes, it's too late," then the response is, "Then I don't have to do anything." Both answers promote a quietist response. Same with "Are we doomed?" because if yes, oh well; and if not, then oh good; but either way, not a spur to action.... We are faced, in other words, with a tremendously serious global emergency, a clear and present danger, right now, and we have to respond well [Rohn].

This is the problem of generic modification in a nutshell. The thriller genre is readily taken up and reproduced by individuals and society, but to the detriment of the social organism's recognition of lived complexity. So long as people experience — live — the crisis in the form of a conventional thriller, no action will result. The genre has the genetic power to generate and explore an emotional threat response, but that power is circumscribed by the concomitant genetic compensation of reductive formal resolution. The culture of modern capitalism, of course, effectively reproduces such genres in the form of addictive commodities that provide simulated compensations for an increasingly disembodied existence; a culture situated in pre-modern environmental contingencies would have less use for this artificial stimulation as well as little ability to reproduce it.[10] A potentially revolutionary generic modification would seek to employ the emotional threat response (and indeed something of the vicarious pleasure of reading as a kind of curiosity) while suppressing the unnaturally simple resolution. No doubt this is partially what Robinson meant by aiming to place a generic "trap door" in the series.

Another genre that encodes crisis is the Robinsonade, the archetypical story of Robinson Crusoe. In this case, crisis is the enabling feature of the fantasy, rather than a source of threat and anxiety. Crusoe, of course, is stranded — more precisely, islanded — by unforgiving fate or nature. Fortunately for the genre's power, he is able to retrieve a cache of modern tools and supplies before his heroic confrontation with nature. Defoe's fantasy is thus also one of a fortunate crisis providing a radical escape from the restrictions of conventional society and enabling a technocratic dream of socioeconomic reinvention. In these senses, its utopian potentials are clear: a foundational break from existing society, a reinvention along new material and ideological lines, a thought experiment or fantasy about a rational reconstruction of life. At the same time, as is well known, the Robinsonade as a generic form is historically and ideologically connected to decidedly undesirable social and political expressions. Most importantly, it is a fantasy of European colonialism over nature and other cultures. It is also a radically masculinist fantasy, an antisocial fantasy of personal acquisition, and so on. It offers a model of heroism as conquest of civilization over nature, with "nature" understood as something both blank and horrible to be mastered or exterminated.

The Robinsonade is thus also a candidate for generic modification — and this is precisely how it is treated in the series. Frank self-consciously lives a Robinsonade as a "project in paleolithic living" (2: 88). In doing so he draws on revolutionary versions of science, on the fortunate crisis, and on intellectual biodiversity. Indeed, this Robinsonade has been returned to the status of a living thought experiment, represented through the fictional crises of Frank's life. From the biological perspective, Frank and the other "ferals" are compared to islanded populations, evolving in distinct environments: "The paleolithics had lived through ice ages, faced cold and storms for thousands of years. A new theory postulated that populations islanded by abrupt climate change had been forced to invent cooperative behaviors in bad weather time and time again, ultimately changing the gene and bringing about the last stages of human evolution.... Maybe they were going to have to do that again" (2: 269). The desired genetic expressions of this postmodern Robinsonade are fairly clear: escaping certain pathologies of modern life, recreating individual and social habits more in line with the entire human organism, exploring new modes of ecological and social self-determination, and making the "feeling of perpetual change ... an aspect of optimodality" (2: 268).

These generic modifications constitute an appropriately postmodern utopian strategy within late capitalism by revitalizing genres that have been commodified and colonized by global capitalism. Frank inherits the Robinsonade form most immediately from the Swiss Family Robinson tree house and the Huck Finn/Frontierland simulations at Disneyland. As a Disneyfied genre, the Robinsonade becomes a childish escape into addictive simulations. In effect, Frank turns the fantasy against capitalism itself by reincorporating it into living thought. Instead of colonizing nature or others, Frank is colonizing the "civilized" spaces of late capitalism, fortunately destabilized by crisis, using the "detritus" of civilized life, things "scavenged from the wreckage of his life, as in any other Robinsonade" (2: 89).

The wreckage of Frank's modern American life includes other genres suitable for generic modification, insertion, and reincorporation into the "optimodal" life — thus allowing Robinson to engineer fragments of other forms of thought into a kind of generic hybrid. Robinson has spoken, for example, of needing to reclaim what was good in the "American experiment" (*Agony Column*). An example of this in the series is the transcendentalism of Emerson and Thoreau. Here again, Frank finds the genre in a postmodern form; in this case, in Googled excerpts at a website called Emersonfortheday.net. In this form they "read like some miraculously profound horoscope or fortune cookie" (2: 335). Frank immediately sees that Emerson "had already sketched the parameters or the route to a new kind of nature-worshipping religion" (2: 335), and so he takes up transcendental thought into his daily routine. Thus transcendentalism (and particularly Thoreau as "a very respectable early scientist" [3: 13]) offers another generic model of an experimental and sublime relationship to nature and the present moment. Like the Robinsonade, however, Emersonian thought has a complex history that has sometimes engendered individualistic and nationalistic behaviors as well as more effectively radical ones.[11] Robinson avoids these aspects by emphasizing journaling and treating transcendentalism as lived immediacy rather than as an abstract philosophical system. Frank admires the writing in Emerson's journals for its quality of "someone thinking on the page" (2: 335) and reinscribes it into his life in a kind of reverse journaling that reactivates its radical potential as living thought.

Political heroism is another element of the American Experiment that Robinson reincorporates as an altered genre. His heroic president Phil Chase is a fantasy constructed out of bits and pieces of political history and mythology. The main political heroes that Robinson invokes, Abraham Lincoln and Franklin Roosevelt, are leaders from times of major crisis. Indeed, FDR rather than science per se provides the novels' injunction of "bold and persistent experimentation." Here again, the genre is necessarily modified in order to extract its utopian potential and neutralize its undesirable effects. Appealing to political heroes is after all an utterly familiar genre used by politicians of all stripes to claim an ideological heritage. To imagine proto-utopian changes in terms of mundane politics is therefore obviously dangerous, and recalls the older utopian literary tradition of big men with big ideas — the tradition rejected by the feminist "critical utopias" with which Robinson is generally associated. Robinson is fully aware of this danger, and has explicitly criticized "great man" versions of history. However, from the perspective of utopian modification the genre of political heroism is appealing for its clear version of a generic/genetic insertion technique: namely elective politics, whereby macro-political messages are incorporated into the vast social organism that is the American government. Combined with the catalyst of a major crisis, then, political heroism and governmental politics provide another possible model for systemic change. Robinson admits that Phil Chase is a fantasy (Gunn 2007), so the novels' modified version of governmental politics is simultaneously realistic and unrealistic. In term of genres as genes, though, we can see that the fantasy involves a modified hero constructed out of elements of American political and philosophical experiment (including transcendentalism and environmentalism) who is then imaginatively inserted into the organism of governmental politics in order to transform it into something new.

One other major element of generic modification in the novels is Buddhism, which Robinson again uses in more or less postmodern ways to further revolutionize science and engender new forms of living thought. The series opens with this seemingly odd insertion of Buddhism into an American near-future science fiction. The first chapter, "The Buddha Arrives," begins with Anna Quibler's weekday routine of waking up and going off to work. Ironically, this "waking up" largely involves unconscious actions: alarms set, routines followed, dream fragments forgotten, sticking to the "behavioral conditioning plan" for their son — "all were actions accomplished without conscious thought" (1: 8), and yet somehow "this was one of the high points of her day." Anna realizes, "not for the first time," that "There were some disturbing implications in that fact," but she simply "banished" these thoughts (1: 7). This routine is especially ironic because Anna, like Frank, is a scientist who likes "quantitative solutions to quantified problems" (1: 118) and considers herself purely rational. Like the scientists at the lecture, Anna's thoughts are described as having "a tropism toward work issues" (1: 6), making her "scientific" mode into a kind of helpless biological reflex. Because of this scientific bias, Anna "doesn't want to know" what is meant by "religious studies," and yet in reference to political leaders who ignore the environment Anna feels "there could be no greater intellectual crime. It was incomprehensible to her: *they didn't want to know*" (1: 123, emphasis in original). Thus Anna's rigid "scientific" habits are subtly revealed to be forms of repression and self-deception that perpetuate the flawed culture of business as usual at NSF and in the country generally.

Into these personal, professional, and ecological habits come the Khembalis, whose Buddhist values stress such things as presence in the moment, direct personal and emotional experience of the universe, compassion for all living things, and an animistic belief in demons and reincarnation. According to Rudra, "On the one hand, science has specialized, through mathematics and technology, on natural observations, finding out what is, and making new tools. On the other hand, Buddhism has specialized in human observations, to find out — how to become. Behave. What to do" (1: 266). Significantly, Anna only establishes a connection to Deprung because she saw a "tiny grimace of distress" on his face and "recognized [his] expression at once" (1: 13) as similar to one her young son once made. In other words, Anna uses an unconscious and emotional method — what Buddhists might call compassion — to decide how to act. Her subsequent efforts to help Deprung and the Khembalis (and ultimately the entire biosphere) grow out of this human observation. Frank's paradigm shift is even more overtly linked to the influence of Buddhism, through the lecture that helps him question his "excess of reason." He comes to believe, as Rudra says, that "science is something like devotion" toward "whatever you find" (2: 110). He thinks of his "optimodal" experiment partially as "inventing a new-but-old world religion" (2: 216) and insists that "if science wasn't helping then it was a sterile waste of time" (2: 162). Thus generic qualities of science and religion are in effect combined to create more ecological and vital forms of thought.

At the same time, Khembali spiritual beliefs in reincarnation and Shambhala are modified in the novels to be more secular. Reincarnation and animism are powerfully attractive forms of thought. They also have obvious utopian potential in their emphasis on compassion, personal spiritual continuity, progress toward enlightenment, and mystical unity with the universe. Their myth of Shambhala is explicitly "the Buddhist idea of utopia" (3: 300), a "shifting kingdom" (1: 358) or "hidden valley" (2: 466), a "place for good" or "buddhafield" where compassion and wisdom increase (2: 466). However, when Charlie starts to believe literally in this animism as an exotic power and asks the Khembalis to perform exorcisms to change his son Joe, the ceremonies they perform are revealed in the end to have been aimed at exorcising Charlie's own "demons" understood as "some bad ideas that had taken root in him" (3: 378). At the end, Deprung says that reincarnation is "a heuristic device only," in the sense that "in any life your body changes, and where you live changes—the people in your life, your work, your habits. All that changes, so much that in effect you pass through several incarnations in any one biological span." Thinking this way "helps you not to have too much attachment" and to remember that "Each day is a new thing" (3: 347). With the chastising of possessive egoism characteristic of Buddhist practice, then, Charlie realizes that he is not the owner of a mystical power, but instead a "de-subjectified" element of the living cosmos.[12] Reincarnation itself becomes secularized as a heuristic device for changing thought or even as a model of history understood as the evolution of living thought. Even the utopian myth of Shambhala becomes secularized and materialized when Rudra says, "Khembalung is not a *place*" but "A name for a way" which "moves from age to age" (2: 555). Thus the series concludes with a ceremony intended to recognize the Khembalis' new farm in Maryland as "the current manifestation of Shambhala" (3: 301).

Again, Robinson's use of these forms of thought amounts to generic modification and experimentation. Robinson's ideal here is biodiversity of thought akin to the ecological complexity of life, with a focus on integrating spiritual and emotional "living thought" with all other forms of living thought. This results in hybrids, an ancient and natural form of genetic modification. In fact, each major aspect of Frank's crisis—science, spirituality, and romantic love—results in hybrids, including the genetic hybrid of an expected child. This is not a model of mere diversity or pluralism, but a coherent examination of genres as living thought scientifically adequate to the intellectual and material environment. No one genre or mode of thought can rise above this ecological context, and simplistic rationalism is inadequate to understanding it. However, on the model of postmodern sciences, forms of thought might be consciously modified and reincorporated into social organisms to engender material transformations better adapted to lived complexity.

Biology and Comedy

Robinson's own generic descriptions of the Science in the Capital series are also strategic hybrids. Robinson describes the trilogy as "inhabiting or inventing a genre that I think of as 'utopian black comedy'" ("Redefining Utopia") and wonders "What would that read like?" (*Science Fiction Weekly*). The biological perspective explains Robinson's peculiar double verb: genres are treated as material structures in and through which one lives, but which can simultaneously (on the model of postmodern science) be (re)invented by modification or combination with other genres. We also see that his goal is overtly experimental: "What would that read like?"

More specifically, the paradoxical neologism "utopian black comedy" seems at first to contradict serious, political, and utopian concerns. Compared to the cerebral genres with which Robinson is frequently associated—not just sf and utopia, but "hard sf" and the "critical utopia"—the suggestion that this series is a comedy or farce is somewhat surprising. However, Robinson has repeatedly asserted that his work is comic, and indeed it is. One thinks, for example, of Oscar's sardonic letters in *Pacific Edge*, or the devastating satire-projection of "autotopia" in *The Gold Coast*, or the Huck Finn–like spoofing of adventure literature in *The Wild Shore*. The "War of the Asuras" chapter of *The Years of Rice and Salt* reads like a cross between great war satires such as Vonnegut's *Slaughterhouse-Five* and Heller's *Catch-22* and the metaphysical playfullness of Borges. Robinson also ends *The Martians* (and thus, in effect, his entire Martian magnum opus) with the self-referential and comically deflating story "Purple Mars." Robinson also consciously works against the "dry" reputation of utopian literature, as for example his emphasis on forms of play (softball, drag racing, pro wrestling) in *Pacific Edge* (Foote 54). Therefore, any surprise at Robinson's invocation of comedy or farce probably says more about critical priorities to date than about any sudden generic shift in Robinson's work.

Invoking black comedy, a genre associated with ruthless social criticism and misanthropic satire, helps to instill a promise of political seriousness to Robinson's neologism, but at the cost of suggesting systematically dystopian or even anti-utopian perspectives that would seem to be difficult to reconcile with utopian goals. Still, utopian literature has historically been a hybrid that entails satire as well as visions of the alternate world, starting with the sly Greek wordplay in More's original, so a certain grim humor is not an unexpected generic component. The Science in the Capital series makes ample use of grim humor and black comedy. Frank's over-indulgence in sociobiological thinking, and the representative article submissions he reads as an editor for the *Journal of Sociobiology*, constitute a spoof of reductive "scientific" explanations while simultaneously drawing attention to the inescapably animal nature of humans. In an interview, Robinson stated that he loves sociobiology "because it's so hilarious" (*Agony Column*). The grim nature of abrupt climate change and global capitalism also evoke black comedy, as for example the outrageous facts that Edgardo posts in the "Department of Unfortunate Statistics" (1: 76). Most obviously, American political blindness and the illogic of late capitalism yield darkly comic satire. The U.S. president is "the happy man" (1: 156) who blandly dismisses carbon dioxide's threat by calling it "the bubbly in my club soda" (1: 161) and insists on a "growth-based approach" (1: 162) to global warming. The president's science advisor, nicknamed Dr. Strangelove in an obvious homage to Kubrick's black comic masterpiece, spouts ironic double-speak worthy of his namesake in the face of global catastrophe: "We've agreed that there is general agreement that the observed warming is real" (1: 159). Charlie summarizes their attitude with grim irony: "Easier to destroy the world than to change capitalism even one little bit" (1: 156). Charlie's meeting with the President and Dr. Strangelove takes place incongruously with his son asleep on Charlie's back and ends with Charlie laughing uncontrollably. There are also slyer examples of black comedy, as for example when Frank and Diane watch the effort to restart the Gulf Stream on an oil tanker named the *Hugo Chavez* (2: 559).

Meanwhile, utopianism obviously has affinities with comedy as a conventional form with a seemingly miraculous happy ending, and in terms of overall shape the series clearly is a comedy, complete with a multiple wedding as its formally happy ending. Here comic resolutions and utopian hopes predominate over black comedy, without at all excluding it — a mixture common to the critical utopia and critical dystopia.[13] In terms of biology, the evolutionary perspective can be both misanthropic (like black comedy) and hopeful and forward-looking (like comedy more broadly). Indeed, black comedy as anti-social satire throws the reader back on a biological or evolutionary perspective in the same way that the fortunate crisis does, while the comic resolution with its hybrid forms and literal marriages also stresses the biological context. Utopian black comedy is another way of characterizing the tragicomedy of biological life and the living thought that we must use to express it. These are no doubt aspects of what Robinson means by calling it a utopian black comedy. "Utopian black comedy" is therefore in the vein of "critical utopia" or "ambiguous utopia" as a complex and radically contingent modern genre.

The Shadow of the Future

The utopian functions of Robinson's other main generic designation for the series, "near-future science fiction," are similarly illuminated from the biological perspective. Locating the attempted sf novum so close to our existing time and place clearly invites difficulties, but Robinson has strategic reasons for embracing those difficulties. He has said that near-future sf "captures the sense of perpetual newness in life these days, that anything is possible." At the same time, however, "it also feels like nothing fundamental will ever change again (capitalism); and in that weird dichotomy of feeling we carry on day by day" (Szeman 181). Near-future sf not only captures this contemporary structure of feeling, but to the extent that (as Robinson has asserted repeatedly) "we in the West ... are already living in a science fiction novel that we are all writing together," then "reading science fiction ... is a way of orienting oneself and examining questions of meaning in the contemporary world" (Rohn).[14] Science fiction, and particularly near-future sf, is thus a form of "living thought." From the biological perspective, we can see that the genre highlights the interactions between material structures (bodies, institutions, social organisms) and consciousness (thoughts, projections, and fictions). Its location as a lived and contingent process of creation "on the future edge of things" (Gunn 2007) is both allegorically and literally a model of history. Indeed, Robinson has asserted that "SF serves as a kind of modeling or climate forecasting" (Jamneck). It can thus be thought of as sharing functions with new sciences like bioinformatics, particularly in the way that the statistical and computer modeling aspects of those new sciences encourage the feeling of chaotic complexity in which present and future reality are seen as radically dynamic and open. Robinson is describing this liberating effect of writing near-future sf when he says that "there is a tremendous pleasure and value in writing about the present as if writing science fiction" (Szeman 181). In fact, Robinson asserts that "science itself is a 'utopian science fiction' working to make itself real" (Szeman 186). The Science in the Capital series calls this function "the shadow of the future"—a feedback loop into the present, rather than mere fiction. Robinson insists, correctly, that he is just a novelist, but he also asserts that "symbolic acts are also real acts" (Szeman 182). The Science in the Capital series demonstrates that complex reality by using the biological, ecological, and evolutionary perspective to link genes and genres, and by enacting that link on the model of postmodern sciences in its own hybrid and dynamic narrative form.

Utopia and/as Generic Modification

The Science in the Capital trilogy thus continues the inventive exploration of the possibilities for thinking utopia that critics now expect from Kim Stanley Robinson. Identifying Robinson with the critical utopia means that generic complication and radical contingency is expected. Such generic dynamism is also in keeping with the dialectical understanding of utopia that Jameson has developed most fully in "The Desire Called Utopia." In fact, as Jameson has pointed out, "Utopian critics, today, are in much the same situation as Utopian creators and storytellers, and are to that degree in a better position to appreciate the achievements of the latter (as the various acknowledgements of the work of Kim Stanley Robinson testify)" (*Politics and Culture*). In trying to keep utopia alive under global capitalism, Robinson is no longer taken to be exceptional; in fact, he has become exemplary, and even a model of critical paradigms.

However, in its use of the biological, ecological and evolutionary perspective, the series also seems to complicate current expectations — because in addition to the largely negative functions of utopia described by Jameson, Robinson's genetic model of genres also appears to offer positive, material, and scientific formulations of utopian representations. This complication can best be seen by examining Jameson's discussions of the utopian "break" at the conclusion of "The Desire Called Utopia." Following up on his assertion in "The Politics of Utopia" that "utopianism emerges at the moment of the suspension of the political" (43), Jameson elaborates on the political function of utopia today:

> Disruption is, then, the name for a new discursive strategy, and Utopia is the form such disruption necessarily takes. And this is now the temporal situation in which the Utopian form proper — the radical closure of a system of difference in time, the experience of the total formal break and discontinuity — has its political role to play, and in fact becomes a new kind of content in its own right. For it is the very principle of the radical break as such, its possibility, which is reinforced by the Utopian form, which insists that its radical difference is possible and that a break is necessary. The Utopian form itself is the answer to the universal ideological conviction that no alternative is possible, that there is no alternative to the system. But it asserts this by forcing us to think the break itself, and not by offering a more traditional picture of what things would be like after the break [*AF* 231–2].

This characterization certainly describes the Science in the Capital series in terms of the lack of a "traditional picture" of utopia and the way Robinson's series forces us instead to think "the break itself."[15] However, Jameson's point seems to be that the "Utopian form proper" achieves this focus primarily by its necessary and constitutive formal flaw: namely, that in positing a closed system beyond some break or trench from existing time and space, the Utopian form proper by definition cannot give a realistic account of the break itself. In the current political situation, then, the moment when both Jameson and Robinson are writing, utopia "now better expresses our relationship to a genuinely political future than any current program of action" only because this "formal flaw — how to articulate the Utopian break in such a way that it is transformed into a practical-political transition — now becomes a rhetorical and political strength — in that it forces us precisely to concentrate on the break itself: a meditation on the impossible, on the unrealizable in its own right" (*AF* 232). Thus Jameson posits that it is the "radical break or succession of Utopia from political possibilities as well as from reality itself" that "now more accurately reflects our current ideological state of mind" (*AF* 232).

In this regard, the Science in the Capital series as I have been characterizing it seems to offer a significantly different approach to the utopian break than the one Jameson suggests. For one thing, Robinson's work seems to be directly *about* the break, rather than indirectly. For another thing, it seems to approach the question of a break from "our current ideological state of mind" in arguably realistic, scientific, and material ways. The comparisons of genres to genetic engineering, bioinformatics, computer modeling, and other feedback loops of postmodern science are not only (as Jameson correctly characterizes utopias in general) "wishfulfillments, and hallucinatory visions in desperate times" (*AF* 233), but also literal reinscriptions of human culture into biological and ecological frameworks. Insofar as Robinson's perspective is biological, ecological, and evolutionary, that is to say, it offers models for revolutionary disruptions that are both discursive and scientific, both generic and genetic.

At this point two objections might be raised against my assertion that Robinson's biological perspective presents a material model of utopianism: namely, that it is not truly utopian, and/or that it is not truly material. The first objection would question how "utopian" the Science in the Capital series is if it insists that real (albeit postmodern) sciences and technologies might materialize the "break" from "our current ideological state of mind"? How much of a break can it be, in other words, if it is connected in an evolutionary or technocratic way to what has come before, and if it relies on science (however humanized) and technology (however ecologized) and even aspects of global capitalism itself, such as the reinsurance industry? Given "the obligation for Utopia to remain an unrealizable fantasy" (*AF* 227), it could be argued that Robinson's near-future sf is too realistic to be properly utopian. Robinson himself usually speaks of his utopianism in relative rather than absolute or formal terms, however, so this objection is perhaps more a matter of definition than substance here. The second objection, meanwhile, would presumably point out that Robinson's series is still only a fantasy, still only a work of literature imagining itself to be material and genetic. Utopian literature has always fantasized a powerful role for itself, and Shelly's dictum that "Poets are the unacknowledged legislators of the world" shows that literature as a whole frequently shares the same fantasy. But as I have tried to show, Robinson has a very material conception of how genres and other forms of thought work in the postmodern world — not just literary genres, but scientific and other "material" genres as well. The novel quotes a neuroscientist, Antonio Damasio, who says of human cognition that "The system is so complex and multilayered that it operates with some degree of freedom" (2: 250). This freedom of complex living systems would seem to be a biological-political version of Althusser's psychological-political concept of overdetermination. In addition, Robinson's evolutionary perspective and experimental mode simply open hope and imagine possibilities — they don't guarantee specific outcomes. Robinson constantly reminds interviewers that he is a novelist. Nevertheless, he seems to offer some very powerful contexts for the novelistic experiments that he conducts, and for asking "what would that read like?"

A useful context for my claim that Robinson's utopianism is both imaginative and material might be Jameson's challenge to find an "absolute formalism" (*AF* 213) that can differentiate "the newer [supposedly postmodern] Utopias from their modernist predecessors" (212). Such formalism, Jameson asserts, would have to go beyond what he calls the modernist "category of reflexivity," which has "constituted one of the fundamental 'solutions' of the modern era as far back as one wishes to go" (*AF* 217), but which in fact merely turns literary self-consciousness into subject matter and asserts that this formal reflexivity is radical in and of itself. By contrast, any "new formal solution" demonstrating that newer (postmodern) utopias go beyond mere reflexivity will "need to take into account both the historic originalities of late capitalism — its cybernetic technology as well as its globalizing dynamics — and the emergence, as well, of new subjectivities such as the surcharge of multiple or 'parcellated' subject positions characteristic of postmodernity" (*AF* 214).

This seems to be precisely what Robinson has attempted — and perhaps achieved — in the Science in the Capital series: a formally and strategically postmodern utopian novel. The series elaborately explores cybernetic technology and parcellated subject positions; indeed, Jameson provides an excerpt from *Fifty Degrees Below* as "some properly science-fictional versions of these well-known post–Lacanian 'multiple subject positions'" (*AF* 192–93, n. 21). It imagines, on the model of postmodern sciences, how reflexivity can function as a formal feedback loop, not as mere disembodied consciousness or recycled subject matter, but as iterations that change chaotic systems or modifications that alter generic/genetic codes. He attacks the "historic originalities" of late capitalism directly, but using the framework of Buddhist-inflected postmodern biology and ecology more than the quintessentially modernist frameworks of psychology and history. Robinson even incorporates Jameson's own expressions into his work. As Frank Vanderwal wonders rhetorically "What could be done if humanity were not trapped in its own institutions?" and makes the most forceful case he can for utopian changes, a phrase pops into his head: "'To wrest Freedom from the grasp of Necessity' ... Who said that?" (3: 171). Although the text itself does not say, this is a paraphrase from Jameson's *Political Unconscious* (19) and an echo of Marx. Thus we know that Jameson's thought is itself part of the generic/genetic heritage of Robinson's utopia. Of course, Jameson insists on the political frameworks of history and psychology, and these frameworks can account for representations of biology as easily as the obverse. And it is certainly true that these desperate times call forth increasingly desperate fantasies and wish-fulfillments. However, as Darko Suvin reminds us, "practice is always slyer than theory" (*Learning from Other Worlds* 251). Or, in terms of biology: life is a very complex system.

Notes

1. Moylan similarly cites Robinson as an exception to the historical primacy of the dystopia in the 1990s; see "'Look into the Dark': on Dystopia and the *Novum*," 57. A very useful history of the concept of the "critical utopia" can be found in "Utopia Is When Our Lives Matter" (20n4). By extension, Robinson's association with the "critical utopia" also suggests his association with the "critical dystopia"; see n12 below. Moylan's evolving critical definitions and historical arguments are striking examples of how Robinson's work has helped to provoke revisions of critical models.

2. For an early exception to this positive critical assessment, see Ernest Yanarella, "Terra/Terror-Forming and Death Denial in Kim Stanley Robinson's Martian Stories and Mars Trilogy." Significantly—given my focus in this essay—Yanarella's objections are primarily eco-critical. It should also be noted that Jameson does not view Robinson (or any other writer) as an exception to his assertion that utopian representations must ultimately and by definition fall short of their goal; in addition to *Archaeologies of the Future*, see "The Politics of Utopia."

3. The informal designation "Science in the Capital" derives from Robinson's working title for the series. Robinson claims that his planned titles for the volumes in the series were "Science in the Capital," "The Capital in Science," and "Global Cooling," but that his publisher insisted on more "novelistic" titles; see Robinson's interview with Moira Gunn. "Science in the Capital" is also an early chapter title in *Antarctica*, the novel in which Robinson first develops the character of Senator Phil Chase. It should also be noted that, as Jameson has said of the so-called Mars trilogy, the Science in the Capital books are not truly a trilogy, but "three books [that] form a single narrative and constitute a single novel" (*AF* 397). Quotations from the series will be cited by volume number and page number.

4. For discussions of the generic designation "sf and utopia," see *Learning from Other Worlds*, especially Carl Freedman, "Science Fiction and Utopia: A Historico-Philosophical Overview." In *Metamorphoses of Science Fiction*, Darko Suvin famously defined utopian literature as "Strictly and precisely speaking, ... not a genre but the *sociopolitical subgenre of science fiction*" (61, emphasis in original). In addition to the re-examinations of this assertion about the genre(s) of sf and utopia in *Learning from Other Worlds* (which is a kind of *Festschrift* dedicated to Suvin), see Jameson's brief meta-criticism of generic classification in *Archaeologies* (18n11).

5. Indeed, biotechnology is perhaps necessarily a kind of lived science fiction; see Hamilton, "Traces of the Future: Biotechnology, Science Fiction, and the Media."

6. In 1819, U.S. Supreme Court Chief Justice John Marshall defined a corporation as an artificial person "invisible, intangible, and existing only in the contemplation of the law." After the passage of the Fourteenth Amendment, business corporations were deemed to have the status of a constitutional "person" and thus to receive protection under the "due process" clause. In legal terms, a corporation is considered a "juristic" or "juridical" person, as opposed to a "natural" person. See Miller, *The Modern Corporate State*, 37–49.

7. Veronica Hollinger points out that this optimistic vision has sometimes been called "participatory evolution"; see "Stories about the Future," 457 and 468n14.

8. For a provocative examination of the experience of postmodern economic information, see Randy Martin, *Financialization of Daily Life*. Coming at the same confluence from another direction, Neil Gerlach and Sheryl N. Hamilton explicitly suggest that "sf and business writing can be read as linked discourses, sharing a commitment to science and technology and the project of positing a credible relationship between present and future" (461).

9. See especially *For a Critique of the Political Economy of the Sign* and the essay "Simulacra and Simulations" in *Selected Writings*.

10. On commodities as addiction and compulsion, see Jameson, "The Politics of Utopia," 52–53.

11. For an example of a critical reading of the Emersonian tradition, see Rowe, *At Emerson's Tomb*.

12. For Jameson's idea of "desubjectification," the "loss of psychic privileges and spiritual private property," see "The Politics of Utopia," 39–40. On "secularization" as an aspect of contemporary utopia (and in Robinson specifically), see *Archaeologies*, 398–99.

13. That is to say, both the critical utopia and the critical dystopia are blended genres. On the critical dystopia, see Moylan, *Scraps of the Untainted Sky*, especially Chapter 6 and 7, and the essays in *Dark Horizons: Science Fiction and the Dystopian Imagination*. Suvin suggests the terms "fallible eutopia" and "fallible dystopia" as more accurate descriptions of what Moylan calls "critical utopias" and "critical dystopias": see "Theses on Dystopia 2001," 195–97.

14. For an interesting examination of the generic and theoretical implications of this asymptotic approach of present and future in science fiction, see Hollinger, "Stories about the Future." In note 20, Hollinger labels the Science in the Capital series "*very*-near-future novels" and places them in a line of recent sf novels confronting this sense of the present as a kind of science fiction (469).

15. It should be pointed out that the Science in the Capital series was only a forthcoming trilogy referenced in a footnote (*AF* 5n7) when "The Desire Called Utopia" was begun. Farther into "The Desire Called Utopia," however, Jameson quotes *Fifty Degrees Below* in a footnote (*AF* 192–93n21). Thus while the Science in the Capital novels are not explicitly considered in "The Desire Called Utopia," Jameson was apparently reading the first two novels as he was writing and/or revising his essay.

Works Cited

Baudrillard, Jean. *For a Critique of the Political Economy of the Sign*. Trans. Charles Levin. St. Louis: Telos, 1981.

———. *Selected Writings*. Ed. Mark Poster. Stanford: Stanford University Press, 1988.

Burling, William J. "Reading Time: the Ideology of Time Travel in Science Fiction." *KronoScope* 6.1 (2006): 5–30.

Clarke, Amy. "'Like a Japanese Paper Flower in Water': An Interview with Kim Stanley Robinson." *Writing on the Edge* 12.1 (2001): 5–14.

Dark Horizons: Science Fiction and the Dystopian Imagination. Ed. Raffaella Baccolini and Tom Moylan. New York and London: Routledge, 2003.

Feyerabend, Paul. *Against Method: Outline of an Anarchistic Theory of Knowledge*. London: Verso, 1975.

Foote, Bud. "A Conversation with Kim Stanley Robinson." *Science-Fiction Studies* 21 (1994): 51–60.

Franko, Carol. "Working the 'In-Between': Kim Stanley Robinson's Utopian Fiction." *Science-Fiction Studies* 21 (1994):191–211.

Freedman, Carl. "Science Fiction and Utopia: A Historico-Philosophical Overview." In *Learning from Other Worlds: Estrangement, Cognition, and the Politics of Science Fiction and Utopia*. Ed. Patrick Parrinder. Durham: Duke University Press, 2001. 72–97.

Gerlach, Neil, and Sheryl N. Hamilton. "Telling the Future, Managing the Present: Business Restructuring Literature as SF." *Science-Fiction Studies* 27 (2000): 461–477.

Hamilton, Sheryl N. "Traces of the Future: Biotechnology, Science Fiction, and the Media." *Science Fiction Studies* 30 (2003): 267–282.

Hollinger, Veronica. "Stories about the Future: From Patterns of Expectation to Pattern Recognition." *Science-Fiction Studies* 33 (2006): 452–472.

Jameson, Fredric. *Archaeologies of the Future: The Desire Called Utopia and Other Science Fictions*. London: Verso, 2005.

———. *The Political Unconscious: Narrative as a Socially Symbolic Act*. Ithaca: Cornell University Press, 1981.

———. "The Politics of Utopia." *New Left Review* 25 (2004): 35–54.

———. "Utopia and Failure." *Politics and Culture* 2000.2 (2000). 13 Apr. 2007 <http://aspen.conncoll.edu/politicsandculture/page.cfm?key=18>.

Kuhn, Thomas S. *The Structure of Scientific Revolutions*. 2nd ed. Chicago: University Chicago Press, 1970.

Learning from Other Worlds: Estrangement, Cognition, and the Politics of Science Fiction and Utopia. Ed. Patrick Parrinder. Durham: Duke University Press, 2001.

Martin, Randy. *Financialization of Daily Life*. Philadelphia: Temple University Press, 2002.

Miller, Arthur Selwyn. *The Modern Corporate State: Private Governments and the American Constitution*. Westport, CT: Greenwood Press, 1976.

Moylan, Tom. "'Look into the dark': On Dystopia and the *Novum*." In *Learning from Other Worlds: Estrangement, Cognition, and the Politics of Science Fiction and Utopia*. Ed. Patrick Parrinder. Durham: Duke University Press, 2001. 51–71.
_____. *Scraps of the Untainted Sky: Science Fiction, Utopia, Dystopia*. Boulder: Westview, 2000.
_____. "'Utopia Is When Our Lives Matter': Reading Kim Stanley Robinson's *Pacific Edge*." *Utopian Studies* 6.2 (1995): 1–24.
Robinson, Kim Stanley. *Fifty Degrees Below*. New York: Bantam, 2005.
_____. *Forty Signs of Rain*. New York: Bantam, 2004.
_____. Interview. *The Agony Column*. 4 June 2004. 5 July 2007. <http://trashotron.com/agony/news/2004/06-14-04.htm>
_____. Interview. *Locus Online*. 6 June 2007. <www.locusmag.com/2007/Issue04_Robinson.html>
_____. Interview. *Science Fiction Weekly*. Nov. 2003. 5 July 2007. <http://www.scifi.com/sfw/issue351/interview.html>
_____. Interview with Lynn Jamneck. *Strange Horizons*. 15 Aug. 2005. 5 July 2007.
_____. Interview with Moira Gunn. *Tech Nation*. ITConversations. 10 Jan. 2006. 5 July 2007 <http://www.itconversations.com/shows/detail935.html>
_____. Interview with Moira Gunn. *Tech Nation*. ITConversations. 4 Apr. 2007. 5 July 2007 <http://www.itconversations.com/shows/detail1773.html>
_____. "Interview with Novelist Kim Stanley Robinson." By Jennifer Rohn. 4 Feb. 2007. 5 July 2007 <http://www.lablit.com/article/208>
_____. "Redefining Utopia: Kim Stanley Robinson Interviewed." 5 July 2007 <http://www.yatterings.com/2007/04/17/redefining-utopia-kim-stanley-robinson-interviewed/>
_____. *Sixty Days and Counting*. New York: Bantam, 2007.
_____. "Wilderness, Utopia, History: An Interview with Kim Stanley Robinson." By Nick Gevers. *infinity plus*. Sept. 1999. 5 July 2007 <http://www.infinityplus.co.uk/nonfiction/intksr.htm>.
Rowe, John Carlos. *At Emerson's Tomb: The Politics of Classic American Literature*. New York: Columbia University Press, 1997.
Suvin, Darko. *Metamorphoses of Science Fiction: On the Poetics and History of a Literary Genre*. New Haven and London: Yale University Press, 1979.
_____. "Theses on Dystopia 2001." In *Dark Horizons: Science Fiction and the Dystopian Imagination*. Ed. Raffaella Baccolini and Tom Moylan. New York and London: Routledge, 2003. 187–201.
Szeman, Imre and Maria Whiteman. "Future Politics: An Interview with Kim Stanley Robinson." *Science Fiction Studies* 31 (2004): 177–188.
Wallerstein, Immanuel. *World-Systems Analysis: An Introduction*. Durham and London: Duke University Press, 2004.
Yanarella, Ernest J. "Terra/Terror-Forming and Death Denial in Kim Stanley Robinson's Martian Stories and Mars Trilogy." *Foundation* 89 (2003): 13–26.

13

"Structuralist Alchemy" in *Red Mars*[*]
William J. White

Kim Stanley Robinson's Mars trilogy has been lauded as a signal achievement in science fiction. Its three parts describe the colonization and terraforming of Mars over the course of more than two centuries, forming a cohesive storyline focused on the "First Hundred," the earliest colonists who, granted extended longevity by virtue of medical technologies, become central to the revolutionary utopian scientific and political project whose unfolding is the heart of the series. The first part, *Red Mars*, won the Nebula Award, and both of its sequels, *Green Mars* and *Blue Mars,* received Hugo Awards. Reviewing *Red Mars* for the *New York Times,* Gerald Jonas called it "an absorbing novel of ideas, notable for the opportunity it provides to watch a scientifically informed imagination of rare ambition at work" (25). Scholars have taken note of the series' rich allusiveness, its awareness of its own textuality (Foote; Franko "Density"), while readers have marveled at its scientific virtuosity and compelling humanistic vision (Amazon.com).

Of course, some of those same readers have expressed dismay at the complexity of the writing and the storyline, a feature that scholars acknowledge as well. Bud Foote, for example, in an appreciative note on the first novel, clearly relishes the prospect that untenured assistant professors and graduate students will be digging out its references for decades to come (66). William Dynes, on the other hand, in discussing his own students' experiences, says that upon finishing *Red Mars,* "even after five hundred pages and at least seven distinct shifts in narrator, the reader cannot feel that he or she has been given a reasonably complete understanding of the events of the novel" because of the contradictions and conflicts between the viewpoints used to develop the story (154). This essay, in seeking to make sense of the novel's structure, is an effort to grapple with the complexity of the Mars books and provide the basis for a more complete understanding of its events.

In order to do so, this essay takes as its starting point the strange musings of Robinson's psychiatrist character Michel Duval in an early section of *Red Mars* as he suffers through homesick alienation from the rest of the Martian colonists he has been sent along to watch over. Following a hint that the "structuralist alchemy" (as Robinson calls it) in which Michel engages is meant to suggest a way of reading the meanings implicated in the novel itself, this essay makes use of the work of the French semiotician from whom Robinson borrows his alchemical procedures, turning them recursively upon the novel itself in order to bring to light

---

[*]First published as "'Structuralist Alchemy' in Kim Stanley Robinson's *Red Mars*." *Extrapolation* (forthcoming). Reprinted by permission of *Extrapolation*.

the thematic discursive structures that underpin the narrative. It then turns to a narrative analysis that explores the "actantial" dimension of *Red Mars;* that is, how characters come to embody or instantiate those discursive structures. It does so by examining the story of John Boone, a charismatic leader of the Martian colony, in structural terms. It then contextualizes that "mythic" (uninflected) narrative analysis in light of the "counter-narrative" afforded by the story of Frank Chalmers, Boone's romantic and political rival, suggesting that an effect of that contrast is both to valorize and problematize Boone's intertwined political and spiritual mission. Finally, the essay concludes by suggesting that it is the tension between the mythic and the ironic that gives the novel much of its resonance, "exploding" (that is, expanding) the myth/irony dualism in order to do so.

The Semantic Rectangle Appears on Mars

Among the "First Hundred" colonists who arrive on Kim Stanley Robinson's *Red Mars*, Michel Duval occupies a singular place. The rest of the settlers are scientists, engineers, and technicians, charged with exploring and building a new world; he is the psychiatrist sent to observe, evaluate, and when necessary counsel the others. Whereas they endured a rigorous winnowing process to join the First Hundred, eager to be among the first to colonize the planet, Michel was included by the selection committee largely at his own insistence to ameliorate the potential social and psychological dysfunctions created through the selection process. But Michel Duval is a reluctant colonist at best, and his alienation is the key issue in the section of *Red Mars* in which he is the viewpoint character (Part 4, "Homesick"). He is withdrawn and melancholy, mechanically going through the motions of his work in a forlorn fugue until "rescued" by Hiroko Ai, the mystagogical leader of the bioscience-oriented "farm team" that splinters off from the colony at the end of Part 4 to pursue in secret their own vision of Mars.

Furthermore, in contrast to the technical and geographical prose that characterizes the "hard science" of earlier and later sections, in "Homesick" there is a description of Michel's use of a "Greimas semantic rectangle" (*Red Mars* 217) to categorize members of the First Hundred, labeling them according to a scheme derived from the ancient theory of the four humours, so that the affable and easy-going astronaut John Boone is "sanguine" while the glowering political operator Frank Chalmers is "choleric," and so forth. The semantic rectangle he uses is a "combinatoire" involving paired contradictions of personality (introvert vs. extrovert) and emotional volatility (stabile vs. labile). Robinson describes how Michel combines different pairs of the four terms to identify "temperaments" as contingencies of those combinations (see Figure 1).

The "Greimas" to whom Michel Duval attributes the semantic rectangle is Algirdas Julien Greimas (1917–1992), a French semiotician whose work was heavily influential upon the structuralist "Paris school" of the 1970s and 1980s; his 1966 *Sémantique structurale* "stood out like a culmination and pinnacle of all previous attempts to produce a systematic theory of meaning" (Budniakiewicz 3). The semantic rectangle (and the "semiotic square" that forms its core set of contrasting terms; see Schleifer 25) is an attempt to grasp the "entanglement" of opposites (Schleifer 30). In other words, Greimassian semiotics recognizes the inadequacy of simple opposed binary pairs (e.g., black/white) and attempts to account for the missing or excluded semantic terms (e.g., *both black and white*, equivalent to "grey" or "striped" or "colored [in]," depending on context, and *neither black nor white*, equivalent to "colorless").

Duval's arcane musings have not attracted much comment in the reviews and criticisms

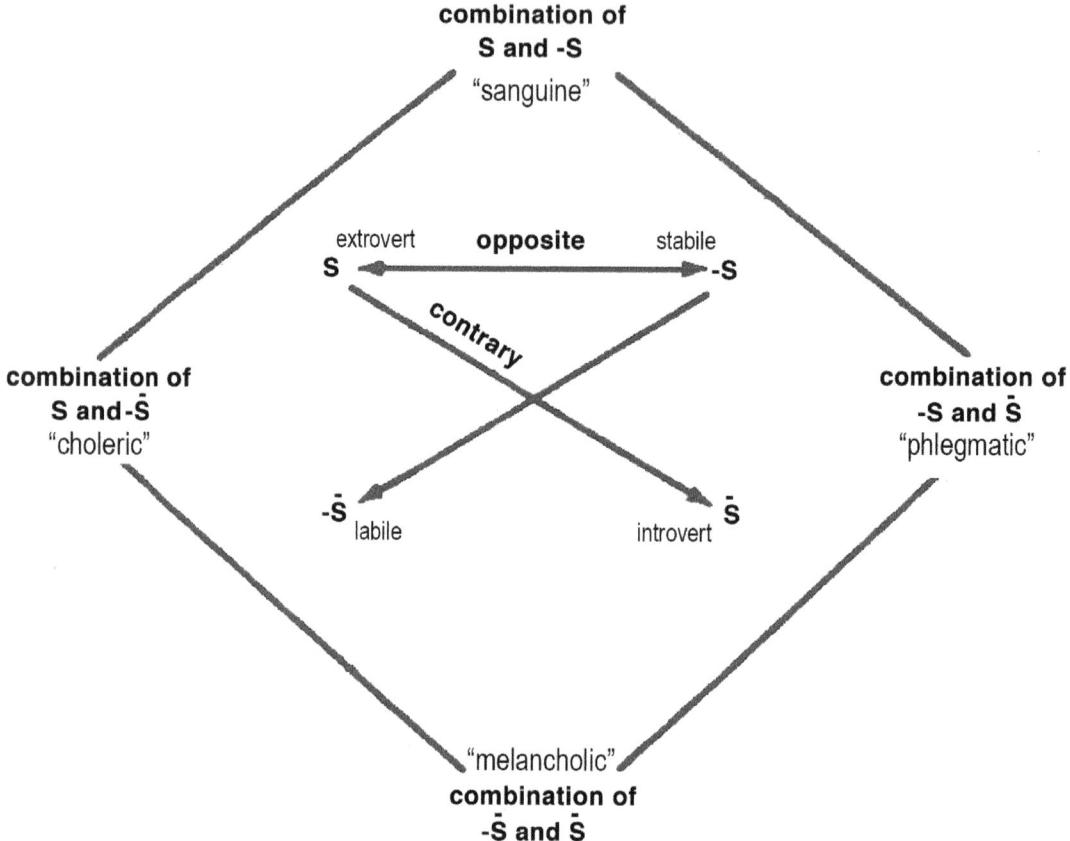

Figure 1. The "four humours" as products of a Greimassian semantic rectangle, in which the inner "semiotic square" situates contradictory extrovert/introvert and stabile/labile pairs. After Robinson, *Red Mars*, 218–219.

of Robinson's trilogy, perhaps because they seem part and parcel with the rest of his psychological "science," which attracts critical derision from other characters whenever it appears: Michel's defense of the personality test used to assess the candidates for the expedition generates a "methodological inquisition" (63), and his off-hand reference to Abraham Maslow's notion of "peak experience" after John Boone's visionary speech on Olympus Mons elicits a groan from one of his friends (381). Michel himself is self-deprecatingly amused when he recognizes the irony of using "a century's [worth of] psychological thinking, and some of the latest laboratory research in psychophysiology, not to mention a complicated apparatus from structuralist alchemy, all in order to reinvent the ancient system of the humours" (219).

Read Mars: A Semantic Rectangular Recursion

Despite this, there is some evidence that Robinson intends for the close reader to take the semantic rectangle seriously at least as a device for illuminating some of the thematic underpinnings of the Mars trilogy. This being the case, it is thus possible that Greimassian semiotics can be employed recursively to decode or at least unpack meanings available in the text. Robinson's academic mentor Fredric Jameson, whose influence Robinson acknowledges in *Red Mars* and whom he cites extensively in his own dissertation on the science fiction writer Philip K. Dick, himself analyzes one of Dick's novels using a semantic rectangle ("After Armageddon") and suggests in his foreword to a translated volume of Greimas's essays that that newcomers to Greimas should feel free to engage in *bricolage* or, more plainly, "simply ... steal the pieces that interest or fascinate us, and ... carry off our fragmentary booty to our intellectual caves" (Greimas viii). Robinson's dissertation, later published as a book (*The Novels of Philip K. Dick*), reveals him to be intensely interested in the structural relationships among characters, at least as a literary scholar, which experience Robinson says he regards as part of his education as a writer (Foote and Robinson).

Besides these contextual cues, the semantic rectangle reappears at least in passing several times in the novels, most notably as sense-making device during the "Dorsa Brevia conference" in *Green Mars*, when many of the factions involved in the underground Martian independence movement meet to hash out a political program:

> One night Michel Duval joined [three other characters] for a drink, and as Nadia described the problem he got out his AI and began to make diagrams based on what he called the "semantic rectangle." Using this schema they made a hundred different sketches of the various dichotomies, trying to find a mapping that would help them understand what alignments and oppositions might exist among them. They made some interesting patterns, but it could not be said that any blinding insights jumped off the screen at them — although one particularly messy semantic rectangle seemed suggestive, at least to Michel: violence and nonviolence, terraforming and antiterraforming formed the initial four corners, and in the secondary combination around this first rectangle he had located Bogdanovists, Reds, Hiroko's areophany, and the Muslims and other cultural conservatives. But what this *combinatoire* indicated in terms of action was not clear [*Green Mars* 368].

This kind of technique for eliciting meaning — for understanding!— seems exactly suited for making sense of *Red Mars*, which seeks to articulate contradictory positions in a way that gives each the opportunity for eloquence (Dynes) and in which characters struggle "to yoke together impossible opposites: mind and body, spirit and matter, nature and culture, and biosphere and technoscience" (Markley 774). As Schleifer explains, the essence of the semiotic square involves exploding a dichotomy in order to reveal hitherto unnoticed levels of signification (30). So beyond the initial dichotomy of *yes* and *no*, for instance, there exists a *complex positive term* that combines the meanings of the dichotomous terms the way that *maybe* does, and a *complex negative term* that rejects or negates the dichotomy the way that *unknown* does. In that expansion of the dichotomy, an additional distinction between certainty (*yes* and *no*) and uncertainty (*maybe* and *unknown*) also appears, with the "positive" and "negative" members of each pair standing as complements to their counterpart in the other pair and as contraries to the complements of their opposite (so that *maybe* is the complement of *yes* and the contrary of *no*).

The Semiotic Square: Red and Green

It thus seems plausible to regard Michel's rediscovery of the four humours in the first half of *Red Mars* Part 4 ("Homesick") as a primer in the use of the semantic rectangle, and an invitation to apply the technique to the dualism that is at the core of the second half of the section. This dualism is the dichotomy between *kami* and *viriditas*, the two metaphysical principles that form the essence of Hiroko's Mars-worshipping "areophany," a kind of "landscape religion" acknowledging, on the one hand, the spirit of place inhering within the landscape of Mars itself (*kami*), and on the other, the fructifying "greening power" (*viriditas*) residing with human beings and life more generally (229). At the climax of "Homesick," Michel finds himself swept up in the ritual of the areophany, a ceremony that Hiroko and her followers among the First Hundred had created together to enable "the combination of these sacred powers that would allow humans to exist [on Mars] in a meaningful way." Struck by the word *combination,* Michel envisions a kaleidoscope of semantic rectangles that collapses "to a single, beautiful rose, the heart of the areophany, *kami* suffused with *viriditas*, both fully red and fully green at one and the same time" (229).

In "Homesick," the opposition of Red and Green as symbolic terms representing commitments on the part of the characters of the Mars trilogy is articulated fully for the first time. Red and Green will also come to be used as labels for political factions respectively opposed to or in favor of terraforming Mars, but those political positions are motivated by an underlying allegiance to respect for Mars as its own place on the one hand and the inherent value of life on the other. Elizabeth Leane, in a critical examination that focuses on the entangled dichotomies of science, colonialism, and literature within the trilogy, observes that the Red/Green dichotomy at its core addresses the aesthetics of Mars: Red Mars is a place whose beauty inheres within itself, while the beauty of Green Mars emerges from what humans see in it (92–93). This is the essence of the persistent debate about terraforming between the single-minded geologist Ann Clayborne and the polymathic physicist Saxifrage Russell that begins shortly after the First Hundred land on Mars (*Red Mars* 176–179) and which continues until their long-delayed rapprochement at the climax of *Blue Mars.*

The Semiotic Square: Green and White

Leane also discusses the Green/White contrast that Robinson introduces in *Green Mars.* Green still represents *viriditas*, the life-force, while White stands for either a gimlet-eyed rejection of the mystical or a solipsistic refusal of the numinous; embracing rather the rational or pragmatic (96–100). Michel Duval, in hiding with other survivors of the failed Martian revolution of 2061 in a terrarium-like refuge tunneled out of the Martian south polar ice cap helps Nirgal, one of the young "ectogenes" (test-tube babies) being raised by Hiroko's team, make sense of the contrast between Hiroko and Sax Russell:

> One morning ... Nirgal stayed behind in the school until he and Sax were the only ones left, and then he said, "Why don't you like it when you can't say why?" The frown returned. After a long silence, Sax said slowly, "I try to understand.... When we can't ... well, I don't like it. It vexes me. Sometimes I call it ... the Great Unexplainable." It was the white world, Nirgal saw suddenly. The white world inside the green, the opposite of Hiroko's green world inside the white.... Looking from the green side, when Hiroko confronted something mysterious, she loved it and it made her happy—it was viriditas, a holy power. Looking from the white side, when Sax confronted something mysterious, it was the Great Unexplainable, dangerous and awful.... She loved the green world, he the white. "But yes!" Michel said when Nirgal mentioned this to him. "Very good, Nirgal. Your sight has such insight. In archetypical terminologies we might call green and white the Mystic and the Scientist. Both extremely powerful figures, as you see. But what we need, if you ask me, is a combination of the two, which we call the *Alchemist*" [*Green Mars* 15].

Leane finds Sax's transformation over the course of the trilogy to be an example of that alchemical bridging, culminating in a vision of an alternative, utopian science that embodies Robinson's appreciation (expressed in Foote and Robinson) of science fiction as an intertwining of facts and values, science and literature (Leane 102). Fittingly, Ann Clayborne's transformation — from the "prototypical Red" in the first novel, angry, alienated, solitary, and obsessed with the stark mineral unlife of the Martian landscape, to a healed, psychologically integrated person finally shut of the Earthly past that had damaged her and capable of feeling joy at the fact of being *on Mars* by the end of the third — is brought about by Sax's persistent efforts to that end. If Nirgal had known Ann as well as he did Sax and Hiroko, he might have ascribed to her the archetype of Hermit: alone in the wilderness, neither Scientist nor Mystic. But it is important to recognize that none of the major characters in the Mars trilogy are pure archetypes, nor are they static. In interacting, they move and complicate one another; additionally, as fictional characters, they stand in contrast and counterpoint to each other.

The Semiotic Square: White and Blue

In Greimassian terms, White serves as the *negative complex term*; it is neither Red nor Green, neither mineral nor animal/vegetable. Instead, it represents a knowing subject interested in the positive ends of science: explanation, prediction, control. The *positive complex term* is associated with the archetype of the Alchemist, who mixes unlike things: the scientific and the mystical, the rational and the irrational, the real and the true. It may be merely convenient that Robinson offers a fourth color for the completion of the semiotic square initiated by the dichotomy of Red and Green, but as *Blue Mars* is the title of the final novel in the series, the label Blue suggests both the culmination of the terraforming process (with the creation of oceans on Mars) and the completion of the utopian political project initiated by the Martian settlers. Robinson nearly says as much, at the end of *Blue Mars*, when Ann and Sax are sailing idly in a small boat upon a Martian sea, "talking or not talking. Many times they came back to what it might mean to be brown [i.e., the synthesis of Red and Green]. 'Perhaps the combination should be called blue,' Ann said one evening, looking over the side at the water. 'Brown isn't very attractive, and it reeks of compromise. Maybe we should be thinking of something entirely new.'" And Sax replies, "Maybe we should" (*Blue Mars* 730). Ultimately, however, "the name for this unnameable color is Utopia, which stares insistently back at us from the Mars trilogy just as it does at Sax" (Jameson "One Good City" 224).

With this in mind, it is interesting to note the way in which the blueness of the sky emerges as both a metaphor for home and a commentary on the other colors. Nirgal's insight about the vastness of Earth — so much greater than Mars that "it out–Marsed Mars itself ... it was greater even at being Martian" (*Blue Mars* 195) — takes place beneath a Prussian blue sky he sees in the Alps during his visit to Earth, so that the green world within the white world is enfolded in a blue one. Later, Nirgal's search for a place to call home on Mars is influenced (but not settled) by the color of the sky in the places he considers (e.g., *Blue Mars* 371). And Sax Russell's and Maya Toitovna's hobby of sitting in an oceanfront café in the Martian city of Odessa and naming the sunset colors (which leads to political discussions of the mixing of reds and greens) culminates in a shared moment of dumbfounded reverence: "[A]s the sun dropped everything drifted over the spectrum into the blue.... Everything was blue, sky blue, Terran blue, drenching everything for most of an hour, flooding the nerve pathways in their brains, no doubt long starved for precisely that color, the home they had left forever" (*Blue Mars* 653).

And while this analysis draws from across all three novels, it is important to recognize that the structure of signification it has produced may apply strictly only to *Red Mars*. As Earth and Mars increasingly come into symbolic deixis (i.e., complementarity by virtue of their contrasts) as well as political antagonism, the fields of meaning seem to shift so that

Blue, via its association with the color of the terran sky, slides into Greimas's negative complex position, allowing White (with its associated archetype of Scientist) to become that which mediates Red and Green. More simply, the semiotic configuration of the first novel isn't fixed: the archetypical scientist of *Red Mars*, Sax Russell, is transformed in multiple ways and becomes increasingly central once the representatives of the old world, John Boone and Frank Chalmers, have left the stage. The inflection point of this inversion, if it is real, may be connected to the "paradigm shift" sought by the conferees at Dorsa Brevia, a reconceptualization of revolution in economic rather than military terms (*Green Mars* 358–362). The implication is that the entirety of *Red Mars* can be seen as a kind of prologue, the final failure of an old political paradigm to bring about a just social order in a new world.

Circling the Square: Fleshing Out the Semantic Rectangle

The Red/Green dichotomy is thus complemented by the White/Blue one in which the four terms occupy the corners of the central square in a semantic rectangle as depicted in Figure 2, at least insofar as the events of *Red Mars* are concerned. The colors represent principles of (1) *kami*, (2) *viriditas*, (3) science, and (4) that alternate value-conscious not-science that Michel calls alchemy. They evoke archetypes of Hermit, Mystic, Scientist, and Alchemist respectively. Motifs of isolation/alienation are associated with the Red-White pair while motifs of connection/integration belong to the Blue-Green. Conversely, Red and Green are connected by their location on an ontological continuum, while White and Blue are located on an epistemological one. In other words, Red/Green has to do with the nature of existence while the Blue/White has to do with the role of consciousness.

Completing the core semiotic square allows the semantic rectangle that surrounds it to be fleshed out. Moving counter-clockwise around the figure from the top, Hiroko Ai stands at the junction of Red and Green, a hermit-mystic who becomes a Martian will-o-wisp, the Persephone of the First Hundred and high priestess of the *areophany*. Geologist Ann Clayborne occupies the Red-White vertex; her *areology* (Martian geology) is directed toward understanding Mars scientifically, a stark and beautiful planetscape, and she is revealed as a hermit-scientist throughout the trilogy, in which she frequently isolates herself from the others, resisting their attempts to connect with her and remaining willing to keep her areological knowledge secret if it will help preserve Mars-as-it-was.

In contrast, Sax Russell's *terraforming* project occupies the junction of White and Blue, as when Sax argues for terraforming Mars because the universe is empty without consciousness: "Science is creation.... We can transform Mars and build it like you would build a cathedral, as a monument to humanity and the universe both" (*Red Mars* 178). The closest to the stereotypical scientist at the beginning of the trilogy, Sax moves toward the ideal of alchemist over the course of the novels, his transformation occupying a significant portion of *Green Mars*.

Finally, John Boone's *Martian syncretism* occupies the final vertex, between Blue and Green, reflecting his efforts to develop a vision or plan for a new Martian society by traveling widely and listening intently to those he meets on Mars. Boone is a mystic alchemist, pursuing an "areoformation" that will shape humans to Mars. That pursuit is the central motif of *Red Mars*, and tracing the discursive (i.e., semiotic) and syntagmic (i.e., narrative) constitution of that motif will occupy the rest of this essay.

The upshot of this analysis is to affirm the usefulness of Greimassian "structural semantics" (Greimas) as a way of making sense of Robinson's densely written, thickly allusive, dissonantly multi-voiced novels. The semantic rectangle suggests potential points of thematic

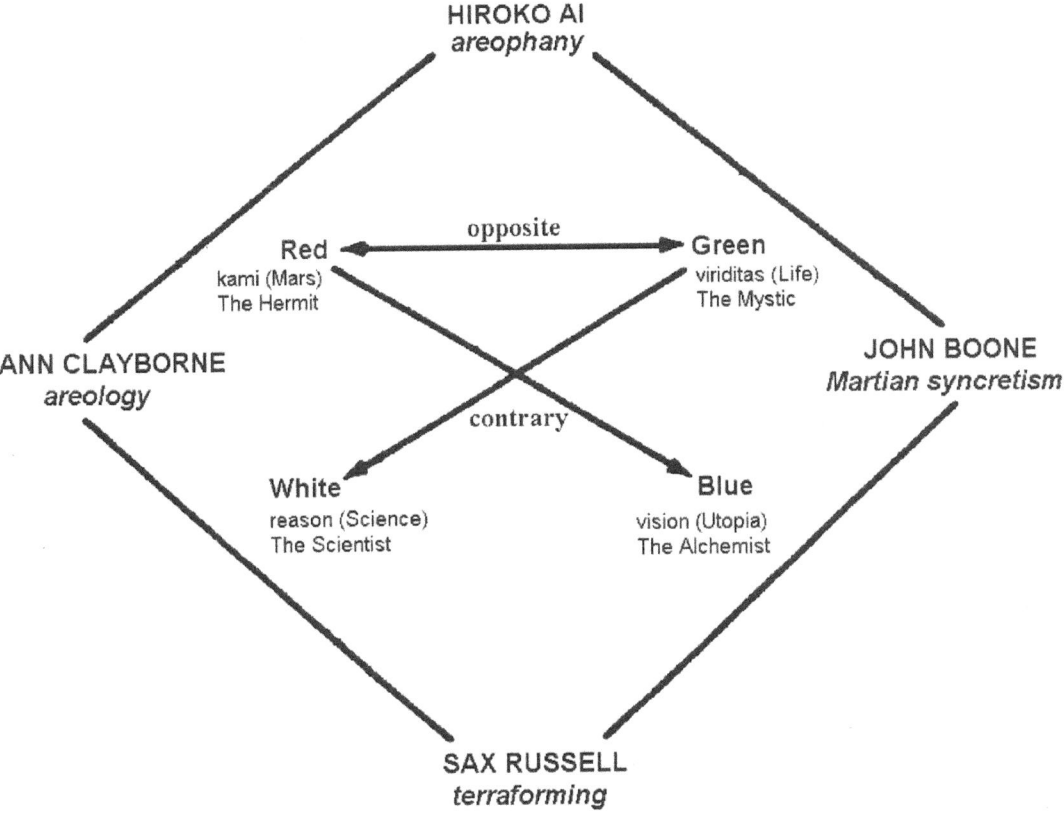

Figure 2. A Greimassian semantic rectangle for characters/projects from *Red Mars*.

conflict between characters. For example, the debate during the early days of the colony between Ann and Sax over whether or not to begin terraforming rests upon arguments about the character of science (*Red Mars* 175–179), while later John urges Sax to greater reflexivity — greater awareness or consciousness — about the role of economic power in the terraforming project (266). Similarly, John takes Hiroko aside after she reappears to a gathering of the First Hundred and friends on Olympus Mons to express his displeasure over his discovery of her use of his frozen sperm to create their test-tube son without his permission or awareness (373–375). And Leane calls Ann and Hiroko "ecofeminists divided over their attitude towards colonialism" (95), that is, over the way in which the Martian rights of place are to be respected by human settlers on Mars.

However, thus far all that has been achieved is an impressionistic albeit suggestive sketch of the discursive structure within *Red Mars*, which is merely the first part of Greimas's method. What is required next is a deeper exploration of the text as narrative. In Greimassian terms, we must turn from the discursive to the syntagmic, from the domain of meaning to that of (narrative) action. Since John Boone is so central to the action of *Red Mars* (and his absence so palpable a loss still in the rest of the trilogy), and since Boone's relationship with his friend and rival Frank Chalmers drives both the plot of *Red Mars* and the utopian political argument at the heart of the Mars trilogy, it is necessary to focus on the story of John Boone to engage in that exploration.

Enacting Character: The Actantial Dimension

In his *Structural Semantics,* Greimas describes the development of a method of narrative analysis in which the analyst (1) "objectifies" the text, reducing it to an abstract that is focused on the plot-related moves or actions of significant "actants" (i.e., the conventional narrative roles occupied by characters in the story); (2) maps that abstract onto a "syntax of description" that amounts to a rationalization of Russian folklorist Vladimir Propp's 31 character functions (which allow fairy-tale plots to be described as a sequence of more-or-less conventional character situations, exchanges, or interactions, e.g.: someone faces a lack; a hero is given a magical gift; a hero struggles with a villain); and (3) goes back into the text in order to produce a "lexematics of description" that shows where and how the "constructed functions" identified via the syntax of description are manifest (i.e., how they instantiate a particular discursive structure). The actantial dimension thus reveals the "narrativization of discourse," in which the intersection of narrative functions and thematic attributions produces a dynamic semiotic system (Greimas *On Meaning* 119–120).

Actantial analysis helps clarify the significance of an important scene involving John Boone from an early section of *Red Mars,* "The Voyage Out," that occurs while the First Hundred are still aboard the *Ares* (their spaceship). This section is seen from the perspective of Maya Toitovna, leader of the Russian contingent and soon to be John's on-again, off-again lover. Maya begins to pay attention to a Sunday morning conversation in the ship's mess hall when she hears John Boone express skepticism about the Christ story he learned in his Lutheran confirmation class to Phyllis Boyle, a geologist who'd just led an Easter service aboard the ship. Boone argues that, since the gospels are the product of a third-century political process in which some versions of the Christ story were excluded, Christ is a "kind of literary figure really, a political construct" (52). When Phyllis disagrees, John insists on his point. They go back and forth until Phyllis, recognizing the impasse, sighs and rises to go. "Outside your rational scientific thought is an important area of consciousness, an area more important than science," she says, and it includes faith (53).

The conversation continues after Phyllis leaves. John apologizes to the onlookers, who begin to comment. Sax says, "Whenever scientists say they're Christian, I take it to be an aesthetic statement," deriving from their belief that there is a spiritual dimension missing from modern life that can be regained via religion. John exclaims, "But that brings in so many absurdities!" and complains that hard-headed scientists become fuzzy-thinking and illogical when they start talking about religion. While he's been speaking, Frank has been egging him on, interjecting "You just don't have faith!" at intervals. Finally, John has had enough. "Well, I hope I never get it!" he says. "It's like being hit by a hammer in the head!" Maya watches him exit, thinking, it must have been a really bad confirmation class (53).

The foregoing abstract can now be fitted into Greimas's syntax of description. This is encapsulated in what he calls the "actantial mythical model," in which important characters and the things that drive them occupy specific roles derived from structural analyses of folk tales (subject, object, sender, receiver, helper, opponent, i.e.) and the actions in which they are implicated are mapped onto "functions" similarly derived (making and breaking contracts, being tested and rewarded or punished, moving in space or circumstances, e.g.). According to Greimas, "this model seems to possess ... a certain operational value. Its simplicity lies in the fact that it is entirely centered on the *object of desire* aimed at by the subject and situated, as *object of communication,* between the sender and the receiver — the desire of the subject being, in its part, modulated in projections from the helper and the opponent" (*Structural*

Semantics 207). The model is "mythic" in the sense that it describes a narrative logic that underlies the causal surface of a story.

Figure 3 recreates the scene from "The Voyage Out" in Greimassian terms as a complete story, in which John Boone is both (a) "subject" pursuing (in a negative way, i.e., renouncing) the "object" of faith and (b) "sender" revealing himself through that vocal renunciation to Maya, who in providing the viewpoint through which we hear the debate stands in for the reader as "receiver." The three other characters who participate in the debate do so in opposition to John, who vehemently rejects religious faith as an intellectually consistent move for a scientist. Phyllis, Sax, and Frank each offer alternatives to John's outright renunciation of religious sentiment. Phyllis supraordinates faith to science while Sax dismisses it as a consolation of sorts, reconcilable with the professional ethos of science as a mere "aesthetic preference." Frank uses it strategically to goad John, needling him by sarcastically declaring that he just doesn't have faith, but also suggesting that hypocritical lip service to piety is acceptable. In all of this, John's only instrument or "helper" is his commitment to a scientific worldview. He explicitly draws upon scientific knowledge to argue against the compatibility of faith with that worldview, saying, "There's a kind of archaeology, an anthropology — a sociology of religion, that makes all of this perfectly clear — how it came about, what needs it fulfilled" (*Red Mars* 52).

These syntactical relations having been established, the final step is to interrogate the "lexematics" (i.e., discursive regularities) of the story, identifying semantic relations among concepts implicated in the text. In this case, an initial dichotomy exists between the value-object that Boone repudiates, *faith*, and *science* (no faith) his helper. The junction *both faith and no faith* that forms the positive complex term of this square can be called *skepticism* (a kind of negative faith, a commitment to doubt) while the negative complex term (*neither faith nor no faith*) that is the opposite of skepticism and the contrary of science deserves the epithet *irrationality*, intimating as it does both emotionality and randomness.

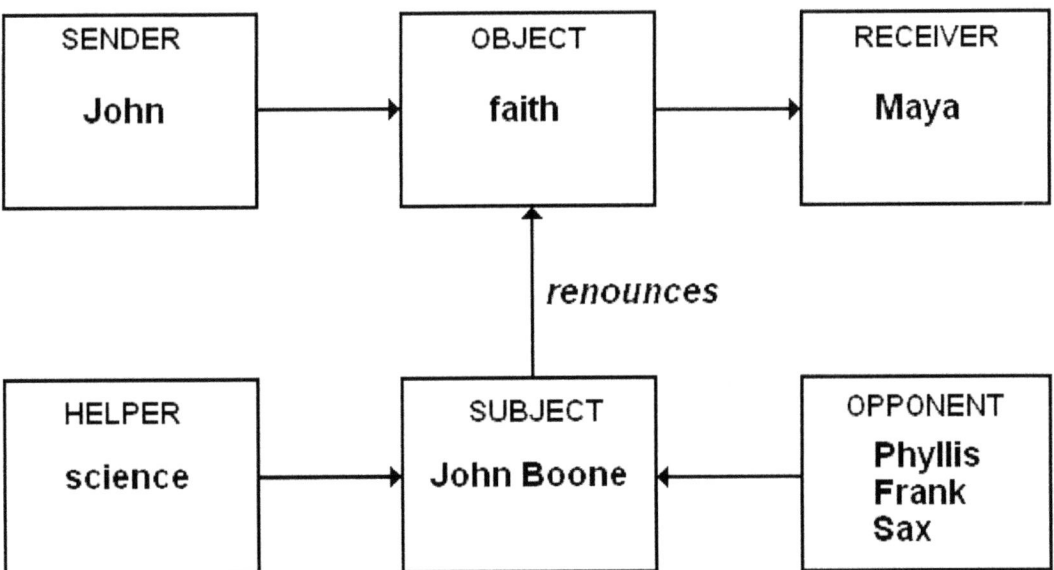

Figure 3. The "actantial mythical model" of the *Ares* debate.

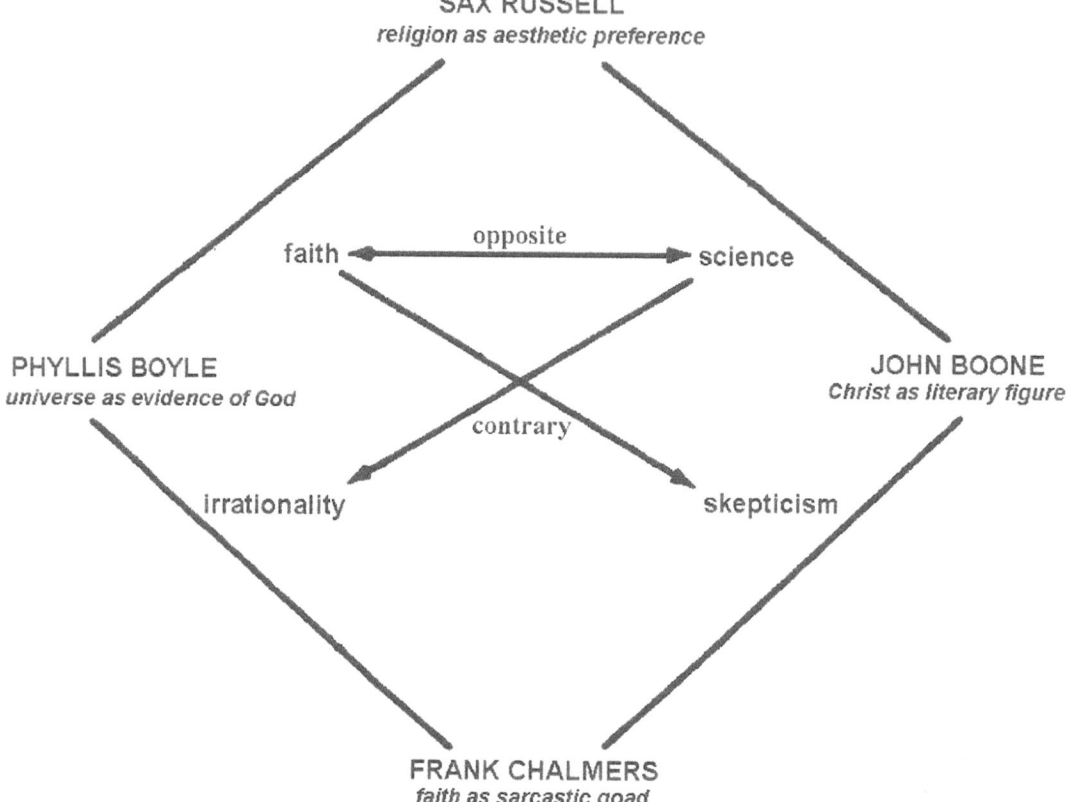

Figure 4. A semantic rectangle of character positions in the *Ares* debate.

As Figure 4 reveals, the four characters who participated in the conversation aboard the *Ares* can be located in a semantic rectangle that sees their positions as combinations of these terms. John's renunciation of faith is a product of his scientific skepticism and his science-derived knowledge of the sociology of religion. Sax is able to reconcile faith and science by reducing the significance of the former. Phyllis's defense of her faith is to John irrational, relying on "all kinds of debaters' tricks, evasions, qualifications, fuzzy thinking of every kind" (*Red Mars* 53); more positively, she is not afraid to accept the possibility of the miraculous, of there being more to consciousness than science. And Frank's egging-on of John in its sarcasm evinces both a cynical kind of skepticism and a malicious (albeit very possibly strategic) unreasonableness.

A Martian Odyssey: The Journey of John Boone

But the debate aboard the *Ares* between John and Phyllis is *not* in fact in and of itself a complete tale; it is one turn of a larger plot in which John's renunciation of faith is the opening move. The story of John Boone, who is the key character of the long central section of *Red Mars* called "Falling into History," has been seen as "pivotal" (Abbott) and "the heart of the series" (Dynes). Its plot can be described as a tale of *conversion* (Wang and Roberts), in which following an initial renunciation of some value-object (in this case, faith), the hero appropriates the object in some fashion, usually by recognizing the value of what he or she had once renounced.

"Falling into History" opens a few decades after the arrival of the First Hundred on Mars. Terraforming and commercial mining are in their initial stages but growing robustly, to the dismay of many early settlers who resent the influx of new colonists and the influence of the large "transnational" corporations that are seeking to grow rich off the wealth of Mars. John Boone, working for Sax Russell's terraforming project, is inspecting a "mohole" (designed to release hot gases from the planet's interior into the Martian atmosphere) when he narrowly avoids being crushed by a truck falling from above: sabotage! (*Red Mars* 233–4)

The bulk of the section details John's peripatetic investigations, which involve two distinct but interwoven threads. The first is his quest for a "new vision of Martian society" that will not let the interests of the Martian colonists be subordinated to those of the transnationals exploiting Mars. The second is the search for the identity of the saboteurs, who may or may not also be responsible for attempts on John's life as he pursues them. John's complicated relationships with Frank and Maya, a romantic and political triangle whose details manifest themselves in this story line, also contribute to an ironical counter-narrative: the reader has already witnessed Frank's culpability for John's death in the prologue-like first section of the novel, "Festival Night."

Taken unto itself, "Falling into History" displays a coherent narrative structure capable of being described in the terms that Greimas borrows from Propp: an initial "break-up of the order and alienation," followed by the dispatch of a hero who is then initiated in a preparatory "qualifying test," faces his or her climactic "main test," and then recognized through a confirmatory "glorifying test." The passage of these tests enables a "reintegration and restoration of order" (Budniakiewicz 220). At the beginning of the story, the hero labors under an interdiction, in this case self-imposed (John rejected religious faith in Section 2, "The Voyage Out"), and from absentation (he broke up with Maya in Section 4, "Homesick"). Additionally, there is villainy (the sabotage) and a lack (a new vision for Martian society is needed). John is dispatched by Sax to solve the mystery of the sabotage, and begins his wanderings (*Red Mars* 240–2). All of these are characteristic elements of the expository stage of a narrative (Budniakiewicz 220).

John then faces a long series of "qualifying tests." He meets with geologist Ann Clayborne, emblem of the Reds he suspects as the sabotage culprits. When he satisfies her as to his political intentions, she tells him to look for "the coyote," a mysterious figure who was supposedly a stowaway aboard the *Ares* and who is now associated with stories of Hiroko, who vanished with her team some ten or so years earlier (*Red Mars* 243–54). He travels across Mars, making use of "magical" gifts (his AI Pauline and his fame as the First Man on Mars) to meet Martian settlers of all kinds (including the coyote) and learn about political and economic philosophy (255–84). He is granted additional gifts that aid his quest: He takes the longevity treatment discovered by biological researchers among the First Hundred, giving him a lifespan perhaps measurable in centuries (285–90). And recognizing his love for Maya, he proposes to her and is accepted (291–4). The culmination of his journey is when he is moved to join some nomadic Sufi explorers in one of their dervish-dances, chanting as he does the varied names of Mars. He has an epiphanous realization: "He stood, reeling; all of a sudden he understood that one didn't have to invent it all from scratch, that it was a matter of making something new by synthesis of all that was good in what came before.... 'Why can't we invent together a new religion. The worship of Al-Qahira, Mangala,

Kasei!'" (314). A Sufi woman gives him an affectionate and prophetic farewell: "'Whether it be of this world or of that,' she said, 'your love will lead us yonder in the end'" (316). This completes the conversion tale, qualifying John to serve as the advocate of a new vision of Mars.

But John's "main test" involves first solving the mystery of the sabotage and the attacks on him personally. Someone tries to frame him for murder, but he uses Pauline's cybernetic capabilities and his own stature as First Man on Mars to outmaneuver them (353–9). He figures out the identify of the saboteurs (some of Hiroko's people) and of his attackers (security agents sent by the transnationals ostensibly to investigate the sabotage), revealing these answers at a gathering he calls on Olympus Mons to celebrate the end of a years-long dust storm (364–82). The celebration includes many of the First Hundred, including the unexpected presence of Hiroko and her followers.

On Olympus Mons, John undergoes his "glorifying test." Hiroko, chanting the names of Mars, suddenly takes his hand and raises it up. Her cry of "John Boone" is taken up by the others there (intermingled with shouts of "Mars!") and John is called upon to speak. "Look, here we are on Mars!" he begins, echoing the words he spoke when he became the First Man on Mars: "Well, here we are" (see Franko "Density"). His speech is an impassioned call to arms and a summary of what he'd learned during his journey, stressing the necessity of creating new institutions and new ways of living by synthesizing the breadth of human experience, wisdom, and knowledge available to them, even in the face of the conflicts and tensions they'd brought to Mars and the ones surrounding them in the approaching showdown between democracy and capitalism. In this speech, John seems to provide the hoped-for alchemical vision, showing how a utopian mixing of unlike things could be achieved. The speech is received with mad cheers and delighted approval from his friends, and leads to plans for John and a few others to draft and advocate a revised treaty during the upcoming negotiations (378–81).

Boone's Journey as Myth and as Irony

John Boone's odyssey evokes the mythological hero-story that Greimas recapitulates in his "actantial mythical model" (see Figure 5). John is the actantial subject, the hero pursuing a utopian vision of Martian society synthesized from history and gifted to the "we" whom he addresses in his speech at Olympus Mons ("Look, here we are on Mars!"). This search is abetted with the aid of the Martian settlers and colonists he meets on his journey and opposed by the transnationals, who see Mars only as a resource to be exploited. The contrast between the two groups is marked. The settlers are earnest, "balanced" in their actions, moderate in their desires, and motivated by a spirit of inquiry and freedom. The agents of the transnationals are duplicitous, extremist and even murderous in their actions, rapacious in desire, and motivated by greed.

Robinson telegraphs Boone's heroic status by his fame, his charisma, and his identification as "astronaut." Our awareness of John's impending death heightens that stature: the rivalry between Frank and John recapitulates that of Cain and Abel, and we see John Boone become the subject of Paul Bunyan–like tall tales after his death (Abbott). Carol Franko calls Boone a "carnivalized Socratic hero" ("Density" 61), invoking both Bakhtin and Plato to suggest both the pride of place given to dialogue in Boone's repertoire of action and the ultimately violent and tragic fate that he meets. Even his name evokes the part of the hero, whose Campbellian task it is to travel into the underworld and return with a gift (a "boon") to bestow upon his people. And John's syncretic, dialogical philosophy does indeed have a profound influence

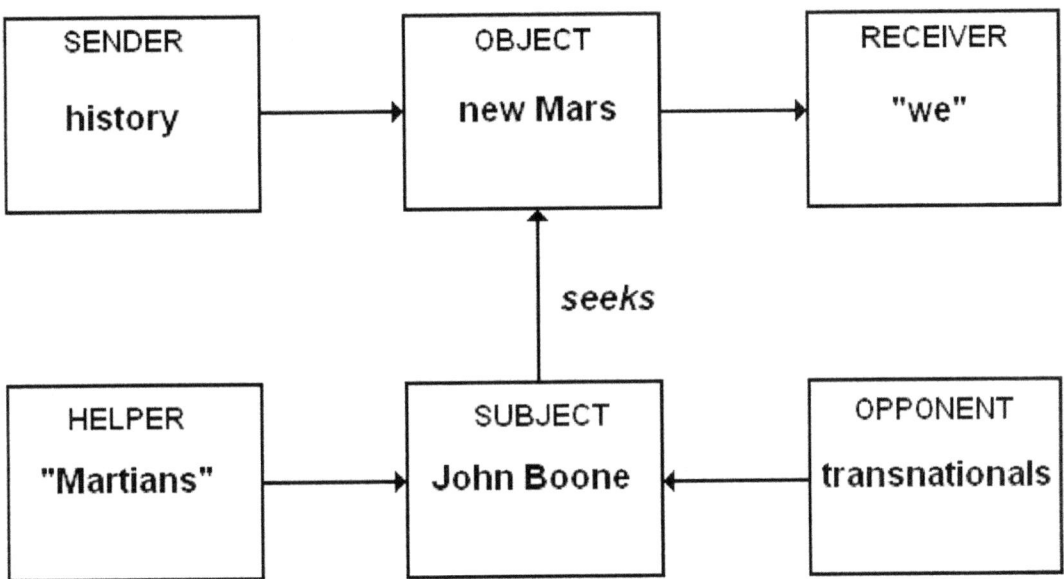

Figure 5. Actantial mythical model of "Falling into History" (*Red Mars* 234–382).

on the Martian constitution as it is eventually formulated during the underground years at the Dorsa Brevia conference (*Green Mars* 355–397) and implemented at the convention on Pavonis Mons after the success of the Martian revolution (*Blue Mars* 114–158), though it is regarded by some critics of the novels as inadequate in that it fails to recognize the possibility of irreconcilable cultural conflict (Abbott; Leane), just as Boone fails to recognize the depth of Frank Chalmers' anger toward him (Dynes; Markley).

On the other hand, there is a heavy irony in regarding John Boone as a mythic hero, in the reductive sense of merely being the uninflected locus of valorized attributes and functioning as the actantial subject. This irony manifests itself in a number of ways, including the novel's sensitivity to the dynamics of history (Abbott) and its self-referential awareness of the processes of story creation, as when John, in his efforts to find the coyote by tracing the tales told about him, thinks that he needs "to find a folklorist, someone who can tell him how stories are born" (*Red Mars* 316). But as Franko observes, he is indeed himself a story being born — even after his death, as is suggested by the interlude in which anonymous voices related where they were and what happened when they heard that John Boone had died (*Red Mars* 384–387; Franko "Density" 64).

In addition, and more importantly, the fact of John's murder means that there is a larger story revolving around Frank Chalmers in which John's quest despite its salience is a mere incident (see Franko "Mars Trilogy"): ultimately, *Red Mars* is Frank's story as much as if not more than it is John's, since it is about the failure or bankruptcy of all the old ways of doing politics. This is not of course to deny the multiplicity of character nor the polyphony of voices contained within the entire trilogy — the story continues past the deaths of both John and Frank. Nor is it to deny the centrality of the larger utopian political vision that informs Robinson's work. In fact, that vision is sharpened by attending to the interplay of two characters fundamentally divided in political outlook and around whom the central conflict of the first part of the trilogy is oriented.

The Shadow of Frank Chalmers

Frank is John's *nafs*, according to one of the Sufis that John meets: his evil self, his Shadow (*Red Mars* 312). As a character, he is constructed in contradistinction to Boone, the model of a political operator to John's charismatic visionary. Physically, he is dark and saturnine where John is fair and apollonian. He pursues policies where John tries to understand; he wields political influence where John makes friends. John is earnest and optimistic (Frank would say naïve), open, passionate, charismatic, and famous; Frank is cynical and angry, manipulative, reserved, pragmatic, and behind-the-scenes, the *éminence grise* of Mars. John's love for Maya is affectionate and honest, "*eros* just a spice in a feast of *agape*" (294); Frank's possessive desire for her is deformed by his guilt over John's death (399–400).

As the series proceeds, another point of distinction between John and Frank emerges. Frank remains an enigma, a cipher to those who once knew him, misrepresented by historians and eventually (perhaps willfully) forgotten. John Boone, on the other hand, is sorely and painfully missed by others throughout the books. That he is turned into a folk hero and so in that sense misunderstood is true, but beyond that children are named in his memory and his absence is marked with regret, as when Sax is reminded of the night of John's murder, and is "distraught at the loss of a friend 153 years before," at the loss of more than a friend: "his brother ... his brother who had laughed at him but loved him as well, loved him before anyone else thought of him at all" (*Blue Mars* 678) or when Nirgal calls up Boone's voice, recorded by his old AI Pauline:

> Nirgal let the tape run ... listening to the hoarse voice with the friendly American accent, a voice unselfconscious about talking to an AI. Listening to the voice made Nirgal wish he could really talk to the man.... It made him laugh to hear the man's voice.... It made him understand the way the issei [first-generation settlers] talked about Boone, the hurt in them that never went away. How much better it would be to have John here than just these recordings in an AI, what a great adventure it would have been to watch John Boone negotiate Mars's wild history! [*Blue Mars* 373]

Festival Night

The opening section of *Red Mars*, called "Festival Night," sketches out the rivalry between Chalmers and Boone. It is clear that Frank regards John as his rival for both Maya and for Mars, and that rather than thinking of himself and John as radically different, he is irritated that they are *much the same*. Frank listens to John give a speech, growing angry at platitudes he takes to be lies; he then takes the podium and finds himself giving a speech that in different words says the same thing because he cannot bring himself to say what he really believes:

> Usually when he spoke to an audience he picked out a few faces and the rest became visual filler, but with the sunlight coursing over his shoulder they all caught his eye at once, and it was nearly too much. Five thousand people in a single Martian town! After all the years in Underhill it was hard to grasp. Foolishly, he tried to tell the audience something of this. "Looking," he said. "Looking around ... the strangeness of our presence here is ... accentuated." He was losing the crowd. How to say it? How to say that they alone in all that rocky world were alive, their faces glowing like paper lanterns in the night? How to say that even if living creatures were no more than carriers for ruthless genes, this was still somehow better than the blank mineral nothingness of everything else? Of course he could never say it. Not at any time, perhaps, and certainly not in a speech [*Red Mars* 6].

What is not clear is what motivates Frank to pursue either Mars or Maya. It may be nothing more than the self-centered will to power that makes Frank say to himself after Boone's death, *Now we'll see what I can do with this planet* (*Red Mars* 23). Later, long after

Frank's death, Maya will read the work of his biographers in order to try to understand him better: she learns of his early career as a public-works administrator in a short-lived "National Service Corps," in which he displayed great idealism and political promise, and his subsequent rise through the administrative ranks at NASA following the demise of the NSC and his divorce from a socialite wife: the events that somehow turned his idealism to anger (*Green Mars* 444–447).

Guns Under the Table

Nonetheless, it is through Frank's eyes that we see the treaty negotiation process that takes place in the late 2050s, with Frank (in the position of the cabinet-level United States Mars Secretary) occupying a pivotal role in that process, in the section called "Guns Under the Table." Drawing upon all of his political skills and diplomatic abilities, he brokers a deal in which the interests of the Martian settlers and of the national governments back on Earth are maintained at the expense of the transnational corporations. But Frank's victory is a hollow one: he learns that the transnationals will simply use a loophole in the revised treaty to continue to pursue their Martian projects. So conditions worsen, as an influx of workers (mostly under contract to the transnationals) creates crowding, crime, and tension in the tent-towns where they are housed, and escalating violence results in outright conflict: the failed "revolution" of 2061, bloodily suppressed by transnational security forces.

We are faced with the destruction through the eyes of Nadia Cherneshevsky, the engineer who was also the viewpoint character during the first phases of building the Martian colony. During the violence of the doomed revolt, she uses her skills to effect what repairs she can by means of remote-controlled robotic construction vehicles. As some of the First Hundred flee together in a ground vehicle called a "rover," Frank goes outside to free the vehicle when it becomes stuck in frozen ground. A flash flood caused by the demolition of a large aquifer nearly catches the rover. It races out of the surge, but the flood waters take Frank; he vanishes, having sacrificed himself to free the rover in time (*Red Mars* 560–2).

So in the end there is another reversal: Frank is ultimately helpless against the forces bearing down on him, metaphorically in the case of the transnationals and literally in the case of the flood in the Marineris valley, despite all his skill, savvy and ruthlessness. A moralist might find a certain justice in this, seeing Frank's failure to be a consequence of his instigation of John Boone's murder, and thus a comeuppance that validates John's heroic status and confirms Frank's villainy. This is naturally enough the view that an actantial mythical model encourages us to take; myths are nothing if not committed to a particular moral order.

However, Robinson has subverted this easy valorization of Boone and demonization of Chalmers by pointing to their equivalence: both of their visions of Mars were ultimately found wanting, and for similar reasons. Frank underestimated the tenacity of the transnationals; John underestimated both Frank's malice and the degree to which old animosities and suspicions would interfere with the tolerant syncretic world he desired (see Markley). And it is possible to see Frank as a mythic hero in his own right, albeit a dark one: his qualifying test is the instigation of Boone's murder, his (ultimately failed) main test is the negotiation of the treaty revisions, and his "glorifying" (better: redeeming) test is his (perhaps unintended) self-sacrifice during the Marineris flood to save the rover his friends were in.

On the other hand, Frank's angry alienation from others and his pessimistic, power-oriented political realism position him in striking contrast to Boone's easy integration with others and his political optimism. More importantly, Boone's apotheietic spiritual journey and martyrdom stand in opposition to Chalmers' spiritual descent, guilt, and (possibly) redemptive sacrifice. This contrast of the two male American astronauts who are viewpoint characters invites a comparison in counterpoint with the two female Russian cosmonauts who are viewpoint characters, Maya Toitovna and Nadia Cherneshevsky, the former characterized by her stormy, manic-depressive moodiness and the latter by her plucky pragmatism. Maya thus stands at the vertex of alienation and integration while Nadia combines a hopeful political optimism with a realistic appreciation of the possible (see Figure 6).

The effect of this duplication is to locate John at the center of conjoined or doubled semantic rectangles with Maya in the position analogous to Hiroko, Nadia to Sax, and Frank to Ann; suggesting interesting structural parallels between the analogous characters in relation to Boone: Maya/Hiroko as hard-to-obtain, Mars-embodying objects of desire; Nadia/Sax as allies and ultimately successors who attempt to fulfill John's vision; Frank/Ann as serious critics of that vision who challenge its tenets at fundamental levels but who are themselves marked and marred by their anger and alienation.

Conclusion

The argument here is demonstrative rather than deductive. I have tried to justify the employment of structuralist methods by pointing to Robinson's sensitivity to structure both

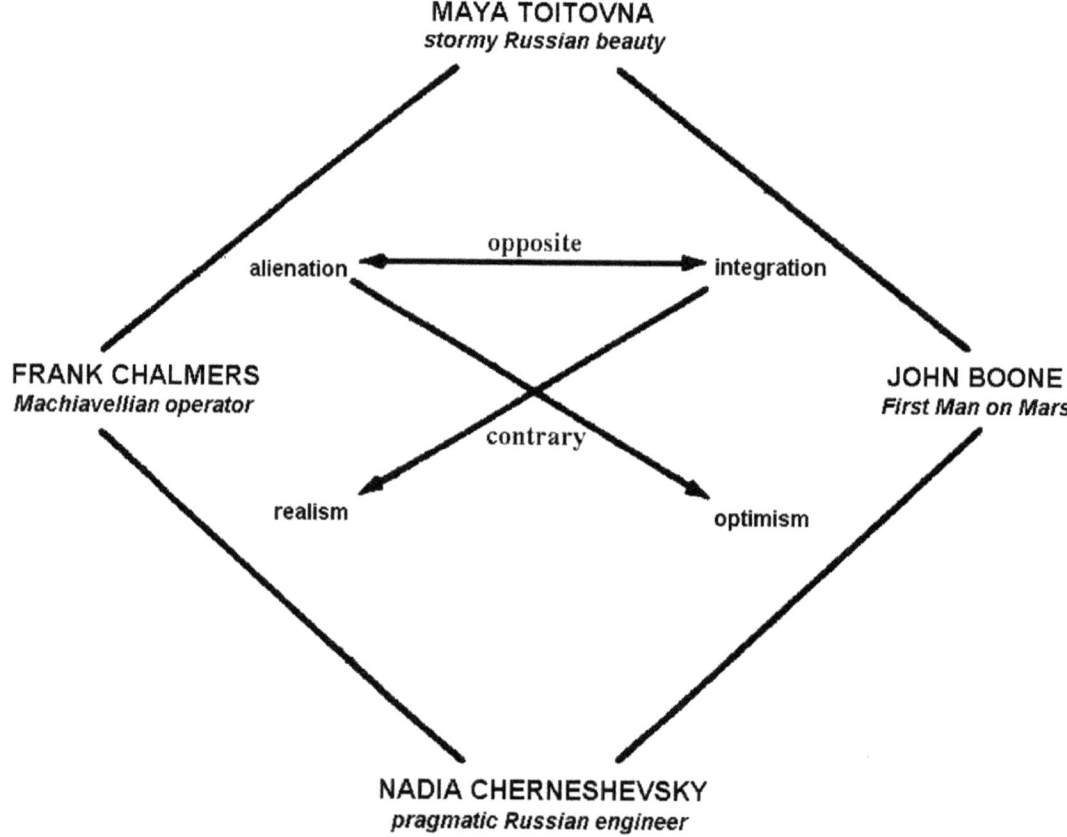

Figure 6. A semantic rectangle of the Boone-Chalmers contrast.

in his scholarship and in the construction of the trilogy itself. Employing the techniques of structural semantics, I have shown how certain characters seemed to embody color-coded and multiply contrasting archetypes of Hermit, Mystic, Scientist, and Alchemist, and closely followed the story of John Boone to see how the metaphor of alchemy played out in the emergence of Boone's utopian vision of a new Martian society enabled by a tolerant syncretism, with Boone as the actantial hero of that emergence. Finally, I have pointed to the ironical counter-narrative to Boone's part in the story that exists in the story of Frank Chalmers, who serves not only as a contrasting character to Boone but also to undermine the reading of Boone's story as myth in an uncomplicated way. John Boone and Frank Chalmers, long gone by the end of the work, nonetheless by their fates reinforce Robinson's social-critique-as-fiction: "history" is kinder by far to the optimistic political visionary who believes in the possibility of utopia via dialogue than to the political realist willing to commit murder in the name of power. But the trilogy garners its literary power not from a simplistic moralizing; rather, it obtains its force from how its components reflect wryly upon each other.

Robinson thus presents us with a final duality which can be called myth/irony. On the one hand, *myth* manifests itself in the structures of the individual stories that the novel comprises, active subjects pursuing the objects of their desire. *Irony* emerges from the layering or nesting of those stories within each other, reversing or inverting meanings seemingly fixed within the mythic narrative taken unto itself. That which is *both myth and irony* is *allusion*, or intertextuality: it is constituted in the reference of one text to another. And that which is *neither myth nor irony* rejects narrative in favor of *fact*.

This semiotic square embodies dimensions of narrativity/referentiality and multiplexity/singularity, so that myth is singular narrative, irony is multiplex narrative, fact is singular reference (i.e., to the objective external world), and allusion is multiplex reference (to the worlds embodied in texts, i.e.). The *Mars* trilogy instantiates the semantic rectangle formed by this *combinatoire*.

We have seen how the interaction of myth and irony work to produce the *fiction*, generating story as pure narrativity folded back upon itself. But the interaction of fact and allusion is also present in the extensive technical descriptions of the Martian landscape and other scientific exposition, including his discussions of a sustainable "eco-economics" (Costanza), generating an image of *science* that at the same time serves to comment upon the social and political developments of the novels (Franko "Mars Trilogy"; Jameson "One Good City"; Leane). In the intersection of fact and myth, complementary singularities, is a notion of *history*: how stories-as-memories come to be made of real lives and to shape the trajectory of events (Franko "Density"). And the intersection of irony and allusion the novel presents itself to us as *rhetoric*, in two senses. The first is that of artifice, as when through its self-conscious evocation of other science fictional texts *Red Mars* "gives the reader an almost continual sense of itself as artifact, in its declaration that it is a story encompassing past stories which, in turn, encompass still older stories" (Foote 65). The second is that of argument, as in the figurative presentation of a political vision that exists as an ideal not merely in the fictional world of Robinson's imaginings but also in our own (Leane; Markley), a metaphor for what we need to do on this planet, since it will be "easier to live sustainably on Earth than to terraform Mars" (Szeman, Whiteman and Robinson 183).

As Figure 7 implies, the multiplexity of *Red Mars* and its sequels can be viewed as the product of the various tensions and sympathies emerging from the entanglement of myth and irony. Robinson has spoken of his appreciation of science fiction as a site of encounter between facts and values (Foote and Robinson), and the ultimate effect of this essay is to explode that

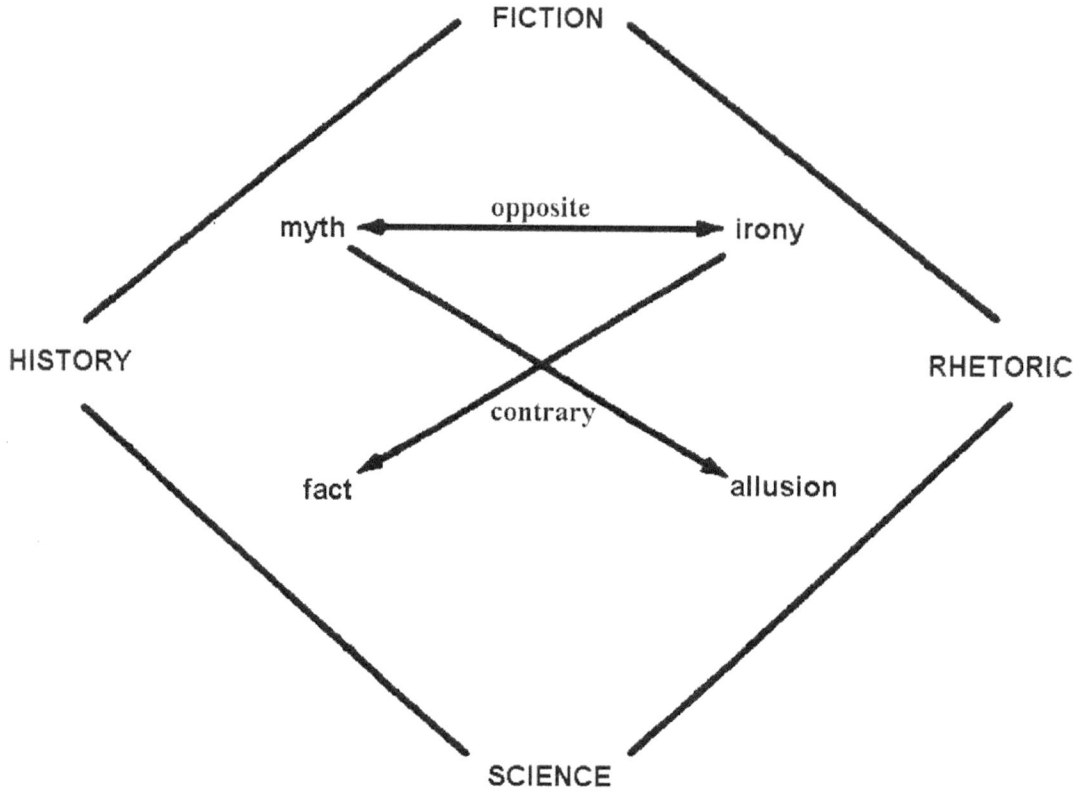

Figure 7. A semantic rectangle of science fictional imperatives in *Red Mars*.

dualism, to reveal and help make sense of the intricate discursive constitution of the Mars trilogy in particular and science fiction more broadly.

WORKS CITED

Abbott, C. "Falling into History: The Imagined Wests of Kim Stanley Robinson in the "Three Californias" and Mars Trilogies." *Western Historical Quarterly*, 2003. 27–47. Vol. 34.
Amazon.com. "Red Mars." Sept. 28 2006. <http://www.amazon.com/Red-Mars-Trilogy-Stanley-Robinson/dp/0553560735/sr=8-1/qid=1159465593/ref=pd_bbs_1/104-4462711-3307119?ie=UTF8&s=books>
Budniakiewicz, Theresa. *Fundamentals of Story Logic: Introduction to Greimassian Semiotics*. Philadelphia, PA: John Benjamins, 1992.
Costanza, R. "Book Reviews." Rev. of Mars trilogy. *Ecological Economics* 33.1 (2000): 167–69.
Dynes, W. "Multiple Perspectives in Kim Stanley Robinson's Mars Series." *Extrapolation* 42.2 (2001): 150–64.
Foote, B. "Notes on Kim Stanley Robinson's 'Red Mars.'" *Science Fiction Studies* 21.1 (1994): 61–66.
_____, and K. S. Robinson. "A Conversation with Kim Stanley Robinson." *Science Fiction Studies* 21.1 (1994): 51–60.
Franko, Carol. "The Density of Utopian Destiny in Robinson's 'Red Mars.'" *Extrapolation* 38.1 (1997): 57–65.
_____. "Kim Stanley Robinson: Mars Trilogy." *A Companion to Science Fiction*. Ed. David Seed. Malden, MA: Blackwell, 2005. 544–55.
Greimas, Algirdas J. *On Meaning*. Trans. Paul J. Perron and Frank H. Collins. Theory and History of Literature. Minneapolis, MN: University of Minnesota Press, 1987.
_____. *Structural Semantics: An Attempt at a Method*. Lincoln: University of Nebraska Press, 1983.
Jameson, Fredric. "After Armageddon: Character Systems in *Dr. Bloodmoney*." *Science Fiction Studies*, 1975. Vol. 2.

_____. "'If I Find One Good City, I Will Spare the Man': Realism and Utopia in Kim Stanley Robinson's Mars Trilogy." *Learning from Other Worlds: Estrangement, Cognition, and the Politics of Science Fiction and Utopia.* Ed. Patrick Parrinder. Durham, NC: Duke University Press, 2001. 208–32.

Jonas, Gerald. "Science Fiction." Review of *Red Mars. New York Times Book Review* January 31, 1993: 25.

Leane, Elizabeth. "Chromodynamics: Science and Colonialism in Kim Stanley Robinson's Mars Trilogy." *Ariel-A Review of International English Literature* 33.1 (2002): 83–104.

Markley, R. "Falling into Theory: Simulation, Terraformation, and Eco-Economics in Kim Stanley Robinson's Martian Trilogy." *Modern Fiction Studies* 43.3 (1997): 773–99.

Robinson, Kim Stanley. *Blue Mars.* London: HarperCollins Publishers, 1996.

_____. *Green Mars.* London: HarperCollins, 1993.

_____. *The Novels of Philip K. Dick.* Studies in Speculative Fiction ; No. 9. Ann Arbor, MI: UMI Research Press, 1984.

_____. *Red Mars.* London: HarperCollins, 1992.

Schleifer, Ronald. *A.J. Greimas and the Nature of Meaning: Linguistics, Semiotics, and Discourse Theory.* Lincoln: University of Nebraska Press, 1987.

Szeman, I., M. Whiteman, and K. S. Robinson. "Future Politics: An Interview with Kim Stanley Robinson." *Science Fiction Studies* 31.2 (2004): 177–88.

Wang, Y., and C. W. Roberts. "Actantial Analysis: Greimas's Structural Approach to the Analysis of Self-Narratives." *Narrative Inquiry* 15.1 (2005): 51–74.

Part III. Ecology and Nature

14

Ecological Newspeak*
Alan R. Slotkin

Recent discussions on the ADS list (January 1997) in relation to the ending *-zine* have underscored again the importance of science fiction writing in creating new words and in changing the usage of already existing words. Kim Stanley Robinson is a science fiction writer whose new words and new usages may similarly have a lasting effect on English. Robinson's work, having won Hugo, Nebula, and John W. Campbell awards, is not only well-respected, but widely read, thereby giving his neologisms a better than average chance of affecting usage outside his novels.

Robinson's *Pacific Edge* (Orb Edition. New York: Tom Doherty Associates, Inc., 1988), a part of his Three Californias trilogy, is a novel which stresses the importance of man living in ecological balance with nature. To underscore his themes, Robinson establishes a number of innovative usages of differing types; but almost all have a common thread, their relationship to the natural world and/or to human beings' attempts to live in harmony with that natural world. First, there are several neologisms that are analogous to already existing words in English that involve geographical terminology: *upcanyon* as in "Upcanyon, yes, in the direction that Kevin and Ramona had gone" (163) *and downcanyon* as in "The ground fell away in a smooth slope downcanyon" (166), The use of *up-* and *down-* with geographical words has long been a feature of English, as words such as *upchannel* (OED2 1893), *upcountry* (OED2 1688), *upfield* (OED2 1951), *uphill* (OED2 1607), *upriver* (OED2 1774), *upslope* (OED2 1920), *upstate* (OED2 1901), *upstream* (OED2 1681), *uptown* (OED2 1802), *downcountry* (OED2 1823), *downhill* (OED2 1591), *downslope* (OED2 1908), *downstate* (OED2 1909), *downstream* (OED2 1706), and *downtown* (OED2 1835) clearly attest. In creating *upcanyon* and *downcanyon*, Robinson has simply extended an already existing use of these locative prefixes.

Similarly, Robinson's usage of *waterscape*, while finding its analogy in words like *landcape, cloudscape,* and *seascape,* expands the domain of the form by providing a nuance of meaning not generally found in either its definition of those of its analogs. As the RH2 notes, *waterscape* denotes "a picture or view of the sea or other body of water" and has done so since the 1850s. Robinson's context, however, goes beyond the association of *-scape* with scenery and/or the artistic representation of it by associating the term with groundwater reservoirs and the management of them: "But groundwater basins paid no heed to county lines, and so use of the groundwater in many cases had to be adjudicated by the courts. In many cases state

---

*First published as "The Ecological Newspeak of Kim Stanley Robinson." *American Speech* 72 (1997): 440–443. Copyright 1998, University of Alabama Press. All rights reserved. Used by permission of the publisher.

control was stronger than ever. The waterscape was simply bigger than local governments could effectively manage" (189). In Robinson's use *waterscape* only peripherally involves "scenery consisting of water," since groundwater is not generally either visible or picturesque.

In the course of the novel, Robinson also creates two new compounds and an interesting blend, all of which enhance his themes of ecological balance and of the reshaping of human ecology to be harmonious with nature. In the first compound, *cloudgel*, Robinson simply couples two already existing forms into one that is essentially self-explaining in the novel's context. As the following citations show, *cloudgel* connotes a form of roofing material/insulation that is light, airy, gelatinously liquid, and which reacts to heat to provide reflectivity on warm days, but allows conduction of sunlight on cool ones:

> Put the skylights in place, boxes into the roofing, bubbles of cloudgel into the boxes, get the seal right, make it all so clean and perfect ... [241];

and,

> As they cut curves in the air Kevin saw buildings he had worked on at one time or another: a house reflecting sunlight from canopies of cloudgel and thermocrete... [16].

The form, then, literally denotes "a semirigid colloidal dispersion of a solid with a liquid or gas, as jelly, glue, etc." (RH2) that *clouds* when heated.

In the second compound, *light-charged*, Robinson again reflects his ecological concern that houses should be a part of nature, in this instance by allowing light to enter and give energy to the room: "Oscar's house had been an ordinary tract house before, but now with the south rooms all made one, and clerestory windows installed at the top of their walls, they formed a long plant-filled light-charged chamber" (240). In creating this form, Robinson uses the past participle of *charge* in one of the OED2's listed senses of "to fill (any substance) *with* other matter, diffused or distributed throughout it (*e.g.* the air *with* vapour, water *with* mineral substances, etc.)," but chooses to create a foregrounded or marked compound rather than use a more frequently occurring phrasal such as *charged with light*. Moreover, Robinson's blended form, *thermocrete* (cited above), again emphasizes the ecological concerns of the book in naming a building material that apparently, like *cloudgel*, contributes to the weather-sensitivity of the house, perhaps by the transference of heat. The first element of the blend, *therm-*, has long functioned as a combining form both in scientific and other contexts; the second element is clearly derived from *(con)crete*.

Most interesting among Robinson's new usages, however, are his functional shifts. The first of these shifts is *thermostat*, a word associated with the properties of *cloudgel*, from verb transitive to verb intransitive, a use unrecorded elsewhere: "At about seventy degrees it begins to cloud up, and at eighty it's white, and reflecting sun away. So it thermostats, just like clouds over the land" (125). While the OED2 does list *thermostat* as a transitive verb meaning "to regulate the temperature of (a substance or a piece of apparatus) by means of a thermostat" and usually occurring in its past participle form, as in the most recent citation: "1979 Nature 25 Jan 29½ The complete reaction chamber was heated in a thermostatted oven." Robinson's intransitive use makes *cloudgel*, with its heat reactant properties, its own thermostat.

The next functional shift is that of *iceberg* from noun to verb, and this particular form has no clearly discernible denotation, although it is highly connotative in context. The present participle *iceberging* appears when several of the more ecologically sensitive characters in the novel are discussing the hiding of a company's growth to avoid government scrutiny:

Apparently Heartech's growth had been even more rapid than it appeared to the public. And some of that growth was being absorbed by a hidden backer, so that Heartech would remain within the legal company size, and avoid any special audits from the IRS. Or so the rumors had it. "They're iceberging in the black..." [140–141].

Like an iceberg that shows only ten percent or so of its surface to the world, Heartech is showing only a portion of its profitability to the government; therefore, *to iceberg* apparently means "to show only what appears within legal limits."

Less abstract is Robinson's use of *pruning* as a present participle. While the verb *to prune* already exists in English with numerous meanings ranging from "to trim foliage" to, when applied to persons, "to trim oneself or to plume oneself," Robinson's verb *to prune up* is clearly a functional shift based on the noun *prune* and not on any of the preexisting verbs because the meaning is clearly that of "to come to look like a prune": "Look at my fingertips.... They're really pruning up" (157).

In addition, Robinson includes two forms which reinforce the book's vision of man living in harmony with all other creatures. Both forms are verbs created from animal names, but only one constitutes a functional shift, since the other just extends the domain of a pre-existing verb. In the first instance, Robinson turns *grunion* "a small fish that spawns in the coastal waters of California and Mexico" into a verb that means "to behave and/or swim like a grunion by hugging the shore": "Nothing but shore break. They grunioned around that for a long time, mindless, lifted up and down by the moon. After that their suits were full of sand, they had to swim out again to flush them clean" (133).

In the second instance, Robinson creates the same sort of verb meaning for *shark*; but, since the verb *to shark* normally means "to fish for sharks" and "to prey like a shark; to victimize," both of which are antithetical to his theme of natural harmony, Robinson uses the verb in a new way: "Kevin sharked over the rippled tawny sand on the bottom, looked up through silver bubbles at the surface, saw its rise and fall" (132).

Clearly, Robinson intends his reader to see Kevin swimming as a shark swims, gliding over the sandy bottom and enjoying his buoyant journey through the sea, so that even a shark, normally a fearsome reminder of nature's viciousness in the minds of many, becomes a symbol for the harmonious, ecologically balanced future that Robinson portrays.

Like other science fiction and fantasy writers, Kim Stanley Robinson often creates new words or uses existing words in new ways to enhance his ideas and themes. In *Pacific Edge*, Robinson bases some of his creations, such as *upcanyon* and *downcanyon*, on analogy, while others, such as *cloudgel*, *lightcharged*, and *thermocrete*, are either new compounds or blends; some, such as *to thermostat (something)* and *waterscape*, extend the domain of already existing words, while others, such as *to iceberg*, *to shark,* and *to grunion* convert already existing words to new uses. In these ways, Robinson not only expands the vocabulary of English, but also emphasizes his vision of man's need to establish ecological balance by creating the using words that have a common thread: humanity's relationship to nature and its need to live in harmony with the natural world.

Notes

1. The author would like to thank Jeffery Triggs of the *OED* for confirming that Robinson is the earliest citation for *to shark, to grunion, to prune, upcanyon, downcanyon,* and *cloudgel.* He notes, moreover, that Robinson subsequently uses *downcanyon* in both *Red Mars* (1992) and *Green Mars* (1993). Apparently *to thermostat, thermocrete,* and *lightcharged* are not attested to in the OED archives. Robinson's use of *waterscape* is apparently not the first usage, since Trigg cites J. McPhee's *Atchafalaya in Control of Nature* (1992) 162 as the

earliest use. However, McPhee's use is slightly different from Robinson's, as the following quotation reveals: "water just poured out ... and flowed on into a distributary waterscape known as Atchafalaya." McPhee's use refers to visible water sources, very much the way *seascape* refers to the visible sea and its environs, while Robinson's use refers not only to streams and rivers, but to underground wells, thereby extending the use of the *-scape* concept to include seen and unseen elements.

WORKS CITED

(AH2.) *The American Heritage Dictionary of the English Language.* 2nd College ed. Boston: Houghton, 1982.
(BDE.) *The Barnhart Dictionary of Etymology.* H. W. Wilson, 1988.
(Chambers.) *Chambers 20th Century Dictionary.* New ed. Edinburgh: Chambers, 1983.
(DAE.) *A Dictionary of American English on Historical Principals.* Chicago: University of Chicago, 1944.
(DSUE.) *A Dictionary of Slang and Unconventional English,* 8th ed. New York: Macmillan, 1984.
(OAD.) *Oxford American Dictionary.* Compiled by Eugene Ehrlich, et al. New York: Oxford University Press, 1980.
(OED2.) *The Oxford English Dictionary,* Rev. ed. Oxford: Clarendon, 1989.
(HDAS.) *Random House Historical Dictionary of American Slang.* Vol. 1. New York: Random House, 1994.
(RH2.) *The Random House Dictionary of the English Language,* Second ed., Unabridged. New York: Random, 1987.
(W3.) *Webster's Third New International Dictionary of the English Language.* Springfield: Merriam, 1981.

15

Murray Bookchin on Mars! The Production of Nature in the Mars Trilogy*

Shaun Huston

While science fiction most often conjures up images of technology and the so-called "hard sciences," writers in the genre also address human social relations. One of the exemplars of this tradition is Kim Stanley Robinson. In his award-winning Mars trilogy, *Red, Green* and *Blue Mars*, Robinson uses the idea of transforming Mars into a habitable planet to explore the ethics and limits of the human ability to (re)produce nature. Philosophically and theoretically, Robinson's writing has particular relevance to the work of social ecologist Murray Bookchin. The Mars trilogy provides a fruitful exploration of what Bookchin refers to as third or free nature, a synthesis of first (bio-physical) nature and second (human social) nature wherein humans "co-operate" with first nature and directly participate in the evolution of life.

This chapter is divided into two main sections. The first sketches out Bookchin's "dialectical naturalism" and considers a particular critique of the idea of third nature. The second section introduces Robinson's Mars trilogy and interprets those works as an exploration of free nature.

Bookchin's Philosophy of Nature

Intellectually, Bookchin falls in the Western tradition of dialectical thought represented by Aristotle, Hegel, Marx and the Frankfurt School. Bookchin's relationship with Marx is largely oppositional; he rejects the centrality of class struggle, focusing on a more general struggle with hierarchy/domination (*Post-Scarcity Anarchism* and "New Social Movements"; Purchase 57–70). At the same time, Bookchin clearly draws insights from Marx's analysis of capitalism (Kovel 37–48). His early work on cities, *The Limits of the City*, directly builds on Marx's observations regarding uneven development between city and country (*Limits of the City* vi–xi, 4, 101). Similarly, Bookchin draws on Adorno and Horkheimer's critique of

---

*First published as "Murray Bookchin on Mars! The Production of Nature in Kim Stanley Robinson's Mars Trilogy." *Lost in Space: Geographies of Science Fiction*. Rob Kitchin and James Kneale, eds. London, New York: Continuum, 2002. 167–179. Used by kind permission of Continuum.

instrumental reason in developing his own critique of domination, both human on human and human on nature, but criticizes their work for reducing nature to a passive, crude object transcended by the human species (*Ecology of Freedom* 270–80). Bookchin develops his notion of "eduction," or reasoning that draws out the developmental potential of things in nature, and nature itself, from Aristotle and Hegel, though he argues that their dialectics require a sense of natural evolution to be truly ecological, that is, a sense of nature as a "flowing continuum" rather than a static "ladder of being" (*Philosophy of Social Ecology* 124, 119–33; Purchase 68–70). Perhaps the critical distinction between Bookchin and his influences, especially Marx and the Frankfurt School, is that Bookchin reasons that the domination of nature by the human species was preceded by, and emerged from, the domination of human by human (hierarchy), rather than in the reverse (Merchant 8–9; Bookchin, *Remaking Society* 154).

Politically, Bookchin's closest predecessor, both historically and substantively, is the anarchist Peter Kropotkin. Kropotkin contributes several historical and theoretical themes to Bookchin's work, notably the rooting of co-operation (mutual aid) and ethics in nature, historical connections between cities and human freedom and the image of a free world are made from regional confederations of cities and towns (which, in turn, are organized as grassroots confederations) (Macauley; Purchase 57–70; Bookchin, *Remaking Society* 154, *Urbanization without Cities* 152–3). It is out of this synthesis of an "ecologized" dialectical tradition and anarchist communism that Bookchin develops his philosophy of nature.

As noted in the introduction, Bookchin conceives of nature as developing through three forms. Initially, there is first or bio-physical nature. In this form, nature strives for self-awareness, providing the basis for the emergence of the human species. With the human species comes second or social nature. In second nature, the development of life, as represented by the human species, and the interaction between life and its environments become self-conscious and self-directed, rather than instinctive and guided primarily by deep evolutionary memory. However, because human and non-human nature do not actually break from one another, but remain intertwined, it is necessary to bring social nature into conscious synthesis with first nature. Bookchin refers to this synthesis as third or "free" nature. Here, human-defined second nature is integrated with first nature so that the human species actively participates in the differentiation and evolution of life.

Third nature is "*free* nature — that is, an ethical humanly scaled community that establishes a creative interaction with its natural environment" (Bookchin, *Urbanization without Cities* xvii, italics in original). This integration of first and second nature heals the (illusory) split between "the social" and "the natural" that occurs in the elaboration of second nature. According to Bookchin:

> Both are in a very real sense *natural*, and their naturalness finds its evolutionary realization in those remarkable primates we call human beings who, consciously responding to a sense of obligation to the ecological integrity of the planet, bring their rational, communicative, richly social, imaginative, and aesthetic capacities to the service of the nonhuman world as well as the human [*Urbanization without Cities* xvii-xviii, italics in original].

Thus, in reaching third nature, humans realize their potential as "nature rendered self-conscious" (Bookchin, *Ecology of Freedom* 315–16). In second nature, humans emerge as a species able to think and act in and for itself. This achievement lays the ground for the human species to think and act in and for the world, or nature, at large (see Bookchin, *Ecology of Freedom, Modern Crisis, Urbanization without Cities* and *Philosophy of Social Ecology*).

Bookchin's account of third nature is heavily weighted towards describing human social relations and structures. His description of how first and second nature can, and will, be integrated is much less developed. This leaves his work open to the criticism that third nature is, at best, recklessly vague, and, at worst, plays to human hubris regarding non-human nature. Eckersley (137) argues that "Bookchin's vision of stewardship does not qualify how and to what extent our responsibility is to be discharged." She proceeds to provide a list of potentially disastrous human interventions into the evolution of life (wholesale introductions of new species, the "greening" of deserts, etc.), not to mentions the cumulative history of past and present human interventions. Furthermore, while acknowledging that Bookchin's social ecology advances beyond a simple anthropocentrism, one that justifies the use of non-human nature for strictly human ends, she questions the extent to which Bookchin's world-view remains focused on humanity to the potential detriment of other species. She asks whether "we now know enough about these processes [of natural evolution] to *foster and accelerate them*" (Eckersley 142, italics in original). In other words, there seem to be grave risks in moving humans to actively, and as a matter of course, intervene in evolution of non-human nature, especially with the intent of promoting certain characteristics.

It can be argued, as Bookchin has (Bookchin, "Recovering Evolution"), that critics such as Eckersley are uncritical skeptics and unimaginative about the reconciliation of first and second nature and the transcendence of inherited histories. Nonetheless, Bookchin's discussions of third nature tend to be either highly abstract, advocating the use of "eductive" reasoning to understand first nature (Bookchin, *Philosophy of Social Ecology*), or superficial and technical (see Bookchin, *Post-Scarcity Anarchism, Toward an Ecological Society* and *Ecology of Freedom*). Significantly, the technical innovations that Bookchin writes about, renewable energy technologies and bioregional urban design and architecture for example, do not directly address what human *participation* in the evolution of nature might be like. Such innovations may adapt second nature to first, but if anything, they are tools for minimizing, rather than heightening, the impact of human development on non-human nature. If Eckersley is too chained to the past or the world as it is, Bookchin appears too confident in his own sense of the *process* of nature (see also Kovel). At the very least, the questions raised by Eckersley suggest a need for a more satisfactory accounting of how third nature is to emerge and what it would mean for humans to overcome their one-sided relationship with first nature.

There is also the issue of the relative specificity with which Bookchin addresses the two dimensions of third nature. While Bookchin's consideration of first nature in third nature tends to take the form of general principles with a smattering of specifics, his account of second nature and its revolutionary transformation is rife with detail (see Bookchin, *Toward an Ecological Society, Remaking Society* and *Urbanization without Cities*; Biehl). Furthermore, in the 1990s, Bookchin turned much of his attention to beating back perceived misanthropic tendencies in the ecology movement, that is, tendencies which blame humans *per se* for ecological and environmental degradation, rather than social structures (see, for example, Bookchin, *Ecology Movement*). Bookchin's extensive effort to articulate the specific conditions for human freedom, while leaving the actual integration of first and second nature to the unfolding of "the Dialectic," underscores the criticism that third nature is hazy, if noble, fraught with potential difficulties if not disasters.

It is in addressing the criticism that his work fails to sufficiently elaborate on the content of third nature that Kim Stanley Robinson's Mars trilogy offers the greatest insight for Bookchin's social ecology.

Robinson and Bookchin

Operating in the realm of social theory and philosophy, it is difficult for Bookchin to get around the largely negative history of human intervention into bio-physical nature and its environments, especially, though not exclusively, since the onset of the Industrial Revolution. Noting a lack of imagination in getting past that history on the part of critics such as Eckersley is not sufficient. By working in fiction, Robinson is able to take the question of third nature into new contexts for examination. Through the literal removal of humans from the bonds of the Earth, he presents the human species with a new beginning in its relationship with first nature.

In Mars, Robinson presents an environment that appears to require outside intervention for life to evolve (or, perhaps, to re-evolve). Mars possesses key elements necessary for life as humans know it, an atmosphere, albeit a thin one, and water, though locked up in ice and permafrost, but there are no signs of actual life or evolution. This puts a new perspective on possible human participation in the production of nature. The biological aspect of bio-physical first nature requires action out of second nature to exist, while second nature is extremely limited without completing first nature. Not surprisingly, in the trilogy, the issue of whether to use human technology and knowledge to release Mars's latent capacity for life, "terraforming," quickly gives way to the question of how to transform the planet. The question thus becomes: will humans terraform Mars in order to reproduce an environment convenient to human activity, or will they choose to terraform in a manner that co-operates with the Martian environment and gives rise to a unique order of life? In more Bookchinist terms, will humans annex Mars to second nature, or will the species foster a third nature that transcends the legacy of human social nature on Earth?

The idea that moving humanity to another planet would be an opportunity to develop new social and physical environments is one that Robinson explicitly introduces in *Red Mars* through the character of Arkady Bogdanov, a space navigator and one of the First Hundred colonists:

> We have come to Mars for good. We are going to make not only our homes and our food, but also our water and the very air we breathe — all on a planet that has none of these things.... This is an extraordinary ability, think of it! And yet some of us here can accept transforming the entire physical reality of this planet, without doing a single thing to change ourselves or the way we live.... And so I say that among the many things we transform on Mars, ourselves and our social reality should be among them [Robinson, *Red Mars* 89].

This statement captures the full sense of third nature: the freeing of humanity from a narrow second nature that fosters domination in both human and non-human nature, and a shift to a (more) fully self-conscious relationship to our own nature, the nature of others and the physical environments that tie all forms of nature together.

Through two devices, a longevity treatment and the benefits of living in a lower gravity environment, Robinson tracks the progress of the human project on Mars (and back on Earth) through a group of characters that live through large sections of the trilogy's 200-year-plus timespan. Two of the trilogy's central characters are physicist Saxifrage Russell (Sax) and geologist Ann Clayborne. The development of these two characters, more than others, captures the transition of Terran-Martian culture from a replicant of Earthly second nature to a unique third nature.

In *Red Mars*, both Sax and Ann are, in different ways, alienated from the Martian environment. Sax's alienation is more straightforward than Ann's. Sax is the archetypal master planner: an ivory tower scientist and technocrat. To Sax, Mars could be any place. What matters is humanity, with its technology, its knowledge and the superiority of sentience and self-consciousness, has arrived. In one of the early exchanges about the human role on Mars, still on the transport from Earth, two proclamations sum up Sax's early relationship with the planet: "We'll change it just by landing" and "It's dead" (Robinson, *Red Mars* 40). Once humans arrive on Mars, the process of change will be underway, it will be irreversible and it will be for the better. Sax elaborates on these sentiments in a debate with Ann.

> Without the human presence it [Mars] is just a random collection of atoms, no different than any other random speck of matter in the universe. It's we who understand it, and we who give it meaning.... Not the basalt and the oxides.... If there are lakes, or forests, or glaciers, how does that diminish Mars's beauty? I don't think it does. I think it only enhances it. It adds life, the most beautiful system of all.... We can transform Mars and build it like you would build a cathedral, as a monument to humanity and the universe both [Robinson, *Red Mars* 177–8].

While Sax's sentiments are suggestive of third nature, the image of a cathedral or monument implies control over the production of nature. For Sax, Mars in itself is irrelevant. What matters is the human ability to turn Mars into a habitable place.

In contrast with Sax, Ann is deeply attached to Mars, or, at least, to what it represents: billions of years of geologic history (apparently) uninterrupted by the chaos and disturbances of life. This attachment puts her in conflict. She wants to see Mars up close. She wants to touch and study it, but to do all that she must alter what makes Mars special to her. On a larger scale, the forces that make it possible for her to be on Mars will not allow the planet to remain as it was found. She lets these contradictions out in a conversation regarding how much time to spend on the surface in the face of radiation allowed in by the planet's thin atmosphere. Ann exclaims:

> I look at this land and, and I *love* it. I want to be out on it traveling over it always, to study it, to live on it and learn it. But when I do that I change it—I destroy what it is, what I love in it.... I'd rather die. Let the planet be, leave it wilderness and let radiation do what it will [Robinson, *Red Mars* 157, italics in original].

For Ann, there is an essential Mars to which humans, herself included, are anathema. To ease this contradiction, she seeks ways to minimize the human impact on Mars even as she realizes that the planet will never be the same now that humans have arrived, no matter how circumscribed their presence.

The early life of the First Hundred is observed by people back on Earth: a live-action soap opera and political thriller. Sax and Ann come to represent different sides of the terraforming debate, with the physicist representing a majority faction on both Mars and Earth that believes in terraforming Mars "by all means possible, as fast as they could," and the geologist standing in for a smaller but committed "hands-off attitude" (Robinson, *Red Mars* 169). In the face of overwhelming odds, Ann commits herself to slowing terraforming down, making the case that humans need to study and understand Mars before changing it.

Ann loses this argument and the human population on Mars grows. Many of the new arrivals possess distinct cultural and political identities and have different goals in mind for Mars: cultural autonomy for individual groups versus universal standards of rights and responsibilities, close ties to Earth versus Martian independence. In the end, the United Nations and corporate authorities that funded the Martian expedition assert their authority over the planet. Many of the First Hundred, identified with movements in favor of an independent Mars, are forced underground, including Sax and Ann. This change in circumstance sets the stage for *Green Mars*.

In *Green Mars*, Ann heads into the Martian outback. It is revealed to her that she has, reluctantly and, it seems, unknowingly, become a focal point and hero to a faction on Mars called the "Reds," essentially a Martian Earth First! who practice ecotage against terraforming. Coyote, an unofficial member of the First Hundred who stowed away on the original transport, persuades her to meet with the Reds. Initially, Ann is skeptical about the efficacy of ecotage and is reluctant to involve herself in a political movement removed from scientific debate. Her turning point comes during a trek to the Red base of operations. Witnessing multiple signs of life and environmental transformation, she decides that she should meet with the Reds and arrives a hero. Ann's turn to the Reds is significant because it is a self-admission that her objections to terraforming are not grounded solely in science — too much has already changed for her arguments for further study of the native landscape to hold. Joining the Reds is an emotional and political decision.

> A bunch of radicals. Not really her type, Ann thought, feeling a residual sensation that her objection to terraforming was a rational scientific thing. Or at least a defensible ethical or aesthetic position. But then the anger burned through her again in a flash.... Who was she to judge the ethics of the Reds? At least they expressed their anger, they had lashed out [Robinson, *Red Mars* 129–30].

After witnessing the land "melting" away from the unlocked water, she decides to lash out as well. At this moment, Ann does not perceive humans to be capable of transcending second nature, and, as a result, rejects the idea of a third nature on Mars.

Contributing to Ann's decision to join the Reds is her skepticism about human nature. She expresses the conviction that humans on Mars, whether they were born there or not, are "human and human we remain." A significant number of humans on Mars take as an article of faith that as humans terraform Mars, Mars "areoforms" human nature. Areoforming is defined as a certain sense or spirit of place and life that is uniquely Martian. To Ann, the terraforming efforts in themselves, and the sameness of the colonists' tent cities, imply that areoforming is a bankrupt idea, one that serves to mask the destructive selfishness of human activity on Mars (see Robinson, *Green Mars* 365–6). This rejection of even the idea behind areoforming represents a rejection of third nature. For Ann, humans should withdraw from Mars as much as possible without leaving entirely. That is the only way to insulate the planet from a selfish and grasping human social nature.

Where Sax is concerned, *Green Mars* is a significant time of transition. Not satisfied with hiding out, he acquires a new identity and a new face. Fundamentally a generalist, he transforms himself into a biologist and goes to work for a biotech company designing plants for Mars's emerging environments. Whereas, before, Sax was the master planner, working with macro-level design and analysis of terraforming, in his new identity, Stephen Lindholm, he is involved in the ground-level work of terraforming. His observations as a fieldworker have a profound affect on his awareness of the Martian influence on human endeavors to change the planet and on the ability of life to develop in unintended or unexpected ways.

In a key passage, Sax takes off on his own to explore a proto-alpine meadow. Dotted with trees and grass, he observes that the trees, mainly white spruce and lodgepole pine, are gnarled and stunted, and this is despite extensive engineering for growth, hardiness and adaptation to Martian soil composition. Taking delight in these trees and the few insects that had been released, he wishes for "Some moles and voles, and marmots and minxes and foxes" (Robinson, *Green Mars* 180). His reasons are practical: many animals provide useful services to plant life and vice versa, but he also begins to realize that not everyone is engaged in the terraforming for the same reasons. He is especially disturbed by an arrangement of solar mirrors and lenses being used to heat the surface and increase the melt of ice and permafrost. This action not only destabilizes the surface, but increases the amount of CO_2 in the atmosphere, intensifying and speeding up the warming of the planet, but making it uninhabitable for animal life. "As if warming the planet was the only goal" (Robinson, *Green Mars* 180). His commitment to life, articulated in *Red Mars*, sharpens here. It is not only human life, but life in general that matters to Sax. However, many of the more drastic, and apparently ascendant, terraforming plans are centered on a heavy industrial model that would heat the surface and thicken the atmosphere as fast as possible. This would make the planet eminently exploitable, unveiling mineral ores and enabling activities on the surface otherwise inhibited by cold, but it would not support the introduction of life in general, most likely only technologically or genetically enhanced humans.

This distinction in terraforming goals illustrates the practical and ethical differences between remaining in second nature and transitioning to third nature. In the former, human knowledge and technology are employed to bend the Martian environment to serve human needs. In the latter, those same capabilities are employed for the benefit of other species and, at some level, preserving the integrity of the Martian landscape.

These differences also come into relief at an annual conference on terraforming. The push to heat and thaw the surface in all haste disturbs Sax. He begins to doubt even his own initial plans for making a fast jump to a human habitable surface. The extent to which terraforming now seemed to be driven by developing an environment exclusively convenient to human purposes and tastes, and by the pursuit of profit, shakes Sax's faith in the political disinterest of science. He becomes aware of the drastic changes to the Martian landscape resulting from terraforming. Significantly, he thinks:

> All of this was as Ann had predicted to him, long ago. No doubt she was noting reports of all these changes with disgust, she and all the rest of the Reds. For them every collapse was a sign that things were going wrong rather than right. In the past, Sax would have shrugged them off; mass wasting exposed frozen soil to the sun, warming it and revealing potential nitrate sources and the like. Now he was not so sure.... The collapse of landforms were considered no more than an opportunity, not only for terraforming which seemed to be considered the exclusive business of the transnats, but for mining [Robinson, *Green Mars* 217–18].

Sax comes to believe that the terraforming effort has become something other than a noble attempt to bring life to Mars, but a means for turning the planet into a raw materials colony for Earth.

Eventually, Sax's identity is uncovered by the Earth-based authorities on Mars. He is tortured and brain-damaged. After he is rescued by the underground, his mind and body are reconstructed, albeit not perfectly. He decides to take down one part of the solar mirror-lens arrangement to slow down the heating of the surface. His success leads to another exchange with Ann, a person that he has come to think about a lot. Until the end, this exchange is much like the others between the two of them. Sax defends the terraforming in principle. He reasserts a plan for a "human-viable surface to a certain elevation" and a slower approach to transforming the surface and the atmosphere. Ann is curious about his decision to knock out the one portion of the heating device, but is still bitter about the terraforming and Sax's commitment. But this time Sax ends with this admission: "I was wrong.... We should have waited. A few decades of study of the primal state. It would have told us how to proceed. I didn't think things would change so fast." Ann, non-plussed, simply responds: "But now it's too late" (Robinson, *Green Mars* 415). This exchange, Ann in bitter alienation from Sax and what she believes he represents, and Sax expressing remorse and a desire to reach out to and understand Ann, sets the scene for *Blue Mars*. Ann continues to be uncomfortable with the idea of integrating the human species with the Martian environment, while Sax has undergone a significant transformation in consciousness, ethical awareness and judgment. No longer overwhelmingly enamored of human capabilities, and freed from the belief that human second nature can freely bend other forms of nature to its will, Sax has moved to an understanding of the ethical and practical limits to human interventions into the production of nature. Most significantly, he has come to appreciate the value and role of the native Martian landscape in guiding the evolution of life on the planet.

Mars itself undergoes yet another revolution in *Green Mars*, only this time Mars breaks free from Earth. In *Blue Mars*, the independence movement must now address issues of Martian governance and what sort of relationship to establish with Earth. Both of these decisions shape the context for addressing Sax's and especially, Ann's personal transformations and their respective relationships with the planet that has become their home. Indeed, in *Blue Mars*, Sax and Ann emerge as the trilogy's principal characters. Sax's focus in *Blue Mars* is on deepening his understanding of Ann's connection to Red Mars and finding an entry to persuade her that life on Mars is not a blight, but a beautiful and right thing.

It is clear in *Blue Mars* that Martian independence from Earth plays an important role in bringing Ann to an accommodation with the human presence on, and even transformation of, Mars. Most sections of the trilogy are introduced by the thoughts and descriptions of an unnamed observer. *Blue Mars* begins with one of these passages. The observer is describing a scene where Ann Clayborne is smiling, addressing a group of Reds. The heart of her message is recorded by the observer:

> *We came from Earth to Mars, and in that passage there was a certain purification. Things were easier to see, there was a freedom of action that we had not had before. A chance to express the best part of ourselves. So we acted. We are making a better way to live* [Robinson, *Blue Mars* 2, italic in original].

While still not persuaded that the terraforming is anything but a small-minded endeavor, it is significant that Ann would be talking not about restricting human action on Mars, but about the possibilities of making a better human life on the planet. The break with Earth distances Mars from what are, in Ann's estimation, the most selfish and grasping aspects of second nature.

There are several places in *Blue Mars* where Ann engages in close observation of human life on Mars. While these observations are not wholly positive, her curiosity about how humans are living on the planet is a crack in her shield against the idea of truly inhabiting, as opposed to simply studying, this new place. She finds herself concluding at one point, "People's faces, staring in concert; this ran the world" (Robinson, *Blue Mars* 16). This thought indicates a recognition that humans have added value to Mars rather than simply taking value from it.

There is one particularly important moment in the book where Ann starts to make a turn away from her alienated relationship with humanity on Mars and the Martian environment. This moment is a conversation with Michel Duval, another of the First Hundred, who, at Sax's urging, has engaged her in conversation about possible suicidal tendencies. Perhaps because he has more distance from Ann, or perhaps because of his psychological training, Michel is able to talk to Ann in ways that Sax is not.

> [Michel:] *There is so much of Red Mars that remains. You should go out and look! Go out and empty your mind and just see what is out there. Go out at low altitude and walk free in the air, a simple*

> dust mask only. It would be good for you, good at the physiological level. Also it would be reaping a benefit of the terraforming. To experience the freedom it gives us — that we can walk on its surface naked and survive. It's amazing! It makes us part of an ecology. It deserves to be rethought, this process. You should go out to consider it, to study the process of areoformation.
> [Ann:] *That's just a word. We took this planet and plowed it under. It's melting under our feet.*
> [Michel:] *Melting in native water. Not imported from Saturn or the like, it's been there from the beginning...* [Robinson, *Blue Mars* 252, italics in original].

Ann resists Michel's arguments but this exchange does send her out on a trip around the planet, both in and out of human company. It is also evident that Michel has raised difficult questions about terraforming. The discussion about water is important because it questions Ann's assumptions about what is and what is not "natural." Her trip prompts further reflection on these lines.

The backdrop to Ann's rapprochement with Sax and with humanity on Mars is the changed political situation on Mars. Early in *Blue Mars*, a new, independent Martian government is established. This government exhibits many Bookchinist characteristics, including a confederal structure, common ownership of land, and a system of human and environmental ethics that is reflected in various institutions and limitations on strictly private enterprise (Robinson, *Blue Mars* 153–8). This new government taps into Ann's hopes about building a better life, a better form of humanity on Mars.

The trilogy winds down with Sax devising a memory treatment to address one of the symptoms of old age made possible by the longevity treatments and Martian gravity. Many of the remaining First Hundred begin to die off, suffering a "quick decline," with memory loss being one of the harbingers. Sax gathers together those who are left at their original settlement to undergo the treatment. Ann uses this as an opportunity to focus on Mars as it was before the terraforming, and emerges fully transformed from the experience. She and Sax sail on one of the inland seas, taking in the emerging Mars, one made blue as well as green and red by an earlier deal between them that resulted in Sax removing the final part of the solar heating arrangement.

As the final chapter begins, the reader is introduced to "A new Ann. A fully Martian Ann at last" (Robinson, *Blue Mars* 754). In a public way, this transformation is represented by Ann speaking in favor of allowing legal Terran immigration to Mars in order to avert a war that would destroy the still-developing, life-sustaining Mars. More privately, the closing paragraphs bring both Ann and, symbolically, humanity into a state of free nature with Mars.

Ann, Sax and a host of family and friends make a home out of the original settlement. On the beach, after bringing ice cream back for everyone and experiencing a brief, terrifying moment where she thinks she is experiencing quick decline, Ann is confronted by a child looking at the water, sky and passing pelicans. "Innit pretty? Innit pretty? Innit pretty?" Eventually Ann answers "Yes," but her reflection continues internally.

> Oh yes, very pretty! She admitted it and was allowed to live. Beat on, heart. And why not admit it. Nowhere on this world were people killing each other, nowhere were they desperate for shelter or food, nowhere were they scared for their kids. There was that to be said. The sand squeaked underfoot as she toed it. She looked more closely: dark grains of basalt, mixed with minute seashell fragments, and a variety of colorful pebbles, some of them no doubt brecciated fragments of the Hellas impact itself [Robinson, *Blue Mars* 761].

Mars is forever changed, but the Mars they inherited is still there, beneath her feet, mixed with what humans have, if not fully created, then set in motion. In the end, for both Sax and Ann, the desire to inhabit this particular place leads them to overcome their original states of alienation.

Conclusion

By making Sax in particular struggle with the threat of Mars being terraformed into a tropical mining colony for Earth, Robinson does address the problematic history of human intervention into the production of (first) nature. Unlike Earth, Mars does not bear the full weight of this history. Mars represents the possibility of a different direction, one that is not marked by an attempt to subsume the rest of nature into the human fold. Sax and Ann, in their own ways, give up the idea that humans can dominate nature. Sax abandons the notion that humans can fully master the evolution of life or transformation of an environment, while Ann comes to accept that human intervention does not necessarily extinguish nature. By tracing the transformation of Sax and Ann, and speculating on the process of terraforming, the Mars trilogy opens a window on third nature, one that makes it possible to perceive the possibilities of a truly integrated relationship between human and non-human nature. Robinson creates a human culture where the central questions are: what does it mean to live in a place, and how can the human species use its abilities to enhance the life of that place? That these questions are asked and the answers are meaningful and consequential. The struggle toward this type of social-cultural context is what Robinson elaborates in *Red, Green* and *Blue Mars*. It is also the struggle, and fundamental basis, for third nature.

Notes

1. The connection between Robinson and Bookchin is more than incidental. The Mars trilogy is peppered with explicit references to Bookchin's work. *Pacific Edge* (1990), one of the Three Californias books, is a slice-of-life story about a Bookchinesque municipality. Robinson's first post–Mars-trilogy book, *Antarctica* (1999), tackles social ecology themes such as what it means to inhabit a place, distinctions between radical, reformist and (arguably) misanthropic ecology, and the promises of collective self-management.

Author's Note

This chapter was prepared and edited with constant help and encouragement from Anne-Marie Deitering. Additional thanks to Rob Kitchin and James Kneale for their efforts in helping me clarify the chapter. And finally thanks to Sarah Coelho for assisting in the copyediting and transcription of the chapter for this current anthology.

Works Cited

Biehl, Janet. *The Politics of Social Ecology: Libertarian Municipalism*. Buffalo, NY, and Montreal: Black Rose Books, 1998.

Bookchin, Murray. *The Ecology of Freedom: The Emergence and Dissolution of Hierarchy*. Palo Alto, CA: Cheshire Press, 1982.

———. *The Limits of the City*. New York: Harper Colophon, 1974.

———. *The Modern Crisis*. Philadelphia: New Society Publishers, 1986.

———. "New Social Movements: The Anarchic Dimension." *For Anarchism: History, Theory, and Practice*. Ed. David Goodway. London and New York: Routledge, 1989, 259–274.

———. *The Philosophy of Social Ecology: Essays on Dialectical Naturalism*. Cheektowaga, NY, and Montreal: Black Rose Books, 1995.

———. *Post-Scarcity Anarchism*. Palo Alto, CA: Ramparts Press, 1971.

———. "Recovering Evolution: A Reply to Eckersley and Fox." *Society and Nature* no. 2 (1992): 144–173.

———. *Remaking Society: Pathways to a Green Future*. Boston: South End Press, 1990.

———. *Toward an Ecological Society*. Cheektowaga, NY and Montreal: Black Rose Books, 1980.

———. *Urbanization without Cities: The Rise and Decline of Citizenship*. Cheektowaga, NY and Montreal: Black Rose Books, 1992.

———. *Which Way for the Ecology Movement: Essays by Murray Bookchin*. San Francisco and Edinburgh, UK: AK Press, 1994.

Eckersley, Robyn. "Divining Evolution: The Ecological Ethics of Murray Bookchin." *Society and Nature* no. 2 (1992): 120–143.
Kovel, Joel. "Negating Bookchin." *Social Ecology after Bookchin*. Ed. Andrew Light. New York: Guilford, 1998, 27–57.
Macauley, David. "Evolution and Revolution: The Ecological Anarchism of Kropotkin and Bookchin." *Social Ecology after Bookchin*. Ed. Andrew Light. New York: Guilford, 1998. 298–342.
Merchant, Carolyn. "Introduction." *Key Concepts in Critical Theory: Ecology*. Ed. Carolyn Merchant. Atlantic Highlands, NJ: Humanities Press, 1994. 1–25.
Purchase, Graham. *Anarchism and Environmental Survival*. Tucson, AZ: See Sharp Press, 1994.
Robinson, Kim Stanley. *Antarctica*. New York: Bantam Books, 1999.
_____. *Blue Mars*. New York: Bantam Books/Spectra, 1997.
_____. *Green Mars*. New York: Bantam Books/Spectra, 1995.
_____. *Pacific Edge*. New York: Tom Doherty Associates, 1990.
_____. *Red Mars*. New York: Bantam Books/Spectra, 1993.

16

The Mars Trilogy and the Leopoldian Land Ethic*
Eric Otto

> and as it yo-yoed back and forth it loomed before them in all its immense potential: tabula rasa, blank slate. A blank red slate. Anything was possible, anything could happen — in that sense they were, in just these last few days, perfectly free. Free of the past, free of the future, weightless in their own warm air, floating like spirits about to invest a material world.
> — Kim Stanley Robinson, *Red Mars*

Set on barren Mars, Kim Stanley Robinson's Mars trilogy speculates about what paradigms the planet's fictional settlers will inscribe on the "blank red slate." Anything is possible for the group of one hundred chosen to establish the first Martian colony. Their sense of freedom from past political constraints and from future Terran political regulation sets up the utopian potential of the new settlement. And Robinson uses all 1900–plus pages of his trilogy to illustrate the challenges of moving beyond a history spawned on Earth and toward a future, Martian history generated by utopian social, political, scientific, and ecological ideas.

The settlers' hopes are indeed utopian in the etymological sense that utopia is always impossible and always existing nowhere. Before the group even lands on Mars, "rival cliques" develop and arguments become "frequent, and vehement" (*Red Mars* 73, 75). As Maya Katarina Toitovna, the settlement's leader of the Russian contingent, reflects, "Interest groups, micropolitics — they really were fragmenting. One hundred people only, and yet they were too large a community to cohere!" (76). These arguments include Phyllis Boyle's defense of Christianity against John Boone's rational, scientific logic; Arkady Bogdanov's insistence that the architecture of the settlement be redesigned to suggest equality rather than hierarchy; and, more generally, the group's disagreements over their job assignments once the Mars colony is established. In short, and to borrow one of the many technological metaphors in *Red Mars*, "the international nature of the equipment meant that there were inevitable mismatches of size and function" (108).[1]

Though we may read the first few chapters of *Red Mars* as fictions about the unlikelihood of materializing utopian visions of new histories, new presents, and new futures, Robinson is not sending the message that utopia is hopeless. Rather, as William Dynes notes, "the

---

*First published as "Kim Stanley Robinson's Mars Trilogy and the Leopoldian Land Ethic." *Utopian Studies* 14.2 (2003): 118–135. Reprinted by permission of *Utopian Studies*.

Mars series evokes a utopian call for community: of wholeness within the self, within interpersonal relationships, within political and economic entities, within the species itself" (151). In fact, in an interview with Bud Foote, Robinson states, "Utopia has to be rescued as a word, to mean 'working towards a more egalitarian society, a global society.' Which means at every point defending it, going to the mat for the term and for the concept of Utopia" (56). "Working towards" is the key expression, here. Robinson's trilogy focuses on the reasons our current paradigms make this brand of critical utopia difficult to achieve and on the things we can do to move toward it more effectively.[2] In other words, Robinson uses his Mars trilogy not to advance a cynical view of humanity and of humanity's inability to improve the conditions of life, but to show us the difficulties inherent in any attempt to do so and to model ways of moving closer to a critical utopian society.

Robinson's concerns include interpersonal relationships, intercultural relationships, political ideologies, and economic systems. Each of these concerns, as well as many others in the trilogy, merit scholarly attention. But my focus in this paper is on Robinson's interest in environmental issues — more specifically, on the ways in which the *Mars* books call to mind Aldo Leopold's critically utopian vision of a land ethic. I suggest that *Red Mars* (1993), *Green Mars* (1994), and *Blue Mars* (1996) work together to envision a contemporary rendering of Leopold's "Land Ethic," as defined in his 1949 book *A Sand County Almanac*. Kim Stanley Robinson gives us a range of perspectives regarding human relationships to the land, from treating the land as an economic resource to leaving the land in its primal state. By the end of *Blue Mars*, the final book in the trilogy, we realize that it is our responsibility to synthesize the environmentally sound and unsound viewpoints that Robinson provides in his critical — indeed, ecocritical — utopian series in order to construct a viable model for ecological sustainability and an egalitarian relationship between all of nature's components.

Aldo Leopold's Land Ethic

Leopold begins his discussion of the land ethic by defining *ethic*. Any ethic "has its origin in the tendency of interdependent individuals or groups to evolve modes of co-operation" (238). He refers to The Golden Rule and democracy as ethical systems that, in the former case, "integrate the individual to society," and in the latter case, "integrate social organization to the individual" (238). Noticing such tendencies between individuals and between groups to evolve these modes of cooperation, Leopold then questions the absence of the land in modern society's ethical paradigms. He complains that while traditional ethics emphasize the obligations humans hold for each other, no ethic as yet — in 1949 — encouraged principled cooperation with the land. By definition, then, "The land ethic simply enlarges the boundaries of the community to include soils, waters, plants, and animals, or collectively: the land" (239).

To arrive at such an ethic involves fundamental changes in the way we view the land, for "No important change in ethics was ever accomplished without an internal change in our intellectual emphasis, loyalties, affections, and convictions" (246). Among these changes, land can no longer be seen only for its economic value. Even justifying conservation on economic grounds is a bad idea, for "most members of the land community have no economic value" (246). While it may be productive for saving economically useful species or landscapes, justifying conservation on economic grounds still fails to change the utilitarian view of the natural environment into the scientific and philosophical views that Leopold feels are necessary for a new ethical system to emerge. An economic view of the environment also does not consider the complexity of natural systems. Any attempt to govern ecology based on its use value tends to overlook those "unusable" components that are essential to the health of the whole system.

This leads to another fundamental change that Leopold advocates: to approach ecology with the aim of understanding the complexity of the environment and what makes the environment healthy. Leopold's central image for discussing a healthy environment is "a tangle of chains so complex as to seem disorderly, yet the stability of the system proves it to be a highly organized structure. Its functioning depends on the co-operation and competition of its diverse parts" (252–53). Developing an understanding of this complexity — developing an ecological consciousness — involves acknowledging that many human alterations of ecological systems result in violent releases of the land's energy that destabilize the environment, making it sick. Not only do the changes humans make to the land often cause environmental problems, they also "[steer] the course of history," as Leopold demonstrates by referring to the settlement of the Mississippi valley.[3] For Leopold scholar James I. McClintock, "History, whether in terms of losses or gains, is understood as humans acting within, not outside or above nature" (30). Cultivating an ecological consciousness, then, requires developing a scientific understanding of the complexity of land and opening up our histories to the idea of ecology.

Leopold's land ethic thus involves reworking paradigms of economics, education, and history. Leopold wants to re-vision the land as valuable not as commodity but as community. He wants to educate individuals about the complexity of the land and about how human alterations of this complexity often infect the environment with instability. Finally, he wants to examine the historical importance of the natural environment. We must ceaselessly interrogate "the same basic paradoxes: man the conqueror *versus* man the biotic citizen; science the sharpener of his sword *versus* science the searchlight on his universe; land the slave and servant *versus* land the collective organism" (260–61). At the root of Leopold's land ethic is a critical utopian vision that recognizes "the land ethic as a product of social evolution," "an intellectual as well as emotional process" (263). This is why in this paper I parallel Leopold's vision with what Kim Stanley Robinson produces in his Mars trilogy. Both writers underscore the economic, political, social, and historical complexity of the evolution of environmentally ethical ways of knowing and being.

As McClintock notes in his book *Nature's Kindred Spirits*, "Rhetorically, Leopold manages to clothe his argument in language that blurs distinctions between scientific, social, and spiritual realms, thus appealing to his audience's longed-for reconciliation between science, social conduct, and spiritual belief" (35). At the heart of McClintock's advocacy of Leopold's land ethic, then, is his realization that an ecological consciousness bridges the gap between the is/ought problem, which places scientific "facts" in opposition to social and religious values. McClintock asserts, "One need not turn to mysticism and against science to defend a land ethic" (44). By the same token, one need not turn to science and against "fiction" to establish a better model of environmental ethics. Rather, the land ethic involves a both/and view of the is/ought problem. Leopold's land ethic is itself a recursive ecological system of ideas involving economic, philosophical, and scientific discourse, which only in dialog can bring about eco-critical utopian paradigms.

The Mars Trilogy and the Economically Based Land Relation

Turning now to Kim Stanley Robinson's Mars trilogy, I suggest that the books dramatize the interplay of economics, philosophy, science, and history that is central to Leopold's land ethic. By critiquing the economic view of the land held by transnational and metanational corporations, demonstrating the complexity of ecological systems, emphasizing the mystical side of the land ethic, and contrasting opposing views of science, Robinson's books promote a critical synthesis of ideas, leading to an ecological consciousness and a view of the land as part of the community.

In an interview, Robinson says, "science fiction is an enjambment of facts and values in a way that our culture desperately needs right now. The fact-value problem is specifically relevant to today's world, because we have a culture that is making developments and cultural changes without much regard for the underlying values that are going to be thereby expressed" (53). Science fiction, for Robinson, is a literary genre that allows readers to see the connections between science-based facts and the cultural values expressed in fiction. This being the case, SF like the Mars trilogy is most appropriate for taking on environmental issues, issues that involve conflicts of both facts and values. What Robinson attempts in his three books, though, is not to make a case either for a fact-based land ethic or for a value-based land ethic, but to show how both fact and value need to be parts of our ecological consciousness.

The subject through which Robinson explores the land ethic is the terraforming of Mars, the alteration of the Martian surface to allow for life. By making terraformation the focus of his fiction, Robinson directly confronts issues that apply to Earth's environment; for the alteration of environments is necessary for human civilization. In terraforming Mars, as in "terraforming" Earth, though, there exist a range of perspectives about the degree to which we should alter the land for human habitation. For Robinson, this range includes contrasting economic and scientific models, mystical perceptions of the environment, and dueling conceptions of stewardship, all of which he explores in the *Mars* books.

Like Aldo Leopold, Robinson spends much time implicating traditional economic systems for disallowing a viable land ethic or land-human symbiosis. Though we learn early in *Red Mars* that the Mars settlement team of one hundred scientists has hopes of beginning a small scientific research station, later, in the chapter entitled "The Crucible," we are introduced to the motives of those higher powers responsible for sending these scientists: to terraform Mars rapidly. As UNOMA (the U.N. Office for Martian Affairs) approves the terraformation of Mars, Earth's own environmental protection policies break down as a previously protected Antarctica starts being mined and drilled for its oil. The parallel between the terraforming of Mars and the treatment of Antarctica is indeed deliberate on Robinson's part; for as an ecologically conscious science fiction writer he wants to suggest that as "'the last clean place on Earth is gone,'" an issue he explores in depth in his book *Antarctica*, so the next clean place, Mars, is becoming the victim of the same economic motives (251). To relate terraforming Mars to the destruction of Antarctica is thus to foreshadow the ultimate motive that UNOMA has for altering the planet — to mine its resources — and to suggest the destructiveness of an economically based land relation.

By the end of "The Crucible" and through the early parts of the next chapter, "Falling into History," we learn that the scientific motives of the first settlers have succumbed to hypercapitalist intentions. Though many of the first one hundred are pleased with UNOMA's decision to support terraformation, it is the subsequent intrusion of transnational corporate interests that instigates many of these settlers to revolt later in *Red Mars*. The first sign of this intrusion is when the German millionaire and UNOMA bureaucrat Helmut Bronski violates a Mars treaty by allowing Armscor, a transnational organization, to begin prospecting on Mars. As John Boone, the settlement's symbolic father, observes the heavy mining operations at Bradbury Point, his thoughts suggest an environmentalist's distress over a relationship to the land based solely on economic motives:

> John shook his head. That afternoon they drove for an hour back to the habitat, past raw pits and slag heaps, toward the distant plume of the refineries on the other sides of the habitat mesa. He was used to seeing the land torn up for building purposes, but this.... It was amazing what a few hundred people could do. [...] wreaking such havoc just to strip away metals, destined for Earth's insatiable demand [276–77].

Though by this point in the book Mars has only recently been settled, the developing industrial landscape already reflects the contaminated atmosphere of a world being torn apart by greedy capitalists.

Robinson's reflections on the capitalist economy and its effects on the environment do not end with John's observation of the Armscor mining project — the "gold rush," as John later calls it (284). One of the most awful (in both senses of the word) technologies created in *Red Mars* is the space elevator, which extends from the surface of the planet far into space and allows the various ores being mined from Mars to be shipped efficiently to Earth. As Phyllis Boyle, the primary visionary of the space elevator, explains,

> It will also be possible to use the cable's rotation as a slingshot; objects released from the ballast asteroid toward Earth will be using the power of Mars's rotation as their push, and will have an energy-free high-speed takeoff. It's a clean, efficient, extraordinarily cheap method, both for lifting bulk into space and for accelerating it toward Earth. And given the recent discoveries of strategic metals, which are becoming ever more scarce on Earth, a cheap lift and push like this is literally invaluable. It creates the possibility of an exchange that wasn't economically viable before; it will be a critical component of the Martian economy, the keystone of its industry [306–07].[4]

Important in Phyllis's defense of the proposed elevator is her argument for an economically based land relation, one that Robinson, like Leopold, questions. Though Phyllis promotes the elevator's cleanliness and its low energy use, her assurance is odd after reading John's observation thirty pages earlier of the "raw pits," "slag heaps," and "distant plume[s]" that litter the Martian landscape and that are the results of the mining that Phyllis sees as key to the developing Martian economy. Furthermore, Phyllis's promotion of the space elevator is even more awkward if we consider her awareness that Earth's own supply of metals is dwindling. Indeed, this economic view of the land lacks a land ethic. The philosophy of "Minimize expenses, maximize profits" excludes both the expenses the land suffers and the non-economic profits of maintaining a healthy ecosystem (442).

Eco-Economics: Toward a Land Ethic

Robinson presents a model of economics that counters the hyper-capitalism ravaging the Martian surface: eco-economics. Thought up by the biological team of Vladimir Taneev and Marina Tokareva, eco-economics places value on individuals according to their biological contributions to the ecosystem: "'Everyone should make their living, so to speak, based on a calculation of their real contribution to the human ecology'" (298). Though Vlad and Marina's eco-economics does not and cannot specifically consider the land of Mars as part of the community — for, the Martian surface is not yet habitable in *Red Mars* and the human community lives underneath large tents — it is the ecological consciousness inherent in eco-economics that makes it applicable to the land ethic developing in the trilogy. Eco-economics posits, as Robert Markley notes, that "Restricting consumption becomes a far more effective means to increase one's value to the system than accelerating production because production invariably strains scarce resources" (776). In imagining such a system, Vlad and Ursula envision a human-land symbiosis based on the imperative to include land in the community.

Robinson thus establishes a tension between the capitalist view of land as an economic resource and a conscientious view of land as a part of the community. As one component in the dialogue that ultimately leads to the land ethic of the *Mars* books, this tension continues through the three books and is resolved in *Blue Mars*. In a manner reminiscent of Leopold, Robinson shows how the rapid alterations of the Martian surface — particularly the heating of the atmosphere and the subsequent melting of the ice in Mars's thick permafrost layers — have caused environmental instability or sickness. The action at the end of *Red Mars* takes place among avalanches and floods, Leopold's "penalties of violence" (255). Furthermore, as in *Red Mars*, the environmental violence of *Green Mars* is also prefaced by Phyllis's faith in an economically based land relation: "'All the stockpiled metals from the last forty years are ready to enter the Terran market, and that's going to stimulate the entire two-world economy unbelievably. We'll see more production out of Earth now, and more investment here, more emigration too'" (183). Soon after Phyllis says this, Sax Russell, a scientist whose view of the land becomes central to the ethic of the trilogy, reflects on the negative effects of the rapid changes to the Martian environment: "Mass wasting was causing many landslides a day, and fatalities and unexplained disappearances were not at all uncommon. Cross-country travel was dangerous. Canyons and fresh craters were no longer safe places to locate a town, or even to spend a night" (217). Here, Robinson again questions the economic view of the land by drawing attention to Leopold's penalties of violence. In *Red Mars* he describes the polluted landscape and the effects of this economically motivated contamination, and in *Green Mars* he continues to show how the altered landscape has erupted with sickness and instability, mostly the result of capitalist interference.

The eco-economic model of land relations becomes, for Robinson, the most viable model for limiting the influence of capitalist institutions on the fragile Martian environment. Having finally gained independence from Earth's metanational corporations, the leaders of Mars in *Blue Mars* organize a congress to establish an official Martian government. Because Mars is a completely new social, political, economic, and environmental situation, it is difficult for these leaders to turn to historical models for help in creating their political system. Indeed, as Carl Abbott notes, one tenet of Robinson's utopian vision is to be "fully aware of the traps in seeing history as sets of analogies, which mislead us as often as they help," to let history describe itself through a dialectical process of ceaseless political communication (par 13). Despite all the possible conflicts inherent in trying to form a new system, though, the issue that provokes the most debate is land-use, an environmental concern. While much of this debate revolves around the terraforming of Mars — the Red/Green debate — the debate over land-use also involves finding an economic system that stresses not the monetary value of the land, as does capitalism, but the importance of a land-human community. Phyllis defends capitalism in both *Red Mars* and *Green Mars*, and her sentiments are repeated in *Blue Mars* by another character, Antar.

At the end of the chapter entitled "A New Constitution," Antar claims that the eco-economic model of the Martian economy "'is a radical and unprecedented intrusion of government into business'" (141). Unconvinced, Vladimir outlines the eco-economic system, which provides the equal rights and self-rule that the hierarchical structure of capitalism cannot. Environmentally, such a true democracy also requires a view of the land that opposes capitalist paradigms. Evoking the ecotopian fictions of Ernest Callenbach and Marge Piercy,

Vladimir states, "'the world is something we all steward together'" (144). Important in the eco-economic model, then, is its synthesis of socialist elements—workers owning the means of production and "'hiring capital rather than the other way around,'" for example—with ecological elements (147). Stewardship becomes everyone's responsibility, and environmental courts "have the power to review all laws passed by the congress for their impact on the Martian environment, and have the right to veto such laws without appeal if their environmental impact is judged unconstitutional" (*Martians* 268). Ultimately, the eco-economic model is voted in. The new Martian system addresses one of Leopold's paradoxes: man the conqueror *versus* man the biotic citizen. Martian civilization becomes a biotic citizenry through a new economic paradigm that values a land-human symbiosis.

Spiritual Aspects of the Land Ethic

Besides portraying characters who support an eco-economy, the Mars trilogy further dramatizes Leopold's ideas by focusing on the religious aspects of environmental thought. In this sense, Robinson, like Leopold, approaches ecology at once through the social science of politics and economics and through the more speculative world of myth. And nowhere is Robinson's interest in the possibilities of mysticism more evident than in his character Hiroko Ai, "the Japanese prodigy of biosphere design" (*Red Mars* 32). As Aldo Leopold asks for "an intense consciousness of land," so Hiroko Ai provides this consciousness (261).

Saying things like "'Mars will tell us what it wants and then we'll have to do it,'" Hiroko is the most religious ecological thinker in the *Mars* books (*Red Mars* 115). Hiroko's "areophany" is "a kind of landscape religion, a consciousness of Mars as a physical space suffused with *kami*, which was the spiritual energy or power that rested in the land itself" (*Red Mars* 229). As the critic William Dynes observes, "The focus of the areophany is a celebration of interdependency with the planet rather than an exploitation of it" (160). Hiroko's "*viriditas*" encourages followers of the areophany to foster the positive feelings of ecological connectedness by spreading life everywhere. Initiated into this areophany, Michel Duval, a French psychologist, must eat dirt in a ritual with other members of Hiroko's group. "'This is your initiation into the areophany, the celebration of the body of Mars,'" Hiroko says to Michel. "'Welcome to it. We worship this world. We intend to make a place for ourselves here, a place that is beautiful in a new Martian way, a way never seen on Earth'" (*Red Mars* 230). That Hiroko's followers eat dirt is symbolic of the connection between humanity and land that Leopold advocates.

Green Mars opens with Hiroko teaching the first generation Martian children about viriditas. On the beach with the children, she says,

> Look at the pattern this seashell makes. The dappled whorl, curving inward to infinity. That's the shape of the universe itself. There's a constant pressure, pushing toward pattern. A tendency in matter to evolve into ever more complex forms. It's a kind of pattern gravity, a holy greening power we call viriditas, and it is the driving force in the cosmos. Life, you see. Like these sand fleas and limpets and krill—although these krill in particular are dead, and helping the fleas. Like all of us. [...] And because we are alive, the universe must be said to be alive. We are its consciousness as well as our own. We rise out of the cosmos and we see its mesh of patterns, and it strikes us as beautiful. And that feeling is the most important thing in all the universe [9].

Thus, Hiroko becomes the ecological philosopher-educator of the Mars trilogy. Her brand of education, though, is rooted not in political ideology, but in religion.[5] She is a philosopher whose ideas are necessary to prompt thoughts of Martian independence and ultimately of ecological connectedness. Markley states, "it is the moral force of [Hiroko's] lived-philosophy of viriditas that brings together the scattered groups of the underground in a loose confederation and that eventually provides the rationale and moral authority of independence" (784).

When Hiroko is forced to leave Sabishii, the capital city of the underground groups who are organizing a revolution against the powerful corporate entities that run Mars, she disappears for the rest of the trilogy, either slain with her closest followers or else choosing voluntary exile. Her presence continues, though, in the form of mythology: Sax Russell believes she rescues him from a cold death in *Blue Mars*, and her son Nirgal hears rumors that she is in England, in Elysium, Mars, and somewhere in the Uranian system. At the end of *Blue Mars*, we even experience a Hiroko sighting: "Down the beach an old Asian woman was surf-fishing" (760). Accordingly, Hiroko's mystical presence in the *Mars* books balances with Robinson's close attention to economics. If as McClintock notes, Aldo Leopold's "'The Land Ethic' essay mythically combines philosophy, religion, science, and political ideology," then Robinson's attention to political ideology and religion positions his trilogy as a contemporary, science-fictional incarnation of the ideas Leopold advocated decades ago (34).

Synthesizing Conceptions of the Land-Human Relationship

Tracing the conflict between the economically based land relation and the eco-economic model of economics in the Mars trilogy gives us insight into one aspect of the ecotopian land ethic that Robinson advocates: the need for conceiving an economic system that encourages environmentally sustainable behavior. And Robinson's presentation of Hiroko Ai as a mystical "Mother-Goddess of the Earth" with a deeply religious view of the connections between land and human life contributes further to the land ethic of the three books. The land ethic advocated by Robinson's trilogy, though, involves further concepts of ecology that the author sees as crucial to developing ecological sustainability, namely, the ways in which we view our relationship with the land. Robinson conceptualizes a viable model of this relationship throughout the trilogy by establishing an extended debate between the philosophical "Red" worldview and the scientific "Green" worldview.

The debate between the Reds and the Greens, addressed throughout the Mars trilogy by pitting Ann Clayborne, a Red, against Sax Russell, a Green, begins as a debate between advocates of pure science and advocates of applied science. Supporting the former, Ann Clayborne wishes to study Mars in its primal form: "'There's as much land on Mars as on Earth, with a unique geology and chemistry. The land has to be thoroughly studied before we can start changing it'" (*Red Mars* 39). Excited about the prospects of applying science to the Martian surface in a vast terraforming effort, Sax rebuts Ann's claim, saying, "'We'll change [the land] just by landing'" (40). With both positions posited so early in *Red Mars*, before we even know the ideological thrusts of the trilogy, we can perhaps accept both Ann's and Sax's positions as credible scientific outlooks. One simply wants to study Mars as a geologist would study rocks or plate tectonics; the other wants to experiment with an entirely new environment to see what can be done to make life there possible. As Bud Foote notes, "the appeals and the honesty and the beauty of both sides are presented with skill and passion," making it difficult to side with either attitude (61). And though Sax's support for terraforming — for using science as a tool of change — may for some science fiction readers foreshadow a fate similar to Victor

Frankenstein's, it is at least qualified when Sax speculates that even human presence on Mars will alter the landscape. Without such a thoughtful, constructionist observation, we may think the terraforming effort is just as impulsive as Frankenstein's promethean effort to generate life in a stitched-up assemblage of human body parts.

Though the terraforming debate begins as a conflict between pure science and applied science, it quickly turns into a philosophical debate that involves a conflict of values. With Ann insisting that Mars "'is *its own place*'" and Sax insisting that the planet is "'dead,'" the pure science/applied science debate develops into a contest between philosophical worldviews (*Red Mars* 40). Does Mars, or by extension, the land, own itself as an individual owns herself or himself in a democratic or eco-economic state? Or, is Mars dead and valueless? Ann believes the former: the landscape has inherent beauty and worth. She claims that Sax's interventionist science is "'just playing around'"; to "'destroy a beautiful pure landscape'" is "'for *nothing at all*'" (177). Sax, on the other hand, believes "'The beauty of Mars exists in the human mind'" (177). He reduces Mars to "'a collection of atoms, no different than any other random speck of matter in the universe'" (177). The argument developing here involves a dichotomy between value and fact that as yet, and for many more pages of the Mars trilogy, shows no hope of resolution or of budding into some other worldview. Ann is ecocentric in believing "'We are not lords of the universe. We are one small part of it'" (179). Sax is anthropocentric in believing "'We are the consciousness of the universe'" (178). Is an ethic that maintains cooperation between humans and the land possible with such diametrically opposed beliefs? The rest of Robinson's trilogy serves to answer this question by ultimately working toward a Red/Green synthesis.

Very little happens in *Red Mars* to suggest this eventual synthesis between the Red and Green worldviews and a viable model of stewardship derived from both. On the contrary, we begin to see an increasing fragmentation between the Reds and the Greens as the Reds begin to sabotage Green attempts to terraform the land. Just as unproductively radical, the Greens approach terraforming like the transnational corporations approach mining—that is, putting no limits on their effort to get what they want out of the land. The key elements of the terraforming debate thus seem too radically divergent and inflexible to promise an eventual synthesis. Sax's terraforming effort—the "Russell program"—"plans to terraform the planet by all means possible, as fast as they could" (169). This view lacks a land ethic because, as Leopold would have it, science becomes the sharpener of man's sword, accommodating the desire to impose human knowledge on the world in order to change it for unsustainable human purposes. Likewise, Ann's "hands-off attitude" lacks a land ethic; for in its fervent defense of the land's natural right to remain in a primitive state, it excludes humanity's inclusion in the biotic community, and in fact, sees humans as expendable burdens on the ecosphere.

It is interesting to consider, here, the symbolic importance of an incident that occurs at the end of *Red Mars*. Driving with eight passengers to escape a massive flood made possible by the Green terraforming efforts and Red sabotage of the mighty space elevator, Ann is distracted by the spectacle of the Martian sky and gets the rover stuck on a boulder. Frank Chalmers, the leader of the American settlement team, attempts to free the car from the rock and dies in the effort. With this incident, Robinson suggests that the Red and Green worldviews are in themselves inadequate ethical paradigms. The flood that washes Frank away is the result of the careless effort to transform the Martian surface as fast as possible. By the same token, and on a more symbolic level, Frank dies because Ann gets stuck on a rock, something that as a Red geologist she loves so much and would defend to the death.

As *Red Mars* ends with a land ethic yet to be established, so does *Green Mars* begin with the same Red/Green tensions that pervade the earlier book. In fact, the distance between Ann and Sax is further established early in *Green Mars*. Ann continues her pure scientific studies of Martian geology or areology; and though she is hesitant to identify herself with the Reds — by now an extremist group — she vows to join them after observing "the planet [...] melting under her feet. Disintegrated. Reduced to mush in some Terran cartel's mining venture" (128). In this same chapter, "Long Runout," we also find Sax pursuing what he believes in — the terraforming effort. He joins a biotech company that is working to change the Martian surface.

Having so strongly established Ann and Sax's differences, Robinson then brings them together in *Green Mars* for what turns out to be a pivotal debate regarding the land ethic of the trilogy. In their conversation, Ann and Sax establish themselves as opposites when they admit their respective support of pure science and applied science. Sax reflects on Ann's position, identifying the ultimate conflict between him and Ann as one between divergent perceptions of what land is: "He knew she believed in some kind of intrinsic worth for the mineral reality of Mars; it was a version of what people called the land ethic, but without the land's biota. A rock ethic, one might say. Ecology without life" (145). Vowing to protect her "rock ethic," Ann declares that "'Red resistance'" will curtail Green attempts to terraform Mars (147). Sax asks, "'what's the point of that, now?'" and Ann replies, "'Mars. Just Mars. The place you've never known'" (147). It is this latter statement that Sax, and readers of the *Mars* books, must consider when attempting to view the land from Ann's radical perspective; for Leopold's land ethic requires foremost that the land be "known" a certain way, a way that the economically based land relation and applied science would fail to see without the critical input of more environmentally conscious worldviews.

Sax begins to consider Ann's position as he studies the Martian surface and develops his own sense of place and being within the Martian environment:

> Looking down the wild cracked surface of the glacier, he found himself thinking of [Ann]. Every little berg and crevasse stood out as if he still had the 20x magnification on his faceplate, but with an infinite depth of field — every tint of ivory and pink in the pocketed surfaces, every mirror gleam of meltwater, the bumpy hillocks of the far horizon — everything was, for the moment, surgically clear and focused. And it occurred to him that this vision was not a matter of accident (the lensing of tears over his cornea, for instance) but the result of a new and growing conceptual understanding of the landscape. It was a kind of cognitive vision, and he could not help but remember Ann saying angrily to him, *Mars is the place you have never seen* [189].

Sax's vision of the landscape displays qualities that are indeed "Red." Its focus on the details of the landscape demonstrates that Sax is becoming aware of Mars as more than a scientific experiment. Sax's "new and growing conceptual understanding of the landscape," however, does not resolve the complicated conflict of perception between him and Ann. For immediately after Sax's seemingly pure scientific observation, he also begins to understand the root cause of their conflict: "he was seeing a Mars he had never seen before. But the transformation had come by focusing for a matter of weeks on just those parts of the Martian landscape that Ann despised, the new life-forms" (190). The conflict is thus one of paradigms, of Sax valuing life and desiring to steward this life, and of Ann valuing the primal landscape and desiring to preserve the areology of the pre-colonial Mars. By themselves, neither of these paradigms is conducive to a sustainable land-human, or in this case, rock-biota ecology.

While Sax may be adopting elements of Ann's Redness — even admitting to Ann, "'We should have waited before we started [terraforming]. A few decades of study of the primal state'" — Ann has yet to accept Sax's views on the value of human life (414). She tries to commit suicide at the end of *Red Mars*, and in *Green Mars* she admits she is no longer taking the gerontological treatments that will significantly prolong her lifespan. Additionally, as the second Martian revolution is underway at the close of *Green Mars*, Ann sees the revolt "as a chance to wreck all terraforming efforts and to remove as many cities and people as possible from the planet, by direct assault if necessary" (581). Ann's "rock ethic" is admirable for its attention to the intrinsic worth of the landscape, but it fails as a viable land ethic, because it does not propose to solve the problem of maintaining a sustainable land-human symbiosis. Instead, it obscures any useful discussion of sustainability by resorting to radical actions, to killing off humans.

Green Mars is thus a book about Sax Russell's intellectual growth and Ann Clayborne's intellectual stagnancy. Ann's contribution to our own thoughts about the land ethic goes beyond simply showing the limits of epistemological inflexibility, though. She makes a point about the historical effects of terraforming that draws our attention to Aldo Leopold's thoughts on landscape and history. As Leopold calls attention to the plant succession of Kentucky and speculates about other possible historical scenarios growing from other possible landscapes, Ann argues that terraforming Mars can only prevent the planet from ever becoming independent of Terran hegemony and overpopulation — in short, of ever supporting a successful revolution: "'When the surface is viable [...] they'll be here by the billions. As long as we have to live in shelters, logistics will keep the population in the millions. And that's the size it needs to be if you want a successful revolution'" (363).[6] Ann's observation, here, is wholly Leopoldian in that she sees the changing landscape as intricately connected — ecologically connected — to the course of political history; and it is this sort of perception that Leopold wants. "Is history taught in this spirit?" Leopold asks; "It will be, once the concept of land as a community really penetrates our intellectual life" (243).

So though Ann seems to hinder the trilogy's development of a viable land-human relationship by refusing to see human life as part of the ecological community, her steadfast attention to the importance of the landscape is instrumental in causing Sax, and us as readers, to see the land in new ways. Her Red paradigms also influence the congress at Dorsa Brevia, which drafts a temporary Martian constitution. Work point six of the document states, "The Martian landscape itself has certain 'rights of place' which must be honored. The goal of our environmental alterations should therefore be minimalist and ecopoetic, reflecting the values of the areophany" (389). Though terraforming will go on, point six does reflect back on Ann's declaration early in *Red Mars* that the planet "'is *its own place*,'" and thus planetary changes will be subtle, localized, and uninfluenced by heavy industry — hence the terms "ecopoetic" and "the areophany."

The land ethic of the Mars trilogy becomes more apparent in *Blue Mars* as Ann and Sax move closer to a romantic union, a union that in a critically utopian way involves not a compromise or a negotiation between the two opposite individuals, but an "intermixture of red and green" (66). Indeed, it is primarily Sax's initiative to achieve this intermixture early in the book that leads to a new ecologically literate paradigm for both parties. He desires that Ann see "the beauty of the new biosphere," to "walk over the land, and let it speak for itself" (96). In this desire, Sax also wants to see the land as Ann does. And he does:

> The primal planet, in all its sublime glory, red and rust, still as death; dead; altered through the years only by matter's chemical permutations, the immense slow life of geophysics. It was an odd concept — abiological life — but there it was, if one cared to see it, a kind of living, out there spinning, moving through the stars that burned, moving through the universe in its great systolic/diastolic movement, its one big breath, one might say [97].

That Sax's thoughts are so imbued with alternative concepts of life suggests a major breakdown in the Red/Green opposition that has thus far pervaded the trilogy. Sax's revelation can be expressed as a syllogism: If life can be abiological, as Ann says and as Sax is beginning to understand, and if to be Green is to value life, then to be Green requires one to value those components of the land previously believed to be dead. The Red/Green binary falls apart under this new reasoning, and indeed a new paradigm, an intermixture, emerges.

But as Sax desires a new intellectual paradigm, so does Ann. Her drive to revision the Reds' revolutionary methods — to avoid the conflict that has killed many Reds and Greens — draws from Green values of biological life. Certainly Ann still advocates preserving Mars's primal state, but her increased political activism, her shift from advocate of radicalism to advocate of less harmful revolutionary methods, suggests that she, like Sax, desires a more viable land-human symbiosis, one in which humanity also has inherent value. That Ann wants "'to stain that green until it turns some other color,'" in fact, demonstrates her and Sax's parallel intentions; for they are both searching for other colors, other views of the land-human relationship (272).

Though much of the remainder of *Blue Mars* is punctuated with moments when both Ann and Sax seem to revert to their respective positions, which attests to the difficulty of synthesizing such opposing viewpoints, the conclusion presents a component of the trilogy's land ethic. As Sax comes to believe that what is important is "Not nature, not culture: just Mars," he finally breaks down the Red/Green, land/culture opposition (679). In his revelation, "Sax felt he had come over the years to love what Ann loved in Mars; and now he wanted her to reciprocate, if possible" (680). Thus he seeks out Ann's company, and as in *Green Mars* he apologizes to Ann for supporting rapid terraforming, which by now has created blue oceans and green life on the formerly red, rocky planet: "'I made mistakes. [...] I didn't see the — the beauty until it was too late. I'm sorry. I'm sorry. I'm sorry. I'm sorry'" (711). As Sax apologizes and advocates a halt to further terraforming efforts, Ann now imagines a future with human life that must be protected: "'Better to die thinking that you're going to miss a golden age, than to go out thinking that you had taken down your children's chances with you. That you'd left your descendants with all kinds of toxic long-term debts'" (728).

Ann and Sax's romantic union represents a union between Red and Green political positions that goes beyond mere compromise. The new paradigm is a combination of the two viewpoints, but it is a synthesized combination that ultimately becomes, as Ann states, "'something entirely new'" (730). In the final chapter — in fact, in the final paragraph of the trilogy — we are left with what ultimately becomes a key component of the Mars trilogy's land ethic. Appropriately, we see this new "Blue" ethic through Ann's eyes. Walking on the beach with a child, Ann reflects,

> Nowhere on this world were people killing each other, nowhere were they desperate for shelter or food, nowhere were they scared for their kids. There was that to be said. The sand squeaked underfoot as she toed it. She looked more closely: dark grains of basalt, mixed with minute seashell fragments, and a variety of colorful pebbles, some of them no doubt brecciated fragments of the Hellas impact itself. She lifted her eyes to the hills west of the sea, black under the sun. The bones of things stuck out everywhere. Waves broke in swift lines on the beach, and she walked over the sand toward her friends, in the wind, on Mars, on Mars, on Mars, on Mars, on Mars [761].

This Blue ethic involves for Ann an appreciation of human life, intermixed with a strong awareness of land. It allows Ann to reflect on the value of humanity while she also reflects on the value of the environment that surrounds her. The Blue ethic represents a symbiosis between humans and the land that moves beyond a Red/Green, either/or binary. Instead, it places humanity and the land — the biological and the abiological — together as necessary components of a living ecology.

Conclusion: A Land-Human Community

Contrary to what Ernest J. Yanarella has argued, the "polyphony of subject-positions" in the *Mars* books does not act "as an authorial ruse to exonerate Robinson of the apparent responsibility for choosing or determining the outcome of the terraforming controversy and the fate of the Martian experiment" (280). Rather, Robinson's multi-positional narrative approach attests to his desire to move closer to utopia by encouraging readers to synthesize continually a complex array of political positions. One such array of positions, as this paper has argued, involves a multiplicity of economic, philosophical, scientific, and historical perceptions of the land. The Mars trilogy, as a series more about Earth than about Mars, requests that we work toward developing an ethic that places the environment and humans within the same community. In fact, we must not draw traditional distinctions between life and land. Instead, it is crucial that we shift our ontological paradigms to include the being of the land, to see community not in anthropocentric terms, but as a complex ecology of ideas, of people, and of places. Certainly, ecotopia — utopia — is such an ever-evolving, ecological state.

According to J. Baird Callicott, "what [Leopold] wishes us to conclude is (i) that *we* are members of a human community (now grown from the savage clan to the 'family of Man,' and in reference to which we have evolved ethical limitations upon our conduct), (ii) that *we* are also members of a biotic, or land, or ecological community, and (iii) that accordingly, *we* should evolve or assume environmental ethical limitations upon *our* conduct" (67). In the Mars trilogy, Kim Stanley Robinson wishes us to envision something similar. The utopia that he strives for through his science fiction places political, religious, philosophical, and scientific ideas into a crucible. And as John Boone becomes the "utopian social engineer" within *Red Mars* by synthesizing the paradigms of various settlement groups, so do we, as readers whose active participation is demanded by the *Mars* books, become utopian ecological engineers by reaching into Robinson's crucible and pulling out a fully synthesized vision of an eco-economic/areophonic/Blue, and altogether Leopoldian, land ethic (Franko 61).

Notes

1. For more on the technological metaphors in *Red Mars*, see Bud Foote, "Notes" 62.
2. In *Scraps of the Untainted Sky*, Tom Moylan distinguishes the "critical utopia" from utopia in general. Critical utopias, emerging with the activist movements of Post–World War II America, "challenged any tendency toward [the] narrowly conceived and enforced utopianism" of earlier utopian fantasies of perfection (83). Robinson's Mars trilogy is of this critical utopian genre, for it refuses to locate faultlessness in any one of its characters' political positions, and instead makes as its project a constant "working towards" the ever-evolving state of utopia. Indeed, as I argue later, the trilogy becomes an *eco*-critical utopia as it engages Aldo Leopold's land ethic, which involves the type of recursive and interdisciplinary knowledge-building system that marks critical utopianism.
3. "Consider," Leopold states, "the settlement of the Mississippi valley. In the years following the Revolution, three groups were contending for its control: the native Indian, the French and English traders, and the American settlers. Historians wonder what would have happened if the English at Detroit had thrown a little more weight into the Indian side of those tipsy scales which decided the outcome of the colonial migration into the cane-lands of Kentucky. It is time now to ponder the fact that the cane-lands, when subjected

to the particular mixture of forces represented by the cow, plow, fire, and axe of the pioneer, became bluegrass. What if the plant succession inherent in this dark and bloody ground had, under the impact of those forces, given us some worthless sedge, shrub, or weed? Would Boone and Kenton have held out? Would there have been any overflow into Ohio, Indiana, Illinois, and Missouri? Any Louisiana Purchase? Any transcontinental union of new states? Any Civil War?" (241).

4. In this passage, and elsewhere throughout *Red Mars* and *Green Mars*, there is also an implicit critique of Christianity; for Phyllis Boyle believes "'God gave us this planet to make in our image, to create a new Eden,'" while at the same time she becomes the foremost advocate of the space elevator and of the capitalist intentions behind it (*Red Mars* 171).

5. Dynes rightly warns readers that Hiroko's areophany suffers from a "narrowness of vision" (160). To develop Dynes's claim, Hiroko does present a dogmatic veneration for abstract values that is similar to the Kakaze, a radical anti-terraforming group. While the parallel may seem extreme, it is significant that as the Kakaze vehemently pursues Red ideology, Hiroko's group religiously pursues the areophany, frequently escaping political involvement by isolating themselves in the Martian south. And indeed, Red ideology and the areophany are both value-laden conceptual positions that disregard recursive modes of building a viable land-human symbiosis. Nevertheless, as I will argue later, it is in a synthesis of the Mars trilogy's various ecological paradigms that we construct the books' ultimate environmental message. So while we must be critical of the areophany's negatives, we must focus on what its ideas contribute to ecological thought.

6. Ann's contention stands in contrast to the earlier politico-scientific opinion of Arkady Bogdanov, who claimed that terraforming Mars would usher in a new era of human freedom, rather than of increased population and corporate control. As Arkady argues:

"We have come to Mars for good. We are going to make not only our homes and our food, but also our water and the very air we breathe—all on a planet that has none of these things. We can do this because we have technology to manipulate matter right down to the molecular level. This is an extraordinary ability, think of it! And yet some of us here can accept transforming the entire physical reality of this planet, without doing a single thing to change our selves, or the way we live. [...] We must terraform not only Mars, but ourselves" [*Red Mars* 89].

Here, as Yanarella notes, Arkady "sees in a terraformed Mars the possibility of a new beginning for the anarchist dream of a decentralized, egalitarian society" (275). Ann's position emerges in *Green Mars* after we understand the impossibility of Arkady's vision; thus her critical view of the landscape and political history is more valid. Nevertheless, both Ann and Arkady's visions are grounded in a Leopoldian awareness of the landscape as a key influence on human culture. Both are thus pedagogical, in a Leopoldian sense.

WORKS CITED

Abbott, Carl. "Falling into History: The Imagined Wests of Kim Stanley Robinson in the 'Three Californias' and Mars Trilogy." *Western Historical Quarterly* 34.1 (2003): 49 pars. 16 Sep. 2003 <http://www.historycooperative.org/journals/whq/34.1/abbott.html>

Callicott, J. Baird. *In Defense of the Land Ethic: Essays in Environmental Philosophy*. Albany: State University of New York Press, 1989.

Dynes, William. "Multiple Perspectives in Kim Stanley Robinson's Mars Series." *Extrapolation* 42.2 (Summer 2001): 150–64.

Foote, Bud. "Notes on Kim Stanley Robinson's *Red Mars*." *Science-Fiction Studies* 21.1 (March 1994): 61–66.

Franko, Carol. "The Density of Utopian Destiny in Robinson's *Red Mars*." *Extrapolation* 38.1 (Spring 1997): 57–65.

Leopold, Aldo. *A Sand County Almanac, with Essays on Conservation from Round River*. 1949. New York: Ballantine, 1966.

Markley, Robert. "Falling into Theory: Simulation, Terraformation, and Eco-Economics in Kim Stanley Robinson's Martian Trilogy." *Modern Fiction Studies* 43.3 (Fall 1997): 773–99.

McClintock, James I. *Nature's Kindred Spirits: Aldo Leopold, Joseph Wood Crutch, Edward Abbey, Annie Dillard, and Gary Snyder*. Madison: University of Wisconsin Press, 1994.

Moylan, Tom. *Scraps of the Untainted Sky: Science Fiction, Utopia, Dystopia*. Boulder: Westview, 2000.

Robinson, Kim Stanley. *Antarctica*. New York: Bantam, 1998.

_____. *Blue Mars*. New York: Bantam, 1996.

_____. *Green Mars*. New York: Bantam, 1994.

_____. Interview. "A Conversation with Kim Stanley Robinson." By Bud Foote. *Science-Fiction Studies* 21.1 (March 1994): 51–60.
_____. *The Martians*. New York: Bantam, 1999.
_____. *Red Mars*. New York: Bantam, 1993.
Yanarella, Ernest J. *The Cross, the Plow, and the Skyline: Contemporary Science Fiction and the Ecological Imagination*. Parkland: Brown Walker, 2001.

17

Dead Penguins in Immigrant Pilchard Scandal: Telling Stories About "the Environment" in *Antarctica*

Sherryl Vint and *Mark Bould*

Kim Stanley Robinson is frequently spoken of as both a Marxist and an environmentalist writer, as if the relationship between red and green politics was straightforward and unproblematic. However, these politics, neither of which is monolithic, often also build from radically different premises, typically resulting in "mutual suspicion, hostility or, at best, indifference" (Benton 1). For example: deep ecologists focus on overall ecosystem health and stability and accept that their views often entail the deaths of many individuals, including humans, in order to serve the health of the ecosystem, while Marxist thought, which rejects capital's reduction of human being to labor-power, is not particularly amenable to reducing humans to their role within the ecosystem; animal rights advocates often conflict with deep ecologists over the wellbeing of every individual animal (rather than prioritizing the ecosystem) and with Marxists over the notion of "rights" (derived from a liberal humanist conception of the rights of the citizen, which Marx correctly criticized as being founded on a concept of self as property and as separating civic and political life from the rest of social and material being). Robinson's fiction, therefore, walks a very difficult line, trying to reconcile divergent red and green politics which should be mutually supportive, especially in the ongoing crisis of environmental destruction and mass extinction caused by capitalist social relations. As such, it should not only be lauded but also recognized as part of the recent re-examination of Marx's conceptualization and treatment of nature and of attempts to develop a "green" Marxism (see Benton, Burkett, and Foster).

In this essay, however, we want to draw attention to one of the key aporia in attempts to bring together environmentalist and Marxist perspectives: the loss of focus on non-human life as an end in itself rather than as a means to human ends. This is not unique to Robinson and in drawing attention to it in his work our aim is to more broadly point to the status of non-human nature as one of the sites of social justice that requires further thought in Marxist analyses. The current historical conjuncture is not merely one of ecological problems (extinctions, habitat destruction, global warming), but also one in which we are finding increasing evidence of animal's cognitive and emotional abilities, their own social lives, and their increasing exploitation as they are further incorporated into capital's production methods in ways which deny or ignore such capacities (for example, pharming and xenotransplantation). A materialist analysis requires that we include non-human nature in our demands for social justice, and we fear that even work as environmentally sensitive as Robinson's is not sufficiently attentive to such matters.

From the Orange County trilogy's (1984–1990) vision of alternative futures and the Mars trilogy's (1993–1995) preoccupation with the ecological and ethical aspects of terraforming, to the Science in the Capital trilogy's (2004–2007) dramatization of global warming, Robinson articulates the urgent need for a new relationship with the natural world that acknowledges our dependency upon and place in it, and concomitantly to develop new human social relations within it. In this, his work is similar to that of environmental philosopher Val Plumwood, who calls for us to develop "an environmental culture that values and fully acknowledges the non-human sphere and our dependency on it, and is able to make good decisions about how we live and impact on the non-human world" (3). The most notable difference between these two thinkers is Plumwood's greater consciousness of the environment not simply as a material backdrop for human lives but as a complex system of non-human subjects with which we share the physical space of the world. In contrast, Robinson's theorizations of environmental relationships typically remain human-centered, concentrating on the damage we do ourselves and our descendents by destroying the biosystem in which we live.

This tendency is perhaps most evident in his remarkable ability as a landscape writer. While unrivalled as such within sf (and most other contemporary writing), he generally remains a writer of landscapes, rather than environments.[1] This is not only an inherently anthropocentric perspective but also one which reproduces the political problems of mastery and possession upon which depend both the capitalism he critiques and the scientific project he champions. As Raymond Williams's analysis of the modern English pastoral tradition demonstrates, the notion of a landscape is intimately connected to ownership of and exclusions from the land, and with the reconstruction of the land for the benefit of a minority class. The divisions of the social and economic order are materialized in both park lands created for aesthetic purposes and the "mathematical grids of the enclosure awards," with the "natural curves and scatterings of park scenery" hiding the fact that they are "related parts of the same process": "in the one case the land is being organised for production, where the tenants and labourers will work, while in the other case it is being organised for consumption — the view, the ordered proprietary repose, the prospect" (Williams 124). Williams later notes that the history of these spatial and material reconstructions performed by capital extends beyond national boundaries, and, in fact, "What was happening in the 'city,' the 'metropolitan' economy, determined and was determined by what was made to happen in the 'country'; first the local hinterlands and then the vast regions beyond it, in other people's lands..... Thus one of the last models of 'city and country' is the system we now know as imperialism" (279).

As will become clear below, Robinson's utopian experiments, Martian and Antarctic, follow precisely this logic, producing fantasies of human community with minimal negative environmental impact that are nonetheless readily recuperable to the discourse of global capital. The settings of both the Mars trilogy and *Antarctica* enable Robinson to emphasize his conviction that our harmful environmental practices are deeply intertwined with the harmful social relations of the capitalist mode of production. This leads him to envision the possibilities for human happiness and fulfillment attendant on the radical social transformations which will follow a changed relationship to nature. However, by selecting such (apparently) empty locations, Robinson's (thought-)experiments in living omit the major groups of non-human actants — plants and animals — which constitute the environment. Like the peasant or worker hidden from sight, they have been cleared from our view so that, like the aristocrat or the new bourgeois landowner, we can savor, untroubled, Robinson's Arcadian prospects. Therefore, this essay will explore Robinson's concept of environmental and social transformation, focusing particularly on the tensions between his critique of capitalist social relations (as the underlying cause of environmental destruction) and its failure to account for non-human subjects and our social relations with them. After a brief examination of *Icehenge* (1984), this paper will focus on *Antarctica* (1997), a novel which most clearly reveals these tensions through its setting on a continent seemingly devoid of life.

Part of the difficulty in imagining a new social relationship with the environment is our ignorance of it. For example, we often think of Antarctica as a climate too harsh to support life because of the absence of many of the species we, from warmer climes, recognize as "nature." It is "a continent without a tree, and with only two species of flowering plants, [...] the only land mass without wasps, beetles, butterflies, worms, or spiders," yet it is nonetheless home to "the world's largest coherent ecosystem" in its Southern Ocean, incorporating species from "phytoplankton [...] up through shrimp-like krill to fish, birds, squid, seals, and whales" (Kimball 1). *Icehenge*, which carefully inter-relates three stories set between 2248 and 2610, directly addresses problems of epistemology and hermeneutics. In the first story, Emma Weil recounts the jerry-rigging and launch of a starship by the banned Mars Starship Association in defiance of the tyrannical and bureaucratic Committee, while on Mars the Committee violently suppresses a full-blown revolution. The second story follows archaeologist Hjalmar Nederland's discovery, in 2547, of Emma's diary, which he uses, along with other artifacts, to "prove" that the Martian revolution, now denied by official Committee accounts, actually happened. From evidence in Emma's diary, Nederland further posits that the Icehenge monument, recently discovered on Pluto, was a marker left behind by the *Lermontov* crew, and is thus further evidence of the reality and extent of the revolution. In the third story, Edmond Doya "proves" that Icehenge was built, for unclear reasons, by reclusive shipping magnate Caroline Holmes, when a fresh expedition to Pluto uncovers new and apparently incontrovertible evidence. However, before they can even begin their journey home, his conclusions are challenged by two fresh hypotheses: that Icehenge was built by the crew of the original Pluto expedition, who then claimed to discover it; and, based on a misunderstanding of Doya's belief that Caroline Holmes wrote Emma Weil's journal, that Weil survived the Committee's mass murder of revolutionaries, and built a new life for herself under the assumed identity of Holmes. The novel ends in this state of indeterminacy, with no "truth" uncovered.

Robinson arranges these multiple interpretations and struggles over meaning to demonstrate the ways in which language and narrative are always-already shaped by existing structures of power and, however much they are deployed in the service of resistance to that power, they are nonetheless always-already susceptible to its recuperation. The novel nevertheless maintains that it does matter which stories are told, and by whom and for what purposes, suggesting that the "truth" of a narrative might be better judged according to the world it creates than by some appeal to an ontological "real" beyond representation. Nederland presents his interpretation of Icehenge as, ultimately, a means of ensuring the memory and praxis of resistance: "The Mars Starship Association had resisted, Emma Weil had resisted, I had resisted, and I would keep resisting; and perhaps one day we would make Mars free" (165). While his passion reveals the complex connections between representation and action, Doya, who regards himself as "not a political person" (234), tries to remove the interpretation of Icehenge from a complex social reality and relocate it in the realm of "pure" science, arguing that "the admissions that the Martian government made about their conduct in the civil war" (234) cannot be recanted even if he proves the monument a hoax. Nederland refuses to accept Doya's asocial and apolitical notion of science as something which can be conducted in a realm purified of human struggle. Insisting that it does matter whether Emma's diary is true or not, Nederland is clear about the political consequences of Doya's theory being accepted.

Antarctica returns to *Icehenge*'s exploration of the connections between research and storytelling, sometimes representing life on the eponymous continent as a utopian, scientific enclave, separated and purified from the messy world of politics, and suggesting that in such a setting we would be able to live a more harmonious life with nature and one another. This romanticized Antarctica is a consequence of its unique, real-world geopolitical situation. Overlapping parts of the continent are claimed by seven nations, but no claim has been recognized by any other nation and thus, under current international law, the territory remains in limbo, occupied by humans but not owned by any of them. Since 1959, Antarctic scientists have operated under a treaty which allows research, forbids militarized occupation, and encourages free sharing of data. As Robinson appreciates, it is a "unique laboratory for international relations" (Kimball 2), as well as "a vast reference zone for measuring contaminants that increasingly pollute Earth" (Speth vii), and for him it provides an ideal site to explore new, more ecologically-sound and less socially-alienating ways of living.

The novel frequently brings together these concerns through its interrogation of storytelling and the search for scientific "truth." For example, characters on an adventure tourism trip following in Amundsen's footsteps begin to compare his expedition to the South Pole with Scott's. Challenging their harsh critique of Scott, one group member, Elspeth, points out that they are all drawing on "the Roland Huntford biography of Scott and Amundsen" (251) which "should really have been called *Scott Was an Idiot*. It's a five-hundred-page list of stupidities" (252). She argues that the Huntford account is not what really happened but a biased interpretation, implying that one can extract the truth of the expeditions from weighing the different accounts' circulations in a complex web of human intentions and meanings which have as much to do with the contexts of their authors and readers as with the events themselves. When she complains that "Huntford made everything black and white, but that's not the way it was" (252), Ta Shu (a Chinese Feng Shui master and the novel's problematically Orientalist spiritual core) explains, "All stories are still alive.... All stories have colors in them.... This present moment — this is clear.... The past — all stories. Nothing but stories. All colored. So we choose our colors. We choose what colors we see" (256). Through this image, Robinson suggests that it is impossible to view the material realm from a perspective-less, disinterested position (what Donna Haraway calls "the god trick"). Like Haraway, Robinson insists that to recognize the relativism, partiality, and interestedness of all perspectives is not to abandon truth but instead to call for "accountability and responsibility for translations and solidarities" (Haraway 196). Acknowledging that we choose the colors we see, that our choices are never entirely conscious, and that they are structured and determined by our multiple contexts, makes for a better account of the world, and a better science — not the myth of science as that which "escapes human agency and responsibility in a realm above the fray" (196) but an engagement with the world that acknowledges "*both* the concrete, 'real' aspect and the aspects of semiosis and production in what we call scientific knowledge" (195).

In *Antarctica*, Robinson focuses on the exchange of material and semiotic elements in human relationships to the environment, and on our relationship to the "scientific" practice of economics (one of the major forces shaping our interactions with the environment). As Plumwood argues, one of the reasons that our economic activity does so much damage to the environment is that we have incomplete stories which excise certain elements (typically labeled "externalities" in cost-benefit calculations; and although she does not explicitly use the language of commodity fetishism, it is evident that these excised elements include the workers whose labor is obscured by the commodity form and its masking of the social relations of production). Plumwood's concern also includes the complex social relations of the ecosystem of which humans are a part. Thus, we need to understand the ways in which our commodities are part of a complex system of production which includes the exploited labor of humans, but which also includes the erasure of habitats for non-humans, the pollution of the air and the water table, and most importantly the destruction of the previously existing ecosystem relations, which were balanced and able to sustain life for many humans and non-humans. As Plumwood argues, "We can find out what is available in the market to meet our desires and at what price, but we cannot without great difficulty trace where it came from or what its real costs are, in terms of the earth" (16). Just as the Huntford biography prompts us to view Scott as an irresponsible fool, so the market encourages us to think of commodities as dis-embedded goods whose origin is of no concern.

Plumwood illustrates the consequences of incomplete stories through the example of a penguin whose body she found washed up on an Australian shore. It was one of a large number of penguins who died because the native pilchards which formed their staple diet were killed by a disease spread by other pilchards which were imported as feed for salmon farms. The fish farms saw only the marginally lower cost of the imported pilchard; the penguins' deaths *appear* unrelated and thus consumers of the salmon were unaware of its tainted history. Robinson makes a similar point through the story of an unnamed character who becomes a radical ecoteur when his defense of forest lands from logging failed because of an agreement made elsewhere: an Arctic slope is made "a national park, with a special provision for oil extraction in case of national emergency; and to balance this 'concession to wilderness,' ninety percent of the hundred million acres were to be opened up to new 'environmental logging'" (51). Environmental groups supported the national park, unaware of the less-incomplete story in which its creation was part of a deal causing a net increase in environmental destruction. While all stories are colored — more complex than black-or-white — Robinson's solution is to invoke a spectrum of many colors and truths. We might choose which colors to see, but in doing so we have an obligation to more complete stories, to reconnecting the parts of our existence compartmentalized by capitalist social relations, and to accepting the multiple consequences of the colors we choose.

Robinson tries to counter the tendency in many of our knowledge-practices toward abstraction (and thus less complete stories). Plumwood considers that the problem of abstraction is fundamental to the rationalist culture which grounds both capitalism and scientific disciplines, arguing that "heavily implicated in both the logic of the global market and the death of the penguins are distorted forms of human rationality whose simple, abstract rules of equivalence and replaceability do not fit the real, infinitely complex world of flesh and blood, root and web on which they are so ruthlessly imposed" (14). Robinson's evocation of Antarctica suggests a similar need to focus on the material. When tour guide Val leads her group to an isolated spot to which Edward Wilson, whose journey they are retracing, had visited in order to study penguins, the group pay no attention to the birds around them. They are interested in the site only as one which Wilson visited, and thus do not experience it for itself. Val grows increasingly weary of clients visiting Antarctica merely to follow in the footsteps of famous expeditions, preferring the continent about which they have read to the rich material reality of the place itself; and she comes to recognize the futility of their desires:

And really, no matter how closely they tried to reproduce the experience — some expeditions had tried wearing the same clothing and using the same gear, with spectacularly unhappy results — it could not truly be done. Because Amundsen and his group had approached a section of the Transantarctics that no one had ever seen before. It was an unknown mountain range that they had to cross somehow, with food supplies so tight that they had not had the luxury of scouting out alternative routes to find the easiest way to the polar cap, which they only knew was there because of Shackleton's trek three years before [232].

The recreation of the original experience is impossible not only because the contextual elements related to the human situation have changed, but also because Antarctica itself has changed. It is not a static and empty space awaiting human "discovery" and exploration, but a complex ecological system subject to changes caused by climate, erosion, and animal behavior; and even if no humans were to venture there, it would still be changed by the human activities elsewhere in the world, not least pollution and global warming. Robinson's critique of the abstraction favored by adventure tourists correctly points out that their attitude strips the experience of context and the concrete materiality which shapes the meaning of both the original and reconstructed journey, but generally falls short of acknowledging that humans are not the only actants who have changed between the original encounter and its reconstructions.

The adventure tourists, caring more for historical recreation than for the experience of actually-existing Antarctica, demonstrate "the economic form of rationalism [that] privileges the abstract over the contextual and experiential, imposes the universal formula on the local, and everywhere exhibits the typical rationalist desire for the permanence and purity of abstraction and mathematisation" (Plumwood 23). This narrow rationalism turns the landscape into grids on a map; the tourists fail to see beauty around them and instead of "climbing in the Asgaards, or wherever, somewhere really spectacular" (152) merely tick off completed stages of earlier journeys. *Antarctica* is repeatedly critical of "[f]ools [...] in love with ideas rather than real places" (152), urging us to recognize that "if the reality of Earth is perceived merely as material to be passed through, then it is not really there for you, and so the imagination becomes impoverished.... Unless you inhabit a place — not stay in one spot, but inhabit a place, as the Paleolithic people inhabited their places, with every bush known and every rock named — then it becomes too decentered and metaphysical; you live in the imagination of an idea" (319–320). Like the simultaneously material and semiotic science advocated by Haraway, Robinson's model for a new relationship with the environment acknowledges the importance of the abstract, the imagination, but insists that we must also be attentive to the materiality of place.

But this vision has its color, and its blind spots, too. Ta Shu calls for us to know a place, yet focuses on the environment as landscape — a passive and empty space without agency — and does not acknowledge the non-human creatures with whom we share the world. Further, while the notion of landscape is inherently proprietorial, rearranging the world from the viewer's perspective, his model of knowing also involves the sort of mastery associated with both Christian concepts of stewardship and enlightenment science: knowing as naming. He advocates a new relationship with the environment that combines knowing with loving: "we must learn this Earth as closely and completely as our Paleolithic ancestors knew it on the savannah; we must know it in the mode they knew it, as scientist and lover wrapped together in one. The loverknower. We must draw the Paleolithic and the postmodern together in a single design" (592). In this call for a science that is not based on distanced, objective mastery and control, but which instead allows for an affective, caring relationship between knower and world there emerges a critique of the destructiveness of abstract rationality consistent with Plumwood's argument. However, Robinson's story of science is colored in such a way as to omit the degree to which science arose as a discourse of distancing oneself from a simultaneously reified nature. *Antarctica* thus treats the continent as a laboratory for experimenting with new social relations in science as well as politics, basing its image of a transformed world on the influence of science practiced outside of capitalist social relations.

Robert Markley notes a similar pattern in Robinson's representation of technology in the *Mars* series, where it is "a crucial means to empowerment by allowing humankind to control nature and improve the quality of life" through embracing a less distanced, more "natural" relationship with the environment, but at the same time a "massive investments of labor, capital, and resources" (774) is necessary to enable and sustain this neo–Paleolithic lifestyle. Likewise, in *Antarctica*, humans must learn new ways of living because the inhospitable continent does not allow humans to take the physical world for granted. So too in *Fifty Degrees Below* (2005), protagonist Frank, embracing the neo–Paleolithic in a rapidly-freezing Washington, observes the wastefulness of a built environment designed to separate people from the world, noting that most people "wore clothing suited to 'room temperature' all the year round, thus sweltering in the summer and shivering in the winter anytime they stepped out of their rooms. [...] They used their buildings as clothing, in effect, and heated or cooled these spaces to imitate what clothing did, no mater how crazy this was in energy terms" (230–231). In contrast, *Antarctica*'s feral humans use clothing "so advanced that in most ways it functions as your house" (512), arguing that "When your clothes are your house, and your tent is your farm, then you can go where you please" (518–19) and that if they "can do it [t]here [...] then everywhere else it can only be easier" (518). Thus, while advanced technology enables humans to live in a way that is less wasteful of energy and less destructive to the environment, it is also the only means by which the neo–Paleolithic lifestyle to which Robinson's fiction repeatedly returns is possible. The Antarctic experiments in new ecological and social relationships depend entirely upon technologies produced by global capitalism, a system which itself depends upon the deformation and devastation of ecologies and social relations. This contradiction is identical to the one which the environmentalists groups supporting the Arctic national park — and thus enabling destructive logging of timber reserves elsewhere — occupied. Looked at in isolation, the Antarctic feral enclave, like these environmental groups, have made "good" choices which benefit the environment, but in the more complete context of the consolidated world market, matters are not so clear-cut. Robinson is not unaware of this problem, as the conflict between the "fundies" and the "prags" demonstrates: the former "want to live down here with no help from the north, using Eskimo and Sami methods to make our food and clothing and shelter" while the prags are "willing to try out all the latest things from the north, to see if they can be useful down here" (486). However, this does not get to the core of the contradiction. While one prag argues that there is "no reason for an artificial exercise" (518) like living on the land in traditional ways, positioning the fundies as akin to the adventure tourist who do not see Antarctica because they are trying to recreate an earlier journey, the romantic notion of bringing together "the Paleolithic and the postmodern" (592) is abstract in a different way. It is structured by a willingness to acknowledge and accept only some of the implications of dependence upon the north and the capitalist mode of production for which it stands. While this technological and economic dependence allows even an Antarctic neo–Paleolithic to develop in ways far more comfortable than a genuine temperate zone Paleolithic, it is only at the cost of capital's ongoing exploitations, depredations and impoverishments in the world to the north — costs which involve environmental destruction, including, through global warming, that of Antarctica itself. The prags' "ecologically-sound" lifestyle demands a contradictory imbrication into a perpetuated global capitalism which excludes questions of where an item "came from or what its real costs are, in terms of the earth" (Plumwood 16).

Plumwood's critique of the rationalized culture of neo-classical economics and enlightenment science — she argues that "such systems conspire to conceal from us our dependency on nature, to overestimate our autonomy and manipulative ability, to claim invincibility so we believe we know no limits, and so devise Promethean projects like growing indefinitely on earth, taming space and terraforming Mars. According to its story, nature has no agency or autonomy of its own and imposes no real limits on us" (35) — is thus applicable to Robinson's fiction, too. In trying to work through the challenge of a radically transformed relationship to the environment, whether on Mars or in Antarctica, Robinson often succumbs to these technophilic atavisms lurking deep in the genome of American sf.

Carlos, the character most closely associated with a defense of science, argues that the needs of an impoverished human population demand priority over wilderness preservation: "there are ten billion people on this Earth and half of them are starving, and it is not some rich well-fed aristocrat son-of-a-bitch hunter-gatherer Disneyland wilderness advocate that is going to feed those people or their children! We have to provide them with food and the energy to make food and shelter and clothing and schools and hospitals and you *cannot do it* with your deep-ecology wilderness dream" (566). As he repeatedly argues, the state of the environment is interwoven with the consequences of the North's colonial exploitation of the South, which continues in many forms, including the situation in which the privileged North can wring its hand over "nature" while bracketing-off the abject impoverishment their privilege causes in the South. Yet his solution is just more techno-optimism: the hi-tech, environmentally-sound extraction of methane hydrates — so as to provide for the South's energy needs while also using up greenhouse gases which would accelerate global warming if released into the atmosphere through the melting of the Antarctic ice in which they are found — rather than any kind of radical social transformation. In Plumwood's scathing dismissal of such "solutions," "Science will save us, provided we do not lose our nerve or our faith in techno-reason and our will to continue along our current path, however precarious it may seem" (6).

Robinson's techno-optimism — of a slightly different color than the technophilic striving beyond limits Plumwood critiques — often suggests that science is based on values that will allow us not merely to resolve problems of scarcity through technological solutions, but also, if embraced, to transform social relations. According to Carlos, science is "the great outsider, the system that capitalism cannot conquer" (349), "a utopian project [that] tries to make a utopia within itself, in the rules of scientific conduct and organization, and [...] tries to influence the world at large in a utopian direction" (349–350). Describing a book-within-the book, *Los Elementos Eticos, Políticos, y Utópicos Incorporados en la Estructura de la Ciencia Moderna*, he sees the utopian Antarctic scientific enclave as the model for a revolutionary transformation of the social world based on the insights of modern science:

> what [the book] demonstrates very clearly is that what we think of as neutral objective science is actually a utopian politics and worldview already. There is a big historical section describing the rise of science, showing that science is self-organizing and self-actualizing, and always trying to get better, to be more scientific, as one of its rules. And there is a big middle section showing how various features of normal scientific practice, the methodology and so on, are in fact ethical positions. Things like reproducibility, or Occam's razor, or peer review — almost everything in science that makes it specifically scientific, the authors show, is utopian. And the final section tells what the ramifications of this fact are, how scientists should behave now, once they realize this truth [350].

That Carlos bases his argument in part on the belief that "Most scientists have analyzed life scientifically, and realized that sufficiency is all that you really need, and that pursuing money beyond the point of sufficiency only degrades life" (347) demonstrates his enthusiastic naïveté. Imagining science as a utopian project is another alluring abstraction; it does not account for the material realities of scientific practice. As X protests, scientists do not behave in the way Carlos wishes: although scientists could be guiding policy in less socially- and environmentally-damaging ways, "they're not even trying! [...] They've got their island utopia [...] and so they just come down here or wherever else and hang out in the field or the lab and do their thing, and they're not doing anything to save the world [...]. They're just part of the capitalist machinery" (349).

Antarctica explores this contradiction between the utopian image of science and science as it is actually practiced, particularly in relation to Robinson's concern with story-telling and the search for more truthful stories. One of the scientific controversies regarding Antarctica concerns the age of certain ice sheets. Stabilist theory insists that the eastern ice cap is an old and stable feature, dating from 40–50 million years ago when the continent detached from South America. Dynamicist theory, arguing from the dating of diatoms in sandstone, contends that it is only three million years old and subject to the same changes which occurred to the western ice sheet. This interpretative struggle, like the struggle over the meaning of Icehenge, requires each group to tell different stories, prioritizing, minimizing or discounting different aspects of the evidence. The stabilists produce alternative narratives about key dynamicist pieces of evidence: "They say the beech forests are older than fourteen million years, perhaps even Cretaceous. They say the diatoms blew in from elsewhere. They ignore the beetles entirely" (174). Furthermore, like Nederland and Doya's conflict over the meaning of Icehenge, the stakes in the debate are not "merely" scientific but are inextricably connected to political and other struggles that are part of the social fabric in which science is practiced. Thus, the stabilists need to defend their view not merely because they think their story is "better science" but because "Whole careers have been given over to [their] position. Grad students are getting Ph.D.s, assistant professors are getting tenure, all on the strength of papers advocating the stabilist position. They can't just admit they were wrong all along" (173–174). The same is, of course, true of the dynamicists.

This understanding of science as being embedded in human social relations, rather than purified and ideally rational, is consistent with Bruno Latour's description of "science in action." The practice of science and the succession of scientific paradigms, he argues, is not merely a matter of which story offers the "better" explanation of the facts observed from nature, but rather are also explained by the networks of colleagues, funding, institutions, and beliefs that combine to promote certain kinds of conclusions over others. Crucially, Latour insists that non-humans (including machines, as well as plants and animals) are among the collaborators who contribute to the creation of scientific "facts." Knowledge, he concludes, is the result of exchanges among the material elements of the world (including human actants) and the semiotic concepts that structure beliefs and behavior. Combining the traditional definition of the fact (that which is "objectively" true) with the fetish (the blank screen upon which we project our desires but in which we can believe only so long as we refuse to recognize that it is fabricated), Latour coins the term "factish." The factish acknowledges that scientific facts have an element of "fabrication in the laboratory" (*Pandora* 273) but at the same takes seriously "the role of actors in all types of activities" (*Pandora* 306), including the "objective" properties of the world under investigation. Latour's understanding of science thus requires us to accept that we cannot purify the semiotic from the material — that the very facts themselves are always permeated by the desires and constructions of multiple agents — but that this does not make them any less "real." Furthermore, he refutes the separation of science from the social world, seeing the defense of "papers, careers, livings" (*Antarctica* 346) as a part of "normal" scientific practice. Robinson, in contrast, renders such activities as a consequence of the practice of science under capitalism, suggesting that science might be otherwise and thus occludes, in pursuit of an abstract ideal, the history of science as institution and methodology.[2]

Carlos's argument that the normal practice of science is in fact a utopian politics tries to purify science and separate it from human contingency. A "fairly large number of scientists ... are not completely scientific," he admits, by which he means that they fail to apply scientific values to "life outside their own field of study" (346). Graham, a less idealistic scientist, learned the hard way that "the simple truth was that science was a matter of making alliances to help you to show what you wanted to show, and to make clear also that what you were showing was important" (309). When his graduate research challenged his supervisor's stabilist position, he found himself never receiving critique of his work, second authorship credits, or the other material supports necessary for publication and a scientific career. When he finally in frustration sent a paper to a journal without his supervisor's approval, "the paper [was] rejected, [the supervisor] informed [...], and Graham basically dismissed from the program, as he was not invited to return to Antarctica" (308). Thus he discovers that "Science was not a matter of automatons seeking Truths, but of people struggling to black-box some facts" (310), and that a scientific career must be spent building "the walls that would box this part of the story up for good, building it brick by brick over years and generations. Because the stones did not speak, not really. They had to be translated" (311). This grasp of science as a highly restricted type of story-telling with rules governing the admission and position of certain "facts" is similar to Latour's "science in action." The world must be "translated" into data that has meaning within a theoretical paradigm, and this translation changes the material object of analysis in that it also becomes part of a semiotic system. Latour uses the example of soil samples — taken from the physical world, translated into a system of rows and grids in a pedocomparator (a suitcase designed for holding soil samples according to a spatial system related to their color, soil density, etc.), and finally translated from the pedocomparator into tables and graphs of data — to argue that the practice of science constantly moves from the concrete to the abstract. The soil samples enter into science through this semiotic reference system that is not "simply the act of pointing or a way of keeping, on the outside, some material guarantee for the truth of a statement; rather it is our way of keeping something *constant* through a series of transformations. Knowledge does not reflect a real external world that it resembles via mimesis, but rather a real interior world, the coherence and continuity of which it helps to ensure" (*Pandora* 58).

The crucial difference between Latour's and Robinson's understandings of the relationship between abstraction and materiality in science has to do with the point at which abstraction and story-telling enter into science. Robinson suggests that the translation of the stones into walls that buttress stabilist or dynamicist positions happen because external concerns with careers and income begin to push scientists toward accepting particular readings as unquestionable black boxes, while Latour recognizes the inevitable intersection of materiality and semiotics in the social relation with nature that we call science. "Knowledge," he argues, "does not reside in the face-to-face confrontation of a mind with an object, any more than reference designates a thing by means of a sentence verified by that thing. [...] The operators are linked in a series that *passes across* the difference between things and words" (69).

Robinson's utopian science desires purification from career-advancement and other "perversions" caused by capitalist social relations, as in the scientist, Harry, whose approach to research is very like Ta Shu's "lovingknowing" relationship to the land. As Harry and Graham search for evidence of vegetation that would support the dynamicist view, Graham thinks of their work as "like a treasure hunt [...] like prospecting for gold. A find like this would result in a paper that would help make a case that would help make a career that would help pay the bills" (314), while Harry imagines the data as evidence of the materiality of the place in which they stand, exclaiming "Can you imagine a beech forest growing down here, what it would have looked like! So *beautiful*. This is a beautiful fjord shoreline [...] like a holy place" (314). For him, the landscape is more than mere data, a place rather than a source of accolades. The contrast between Harry and Graham recalls Ta Shu's criticism of Amundsen's expedition. Although Amundsen was the first to reach the South Pole, his choice of Antarctica was based not on the place itself but on the fact that no one had been there before. His original goal of the North Pole was abandoned when he learned that both Cook and Perry had already succeeded in reaching it because "he had no desire to be the third man to the North Pole, nor even the second.... What he wanted then was not the North Pole, center of his life's work and placement. He wanted to be first. It is not at all the same thing. Not a hunger for place, but for position. A concentration on time rather than space; a desire to write one's name on history, rather than to occupy a place on Earth" (317). For Robinson, the better scientists — and better humans — are those who care for the place, and refuse to abstract or reduce it, and he suggests that science, uncorrupted by capital, can lead us to such a relationship to the Earth. However, his position is inconsistent with the rise of scientific methodology itself, which as Latour outlines emerged on the model of Clarendon's 1661 Treason Act, which required two witnesses for conviction. Boyle adapted this standard for the observer in the laboratory, valued not for his opinion or subjectivity but for his "objective" and "neutral" ability to witness. "Facts" were thus established by observation, not interpretation or argument, in a realm supposedly devoid of politics and semiotics, witnessed by a male observer of a certain class (someone whose word could be trusted because financial need would not lead him into misstatements). This class and gender bias, fundamental to the development of the experimental method is never acknowledged by Boyle, who takes Nature to speak truths that are true in all times and places. Scientific practice thus defines itself in a way that erases the translation activities of humans as the world is transformed into data in the isolated laboratory setting (*Never Been Modern* 20–27).

Thus, for science to serve the utopian role for which Carlos argues, its very methodology must be transformed because the abstract ideal of science-outside-of-interpretation is a fabrication. As Plumwood argues, "What we *need* for a viable future is an integrated democratic science that is dialogical, non-reductionist and self-reflective — a science that can bring itself and its ends under critical and democratic scrutiny. We need above all an *ethical* science: sado-dispassionate science has used the ideology of disengagement to wall itself off from ethics just as effectively as capitalism has done through the ideology of the private sphere" (53). Robinson lacks Plumwood greater awareness of the problems of science itself as a rationalist discipline whose methodology forbids affective engagement with the world under investigation, and her sense of the crucial need for an ethical stance toward the non-human world as part of a transformed science. Characters such as Ta Shu, Harry, Val and X come to love Antarctica and begin to live in the place itself rather than treat it as an abstraction or part of their own projects. Yet this vision of a loved continent is disturbingly devoid of non-human life. It is as if Robinson advocates caring for the environment for the same reason Kant suggested we should be kind to animals: not for the sake of the non-human world, but because of the damage an instrumental attitude does to humans.

As a result of the urgency with which Robinson views our need to transform capitalist social relations, he focuses on the environment to the extent that it serves human beings.[3] Transformed relationships of employment are as much a part of *Antarctica*'s utopian vision as a more loving relationship to the environment. The conclusion imagines McMurdo Station run not by employees of a corporation based elsewhere but as part of a worker-owned collective, better able to address ecological concerns "because of increased worker tenure, involvement, satisfaction, awareness, esprit de corps, and so on" (613). The novel suggests that "Social justice is a *necessary part* of any working environmental program" (604) and thus what is best for the Antarctic environment is better social relations among the humans who live and work there. *Antarctica* tries to find a way past the polarized opposition between deep ecologists sabotaging human activity in Antarctica and those who believe that developing its resources is essential to alleviate human impoverishment elsewhere. As X points out, advocates on both side of this debate "had been attacking the practices of Götterdämmerung capitalism without seeming to notice the complementarity, and thinking instead that they were attacking each other" (572), suggesting that the division between the needs of humans and those of the environment is a false one used by capitalism to disrupt solidarity among its opponents. Plumwood similarly suggests that the hostility between animal rights groups and those concerned with "human" problems should be transcended in favor of a eco-social justice movement which would include coalitions with workers (on wages, conditions and use of prison labor in slaughter facilities), consumers (on health issues, antibiotics in milk, problems with BSE), local environmental movements (on water pollution and other ecological consequences of intensive farming), small farmers (on destruction of family farms in favor of agribusiness), and activists against neoliberalism (on issues of ethics, community empowerment and compassion in trade) (154). To see the needs of the environment and the needs of humans as opposed within a zero sum game of advantage only increases the power of global capitalism.[4]

The environmentally sound lifestyle combined with worker ownership proposed at the end of *Antarctica* is similar to Plumwood's vision, but limited by its failure to attend to non-humans' limits. This version of eco-social justice sees the environment as meeting humans' needs (food, shelter, aesthetic stimulation) but does not recognize it as having worth beyond its ability to meet these needs. Plumwood, in contrast, emphasizes that "Interspecies distributive justice principles should stress the need to share the earth with other species (including difficult and inconvenient ones like snakes, crocodiles, and bears — animals that are predators of humans or of animals under human protection) and provide adequate habitat for species life and reproduction" (117). By not including the needs of non-humans, Robinson creates a version of environmentalism easily co-opted into the discourse of "Natural Capitalism."[5]

Natural Capitalism's proponents contend that "the environment is a form of capital" (Prugh et al. xix) and that "*The primary value of natural capital is life support.* [...] At the local, regional and global levels, the functionality of ecosystems ultimately depends on their integrity, or the intactness of the complicated web of interconnections that link species with one another" (54). Extinctions and the strains put on non-human species by human economic activity threaten to disrupt the effective functioning of this life support web. Natural Capitalism's advocates argue that because neo-classical economics failed properly to include natural capital on the balance sheets, we have been operating under a system of faulty accounting which has not measured the true costs of some of our economic decisions, thus depleting or devaluing our stock of natural capital. Their solution is a better system of capitalism that understands and accounts for natural capital, and which would see a forest as something that "produces a flow of goods in the form of new trees *and a flow of services* in the form of oxygen, erosion control, wildlife habitat, etc." (51). Although Robinson's representation of the environment is clearly not as instrumentalist as this, his characters at times come close to reproducing natural capitalism's logic. For example, Mai-lis, the prag leader of the feral community, argues that "It is a matter of doing a true-cost true-benefit analysis, which is to say that all costs and benefits are included, including the so-called exterior costs, while the unpriceable aspects of the situation are also acknowledged and included" (570). She goes on to argue for "Environmentally safe technologies, green technologies, applied according to a humane green analysis of the costs and benefits of our various activities" (570) but it is not at all clear that her analysis will include the costs and benefits to non-human actants—and the prags already exclude the full range of costs associated with the production of the imported technologies upon which their lifestyle depends. This is far from Plumwood's vision of interspecies distributive justice, and uncomfortably close to natural capitalism's view of nature as life-support system.[6]

Robinson's reluctance to take account of the needs and perspectives of non-humans is indicative of a much graver limitation than mere anthropocentrism. To continue to see the environment only as resource for human ends is to perpetuate exploitative social relations homologous to those under which capital reduces workers to labor power for its own ends. Such an attitude toward the environment feeds into and supports the logic of equivalence underpinning capitalism's exploitative social relations, as Plumwood indicates: "nature represented in mechanistic terms as inferior, passive and mindless, whose only value and meaning is derived from the imposition of human ends, is simply replaceable by anything else which can serve those ends equally well—it can be reduced and regimented, the more so as those ends are defined in monological and minimally interactive terms. As you wipe out one species of fish, it can be replaced with another, in theory without limit" (49). This is obviously inconsistent with *Antarctica*'s arguments about lovingknowing an environment in its particularity and specificity, but the degree to which the novel's environmentalism remains an abstract idea of "love of place" does support this sort of logic of substitution. Just as capitalism seamlessly substitutes human and machine labor without taking into account their very different contingent materialities, so Robinson's representation of the environment subsumes differences and particularities under the notion of "landscape" by failing to represent any agency or subjectivity for the non-human others who also constitute the environment. The environment is more than a landscape organized around the proprietorial human subject. And it is more than a place. It is a community of non-human and human actants, of complexly interrelated intersubjects.

Plumwood points out that "The term 'natural' in 'natural capitalism' is meant to indicate both the movement of capitalism to less wasteful technology and its moving in that direction 'naturally,' without political effort, which is carefully discounted by proponents of Natural Capitalism" (6). Robinson is clearly concerned with political action and his model of utopian science is premised on the ideal that the rational and sufficient lifestyle embraced by scientific principles can inspire global social and political transformation. The eight principles for the future occupation of Antarctica postulated towards the end of the novel are an anthropocentric plan for improving preservation of the environment *and* a political framework for developing a new way to live with nature. They include: renewal of the Antarctic Treaty, which promotes friendly scientific cooperation among nation without recognizing territorial claims;

the designation of Antarctica as a "world site of special scientific interest" (624); debt-for-nature exchange agreements with energy-poor South nations which would enable them to improve their infrastructure while holding-off on Antarctic fuel-extraction as green technologies are developed; protection of indigenous animals that should not be harvested as food beyond levels consistent with the continent's "human carrying capacity" (626); strict rules limiting pollution caused by human habitation; a system of "social structures" (628) that will ensure "cooperative, nonexploitative economic models" because zero-impact lifestyles are "not merely a matter of the technologies employed" (628); and the renunciation of "violence against humanity or its works" (628). Building a new society from these principles, one "intent on cooperation in a communal enterprise" (600), is necessary to arrest, and hopefully reverse, the environmental damage that destructive human practices have already done.

These principles represent the complex interconnections among economic structures, human social relations, and the environmental impacts of human activity that are the core of Robinson's new social relationship with the environment. The eighth principle declares that "What is true in Antarctica is true everywhere else" (628). While the novel presents a possible new social relation with nature as something (relatively) sealed away from the world in an Antarctic enclave, it is always conscious of this utopian venture as an experiment in living intended to prove the possibility of generalizing and globalizing its revolutionary results. The utopianism of science thus does not require a PhD or similar training because "to the extent that we know well, and love deeply, we are all true scientists" (600). The novel ends on a very optimistic note, with X embracing a new and more active lifestyle in Antarctica, truly loving and knowing the place. He has moved from the novel's opening lines that "First you fall in love with Antarctic, and then it breaks your heart" (1) to a recognition that "First you fall in love. Then anything could happen" (651).

As his example suggests, the novel's ideal seems to be that we will fall in love with the Earth and consequently we will learn to cooperate and save it as part of the process of repairing our competitive and alienating social relations. However, the environment with which we are to fall in love remains, in *Antarctica*, suspiciously abstract and empty, depicted predominantly as backdrop for human activities (if one about which we should take more care than is typical of western industrialized culture). Plumwood's vision of a natural world with whom we share subjectivity gets us closer to the radically new social relations necessary to move beyond structures of exploitation — with non-humans as well as among humans. As long as we see humans as the only social actors of consequence, our environmental politics are too easily co-opted back into the logic of capitalism — as the correspondence between some of Robinson's ideas and the rhetoric of Natural Capitalism reveals. Plumwood argues that the radical separation of nature from culture produces a "Hyperbolised autonomy and the backgrounding of the earth" which creates "an illusory sense of detachability from the earth, and presents as 'rational' a project where every venture outwards further damages the earth we depend on. When we have learnt the true nature of our being as earth-dependent and have learnt both to cherish the earth and to go beyond it without damage, it may be time for us to try to leave for the stars — but not before" (240). To the extent that Robinson's Antarctic enclave of environmentally-sound feral humans limit the stories they tell about the environment to their immediate lifestyle in Antarctica, and fail to account for the damage caused by the technologies manufactured in the north upon which they depend, they operate according to a logic that is similar in kind — if different in degree — to the position Plumwood critiques. Moreover, they idealize an anthropocentric vision of an ecologically-sound lifestyle where other species must be protected only to the extent that their continued presence is necessary to support human life in Antarctica. Perhaps we might see in the centripetal trajectory of Robinson's work from the *Mars* series, through *Antarctica*, to the Science in the Capital trilogy some inkling of this need to stay on the earth and fix the damage we have done rather than strive for the stars through terraforming Mars or developing experimental communities in Antarctica. When we can live cooperatively with human and non-human species, making room for more than our own ends, perhaps we will then truly have developed a new social relationship with nature. *Antarctica* tells us the necessary first chapter of this story, our need to recognize the connections between social justice and ecological conservation, to abandon our abstractions and come back down to Earth. The subsequent chapters, which fall to all of us, must now tell more stories, and they must feature far more radical coalitions among humans and non-humans.

NOTES

1. Most of the published criticism on Robinson fails to make this distinction. For example, Shaun Huston reads the Mars trilogy in terms of Murray Bookchin's idea of third or "free" nature, "a synthesis of first (bio-physical) nature and second (human social) nature wherein humans 'co-operate' with first nature and directly participate in the evolution of life" (167). While we agree with much of Huston's assessment, we would argue that "third nature" mistakenly posits that only humans have a social nature. In Bookchin — and often in Robinson — first nature is passive and so our social relationship to it can be, at best, akin to stewardship. Following Plumwood, we argue for the significance of seeing non-humans as possessing lives entirely unconnected to human concerns. Similarly, Eric Otto reads the Mars trilogy in terms of Aldo Leopold's land ethic, which "questions the absence of the land in modern society's ethical paradigms" (119) and argues that we should "re-vision the land as valuable not as commodity but as community" (120). This is closer to our position, but is nonetheless limited in its reduction of complex ecosystems to the singular "land" and in its insistence that humans are a necessary part of any ecosystem. Critiquing Ann Clayborne's defense of an unterraformed Mars, Otto argues her "'rock ethic' is admirable for its attention to the intrinsic worth of the landscape, but it fails as a viable land ethic because it does not propose to solve the problem of maintaining a sustainable land-human symbiosis. [...] *Green Mars* is thus a book about Sax Russell's intellectual growth and [her] intellectual stagnation" (130). Otto's reading reveals the degree to which Robinson's environmentalism is premised upon the privileging of human needs — on landscape rather than environment.

2. Elizabeth Leane argues that there is a close connection between Robinson's critique of colonialism in the Mars trilogy and his articulation of a new version of science, which she sees as consistent with feminist and postcolonial critiques of Western scientific practice. She argues that the character of Sax Russell "can be read as the working through of a utopian vision of science — the kind of 'successor science' that, according to feminist critics, is increasingly necessary. This successor science [...] is based on a desire to accept the agency of the other — to nurture what Barbara McClintock has termed 'a feeling for the organism'" (88). However, Robinson's utopian vision of science fails to account for non-humans and the material world as agent rather than as object, or for the way that modern science is premised on the subject/object division which creates the damaging social relations with the environment he elsewhere critiques, and thus falls short of being a successor science.

3. In this, Robinson reproduces the familiar error of treating capitalist social relations as something to be abstracted from the material and historical complexities through which they inextricably run; and, once fixed, to be reinstalled, thus transforming social reality. Historically, this has resulted in a tendency to prioritize economic structures and to postpone dealing with racist, sexist and other structural hierarchies until after the revolution. In limiting his conception of nature and non-human life to their relevance to humans, Robinson is consistent with mainstream Marxism, including recent attempts to bring together ecological and Marxist thought. Paul Burkett articulates the view most consistent with Robinson's environmentalism, arguing that our damaged social relations with nature result from the capitalist mode of production, which "requires nature only in the form of 'separate' material conditions for its appropriation of labor power's use value, not in the form of an organic social and material unity between the producers and their natural conditions of existence" (1999: 62). Capital's "damaging effects on labor power and nature" are parts of the same process, with "the pressure of competitive monetary accumulation stretch[ing] human and extra-human forces to the breaking point" (133–34). However, both Robinson and Burkett tend to reduce nature to its use-value for human happiness, just as capitalism reduces nature to its exchange-value. Burkett explains that "For Marx, the fundamental contradiction of capitalism is that between wealth for capital versus wealth for the produc-

ers and their communities — where the latter is defined not in terms of the minimalist material and social requirements of capital accumulation but rather in terms of the conditions for a less restricted and more sustainable human development" (197). This implies a commitment to improving the environment but only because it is the site of human development and happiness, not because its non-human inhabitants have worth in themselves and beyond their capacity to sustain/develop humanity. Burkett argues that "labour's use-value orientation means that its struggles against capital's degradation of nature are just as inevitable as its resistance to capital's exploitation of labor" (216). However, as in *Antarctica*, non-human life only appears here in its relation to human needs. Likewise, Robinson's environmentalism seems, in the last instance, to be subsumed to a Marxism we fear is too anthropocentric to serve the current historical situation. John Foster Bellamy offers a more promising approach, arguing that Marxism and environmentalism, which do share common concerns, should resist the binaries of "anthropocentrism vs. ecocentrism — indeed such dualisms do little to help us understand the real, continuously changing material conditions of human existence within the biosphere" (11). Similarly, Ted Benton's attempts to reconcile socialism and environmentalism are attentive to their sometimes diverging priorities.

4. Similar arguments about the mutual benefit to humans and non-humans that result from bringing together ecological and class concerns can be found in the more explicitly Marxist work of Benton, Burkett, and Foster. Benton argues that broadening the concept of social relations to include our social relations with animals would not only lead to more just treatment of animals, but also enables the Marxist critique of capital to encompass other sites of damage to humans, including our alienated social relationship with nature. Focusing on the concept of species being, he suggests ways of enriching Marxist thought by thinking about human needs that we share with other species and critiquing the damage done by capitalism through its denial of our ecological interdependence with non-human life. Burkett critiques the commonly accepted view that Marx ignores the role of natural conditions in material production. He demonstrates the instrumentalist attitude that capital takes to both labor *and* nature, and argues that capital reduces humans to dependence on wage labor in part by separating us from our social relation with a nature not conceived of in terms of ownership. Foster argues that Marx's critique of capital was as concerned with changing social relationships to nature as with changing social relationships among humans, and that we need to focus on the co-evolution of humans and non-human nature in order to be consistent with Marx's materialist method. He also sees connections among the exploitation of labor, the severing of human ties with the land, and the destruction of non-human nature for profit.

5. In *Fifty Degrees Below* there is some acknowledgement that this is a limited way to think about nature: "All the discussion in the meeting that day had centered on the impact to humans. That would be the usual way of most such discussions; but whole biomes, whole ecologies would be altered, perhaps devastated. That was what they were saying, really, when they talked about the impact on humans: they would lose the support of the domesticated part of nature. Everything would become an exotic; everything would have to go feral" (70–71).

6. On May 7, 2007, the World Resource Institute published a report entitled *Restoring Nature's Capital: An Action Agenda to Sustain Ecosystem Services*. This report concludes with a vision of earth as "Planet Earth Ltd. ... an integrated global conglomerate that provides products and services to customers all over the world" (61), a company that is in deep trouble as a recent audit reveals. It then argues for the transformation of "civil society, business, the education and research communities, local communities, national government, and international organizations" (62) in order to create a culture of ecosystem stewardship and a better financial audit for Planet Earth Ltd. A chilling example of Jameson's contention that "It seems to be easier for us today to imagine the thoroughgoing deterioration of the earth and of nature than the breakdown of late capitalism" (xii), this report demonstrates the resilience with which capital can incorporate resistance into its own agenda. The ease with which Robinson's ideas might be so incorporated is particularly evident in his Science in the Capital trilogy. In *Sixty Days and Counting* (2007), President Phil Chase argues that because of the urgency with which they must implement radical measures to stop global warming "*we have to look to what we have now. And right now we have capitalism. So we have to use it*" (266). Thinking like a Heinlein/Campbell engineering-hero, he sees capitalism as a technology from which solutions can be jerry-rigged. He suggests that in the short term, they can focus on capital's strengths — having a lot of capital that they need to invest and overproduction — and leverage those strengths into making "*saving the environment ... the next undeveloped country*" (268) for capital. While aware that capitalism's desire for unrestrained growth is what produced the environmental crisis, he claims that ultimately capital is controlled by government and so if the majority of the people choose then "*we the people can aim capitalism in any direction we want*" (269). And in true Heinlein-style, this concluding volume offers few voices to challenge Chase's perspective. However, once capital enters a space, it is loath to leave it, and like any other technology it has consequences which cannot be predicted or controlled.

WORKS CITED

Bellamy, John Foster. *Marx's Ecology: Materialism and Nature.* New York: Monthly Review Press, 2000.
Benton, Ted. *Natural Relations: Animal Rights, Human Rights, and the Environment.* London: Verso, 1996.
Burkett, Paul. *Marx and Nature: A Red and Green Perspective.* Basingstoke: Palgrave Macmillan, 1999.
Dynes, William. "Multiple perspectives on Kim Stanley Robinson's Mars Series." *Extrapolation* 42.2 (Summer 2001):150–164.
Haraway, Donna. "Situated Knowledges: The Science Question in Feminism and the Privilege of Partial Perspective." *Simians, Cyborgs and Women: The Reinvention of Nature.* New York: Routledge, 1991. 183–201.
Huston, Shaun. "Murray Bookchin on Mars! The Production of Nature in Kim Stanley Robinson's *Mars* Trilogy." *Lost in Space: Geographies of Science Fiction.* Edited by Rob Kitchin and James Kneale. London: Continuum, 2002. 167–179.
Irwin, Frances, and Janet Ranganathan. *Restoring Nature's Capital: An Action Agenda to Sustain Ecosystem Services.* Foreword by Jonathan Lash and Walter Reid. Washington: World Resource Institute, 2007.
Jameson, Fredric. *The Seeds of Time.* New York: Columbia University Press, 1994.
Kimball, Lee A. *Southern Exposure: Deciding Antarctica's Future.* Foreword by James Gustave Speth. World Resources Institute, November 1990.
Latour, Bruno. *Pandora's Hope: Essays on the Reality of Science Studies.* Cambridge: Harvard University Press, 1999.
_____. *We Have Never Been Modern.* Trans. Catherine Porter. Cambridge: Harvard University Press, 1993.
Leane, Elizabeth. "Chromodynamics: Science and Colonialism in Kim Stanley Robinson's *Mars* Trilogy." *Ariel* 33.1 (2002):83–104.
Markley, Robert. "Falling Into Theory: Simulation, Terraformation, and Eco-Economics in Kim Stanley Robinson's Martian Trilogy." *Modern Fiction Studies* 43.3 (1997): 773–799.
Otto, Eric. "Kim Stanley Robinson's *Mars* Trilogy and the Leopoldian Land Ethic." *Utopian Studies* 14.2 (2003):118–135.
Plumwood, Val. *Environmental Culture: The Ecological Crisis of Reason.* London: Routledge, 2002.
Prugh, Thomas, with Robert Costanza, John H. Cumberland, Herman Daly, Robert Goodland, and Richard B. Norgaard. *Natural Capital and Human Economic Survival.* Foreword by Paul Hawken. Solomons, MD: International Society for Ecological Economics Press, 1995.
Robinson, Kim Stanley. *Antarctica.* New York: Bantam Books, 1998.
_____. *Fifty Degrees Below.* London: HarperCollins, 2005.
_____. *Icehenge.* New York: Ace Books, 1984.
Slotkin, Alan R. "The Ecological Newspeak of Kim Stanley Robinson." *American Speech* 72.4 (1997):440–443.
Speth, James. "Foreword." *Southern Exposure: Deciding Antarctica's Future.* Foreword by James Gustave Speth. World Resources Institute, November 1990. vii–viii.
Williams, Raymond. *The Country and the City.* London: Chatto & Windus, 1973.

Part IV. Interview and Select Bibliography

18

A Conversation with Kim Stanley Robinson*
Irving F. "Bud" Foote

During last June's SFRA Convention in Reno, Stan and I sat down for an hour for a wide-ranging conversation about his work and his ideas. It was June 19, 1993, the day after he and I had appeared in the same session, he to present his ideas on postmodernism in the genre, and I to discuss his novel *Red Mars* in the context of his other work. (*Red Mars* is, of course, the first of a trilogy; *Green Mars* should appear early in 1994, *Blue Mars* in 1996.) I transcribed the whole conversation and edited it down to manageable form; Stan made a few amendments before I produced this final version. Nothing substantial has been added, but peripheral matters we judged interesting only to the two of us have been largely eliminated, or at least I hope so.

Bud Foote (BF): Stan, I note that *Red Mars* is set in the same future history as the novella "Green Mars" and the novel *Icehenge*.

Kim Stanley Robinson (KSR): Very roughly. In the earlier works I didn't have the complete conception of what I wanted to do in mind, and I don't think of myself as building a future history. Each of those works attempts to be a complete thing. It is true that in *Icehenge* people are excavating the evidence of a failed Martian revolution, and that revolution bears some resemblance to the one in the final chapters of *Red Mars*, but the details are generally different. I think of these things as different takes that don't add up to a coherent future history.

BF: But wouldn't you say that the discrepancies in this future history echo the discrepancies in *Icehenge*, which gives us three different takes on a given set of events?

KSR: No. In *Icehenge* the discrepancies are part of a deliberately planned structure, and part of a point that I wanted to make. The discrepancies between *Icehenge* and "Green Mars" and *Red Mars* are simply me at different points in my life, wanting to make the most coherent individual work that I could, and not caring about the relationships with the other ones. So the discrepancies are accidents; I'm not making anything out of those contradictions that I think people can decode or find anything in. For instance, the lengths of

---

*The interview first appeared in *Science Fiction Studies* 21.1 (March 1994): 51–60, and is reprinted by permission of the Managing Editor and Publisher.

time in *Icehenge* are enormously long compared to what I now think makes sense, and so I've just abandoned them.

However, *The Memory of Whiteness* has a chapter set on Mars, and by chance that does fit in more or less, because it's so far off in the future that you can imagine it following the Mars books.

BF: What you're describing is a little bit like what happened to William Faulkner; although eventually he tried to make a unified history, it seems as if, early on, he just ignored any contradictions among individual stories.

KSR: Yes. But I think that of the two places I've set a lot of tales in, the one that is the best analog to Yoknapatawpha County is Orange County, which is my own home ground and my own mythic space. Faulkner did things that were not common to science fiction but that are very important to most literature, connected to a very intense attachment to place and an exploration of what that place meant to the people who lived in it. And science fiction, being often set in imaginary spaces, just didn't have that quality. So I thought that if I set three science fiction novels in the near future in my home town, this might give it the sort of density and weight of landscape and place that I value.

BF: You conceived of the Orange County Trilogy as a trilogy, from the start?

KSR: Yes. It came to me as a trio, a trilogy with a new structure, and one thing which interested me from the start was the structure itself—a sort of a tripod arrangement, where the base of the tripod, so to speak, was the present moment, and then the three legs would head off in three different directions that were as far apart from each other as I could imagine, each of them taking a basic science fiction scenario—the after-the-fall, the dystopia, and the utopia. They would have their relationships not as sequels to each other, but as a harmonic chord, so to speak.

BF: With many of the same people, and many of the same places, and many of the same events: for instance, all three books begin with digging up something, but for different reasons.

KSR: Yes. I wanted to make as many overtones in this chord as possible. And there is one character who is literally in all three novels, which is the old man, who is a young man before history makes its split in these three directions, and who lives different lives in the three different histories. I think it is an interesting way to talk about how much history impacts our individual lives, how we don't have as much control over our individual histories as we might think.

BF: Of course, in the structure of the three books, you have echoed another one of the key scenarios of science fiction, which is the alternative history.

KSR: Yes. I think the alternative history fits into science fiction because of the historical definition, that science fiction stories have historical links to our present, either implicit or explicit. It seemed to me that I could make that manifest with these three books, drawing links back to our present from three near-futures. Science fiction is the history that we cannot know, the future history and the alternative history. And that's why, I think, we incorporate prehistoric romances into science fiction, that we draw it instinctively into the genre because it is yet another history that we cannot know, a history that's lost to us.

BF: So science fiction — science fiction is a bad name for it, but we're stuck with it, I suppose —

KSR: I like the name science fiction partly because of something I've been thinking about recently, the is-ought problem, or what people in the environmental movement call the fact-value problem; we have a world of facts, of which science is the exemplar and the discoverer, and then there's our world of value, which we take out of religion, or psychology, or literature.

BF: Or science.

KSR: Yes, but a lot of scientists would claim that the values don't actually come out of the facts, that they're disconnected, they're separate worlds — although sociobiology tries to talk about values as coming out of facts, and from the other direction there are culture critics who insist over and over again that science is imbedded with values that it's not quite aware of. But that's something that a lot of scientists would disagree with; they would say that the scientific method is not a value system, but just an investigative method, an epistemological system.

BF: I suppose that here would be the place to put in a plug for Georgia Tech's two new degrees, one in literature and science and one in history and science.

KSR: Yes, I think that the programs you've got are an attempt to investigate the links between facts and values, which is important work. The very name science fiction includes science, which is the world of facts, and fiction, which is for me the main repository of our values. So you could say that our genre is called fact-values. Now for a genre to proclaim that we can yoke these two disparate worlds together, is a very powerful statement; and I think that people come to science fiction instinctively thinking that they're going to learn about how facts and values are connected, and then they read a dumb space-opera and they're disappointed in science fiction, because the name itself proclaims that it can do more than the actual texts usually do. But when it works right, science fiction is an enjambment of facts and values in a way that our culture desperately needs right now. The fact-value problem is specifically relevant to today's world because we have a culture that is making developments and cultural changes without much regard for the underlying values that are going to be thereby expressed.

BF: Then shouldn't we call it technology fiction instead of science fiction?

KSR: Yes, but science is the larger term within which technology exists as kind of the activist arm, so I think it's more powerful to call it science fiction than technology fiction.

BF: But it's all mostly about history.

KSR: And that takes it into an even larger sphere than science itself, history being at this point humanity's attempt to take charge of its own fate. If technology exists within science, then science exists within history, and science fiction is capable of taking on historical questions.

BF: The image in "Festival Night" [the introductory passage of *Red Mars*] that struck me most strongly occurs when Frank pokes his finger into the plastic material of the dome which covers the city and reflects that his anger is transferred into energy to fuel the city. That, I suspect, on your part was a quite conscious metaphor integrating the things that we've been talking about, the emotional, the human, the individual, with the larger context of science and technology.

KSR: Yes. In graduate school I wrote a bit about Proust, concentrating on his metaphors. Proust was quite aware of the science of his time, and of the thousands of metaphors that he uses, many of them are directly out of the sciences. It's one of the many aspects of Proust I admire. And it seemed to me in science fiction, there was room for integrating more of contemporary science into the metaphor system. I make an effort to make as many scientific metaphors as I can possibly think of. And once you set yourself that as a task, they begin to pop up everywhere. The mind is intensely metaphoric anyway, but these metaphors for our human lives out of the scientific world, it's not as if you have to hunt for them very hard, after you set yourself the task: they just begin to jump out at you.

BF: The use of softball, as metaphor and otherwise, in *Pacific Edge* really impresses me. Did you yourself play softball and baseball?

KSR: I played both, yes, and I still play softball. And when I was writing a utopian novel I was wondering why Utopias seem a bit dry, why people will make the common complaint that they wouldn't want to live in a Utopia, that there's something life-dampening about them. I wanted to write a Utopia that people might want to live in. I knew I couldn't please everybody, but I could suggest that Utopia is a world in which most pleasures will be pursuable. But in order to make a really concrete example of that, I had to choose something that I myself love. And there's an inherent drama and beauty in softball and baseball; so I thought, I will make it part of this world, and then people who like softball will say, "Oh, that would be fun," and as for the many readers who I suppose are not into it, they can say, "Okay, that's Stan's obsession, but he seems to be suggesting that this world will also include my obsession as something that I could do."

BF: Soccer fields, chess tournaments —

KSR: Heroin dens — I tried to suggest a little bit of all that with the professional wrestling and the drag racing, which are both things that I myself find ludicrous, but are flourishing in this world; and they're particularly American, they're Great American Stupid Sports.

BF: One of the questions people ask is: you're a Ph.D. in English, and you've taught English. You're one of us academicians. There aren't too many Ph.D.s in English who write very well. Somebody asked me today, does Stan think that being a Ph.D. in English has hurt his writing?

KSR: Ah! Well, no no no. For a while I was scared of the university; you know that split in American literature between the palefaces and the red Indians — I believed in that split, and I would identify myself with the red Indians of American literature — Faulkner, Hemingway, Twain, Snyder — rather than palefaces like Eliot and Henry James and their need to go back to Europe, to look backward. And so as a red Indian I was nervous about being in the university. But I had a very sympathetic group of advisors, mentors, professors at UC San Diego, particularly Donald Wesling and Fredric Jameson. And I also thought: the more you know, the better off you're going to be when it comes time to write that next sentence. And so, I think it helped.

BF: When did you know that you were going to become a writer?

KSR: I discovered SF in 1971, and I was excited about it, because it spoke to my experience in Orange County, as someone who was brought up in an agricultural community that got ripped out and replaced by the apartment-and-freeway nightmare that's there now. When I ran into science fiction, it was explaining myself to myself. So, in college I started writing SF short stories, and I liked the work.

BF: This is a standard question that people always ask; but I think it's an essential question. Of the writers in the field, both twentieth-century and nineteenth-century, whom do you see as the largest influences on your own craft?

KSR: It's hard to talk about influence. This is the standard answer to this standard question. I read a lot of writers, and I like a lot of them, and then when I write my works I very seldom feel that I'm doing a pastiche. I've only done a couple of pastiches in my entire career, and those not of the writers I like most to read. But of the pre–sixties science fiction, I enjoy particularly Clifford Simak and Walter Miller, Edgar Pangborn and Cordwainer Smith, and in England Olaf Stapledon and H.G. Wells. The thing that really excited me when I first discovered science fiction was the writing of the sixties, the New Wave. Delany was very important for me. And Le Guin. Disch. Lem. Gene Wolfe, very much so. The Strugatsky brothers. Joanna Russ. I had very important teachers in Damon Knight and Kate Wilhelm. I admire Phil Dick, especially his protagonists, ordinary people who are struggling in difficult situations, trying to prevail. I like that even more than his more celebrated reality breakdowns and his hallucinogenic quality and his amazing insight into American culture, especially in its dysfunctional Reno-Nevada aspects.

BF: It strikes me that that little guy somehow struggling to maintain a dignity harks back to a lot of the early H.G. Wells.

KSR: Yes. Wells still towers over science fiction, not only for the famous short scientific romances, but for the Utopias. He was a man with a dark streak in him, but he made his attacks on the problem time after time, with an inherent optimism, saying let's get our priorities straight: first let's talk about social justice and equal rights, and then after that we'll talk about transcendence and metaphysical and ontological problems. H.G. Wells fits in very well with Fredric Jameson, who in his criticism is also constantly emphasizing social issues. I love this part of the literature: the thought-experiment which attacks social problems and suggests solutions, utopian goals, or envisions societies that we might then work towards. It seems to me that's one of the most important things that it does, and it doesn't necessarily have to be like taking castor oil. It can be playful, and it can be fun to read, and yet still be a way of increasing the meaning of our lives and sharpening our political will.

BF: A lot of the canonized literature of the twentieth century doesn't do that.

KSR: But Wells does.

BF: Yes. But we've canonized him. The mainstream hasn't.

KSR: That's right; in fact, they've marginalized him.

BF: The part of Wells that the mainstream likes is the early, black, despairing Doctor Moreau Wells. The later stuff, people ignore. And both utopian and idealistic have become dirty words.

KSR: Yes, but that in itself is a political stance. The people who put down Utopia as "pie in the sky," impractical, and totalitarian — all that is a political stance aiding the status quo, which itself is clearly unjust and insupportable. Utopia has to be rescued as a word, to mean "working towards a more egalitarian society, a global society." Which means at every point defending it, going to the mat for the term and for the concept of Utopia. In a way, it's an antidote or a response to post-modernism, to post-modernism's fragmentation, anomie, apoliticism, stupidity, quietism, and capitulationism.

BF: The present order, you say, is indefensible. What, in the present order, would you retain, outside of softball?

KSR: I would retain science, as a method. The pure play of science, I think, is one of the best expressions of human values. Also the insistence on individual rights as being the basis for the state; I think it needs to be insisted on when you look back at the history of the twentieth century. What I would want to get rid of, however, is capitalism, an economic system that (1) insists on perpetual growth in an ecology that is limited, and (2) sanctions people ripping off other people's labor with police protection. I say of the notion that somebody's work can have its value appropriated by someone else, "Look, this is something that everybody seems to take for granted, people think it's part of the natural order, but it's actually crazily unjust." So is the notion that somebody could own land, water or air, and extract a profit from it from other human beings.

BF: Let me be devil's advocate. Obviously, the kind of capitalism I grew up with is a long haul from the mass capitalism of today. Still, I grew up with the idea that your house is your castle, that owning a piece of land was an investment in the community to be handed down to your children, that you could put together a business, whether you were fixing plumbing, repairing TVs, or running a general store, and that if it was a valid service to the community, it entitled you to make a buck.

KSR: And you would benefit from it.

BF: And the community would benefit.

KSR: Yes, I see your point, and I think that taking the position that people do not have self-interest is wrong, in that it's a statement that doesn't match, in fact, with what we observe in other animals. And here this gets into sociobiology, but I think you can construct a sort of a leftist sociobiology which says that self-interest obviously exists, that we're animals, and that we're strongly motivated genetically to protect our offspring.

BF: And to hang on to what our parents gave us.

KSR: Yes, but what I would say is that you ought to be able to allow for self-interest up to a certain point, and then set a limit. There are a lot of things that are good up to a certain point, but beyond that point become poisonous.

BF: Like beer.

KSR: [Laughs.] And another of them is self-interest, and the ability to make a profit from your work! If it was just your work, as an electrician, say, and you did your work and you made your profit from it, then that's legitimate, almost biological self-interest. But if it goes beyond that, and you begin to be able to take the value of other people's work, and accumulate capital, what you get back into is feudalism. Capitalism now is simply feudalism in disguise, with an aristocracy that gets to rip off and live on the efforts of their peasants.

BF: Now wait a minute: are you telling me that if I'm a master plumber, I can't take an apprentice and teach him the trade, and get him to where he can be a master plumber? that I can't have a journeyman?

KSR: No — it's an interesting question because it says where are the limits? and I think they have to be human scale. You're a teacher to your apprentice, and you're making an exchange. He's doing some work for you, you're doing some work for him, and this is a human exchange that goes back into a human past that must have happened for more generations than we know about, by a long shot. But, if there's a class of people who are going off to their offices, and making decisions, and ordering around a group of perhaps ten thousand people, none of whom they know, and all of whose work they're taking a cut from, and they are living on a salary of two million dollars a year, whereas the people who are at the bottom end of this pyramid system are making twenty thousand a year, and hurting day in and day out to keep their kids healthy, then that's where — it's gone too far. It clearly has gone too far.

BF: One of the major problems that I see in the sort of Utopia that you're talking about is that there are too many people in the world.

KSR: Yes, one big part of our political-environmental crisis is overpopulation. We have to look to those countries with severe population problems that have managed to ameliorate them very quickly, by methods that are not over-controlling or violent — I'm talking about China, Indonesia, and Thailand, three countries that have made concerted efforts to cut their population growth and have had success. In each one of these countries there have been occasional abuses, but in the main, what they have used is social pressure, tax laws and the like, and they've had success in convincing their populace to cut down on the number of children they have. I'd like to see science fiction begin to address this, by portraying futures that are less populated or futures that are working to reduce population, and the kind of dramas that would result from that. Because you get good narratives, right off the bat. I mean, if the governments of the world would say, "OK, everybody has the legal right to three-quarters of a child, and so you and your partner have the right to a child and a half when you add 'em up, and so after you've had one child you've got a half-credit left, and then you either have to buy another half, or you can sell your half," the soap operas that result from this scenario are fantastic! They're funny, they're interesting, they're entertaining thought-experiments, and they're also suggestive — they bring into the consciousness of the public the overpopulation problem, which is so severe. Science fiction ought to be playing with these ideas more, bringing them into our mind more, so that when the Vatican prevents the Rio Earth Summit meeting from discussing population problems, for instance, the public can say, "Oh yes, I know about that; I've read about it in a novel by David Brin," or someone else. David is very good at bringing these questions to a wider audience, as he does in his novel *Earth*.

BF: Every society makes a division: here are the things that are your own business, and here are the things that are the business of the society. And for several thousand years in western history, the crucial thing on the border has always been sex, because it's an intensely personal business, and also it's very much the business of the society as a whole, because of the results thereof.

KSR: Right. But now, because of technology, we can separate sex from reproduction, from child-creation—

BF: But we can't make people separate it.

KSR: No, but Faye Wattleton, who used to be the president of Planned Parenthood, said that in every country she's gone to on Earth, there has been a group of women who have said, "Look, we would love to have birth control and have control over this aspect of our lives." And this includes the Moslem countries, and it includes the countries in which women have the approximate status of cattle. And so it isn't as if a government's going to have to come in and force people to do something they don't want to do. It's giving people, especially women, more control over their own destinies. One of the greatest methods of slowing population growth is simply empowerment of women. In every country in which women have gotten more education and more power over their own lives, the population growth rate has dropped. What's nice about this is, we see a problem environmentally, and the best solution to it is more human power, more human freedom. So we have a win-win situation, in that the more we can empower human beings who are female, the better off the environment of the planet's going to be.

BF: It takes on an almost mythic quality.

KSR: Yes. And I'm sure that there are going to be feminists who would want to divide this mythic Gordian knot and say, "It's just a coincidence, it's not an archetypal thing," but whether it's a coincidence or some Mother-Goddess-of-the-Earth thing, it's still true. One of the best ways to help our grandchildren live in a better world is to increase the rights of women right now.

BF: "Help our grandchildren live in a better world" is an echo of Vonnegut, who says science fiction people are really the only people who give a damn about what's going to happen a thousand years down the line. What makes us do that?

KSR: Imagination, I think. People who have the ability to imagine what the other is like, what the life of the other is like, put themselves in the place of the other—they can imagine that these future generations are going to look back at us and either curse us or say, "Well, they tried their best." And it would be better if they were to say that we tried our best. So I think it's the power of the imagination. One thing I find encouraging is that of my three Orange County books, by far the one that people are most interested in talking to me about is the Utopia. I find this encouraging and a sign that people have a hunger for this kind of imaginative project.

BF: The person you remind me of most, strangely enough, in your intellectual stance, is Fred Pohl; he has a kind of a modest optimism, a very qualified optimism, a cynical optimism—

KSR: I admire Fred greatly, because he's very high-spirited and playful, full of fun, but also politically engaged. He's always been a leftist, in a field that doesn't have all that many of them. And he has a very practical bent, a realistic view of institutional inertia and the various things that might slow us up. I hesitate to say "human nature" because I think human nature is fairly malleable, although this is a question that sociobiology and SF as well are investigating: how malleable is human nature?

BF: Well, neither you nor Fred have demanded that perfect people come into being in order to inhabit a utopia.

KSR: Joanna Russ, I think, made up the term the optopia, which is not that you go for the perfect society, but that you go for the optimum society, the best one possible, given — everything. And I think that's a nice reworking of the utopian notion. In *Pacific Edge* I tried to show that even if we were to reach a fairly just society, we would still have tragedies left, just because of the nature of biology and of the cosmos, that between death and the various failures of human relationships, even in Utopia there would be a lot of unhappiness — but it's still important to try for Utopia, because then we would be experiencing the most human unhappinesses; it wouldn't just be war, famine, and meaningless death, but it would be unrequited love, and death at the end of a meaningful life. And that's a big difference.

BF: But human beings seem to have a sort of original sin, or innate depravity —

KSR: When you say "original sin," you invoke a whole system that I reject. But when you say "innate depravity" I say, yes, there is perversity, there's the cross-grained streak, there's the Jungian shadow — there's a dark streak in us. Or so it seems! I'm very interested in the scientific view of this stuff, in studying ourselves as animals, and so I'm very interested in sociobiology, although I would insist that it's more a philosophy, or a speculative fiction, than it is a science, because it's making analogies from ants and termites and other animals to the human, analogies that are simply leaps, analogs, metaphors. But still it's interesting to look at sociobiology as a way to think about our natures. Because we evolved from primates, and we have to think about ourselves and our brains and our values as having evolved from a certain lifestyle on the savannah that lasted over millions of years. This being the case, I think we ought to be shooting for a society that satisfies the brains that were grown in those years of evolution, a society which would include simple things like walking or spending most of the day outdoors or looking at fire, because these were things that over a million years were profound pleasures to us, and still are, and when we sit in our little boxes in the urban environment and don't give ourselves these pleasures, we begin to go perverse. And my feeling is that, if over the next five hundred years, we reduced our population and started living in tree-houses with little computers in them and spent a lot of time outdoors throwing rocks or softballs, and doing work outdoors, growing our food or even hunting our food, I suppose, although I haven't thought about that one very deeply, then I think a lot of this so-called innate depravity would begin to slip away, and what we would show is what animals show. Very few animals kill just for pleasure; the wantonness of the minx is a problem —

BF: Or shrikes.

KSR: Yes. But we're not sure that these things are true. I mean, this is a metaphor for ourselves, these observations of these animals. And so I say what we ought to do is run a consistent experiment even if it takes 500 years. Let's give ourselves a utopian society and run it for a while, and see how depraved we are. Right now we don't know.

BF: Most of the hunters I know are like everybody else; but people who are gardeners have, in a lot of ways, more pleasant personalities than people who are not. The Carlos Casteneda books, strange books, fiction, but interesting —

KSR: Science fiction, in fact —

BF: He has Don Juan say, "You must think like a warrior," which doesn't mean you should go out and kill people; it's more like what you're saying: you must think like a primate on the savannah.

KSR: Yes.

BF: I teach people to read fast and I tell people, "You must read like a warrior." And I see the act of reading as very much like hunting — it involves the eyes, it involves the brain, it makes the same kinds of demands. So the reader is in a way a savannah hunter.

KSR: It's a wonderful metaphor. The more I think of us as animals, the easier it becomes for me to understand things that I didn't understand before. I can better frame the goals that I'd like society to be working for when I think of us as primates, as large mammals, existing as predators at the top of the predator heap. And I can see a lot of the arguments that go on amongst us as primate-dominance dynamics, with all their triviality and their day-to-day swipes with the back of the hand. One of my definitions of Utopia is that if we could just satisfy ourselves as animals, then the part of us that is human, the consciousness, the awareness of the cosmos, would then begin to flower even more than it has now. It would not take tragedy out of our lives, but it would bring a lot more joy into them.

Notes on Kim Stanley Robinson's *Red Mars*

[Editor's Note: I have deleted the first two sentences from Professor Foote's original introduction to this section, concerning when *Green Mars* might be published.]

At the moment I write one can only speculate about what *Green Mars* will add to *Red Mars*, and what will be added a year or so later by *Blue Mars;* and, furthermore, *Red Mars* is itself so long and so rich in so many ways that no paper of this length can do more than suggest some approaches to the first novel of the trilogy.

Having read the earlier work of Stan Robinson, we come to *Red Mars* with certain expectations. We have read the careful hard-core presentation of the life-support system of a starship in *Icehenge*, and we therefore anticipate a similarly careful treatment of the technology Robinson will hypothesize as desirable, first, for the establishing of a permanent colony on the red planet, and, second, for making the naked Mars inhabitable for Terran life. We get them.

We have read *Pacific Edge*, and we therefore expect ecological concerns. It is not simply an easy irony which makes those who would keep Mars as it is — stark, and dead, and beautiful — those who on Earth would be those most concerned with the preservation of the living environment: the aesthetes, the nature-lovers, the artists, the humanists. Those who wish to bring life, in all its peculiar and multiple beauties, to Mars are, on the other hand, the technicians, the scientists, and the engineers. There is no easy judgment to be made between these positions: both in *Red Mars* and in the earlier books, the appeals and the honesty and the beauty of both sides are presented with skill and passion.

It was Asimov, I believe, who noted that most SF is political, explicitly or implicitly: that postulating a new society of necessity involves a comment on our present society. *Pacific Edge,* an ambiguous enough Utopia, certainly gives us politics in abundance; and as soon as we enter the first part of *Red Mars* we are in the middle of a power struggle. *Pacific Edge,* like the rest of Robinson's fiction — and like much of Le Guin's — has a mainstreamish quality about it. Unlike Le Guin, Robinson has taken a certain amount of grief from some readers for this mainstreamishness: what sort of a SF novel is it, after all, we are asked, that spends so much time worrying about how many times the protagonist has hit safely in softball games, and what it is doing for his head?

In his concerns for the ecology, Robinson is very contemporary, but not contemporary SF, which puts some people off. In his concern for human struggles, interior and exterior, he returns to the example of the great SF writers of the nineteenth century; and in his scrupulousness about technological possibility, he belongs to the generic SF hard-core of the Campbell era.

We are barely into *Red Mars,* when a Swiss guide explains to tourists the structure of the dome under which the new city has been built: "An outer membrane of piezoelectric plastic generates electricity from wind. Then two sheets hold a layer of airgel insulation. Then the inner layer is a radiation-capturing membrane, which turns purple and must be replaced ..." (§1:8). That is the sort of explanation which ought to be hard-core enough for anyone this side of Hugo Gernsback; but note how Robinson immediately turns the technology into metaphor, with one of the political players as his focus: "Frank reached out and pushed at the inner membrane.... He poked the tent wall so hard that he pushed out the outermost membrane, which meant that some of his anger would be captured and stored as electricity in the town's grid" (§1:8). It is human motion which powers the colonization of Mars; it is human emotion which is turned into energy. Robinson returns briefly to chemistry, only to link the fragility of molecular structure with the affairs of the human colony: "It was a special polymer in that respect — carbon atoms were linked to hydrogen and fluorine atoms in such a way that the resulting substance was even more piezoelectric than quartz. Change one element of the three, however, and everything shifted; substitute chlorine for fluorine, for instance, and you had saran wrap" (§1:8). Change one atom, or one person, and what you have is saran wrap; remove the human emotion from the equation, and you remove just that much power. (Robinson discusses this kind of metaphor in our conversation.)

If, as I have noted above, Kim Stanley Robinson seems in various ways to be simultaneously contemporary, Campbellian/Gernsbackian, and Wellsian, he is also, using a conventional if finely crafted prose, surprisingly New-Wavish. And he accomplishes this largely by nods at earlier literature of Mars. If a reader misses this fact earlier in the book, he or she will have their nose rubbed in it on page 19: Mars revolves, as chance would have it, in just a bit over the same time that Earth does: 12 [*sic* 24] hours, 39 minutes, 30 seconds. But the first colonists of Mars, dedicated and accustomed to the old 24-hour day, decide to keep it; and so at midnight, every day, the clocks all stop for thirty-nine and a half minutes. And what do they call this interval? You guessed it: *The Martian Time Slip.*

And isn't that a nice family joke, the younger writer sweeping off his hat in a half-bow across three decades toward Phil Dick as if to say, "Look, uncle, what I have done with your bad dream."

But most of us have learned to take Stan Robinson seriously, even and maybe especially when he is joking. And so we back up, hardly having started reading *Red Mars,* and start over again. But before we do that, we stop and think a bit, in both historical and symbolic terms, about those thirty-nine minutes.

Over the last several thousand years, a good bit of the intellectual energy of our species has gone into trying to make mathematical sense out of the timekeepers the universe has given us. The lunar year and the solar year just will not fit conveniently together, and that fact gave our ancestors not only fits but a lot of good mythic material. Prechristians knew perfectly well that 28 went into 365 thirteen times and a bit; hence the very old rhyme,

> How many merry months are there in the year?
> There are thirteen, I say.

But thirteen is a terrible number; for all sort of reasons, astronomical, theological, and mathematical, twelve is much more to be desired, and so the old rhyme was modified to read "There are but twelve, I say." And all of that makes what might be called a Terran time-slip.

Worse still is the fact that the rotation of the Earth and its circuit around the sun just won't come out even. Now we have a formula which will work for several thousand years, which gives us a time-slip of a day every four years, *except* when the year is evenly divisible by 100, *except* when the year is evenly divisible by 400. But this solution is messy and somewhat offensive. *Things are supposed to come out even,* we think, echoing Judah Asimov at the candy-store cash drawer.

Humans keep pounding on the universe, demanding that it come out even, finding that *coming out even* demands more and more complicated systems of thought, shifting scientific paradigms every time the slips get too much to bear. If the history of science tells us anything, it is that shifts in paradigm are coming thicker and faster all the time. Most of us manage to live, somehow, in four different systems: the pre–Copernican ("The sun rises in the east and sets in the west"), the Newtonian, the world of Heisenberg and quantum theory, and the world of Hawking in which black holes may leak naked singularities and anything may happen, any time, and make total hash out of all our mathematics.

It is clear that the biggest part of the lives of the characters in *Red Mars,* like most of our daily lives, is lived in the sensible world of the pre–Copernican and the Newtonian. That world is Premodern, as Heisenberg is Modern and Hawking is Postmodern. But as we think about the calendar and timekeeping through human history, that struggle to reduce the universe to comprehensible mathematics, we recognize that nothing is ever going to come out quite even, that even in the middle of a history of the conquest of Mars which pays enormous attention to the scientific and technical realities of the whole business, there is going to be the occasional reality-slip in which, for just a moment, the nightmarish and schizophrenic world of Phil Dick flickers into being.

But let's go back to the beginning of the book. The reference to Phil Dick makes us wary, makes us wonder: to what extent is this book going to be *recursive,* to use Anthony Lewis's term? (I'm going to restrict my comments, very largely, to the very first section of the book, "Festival Night," because the book is so vast in its range that there is material there for dozens of papers; and if the *Green Mars* and *Blue Mars* to come live up to the promise of this book, graduate students and untenured assistant professors will bless the name of Stan Robinson for decades to come.)

Consider the introduction to "Festival Night"; it consists of two pages, apparently drawn from the speech which John Boone is giving to his fellow colonists as the narrative proper begins. "Mars was empty before we came," he says. "We are all the consciousness Mars has ever had" (§1:2).

A couple of years ago, at the International Association of the Fantastic in the Arts convention, I dealt with Stan's novella "Green Mars" in which, incongruously, in the middle of climbing Olympus Mons, a couple of characters begin discussing Jean-Paul Sartre and his notion that we change the past by what we do in the present. Since the past exists only in our memories and our records and in the relative importance we attach to different segments of those memories and those records, the past of a devout Marxist is going to be quite different than the past of a convicted Christian.

And therefore, going back to the speech of John Boone, the past of Mars is whatever present consciousnesses make it. As Sartre says,

> The past is ... the past of something or somebody.... There is not first a universal past which would later be particularized in concrete pasts. On the contrary, it is particular pasts we discover first. The true problem ... will be to find out by what processes these individual pasts can be united so as to form the past [88].

John Boone goes on to appeal to all the stories that have ever been told about Mars and all the names it has had — Nirgal, Mangala, Auquakuh, Harmakhis — from the Ice Age down to our present. Through his mouth, Robinson invites us to see the multiple symbolism of his use of color (almost an echo of John D. MacDonald's Travis McGee books):

> Yes, for thousands of years Mars was a sacred power in human affairs; and its color made it a dangerous power, representing blood, anger, war and the heart.
> [But] then the first telescopes gave us a closer look, and we saw the little orange disk, with its white poles and dark patches spreading and shrinking as the long seasons passed [§1:2].

Just as Hawking's world-view encompasses that of Heisenberg, and Heisenburg's that of Newton, and Newton's that of Ptolemy, so Boone's new story of Mars is made to encompass all the stories told about Mars all the way back to Ice-Age campfires. Fossil stories they are, as the names for Mars are fossils:

> perhaps it is not surprising that all the oldest names for Mars have a peculiar weight on the tongue ... they sound as if they were even older than the ancient languages we find them in, as if they were fossil words from the Ice Age or before [§1:2].

But some of those fossils, we are given to understand, come to life rather like the dinosaurs of *Jurassic Park,* one of the *past* pasts of Mars is evoked in terms which are obviously meant to apply to the colonists whom Boone is addressing:

> ... the best Earthbound images gave Lowell enough blurs to inspire a story, the story we all know, of a dying world and a heroic people, desperately building canals to hold off the final deadly encroachment of the desert.
> It was a great story. But then Mariner and Viking sent back their photos, and everything changed. Our knowledge of Mars expanded by magnitudes, we literally knew millions of times more about this planet than we had before. And there before us flew a new world, a world unsuspected [§1:3].

But, Boone goes on to say, even after the arrival of colonists on the planet, the old stories keep reviving themselves, like "elusive little red people, always glimpsed out of the corner of the eye." They are, he says, "an attempt to give Mars life, or to bring it to life." And here it has to be noted that this whole introductory section, the speech of John Boone, is a deliberate echo — Robinson has confirmed this in conversation — of, and contrast to, the introduction to one of the best-known Mars stories, C. L. Moore's "Shambleau" (1933):

> Man has conquered Space before. You may be sure of that. Somewhere beyond the Egyptians, in that dimness out of which come echoes of half-mythical names — Atlantis, Mu — somewhere back of history's first beginnings there must have been an age when mankind, like us today, built cities of steel to house its star-roving ships and knew the names of the planets in their own native tongues — heard Venus' people call their wet world "Shaardol" in that soft, sweet, slurring speech and mimicked Mars' gutteral "Lakkdiz" from the harsh tongues of Mars' dryland dwellers. You may be sure of it. Man has conquered Space before, and out of that conquest faint, faint echoes run still through a world that has forgotten the very fact of a civilization which must have been as mighty as our own. There have been too many myths and legends for us to doubt it [7].

These myths, these legends, these stories, all — in Sartre's terms — parts of the *past* pasts of Mars are told, Boone says, to give Mars life, or to bring it to life.

But giving Mars life, and bringing it to life, are the central concerns of the book. As in the novella "Green Mars" and as in *Icehenge,* as we have already noted, the colonists are divided into those who would leave Mars as it is — red, and lifeless, and barren, and majestic in a way that no Earthly landscape can be majestic — and those who want a green Mars, gradually filling up with genetically tailored flora and fauna which will slowly push back the deserts which threatened the pathetic and heroic Martians in Percival Lowell's *past* past of Mars.

Like many of the writers of the Golden Age, Robinson is himself a great reader of SF; and he says that before beginning the trilogy he went back and read heavily in the literature. *Red Mars* gives the reader an almost continual sense of itself as artifact, in its declaration that it is a story encompassing past stories which, in turn, encompass still older stories. The enraged Arab, Selim, mutters about "the Koran or Camus, Persepolis or the Peacock Throne, references scattered nervously among non sequiturs" (§1:11), and we are once again back to Philip K. Dick. Boone says,

> what they didn't realize was that by the time we got to Mars, we would be so changed by the voyage out that nothing we had been told to do mattered anymore ... we became *fundamentally different beings* [§1:4].

And we are reminded not only of Bradbury's *Martian Chronicles* but also, less happily, of Pohl's *Man Plus.* The underground colony which preceded the domed city was called, we are told (§1:18), Underhill, and all of a sudden, out of the corner of our eye, there is Bilbo Baggins, like an elusive little red native. Nadya (§3:118) is Nadya Nine-Fingers, an echo of Frodo. In Edgar Rice Burroughs' *Gods of Mars* (§13:206–08), John Carter flies his airship straight up a shaft, amazing everybody; and so does Hiroko in *Red Mars* (§2:60). And it just goes on and on: people will be digging references out of this book for decades. If Robinson's short fiction reminds us of *Dubliners* in an SF mode, *Red Mars,* beneath its deceptively conventional surface, is as recursive and rich in allusion as *Ulysses.*

And, like *Portrait of the Artist, Red Mars* is, among other things, a manifesto. At the end of "Festival Night," Frank Chalmers, who has had Boone killed so that he may assume power over the colony, says to himself, in words that seem to come from the author himself, looking back over the accumulation of Mars fiction of the past several hundred years, "*Now we'll see what I can do with this planet*" (§1:22).

Works Cited

Bradbury, Ray. *The Martian Chronicles.* NY: Doubleday, 1950.
Burroughs, Edgar Rice. *The Gods of Mars.* Chicago: McClure, 1918.
Dick, Philip K. *Martian Time-Slip.* NY: Ballantine Books, 1964.
Lewis, Anthony R. *An Annotated Bibliography of Recursive Science Fiction.* Introduction by Barry N. Malsberg. Cambridge, MA: NESFA Press, 1990.
Moore, C.L. "Shambleau." (*Weird Tales,* November 1933). *The Best of C.L. Moore.* Ed. Lester del Rey. Garden City, NY: Nelson Doubleday, 1975. 7–32.
Pohl, Frederik. *Man Plus.* NY: Random House, 1976.
Robinson, Kim Stanley. *The Gold Coast.* NY: TOR, 1988. Part of the so-called Orange County Trilogy, along with *Pacific Edge* and *The Wild Shore.*
_____. *Green Mars.* NY: TOR, 1988. A TOR double with Arthur C. Clarke's *Meeting with Medusa;* first published in 1985. A novella, not to be confused with *Green Mars* as the sequel to *Red Mars.*
_____. *Icehenge.* NY: Ace, 1984.

_____. *Pacific Edge*. Norwalk: Easton, 1990. Also NY: TOR, 1990.
_____. *Red Mars*. NY: Bantam, 1993.
_____. *Remaking History*. NY: TOR, 1991.
_____. *The Wild Shore*. NY: Ace, 1984.
Sartre, Jean-Paul. *Being and Nothingness*. Trans. Hazel E. Baines. Secaucus NJ: Citadel Press, 1977. First published in Paris by Gallimard, 1943.

19

A Select Secondary Bibliography
William J. Burling

Critical Scholarship

Abbott, Carl. "Falling into History: The Imagined Wests of Kim Stanley Robinson in the 'Three Californias' and Mars Trilogy." *Western Historical Quarterly* 34.1 (2003): 27–47. Reprinted in *Frontier Past and Present: Science Fiction and the American West*. Lawrence: University Press of Kansas, 2006.

Bailey, K. V. "Mars Is a District of Sheffield." *Foundation* 68 (Autumn 1996): 81–86.

Buhle, Paul. "Green Dreams of Space." *Capitalism, Nature, Socialism* 9.2 (June 1998): 125–128.

———. "Kim Stanley Robinson, Science Fiction Socialist." *Monthly Review* 54.3/4 (July 2002): 87–90.

Burgess, Helen J. "'Road of Giants': Nostalgia and the Ruins of the Superhighway in Kim Stanley Robinson's Three Californias Trilogy." *Science Fiction Studies* 33.2 (2006): 275–290.

Burling, William J. "The Theoretical Foundation of Utopian Radical Democracy in Kim Stanley Robinson's *Blue Mars*." *Utopian Studies* 16 (2005): 75–96.

Bush, Fred. "The Time of the Other: Alternate History and the Conquest of America." *Strange Horizons* (15 July 15, 2002). www.strangehorizons.com

Butler, Andrew M. "Heading Toward Utopia: Kim Stanley Robinson's 'Mars' Trilogy." *Vector* 189 (September/October 1996): 7–8.

Clarke, Amy. " Martian Odysseys: Travel and Narrative Unrest in Kim Stanley Robinson's *Red Mars*." *Fantastic Odysseys: Selected Essays from the Twenty-Second International Conference on the Fantastic in the Arts*. Mary Pharr, ed. Westport, CT: Praeger, 2003. 133–138.

Dynes, William. "Multiple Perspectives in Kim Stanley Robinson's Mars Series." *Extrapolation* 42 (2001): 150–164.

Foote, Bud. "Assuming the Present in SF: Sartre in a New Dimension." *Functions of the Fantastic: Selected Essays from the Thirteenth International Conference on the Fantastic in the Arts*. Joe Sanders, ed. Westport, CT: Greenwood; 1995. 161–67.

———."Kim Stanley Robinson: Premodernist." *Imaginative Futures: Proceedings of the 1993 Science Fiction Research Association Conference*. Milton T. Wolf and Daryl F. Mallett, eds. San Bernardino, CA: Jacob's Ladder Books, 1995. 329–340.

———. "Notes on Kim Stanley Robinson's *Red Mars*." *Science Fiction Studies* 21.1 (1994): 61–66.

Franko, Carol. "The Density of Utopian Density in Robinson's *Red Mars*." *Extrapolation* 38 (1997): 57–65.

———. "Dialogical Twins: Post-patriarchal Topology in Two Stories by Kim Stanley Robinson." *Science Fiction Studies* 22 (1995): 305–322.

———. "Working the 'In Between': Kim Stanley Robinson's Utopian Fiction." *Science Fiction Studies* 21 (1994): 191–211.

Frisch, Adam J. "The Subjective Objective in *The Years of Rice and Salt*." *Foundation* 34.4 (2005): 31–38.

Huston, Shaun. "Murray Bookchin on Mars! The Production of Nature in Kim Stanley Robinson's Mars Trilogy." *Lost in Space: Geographies of Science Fiction*. Rob Kitchin and James Kneale, eds. London, New York: Continuum, 2002. 167–179.

Jameson, Fredric. *Archaeologies of the Future: The Desire Called Utopia and Other Science Fictions*. New York: Verso, 2005.

———. "'If I Find One Good City, I Will Spare the Man': Realism and Utopia in Kim Stanley Robinson's

Mars Trilogy." *Learning from Other Worlds: Estrangement, Cognition and the Politics of Science Fiction and Utopia*. Patrick Parrinder, ed. Liverpool, UK: Liverpool University Press, 2000. 208–233.

Leane, Elizabeth. "Antarctica as a Scientific Utopia." *Foundation* 32.89 (2003): 27–35.

_____. "Chromodynamics: Science and Colonialism in Kim Stanley Robinson's Mars Trilogy." *ARIEL* 33.1 (2002): 83–104.

Markley, Robert. "Falling Into Theory: Simulation, Terraformation, and Eco-Economics in Kim Stanley Robinson's Martian Trilogy." *Modern Fiction Studies* 43 (1997): 773–799. Essay reprinted in *Dying Planet: Mars in Science and the Imagination*. Durham: Duke University Press, 2005: chapter 9.

McVeigh, Kevin. "The Edge of Utopia? Kim Stanley Robinson's *Pacific Edge*." *Vector* 189 (September/October 1996): 8–9.

Michaels, Walter Benn. "Political Science Fictions." *New Literary History* 31.4 (2000): 649–664.

_____. "The Shape of the Signifier." *Critical Inquiry* 27 (2001): 266–83.

Miller, Ryder W. "Reflections on the 100-Year Anniversary of 'The War of the Worlds': A Frontier and Literary History of Mars." *Mercury* 27.3 (May/June 1998): 12–16.

Morton, Oliver. *Mapping Mars: Science, Imagination, and the Birth of a World*. New York: Picador, 2002.

Moylan, Thomas P. "The Moment Is Here ... And It's Important: State, Agency, and Dystopia in Kim Stanley Robinson's *Antarctica* and Ursula K. Le Guin's *The Telling*." *Dark Horizons: Science Fiction and the Dystopian Imagination*. Rafaella Baccolini and Tom Moylan, eds. New York: Routledge, 2003. 135–154.

_____. *Scraps of the Untainted Sky: Science Fiction, Utopia, Dystopia*. Boulder, CO: Westview Press, 2000.

_____. "Utopia Is When Our Lives Matter: Reading Kim Stanley Robinson's *Pacific Edge*." *Utopian Studies* 6.2 (1995): 1–25.

Nicholls, Stan. "The Colors of Mars." *Starlog* 191 (June 1993): 58–67.

Otto, Eric. "Kim Stanley Robinson's Mars Trilogy and the Leopoldian Land Ethic." *Utopian Studies* 14.2 (2003): 118–135.

Quinones, Peter. "Kim Stanley Robinson on Mars." *Firsts: The Book Collector's Magazine* 9.10 (1999): 24–31.

Robinson, Kim Stanley. "Cities in the Overshoot." *Paradoxa: Studies in World Literary Genres* 2.1 (1996): 44–45.

_____. "Notes for an Essay on Cecelia Holland." *Foundation* 40 (1987): 54–61.

_____. "The Profession of Science Fiction, 34: Me in a Mirror." *Foundation* 38 (1986–87): 58–63.

Robson, Justina. "The American Planet: Kim Stanley Robinson's Martian Melting Pot." *Nova Express* 4.4 (Winter/Spring 1998): 18–20.

Slotkin, Alan R. "The Ecological Newspeak of Kim Stanley Robinson." *American Speech* 72 (1997): 440–443.

Smith, Jeremy. "A World, Not a Nation: The Martian Utopias of Kim Stanley Robinson." *Dollars and Sense* 237 (September 2001): 55–56.

Stratton, Susan. "The Messiah and the Greens: The Shape of Environmental Action in *Dune* and *Pacific Edge*." *Extrapolation* 42 (2001): 303–16.

Swidorski, Carl. "Kim Stanley Robinson's Martian Vision." *The Utopian Fantastic: Selected Essays from the Twentieth International Conference on the Fantastic in the Arts*. Martha Bartter, ed. Westport, CT: Praeger, 2004. 43–56.

Voermans, Paul. "Scripts Deep Enough: Kim Stanley Robinson's *Antarctica*." *New York Review of Science Fiction* 125 (January 1999): 1, 4–5.

Wegner, Philip E. *Imaginary Communities: Utopia, the Nation, and the Spatial Histories of Modernity*. Berkeley: University of California Press, 2002.

White, William. "'Structuralist Alchemy' in Kim Stanley Robinson's *Red Mars*." Forthcoming. *Extrapolation* 42 (2007): 578–603.

Winthrop-Young, Geoffrey. "The Rise and Fall of Norse America: Vikings, Vinland and Alternate History." *Extrapolation* 43 (2002): 188–203.

Yanarella, Ernest J. "Terra/Terror-Forming and Death Denial in Kim Stanley Robinson's Martian Stories and Mars Trilogy." *Foundation* 32.89 (2003): 13–26.

Interviews

Clarke, Amy. "Like a Japanese Paper Flower in Water: An Interview with Kim Stanley Robinson." *Writing on the Edge* 12.1 (Fall/Winter 2001): 5–14.

Foote, Bud. "A Conversation with Kim Stanley Robinson." *Science Fiction Studies* 21.1 (March 1994): 51–60.

Gevers, Nick. "The Spin of a Coin, An Anthology of Souls, Kim Stanley Robinson Interviewed." *Interzone* 177 (March 2002): 15–19.
"An Interview with Kim Stanley Robinson." Space.com [5pp.] June 28, 2000. http://www.space.com/scienceficition/kim_stanley_robinson_interview_000626.htmlJackson, Thomas E. "Interview with Kim Stanley Robinson." *New York Review of Science Fiction* 117 (May 1998): 15–18.
Jamneck, Lynne. "Interview: Kim Stanley Robinson." *Strange Horizons* (15 August 2005). www.stangehorizons.com
McVeigh, Kevin. "Red Prophet, Green Man, Blue Adept: Kim Stanley Robinson in Conversation." *Vector* 189 (September/October 1996): 3–6.
_____. "The Red Prophet: Kim Stanley Robinson, an Interview." *Vector* 176 (December 1993/January 1994): 5–8.
Nicholls, Stan. "Green Light for Red Planet Blues: Kim Stanley Robinson Interviewed." *Interzone* 70 (April 1993): 24–25.
_____. "Kim Stanley Robinson Says Mars Is Making Eyes at Him." *Wordsmiths of Wonder: Fifty Interviews with Writers of the Fantastic*. Stan Nicholls, ed. London: Orbit, 1993. 218–226.
Seed, David. "The Mars Trilogy: An Interview with Kim Stanley Robinson." *Foundation* 68 (1996): 75–80.
Sellars, Nigel. "From the Shores of California to the Sands of Mars: An Interview with Kim Stanley Robinson." *Pirate Writings* 4.1 (1996): 11–13.
Szeman, Imre, and Maria Whiteman. "An Interview with Kim Stanley Robinson." *Science Fiction Studies* 31.2 (2004): 177–188.

News, Notices, and Reviews

"Campbell Award for Kim Stanley Robinson; Terry Bisson Takes Sturgeon Award." *Science Fiction Chronicle* 12 (September 1991): 4.
Fintushel, Eliot. "Kim Stanley Robinson: Götterdämmerung on Ice." *Publishers Weekly* 245.25 (22 June 1998): 72–73.
Gevers, Nick. "*The Martians*." *The New York Review of Science Fiction*. November 1999. 10–11.
Interview. *The Agony Column*. 4 June 2004. 5 July 2007. <http://trashotron.com/agony/news/2004/06-14-04.htm>
Interview. *Locus Online*. 6 June 2007. <www.locusmag.com/2007/Issue04_Robinson.html>
Interview. *Science Fiction Weekly*. Nov. 2003. 5 July 2007. <http://www.scifi.com/sfw/issue351/interview.html>
Interview with Lynn Jamneck. *Strange Horizons*. 15 Aug. 2005. 5 July 2007.
Interview with Moira Gunn. *Tech Nation*. ITConversations. 10 Jan. 2006. 5 July 2007 <http://www.itconversations.com/shows/detail935.html>
Interview with Moira Gunn. *Tech Nation*. ITConversations. 4 Apr. 2007. 5 July 2007 <http://www.itconversations.com/shows/detail1773.html>
"Interview with Novelist Kim Stanley Robinson." By Jennifer Rohn. 4 Feb. 2007. 5 July 2007 <http://www.lablit.com/article/208>
"Kim Stanley Robinson: Antarctica and Other Alien Landscapes." *Locus* 39.3 (September 1997): 4–6, 83–84.
"Kim Stanley Robinson at the South Pole." *Locus* 36.2 (February 1996): 4
"Kim Stanley Robinson: Green Thoughts." *Locus* 28.2 (August 1992): 4, 69–70.
"Kim Stanley Robinson: Mars on Earth." *Locus* 36.3 (March 1996): 4–5, 79–80.
"Kim Stanley Robinson: The Alien and the Outsider." *Locus* 21.7 (July 1988):5, 64.
"Kim Stanley Robinson: *The Years of Rice and Salt*." *Locus* 48.1 (January 2002): 6–7.
"Redefining Utopia: Kim Stanley Robinson Interviewed." 5 July 2007 <http://www.yatterings.com/2007/04/17/redefining-utopia-kim-stanley-robinson-interviewed/>
Szeman, Imre and Maria Whiteman. "Future Politics: An Interview with Kim Stanley Robinson." *Science Fiction Studies* 31 (2004): 177–188.

Reference Entries

Bogstad, Janice M. "Red Mars by Kim Stanley Robinson (1992)." *The Greenwood Encyclopedia of Science Fiction and Fantasy: Themes, Works, and Wonders*. Gary Westfahl, ed. Westport, CT: Greenwood, 2005. 1221–1223.

Franko, Carol. "Kim Stanley Robinson: Mars Trilogy." *A Companion to Science Fiction*. David Seed, ed. Malden, MA: Blackwell, 2005. 544–555.

Grant, John. "*The Years of Rice and Salt* by Kim Stanley Robinson (2002)." *The Greenwood Encyclopedia of Science Fiction and Fantasy: Themes, Works, and Wonders*. Gary Westfahl, ed. Westport, CT: Greenwood, 2005. 1358–1360.

"Kim Stanley Robinson." *Contemporary Literary Criticism*. Vol. 34. Detroit: Gale, 1985. 105–107.

Stephens, Christopher P., and Tom Joyce. "A Checklist of Kim Stanley Robinson." Revised ed. Hastings-on-Hudson: Ultramarine, 1991. 28pp.

About the Contributors

Carl Abbott is a professor of urban planning at Eastern Oregon University. He has published extensively on the history of city planning, the evolution of U.S. urban policy, and the relationships between urban growth and regional development. He served as president of the Urban History Association for 1995 and is currently co-editor of the *Pacific Historical Review* and of the *Journal of the American Planning Association*. He is the author of several books including *The Metropolitan Frontier: Cities in the Modern American West*, which received the best-book award of the Urban History Association.

Mark Bould is a senior lecturer in film studies at the University of the West of England. A founding co-editor of the journal *Science Fiction Film and Television*, he is the author of *Film Noir: From Berlin to Sin City* (2005) and *The Cinema of John Sayles: A Lone Star* (2008) and co-editor of *Parietal Games: Critical Writings By and On M. John Harrison* (2005). He is currently co-editing *Neo-Noir*; *The Routledge Companion to Science Fiction*; *Fifty Key Figures in Science Fiction*; and *Red Planets: Marxism and Science Fiction*; co-writing *The Routledge Concise History of Science Fiction*; and writing *The Routledge Film Guidebook: Science Fiction*.

William J. Burling is a professor of English at Missouri State University. After twenty years in seventeenth- and eighteenth-century studies and publishing four books and more than fifty articles, notes, and reviews in major journals, he has now turned to science fiction, fantasy, and Critical Theory. Recent essays have appeared in *Utopian Studies* and *Kronoscope*, and forthcoming essays will appear on China Miéville in *Fifty Key Figures in Science Fiction*, music in utopian science fiction (in Bould and Miéville's *Red Planets*), and Marxist theory (in *The Routledge Companion to Science Fiction*).

Irving F. "Bud" Foote was a professor emeritus at Georgia Tech University's School of Literature, Communication, and Culture at the time of his death in 2005.

Carol Franko is an associate professor of English at Kansas State University. She specializes in utopian and science fiction, and her articles have appeared in *Science-Fiction Studies*, *Extrapolation*, *Journal on the Fantastic in the Arts*, and *Mythlore*. She has also contributed an entry on Kim Stanley Robinson's Mars trilogy to *A Companion to Science Fiction*, ed. by David Seed, in the Blackwell Companions to Literature and Culture series.

Nick Gevers is a South African science fiction editor and critic whose work appears frequently in numerous venues, including *Locus*, *The New York Review of Science Fiction*, *Nova Express*, *Infinity Plus*, *Interzone*, and *SF Weekly*.

Shaun Huston is an associate professor in the Department of Geography and the Film Program at Western Oregon University. He has published essays in *The Journal of Popular Culture*; *Anarchist Studies*; *Capitalism, Nature, Socialism*; and *Society and Nature*.

Fredric Jameson is the William A. Lane Professor of Comparative Literature and Romance Studies at Duke University. He has published eighteen books, including most recently *The Modernist Papers* (Verso, 2007); *Archaeologies of the Future* (Verso, 2005); *A Singular Modernity* (Verso, 2002), *The Cultural Turn* (Verso, 1998); and *Brecht and Method* (Verso, 1998).

John Kessel is a professor of English at North Carolina State University and world-renowned author whose honors include the Nebula, Sturgeon, and Tiptree Awards. He has also published criticism in *The Los Angeles Times Book Review, The New York Review of Science Fiction, The Magazine of Fantasy and Science Fiction,* and *Foundation*.

Elizabeth Leane is lecturer in the School of English, Journalism, and European Languages at the University of Tasmania. She has particular interests in the representation of Antarctica in literature, and the relationship between literature and science, and has published in a diverse range of journals, including the *Review of English Studies, Ariel, Theatre Notebook* and *Polar Record*.

Roger Luckhurst is a senior lecturer in the School of English and the Humanities, Birkbeck, University of London. He has published extensively on science fiction and is the author or editor of numerous books, including *Science Fiction* (Polity, 2005); *The Invention of Telepathy* (Oxford University Press, 2002); and *"The Angle Between Two Walls": The Fiction of J. G. Ballard* (Liverpool University Press/St. Martin's, 1997).

Robert Markley is a professor of English at the University of Illinois–Campaign-Urbana. He has published extensively on eighteenth-century literature and drama, cultural studies, film, and science fiction. He is the author or editor of seven books, including *The Far East and the English Imagination 1600–1730* (Cambridge University Press, 2006); *Dying Planet: Mars in Science and the Imagination* (Duke University Press, 2005); *Fallen Languages: Crises of Representation in Newtonian England, 1660–1740* (Cornell University Press, 1993); and *Two-Edg'd Weapons: Style and Ideology in the Comedies of Etherege, Wycherley, and Congreve* (Clarendon Press, 1988). He also edits the scholarly journal *The Eighteenth Century: Theory and Interpretation*.

Thomas P. Moylan is the Glucksman Professor of Contemporary Writing at the University of Limerick and director of the Ralahine Centre for Utopian Studies. He is the author or editor of several notable books, including *Dark Horizons: Science Fiction and the Dystopian Imagination* (Routledge, 2003); *Scraps of the Untainted Sky: Science Fiction, Utopia, Dystopia* (Westview Press, 2000); *Not Yet: Reconsidering Ernst Bloch* (Verso, 1997); and *Demand the Impossible: Science Fiction and the Utopian Imagination* (Methuen, 1986).

Erik Otto is an assistant professor of environmental humanities and English at Florida Gulf Coast University. He is currently working on a book that examines the intersections between science fiction and environmentalism.

Gib Prettyman is a program coordinator and associate professor of English at Penn State Fayette. His articles on utopianism and the Gilded Age have appeared in such journals as *American Literary Realism, American Periodicals, Utopian Studies,* and *Resources for American Literary Study*, where he currently serves as associate editor.

Alan R. Slotkin is a professor of English at Tennessee Technological University. His published work, which focuses on linguistics and literature, includes *The Language of Stephen Crane's Bowery Tales: Growing Mastery of Character Diction* (Garland, 1993) and essays in *American Literary Realism, Language and Literature, Notes on Contemporary Literature,* and *American Speech*.

Sherryl Vint is an assistant professor of English at Brock University. She is writing *Animal Alterity: Science Fiction and the Question of the Animal* and co-editing *The Routledge Companion to Science Fiction* and *Fifty Key Figures in Science Fiction and Fantasy*. Ms. Vint in on the editorial boards of *Science Fiction Studies* and *Journal of the Fantastic in the Arts* and with Mark Bould is a founding co-editor of the journal *Science Fiction Film and Television*.

Phillip E. Wegner is an associate professor of English at the University of Florida. He has published widely on theory and culture, including *Imaginary Communities: Utopia, the Nation, and the Spatial Histories of Modernity* (University of California Press, 2002), and essays in *Genre, Rethinking Marxism, Utopian Studies*, and numerous critical anthologies.

William J. White (Ph.D., Rutgers University) is assistant professor of communication arts and sciences at Penn State–Altoona, where he teaches courses in public speaking and media studies. His fields of inquiry include the rhetoric of science, public understanding of science, and scholarly communication. His research concerns the role of science in public and popular discourse and the place of disciplinarity in the communication of knowledge.

Index

Abbott, Carl 67–82, 247
abrupt climate change 190
Adorno, Theodor 45
Advancement of Sound Science Coalition 173
Albanese, Denise 145, 148
Aldiss, Brian 60, 142n6, 144, 147
Alexandria Quartet tetralogy 71
Allaby, Michael 127
Almayer's Folly 70
Althuser, Louis 50
Always Coming Home (1985) 97
American Petroleum Institute 173
Anderson, Benedict 42, 109
Angenot, Marc 109
Antarctica 3, 96, 148, 257–273
Appadurai, Arun 42
Aronowitz, Stanley 161, 168
"Arthur Sternbach Brings the Curveball to Mars" 96
Autry, Gene 68

Badiou, Alain 162
Bakhtin, Mikhail (M.M.) 78, 115, 116, 118, 119, 120
Bechet, Sidney 84
Benjamin, Walter 100
Bioinformatics 191, 198
Bisson, Terry 100
"Black Air" 84
Blade Runner 25, 70, 72
Bloch, Ernst 36, 107
Blue Mars (1996) 6, 68, 70, 73, 74, 78, 83, 96, 132, 135, 137, 138, 139, 140, 152, 154, 155, 157–169, 204, 208, 247, 249, 252, 253
Bogdanov, Alexander 74, 124
Bone by Bone 73
Bookchin, Murray 71, 157, 234–241, 271n1
Bould, Mark 257–273
Boyer, Paul 178
Bradbury, Ray 74, 96, 290
Brazil 25
Brecht, Bertolt 106
Brevia, Charlotte Dorsa 97
Brin, David 11, 69

Bring the Jubilee (1955) 100
Buddhism 189, 195
Buell, Lawrence 179
Burkett, Paul 271–272n3
Burling, William J. 157–169, 191
Burroughs, Edgar Rice 74, 117, 124, 290
Bush, George W. 172, 174
Butler, Octavia E. 25

Callenbach, Ernest 78, 158
Callicott, J. Baird 254
Camp Concentration 45
Card, Orson Scott 11
Carnivalization 119–121
The Case for Mars 74
The Castle of the Otter 95
Catch-22 196
Cavalcanti, Ildney 45
Chabon, Michael 98
chaos theory 49
Cheap Truth 89
Cherneshevsky, Nikolai 74, 116
Chevengur 105
City of Quartz 72
"The City on the Edge of Forever" (1967) 100
Clarion Writers' Workshop 84
The Comedy of Survival 179
"Coming Back to Dixieland" (1976) 84, 91
Conrad, Joseph 70
"The Constitution of Mars" 97
Corrupting Dr. Nice (1997) 4
Crichton, Michael 173
The Crisis in Historical Materialism (1981) 168
The Crying of Lot 49 70

Damasio, Antonio 177, 200
Davis, Mike 72
The Day After Tomorrow 179
Dear, Michael 72
De Camp, L. Sprague 99
Delany, Samuel R. 11, 15, 31, 45n18, 63, 78
Deleuze, Gilles 63
Descartes' Error 177

"The Desire Called Utopia" (2005) 181, 198, 199
dialogization 116
Dick, Philip K. 11, 15, 20, 70, 100, 124, 207
The Difference Engine (1991) 101, 103, 106
Disch, Thomas 45, 92
"The Disguise" (1977) 84
The Dispossessed 13, 60, 165
Down and Out in Paris and London 88
"Down and Out in the Year 2000" (1986) 88
Dubliners 92
The Dune Encyclopedia 95
Durrell, Lawernce 71
Dynes, William 204, 248

The Ecology of Fear 72
ecopoeisis 127, 128
Ecotopia 158
Einstein Intersection 31
Elkin, Stanley 77
Elliott, Robert C. 64
Ellison, Harlan 100
Elman, Richard 72
Emerson, Ralph Waldo 194
Empire (2000) 167
"The End of History" 5
"Enough Is as Good as a Feast" 97
"environmental thrillers" 192
"Exploring Fossil Canyon" (1982) 95, 96, 123
Eye in the Sky 86

fact-value problem 279
Faulkner, William 278
Fellowship of the Downtrodden 89–91
Fifty Degrees Below (2005) 43, 170, 182, 184, 200, 263, 275n5
Fire on the Mountain (1988) 100
First Landing 75
Fogg, Martyn 127
Foote, Irving F. "Bud" 116, 181, 204, 249, 277–290
Forrest Gump 106

Forster, E.M. 17
fortunate crisis 192
Forty Signs of Rain (2004) 43, 170, 182, 184, 185, 186, 189
"Fossil Canyon" 124, 133
"Four Teleological Trails" 97
Franko, Carol 45, 77, 157, 181, 216
Freedman, Carl 165
Fugard, Athol 23
Fukuyama, Francis 5, 16, 101
Future Primitive: The New Ecotopias 122

Gaia Hypothesis 127
Galaxy magazine 68
Gardiner, Michael 39
Genesis (Turner) 128
genre as biological metaphor 185–187
George C. Marshall Institute 173
Gevers, Nick 95–97
Gibson, William 69, 89, 101
Gilliam, Terry 25
Gingrich, Newt 173
"Glacier" (1988) 90
Glenn, John 68
Gods of Mars 290
Gold, H.L. 68
The Gold Coast (1988) 4, 6, 11, 12, 14, 15–27, 68, 71, 72, 83, 96, 171, 176, 179, 196
The Golden Coast 141
Goldwater, Barry 173
A Good Man Is Hard to Find 92
Gordon, Flash 68
Gramsci, Antonio 158
"Green Mars" (1985) 95, 96, 123, 125
Green Mars (1993) 6, 43, 68, 69, 73, 74, 83, 96, 120, 132, 133, 135, 136, 137, 138, 152, 204, 207, 208, 236–238, 247, 248, 250, 251, 252, 271n1
The Greening of Mars 127–128, 139
Greimas, Algirdas Julien 7, 205
Greimassian semiotics 205–222
Gribbin, John 146
Grinspoon, David 130

Hansen, James 173
Harding, Sandra 145
Hardt, Michael 45, 167
Harraway, Donna 260
He, She and It 27, 31, 43
Hegel, Georg 104
Hegemony and Socialist Strategy: Towards a Radical Democratic Politics (1985) 6, 158
Heinlein, Robert A. 61, 69
Heritage Foundation 173
Hine, Robert 77
"A History of the Twentieth Century, with Illustrations" 93
Hofstadter, Richard 170

Holland, Cecelia 70
Human Genome Project 190
Huntington, Samuel P. 109
Huston, Shaun 157, 231–241

Icehenge (1984) 88, 134, 135, 259–260, 277
"If Wang Wei Lived on Mars" 97
Ihde, Don 122
In Scraps of the Untainted Sky 254n2
In the American Grain 26
In the Wake of Cook 152
Intergovernmental Panel on Climate Change (IPCC) 172, 173
Irigaray, Luce 45

Jameson, Fredric 48–66, 70, 99, 101, 102–103, 108–109, 146, 147, 157, 168, 181, 198, 199, 200, 201, 207
Joyce, James 92

kami 207, 208, 248
"Keeping the Flame" 97
Keller, Evelyn Fox 154
Kennedy, John F. 68
Kessel, John 83–94
Killing Mr. Watson 73
Knight, Damon 84
koan 189
Kornbluth, Cyril 124
Kropotkin, Peter 232

Laclau, Ernesto 6, 158–169
land ethic 243–244
Landis, Geoffrey A. 74
language as genes 186–187
Last and First Men 105
The Late Great Planet Earth 178
Latour, Bruno 175, 265, 266
Leane, Elizabeth 144–156, 208, 271n2
Lefanu, Sarah 45
Lefebvre, Henri 111
LeGuin, Ursula K. 11, 60, 78, 92, 97, 165
Leinster, Murray 99
Leopold, Aldo 243–256
Leopold, Leo 7
Lest Darkness Fall 100
Limerick, Patricia 75
Lindsay, Hal 178
Lord Jim 70
Lost Man's River 73
Lovelock, James 127
"The Lucky Strike" (1984) 85–86, 90, 96, 100, 101, 103, 134
Lukács, Georg 99, 172, 177
"The Lunatics" (1988) 90, 92

MacDonald, John D. 289
Mackey, David 152
MacLeod, Ken 69

Magazine of Fantasy and Science Fiction 68
The Man in the High Castle (1962) 86, 100
Marcuse, Herbert 32
Markley, Robert 67, 122–143, 263
Marriage of Figaro 107
Mars Crossing 74–75
Mars Direct (Mars Mission Proposal) 128–130, 136
The Martian Chronicles 74, 290
"A Martian Romance" 96, 141
The Martians (1999) 95–97, 123, 126, 140, 197
McClintock, Barbara 154
McClintock, James I. 244, 249
McKay, Chris 127, 128, 131
McKitrick, Eric 77
McWilliams, Carey 72
Meeker, Joseph 179
The Memory of Whiteness 278
"Mercurial" (1985) 87
Merril, Judith 124
Metahistory: The Historical Imagination in Nineteenth Century Europe (1973) 102
Meyer, Thomas 127
"Michel in Provence" 96
Miller, Walter 281
Mist 54
Moby-Dick 73
A Modern Utopia 30, 32
Monbiot, George 174
Moore, C.L. 121, 289
Moore, Ward 100
Moral Majority 173
More, Thomas 62
Morgan, Neil 72
Morris, William 62, 57
Mouffe, Chantal 6, 158–169
Moylan, Thomas P. 11–47, 157, 171, 181, 254n2
Mozart, Wolfgang Amadeus 107

National Science Foundation 183
Natural Capitalism 268–270
Nature's Kindred Spirits (McClintock) 244
Nausea 52
"near future science fiction" 198
Negri, Antonio 45, 167
The Neuromancer (1984) 89, 103
New Science, New World 145
News from Nowhere 57, 62
Nietzsche, Friedrich 103
"Night Meeting" 97
Niven, Larry 62, 124
Nixon, Richard 173
Norris, Frank 54
Nostromo 70
The Novels of Philip K. Dick (KSR Ph.D. dissertation) 86

O'Connor, Flannery 92

The Octopus 54
Office of Technology Assessment 173
Orbit 84
Orwell, George 88
Otto, Eric 242–256
Outpost Mars (1953) 124

Pacific Edge (1990) 4, 11, 12, 14, 28–42, 68, 69, 70, 71, 72, 73, 78, 83, 96, 181, 196, 197, 227–238, 286
paleoclimatology 190
Palladino, Paolo 145
Pangborn, Edgar 281
The Parable of the Sower 25, 31
"The Part of Us That Loves" (1989) 91
Passos, John Dos 73
Penrose, Roger 142n6, 144
People Are Living Here 23
The Phantom Empire 68
Piercy, Marge 27, 78
The Planet on the Table (1986) 4, 83
Planned Parenthood 284
A Pliocene Companion 95
The Plot Against America 98
Plotanov, Andrei 105
Plumwood, Val 258, 260, 261, 264, 267, 268, 269
Political heroism 194
Political Unconscious 201
"The Politics of Utopia" 199
"Postmodernism: The Cultural Logic of Late Capitalism" 70
Prettyman, Gib 181
"Prisoners Dilemma" 188
"Progress Versus Utopia; or Can We Imagine the Future?" 99
Proleptic, Realism 170–172, 178, 179
Propp, Vladimir 212
"Purple Mars" 97, 197
Pynchon, Thomas 70

Quinby, Lee 178

Rainbow Mars (1999) 124
Red Mars (1992) 7, 67, 68, 70, 73, 74, 83, 96, 126, 130, 132, 135, 136, 139, 148, 149, 181, 204, 243–235, 245, 246, 247, 250, 252, 277, 286–290
Red Star (1924) 74, 124
Reese, William 120
"Remaking History" (1989) 87, 92
Remaking History (1991) 4, 83
Remaking History (1994) 83
"Ridge Running" (1984) 88
Ringworld 62
Roberts, Keith 92
Robinsonade 193, 194
Roddenberry, Gene 68
"Roger Clayborne and Eileen Monday" stories 96

Rogers, Buck 68
Roth, Philip 98
Russ, Joanna 44n6, 78, 281, 285

A Sand County Almanac (Leopold, 1949) 243
Sargent, Lyman Tower 44n4
Sartre, Jean-Paul 52, 288, 289
"Saving Noctis Dam" 97
Schismatrix 63
Schumacher, Ernst 71
Science in Action 175
Scientists and Engineers for Johnson 173
Scott, Allen J. 72
Scott, Ridley 25, 70, 99
Scott, Walter 99
Scraps of the Untainted Sky (2000) 4
The Search for Life on Mars 144
The Secret Agent 70
Seed, David 45
Sémantique structurale (1966) 205
"A Sensitive Dependence on Initial Conditions" (1991) 85–86, 96, 101, 134
"Sexual Dimorphism" 95, 97
Shambhala 195, 196
Shambleau 121
Shaviro, Steve 123
The Shawshank Redemption (1994) 106, 107, 108
Shklovsky, Viktor 109
"Sidewise in Time" (1934) 99
Simak, Clifford 281
Sixty Days and Counting (2007) 43, 170, 182, 272n6
Slaughterhouse-Five 196
Slotkin, Alan R. 227–230
Smith, Cordwainer 281
Smythe, William 75
Snyder, Gary 75
Soja, Edward 72
"Some Worknotes and Commentary on the Constitution" 97
Sontag, Susan 170
"Space Operas" 68
Stapledon, Olaf 63, 105, 281
Star Trek 68, 100
State of Fear 173, 174
Stephenson, Bruce 69
Sterling, Bruce 63, 89, 101
Strategic Defense Initiative 173
Structural Semantics 212
Suvin, Darko 60, 63, 108, 201
syncretism 115, 120

The Terminator 103
Terraforming 127
Thoreau, Henry David 194
Three Californias Trilogy (Orange County Trilogy) 11–47
The Three Stigmata of Peter Eldrich 86

thriller genre 192, 193
Toon, Owen B. 127
transcendentalism (Emerson and Thoreau) 194
"A Transect" (1987) 90
"The Translator" (1990) 87
Triton 11, 45
trope 188–190
Trotsky, Leon 165
Trouble on Triton 63
Turner, Frederick Jackson 74, 77, 128
"The Two Drovers" 99

Ubik 86
Unamuno, Miguel de 54
"Under the Moons of Mars" 74
U.S. National Commission on Space 68
Universe 84
USA 73
Utopian Black Comedy 184, 196

"Venice Drowned" (1981) 84, 90
Vineland 70
"Vinland the Dream" (1991) 87, 92
Vint, Sherryl 257–273
The Virginian 74
viriditas 58, 59, 131, 132, 133, 134, 137, 140, 150, 207, 208, 248

Walters, Malcolm 144
Wattleton, Faye 284
"The Way Land Spoke to Us" 97
Wegner, Phillip E. 98–112, 157
Wells, H.G. 30, 32, 124, 281
Western Historical Quarterly 75
What Is to Be Done 74, 116, 117
"What Matters" 96
White, Hayden 102
White, William J. 204–223
White Mars 142n6, 144
The Wild Shore (1984) 4, 11, 12, 14, 23, 44, 68, 70, 71, 72, 83, 88, 96, 196
Wilhelm, Kate 92
Wilhelm, Friedrich 104
Williams, Raymond 258
Williams, William Carlos 26
Wister, Owen 74
Worboys, Michael 145
World Fantasy Award 84
World Rescue Institute: An Action Agenda to Sustain Ecosystem Services 272n6

Yanarella, Ernest J. 254
The Years of Rice and Salt (2002) 3, 5, 83, 98–112, 196
The Yiddish Policemen's Union 98

Zubrin, Robert 74, 75, 128–130
"Zurich" (1990) 91